ENGLISH GOVERNMENT AND POLITICS

By THE SAME AUTHOR

The Opening of the Mississippi

Social Progress in Contemporary Europe

The Governments of Europe

National Governments and the World War (with *Charles A. Beard*)

Economic Development of Modern Europe (with *Walter R. Sharp*)

ENGLISH GOVERNMENT AND POLITICS

BY

FREDERIC AUSTIN OGG, PH.D., LL.D.

PROFESSOR OF POLITICAL SCIENCE IN THE UNIVERSITY OF WISCONSIN

New York

THE MACMILLAN COMPANY

1929

Set up and electrotyped. Published September, 1929

SET UP AND ELECTROTYPED BY J. J. LITTLE & IVES
PRINTED IN THE UNITED STATES OF AMERICA

TO MY STUDENTS IN
"POLITICAL SCIENCE 250"
UNIVERSITY OF WISCONSIN

PREFACE

There is a tendency nowadays in the study of government to stress functional rather than historical or descriptive approach; and much is to be said for it. The new method or emphasis, however, cannot serve us so well that it will cease to be useful to fasten the gaze upon a single governmental system and endeavor to comprehend it as a great unit or chapter in the sum total of man's political experience and achievement—particularly if the system be one not only of large inherent interest but also of world-wide influence and renown. The English system is undoubtedly such a one; and it is the purpose of this book to give an account of that system on lines which will render it not only a reservoir of data on principles and processes but a living reality as a going concern. Of function, much is said; of institutions, considerably more. It is hoped that the two have been kept in clear and true relation; likewise that the most pregnant opportunities have not been overlooked to suggest, even if not always to treat at length, interesting and meaningful comparisons with governments of other lands, especially the United States.

A new book on English government is perhaps justified by the remarkable changes in mechanism, function, and method which recent years have witnessed, and particularly by the fluidity of political arrangements in Britain today and the probability of further significant experiments and reconstructions in times immediately ahead. "This island," averred Charles Dickens' egregious Mr. Podsnap, "is blessed, Sir, by Providence, to the direct exclusion of such other countries as there may happen to be." It is doubtful whether even Mr. Podsnap would have been capable of such complacency had he been a contemporary of Stanley Baldwin and Ramsay MacDonald. Certainly the Britain of our time is none too sure about its monopoly of Providential favor, whether in the domain of sea-power, of trade, or even of law and government. Vast political problems have been met and solved in the past hundred years. But their places have been taken by others, even more challenging and baffling. Often thought of as a peculiarly "finished" and static governmental system, the English is, in point of fact, dynamic and shifting—ever feeling its way, by its own cautious methods to be sure, along new lanes into uncharted areas. The chapters that follow will have failed in their purpose if they do not create the picture of a great, expanding, living political organism whose interest for the world flows quite as much from the novel things that it is about to do as from those which it has already done. We ought, as Burke long ago remarked, "to understand it according to our measure," even if we do not admit the force of the statesman-philosopher's further injunction "to venerate where we are not able presently to comprehend."

FREDERIC A. OGG.

UNIVERSITY OF WISCONSIN,
April, 1929.

CONTENTS

ENGLISH GOVERNMENT AND POLITICS

ENGLISH GOVERNMENT AND POLITICS

CHAPTER I

THE ORIGINS OF ENGLISH POLITICAL INSTITUTIONS

It is not necessary to tax the resources of the English language as did Fortescue in the fifteenth century and Blackstone and Burke in the eighteenth [1] to establish the fact that the political institutions of England, and of modern Britain, have played an exceptionally important rôle in the making of our twentieth-century civilization. This would be true if their influence had been confined to those portions of the world which have been peopled principally from Britain and where English is the mother tongue; for these alone embrace more than a sixth of the total land area of the globe and include, besides Britain herself, the United States, Canada, Australia, New Zealand, and considerable parts of Africa. In almost equally extensive lands, however, which are not ethnically or culturally English, but in which British political power has been planted, the marks of English constitutional and political experience are plainly to be seen; while in long lists of countries not English at all—from France and Germany and Belgium to Japan and China at one end of the earth and Chile and Peru at another—the effects of this same experience, while not always definitely measurable, meet the observer at every turn.[2] The Hebrews did not create all religion, nor the Greeks all philosophy or art, nor the Romans all law, nor the English all principles and

[1] Sir John Fortescue, *De Laudibus Legum Angliae;* Sir William Blackstone, *Commentaries on the Laws of England;* Edmund Burke, *Reflections on the French Revolution.*

[2] "The English constitution has made the circuit of the globe and become the common possession of civilized man." G. B. Adams, *The Origin of the English Constitution* (enlarged ed., New Haven, 1920), 1.

forms of government. In each of these fields the world has been enriched by weighty contributions from widely scattered and largely unrelated sources. England, however, looms as prominently in the political realm as Greece in the domain of thought or Rome in that of law; and no one can progress far toward an understanding of the government under which he lives without knowing its English antecedents or connections. Particularly is this true of the American, whose government as it stands today does indeed offer plenty of contrasts with the English, but is none the less deeply rooted in English experience and tradition. In the words of the late Professor Adams, "the history of the formation of the British constitution is a part of our history. . . . The creation and establishment of our judicial institutions and common law, of the supremacy of law over government, of our representative system, of the popular control of taxation, of the responsibility of ministers of government to the legislature, and finally of the principle, fundamental to all else, of the sovereignty of the people, were the work of our English ancestors." [3]

Not only do the political institutions of the United States rest back upon those of England; the institutions and usages of the "tight little island," as we view them today, are the products of long centuries of development. Doubtless it is true that there have been so many changes, even since the eighteenth century, that a Pitt or a Burke, wandering about Whitehall and Westminster today, would feel himself almost a stranger. What he would encounter would, however, be strongly reminiscent of the past; much would be essentially as it was when he first walked the earth. A main characteristic of English constitutional and political experience has been its long and relatively unbroken sweep through the ages.

The primary purpose of this book is to describe the English system of government as it is today, i.e., as a "going concern." To describe, however, means also to explain, which in turn entails taking account of how political forms and practices came to be as we find them. Historical antecedents not only furnish the clue to much that otherwise would be inexplicable,

[3] G. B. Adams, *Outline Sketch of English Constitutional History* (New Haven, 1918), 4-5.

but, in the case of England at all events, often come close to supplying the whole explanation. No apology is required, therefore, for prefacing our study with an outline of the process by which the English constitution came into being and, in the long course of time, took on its present form.

Anglo-Saxon Institutions

To begin at the beginning, one must turn his eyes all the way back to the primitive Britain of the Celts, the Romans, and the Saxons. He will not need to concern himself much with the Celtic tribes which Cæsar, at his famous crossing of the Channel in 54 B.C., found in sole possession of Britain and its sister island on the west; because they contributed nothing of which we are aware to the political system of today. Nor did the Romans, who almost a century later carved out a province in the south and center, leave anything behind them on their final withdrawal in 407 A.D. which affected political institutions of later times.[4] The earliest period to which the making of the modern British constitution can be traced is, rather, that which begins with the invasions and settlements of the Angles and Saxons, at the middle of the fifth century and after, and terminates with the Norman Conquest in 1066. This Anglo-Saxon epoch, covering some six hundred years, counted for considerably less in the making of the political system of later days than was once supposed. Nevertheless, it contributed one institution which, even now a conspicuous feature of the political landscape, was for centuries the most prominent of all, i.e., kingship; [5] and, besides, it covered the country with a network of areas of local government which survive in part to this day.

Kingship, it is interesting to notice, arose among the Angles

[4] Roman influences re-entered the country indirectly in the Middle Ages through the study of the Roman law. But the effects upon political institutions, as distinguished from legal principles, were negligible.

[5] Kingship was, indeed, the great central institution around which the English constitution grew up. Not only that, but the monarchy has been, from first to last, the most deeply rooted and continuous part of the constitution and the whole course of constitutional history a progressive adaptation of the concepts and actualities of the monarchy to altered needs and conditions. As will appear, the crown—no longer, of course, the king in person—is still in a very real sense "the government."

and Saxons after their settlement in the new home, and not before; at their coming, the leaders were only *principes,* or chieftains. Monarchy in Britain is therefore an indigenous institution, not an importation. Many chieftains of victorious war bands attained the regal dignity, and, as every student of English history knows, eventually the scattered little dominions gravitated together into the seven kingdoms comprising the "Heptarchy"—East Anglia, Mercia, Northumberland, Kent, Sussex, Essex, and Wessex. One by one, these were absorbed into larger areas, until at length, in the ninth century, Wessex emerged supreme and the entire occupied portion of the country was brought under the sway of a single sovereign.

This "sway" was not, however, very impressive, especially when the king did not happen to be a man of wisdom and vigor. In the first place, the monarch occupied the throne, not by strict hereditary right, but by election. The people who chose him belonged to the *witenagemot,* or "council of wise men," and while they commonly showed preference for members of a given family, they did not hesitate to pass over an eldest son if they considered him incompetent or otherwise undesirable. In the second place, the king, although a lawgiver, issued his "dooms" only with the concurrence of the witan; and they were few and simple, rarely extending beyond the fixing of penalties for offenses to which his red-blooded subjects were specially prone, i.e., breaches of the peace. In the third place, the king was limited in his acts by a steadily growing body of "customs of the people." The king was regarded as supreme judge, and all crimes and misdemeanors came to be looked upon as offenses against him. Here again, however, his actual powers were slight, for with the routine administration of justice locally he had little or nothing to do. In fact, he had scant control over local affairs of any kind. He presided over the assemblies or synods of the church. But the main thing expected of him was that he should lead his people bravely and effectively in time of war. Originally, kingship was only a sort of permanent war-chieftainship; and although it became a good deal more than that before the end of the Saxon period, it was far from absolute in the hands of even so redoubtable a monarch as Cnut.

The *witenagemot* was an assembly of the most important

men of the kingdom, lay and ecclesiastical. It had no fixed membership, but consisted of such persons as the king chose to summon to the three or four meetings commonly held each year.[6] There were no elected members, and the body had no representative character except in the general sense that it spoke for the interests and classes from which its members were drawn and, through them, for the nation. Of course the king was not exactly free in deciding who should be summoned. There were always people who could not possibly be left out; and, broadly, we may say that those present pretty regularly included the chief officers of the royal household, the *ealdormen* who represented the central government in the shires, bishops and other leading churchmen, sundry high officers of state, and the principal men who held land directly of the king. The functions of the witan were almost as ill-defined as its composition, and its actual power was likely to be inversely proportionate to that of the king at any given time. But it had a right to be consulted on all important affairs of both state and church; it gave its assent to the king's "dooms," or laws; it sat with the king as the supreme court of justice; it agreed to treaties and land grants, but had little to do with finance, since there was no national taxation in the modern sense. As has been stated, it elected the king. Similarly, it had power to depose him; and this is one of the reasons why kingship never became absolute in the Anglo-Saxon period. "It has been a marked and important feature of our constitutional history," an English scholar reminds us, "that the king has never, in theory, acted in matters of state without the counsel and consent of a body of advisers."[7] As a prototype of the Great, or Common, Council of later times, and even, more remotely, of the present cabinet, the *witenagemot* is interesting and important. But we should not make the mistake of reading back into it the character of either a modern royal council or a parliament.

Aside from kingship, it was in the field of local government that the Anglo-Saxon period made its largest and most lasting

[6] There was no national "capital," and these meetings were held from place to place around the country as convenience dictated.

[7] W. R. Anson, *Law and Custom of the Constitution* (3rd ed., Oxford, 1907-11), II, Pt. i, 7.

contribution to the British political system of today. Practically the whole population lived in one-roomed, thatched cottages, grouped in little villages, each with a surrounding area of pasture, woodland, and plowed ground; and, naturally enough, every such *tunscip,* or township, had its own bit of local government machinery, consisting as a rule of a *mote*, or town meeting, and a reeve and other elected officers. Some hamlets, favorably situated at meeting points of trade routes or adjacent to fortified posts, grew into *burghs,* or boroughs, enjoying large rights of self-government. London, for example, arose early in this way. The number of such places did not, however, exceed a hundred when the period ended. A group of townships formed a hundred (manifestly having some numerical significance, although nobody now knows precisely what it was); and a hundred had a *mote,* or court, of its own, together with a hundred-man, sometimes elected, sometimes appointed by a landowner who was lord of the region. Here, it is interesting to observe, the principle of representation made its appearance in a limited way; for to the sessions of the hundred court came the reeve, the parish priest, and four "best men" from each of the townships and boroughs within the hundred's bounds. As a rule, the hundred court met once a month and devoted its time to hearing and deciding cases at law—civil, criminal, and ecclesiastical.

Above the hundred was the shire. Not much is known about how the shires came into existence, but it is probable that most of them originated as areas occupied by small independent tribes. At all events, they ultimately appear as the largest judicial and administrative subdivisions of the united kingdom. The shire also had its *mote,* or court, which seems at one time to have consisted of all the freemen who cared to attend, although in later days it was actually made up—whatever the theory may have been—of the reeves and other representatives of the townships, together with the larger landowners and principal church officials. The body met twice a year and, like the hundred court, transacted judicial business chiefly, although sometimes with a trace of legislative, or even administrative, work. In earlier times the chief officer of the shire was the alderman, who presided over the shire court and constituted the local head of a real local government. But later he was drawn under closer royal control, being appointed by king and witan; and eventually he was quite eclipsed by the shire-reeve, or sheriff, who became the king's representative in a very special sense and as such had charge of the royal lands in the shire, collected the king's revenue, received the king's share of the fines imposed in the courts, and even took over the alderman's duties of presiding over the shire court and calling out and commanding the local militia. The alderman's office dropped out altogether after the Norman Conquest, but the office of sheriff went on developing in power and importance and, under greatly altered conditions, has survived to this day.[8] The shire, as a rule, formed a diocese of the church, and accordingly the bishop was accustomed to attend the sessions of the court and take a prominent part, apparently presiding when ecclesiastical cases were up for adjudication.

The significance of this general scheme of local government and administration lies not so much in the modern survival of ancient jurisdictions like the shire (rechristened the county after the Conquest), or of ancient offices like the sheriff's, as in the formation of an ineradicable habit of local autonomy, which has ever been one of the most conspicuous characteristics of the British people. Centuries of relatively weak national government gave opportunity for local institutions to take root so firmly that no amount of centralizing pressure in Norman, Tudor, or other times could squeeze out the life and vigor of county, town, and village, as happened, for example, in Bourbon France. Furthermore, as a recent writer properly emphasizes, the governments of hundred and shire first called into play the principles of representation and so habituated the people to its workings that, when later the time was ripe, it could be made the basis of parliamentary organization on a national scale.[9]

[8] See p. 243 below.

[9] W. B. Munro, *The Governments of Europe* (New York, 1925), 17. For fuller accounts of Anglo-Saxon institutions, the reader may be referred to G. B. Adams, *Constitutional History of England* (New York, 1921), 5-49; A. B. White, *The Making of the English Constitution* (rev. ed., New York, 1925), 3-71; and H. Taylor, *Origins and Growth of the English Constitution* (new ed., Boston, 1900), II, Bk. I, Chaps. iii-v. A

Norman-Angevin Contributions

A new stage in the development of English political institutions was opened when, upon the death of Edward the Confessor in 1066, William of Normandy crossed over from his well-ordered duchy in the northwest of France and, defeating the Saxon claimant on the field of Senlac (or Hastings), assumed the royal title and launched a series of campaigns which in due time left him undisputed master of the country. The precise significance of this event and its aftermath has long been warmly debated by the ablest historians and legal scholars. By a somewhat curious turn, the Oxford professor who, some sixty years ago, wrote the fullest account of the Conquest that we possess attached less importance to the matter than do most authorities today.[10] He was obsessed with the idea that Anglo-Saxon institutions survived the Conquest almost intact and that the English constitution of our own time rests back solidly upon those institutions—even, indeed, in its central principle of popular government, upon the ideas carried over by the Saxons from the German forests.[11] The contemporary historian Stubbs attached somewhat greater weight to the changes wrought by William and his successors, and to the feudal character of the Anglo-Norman period in general;[12] and in later days the permanence of the Saxon institutions has been more and more discounted, until some very good authorities have been led to declare, to all intents and purposes, that the history

classic treatment of the subject is W. Stubbs, *Constitutional History of England in its Origin and Development* (6th ed., Oxford, 1897), especially I, 74-182. J. Ramsay, *Foundations of England,* 2 vols. (London, 1898), is a mine of information. Political and institutional history is narrated fully in T. Hodgkin, *History of England to the Norman Conquest* (London, 1906), and C. W. C. Oman, *England Before the Norman Conquest* (London, 1910). C. Gross, *Sources and Literature of English History* (London, 1900), is an admirable bibliography.

[10] E. A. Freeman, *The Norman Conquest,* 6 vols. (Oxford, 1867-69).

[11] He set forth this view with particular cogency in *The Growth of the English Constitution* (London, 1872, and numerous later editions). Professor Vinogradoff once applied to the doctrine the pregnant phrase "retrospective nationalism."

[12] In the work already mentioned. Emancipation from Freeman's notion of the uninterrupted survival of Saxon institutions began, indeed, with Stubbs, although, as is stated above, it was carried much farther by other and later writers.

of the English constitution really starts only in 1066. Much depends, of course, upon what is meant by "the constitution." If the ground-work of the national government alone is referred to, there is reason for regarding the Conqueror's incursion as the beginning; and, proceeding from that point of view, the most important American writer on the subject, the late Professor George B. Adams, has devoted a very convincing book to proving that "the history of the English constitution upon English soil begins with the Norman Conquest." [13]

Granted that the establishment of Norman rule was a cardinal event, and that the roots of the modern English governmental system run back into William's Continental domain rather more than into the England of pre-Conquest days, there is still danger of over-stressing the point; for local institutions, as above described, went on after 1066 substantially as before, and even the general, or national, government was not completely reconstructed. The Conqueror wanted the good-will of his new subjects and was of no mind to sweep away their cherished laws, forms, and usages except for very urgent cause. Upon one thing, however, he was bent unshakably, i.e., to establish in England the same vigorous centralized rule to which he was accustomed in his Continental dominion; and with unfailing astuteness he manœuvred the entire situation following the invasion in such a way as to make the king the real master—as few Saxon kings had ever been—of the land. Thus, whereas the king until now had frequently been defied and overshadowed by the great earls, William confiscated the estates which formed the basis of their strength and parcelled them out among his own supporters, to be held under a form of feudal tenure so devised that the tenant's foremost obligation was to be obedient to the king. Hitherto feudalism in England was only incipient and chaotic, involving relationships chiefly of an economic nature. But now it took on a highly organized and decidedly political character, quite definitely in the interest of the crown.[14] Reaching out likewise in the direction of the church, the Conqueror assumed the right to appoint

[13] *The Origin of the English Constitution.* See p. 16.

[14] "The fiefs of the English crown never became rival sovereignties to be absorbed one by one in the process of national unification as in France,

bishops, exercised a veto on the acts of ecclesiastical councils, and otherwise asserted a supremacy of the state which, although often seriously threatened in later times, was never overthrown.

It was, however, in the domains of justice and administration that the supremacy of the national government was vindicated most effectively. The later Saxon period had seen the rise of a great variety of courts, e.g., feudal courts, ecclesiastical courts, and courts merchant, in addition to the regular courts of the hundred and the shire, and justice was administered in them on widely divergent lines. These local and private courts by no means disappeared with the Conquest. But a system of royal justice was gradually superimposed, under which king's justices went out into the counties [15] hearing cases, deciding them on uniform lines, harmonizing local customs, and fusing them into a great and steadily expanding body of "common law." [16] Similarly, in the field of administration the long arm of the royal government reached out with a force and effectiveness not previously known. Here the means of centralization lay ready to hand in the office of the sheriff. Important even in Saxon times, this official—appointed and controlled, of course, by the king—now became the vigilant enforcer of the royal will in the county, charged with maintaining law and order and with collecting the revenues due the king, which twice a year were carried to the designated place and turned over to the custodians of the treasury. Frequently, too, the sheriff was commissioned as a justice in the king's court set up in the county. The sheriffs, as Professor Munro has remarked, became the prefects of medieval England.[17]

until all were gone and only royal absolutism was left. The English barons were administrative subordinates of the crown, dangerous to weak kings through casual combinations, but never able to act in opposition to the crown save by joining their forces and appealing for general support, a process which involved terms and conditions, the setting forth of which produced constitutional documents." H. J. Ford, *Representative Government* (New York, 1924), 97-98.

[15] The Norman term now supersedes the Saxon "shire."

[16] On the local king's courts in the reign of William I, and the origin of the common law, see G. B. Adams, *Council and Courts in Anglo-Norman England* (New Haven, 1926), Chaps. iii, v. Cf. W. A. Morris, *The Early English County Court* (Berkeley, 1926).

[17] *Governments of Europe,* 18.

It goes without saying that no king, however vigorous and industrious, could supervise and direct so vast a mechanism of government single-handed. In Norman-Angevin times the assistance which was required was furnished chiefly by two agencies, whose relations and functions it is important to understand. One was the *Magnum Concilium,* or Great Council; the other, the *Curia Regis,* literally, the King's Court. The Great (or Common) Council was, in a manner, the successor of the old *witenagemot;* contemporary chroniclers for a good while continued to call it by the old name. As such, it was composed of the leading men of the realm, lay and ecclesiastical, none of them elected, but all singled out for the purpose by individual summons of the king. "Thrice a year," the Saxon Chronicle tells us, "King William wore his crown every year he was in England; at Easter he wore it at Winchester; at Pentecost, at Westminster; and at Christmas, at Gloucester; and at these times all the men of England were with him—archbishops, bishops, and abbots, earls, thegns, and knights." [18] "All the men of England" means simply, of course, those whose importance in church or state was such that they were naturally invited when any gathering of magnates took place. With few exceptions, they came, however, not simply as churchmen or high civil officials (as was the case in Saxon times), but also as tenants-in-chief, i.e., vassals owing allegiance to the king; attendance was a feudal duty. Presided over and guided by the king, the Council helped decide upon policies of state, supervised the work of administration, sat as the highest court of justice, and made or modified laws on the rather rare occasions when such action was required. An august body it obviously was, with functions which spread promiscuously over the entire field of government.

The Council met on call of the king, but as a regular thing only three times a year, and for no very long periods. Much of the work devolving upon it, however, had to go on all of the time, and hence there arose the Curia Regis, or "little council," whose function it was to help the sovereign carry on the government during the intervals. In a sense, the Curia was not a separate body. It was, in fact, only a sort of inner circle of the

[18] Trans. by J. A. Giles (London, 1847), 461.

Council, consisting of the chamberlain, the chancellor, the constable, the steward, and other officers of the royal household who accompanied the king wherever he went and gave their time continuously, instead of only now and then, to the business of the state. And the Curia's powers were just as great as those of the Council itself. It could do anything that the Council could do, even though, not unnaturally, there was some tendency to hold up weightier matters of business for consideration by the larger body. This was, however, entirely optional with the king, who could refer questions indiscriminately to either body, or indeed to neither of them if he so preferred.

How much real power did the Council and Curia have? Speaking broadly, we do not know. Certain it is, however, that it varied according to whether the king was strong or weak; from which we may deduce that since most of the Norman-Angevin rulers were vigorous men, Council and Curia were rather less of a check upon the sovereign than the witan of Saxon times had usually been. It is a matter of great importance, however, that central machinery of administration and justice, and even law-making, was being built up alongside the kingly office—that strong and weak kings alike followed the practice of calling the leading people of the country together, seeking information and advice from them, turning over much of the public business to them, and, in many matters at least, deferring to their wishes and opinions. The growth of strong kingship was doubtless essential to the orderly development of the nation; it was essential, even, to the rise, in due time, of parliamentary government. But it was also essential to these ends that great permanent administrative and judicial agencies be built up, and that the habit of consulting the nation be hardened into a constitutional principle or rule. As we shall see presently, the Curia became the parent of the Privy Council (and hence of the cabinet), the Exchequer, and the great courts of law; while from the Council was destined to spring the House of Lords, and hence, in a sense, Parliament itself.

For half a century after the death of the Conqueror (1087) the ingenious Anglo-Norman system for which he was responsible held up reasonably well, although rather because of the momentum that its founder had imparted to it than because of any contributions made by his successors of this period; indeed, the anarchy of the reign of Stephen (1135-54) almost wrecked the entire mechanism. Then came the astute and energetic Henry II (1154-89), who recovered all that had been lost and added not a little on his own account. "Henry II," it has been said, "found a nation wearied out with the miseries of anarchy, and the nation found in Henry II a king with a passion for administration." [19] With a view to bringing all of his subjects into due obedience, the great Angevin sovereign waged determined war upon both the rebellious nobility and the independent clergy. He was not entirely successful, especially in his conflict with the clergy; but he at least prevented a permanent reversion of the nation to feudal chaos. Furthermore, he brought the king's law into a stronger position than at any preceding time. This he did by reviving the scheme of itinerant or circuit justices, extending the use of the jury, and so developing a system of adjudication generally that his reign has been declared by a leading authority to "initiate the rule of law." [20] Sending into the counties as sheriffs men who were trained lawyers or hardy soldiers, rather than nobles of the type often employed previously, he toned up administration and extended the influence of the central government in local affairs. Commuting military service for a money payment (*scutage*), and reviving the ancient militia system (the *fyrd*), he brought the armed forces of the nation completely under control. Calling the Great Council into session more frequently, and making larger use of it generally, he contributed to the growing importance of that forerunner of Parliament.[21]

[19] W. R. Anson, *Law and Custom of the Constitution* (3rd ed.), II, Pt. i, 13.

[20] W. Stubbs, *Select Charters . . . of English Constitutional History* (8th ed., Oxford, 1895), 21. Cf. the remark of G. B. Adams: "The reign of Henry II is the first great age of constitutional advance in the history of England." *The Origin of the English Constitution,* 106.

[21] The political and legal institutions of the Norman-Angevin period are treated at greater length in G. B. Adams, *Constitutional History of England* (New York, 1921), 50-143, and *The Origin of the English Constitution,* Chaps. ii-iv; A. B. White, *The Making of the English Constitution* (rev. ed.), 72-452; H. Taylor, *Origin and Growth of the English Constitution,* I, Bk. 2, Chaps. ii-iii; W. Stubbs, *English Constitutional History,* I, 315-682, II, 1-164. Cf. C. H. Haskins, *The Normans in European History,*

The Great Charter

William the Conqueror and Henry II fell but little short of being absolute monarchs; certainly the country in their day was as definitely headed in the direction of autocracy as was any Continental state. The masterful way in which they handled affairs and the general justice of their rule (so far, at all events, as the politically important portions of the population were concerned) won them the support of a majority of their influential subjects, and if their successors had been men of like caliber there might have been a different story of English constitutional development to tell. Autocratic power, however, in the hands of weak or vicious kings—notably Henry's sons Richard I and John—provoked rebellion; and after John, by a series of highhanded acts and humiliating surrenders, had alienated most of his support, the strong men of the country took advantage of his predicament to place in his hands a lengthy list of demands for reform, with the alternative of civil war if he refused them. Evasion proved possible for a brief time only; and on June 15, 1215, in the plain of Runnymede, between London and Windsor, the document in which the terms were set forth—*Magna Carta,* the Great Charter, it has ever since been called—was agreed to on both sides. It was not "signed" in the usual sense of the term; John could not write his name, and few if any of his opponents were more proficient. But the same purpose was served by the affixing of the great seal of the realm and of the individual seals of the victorious barons.

Bishop Stubbs once said of the Charter that the whole of English constitutional history is merely one long commentary upon it, and writers and orators often refer to the document as

Chap. iii. On the Great Council and Curia Regis, see also G. B. Adams, *Council and Courts in Anglo-Norman England,* Chaps. i, ii, iv, and on the sheriff, W. A. Morris, *The Medieval English Sheriff* (Manchester, 1927). The government of the duchy of Normandy, bearing much interesting relation to Norman rule in England, is treated in scholarly fashion in C. H. Haskins, *Norman Institutions* (Cambridge, 1925). General narratives will be found in T. F. Tout, *History of England from the Accession of Henry III to the Death of Edward III, 1216-1377* (London, 1905), and H. W. C. Davis, *England under the Normans and the Angevins* (London, 1904).

the most important one of a political nature in all English history, if not in the history of the world. These estimates do not greatly exceed the truth. It is, however, necessary to observe rather carefully wherein the instrument's real importance lay. In the first place, the Charter, being intended primarily as a statement of existing feudal law, contained little that was new. To some extent, the principles and usages that found expression in the document went back to Saxon times—to Edward the Confessor, and even to Alfred. To a large extent, they had been set forth in a comprehensive charter of liberties granted by Henry I at his accession in 1100.[22] There was no thought of a new form of government, or of a new code of law, but only of a redress of the grievances flowing from the misrule of Richard and John. Not a new system of law, but good government under an old one, was the object. In the second place, the rights claimed in the Charter were not peculiar to England; on the contrary, almost every one was recognized in the contemporary law of France and of most other Continental states.[23] Finally, it must not be forgotten that the agreement was wrested from the king, not by "the people" in any literal sense, but by a single baronial class—by a handful of strong men whose object, naturally, was to secure as large advantages for themselves as they could get. Hence it re-stated the feudal obligations and customs which late kings had ignored; it stipulated that no earl or baron should be fined except by judgment of his peers, and in proportion to his offense; it forbade issuance of writs removing cases from private courts to a king's court; it prescribed that no new tax or feudal "aid" should be laid except with the assent of the Great Council, which, as we have seen, consisted chiefly of the very men who obtained the Charter; and it actually undertook to provide a lawful way by which the barons could proceed against the king, with arms if necessary, in order to compel him to keep his promises. Few of the provisions pertained in any direct fashion to the rights and liberties of humbler folk.[24]

[22] G. B. Adams and H. M. Stephens, *Select Documents of English Constitutional History* (New York, 1906), 4-6.

[23] G. B. Adams, *Constitutional History of England,* 128.

[24] E. Jenks, "The Myth of Magna Carta," *Independent Rev.,* IV, 260 ff.

And yet, the Charter was tremendously important, for three or four main reasons. First, if England was to go on developing as a nation ruled by law rather than by caprice, it was essential that somebody should take the situation in hand, call the tyrannical kings to account, and hold them to their contracts. Only the barons were as yet powerful enough to do this. From the Conquest to 1215, the whole trend was toward more autocratic and powerful, rather than more limited, monarchy. After that date, however, it came to be a cardinal principle of the English constitution that there is a body of law above the king which he may be compelled to obey if he will not do so voluntarily. The Charter not only voiced this principle but went far toward converting it from a mere feudal rule into a rule of the national constitution that was to be. Second, the Charter was, after all, by no means devoid of provisions that were in the interest of other people besides the barons. The rights of the church surviving the Conquest were guaranteed; cities, boroughs, and villages were pledged their "ancient liberties;" security of property and trade was protected; buying and selling of justice was prohibited; and barons and clergy were pledged to extend to their dependents the same "customs and franchises" that they were themselves promised by their lord, the sovereign.

Finally, the Charter has importance because of the way in which it became the age-long touchstone and bulwark of the nation's liberties. To it, as a grand recital of their rights, Englishmen habitually harked back whenever they felt that the king was breaking over the bounds that custom had fixed for him. More than one sovereign in later times was compelled to issue specific "confirmations" of the historic contract.[25] And such portions of the instrument as are still applicable—relatively few though they are—form recognizable parts of the law of the British constitution today. "What the Great Charter did," says Professor Adams, "was to lay down two fundamental principles which lie at the present day, as clearly as in 1215, at the founda-

[25] As late as 1667 a chief justice of the King's Bench was called to the bar of the House of Commons and forced to offer humble apology because in a moment of anger he had let fall a contemptuous remark about the Charter.

tion of the English constitution and of all constitutions derived from it. First, that there exist in the state certain laws so necessarily at the basis of the political organization of the time that the king, or as we should say today the government, must obey them; and second that, if the government refuses to obey these laws, the nation has the right to force it to do so, even to the point of overthrowing the government and putting another in its place. . . . In every age of English history in which the question has risen, in every crisis in the development of English liberty, this double principle is that upon which our ancestors stood and upon which, as a foundation, they built up little by little the fabric of free government under which we live." [26]

Expanding Agencies of Administration and Justice

If one were to read into the term all of its present-day meaning, it would be misleading to talk about an English "constitution" in the thirteenth century. The idea of a national constitution, or of constitutional law in our sense, was quite beyond the barons of Runnymede. Nevertheless, the elements were gradually being assembled out of which a constitution could be, and was, made; and during the next two or three hundred years the country moved steadily toward this objective, even though by no conscious design. Of chief importance in further preparing

[26] *Constitutional History of England,* 138-139. Chap. v of this book, and the same author's *Origin of the English Constitution,* Chaps. iv-viii, afford excellent reading on the subject. The second of these volumes is devoted mainly to showing how it was that, whereas England started with constitutional equipment practically identical with that of France, the former came out of the Middle Ages with a limited, and the latter with an absolute, monarchy (see p. 150). Professor Adams's latest published discussion of the subject is *Council and Courts in Anglo-Norman England,* Chap. ix. The Latin text of the Charter is printed in W. Stubbs, *Select Charters,* 296-306. English versions will be found in G. B. Adams and H. M. Stephens, *Select Documents of English Constitutional History,* 42-52, and Univ. of Pa. *Translations and Reprints* (translation by E. P. Cheyney), I, No. 6. The principal special work on the subject is W. S. McKechnie, *Magna Carta; a Commentary on the Great Charter of King John* (Glasgow, 1905). H. E. Malden (ed.). *Magna Carta Commemoration Essays* (London, 1917), is also of interest, and the history of the Charter as a document during the thirteenth century is well told in F. Thompson, *The First Century of Magna Carta: Why it Persisted as a Document* (Minneapolis, 1925).

the way in this period were two cardinal developments. The first was the emergence of separate, permanent central organs of administration and justice. The second was the rise of Parliament.

It will be recalled that the Curia Regis was an inner circle composed of the more or less professionalized members of the Great Council. Meeting only infrequently and for brief periods, the Council saw more and more of its administrative and judicial labors pass into the hands of the smaller, actively working body, and eventually it practically lost such functions on its own part altogether. It did not cease to exist, indeed, or lose its importance. It simply was turned, by force of circumstances, into a different channel. It developed in a legislative direction, and, by a curious process to be described presently, ended by becoming Parliament. For a time, the Curia kept up advising the king and transacting administrative (including financial) and judicial business without any division of labor, on functional lines at all events. But the infusion of growing numbers of trained lawyers, expert financiers, and other men of special aptitudes, together with the mounting volume of matters to be attended to, inevitably suggested the economy and convenience of splitting up the Curia's multifarious duties into segments and developing a distinct branch or section to take charge of each. It is not meant to imply that anybody ever planned out such a reorganization, as a modern economy and efficiency commission might do it. What happened was simply that by slow and intermittent stages, with chance circumstance playing no small part, there were finally split off from the Curia four great judicial organs, namely, the courts of (1) Exchequer, (2) Common Pleas, (3) King's Bench, and (4) Chancery. Although greatly modified by the effects of time, all of these appear in the English governmental system today.[27]

Advisory functions and general administrative work remained in the hands of that portion of the Curia not drawn off in judicial directions. Under the newer name of the Permanent Council, this body went along for generations. But by the time of Henry VI (1422-61) it had grown so large as to be unwork-

[27] See Chap. xxvi below.

able, and what ultimately happened was that, precisely as the Permanent Council and its parent, the Curia Regis, had been derived by a sort of automatic selection from the original Great Council, so from the overgrown Permanent Council was split off, in the fifteenth century, a smaller and more compact administrative body known to historians as the "Privy Council."[28] By curious analogy, when, in the seventeenth and eighteenth centuries, this Privy Council grew too large for convenient use, an inner circle was, in turn, detached from it; and, although the Privy Council has never wholly disappeared, this smaller group, under the name of the cabinet, became the working head of the government as we know it today.[29]

The chain of developments by which the handling of administrative and judicial business was drawn off into the Curia Regis, and, later, the great courts derived from that body, might be supposed to have left the Great Council high and dry, portending its final dropping out of the picture. But, as has been indicated, such was by no means the case. On the contrary, the Council was saved by a parallel line of development, and not only saved but brought into a new, even if widely different sort of, importance. For, gradually gathering powers of fiscal control and general legislation, it became, in time, the great dominating organ of national government which we know today as Parliament. The Great Council is, in fact, still present in one branch of Parliament (the House of Lords) "almost exactly as it existed under Henry II."[30] How this came about—one hardly knows whether the transformation wrought or the continuity preserved is the more remarkable thing about it—requires some explanation.

[28] See p. 118 below. On the structural and functional changes affecting the Curia Regis, see G. B. Adams, *Constitutional History of England,* 230-239; E. R. Turner, *The Privy Council of England in the Seventeenth and Eighteenth Centuries* (Baltimore, 1927), I, Chap. i; A. B. White, *Making of the English Constitution* (rev. ed.), 114-119, 293-306; and M. Fitzroy, *The History of the Privy Council* (London, 1928). The principal special work is J. F. Baldwin, *The King's Council in England during the Middle Ages* (New York, 1913). T. F. Tout, *Chapters in the Administrative History of Medieval England* (Manchester, 1920), is a mine of information.

[29] See pp. 47-53 below.

[30] G. B. Adams, *Constitutional History of England,* 169.

The Rise of Parliament

To come at once to the plot of the story, Parliament as we know it arose through the broadening out of the old Council by the introduction of chosen representatives of certain newer elements of English society, followed by the gravitation of the resulting heterogeneous mass of members into two distinct branches or houses, Lords and Commons. Nobody planned it in advance; to this day, even the organization in two houses is merely a matter of custom, enjoined by no positive law. To review the stages or steps very briefly, the development begins —for all practical purposes—when King John, hard pressed by both domestic and foreign difficulties, addressed writs to the sheriffs in 1213 ordering that four "discreet knights" be sent from each county to attend a meeting of the Great Council at Oxford. The point to this procedure was that the king, in straits for money, had decided to reach down to the lesser landholders, who in the aggregate held much of the wealth of the country, and require them to agree to a royal levy upon their possessions; and since they were too numerous to be assembled *en masse,* the plan was hit upon of having them designate in each shire four of their number to go to Oxford to speak for them. The expedient did not save the situation for John; but it held a good deal of promise and was not forgotten.

Henry III, urgently needing money for his wars in Gascony, was glad to follow the same plan in 1254, and two knights from each county sat in the "parliament" convoked in that year.[31] The desired grants were, however, not forthcoming,

[31] It must be noted that the central and indispensable part of such a parliament was the Council. Anything that the parliament could do the Council itself could do quite independently. A parliament was simply a Council meeting—the "King's Council in Parliament"——attended by elements not ordinarily present; and for a long time the Council was free to go right on with its business "in parliament" after the outsiders had departed for their homes. For that matter, the term "parliament" long had so indefinite a meaning as to be applied to meetings indiscriminately, whether or not representatives of counties or boroughs were present. The word comes, of course, from the French *parler,* "to speak." Originally it signified the talk itself, but by degrees it came to be applied to the body of persons assembled for conference. In the form *parlement,* the term appears prominently in French institutional history, but as denoting a court of law rather than, as in English-speaking lands, a legislature. In point of fact, the English Parliament, too, was originally conceived of as primarily a court.

and king and barons fell to quarreling, and eventually to fighting, with the result that in 1264 the barons were victorious at Lewes and their leader, the foreign-born Simon de Montfort, emerged as regent of the country. No less in need of money than the king himself, Montfort thereupon convened a parliament in 1265 which was attended not only by the barons, clergy, and two knights from each shire, but also by two burgesses from each of twenty-one boroughs known to be friendly to the barons' cause. Of course the proceeding was revolutionary; and the gathering was only a partisan conclave, which, so far as we know, the regent had no expectation of convoking a second time. To say that Earl Simon was the Father of the House of Commons is to give him rather more than his due. Nevertheless, the meeting for which he was responsible brought the towns into a form of coöperation with barons, clergy, and country gentry not previously attempted, and came nearer to being a genuine national assembly than anything theretofore known.

During the next thirty years several parliaments were held, although apparently none in which the boroughs were represented. But the practice was fast establishing itself, and in 1295 it received notable impetus from the so-called "Model Parliament" of Edward I.[32] Once more the king was engaged in war and needed money; and once more, as in 1265, all elements of the nation in a position to help were called upon—barons, clergy, knights of the shire, and burgesses—with the result that the gathering was by far the largest and most representative that had been held. Two archbishops, eighteen bishops, sixty-six abbots, three heads of religious orders, nine earls, forty-one barons, sixty-one knights of the shire, and 172 citizens and burgesses from the cities and boroughs—upwards of 400 persons in all—were present. The councillors were there,

[32] This parliament was a "model" only in that it summed up the progress of the past and embodied an unusually complete representation of the nation. Only three of Edward's twenty later parliaments contained representatives of the counties and towns. Eventually, however, the plan of 1295, in its essential features, became a matter of regular practice. The parliaments of Edward I are discussed at length in D. Pasquet, *An Essay on the Origins of the House of Commons,* trans. by R. G. D. Laffan and with preface and notes by G. Lapsley (Cambridge, 1925), chaps. iii-iv.

as usual, but they were only a handful as compared with the outsiders brought in to deliberate with them.

Thereafter "Parliament" rapidly became a regular feature of the governmental system. It was, of course, at no time definitely "established;" it merely grew up—by nobody's planning in advance—because the kings found occasional meetings of the kind useful for their purposes. Certainly the plan of calling in representatives of the counties and boroughs to participate in the public business along with the councillors flowed from no popular movement or demand. Parliament did not "break out" spontaneously, as we are told the Virginia House of Burgesses did in 1619. On the contrary, knights and burgesses took their places along with the magnates grudgingly, under the impact of royal command, knowing full well that all that was expected of them was that they obediently saddle themselves and their fellows with new tax burdens.[33] The day was still far distant when representation was to be regarded as a privilege, a benefit and source of power. Fundamentally, knights and citizens and burgesses were brought in because they represented two great classes or groups in English society which by the thirteenth century had so grown in numbers, resources, and prosperity as to make them nearly, if not quite, as good subjects for taxation as the nobles and churchmen. The object was not popular, or democratic, government; it was merely increase of the royal revenues.

The introduction of the representative principle, even under circumstances such as these, was, however, a matter of the utmost significance. Much study has been devoted to the origins of representative institutions, and scholars continue to disagree on the subject. But at all events it was in England that the representative idea first took root, and it was the upbuilding of Parliament on representative lines that has given that country its proud position as the mother of representative government. The representative principle was not altogether a novelty when we first hear of it as a feature of thirteenth-century par-

[33] This involuntary basis of the commoners' presence in the meetings is suggested etymologically by the fact that "common," "community," and similar terms are derived from the Latin *communis,* meaning "bound" or "obligated."

liaments.[34] Although there is no reason to believe that it was known to the Germans before the migrations, it was employed in a limited way, as we have seen, in Anglo-Saxon local government. It was used extensively by the church, notably by the Dominican order, whose organization covered the country by 1250. And it was unmistakably involved in the practice—common in the twelfth and thirteenth centuries—of electing assessors to fix the value of real and personal property for purposes of taxation, and jurors to present criminal matters before the king's justices. The Great Council contained no elective, representative elements; and Magna Carta's provision that the Council's advice should be sought before new taxes were levied was not meant to institute a representative system. Already, however, the advantages to be derived by enlisting the active co-operation of all substantial elements of the nation in meeting the fiscal needs of the government were becoming apparent; and what happened was simply that, under the impetus supplied by royal embarrassment, the principle of popular representation which lay ready to hand in the ecclesiastical organization and in the procedures of local justice and finance, and was doing good service in both, was carried over into the domain of national affairs and gradually given a permanent place in the growing constitution. An ancient gathering of feudal magnates was by stages converted into a national parliamentary assembly.[35]

[34] The best survey of the origins of representative institutions in England, and of the various theories on that subject, is H. J. Ford, *Representative Government,* Pt. i, Chaps. i-x. The author disproves at length the "Teutonic theory" originated by Turner and Kemble and brought into general vogue forty or fifty years ago by Freeman, Green, and other historians. His own views are, mainly, (1) that "representative government originated as a bud put forth by monarchy;" (2) that it developed first in England, not because people were more free there but because monarchy was stronger there than elsewhere; and (3) that in making its start it got its mode and form from the church (p. 88). In the main, the argument is convincing. The author, however, is at fault in taking no account whatever of representative institutions in the Anglo-Saxon period. Cf. A. F. Pollard, *The Evolution of Parliament,* Chap. viii, and D. Pasquet, *op. cit.* (ed. of 1925), Chap. ii.

[35] A *single, national* parliamentary assembly, be it noted; for a series of local or regional parliaments might have grown up, and in fact Edward I did set a perilous precedent in 1282 by convoking a double parliament, one for the north and the other for the south. It is hardly necessary to sug-

In 1295 the members of Parliament first assembled as one body, but afterwards broke into three groups or "estates"—nobles, clergy, and commons—to hear separately the king's plea for money and to make such response as they individually chose; and when the three fell into the way of meeting, as well as transacting business, apart from one another, they seemed to be on the road to developing into a tricameral, or three-house, assemblage, just as did the contemporary Estates General of France. Had that happened, the nobles and clergy—after the point was reached where all of the groups were expected to act upon the same questions and proposals—would very likely have outvoted the commoners on most matters, just as the corresponding orders usually did in France; and that would have cut the commoners out of any real chance for control.

Gradually, however, practical interests led to a different arrangement. Already accustomed to sit and work together in the Great Council, and having many interests in common, the greater barons and greater clergy easily coalesced in a single body; the greater clergy, it must be remembered, were not simply clerics, but feudal lords and landholders. The lesser clergy, deriving no clear benefit from attendance, and preferring to vote their contributions in the special ecclesiastical assemblages known as the convocations of Canterbury and York, dropped out. Similarly, the lesser barons, after wavering between the major and the minor aristocracy, found their interests essentially identical with those of the latter, i.e., the country freeholders, represented by the knights of the shire, and with those of the burgesses. The upshot was a gradual realign-

gest that had permanent development been on these lines, the results would have been very different from those which followed the rise of a single parliament for the whole nation. England's parliamentary history would probably not have been any more impressive than that of Spain, Prussia, or pre-revolutionary France. On medieval estates and their relation to the development of representative parliaments, see R. Muir, *National Self-Government* (New York, 1918), Chap. ii. Cf. A. F. Pollard, *The Evolution of Parliament,* Chap. vii. In these days of keen interest in occupational or functional, as opposed to geographical, representation, it is worth while to note that in the fourteenth century Parliament, then in the making, wavered between these same two principles—that of locality and that of function or vocation. In the outcome, the one principle triumphed in the House of Commons and the other in the House of Lords.

ment of the membership in two great groups, of which one became the House of Lords, the other the House of Commons —the one composed of men who attended in response to an individual summons, the other of persons who attended in a representative capacity. The former practically perpetuated the Great Council of feudal times; the latter was composed mainly of the new elements representing the non-feudal classes. By the close of the reign of Edward III (1377) this bicameral, or two-house, organization seems to have been complete. It arose, not from any definite opinion that two houses are better than one or than three, nor indeed from any clear plan or purpose, but rather by force of social and economic circumstances, and especially because of the failure of the church as a whole to insist upon maintaining a separate and coördinate position on Continental lines.[36] The whole course of English history since the fourteenth century, however, has been profoundly affected by the fact that the national assembly thus took the form of two houses rather than one, as did the Scottish, of three as did the French, or of four as did the Swedish; and not only English history has been affected, but constitutional development the world over, since the bicameral system found almost everywhere today is traceable, directly or indirectly, to English influence and example.

The most striking feature of the British system of government today is the vast powers possessed by Parliament. But this has been a matter of long development, principally since the seventeenth century, and at the outset there was hardly any power at all in the body as a whole. This appears clearly enough from contemporary accounts of how the few, irregular meetings of the early fourteenth century were conducted. The usual meeting place was the Great Hall of the Palace of Westminster,

[36] G. B. Adams, *Constitutional History of England,* 194-195. The beginnings of the House of Commons are described in a scholarly manner in A. F. Pollard, *The Evolution of Parliament,* Chap. vi; A. B. White, *Making of the English Constitution* (rev. ed.), 346-396; Adams, *op. cit.,* Chaps. vii-viii; and D. Pasquet, *op. cit.* The last-mentioned book contributed heavily to the overthrow of traditional views on parliamentary beginnings as set forth in the writings of such authorities as Hallam and Stubbs. The new edition sketches the results of work done on the subject since about 1885.

dating from the reign of William Rufus.[37] Here, when a parliament was convened, the king took his place upon a throne surrounded by his councillors, and faced by the bishops and barons seated in rows. Standing at the rear were to be seen the lowly knights and burgesses.[38] Business was presented by the king exclusively, usually by the voice of his chancellor; and at suitable intervals the three groups of members—two after the bicameral arrangement came in—retired to deliberate. Many matters were considered by the magnates that were never referred to the commons at all; and beyond making their replies, through a spokesman who becomes the prototype of the modern speaker, the commoners, whose presence seemed to be endured rather than enjoyed, had little opportunity to make themselves heard.

The same general conditions, however, that had led to bringing in the knights and burgesses in the first place operated to give them a gradually increasing importance. First of all, they gained the power of controlling, and eventually also initiating, financial actions. Omitting details, we may note that just a hundred years after Edward I's Model Parliament, the formula appeared which is used to this day in making parliamentary grants, i.e., "by the Commons with the advice and assent of the Lords Spiritual and Temporal;" also that in 1407 Henry IV gave formal consent to the principle that money grants should be initiated by the commoners, agreed to by the lords, and only then reported to the king. Already that mighty lever in public business, the power of the purse, had come into the grasp of the popular branch.[39]

Likewise with legislation. Originally, Parliament was not a law-making body at all; such laws as were made still emanated from the king, with the assent of his councillors only.[40] But,

[37] The Palace ceased to be a royal residence in the reign of Henry VIII, although it is still such nominally. The Great Hall was saved from the fire of 1834 and stands today practically as in the Middle Ages. See p. 364 below.

[38] The picturesque ceremony of opening a parliament today preserves features dating from these early times. See p. 371 below.

[39] H. J. Robinson, *The Power of the Purse; a Brief Study of Constitutional History* (London, 1928).

[40] As late as the Tudor period, Parliament—retaining then, as it does even yet to some degree, the varied functions of the old Council—was

starting with a mere right of individual commoners to present petitions, the commons as a body gained, first the right to present united petitions, and later the right to help give their requests the form of law. The costs of government and war compelled the king to appeal to Parliament for supplies; before supplies could be had he, in turn, was likely to be called upon through petitions for a redress of grievances; and this usually meant some kind of legislation, with the result that both the taxing power and the law-making power passed into parliamentary hands. Late in the fourteenth century laws were still being enacted *by* the king with the *assent* of the lords at the *request* of the commoners, and it often happened that the completed measure was something very different from the original request on which it was based. In 1414 Henry V granted that "from henceforth nothing be enacted to the petitions of his commons that be contrary to their asking, whereby they should be bound without their assent." [41] The rule was often violated; but late in the reign of Henry VI (1422-61) a change of procedure was brought about under which measures were henceforth to be introduced in either house in the form of drafted bills. Statutes now began to be made "by the King's [or Queen's] most Excellent Majesty by and with the advice and consent of the Lords Spiritual and Temporal, and Commons, in this present Parliament assembled, and by the authority of the same;" and every act of Parliament begins with these words today unless passed under the terms of the Parliament Act of 1911, in which case mention of the Lords is omitted.[42] Once merely a modest petitioner for laws redressing grievances, the House of Commons, by the end of the fifteenth century, had become—legally at all events—a coördinate law-making assemblage.[43]

thought of as primarily a court rather than a legislature. It was still in reality the "High Court of Parliament." See C. H. McIlwain, *The High Court of Parliament and its Supremacy: an Historical Essay on the Boundaries between Legislation and Adjudication in England* (New Haven, 1910), Chaps., iii-iv.

[41] G. B. Adams and H. M. Stephens, *Select Documents of English Constitutional History,* 182.

[42] See p. 342 below.

[43] The best general history of Parliament is A. F. Pollard, *Evolution of Parliament,* although the author says of the book that it is "less a history of

Parliament than a suggestion of the lines upon which it should be written." The treatment is rather topical than strictly chronological. Good accounts of parliamentary beginnings are G. B. Adams, *Constitutional History of England,* 169-215; W. Stubbs, *Constitutional History,* II, Chaps. XV, XVII; D. J. Medley, *Students' Manual of English Constitutional History* (6th ed.), 137-188; H. Taylor, *Origins and Growth of the English Constitution,* I, 428-616; and A. B. White, *The Making of the English Constitution* (rev. ed.), 337-452. Cf. C. H. McIlwain, *The High Court of Parliament and its Supremacy,* Chap. i.

CHAPTER II

CONSTITUTIONAL DEVELOPMENT

In the year 1485 a long dreary period of civil strife was brought to a close by the victory of Henry of Lancaster over his Yorkist foes on Bosworth Field, followed by his accession as Henry VII, first of a new and illustrious line of monarchs, the Tudors. The Wars of the Roses had really been nothing more than a struggle between rival groups of nobles, with the crown as a pawn. But they kept the country in wasteful disorder and left the people prepared to support any government that was strong enough to keep peace and protect life and property. Such a government the rule of the Tudors quickly proved to be; and through five successive reigns, closing with the death of Elizabeth in 1603, it enjoyed the nation's confidence and respect as well as obedience.

Tudor Government

Speaking broadly, one may say that by 1485 the great institutional foundations of the modern British constitution had been laid, and that what came after that date was in the nature of further growth and elaboration of these institutions, and especially the working out of new relations among them, leading to altered balances of power and mechanisms of control. Already, kingship rested upon the secure foundations of centuries of sovereign authority. The common law had reached an advanced stage of development. The high courts of justice which we know today were functioning actively. The sheriffs and other administrative agencies were at work. County and borough courts were serving both as organs of local self-government and as instrumentalities of central control. The House of Lords, composed of some 150 principal tenants of the crown, lay and ecclesiastical, was, by virtue of its continuity with the earlier Great Council, a vigorous and powerful body. The House of Commons, numbering now some 300 knights and burgesses, had won recognition for the principle that no new taxes might be laid without its consent and had gained considerable powers of general legislation.[1] A long road was to be travelled before these various instrumentalities of government and law should have been fitted into their present positions in the British constitutional system. But their existence at so remote a day shows us how necessary it is for one who would understand that system to take a long look backward across the centuries when he begins.

Tudor days were not themselves a period of great outward change. In a sense, they were a time of reaction, at all events of consolidation of the governmental system as it had stood in earlier generations. The thing chiefly notable about them is the vigorous rule of Henry VII, Henry VIII, and Elizabeth—monarchs who were powerful enough to impose their will unsparingly on the nation and tactful enough to do it in ways that stirred a minimum of resentment and opposition. Existing machinery of royal rule was utilized to the full, and some new devices were introduced. In particular, the Privy Council (derived, as has been seen, from the Great Council of former centuries) was employed as an agency of centralized control over economic life, the church, justice, and administration.[2] Its ordinances, issued in the name of the crown, had the practical effect of law. And various new bodies of the kind—notably Henry VII's Court of Star Chamber and Elizabeth's Court of High Commission—wielded judicial and other powers so sweeping as to give some point to the characterization of Tudor

[1] The county members were elected by the freeholders attending the county court, under the restriction, after 1429, that they must be able to show that their lands had a rental value of forty shillings a year (equivalent, perhaps, to £30 or £40 in present values). Borough members were chosen originally by the "freemen of the town;" though as time went on the right of suffrage was restricted, in most places, to smaller numbers of people, even occasionally to members of a particular guild. See pp. 248-250 below.

[2] E. R. Turner, *The Privy Council of England in the Seventeenth and Eighteenth Centuries,* I, Chaps. ii-iii; A. F. Pollard, "Council, Star Chamber, and Privy Council under the Tudors," *Eng. Hist. Rev.,* July, Oct., 1922, and Jan. 1923; E. Percy, *The Privy Council under the Tudors* (Oxford, 1907).

government as "government by council."[3] Parliament, of course, survived, but it placed no very serious obstacles in the pathway of royal despotism. The center of gravity lay in the aristocratic House of Lords, which in most matters could be depended upon to see eye to eye with the king; and if the commoners developed a will of their own, there were ways of bringing them to terms. There was an obvious tactical advantage in having the great policies upon which the crown was bent (the separation from Rome, for example, under Henry VIII) cast into the form of statutes. This gave them the appearance of being the decisions of the nation, and not simply of the king. No Tudor would have cared to dispense with Parliament, even if he could safely have done so. It was too useful. But it was useful in proportion as it was a tool; and independent-minded commoners were habitually threatened, bullied, and otherwise coerced into confining themselves to the rôle which belonged to them in the monarch's general scheme of things. Freedom of speech, freedom from arrest, and other immunities of the present-day parliamentarian found scant recognition. Sessions were infrequent and brief,[4] and elections—held only when conditions were considered favorable—were often shamelessly manipulated by royal agents to prevent them from going against the king. A parliament that proved amenable was likely to be kept for years; one that showed independence was summarily dismissed. After all, laws that Parliament could not be induced to pass could be contrived through royal proclamations; and the sources of revenue over which Parliament as yet had no control were so numerous that the government could be carried on for years without a subsidy.

On these lines, the nation was governed firmly, but also most of the time wisely; and, in the main, it was content. Parliament

[3] A. T. Carter, *Outlines of English Legal History* (London, 1899), Chap. xii; A. Todd, *Parliamentary Government in England,* ed. by S. Walpole (London, 1892), I, Chap. ii; R. G. Usher, *The Rise and Fall of the High Commission* (Oxford, 1913). Cf. p. 19 above.

[4] Even during the forty-five years of Elizabeth, when Parliament counted for more than earlier, the houses were in session, in the aggregate, something less than three years, an average for the reign of slightly over three weeks a year. One of the ten parliaments of this reign lasted eleven years, but met only three times.

did not rule. But Englishmen as yet had no notion of a scheme of polity under which it should do so. So far as they could see, the alternative to strong royal government was, not parliamentary rule, but baronial anarchy, such as that from which the vigor of the Tudors had delivered them; and they had no mind to live through that sort of thing again. Paternalistic, and even despotic, as it was, the Tudor monarchy "rested on the willing support of the nation at large, a support due to the deeply rooted conviction that a strong executive was necessary to the national unity, and that, in the face of the dangers which threatened the country both at home and abroad, the sovereign must be allowed a free hand." [5] Royal self-interest and public well-being happened to run in the same channel.

The succeeding period of the Stuart kings (1603-88) brought, however, a very different situation. For more than a hundred years the country, although stirred by religious controversies, had enjoyed political unity and peace, and the danger of reversion to feudal chaos was no longer felt. Strong monarchy had served a useful purpose, but that purpose seemed now to have been largely fulfilled. In a quiet way, Parliament had been steadily developing as a medium for the expression of broadly national, as well as merely personal and class, interests and opinions. As a result of the suppression of the monasteries by Henry VIII, the House of Lords became for the first time a predominantly secular body, and in various ways—chiefly the enfranchisement of new counties and boroughs—the House of Commons was increased in membership by more than a third. Not infrequently, particular boroughs were selected for separate representation for the reason that their spokesmen could be depended upon to support the policies of the crown; Elizabeth was especially guilty of this sort of favoritism. Yet, in general, the explanation of the greatly increased borough representation is simply the growing population and prosperity of the country and the disposition of the Tudors to ground their government fundamentally upon the support of the commercial and industrial elements of the population. Not only in numbers, but also in spirit and morale, the House of

[5] G. W. Prothero, *Select Statutes and Other Constitutional Documents Illustrative of the Reigns of Elizabeth and James I* (Oxford, 1898), p. xvii.

Commons made steady progress in the Tudor period. Toward the end, there was a tendency to increased frequency of meetings and longer sessions, and this gave members a better chance to develop common viewpoints and the habit of working together; and Elizabeth found it expedient to consult Parliament and at least make a show of deferring to its judgment to a greater extent than did any of her predecessors. Tense situations that rose during the last ten years of her reign showed that her successor would have to be a person of discernment and tact, else he would run perilously afoul of the rising sense of importance and independence which the Commons now felt as mouthpiece of a prosperous and spirited nation.[6]

Constitutional Conflicts in the Seventeenth Century

It so happened that Elizabeth's successor, James VI of Scotland, who in 1603 became James I of England, was not a person of either discernment (though clever enough in some respects) or tact. As might have been expected, his sturdy insistence upon absolutist rule, based upon divine right, promptly brought to a head the already ripening issue between autocracy and constitutional government; and a chain of events was started that found no terminus until the Stuarts had been driven from the throne and parliamentary supremacy completely vindicated. The Stuart point of view was clearly enough set forth in a pedantic tract, entitled *The True Law of Free Monarchies* which

[6] The constitutional system of the Tudor period is well described in G. B. Adams, *Constitutional History of England,* 240-264, and more fully in H. Taylor, *English Constitution,* II, Bk. IV, and T. Taswell-Langmead, *English Constitutional History,* Chaps. x, xii. Much information can be gleaned from A. F. Pollard, *Evolution of Parliament, passim,* and the growth of the House of Commons is described in R. G. Usher, *Institutional History of the House of Commons, 1547-1641* (St. Louis, 1924), and W. Notestein, *The Winning of Initiative by the House of Commons* (London, 1926). An excellent survey of English public law at the death of Henry VII is contained in F. W. Maitland, *Constitutional History of England* (Cambridge, 1909), 165-236. The general history of the period may be read in H. A. L. Fisher, *History of England from the Accession of Henry VII to the Death of Henry VIII* (London, 1906); A. F. Pollard, *History of England from the Accession of Edward VI to the Death of Elizabeth* (London, 1910); and A. D. Innis, *England under the Tudors* (London, 1905). A. F. Pollard, *Henry VIII* (London, 1902), is an informing biography.

James himself wrote shortly before his accession.[7] The sovereign, so ran the argument, rules by the will of God; his subjects have no recourse against him; if tyranny is a menace, anarchy is still more to be feared; there is no appeal against tyranny save to God. As James bluntly put it a few years later in a speech before Parliament, "Monarchy is the supremest thing upon earth. . . . As to dispute what God may do is blasphemy, . . . so is it sedition in subjects to dispute what a king may do in the height of his power." [8] This was not altogether novel doctrine. Certainly Henry VIII and Elizabeth would have found something in it to approve. But they would have had the good sense to be content with the substance of power, without proclaiming from the housetops principles or theories which were bound to be unpopular.

For by the opening of the seventeenth century there were plenty of people to take strong exception to James's ideas. The purport of his doctrine was that the king was independent, irresponsible, outside the pale of law; whereas the principle had long been developing that, though subject to no man, the sovereign was bound equally with other men by the law. Glanvil and Bracton, great legal writers of the twelfth and thirteenth centuries, had plainly said so; and shortly before the Tudor period, Sir John Fortescue, titular chancellor of Henry VI though he was, had written a book expounding the advantages in the English system of polity accruing from the fact that the king could make law and lay taxes only with the consent of the estates of the realm, and that the judges were sworn to act according to the law of the land even though the king commanded to the contrary.[9] In the Roman system, as reflected in contemporary France and other Continental countries, said the writer, it was the will of the prince that made law, whereas in the English system the will of the prince was only a single

[7] C. McIlwain, *Political Writings of James I* (Cambridge, 1919). See J. N. Figgis, *The Theory of the Divine Right of Kings* (Cambridge, 1896), and H. J. Laski, "The Political Ideas of James I," *Polit. Sci. Quar.*, June, 1919.

[8] G. W. Prothero, *Select Statutes and Constitutional Documents*, 293-304.

[9] *De Laudibus Legum Angliae* ("On the Excellence of the Laws of England"). On Fortescue's political writings, see W. A. Dunning, *Political Theories from Luther to Montesquieu* (New York, 1905), 201-205.

and subordinate element. Tudor high-handedness by no means banished this view of things from the popular mind, and James's pronouncements were challenged from the first, notably by the great jurist Coke in decisions asserting the unrestricted supremacy of law as against the king equally with the least important subject.[10]

If the king was to be held to observance of the law, who was to apply the necessary compulsion? And if he was not to be permitted any longer to take liberties with the substance of the law itself, through his power of proclamation, who was to make and amend law hereafter? The answer to both questions was, of course, obvious: the nation, as represented in Parliament. And the first Stuart had not proceeded far before issue was squarely joined between a king determined to go on with a virtual absolutism and a parliament determined that the king should be limited by law. For three hundred years the claim of Parliament to a controlling voice in taxation and other public matters had been gradually growing more definite and insistent, and now the time had come to assert that claim unqualifiedly, and even to force the nation into civil war in the effort to make it good. Back in the days of Elizabeth, a court secretary, Sir Thomas Smith, had been bold enough to assert that "all that the people of Rome might do, either *Centuriatis Committiis* or *Tributis,* the same may be done by the Parliament of England, which representeth and hath the whole power of the realm, both the head and body." [11] When written, this was rather ahead of the times. But the seventeenth century was to see it become literal truth.

The relations of James and his parliaments were stormy enough. A complete break, however, was staved off until Charles, having got along for eleven years without any parliament at all, was driven by his Scottish wars to resort to the houses for funds. Then the angry controversy came to a head, and the greatest civil war in the country's history was waged to determine whose theory of the constitution was to prevail.

[10] See the Case of Proclamations, reported in B. A. Bicknell, *Cases on the Law of the Constitution* (London, 1926), 6-7.

[11] *De Republica Anglorum; the Maner of Government or Policie of the Realme of England.* There is a convenient edition of this book by L. Ashton (Cambridge, 1906).

Even in 1640 when the Long Parliament began its strenuous work, and in 1642 when the king raised his standard at Nottingham, the parliamentary party had no intention of setting up a government by Parliament alone, in form or in fact. The Grand Remonstrance of 1641 [12] shows that what it had in mind was only to compel the king to live up to the law in such matters as taxation and justice, and to carry out certain "reforms" like the abolition of episcopacy. The military victories of the next few years, however, and the unforeseen shifts of circumstance and opinion, threw open the doors for every sort of constitutional innovation, and between 1649 and 1660 the nation was carried along on a tide of political experimentation such as it had never known and has not witnessed since. Charles having been executed, and kingship and the House of Lords having been abolished, as equally "useless and dangerous," [13] Parliament formally proclaimed a "commonwealth," or republic, in 1649; and on the great seal was inscribed the legend, "In the first year of freedom by God's blessing restored."

Like revolutionists everywhere, seventeenth-century Englishmen found it easier to destroy than to build. All manner of schemes were brought forward for equipping the Commonwealth with a coherent and permanent frame of government. Radical-minded elements in the army were for setting up a parliament elected by manhood suffrage.[14] Cromwell, however, and other leaders frowned on this proposal; for, whatever their precise political views, the men who held the offices and kept things going certainly were not democrats in the present-day sense of the term. They quite agreed with Thomas Baillie when he wrote that "popular government bringeth in confusion, making the feet above the head." Eventually, in 1653, a cautious, conservative frame of government was devised, under the name of the Instrument of Government; and it became the first written constitution to be put into operation in modern

[12] S. R. Gardiner, *Constitutional Documents of the Puritan Revolution* (Oxford, 1899), 202-232.

[13] *Ibid.*, 384-388.

[14] T. C. Pease, *The Leveller Movement* (Washington, 1916), especially Chaps. iii, vi.

Europe.[15] Intended to apply to Scotland and Ireland as well as England, it set up as the executive power a life "protector," assisted by a council of thirteen to twenty-one members, and as the legislative organ a one-house parliament of 460 members elected triennially by all citizens owning property to the value of £300. Cromwell accepted the office of protector; and the ensuing six years form the period commonly known as the Protectorate.

Government under the Instrument was only moderately successful. Cromwell had almost as much trouble with his parliaments as James I and Charles I had experienced with theirs, and, in particular, could not agree with them on the question of whether they had a right to revise the constitution, already felt to be unsatisfactory. In 1657 the Protector was asked to assume the title of king. This he refused to do, but he did accept a new constitution, the "Humble Petition and Advice," in which a step was taken toward a return to the governmental system swept away in 1649.[16] This step consisted principally in the reëstablishment of a parliament of two chambers—a House of Commons and, for lack of agreement upon a better name, "the Other House." [17] Republicanism, however, failed to strike root. Shrewder men, including Cromwell, had recognized from the first that the English people were monarchist at heart, and it is not putting it too strongly to say that from the start the restoration of kingship was inevitable. Even before the death of Cromwell, in 1658, the trend was decidedly in that direction, and after the hand of the great Protector was removed from the helm the change was only a question of time and means. On May 25, 1660, Charles II, the third Stuart, having engaged to grant a general amnesty and to accept such measures concerning a settlement of religion as Parliament should later agree

[15] S. R. Gardiner, *Documents of the Puritan Revolution,* 405-417; G. B. Adams and H. M. Stephens, *Select Documents of English Constitutional History,* 407-416. A constitution known as the "Agreement of the People" was drawn up by members of the army in 1647, but was never put into operation. T. C. Pease, *The Leveller Movement,* Chap. vi.

[16] S. R. Gardiner, *Documents of the Puritan Revolution,* 447-459.

[17] The country's brief and unsatisfactory experience with a unicameral parliament is described in J. A. R. Marriott, *Mechanism of the Modern State* (Oxford, 1927), I, 392-399, and *Second Chambers; An Inductive Study in Political Science* (rev. ed., Oxford, 1927), Chap. iii.

upon, landed at Dover and was received with general acclaim.[18]

Parliamentary Supremacy Established

The larger and lasting significance of the Restoration has been stated admirably by an American historian as follows: "The result in 1660 . . . was a compromise; not less truly a compromise because it was expressed in facts rather than in words. The question which had arisen at the beginning of the reign of James I, whether it would be possible to make the strong monarchy of the sixteenth century and the strong parliamentary control of the fifteenth work together in practice—what boundary line could be found between king and constitution—had been answered by the discovery of a compromise. But it was a compromise of a peculiar type. As developed in the next hundred and fifty years, it meant that form and appearance remained with the king, the reality with Parliament. The words in which the modern constitutional lawyer states the result are as accurate as can be found: 'Sovereignty resides in the king and his Parliament.' The king is in theory sovereign,

[18] An excellent analysis of the system of government which the Stuarts inherited from the Tudors is contained in the introduction to G. W. Prothero, *Select Statutes and Constitutional Documents,* pp. xvii-cxxv. A good brief account of the constitutional developments of the period 1603-60 is G. B. Adams, *Constitutional History of England,* 265-333. The executive side is treated fully in E. R. Turner, *The Privy Council of England in the Seventeenth and Eighteenth Centuries,* I, Chaps. iv-xiii. The best books on the political theory of the time are J. N. Figgis, *The Theory of the Divine Right of Kings* (Cambridge, 1896), G. P. Gooch, *History of English Democratic Ideas in the Seventeenth Century* (rev. ed., Cambridge, 1927), and T. C. Pease, *The Leveller Movement,* as cited. A satisfactory brief survey is R. G. Gettell, *History of Political Thought* (New York, 1924), Chap. xi. The best of the general histories covering the period are F. C. Montague, *History of England from the Accession of James I to the Restoration* (London, 1907), and G. M. Trevelyan, *England Under the Stuarts* (London, 1904). The monumental works are those of S. R. Gardiner, i.e., *History of England, 1603-42,* 10 vols. (new. ed., London, 1893-95); *History of the Great Civil War,* 4 vols. (London, 1894); and *History of the Commonwealth and Protectorate,* 3 vols. (London, 1894-1901). Gardiner's studies were continued by C. H. Firth, who has published *The Last Years of the Protectorate, 1656-1638,* 2 vols. (London, 1909). Of the numerous biographies of Cromwell, the best is C. H. Firth, *Oliver Cromwell* (New York, 1904). J. R. Tanner, *The Constitutional Conflicts of the Seventeenth Century* (Cambridge, 1928), is a good general survey, without particular claim to distinction.

but his sovereignty can be declared and exercised only in Parliament. The king gave up the power to determine by his individual will the policy of the state, but the surrender was disguised by an appearance of power and for a long time by the exercise of very substantial powers and the permanent possession of important rights and influence. It was more than a hundred years before all that the compromise implied was clearly recognized and the balance established at its present level. But it was really made in 1660.

"In the history of government in the world no event has ever happened of greater significance or of wider influence than the making of this compromise. Upon it depended the spread of the English constitution throughout the civilized world which is one of the chief characteristics of the nineteenth century. . . . In this respect it is difficult to overstate the influence of this compromise. Had the course of English history led to a constitution in which in form and law the ministry was directly responsible to Parliament instead of to the king, not merely would it have been immensely more difficult to reconcile the sovereign to a loss of the substance of power, but the adoption of the constitution by other and unwilling monarchies would have been made a practical impossibility. The compromise feature of the present constitution by which in theory and in form the ministry, though supreme, seems to be the creature of the king and responsible to him, would have had no existence. The choice which, without this compromise, a successful revolution might offer to a sovereign between a formal direct responsibility of all the organs of actual government to the legislative assembly on one side, and an out-and-out republic on the other, would have been an even choice with no particular attractiveness or significance. . . . The world influence of the English constitution depended for its existence upon the fact that Parliament came to control the actual government in fact rather than in form, indirectly, not directly; that an actual republic was concealed under all the ceremonial and theoretical forms of a continued monarchy." [19]

The years 1660-88 were a time of experiment, the object being to find out, once for all, whether a Stuart on the throne

[19] G. B. Adams, *Constitutional History of England,* 335-337.

could, or would, keep within the bounds fixed by the vindicated historic constitution. That Charles II (1660-85) contrived to do so most of the time was due not alone to his somewhat indolent disposition but to a political insight which enabled him to see how far it was safe to go and what the consequences of transgression would be. His brother and successor, James II (1685-88), was a man of different temper. He was a Stuart of the Stuarts, irrevocably attached to the doctrine of divine right and sufficiently tactless to take no pains to disguise the fact. He was able, industrious, and honest, but obstinate and intolerant. He began by promising to preserve "the government as by law established." But the ease with which an uprising in 1685 was suppressed deluded him into thinking that through the exemption of the Catholics from the operation of existing laws unfavorable to them he might in time realize his ambition to reestablish Roman Catholicism in England. He proceeded, therefore, to issue ordinances dispensing with statutes that Parliament had passed, to revive the arbitrary ecclesiastical Court of High Commission abolished by Parliament in 1641, and, in 1687, to promulgate a declaration of indulgence undertaking to give Catholics and Nonconformists far more freedom in religious matters than was permitted by the laws of the land.[20] Such resumptions of ancient prerogative violated, of course, the entire agreement on which the Restoration was based.

Foreseeing no relief from absolutist practices, and urged on by the birth, in 1688, of a male heir to the king, a group of leading men representing the various political elements in Parliament invited the stadtholder of Holland, William, Prince of Orange, husband of Mary, James's eldest daughter, to come over to England to aid in upholding and protecting the constitutional liberties of the realm. The result was the bloodless revolution of 1688. On November 5, William landed at Torquay and advanced toward London. Finding himself without a party, James offered vain concessions and afterwards fled to the court of his ally, Louis XIV of France; whereupon an "advisory assembly" composed of the lords, some former commoners,

[20] H. Gee and W. J. Hardy, *Documents Illustrative of English Church History*, 641-644; G. B. Adams and H. M. Stephens, *Select Documents of English Constitutional History*, 451-454.

and certain officers of state requested William to act as temporary "governor" until the people should have chosen a "convention parliament." This body—not in form a parliament, because not summoned in the regular way by a king—met on January 22, 1689, decided that James, by reason of having "withdrawn himself out of the kingdom," should be construed to have abdicated, and established William and Mary on the throne as joint sovereigns.[21] The Stuart monarchy had had its last chance.

Having had unpleasant experience with mere understandings and promises, those who had matters in hand now proceeded to make the terms of acceptance of the new dynasty "watertight" by setting them down in black and white and causing the convention to enact them, and the sovereigns to agree to them, as a "declaration of right." The convention had by now proclaimed itself a full-powered parliament. But to guard against any slip on a technicality, the body, at its second session, in February, 1689, incorporated the declaration, with some additions, in a statute and adopted it as law; and in this form it has ever since been known as the Bill of Rights.

With the possible exception of the Great Charter, the Bill of Rights is the most interesting document in English constitutional history; and, unlike the earlier instrument, most of which is now obsolete because of changed conditions, practically every line of the later one is still applicable and in full operation. It did not create a government, or prescribe the organization and powers of a government, or specify in detail the rights of citizens under a government. Like any other enactment, it could be amended or repealed by Parliament at any time. Nevertheless, as Professor Adams pointedly observes, it is "most nearly of the nature of a written constitution of anything in English history." [22] Without any attempt at theory, such as abounds in the French Declaration of Rights of 1789 and in most of the bills of rights found in American constitutions, it goes straight at the difficulties which twenty-five years of restored Stuart rule had brought to light, and, enumerating previous unlawful prac-

[21] On the legal aspects of the Revolution, see F. W. Maitland, *Constitutional History of England,* 281-288, and W. R. Anson, *Law and Custom of the Constitution* (5th ed.), I, 38-41.

[22] *Constitutional History of England,* 358. Cf. W. R. Anson, *op. cit.* (5th ed.), I, 38.

tices one by one—somewhat after the staccato manner of the American Declaration of Independence later on—forbids their repetition as unequivocally as the English language can be made to do it. It brands as "illegal," or as "illegal and pernicious," the "pretended" royal power of suspending or dispensing with laws, the levying of imposts without Parliament's assent, the arbitrary erection of royal commissions and courts, the raising or keeping of a standing army in time of peace unless Parliament agrees. Still harking back to actual abuses of past years, it affirms the right of subjects to petition the king, the right of Protestant subjects to bear arms for their own defense, the right of members of Parliament to full liberty of speech and debate.[23] It says that the election of members of Parliament ought to be "free," and that parliaments "ought to be held frequently." In short, it lays down definite constitutional rules and principles every one of which could be invoked instantly today if occasion should arise.[24] Even in the matter of succession to the throne, it imposed the limitation, still in effect, that no Catholic nor any person marrying a Catholic should be allowed to inherit.

What the Bill of Rights therefore did was to sum up, very concretely, the results of the Revolution and of the entire seventeenth-century liberal movement, and to put them in legal form so unmistakable that they could never again be misunderstood or challenged. The document, and the political overturn that lay behind it, marks the culmination of the country's constitutional development; all that followed was but the detailed application of established principles, the elaboration of the machinery of the finally vindicated and irresistible parliamentary control. The sovereignty of the nation, the supremacy

[23] Already on the statute book was the Habeas Corpus Act of 1679, which guaranteed the right of an individual, upon arrest, to have his case investigated without delay. The text is in G. B. Adams and H. M. Stephens, *Select Documents of English Constitutional History,* 440-448, and comment will be found in E. Jenks, *Select Essays on Anglo-American Legal History* (Boston, 1908), II, Chap. XXXV.

[24] A related measure is the Toleration Act of May 24, 1689, which provided "some ease to scrupulous consciences in the exercise of religion," i.e., a larger measure of liberty for Protestant Nonconformists. Adams and Stephens, *op. cit.,* 459-462; H. Gee and W. J. Hardy, *Documents Illustrative of English Church History,* 654-664.

of law, the legal omnipotence of Parliament—no one of these was ever again called in question by any persons or elements of sufficient strength to threaten the work that had been accomplished. Kingship went on, regarded, indeed, as a natural and useful institution. But henceforth the royal tenure was not by inherent or absolute right; on the contrary, it was conditioned upon the consent of the nation as expressed through Parliament. For all practical purposes, divine right was dead.[25]

Surviving Problem of Relations Between Crown and Parliament

The events of 1688-89 marked the culmination of English constitutional development truly enough in the sense that the cardinal principles which make the system what it is today were then put beyond danger of successful challenge. But of course there has been a great deal of constitutional development since. Many rules and practices that go to make up the working constitution as we now observe it date from within the past two hundred years. Much present-day machinery, too, is relatively new. To follow the introduction and readjustment of institutions, rules, devices, and methods continuously through to 1929 is not desirable at this point, because most of them will have to be dealt with rather fully later on. The bird's-eye view of constitutional growth which these introductory chapters are meant to supply may, however, be brought to completion by brief surveys of four or five main lines of change since 1689. All center in the ripening of that great scheme of cab-

[25] The text of the Bill of Rights is in W. Stubbs, *Select Charters,* 523-528, and in G. B. Adams and H. M. Stephens, *Select Documents of English Constitutional History,* 462-469. The constitutional developments of 1660-89 are described clearly in G. B. Adams, *Constitutional History,* 334-361; on the more purely executive side, in E. R. Turner, *The Privy Council of England in the Seventeenth and Eighteenth Centuries,* I, Chaps. xiv-xvi, II, Chaps. xvii-xx. General accounts will be found in R. Lodge, *History of England from the Restoration to the Death of William III* (London, 1910), Chaps. i-xv, and in G. M. Trevelyan, *England Under the Stuarts,* Chaps. xi-xiii. The principles on which the parliamentary cause throughout the seventeenth century was based, and on which the revolution of 1688-89 proceeded, were ably expounded and defended by John Locke in his famous *Two Treatises of Government,* published at London in 1690 (convenient edition, by W. S. Carpenter, in Everyman's Library, London and New York, 1924).

inet-parliamentary government which gives English polity its exceptional interest and importance today; hence all are vitally interrelated. In summary, they are: (1) the decline of the personal rule of the king; (2) the growth of the cabinet and of the "cabinet system;" (3) the winning of ascendancy by the House of Commons as against the House of Lords; (4) the conversion of the House of Commons into a broadly representative, democratic body; and (5) the rise of political parties and of the party system. On a somewhat different line, the union of England-Wales and Scotland in 1707 to form what we know as Great Britain, and of Great Britain and Ireland in 1801 to form the United Kingdom (followed by the erection of more than four-fifths of the smaller island into the self-governing Irish Free State in 1922) are developments of high importance. The constitutional system, in its fundamentals, was not, however, affected directly by these readjustments, and consideration of them may be deferred to subsequent chapters dealing with portions of the realm which are governed under special régimes.[26]

The Revolution of 1688-89 established firmly enough the principle of parliamentary supremacy. But it did not set up any rules by which this general principle could be reduced to a practical workaday basis of government, or create any machinery through which crown and Parliament could be prevented from again falling into conflict. Doubtless it could not have been expected to do these things. The need was hardly apparent at the time; besides, the elaborate and delicate mechanism of institutions and traditions through which parliamentary government functions today could not possibly have come into being otherwise than as the fruit of generations of experiment and readjustment, with a certain amount also of historical accident.

But as we can now look back on the situation in the first generation after the Revolution, the facts were substantially these. Notwithstanding the hard knocks he had suffered, the king was still in the center of the picture. After all, he had merely been forbidden by the Bill of Rights to do certain specified things; otherwise, he had not been shorn of power. He

[26] See Chaps. xxix-xxx.

was no longer absolute, but he remained the real executive, selecting the members of the Privy Council as he liked, and also the principal officers of state, or ministers. He controlled the ministers' policies, with no necessary regard for Parliament's opinion—indeed, with no obligation to consult Parliament at all in advance of a decision, in either foreign or domestic affairs. The ministers need not be members of Parliament; they need not be chosen so as to reflect the party situation in Parliament; and the king could act on their advice if he liked, or on that of other people, or on none at all. More important still, if Parliament disliked the policies embarked upon by the ministers, it could get them out of office only by the difficult process of impeachment, and it could thwart the king's general management of the affairs of state only by precipitating an open breach and running the risk of stopping the wheels of government. In short, parliamentary supremacy, while unchallenged as a general principle, was subject in practice to limitations that threatened to reduce it to a nullity. King and Parliament confronted each other, as of old, without the intermediation of any buffer or screen such as nowadays shields them from all possibility of conflict.

As has been suggested, contemporaries of William III had no clear perception of the problems involved in carrying the settlements of 1660 and 1689 to their logical conclusion; indeed, they were inclined to look upon the arrangements that had been made as complete, adequate, and final. Nobody, either then or later, planned a solution. As difficulties multiplied, the way out was gradually discovered; and it proved to be the gradual relinquishment of most of his surviving prerogatives by the king and the lodgment of policy-making and administrative control in a group of ministers selected from Parliament in such a way as to be in agreement with the party in control of the House of Commons, and recognizing complete responsibility, singly and collectively, to that chamber. In other words, the solution was found in the cabinet system. But it should be repeated that, like most features of English polity, the cabinet system was a growth and not an invention.[27]

[27] The best brief exposition of the rise of ministerial responsibility, and of the effects of this principle upon the developing constitution, is G. B. Adams, *Origin of the English Constitution,* Chap. viii.

William III understood well enough the conditions on which he had been received in the country, and he never tried to evade them. But he also had a lively appreciation of the royal prerogatives that had not been cut off, and throughout his reign he wielded powerful personal control over public acts and policies. His successor, Anne, although less forceful, held to the same course. After the accession of the Hanoverian dynasty in 1714, however, the situation changed completely. George I (1714-27) and George II (1727-60) were not the nonentities they have sometimes been painted. But the one was a total alien, speaking no English,[28] knowing nothing of English ideas and ways, caring only for the prestige and military strength which being king of England brought him; and the other, although more interested in his adopted land and sometimes resentful because (as he said) "ministers are the king in this country," lacked the ability to make himself felt in governmental affairs. Both thought of themselves primarily as kings of Hanover and looked upon England as hardly more than a dependency. Under these circumstances, the powers which their predecessors had jealously guarded—at all events, the actual exercise of them—slipped rapidly into the possession of those governmental agencies that were actively functioning, i.e., the ministers and the houses of Parliament. George III (1760-1820), better acquainted with the country, keenly interested in it, and "glorying in the name of Englishman," tried hard to regain what had been lost—not, it should be observed, what had been lost back in the seventeenth century, but what had trickled away since 1688—and for a score of years he was measurably successful. His influence upon government and politics [29] went far beyond anything witnessed since the reign of William III, and in 1780 the House of Commons took apprehensive note of the fact by passing a series of resolutions, of which the first declared boldly that "the influence of the crown has increased, is increasing, and ought to be diminished." [30]

[28] His only medium of communication with Walpole, chief minister after 1721, was Latin, of which neither man had any real mastery.

[29] Americans have reasons for knowing something of what it was.

[30] On the monarchical revival under George III, see T. E. May, *Constitutional History of England since the Accession of George III,* edited and continued by F. Holland (London, 1912), I, Chaps. i-ii, and A. M. Davies,

After the resignation of Lord North in 1782, however, the tide turned, and during the later decades of the reign, clouded by the king's insanity, the whole effort was brought to naught. A satisfactory way of running the government without the active participation of the king had been worked out, and no monarch could have induced or compelled the country to abandon it. During the Regency (1810-20) and the reign of the scandal-smirched George IV (1820-30) loss of popularity was joined to loss of power. Popularity was partly recovered in the days of the genial William IV (1830-37), but not power; and the long reign of the virtuous Victoria (1837-1901), while raising the royal family to new heights in the respect and affection of the nation, removed any lingering doubt as to what the position of the sovereign in the governmental system was henceforth to be. Edward VII and George V have kept up the best traditions of the dynasty, but have left the prerogative where they found it.[31]

Rise of the Cabinet

As the king receded into the background, the center of the stage was taken by the ministers—in particular, those of them who, as a group, came to be known as the cabinet. The cabinet came into being slowly, and the *cabinet system,* with all that it involves nowadays, still more so; and neither the process nor the product is to this day known to the letter of English law.[32] It is customary to regard as the immediate forerunner of the cabinet the so-called "cabal" of Charles II, i.e., the shifting group of persons whom that sovereign selected from the Privy Council and took advice from informally, in lieu of the Council as a whole, just as the Privy Council itself had been detached from the Great Council of Norman-Angevin times. In point of fact, the practice of referring important matters to standing or temporary committees of the large and unwieldy Council antedated Charles II; both the practice and the name

Influence of George III and the Development of the Constitution (Oxford, 1921).

[31] The position occupied by the king today and the opportunities which exist for him to influence the work of the government are dealt with below. See pp. 106-117.

[32] See p. 119 below.

"cabinet council" existed under Charles I.[33] Not, however, until after 1660 were the conditions right for the cabinet to gain a definite place in the machinery of government; not until after that date would it have been possible for the cabinet system to become the central fact and chief glory of the constitution.

Development under Charles II did not go far. On the theory that the "great number of the Council made it unfit for the secrecy and dispatch that are necessary in many great affairs," the king drew round himself a half-dozen ministers who had his confidence and who also were influential with Parliament. To them he referred the principal questions that came up, and to them he looked to procure from Parliament the legislation that he desired. These ministers, the Earl of Clarendon (who for a time belonged to the group) tells us, "had everyday conference with some select persons of the House of Commons, who had always served the king, and upon that account had great interest in that assembly, and in regard of the experience they had and of their good parts were hearkened to with reverence. And with those they consulted in what method to proceed in disposing the house, sometimes to propose, sometimes to consent to, what should be most necessary to the public; and by them to assign parts to other men, whom they found disposed and willing to concur in what was to be desired: and all this without any noise, or bringing many together to design, which ever was and ever will be ingrateful to Parliaments, and, however it may succeed for a little time, will in the end be attended by prejudice."

Herein may be discerned the germ of the later cabinet system: a single, small group of the king's principal ministers, now giving collective advice to the sovereign, now introducing and urging forward legislation that the "government" desired. However, the system itself did not yet exist. As has been explained, the king chose his ministers with no necessary consideration of the political complexion or the wishes of Parliament; practically, if no longer theoretically, these ministers were re-

[33] Privy Council committees to the end of the eighteenth century are treated fully in E. R. Turner, *The Privy Council of England in the Seventeenth and Eighteenth Centuries,* II, Chaps. xxii-xxix. Cf. M. Fitzroy, *The History of the Privy Council* (London, 1928).

sponsible, not to Parliament or the nation, but to the king himself. And it is interesting to observe that, far from recognizing in the little ministerial group an agency that might be turned to account in bringing the king still further under restraint, the leaders of liberal thought attacked it as being an instrumentality of intrigue in the sovereign's interest. The name "cabinet" (arising from the king's habit of receiving the members in a small private room, or cabinet, in the palace) first came into use as a term of reproach.

The device, none the less, met a serious need; in truth, it may be said to have been ultimately indispensable. "If fully carried out in practice," we may remind ourselves, "the compromise [involved in the Restoration of 1660] would mean the direct supervision and control of all lines of government policy and executive action by the legislative assembly. Such an arrangement was new to all human experience and naturally there existed no machinery by which it could be carried out in practice, no institutional forms through which a legislature could exercise an executive authority which in theory it did not have. Constitutional machinery for the practical operation of the compromise must be devised, and the origin and growth of this machinery is the origin and growth of the cabinet with the principle of ministerial responsibility to Parliament. Or we may state the fact in another way: the English system of vesting the executive authority in a cabinet virtually chosen by the legislature and held under a close control by it, was the method finally devised to carry out in the practical operation of the country the sovereignty of Parliament which had resulted from the constitutional advance of the seventeenth century." [34]

Development of the Cabinet System

In 1688 the cabinet was still a half-formed and misunderstood institution, and the "cabinet system" was not conceived of at all. But the events of that and the succeeding year, paving the way for the permanent supremacy of Parliament, made the development of cabinet government inevitable. We have seen that William III retained complete freedom in the choice of ministers and considerable control over their actions. But his

[34] G. B. Adams, *Constitutional History of England,* 363.

reign brought one important step forward. Failing in the attempt to govern with sundry ministries composed of both Whigs and Tories, the king, in 1693-96, gathered around himself a body of advisers containing only Whigs; and although this was at first only a matter of convenience and not of principle, it gradually became the regular practice to take the chief ministers exclusively from the party or faction having effective control of the House of Commons.

Perceiving, but not fully understanding, what was going on, Parliament continued to be apprehensive; and in the Act of Settlement,[35] passed in 1701, it sought to turn the course of events in a different direction. This it did, in the first place, by requiring that all council business should be transacted in the Privy Council, not in a cabal or cabinet, and that the members should evidence their responsibility for what was done by attaching their signatures. In addition, the act made any person holding an office or place of profit under the crown or receiving a pension from the crown ineligible to sit in the House of Commons, the object being to prevent the king from trying to dominate the popular chamber (as William III had freely done) by passing out offices and pensions to its members. Had the provisions taken effect, no place would have been left for anything in the nature of the cabinet as we know it. But in point of fact neither of them was ever in operation; for before the time came for the law to become effective (i.e., at the accession of the House of Hanover) both had been repealed. Parliament at last came to understand how ill-advised it would be to exclude the great officers of state from the chamber in which they could most effectively be held to account. The attempt to keep the public business in the hands of the Privy Council as a whole was also entirely abandoned. The effort to free the House of Commons of office-holders and pensioners was not, indeed, given up, but a Security Act of 1705 and a Place Act of 1707 [36] restricted the prohibition substantially to holders of offices or places created after 1705, while permitting the holders of older

[35] G. B. Adams and H. M. Stephens, *Select Documents of English Constitutional History,* 478. Cf. p. 99 below.

[36] G. B. Adams and H. M. Stephens, *Select Documents of English Constitutional History,* 483-485.

offices, after vacating their seats on receiving appointment, to resume them if reëlected by their constituents.[37] Moreover, it became the practice when an important new office of a political nature was created to make a special statutory provision permitting the holder to sit in the House of Commons. Later acts unconditionally barred from Parliament entire classes of subordinate officials, including holders of many places created before, as well as after, 1705. But officers of a ministerial grade were never touched by this legislation; and thus the way was kept open for the long line of developments which finally gave the country the cabinet system.[38]

For reasons that are apparent from what has been said about the changing fortunes of kingship, the reigns of George I and George II became the great formative period in cabinet history. Successive groups of Whig ministers banded themselves together to keep up a Whig majority in the House of Commons and to uphold the Hanoverian line against the Tories and Jacobites; and in 1742, when Sir Robert Walpole—the first man who can properly be called prime minister—lost the support of this majority, he promptly, and as a matter of course, resigned. In this same period the king ceased to attend cabinet meetings, and Parliament, now seeing clearly enough how the cabinet system enabled it to enforce the responsibility of the actual, working executive, i.e., the ministers, for the first time became willing to permit the old devices of impeachment and attainder to fall into disuse.[39] Simultaneously, the royal veto also fell into abeyance, as being out of harmony with the new relations of king, ministers, and Parliament.[40] The old weapons, freely employed when king and Parliament fought hand to hand for supremacy, were no longer needed. George III disliked the cabinet and its implications and missed no opportunity to put

[37] See p. 137 below.

[38] Cf. *ibid.*

[39] Since 1714 there have been only three cases of impeachment, i.e., the Earl of Macclesfield (1725), Warren Hastings (1788-95), and Lord Melville (1805). The practice is now regarded as obsolete. An act of attainder might still be passed; but a statute of 1870 removing all disabilities from the heirs of an attainted person has taken away some of the earlier terrors of this weapon.

[40] William III used the veto four times, and Queen Anne once (in 1707), which was the last to this day.

obstacles in the way of its development. But his efforts resulted only in prolonged ministerial instability and confusion which emphasized the advantages of the homogeneous and responsible cabinet group. Still, everything indicates that even as late as the last quarter of the eighteenth century there was no general understanding of what we now call cabinet government. The framers of the constitution of the United States made no known reference to it in the Philadelphia convention. The Constitutional Act of 1791, which undertook to give Upper and Lower Canada the same kind of government that England had, made no provision for a responsible ministry. Blackstone wrote his Commentaries[41] and DeLolme his interesting description of the English constitution[42] without saying a word about the cabinet system. Only in the first quarter of the nineteenth century did a real comprehension of the ins and outs, and the ultimate implications, of the system come into view; and not until 1867, when Walter Bagehot's *English Constitution* was published, was it for the first time described clearly and fully in print.[43]

In the nineteenth century the cabinet definitely took on the characteristics which we recognize in it today, as a body consisting (a) of members of Parliament (b) of the same political views (c) chosen from the party having a majority in the House of Commons (d) carrying out a concerted policy (e) under a common responsibility to be signified by collective resignation in the event of parliamentary censure[44] and (f) acknowledging a common subordination to one chief minister.[45] In the nineteenth century, too, the English cabinet system began to wield the very great influence abroad which it still exerts: it was extended to the British dominions beyond seas; France copied it in her constitution of 1814; Belgium did likewise in

[41] *Commentaries on the Laws of England, in Four Books* (London, 1865).

[42] *Constitution de l'Angleterre* (Amsterdam, 1771). The author was a Swiss writer who left his own country on account of political difficulties and settled in England. An enlarged and improved edition of his book appeared in England in 1772.

[43] See p. 76, note 26, below.

[44] A ministry resigned for the first time in 1830 because of defeat suffered on the floor of the House of Commons.

[45] H. D. Traill, *Central Government* (London, 1881), 24-25.

1831; Italy and other states followed, including Japan in 1889. Eventually, in the great era of constitution-making following the World War, cabinet organization, modelled directly or indirectly on the English, was set up in Germany, Austria, Czechoslovakia, Poland, and most other countries of central and eastern Europe. How the system has fructified on its native soil, and what changing phases it presents from generation to generation, and almost from year to year, will presently be described.[46]

Shift of Power to the House of Commons

The king's personal power would hardly have fallen off so heavily, and the cabinet system would certainly never have arisen, had not Parliament also been undergoing some very important changes. There was, of course, a steady accumulation of sovereign authority, implicit in the terms of the settlements of 1660 and 1689, and progressively realized as the scroll of events unrolled through the next two hundred years. But beyond this were two great developments which have largely made Parliament what it is today. One was the gradual shift of the center of gravity of legislative and other power from the House of Lords to the House of Commons. The other was the reconstruction of the suffrage and other electoral arrangements, giving the House of Commons for the first time a broadly popular basis and thus making it more truly representative of the nation as a whole.

All of these different developments went along together, each

[46] See Chaps. vi-vii. On the rise of the cabinet see, in addition to the general histories, G. B. Adams, *Constitutional History of England,* Chaps. xv-xvi; M. T. Blauvelt, *Development of Cabinet Government in England* (New York, 1902), Chaps. i-viii; E. Jenks, *Parliamentary England; the Evolution of the Cabinet System* (New York, 1903); H. B. Learned, "Historical Significance of the Term 'Cabinet' in England and the United States," *Amer. Polit. Sci. Rev.,* August, 1909; H. W. V. Temperley, "The Inner and Outer Cabinet and the Privy Council, 1679-1683," *Eng. Hist. Rev.,* Oct., 1912; W. R. Anson, "The Cabinet in the Seventeenth and Eighteenth Centuries," *ibid.,* Jan., 1914; E. R. Turner, "The Development of the Cabinet, 1688-1760," *Amer. Hist. Rev.,* July and Oct., 1913, and "Committees of Council and the Cabinet," *ibid.,* July, 1914, and "The Cabinet in the Eighteenth Century," *Eng. Hist. Rev.,* Apr., 1917. An extensive systematic treatise by Professor Turner on the origin and development of the cabinet has been announced.

reënforcing the others. Particularly was there interrelation between the growth of the cabinet system and the ascendancy of the House of Commons. The two were, indeed, only phases of one great process—a process that has been aptly described as follows: "It comprised not merely the transfer of the supreme authority in the immediate formation and execution of policy to the cabinet, but also the transfer of the final determining authority in the state to the House of Commons. As soon as the cabinet found itself able to fix the policy of the government independently of the king, it found that its policy must have the approval of the House of Commons or it could not carry it out. In other words, the cabinet wins its position in the modern constitution, not as an independent institution, but as the instrument of parliamentary supremacy. These two changes were clearly intertwined in process and result. Each was dependent on the other. Neither could go beyond a certain point unless the other advanced with equal step. What happened when this double result was fully reached was that the compromise of 1660 was now embodied in the working constitution of the state. The sovereignty of Parliament had found the institutional means through which it could make itself actually effective in the government of the state, and as a consequence, because in truth the sovereignty of Parliament rested upon the ultimate sovereignty of the people, there was a decline in the practical power of the House of Lords as well as of the royal prerogative." [47]

This transference of power began within thirty years after the Revolution of 1688-89 and proceeded, by stages that can be measured roughly, during the next century and a half. Under William and Anne, the House of Lords had not only greater prestige, but greater influence, than the other branch. But the future lay with the latter. The right of prior consideration of all proposals relating to finance would alone have been enough sooner or later to give the Commons the upper hand; nothing in the realm of government carries you farther than the power of the purse. But other circumstances contributed to the same end. One of them was the fact that during the plastic period of the early Georges, the dominating figure in the government,

[47] G. B. Adams, *Constitutional History of England,* 387.

Walpole, was all of the while a member of the House of Commons and made it the recognized center of legislative and political leadership. Another factor was the Septennial Act of 1716, lengthening the maximum life of a parliament from three years to seven, and hence making a seat in the elective branch more attractive to able men and ensuring greater experience and morale on the part of members.

One other contributing cause brings us to the second great change which Parliament underwent, namely, the democratization of the House of Commons. That branch could hardly have gone so far had it not gained the immense moral and practical advantage of a deep popular rootage. From its earliest days, the House of Commons had consisted chiefly of men who had no claim to be representatives of the general mass of the people in the several counties and boroughs. County members were elected by the rural gentry; borough members more variously, but usually by a mere handful of the borough residents. Many seats had fallen under the control of great landlords or other magnates; many, by 1800, were openly bought and sold. Long after the nineteenth century dawned, the House of Commons was hardly less aristocratic in temper, and hardly more representative of the nation in any true sense, than was the House of Lords; and until 1832 it was, on the whole, growing less representative rather than more so. Rising discontent, however, gradually brought the country to a new and vigorous line of policy, and, beginning at the date mentioned, a long series of hard-won statutes extended the suffrage to successive groups of people who had been politically powerless, reapportioned parliamentary seats so as to distribute political influence with greater fairness among the voters, and regulated the conditions under which campaigns were to be carried on, elections held, and other operations of popular government performed. Culminating in the Representation of the People Act of 1918, enfranchising upwards of twelve million men and women, and a supplementary equal franchise law of 1928 adding five million more, these measures made the House of Commons one of the most democratic parliamentary bodies in the world.[48]

[48] Not quite, however, the most democratic of all; for example, in the German republic the electorate is broader in that men and women vote

Unhappily, the House of Lords underwent no corresponding change. The nation occupied new ground politically and carried the House of Commons with it from stage to stage as it advanced. In its structure, and largely in its temperament, the House of Lords, however, stood still. So long as that chamber was content to play a distinctly secondary rôle, passing finance measures unfailingly as they came to it from the House of Commons and rarely blocking general legislation of any importance, serious consequences were rare. When, however, in the early years of the present century it began to show a more vigorous and independent attitude, even going so far as to refuse in 1909 to pass the annual revenue bill, a critical situation was produced, the outcome of which was the Parliament Act of 1911 bringing to an end the historic legal parity of the two houses.[49] Henceforth all money bills could be made law quickly by action of the popular branch alone, and bills of other kinds could be enacted by a slower, but perfectly feasible, process. The House of Lords remains as a checking and revising authority, but legislative power, in the last analysis, has been gathered almost completely into the hands of the reconstructed House of Commons.

Rise of Political Parties

The last notable development to be touched upon in this outline is the rise of political parties and of what may be broadly termed the party system. Parties and party machinery remain to this day quite unknown to the law of the constitution,[50] and they are recognized only slightly by statute. Nevertheless they make up so large and important a part of the actual governmental system that it would be almost impossible to conceive of it, or, indeed, of any scheme of representative government, without them. The origins of political parties in England are not easy to trace. Much depends, of course, upon what one considers as constituting a "party." Macaulay thought of the Cavalier and Roundhead elements, as aligned after the adoption

for members of the Reichstag at the age of twenty, as compared with the voting age of twenty-one in Britain. British suffrage history is related at some length in Chap. xii below.

[49] See pp. 342-347 below.

[50] See p. 482 below.

of the Grand Remonstrance by Parliament in 1641, as the first English parties. But, clearly, they were not parties in our modern sense of the term. They were, rather, mere factions, mutually regarding each other as enemies of the state, to be shown no quarter, and, if possible, to be squeezed out of existence. Speaking properly, we have parties when the people are found divided into two or more groups or followings, each with its leaders, principles, and programs, each seeking to gain and hold control of the government, but each willing to concede that the others are just as much entitled to exist as is itself and just as capable of being entrusted with the running of the government without bringing down the whole political structure in ruins. Certainly the so-called Court and Country parties of the reign of Charles II did not measure up to these standards. No more did their successors, the Petitioners and Abhorrers, who divided so sharply on the question of the exclusion of the Duke of York—the later James II—from the throne. They, too, were only factions. The Whigs and Tories of the later Stuart years have better claim. They, at all events, had definite programs and machinery, although not until long after 1689 were they able to arrive at that mutually tolerant attitude which is a proper basis of distinction between a party and a faction. Perhaps we shall not strike far from the truth if we say that the Whigs and Tories were the first English parties, adding that the process of their conversion from factions into real parties was very gradual and was hardly completed before the middle of the eighteenth century. Scarcely, indeed, before the nineteenth century was the party system fully understood and accepted; only then, as a recent writer has reminded us, did the minority in Parliament come to be thought of as no longer the king's enemies but as "His Majesty's loyal opposition." [51]

What particular groups are the first entitled to be called parties is really of little consequence. The important thing is the gradual ripening of the party system through the eighteenth and nineteenth centuries, in close conjunction with the building up of cabinet government. Cabinet government might conceivably exist without parties, but it would certainly be something very different from any type or form with which we are

[51] W. B. Munro, *Governments of Europe*, 35.

familiar; in England, the whole course of its development was shaped by the growth of parties, and notably by the rise of two, and only two, great parties which divided the allegiance of the country between them. As we progress with our analysis of the law and practice of the present English political system, we shall find ourselves growing in the conviction that few influences have had more to do with making them what they are than those of party.[52]

[52] Cf. Chaps. xx-xxiv below. On the rise of political parties, see especially W. C. Abbott, "The Origin of English Political Parties," *Amer. Hist. Rev.*, July, 1919; M. H. Woods, *A History of the Tory Party in the Seventeenth and Eighteenth Centuries* (London, 1924), Chaps. i-x; and K. G. Feiling, *A History of the Tory Party, 1640-1714* (Oxford, 1924). A good monograph is W. T. Morgan, *English Political Parties and Leaders in the Reign of Queen Anne* (New Haven, 1920).

CHAPTER III

THE CONSTITUTION AND THE GOVERNMENT TODAY

THE accumulated result of the thirteen or fourteen centuries of political growth outlined in the two preceding chapters is that remarkable ground-work, or frame, of government known as the British constitution. This term "constitution," it must be confessed, is one which has often injected a good deal of confusion into the discussion of political matters. Etymologically, it denotes something *constituted,* or established—the fundamental basis or lines upon which, and to some extent the equipment with which, affairs are organized and carried on. We speak of a man as having a "good constitution," meaning that his make-up is such that he has good health, steady nerves, and a sound mind. We speak of a state as having a good constitution, and mean that it has a body of fundamental principles and rules which ensure it a form of organization suited to its needs and put it in a position to enjoy wise and effective government. In the sense that no state, however backward, is ever without some recognized scheme of organization—some accepted bases and modes of political action—every state may be said to have a constitution, of one sort or another, just as has every other form or type of human association.

In its political applications the term has caused difficulty because it is employed in two quite different senses, one narrow and the other broad. Questioned as to what is the constitution of the United States, the average American would be very likely to point to the instrument drawn up at Philadelphia in 1787, put into operation in 1789, later modified and enlarged by nineteen amendments, and printed as an appendix in every text-book on United States government. He would be thinking of a constitution as a document, prepared and adopted at some given time, solemn and weighty in the matters with which it deals, orderly in arrangement, precise in terms, subject to change only on rare occasions and for urgent reasons. And he would be right. There *is* an American constitution which, as James Bryce remarked a generation ago, can be read in twenty minutes; there is a French constitution consisting of three brief fundamental laws (with amendments) adopted by a National Assembly at Versailles in 1875, a German constitution made at Weimar in 1919, a constitution of the Irish Free State voted by the British Parliament in 1922.

But nothing would be wider of the mark than to suppose that one could get an adequate understanding of the American system of government merely by pondering a ten-page document printed in a book. From such a study he would never know that presidential electors are pledged in advance to vote for certain candidates and no others, that the Senate can in effect originate revenue bills, that there is such a thing as a congressional caucus or a political party or a national bank, or scores of other things of major importance about our actual working governmental system. The truth is that our written constitution—*any* written constitution that has been in operation even a few years—has come to be overlaid with, or enveloped by, a mass of rules and usages, not set forth at all in the basic text, yet contributing in many instances quite as much to making the government what it is as anything within the four corners of the formal document. Some of these added features arise from interpretation, more or less far-fetched, confirmed by judicial opinion. Many rest upon statute. Still others flow only from precedent or custom. But the result is that, in a broad and proper sense, the constitution of the United States (and the same is true in France or Germany or Czechoslovakia) comes to be the whole body of rules and practices by which the structure and powers of government, the interrelations of parts, and the ways of doing things are determined, irrespective of whether these rules and methods are written or unwritten, and therefore of whether or not they are to be found in the "constitution" printed in the books.[1]

[1] For further consideration of this matter in connection with the constitution of the United States, see F. A. Ogg and P. O. Ray, *Introduction*

Nature of the English Constitution

What would an Englishman say if asked to produce the constitution of *his* country? That would probably depend on the degree of politeness with which he sought to conceal amusement at the naïveté of the request. He could, of course, bring forward some documents—many of them, in fact —which embody fundamental laws unquestionably forming parts of the national constitution. We have already mentioned certain ones, e.g., the Bill of Rights and the Act of Settlement. But he would hasten to explain that no one of these, nor all of them together, should for a moment be thought of as comprising *the constitution*—that they are only pieces or parts of it, merely scattered stones in the mosaic. For there is no British constitution except in the second of the two meanings of the term indicated above.

For some people, this has meant that there is no English constitution at all. Of this view, for example, was Thomas Paine, who categorically declared that where a constitution "cannot be produced in visible form, there is none." "Can Mr. Burke," he asked, in replying to that eminent statesman's powerful defense of the English constitution in his *Reflections on the French Revolution,* "produce the English constitution? If he cannot, we may fairly conclude that though it has been so much talked about, no such thing as a constitution exists or ever did exist." [2] Similarly, the eminent French student of foreign governments, Alexis de Tocqueville, a generation later, said of the English constitution that it did not exist (*elle n'existe point*), although he was thinking not so much of the absence of a written frame of government as of the fact that Parliament can, by process of ordinary legislation, make any change, at any time, in the country's fundamental law.[3]

to American Government (3rd ed., New York, 1928), Chap. xi, and H. W. Horwill, *The Usages of the American Constitution* (Oxford, 1925), Chap. i. The nature, classes, and modes of growth of constitutions in general are discussed in J. W. Garner, *Political Science and Government* (New York, 1928), Chap. xviii, and W. F. Willoughby, *Government of Modern States* (New York, 1919), Chaps. vi-vii.

[2] *Writings* (ed. by M. D. Conway), II, 309-310.

[3] *Œuvres Complètes,* I, 166-167. De Tocqueville's best known work was *De la Démocratie en Amérique,* published at Paris in 1835 (trans. by H.

Paine's view was one not unlikely to be taken by champions of human liberty in an age when it was the fashion, outside of England, to regard a written constitution as an indispensable condition and guarantee of "the rights of man." De Tocqueville's opinion was an equally natural one to be held by a Frenchman, accustomed to a written fundamental law with which the legislature was supposed not to tamper. Both men, however, misconceived the real situation in England. There was in their day, and assuredly is now, in a very real sense, an English constitution—one which is at once the oldest and the most influential of all constitutions of modern times. From as far back as the reign of Henry II, the term had been applied to exceptionally solemn and important statutes,[4] and in the sixteenth and seventeenth centuries the concept of a body of fundamental law (whether written or unwritten did not matter), superior in authority and dignity to the ordinary law, gained permanent lodgment in both English and Continental political thought. By the time when Paine and De Tocqueville wrote there not only was an English constitution, but Englishmen were equally conscious of its existence and proud of its history.

What, then, is the English constitution of today? Briefly, it is the general body of rules and principles controlling the distribution and regulating the exercise of governmental power and defining the relations of the governing authorities with the people. Some of these rules and principles have been reduced to writing. Indeed, as the practice grows of settling great disputes or problems in documents rather than merely by word of mouth, steadily increasing proportions of the fundamental law take on written form; and to that extent Britain slowly approaches the position of a state with a written constitution. No attempt has ever been made, however, to bring together even the most weighty of the constitution's principles in a single document, or in a group of documents, and consequently the greater part is still simply carried in men's minds

Reeve as *Democracy in America,* 2 vols. 2nd ed., Cambridge, Mass., 1863). Cf. p. 73 below.

[4] For example, the "Constitutions of Clarendon" of 1164 regulating the relations between the king and the clergy.

as precedents, decisions, practices, and habits. Needless to say, a constitution such as this is not the handiwork of any special constitution-framing body or power; far from being adopted at any given time, it is, as has been said, a product of many centuries of political growth, and much of it was never formally "adopted" at all; it can be amended at any time, to any extent, by simple action of the government, i.e., Parliament. "The child of wisdom and chance" (as Mr. Strachey has called it in his *Queen Victoria*), it is a compound of elements which one could hope to bring together only by exhaustively surveying a thousand years and more of history, by laying hold of a statute here and a judicial decision there, by taking constant account of the hardening of political practices into established customs, and by probing to their inmost recesses the mechanisms of law-making, administration, public finance, justice, and elections, as they have been in the past, and as they are actually operated before the spectator's eyes.[5] Small wonder that Englishmen have shrunk from any effort to reduce the thing to systematic codified form, particularly considering how nebulous many parts of it are, and how shifting from generation to generation and almost from year to year! Wisely have they, as a French publicist once remarked, "left the different parts of their constitution where the waves of history have deposited them," without ever attempting "to bring them together, to classify or complete them, or to make of it a consistent or coherent whole." [6]

[5] Lord Bryce's way of stating the matter is that the constitution is "a mass of precedents carried in men's minds or recorded in writing, of dicta of lawyers or statesmen, of customs, usages, understandings, and beliefs bearing upon the methods of government, together with a certain number of statutes, . . . nearly all of them presupposing and mixed up with precedents and customs, and all of them covered with a parasitic growth of legal decisions and political habits, apart from which the statutes would be almost unworkable, or at any rate quite different in their working from what they really are." *Studies in History and Jurisprudence* (New York, 1901), 134.

[6] *Studies in Constitutional Law: France—England—United States,* trans. by A. V. Dicey (London, 1891), 6. Cf. A. B. Keith, *The Constitution, Administration, and Laws of the Empire* (New York, 1924), 1-7; J. O. Taylor, "A Written Constitution for Britain," *Jurid. Rev.,* Dec., 1914. As Dicey points out, the law of the constitution could perfectly well be reduced completely to writing and enacted in the form of a constitutional

The result, of course, is a constitutional structure which lacks symmetry, a governmental system which abounds in the illogical. But this does not trouble the Englishman as it would a Frenchman or a German. Writing from doctrinaire France seventy-five years ago, Walter Bagehot thanked God that the English are not logical; and in our own day a member of the House of Commons stirred applause by declaring, in rebuttal of a colleague's argument that a given bill should be passed because it "removed certain anomalies," that he and Englishmen generally "liked anomalies," that Britain had been able to operate democratic institutions because she is an illogical country, and that the Latin races have failed at this point precisely because they are "troubled by logic." Certainly it is true that the Anglo-Saxon method of political advance has been largely that of taking a venturesome step and then stubbornly refusing to take the steps which by all sound principles of deduction ought next to be taken. Constitutional changes calculated to result in greater actual working efficiency are rather easily made, but those which look no farther than the suppression of incongruities and inconsistencies get scant hearing.

code. But he adds that there is no particular point to doing this unless it were desired to isolate the fundamental law and invest it with a permanence and changelessness not belonging to the ordinary law—which is not the case in Britain. See *Introduction to the Study of the Law of the Constitution* (8th ed.), 86. France, which up to 1789 had been developing a recognized and accepted body of fundamental political maxims and principles (*les lois fondamentales*), largely unwritten, precisely as had England, opened at that date a new era in her history in which it became desirable to put her constitution into written form. She, therefore, took to writing out her constitutional laws, while England simply went on as before. A nation that cuts entirely loose from its political moorings is almost obliged to fall back upon the device of a written constitution. Having repudiated its political past, it can avoid chaos only by supplanting custom and tradition with a body of deliberately prepared and agreed rules. England has had her revolutions. But one great institution—her central and most important "convention"—namely, the monarchy, always remained as a core around which the old constitution could readjust itself and continue developing. The only exception was the period following the execution of Charles I in 1649; and, as has appeared, at that time alone in all her long history did England attempt to fit herself out with an integrated and comprehensive constitution. The experiment was tied up with a series of revolutionary changes which in the nature of the case could not be permanent, and therefore was foredoomed to failure.

Elements Composing the Constitution—the Law

Diverse as they are, the elements that go to make up the constitution fall rather readily into some five main categories or groups. First, there are certain historic documents embodying solemn agreements, or engagements, entered into at times of political crisis or change. Of such a nature are the Great Charter (those portions of it, at all events, which are still applicable), the Petition of Right, and the Bill of Rights. Second, there are parliamentary statutes[7] defining the powers of the crown, guaranteeing private rights, regulating the suffrage, establishing courts, and creating other new governmental machinery—obvious examples being the Habeas Corpus Act of 1679, the Act of Settlement of 1701, the Septennial Act of 1716, Fox's Libel Act of 1792, the Reform Acts of 1832, 1867, and 1884, the Municipal Corporations Act of 1835, the Parliamentary and Municipal Elections Act of 1872, the Judicature Acts of 1873-76, the Local Government Acts of 1888, 1894, and 1929, the Parliament Act of 1911, the Representation of the People Act of 1918, and the Equal Franchise Act of 1928. Third, there are judicial decisions fixing the meanings and limits of charters and statutes, very much as do judicial decisions in the United States, with the important difference that in England, as we shall see, no act of legislation is ever pronounced "unconstitutional." Good illustrations are the decision in Bushell's Case (1670), establishing the independence of juries, and that in Howell's Case (1678), vindicating the immunity of judges.[8] Fourth, there are principles and rules of common law—many of them—pertaining to functions, powers, methods, and relationships of government.[9] These principles and rules grew up entirely on the basis of usage and were never enacted by Parliament, but they include many of the most important features of the governmental and legal

[7] The Bill of Rights was, of course, cast in the form of a statute.

[8] For thirty or more judicial decisions of constitutional significance between 1666 and 1884, see C. G. Robertson, *Select Statutes, Cases, and Documents to Illustrate English Constitutional History* (London, 1904), 217-415. Other convenient collections are B. A. Bicknell, *Cases on the Law of the Constitution* (London, 1926), and D. L. Keir and F. H. Lawson, *Cases in Constitutional Law* (Oxford, 1928).

[9] See pp. 599-602 below.

system. The prerogative of the crown, for example, rests almost entirely on common law; likewise the right of trial by jury in criminal cases, the right of freedom of speech and of assembly, the right to redress for tortious actions of government officers. The first three elements mentioned, i.e., solemn political engagements, statutes, and judicial decisions, exist solely, or almost so, in written form. The rules of the common law, however, have not been reduced to writing, save in so far as they are contained in reports, legal opinions, and, more particularly, formal decisions of the courts, such as those on the rights of jurymen, on the prerogative of the crown, on the privileges of the houses of Parliament and of their members, and on the rights and duties of the police. Not infrequently, statutory additions to the written portions of the constitution are merely declaratory of what was already law by force of custom.[10]

Elements Composing the Constitution—the Conventions

Finally, there are those portions of the constitution which we have been taught by Professor Dicey to call "the conventions." [11] The "law" of the constitution, composed of the four elements that have been enumerated, is law in the strictest sense, and, whether written or unwritten, is enforceable through the courts. It is, for example, a law that the crown may not dispense with the obligation to obey an act of Parliament, and if a court were called upon to deal with a case involving an attempted dispensation of the sort, it would proceed accordingly. The conventions, on the other hand, although they may, and frequently do, relate to matters of the utmost importance, are not so enforceable. They consist of understandings, habits, or practices, which by their sole authority regulate a large proportion of the actual day-to-day relations

[10] J. W. Garner, *Political Science and Government,* 514.

[11] In his *Introduction to the Study of the Law of the Constitution,* already cited. This great work, by a former Vinerian professor of English law at Oxford, was first published in 1885. An eighth edition, prefaced by an extended introduction surveying English constitutional developments since 1884, was issued in 1915. The treatise's main contribution was a luminous exposition of the relations between the "law" and the "conventions" of the constitution.

and activities of even the most important of the public authorities. Most of them will be found described in text-books and treatises. But they do not appear in the statute books or in any statement of the law, written or unwritten—rightly enough, because, although parts of the constitution, they are not law. It is, for example, by virtue of conventions of the constitution (not laws) that Parliament is convoked at least once a year, that it is organized in two houses, that all measures passed by it must be assented to by the crown,[12] that the prime minister is the leader of the party having a majority in the House of Commons, and that a ministry which has lost the confidence of the House of Commons must retire from office unless it makes a successful appeal to the country at a general election. The cabinet and all that the cabinet, as such, stands for, rests entirely upon convention. In short, the conventions have to do with many of the most fundamental and conspicuous features of the constitutional system, which without them would be quite unrecognizable. Of course, as has been suggested above, usage or convention plays a very large part in all political systems, and plays indeed a major rôle in all constitutions (in the broader sense) which have had time to mature. Certainly it is so in the United States, where, indeed, convention forms, in the opinion of Professor Dicey, quite as large a part of the actual working constitution as in England.[13] After all, however, England is the classic land of convention, partly, no doubt, because there it has had more time than anywhere else in which to develop, partly because of a national temper which is peculiarly favorable to that sort of thing. It goes without saying that any one who desires to know the British constitution as it is—even one who comes at it primarily as a student of law, as did Dicey—must study the

[12] On the question of whether the veto power is absolutely extinct there is difference of opinion. See G. Wallas, *Our Social Heritage* (New Haven, 1921), Chap. x.

[13] *The Law of the Constitution* (8th ed.), 28, note. On the conventions of the American constitution, see J. Bryce, *The American Commonwealth* (3rd ed.), I, Chaps. xxxiv-xxxv, and H. W. Horwill, *The Usages of the American Constitution,* cited above. It is interesting to note that both of these discussions of the subject are by English authors. On usage or convention in France, see H. Chardon, *L'Administration de la France; les fonctionnaires* (Paris, 1908), 79-105.

conventions quite as carefully as the positive rules of law.

What is it that gives the conventions force? They are not law, but only a species of constitutional "morality." No court can be invoked to give them effect, and yet the government would become something very different from the thing it is—indeed could hardly go on at all—if they were not observed. What is the sanction, as the lawyers would say, behind them?

At the outset, it should be observed that the recognized conventions or usages are not, as a matter of fact, equally inviolable. All are of the essence of custom, and it goes without saying that some customs are regarded as more important than others, and that some are more, some less, irrevocably established. On all hands, customs are on the road to becoming fixed conventions. Some, however, are deflected and never arrive at the goal. A practice believed to have established itself so securely that it will never be departed from may, after all, some day be disregarded. By 1924 it might have been accepted as a constitutional principle (indeed Dicey in 1915 spoke of it as a "new convention" [14]) that a ministry appealing to the country at a general election and losing its appeal should resign without waiting to suffer a defeat at the hand of the new House of Commons. Following the country's rejection of their program at the election of 1923, however, Mr. Baldwin and his associates remained in office until, the new parliament having assembled, they were definitely voted down on a motion.[15] Whether a particular custom is to be regarded as having definitely taken its place as a part of the constitution is often a matter of sheer guess-work—which is another way of saying that any one who should attempt to stake out the exact boundaries of the English constitution, conventional and legal, would indeed have an unenviable task.

But there are many great maxims which are never violated, and are universally admitted to be inviolable. What is it that gives these their binding character? It is not easy to answer the question to one's entire satisfaction, but two or three considera-

[14] *Law of the Constitution* (8th ed.), p. xlix.

[15] Under the unusual circumstances that existed (see p. 509 below), this was decidedly the honorable thing for them to do.

tions help to an understanding of the matter. The first of these is that many of the most important conventions are so bound up with the laws that they cannot be violated without infraction of law itself, or at any rate without entailing other grave consequences. Mr. Dicey found in this the conventions' principal sanction. The illustration which he was fond of using was the maxim that Parliament shall assemble at least once a year. Suppose, he said, that Parliament should be prorogued in such a manner that a full year should elapse without a meeting. The annual Army Act would expire and the government would lose all disciplinary authority over the troops. Furthermore, although most of the revenue is collected and some of it is spent without annual authorization, certain taxes would lapse and there would be no authority to lay out a penny on the army, the navy, or the civil service. An annual meeting of Parliament, although only a custom which no court would attempt to enforce, is therefore a practical necessity; without it, public officials would find themselves performing illegal acts—or the wheels of government would simply stop. And the violation of other conventions would lead to equally bad consequences.[16]

This is, indeed, a weighty argument. It does not, however, quite cover the case. For, as Lowell suggests, England is not obliged to continue forever holding annual sessions of Parliament because a new mutiny act must be passed and new appropriations made every twelve months; Parliament, with its plenitude of power, could as well as not pass a permanent army act, grant the existing annual taxes for a term of years, and make all ordinary expenses a standing charge on the Consolidated Fund, out of which much is paid now without annual authorization.[17] The conventions are supported by something more than merely the realization that to violate them might mean to collide with the law; the law itself could be changed. For this additional sanction we must look mainly to the power of tradition, perhaps better, the force of public opinion. "In the main," says Lowell, "the conventions are observed because they are a code of honor. They are, as it were, the rules of the game, and the single class in the community which has hitherto had

[16] *Law of the Constitution* (8th ed.), 441-450.
[17] *Government of England,* I, 12. Cf. p. 170 below.

the conduct of English public life almost entirely in its own hands is the very class that is peculiarly sensitive to obligation of this kind. Moreover, the very fact that one class rules, by the sufferance of the whole nation, as trustees for the public, makes that class exceedingly careful not to violate the understandings on which the trust is held." [18] The nation expects, and has a right to expect, that Parliament will be convened annually, and that a ministry that cannot obtain majority support in the House of Commons will resign. The outburst of feeling that would follow if these expectations were not met is a very good guarantee that they will be met. There are other guarantees, but this is certainly one of the number. With the broadening of the popular basis of government in later times, to some extent breaking the monopoly which the aristocracy of birth and education formerly enjoyed in managing the nation's affairs, the effectiveness of tradition and opinion might conceivably decline; and some apprehension has been felt lest, in the new era which Britain has entered, the conventions will be less scrupulously upheld than they have been in the past. Upwards of a year of Labor government (in 1924), however, furnished little evidence of any tendency of the sort, and the new Labor government of 1929 started off in a manner calculated to overcome any lingering fears on the subject. To disregard the essential conventions would only mean to court disaster. Besides, Labor men are, after all, Britishers.

How the Constitution Grows

Enough has been said about the origins and content of the British constitution to establish the fact that, while deeply rooted in the past, it is nevertheless a living organism, changing all of the time before our very eyes. How it grows, and wherein its mode of development resembles or differs from that of other constitutions, is an interesting matter to consider. In the first place, speaking broadly, it does not move forward by a succession of sudden leaps after the manner of the constitution of France since 1789, or even that of Germany or other states which, as a result of wars or revolutions, have swung abruptly from one form of polity to another. On the

[18] *Government of England,* I, 12-13.

contrary, transitions have as a rule been so gradual, deference to tradition so habitual, and the disposition to cling to accustomed names and forms, even when the spirit has changed, so deep-seated, that the constitutional history of Britain displays a continuity hardly paralleled in any other land. At no time, as Freeman wrote, "has the tie between the present and the past been rent asunder; at no moment have Englishmen sat down to put together a wholly new constitution in obedience to some dazzling theory."[19] Even when, as in the seventeenth century, war and revolution seemed to precipitate both sudden and fundamental change, closer examination reveals that what was really happening was only the winning of full and lasting triumph for principles and usages that had long been growing up. Even in his revolutions, as one writer has put it, the Englishman is conservative.

So far does this characteristic prevail that some curious things result. Practice quite outruns theory, and there come to be, in a sense, two constitutions rather than one—the constitution that represents the system as it is supposed to be and the constitution that represents it as it actually is. Take, for example, a matter to be dealt with more fully later, i.e., the relation between the crown and Parliament. Seven or eight centuries ago, England was, to all intents and purposes, an absolute monarchy. For many generations past she has now, however, been not only a limited monarchy, but (in the phrase of Mr. and Mrs. Webb) a "crowned republic," with one of the most democratic systems of government in the world. As great a change has come over her actual political character as can readily be conceived. Nevertheless, the theory has never been dropped off that the government is the king's and not the people's. The law is the king's law; justice is the king's, and is dispensed by the king's judges; the ministers and all their subordinates are "servants of the crown;" no parliamentary election can be held except by the king's writs, no parliamentary statute is enforceable without the king's assent, no civil or military officer is capable of being appointed except in the king's name. The fleets form His Majesty's navy; government documents are published by His Majesty's stationery office; the peo-

[19] *Growth of the English Constitution,* 19.

ple are His Majesty's "loyal subjects." All this, of course, is sheer legal theory, separated from the actualities as one pole from its opposite. The simple truth is that Parliament decides what new law shall be made, makes and unmakes ministries, controls the army and the navy, levies taxes and appropriates money, and, in general, rules the realm, quite without interference from the titular head of the state. The wary student will not be misled, but in threading his way through the glacial drift of history he has to be constantly on his guard. There are sharp contrasts of theory and fact in all governments. But in none do they form the very warp and woof of the system as in the British. To change the figure, a rolling stone may gather no moss, but that mighty boulder which we know as the British constitution has shaken off but little as it has come revolving through the centuries.

What are the ways in which the actual, working constitution progressively adapts itself to changing ideas and needs? Sometimes war and revolution have played a part. But for more than two hundred years no resort to violence has proved necessary.[20] From what has already been said about the elements of which the constitution is composed, the answer to the query can readily be inferred. Judicial decisions contribute something, and even administrative practices. But, in the main, the instrumentalities of change are two—custom and legislation. Of the former, enough has been said to impress the fact that the growth of conventions is not something merely historical, a chapter that is closed, but a continuing process still actively building constitutional principles and rules. Statute as a mode of constitutional growth requires, however, a word of comment—the more by reason of the fact that nowadays it is considerably the most important of all. It involves, of course, constitutional amendment by act of Parliament.

It will strike the American student as strange that Parliament can amend the constitution at all. For in this country we have proceeded on the theory that constituent, i.e., constitution-making or amending, powers should be kept distinct from the powers of ordinary law-making and entrusted to different

[20] A possible exception might be the events which led up to the creation of the Irish Free State in 1922. See Chap. xxx below.

hands. Our national Congress may, indeed, propose constitutional amendments, by a two-thirds vote in both houses; but no amendment can become effective until it has been ratified by the legislatures of three-fourths of the states.[21] In France a constitutional amendment can be adopted only by the senators and deputies sitting together in National Assembly, not by the two houses of Parliament deliberating separately as upon statutes; and in many other countries special devices or processes, of one kind or another, are required to be brought into play before the fundamental law can be changed.

Great Britain, however, knows nothing of such distinctions. There, the unlimited legal power which Parliament possesses to pass ordinary statutes is matched only by the power to enact measures adding to or otherwise modifying the constitution. No variations from the usual organization and procedure are required, and there are no legal limits whatever to the changes that may be provided for. "Our Parliament," observes Anson, "can make laws protecting wild birds or shell-fish, and with the same procedure could break the connections of Church and State, or give political power to two millions of citizens, and redistribute it among new constituencies." [22] Parliament has, of course, actually done these last mentioned things, and more; and it might as well have been added that it could depose the king, abolish the monarchy, deprive all peers of seats in the House of Lords, or suppress that chamber altogether, or, in fact, do any one or all of a score of other things that would leave the British scheme of government unrecognizable by those who know it best. This is really the ground on which De Tocqueville averred that there is no such thing as an English constitution at all.[23] As a Frenchman, he was accustomed, as is an American, to think of a constitution as a document or

[21] An alternative mode of ratification is by conventions, acting favorably in three-fourths of the states. But this method has never been employed.

[22] *Law and Custom of the Constitution* (5th ed.), I, 380. See also A. V. Dicey, *Law of the Constitution* (8th ed.), Chap. i, and F. Pollock, *First Book of Jurisprudence for Students of the Common Law* (London, 1896), Pt. ii, Chap. iii.

[23] "In England," he says, "the Parliament has an acknowledged right to modify the constitution; as, therefore, the constitution may undergo perpetual changes, it does not in reality exist; the Parliament is at once a legislative and a constituent assembly." *Œuvres Complètes,* I, 166, 167.

related group of documents, not only promulgated at a given time and setting forth in logical array the framework and principles of a scheme of government, but subject to amendment, not at the hand of the government itself, but only by the same ultimate agency—distinct from and superior to the government—which made the instrument in the first place. He could discern nothing of this nature in England; on the contrary, every feature of the governmental and legal system there was open to change at any time, to any extent, by simple action of the government—really only one part of the government at that, i.e., Parliament. Hence it seemed to him that there was nothing in England really capable of being considered a constitution.

De Tocqueville would not have been so far wrong, save for one important consideration, namely, that legal power to amend and actual, useable power to do so are two very different things. It does not follow that merely because kingship and jury trial and private property and the suffrage are legally at the mercy of Parliament, they are in danger of being swept away. Parliament, after all, is composed of men who, with few exceptions, are respected members of a well-ordered society, endowed with sense, and alive to their responsibility for safeguarding the country's political heritage. They live and work under the restraint of powerful traditions and will no more run riot with the constitution than if it were weighted down with guarantees designed to keep it out of their control. Legally, the constitution is undeniably the most flexible on earth; but actually, it is considerably less fluid than might be inferred from what the writers say. History shows that few systems of government are more grudgingly and conservatively reconstructed by deliberate legislative act. The flexibility of a constitution, in point of practical fact, depends far less upon the procedure of amendment than upon the political temperament of the people.

Of late, some effort has been made to put Parliament under somewhat greater formal restraint by developing the principle that no far-reaching changes in the governmental system should be made until the voters have had a chance to pass judgment upon the proposals at a general election. Theoretically, of course, Parliament merely carries out the will of the electoral majority in all that it does. But it can easily happen that a constitutional question of the first magnitude will come to a head at a time when a new House of Commons has not been elected in three or four years; and even if there has been an election within less time than that, the question at issue may not have been prominently before the voters. The proposal is that, especially when the latter circumstance obtains, Parliament shall not proceed with important constitutional changes without taking positive steps to ascertain the public will.[24] On certain historic occasions the plan has been followed, notably in 1910 when Mr. Asquith's Liberal government went to the country with the scheme of second chamber reform later embodied in the Parliament Act of 1911.[25] But, although the Conservative party generally and many prominent members of other parties individually have declared for it, the principle of the referendum cannot be said to have established itself, as is evidenced by the enfranchisement of eight and a half million women—not to mention other drastic changes in the electoral system—under legislation passed in 1918 by a parliament dating from 1910 and entirely without formal popular mandate, and, equally, by the creation of the Irish Free State in 1922 under a plan never passed upon by the voters. Not only does the electorate continue to have no formal method of proposing constitutional changes, such as the initiative provides in Switzerland, Germany, and some of the American states, but it has no way of collectively expressing its opinion of such proposals when made by Parliament, save in the uncertain event of a dissolution, followed by a general election, before a final decision is reached. If the idea of the referendum were to gain general acceptance, it would afford a new and excellent illustration of the rise of a great custom or convention of the constitution. But matters have not yet gone this far, and the English system still furnishes a perfect example of a form of polity under which the electorate has "not only wholly surrendered to the government the exercise of constituent powers, or, to speak more correctly, has acquiesced in the complete exercise by that body of constituent

[24] The referendum might, of course, be applied after Parliament had acted but before the legislative process had been completed by the king's assent. The plan, in this form, is discussed in A. V. Dicey, *Law of the Constitution* (8th ed.), pp. xci-c.

[25] See pp. 341-342 below.

powers, but has imposed upon that body no obligation to exercise these powers in any manner different from that followed in the enactment of ordinary law." [26]

Basic Features of the Governmental System

The constitution being what it is, certain great features of the British governmental system naturally follow. The first is its unitary, or non-federal, form. A federal system of government prevails where the political sovereign (whatever it may be in the particular case) has distributed the powers of government among certain agencies, central and divisional, and has done so through the medium of constitutional provisions which neither the central government nor any divisional government has power to alter. The important thing is not the territorial distribution of powers, because such a distribution has to be made under all forms of government, nor yet the amount or kinds of power distributed, but the fact that the distribution is made and maintained by some recognized authority superior to both central and divisional governments. The United States has a federal form of government because the partition of

[26] W. F. Willoughby, *Government of Modern States,* 123. Among the best brief discussions of the British constitution are A. L. Lowell, *Government of England,* I, 1-15; W. R. Anson, *Law and Custom of the Constitution* (5th ed.), I, 1-13; S. Low, *The Governance of England* (new ed.), 1-14; and J. A. R. Marriott, *English Political Institutions* (new ed., Oxford, 1925), Chap. ii. A more extended analysis is A. V. Dicey, *Introduction to the Study of the Law of the Constitution* (8th ed.), already cited. A highly interesting and significant work on the subject is W. Bagehot, *The English Constitution,* first published as a series of articles in the initial numbers of the *Fortnightly Review* in 1865-66 and brought out in book form at London in 1867. When a second edition of this book appeared in 1872, the author seized the occasion to add a lengthy and suggestive introduction discussing the effects of the Reform Act of 1867. Bagehot was a keen-minded journalist who took pleasure in writing of the constitution as it actually was in his day, rather than of its theoretical and legalistic aspects only, as the lawyers, e.g., Blackstone, were wont to do. Dicey remarks (*op. cit.,* 19) that no author of modern times has done so much to elucidate the intricate workings of English government as Bagehot. The most recent edition of *The English Constitution* (London, 1928) contains an illuminating introduction by Lord Balfour. Lord Bryce's famous discussion of flexible and rigid constitutions will be found in his *Studies in History and Jurisprudence,* Chap. iii. American readers will be interested in J. H. Whitehouse, "The Constitutional Systems of England and the United States," *Contemp. Rev.,* Oct., 1926.

powers between the national government and the state governments is made by the sovereign people, through the national constitution, and cannot be changed by the government at Washington any more than by that at Albany or Harrisburg or Indianapolis.[27] On the other hand, the government of England is unitary, because all power is concentrated in a single government, centering at London, which has created the counties, boroughs, and other local political areas for its own convenience, which has endowed them, as subordinate districts, with such powers as it chose to bestow, and which is free to alter their organization and powers at any time, or even to abolish them altogether.[28] The governmental systems of France, Italy, Belgium, Japan, and most other states are of this same character.

A second feature of the British constitution, already obvious, is the supremacy of Parliament. As pointed out above, the combination of king and two houses is, indeed, legally omnipotent.

[27] This definition of federalism is frankly legalistic and does not seem in every case to square with the facts. No one needs to be told that in all federally organized countries the powers of the central government steadily grow at the expense of those of the divisional governments, by usage and by legislation, and quite without any amendment of the formal constitution. Certainly this is true in the United States. Nevertheless, in the eye of constitutional law these changes represent, not accretions of power not previously possessed, but only amplifications or fulfillments of powers already conferred. On the nature and uses of federal government, see J. W. Garner, *Political Science and Government*, 417-422; W. W. Willoughby and L. Rogers, *Introduction to the Problem of Government* (Garden City, 1921), Chap. xxiv; J. Bryce, *The American Commonwealth* (4th ed., New York, 1910), I, Chaps. xxvii-xxx; and J. A. R. Marriott, *The Mechanism of the Modern State* (Oxford, 1927), II, Chap. xxxviii. The tendency of the central government to acquire more and more power is discussed in J. Bryce, *Studies in History and Jurisprudence*, Chap. iv.

[28] This statement is made primarily with reference to England alone. Even Great Britain and the United Kingdom, however, are not federal, for the reason that the special positions occupied by Scotland and Northern Ireland rest entirely upon statutes passed by the parliament at Westminster and repealable by its sole action. Various proposals for "devolution," "home rule all round," etc., look in the direction of federalism, although if they were adopted the result would not necessarily, or even likely, be a true federal system (see pp. 469-477 below). On the other hand, the Irish Free State has too much autonomy to be regarded as joined with the rest of the British Isles in such a system. On "the characteristics of federal government in relation to home rule all round," see A. V. Dicey, *Law of the Constitution* (8th ed.), pp. lxxxvii-xci.

Leaving out of account practical and moral restraints which operate powerfully upon it, and thinking only of what may be done under the law, Parliament can alter or rescind any charter, agreement, or statute; it can cause any official of the government to be dismissed and any judicial decision to be made of no effect; it can put an end to any usage and overturn any rule of common law; it can, at will, bend the constitution in any conceivable direction. An English publicist once remarked that the only thing it cannot do is to make a man a woman. Perhaps it would have been more to the point to say that the thing it cannot do is to make a law or set up a principle which will prevent succeeding parliaments from exercising an equal plenitude of power. In other words, its power is a present one and cannot be so projected into the future as to stereotype a rule or practice beyond possibility of change by a later parliament.[29]

It follows that every act of Parliament is "constitutional," if a measure is passed which is contrary to the constitution as it has hitherto stood, the constitution simply becomes something different in that regard. One who follows English political discussion, even from afar, will not infrequently hear it charged that a legislative proposal, or even a new law, is unconstitutional. But this means only that somebody considers the offending proposal or act to be inconsistent with previously accepted fundamental law, or with an established usage, or with international law, or perhaps only with the accepted standards of morality. An act so regarded is legally quite as valid and enforceable as if no question had been raised. No one can allege that it is *ultra vires.* The word of Parliament, i.e., the *latest* word, is law, however it may cut across existing constitutional arrangements; and as such it will be enforced by the courts. The only way of getting round it is repeal by the same or a succeeding parliament. Something like the American prac-

[29] More than one statute has solemnly declared various of its provisions perpetual—only to be amended in these respects, or even stricken from the books, when circumstances changed. Thus an act of 1869 disestablished the church in Ireland, notwithstanding that the maintenance of the established church there had been made a fundamental condition of the union of 1800. Likewise, notwithstanding that the statute of 1800 specified that the union should last "forever," the Irish reorganization of 1920-22 brought the arrangement effectually to an end—even though, curiously, Pitt's famous measure has never been repealed.

tice of judicial review has gained a considerable foothold in certain Continental countries,[30] but Britain has remained totally unaffected.[31] There, the principle still holds full sway that whatever Parliament decrees is law and remains such until repealed by legislative process. So far as England alone is concerned, the unitary form of the government has averted those clashes between rival authorities, central and divisional, which made judicial review a practical necessity in the United States. The complicated, and sometimes tense, relations between England and Scotland, and between Great Britain and Ireland, might, however, have given rise to something of the kind, but for the one great barrier which has always stood, and still stands, in the way, i.e., the idea of the supremacy of Parliament naturally held in a country devoted to popular government yet uncommitted to any doctrine of separation of powers. As it is, the courts merely accept the statutes put forth at Westminster and enforce them. In applying them to particular cases, the judges have to determine what they mean; and sometimes this involves a rather important power of interpretation.[32] Beyond this, however, the courts have no discretion. Punctuated at every turn by Supreme Court decisions on the constitutionality of acts of Congress and of the state legislatures, the constitutional history of the United States presents an appearance altogether different from that of the mother land.[33]

The foregoing remarks about the legally unlimited powers of Parliament may lead one to wonder what protection the

[30] For a brief account of this development, see J. W. Garner, *Political Science and Government*, 759-770. Cf. p. 628 below.

[31] Except as it is applied to orders in council and administrative rules. But this does not touch the matter of constitutionality of statutes. See p. 202 below.

[32] On the exceptional demands of this nature likely to be made by the Trade Disputes and Trade Unions Act of 1927, see an article by A. T. Mason in *Amer. Polit. Sci. Rev.*, Feb., 1928. Cf. p. 516 below.

[33] The only trace of judicial review of laws in all British practice is the right of the Judicial Committee of the Privy Council (see p. 755 below) to advise the crown to declare unconstitutional an act of a dominion, or other colonial, legislature. This, of course, in no wise affects legislation at Westminster. It is interesting to note that judicial review is fully established in Canada, Australia, South Africa, and the Irish Free State. See, for example, C. G. Haines, "Judicial Review of Legislation in Canada," *Harvard Law Rev.*, Apr., 1915.

individual citizen, or "subject," has against laws curtailing or permitting arbitrary infringement of his personal liberties. On what basis, indeed, does he enjoy any liberties at all? Royal tyranny is a thing of the past. But what about the tyranny that might conceivably be practiced by an omnipotent legislature? Two main facts supply the answer. The first is that there is no lack of solemn guarantees of personal liberty in the constitution. Some of them, e.g., the privilege of the writ of habeas corpus, the right to bear arms, the right of petition, and immunity from excessive bail and from cruel and unusual punishments, are expressly covered in important statutes like the Bill of Rights. Others, as freedom of speech and assembly and freedom of religion, rest equally solidly upon rules of the common law. Hardly a right or liberty which men have learned to hold dear will fail to be found unequivocally guaranteed somewhere within the four corners of the fundamental law.

The second fact is that, while Parliament admittedly has the power to restrict, suspend, or rescind these guarantees at will, all the force of tradition and public opinion militates against such action except in cases of gravest necessity, and in actual practice Britain is one of the freest of lands in this important particular.[34] Other countries have employed different specially devised methods of protecting private rights. Here in the United States our favorite device is a lengthy and detailed "bill of rights" incorporated somewhere in the text of the written fundamental law. The first eight amendments furnish such a feature in the national constitution, and almost every state constitution made from Revolutionary times to the present has articles of the kind. Most of the new post-war constitutions in European countries, notably those of the German republic and the Irish Free State, abound in similar provisions. Even where such formal specifications in the written fundamental law seem most iron-clad, however, they are no more effective in practice than the British guarantees; for in the one case as in the other the thing that really gives force and sanction is not so much the form that the pledges take as the consensus of opinion that lies back of them and keeps the government on its mettle in

[34] The privilege of habeas corpus, for example, has not been suspended in a century, not even during the World War.

living up to them. As recently as 1900 and 1909, the Commonwealth of Australia and the Union of South Africa, respectively, were content to adopt written constitutions in which the principles safeguarding private rights were merely implicit and not expressly stated.[35]

[35] On the history of personal liberty in England, see T. E. May and F. Holland, *Constitutional History of England,* II, Chaps. ix-xiv. Full discussion of the subject will be found in A. V. Dicey, *Law of the Constitution* (8th ed.), Chaps. iv-viii, and E. Jenks, *The Book of English Law* (London, 1928), Chaps. x-xii, and in many of its phases in F. E. Baldwin, *Sumptuary Legislation and Personal Regulation in England* (Baltimore, 1926). Cf. A. B. Keith, *Constitution, Administration, and Laws of the Empire,* 136-144, and D. J. Medley, *Manual of English Constitutional History* (6th ed.), 465-525. There is comment on the disadvantages of a written bill of rights in W. F. Willoughby, *Government of Modern States,* 151-157. Some judicial decisions relating to the rights and duties of the British subject are presented in B. A. Bicknell, *Cases on the Law of the Constitution,* 153-171.

CHAPTER IV

THE CROWN AND ITS POWERS

THE British constitution is, beyond all others, intangible and elusive. Certainly one would be hard put to it to reduce it—custom as well as law—to the captivity of a printed statement; and even if one were to succeed in doing so, changes of content and meaning would invalidate the document in some particulars almost overnight. We have, however, brought to light the chief processes of its growth and a number of its major characteristics: its antiquity, its flexibility, its inherent vigor, its amazing contrasts of legal theory and actual fact. By so doing we have prepared ourselves to analyze and interpret the great system of government carried on from day to day in accordance with its rules and principles. There would be some logic in beginning with Parliament; for that is where the supreme power in the government is to be found. Practical convenience, however, suggests a different plan. We must know the rôles played by the king, the ministry, and especially the cabinet, before we can really understand what Parliament is and does; besides, there is advantage in passing directly from the study of Parliament to that of political parties. Accordingly, we shall begin with the parts of the system that have to do with executive authority and agencies, policy-framing, and administration.

The King and "the Crown"

At the outset we are confronted with one of the most striking illustrations of the constitution's penchant for disguises. This is the contrast between the theory and the reality of the position occupied by the king—the distinction between king and crown which Gladstone once pronounced the most vital fact in British constitutional practice. Various writers in times past have rather enjoyed startling their readers with staccato sentences enumerating the weighty and devastating things that the sovereign is still competent to do. In the first book in which the true character of cabinet government was ever explained, Walter Bagehot, two generations ago, wrote that Queen Victoria could disband the army, dismiss the navy, make a peace by the cession of Cornwall, begin a war for the conquest of Brittany, make every subject a peer, pardon all offenders, and do other things too fearful to contemplate.[1] And Gladstone himself, a decade later, spoke of the sovereign as receiving and holding all revenues, appointing and dismissing ministers, making treaties, waging war, concluding peace, pardoning criminals, summoning and dissolving Parliament, "for the most part without any specified restraint of law," and under "an absolute immunity from consequences." [2] Legally, all this was true; and one would not have to go back many centuries to come upon a time when it would have been true actually and literally. But of course neither the journalist nor the statesman meant for a moment to suggest that the queen, or any other British sovereign in these days, would dream of doing any of the things mentioned. They meant only to call attention to an ultimate historic and legal principle of the constitution which never has been quite extinguished, even though nowadays as obsolete in practice as the belief in Thor and Woden. If speaking in terms of actualities, they would have said that the acts enumerated could be performed, not by the sovereign, but by the *crown*.[3]

What is the crown? Mr. Sidney Low says that it is "a convenient working hypothesis." [4] That, however, is not very satisfying. Elsewhere he calls it "a myth"—yet immediately he goes on to say that it might almost as well be called the Nation, or the Will of the People, or any other suitable abstraction." [5]

[1] *The English Constitution* (2nd ed., London, 1872), Introd., p. xxxiii.

[2] *Gleanings of Past Years* (New York, 1889), I, 227.

[3] Blackstone, in his day—with far less perception of the real situation than such men as Bagehot and Gladstone possessed—wrote extravagantly of the powers of "our sovereign lord, thus all-perfect and immortal in his kingly capacity" (*Commentaries*, I, 250). On the other hand, the philosopher Paley, in his *Principles of Moral and Political Philosophy*, published in 1785, anticipated Bagehot to some extent by calling attention to the wide gap between the theory and the fact of the kingly powers (Bk. vi, chap. 7).

[4] *The Governance of England* (new ed., London, 1914), 255.

[5] *Ibid.*, 256.

Briefly and concretely, it is the supreme executive and policy-framing agency in the government, which means, practically, a subtle combination of sovereign, ministers (especially cabinet members), and to a degree Parliament. It is the institution—if so abstract a thing can be called an institution—to which substantially all prerogatives and powers once belonging to the king in person have gradually been transferred; and its nature will be clarified in proportion as the manner of that transference is understood.

The process passed through two main stages. The first was what we may term the "institutionalizing" of the king. Originally, the kings were elective; each ruled largely independently of his predecessors; and when a king died there was an "interregnum"—a cessation of all government—when, as the chronicler frankly tells us, "every man that could robbed another." After the Conquest, however,—mainly in the twelfth and thirteenth centuries, and under the influence of feudal ideas—the royal dignity became definitely hereditary. Infants, who manifestly could not rule personally, succeeded if next in line, and the reign of one king (Edward I) was recognized as dating from the death of his predecessor even though he remained abroad, uncrowned, for four full years after the event. Through regencies and stretches of absentee kingship laws were enforced, cases tried, taxes collected, precisely as if the throne were actively occupied. The "king's writ was running," because kingship had become a continuous institution, an office, a function, quite unaffected by the coming and going of individual monarchs. When a king died, there was no interregnum. "The king is dead," was now the doctrine; "long live the king."

This change alone brought the king into a wholly new position. No longer a purely personal monarch, owing his place to his prowess or cleverness, and free to do what he liked, he had become a link in a chain, a part of a continuous political system, custodian of the heritage of his predecessors and bound by their acts. People with legal minds grew accustomed to a sharp distinction between the king as an individual and the king as an institution; and so the way was prepared for the second great stage or phase, notably in the seventeenth and eighteenth centuries, when powers of legislation, administration, and finance were stripped from the king as a man and put beyond his control, while yet remaining in the king as an institution, or, as we would say today, in the crown. These processes have been described and require no further comment here. Literally, the "crown" is, of course, an inanimate object which is kept in the Tower of London. But, as an English writer puts it, by the simple process of using a capital letter in writing it, we make it stand for the kingship as an institution.[6]

Thinking, then, of the crown as, primarily, the supreme executive head of the nation (in somewhat the same broad sense in which the president is the chief executive in the United States), and bearing in mind that the king is not even yet entirely dissociated from it in actual practice, as he certainly is not in legal theory, we may first take some note of the origins, scope, and nature of the powers of the crown, and then consider the position which the sovereign himself occupies and the reasons why monarchy survives as a feature of the political system.

Powers of the Crown—General Aspects

As they stand today, the powers of the crown are derived from two great sources, i.e., prerogative and statute. The nature of statute is obvious enough. Any act of Parliament that assigns new duties to the executive authorities, provides for the appointment of new administrative officers, or in other ways increases the work of the government adds by so much to the powers wielded in the name of the crown; and it goes without saying that such increases are numerous and important. But what is prerogative? As conveniently defined by Dicey, it is "the residue of discretionary or arbitrary authority which at any time is legally left in the hands of the crown." [7] Originally, before the days of parliamentary control of public affairs—when, indeed, there was no Parliament at all—all powers rested upon this basis; all were conceived of as "prerogatives" inhering in the person of the king. Later, Parliament began stripping away powers, even while sometimes also bestowing new ones; in addition, old powers fell into disuse and became obsolete.

[6] E. Jenks, *Government of the British Empire,* 23-24.
[7] *Law of the Constitution* (8th ed.), 420.

Such powers, however, as survived on the earlier basis, together with such newer ones as were picked up by usage as distinguished from statute, continued to form the prerogative; and to this day these powers constitute a very large and important part of the sum total possessed. Prerogative, therefore, means, substantially, those powers which have not been granted—those which have been acquired by sheer assumption, confirmed by usage, and tolerated or accepted as features of the governmental system even after Parliament came into a position to abolish or alter them at will. Many crown powers as we find them today rest, indeed, upon neither prerogative nor statute exclusively, being rather derived from prerogative as modified by statute. In such cases it is sometimes difficult to say whether the power exists primarily by virtue of a statute which limits and defines it, or by virtue of an anterior prerogative which may be capable of being stretched or interpreted more or less arbitrarily. No principle of the working constitution is established more securely than that crown prerogative may be defined, restricted, suppressed—or, indeed, given statutory confirmation or extension—by act of Parliament.[8] Naturally, powers that rest upon simple statute are rather easier to ascertain and measure than those in which the element of prerogative survives.[9]

From what has been said it follows that the powers of the crown are continuously in flux; they are now being cut down at certain points and again carried to new heights at others.

[8] "The essential and peculiar character of the English constitution is that the king has remained in theory and in the letter of the law absolute; he is still in form the source of all authority, the acts of the government are his acts, the officers of the state are his servants, while in reality, by various institutions, statute laws, and conventional practices having the force of law, he has been hedged about by limitations, and the true sovereignty, the final power of decision in all questions of importance, has been transferred to the people who form the nation and who act through their elected representatives. The constitution as a whole is made up of the institutions, laws, and practices through which the nation acts and expresses its will, but the one thing which gives unity and system to all these is the limited monarchy, or, to use the other term by which we commonly call it, the constitutional monarchy—a monarchy acting under a constitution." G. B. Adams, *The Origin of the English Constitution,* 41.

[9] A number of judicial decisions having to do with the relation of the prerogative to statute are presented in B. A. Bicknell, *Cases on the Law of the Constitution,* 69-90.

Curtailment has come in three principal ways. The first is great contractual agreements between king and nation (or some part of the nation), best illustrated by Magna Carta. The second is prohibitive legislation, of such nature as the clauses of the Bill of Rights forbidding suspending or dispensing with laws, or the measures putting an end to debasement of the coinage, pre-emption, purveyance, and other earlier royal practices. The third is simple disuse, illustrated by the lapse, since the Tudor period, of the power of the crown to add to the membership of the House of Commons by arbitrary enfranchisement of boroughs, and the disappearance, since a somewhat earlier period, of the power to create peerages for life except by express authorization of Parliament.[10] On the other hand, the crown's powers have been steadily augmented both by custom (which may be regarded as adding something to the prerogative) and by legislation—in later centuries, chiefly, of course, the latter. When, for example, Parliament adds an air service to the army, establishes a system of old age pensions, authorizes a new tax, or passes a new immigration act, it imposes fresh duties of administration upon the crown and thereby perceptibly enlarges the volume of its power; or the grant may look to the exercise of legislative rather than executive functions, by means of the device known as "statutory orders," to be explained presently. The powers of the crown at any given moment represent, therefore, the net product of this pull and haul of forces, tearing down here and building up there.

Two further general facts about these powers are to be noted. The first is that crown authority, instead of being smaller and weaker than in generations past, is greater and stronger, and is still growing. A remarkable feature of democratic development throughout the world in the past hundred years has been the expansion of the sphere which government undertakes to occupy, and accordingly of authority wielded and functions performed; and in Britain, as elsewhere, this has meant a steady augmentation of powers and activities of those parts of the government which execute and administer, equally with that

[10] See p. 322 for the case of Baron Wensleydale in 1856 and for the authorization of non-hereditary peerages by Parliament in 1876 and later years.

which legislates. "We must not confound the truth," says Maitland, "that the king's personal will has come to count for less and less with the falsehood . . . that his legal powers have been diminished. On the contrary, of late years they have enormously increased."[11] "This is simply a natural consequence," remarks an American authority, "of the transformation of the royal office into a public trust, and as the duties of the trusteeship enlarge its activity is correspondingly increased since it has so much more to attend to."[12] "All told," writes another American student of the subject, "the executive authority of the crown is, in the eye of the law, very wide, far wider than that of the chief magistrate in many countries, and well-nigh as extensive as that now possessed by the monarch in any government not an absolute despotism; and although the crown has no inherent legislative power except in conjunction with Parliament, it has been given by statute very large powers of subordinate legislation. . . . Since the accession of the House of Hanover the new powers conferred upon the crown by statute have probably more than made up for the loss to the prerogative of powers which have either been restricted by the same process or become obsolete by disuse. By far the greater part of the prerogative, as it existed at that time, has remained legally vested in the crown, and can be exercised today."[13]

A second fact of major importance is that while the powers of the crown have been spoken of as mainly executive, they are by no means exclusively such. Even in the United States, where government is organized fundamentally according to the principle of separation of powers, functions of different kinds are not kept altogether in different hands; the chief executive participates in law-making, the Senate acts on proposed appointments, and so on. In Great Britain, the principle of separation has never really established itself at all. It is true that the French *litterateur* Montesquieu, at the middle of the eighteenth century, extolled the English constitution on the ground that it provided for the separate exercise of executive, legislative, and judicial powers—by the king, Parliament, and the courts,

[11] *Origin and Growth of the English Constitution,* Pt. I, p. x.

[12] H. J. Ford, *Representative Government,* 124.

[13] A. L. Lowell, *The Government of England,* I, 26.

respectively; and that he held up this supposed system, tempered with a set of checks and balances, as a model for his own country.[14] But he was deceived. Then, as now, Parliament was the one supreme authority in the realm, and, as such, exercised full legislative power, controlled the executive by holding ministers responsible for their acts, and regulated (or at all events was capable of regulating) the conditions under which justice was administered. Similarly, what we know as the crown had to do then, and still has to do, not only with matters of an executive nature but also with legislation and justice. The entire cabinet system, ripening rapidly when Montesquieu wrote, makes for union of powers and functions rather than separation. The crown's place today, in the legislative and judicial, as well as the executive and administrative, mechanism will be apparent if we take a bird's-eye view of the powers which now actually belong to it.

Executive and Administrative Powers

To put it bluntly, the crown is the executive. As such, it, first of all, enforces all national laws, supervises and directs all national administration (for example, the postal service), collects all national revenues, and expends all moneys appropriated by act of Parliament. It appoints and commissions substantially all higher executive and administrative officers, all judges, and the officers of the army, navy, and air service. Judges can be removed only on joint address by the two houses of Parliament, but aside from them (and a small number of other officials on a special basis), any officer who is similarly commissioned in the name of the crown can be removed, even though, in practice, orders in council, usage, and rules of the Civil Service Commission actually give the mass of non-political officers and employees full protection from removal so long as they are efficient and abstain from activities of a partisan nature. The

[14] *De l'Esprit des Lois* (published at Geneva in 1748), Bk. XI, Chap. vi. See W. A. Dunning, *Political Theories from Luther to Montesquieu,* 412-415. Montesquieu's idealized picture of English political institutions profoundly influenced the thought of writers like Blackstone and the acts of statesmen, notably the framers of the constitution of the United States. It developed into what may be termed the literary theory of the English constitution, first seriously shaken by Bagehot's *English Constitution.*

crown thus controls the entire personnel of civil administration and of the defense services.

In the next place, the crown supervises, and to some extent directs, the work of local government and administration as carried on by the authorities of counties, boroughs, rural and urban districts, and other areas. This central control is less extensive than in France and other Continental countries, and it is exercised, not through a single channel like the French Ministry of the Interior, but through the Home Office in matters of police, the Ministry of Health in matters of sanitation, the Board of Education in the domain of public instruction, the Board of Trade in the field of public utilities.[15] The present point is that, however wielded, these powers of supervision and control are strictly powers of the crown.

The crown also manages the country's foreign relations. All ambassadors, ministers, and consuls accredited to foreign states are appointed in its name, and the diplomatic and consular representatives of such states are received in the same way. All instructions to official representatives abroad go out as from the crown; all delegates to international congresses and conferences of a diplomatic character are so accredited; foreign negotiations are carried on in the crown's name. War is declared and peace made as if by the king alone. Of course it is futile to declare war unless there is assurance that Parliament will supply the funds requisite for carrying it on, and either house, or both, may express disapproval of the government's policy or in other ways make its position untenable. But Parliament itself has no direct means of bringing about a war or of bringing a war to an end.[16] When on the fateful fourth of August, 1914, Great Britain cast her lot with France and Belgium in the titanic conflict with Germany, it was the ministers, acting in the name of the crown, who made the decision. Parliament happened to be in session at the time, and the Foreign Secretary explained the diplomatic situation in an extended speech (August 3) in the House of Commons, and received impressive evidences of sup-

[15] See pp. 646-650 below.

[16] W. R. Anson, *Law and Custom of the Constitution* (3rd ed.), II, Pt. ii, 103. See especially F. R. Flournoy, *Parliament and War: the Relation of the British Parliament to the Administration of Foreign Policy in Connection with the Initiation of War* (London, 1927).

port. But had the ministers chosen to send no ultimatum to Berlin, and to hold to a policy of neutrality, the country would not have become a party to the war.

From what has been said, it follows that the treaty-making power belongs to the crown. It is true that treaties are sometimes made expressly subject to parliamentary approval. Examples are the Anglo-German convention of 1890 ceding Heligoland in return for a desirable East African boundary, and the Anglo-French convention of 1904 relating to Morocco and Egypt. It is true, also, that a treaty may lay a financial obligation upon the country of such nature that, unless Parliament acts, the crown is, in effect, put in the position of taxing the people. Treaties which cede territory or pledge money payments are therefore very likely to be submitted to Parliament for endorsement. Yet even here there is no fixed rule; the treaty of Paris in 1783, relinquishing thirteen colonies in America, was not put before Parliament at all. It was considered significant that the treaty of Versailles was laid before Parliament in its entirety in 1919, and that only after being explained, debated, and voted upon there was the royal signature attached and ratification notified to the world. Some people jumped to the conclusion that the submission of treaties to Parliament was going to become the regular practice. Such, however, has not been the outcome; on the contrary, it would appear that the method of handling treaties has undergone no real change. Unless a treaty is made contingent on parliamentary approval, or unless it alters the law of the land (e.g., by reducing customs duties), the assent of Parliament is not necessary to its validity —however essential it may be to procure parliamentary appropriations before its terms can be actually carried into effect.[17]

Another important field of executive control is the colonies. The self-governing dominions—Canada, Australia, New Zealand, and the others—are subject to but little restraint from

[17] A. B. Keith, *Constitution, Administration, and Laws of the Empire,* 56. Cf. W. R. Anson, *op. cit.* 102-112. It may, however, be added that treaties of exceptional interest, and especially those of high moral importance, are likely to be submitted, irrespective of their specific terms. Thus, the Locarno treaty was presented for ratification in 1925. The program of the Labor party demands that "all international engagements" be so submitted.

either crown or Parliament; yet even here the governor-general is a crown appointee and, under new principles adopted in 1926, is regarded as the immediate representative of the sovereign. The same thing is true in the case of the Irish Free State. The dependent empire of India is administered by agents of the crown, as are also the numerous crown colonies, such as Jamaica and Malta. Protectorates and mandated regions are taken care of similarly.[18]

Finally may be mentioned the power of pardon and reprieve, which although sometimes thought of as judicial in nature, is really executive. No pardon can be granted for a civil wrong which has brought injury to a person or group of persons; but in connection with criminal offenses the power can be, and is, exercised at discretion.

The Crown and Legislation

A second general group of crown powers pertains to legislation. It is less imposing than in earlier times, but nevertheless important. Technically, indeed, all power of law-making is vested in "the king in Parliament," which means, historically, the king acting in collaboration with the two houses; and, as has been observed elsewhere, to this day every statute declares itself to have been enacted "by the King's Most Excellent Majesty, by and with the advice and consent of the Lords Spiritual and Temporal, and Commons, in this present Parliament assembled, and by the authority of the same," [19] even though, actually, the king may have had nothing whatever to do with the matter and even the crown may have done nothing more than give formal assent.

It is, of course, on the legislative, rather than the executive, side that most of the losses of power by the crown have taken place. There was a time, before the rise of Parliament, when the crown had practically unlimited law-making power. As Parliament gathered strength, this power was progressively pared down, although for a long time after the general principle of parliamentary control over legislation was established the crown clung to the prerogative of issuing proclamations and

[18] See pp. 746-751 below.

[19] Cf. p. 413, note 27, below.

ordinances with the force of law. In the seventeenth century, however, even this had to be given up, and nowadays the crown has, apart from Parliament, no power to make, repeal, suspend, or alter laws anywhere outside of the crown colonies.[20]

This does not mean that the crown does not, actually as well as theoretically, have a great deal to do with the work of legislation; indeed, without the crown there could be, as the constitution stands, no legislation at all. In the first place, it is the crown that bestows peerages, thus largely determining the composition and character of the House of Lords.[21] In the second place, it takes the initiative in summoning Parliament, subject only to the practical requirement that there shall be at least one session a year.[22] It also prorogues and dissolves Parliament and sets in motion the process by which a new House of Commons is elected. In a very real sense, Parliament transacts business only during the pleasure of the crown. Furthermore, men who are officers of the crown guide and control in practically all that Parliament does. They prepare the king's speech which sets forth the government's program at the opening of a session; they decide what bills shall be introduced, and when (leaving little time for measures emanating from non-governmental sources); they lead in explaining and defending these bills, and pilot them through to enactment. It is true that these men are also members of Parliament. But the circumstance that gives them their power is the fact that they are ministers of the crown. Still further, no bill passed by Parliament gains the character of law, or is of effect in any way, unless and until it has received the crown's assent. Here again it is true that such assent has not been withheld from a measure in more than two hundred years, and that the ceremony by which it is extended to bills, commonly in batches, in these days is nothing more than a picturesque formality.[23] Nevertheless, it is indis-

[20] H. Jenkyns, *British Rule and Jurisdiction Beyond the Seas* (Oxford, 1902), 4-6, 95; A. B. Keith, *The Constitution, Administration, and Laws of the Empire*, 267-270.

[21] See pp. 317-318 below.

[22] See p. 369 below.

[23] The ceremony is described below (see p. 421). The veto was last employed in 1707, by Queen Anne in defeating a bill for settling the militia in Scotland. On the question whether the veto is to be considered obsolete, see Auditor Tantum, "The Veto of the Crown," *Fort. Rev.*, Sept., 1913.

pensable, and could still be denied. The veto has fallen into disuse for the reason that the king is no longer in a position to wield it himself (for reasons that must have become apparent), and because all important bills that ever get through Parliament have originated with, or at all events have been endorsed by, the ministers, who alone could bring the veto into play (in the name of the crown) if it were to be employed at all.

In one other important way the crown has to do with legislation. It has been stated that, except in the non-self-governing colonies, the crown no longer makes laws by inherent power. This is entirely true. Nevertheless, measures having the force of law, and applicable in Britain itself, do today emanate from the crown. These measures take the form of orders in council, being, as the name indicates, orders issued by the king-in-council, i.e., the king and the Privy Council—in effect, though not in form or theory, the cabinet. In the main, such orders deal with matters which are beyond the competence of the crown acting independently, and are issued in pursuance of power conferred by Parliament. Their promulgation by the crown is, nevertheless, as Lowell puts it, "a species of subordinate legislation." [24]

Other Crown Powers and Functions

Turning to the domain of justice, we find that whereas in ages past the "king's law" was enforced in the "king's courts," and the sovereign himself did not scruple to intervene and upset the judgments of his tribunals, the crown nowadays plays a relatively minor rôle. It cannot create new courts, or alter the organization or procedure of any existing court, or change the number, tenure, or pay of judges, or substitute different modes of appointment. All these matters are under the jurisdiction of Parliament. Judges are appointed, indeed, by the crown; and all appeals coming from the tribunals of India, the colonies, and the Channel Islands are decided by the crown through the fiction of advice tendered by the Judicial Committee of the Privy Council, by which authority the appeals are actually heard and considered. But judges can be removed by the crown

[24] This matter of orders is dealt with more fully at later points. See pp. 120-121, 201-203 below.

only at the request of both houses of Parliament; while in office they cannot be controlled in any way; and the court of last resort for Britain itself is, not the crown, but the House of Lords. By hoary custom, the crown is still spoken of, often proudly, as "the fountain of justice." Obviously it is such, in reality, to only a very limited extent.

In greater degree the crown is "the fountain of honor;" for it is the ministers (chiefly the prime minister) acting in the crown's name that single out men for various titles and distinctions, arrange their names in lists for announcement at New Year's and other suitable occasions, and cause the proper patents or other papers to be issued. Some of these honors, e.g., peerages, have a political import; others, like knighthood, are of social significance only.

Finally may be mentioned the connections between the crown and the established churches of England and Scotland.[25] Churches other than the Anglican in England and the Presbyterian in Scotland are voluntary associations, without state connections and free to regulate their creeds and rituals as they like. But the two bodies mentioned are built (in different ways) into the fabric of the state, and both crown and Parliament have large powers of control over them. In the case of the English Church, the archbishops and bishops are appointed by the crown, which means in effect by the prime minister; for although it is true that when a vacancy arises a *congé d'élire,* or writ of election, is sent to the canons of the cathedral concerned, it is always accompanied by a "letter missive" designating the person to be chosen. Deans, too, are regularly, and canons frequently, appointed by the crown, although sometimes by the bishop. The "convocations" of Canterbury and York—bicameral legislative bodies composed of ecclesiastical persons of various grades—meet only by license of the crown, and their acts require assent of the crown just as do acts of Parliament. Since 1919, clergy and laity have both been represented in a National Assembly of the Church of England,[26] and under cer-

[25] The Anglican Church was disestablished in Ireland in 1869 and in Wales in 1920. There are now no established churches in those countries.

[26] Church of England Assembly (Powers) Act, 1919 (9 & 10 Geo. v., c. 76).

tain limitations this body can enact measures which, upon receiving the sanction of a joint ecclesiastical committee of Parliament,[27] and later of Parliament itself, can be presented to the crown for assent. The statute of Henry VIII (1534) which declared the king to be the "only Supreme Head in earth of the Church of England" [28] was repealed under Mary and was not later revived. An Elizabethan Act of Supremacy (1559), however, asserts the supremacy of the crown over all persons and causes ecclesiastical and temporal; [29] and in a score of ways the crown remains the effective head, as is further illustrated by the power (actually exercised since 1833 through the Judicial Committee of the Privy Council) to hear and decide appeals from ecclesiastical courts, diocesan and provincial, growing out of disciplinary cases under the Church Discipline Act (1840), the Public Worship Act (1874), and similar statutes. Crown functions in relation to the established Presbyterian Church in Scotland are not entirely non-existent, but are so purely nominal as to require no comment here.[30]

Such, in outline, are the powers of the crown today. How are they actually exercised? The answer is, in a variety of ways—some by the cabinet, some by the Privy Council and its committees, some by this or that board or other group of ministers, or even by a single minister—in almost every way, in fact, except that in which under historical and legal theory they should be exercised, i.e., by the king himself. Several chapters will presently be devoted to a description of the executive and administrative machinery through which the crown now functions. The sovereign in person, however, is still far from being a negligible part of the governmental system; and before passing on to the actualities of workaday administration we must give some attention to the position which he occupies, both

[27] Fifteen members of each house, named by the Lord Chancellor and speaker, respectively.

[28] G. B. Adams and H. M. Stephens, *Select Documents of English Constitutional History,* 239-240.

[29] *Ibid.,* 296-302.

[30] On the general subject of the relations of crown, Parliament, and the churches, see A. B. Keith, *Constitution, Administration, and Laws of the Empire,* 145-148; W. R. Anson, *Law and Custom of the Constitution,* (3rd ed.), II, Pt. ii, Chap. ix; A. L. Lowell, *Government of England,* II, Chaps. li-lii.

legally and in practical fact, noting the ways in which he helps carry on the business of state, and bringing to view some of the reasons why the great majority of Englishmen feel that the sort of kingship that has been arrived at is useful and ought to be perpetuated.

CHAPTER V

KINGSHIP AND WHY IT SURVIVES

Title and Succession to the Throne

As has been pointed out, kingship in Anglo-Saxon days was elective.[1] It is true that the choice of the electing body, the *witenagemot,* was normally restricted to the members of a single family, falling presumably upon that one who was deemed best fitted. But no definite rule or order of inheritance was allowed to establish itself; and the elective principle was from time to time reënforced by use of the power of deposition. William the Conqueror put forward a claim to the throne on the ground of relationship to the family of Edward the Confessor; and of course his title rested, in practical fact, upon victory in arms. Nevertheless he considered it worth while to submit himself to election by the witan; and for some generations longer the elective principle was held in at least outward respect.

Gradually, however, as kingship became less a matter of personal lordship and more a matter of territorial sovereignty, the hereditary principle gained the upper hand. By the thirteenth century, if not earlier, succession by right of inheritance was the rule—though even now the power of deposition, as employed in 1399 against Richard II, forbade any person to be regarded as having an indefeasible right to reign. Henry VII, the first Tudor, claimed the throne by hereditary right, yet his title was derived from an act of Parliament settling the crown on him and his heirs.[2] Indeed, throughout the Tudor period Parliament, while not seeking to elect every time the throne fell vacant, steadfastly clung to the right to fix the succession when the line was broken or when there was uncertainty or dispute.

[1] See p. 4 above.

[2] G. B. Adams and H. M. Stephens, *Select Documents of English Constitutional History,* 213.

Thus an act of 1533 established the succession upon the issue of Henry VIII and Anne Boleyn,[3] and another of 1544 fixed it, in event of the death of Edward [VI] without heirs, upon Henry's daughter Mary and her heirs, and next upon Elizabeth.[4] Though seemingly irreconcilable, the two principles of heredity and election were therefore brought into reasonable accord: election meant only occasional parliamentary regulation of the order of succession; that order once determined, sovereign followed sovereign by hereditary right.

And this is the situation today. The execution of Charles I, the restoration of the Stuarts in 1660 on terms in effect imposed by Parliament, the flight (construed as abdication) of James II in 1688, and the accession of William and Mary in 1689 by action of the national convention [5] removed any lingering doubt as to the conditional basis on which the throne is held. Whatever the case before 1689, since that time the tenure of English kings and queens has rested frankly upon the will of the nation as expressed in parliamentary enactment.

The statute by which the succession is now regulated is the Act of Settlement, dating from 1701. It provided that, in default of heirs of William III and of his expected successor, Anne, the crown and all prerogatives thereto appertaining should "be, remain, and continue to the most excellent Princess Sophia, and the heirs of her body, being Protestants." [6] Sophia, a granddaughter of James I, was the widow of the ruler of one of the smaller German states, the electorate of Hanover. There were other heirs whose claims, in the natural order of succession, might have been considered superior to hers. But the

[3] G. B. Adams and H. M. Stephens, *Select Documents of English Constitutional History,* 235-239.

[4] *Ibid.,* 264-267.

[5] See p. 40 above.

[6] For the text of the act, see G. B. Adams and H. M. Stephens, *Select Documents of English Constitutional History,* 475-479. As safeguards against dangers which might conceivably arise from the accession of a foreign-born sovereign, the act stipulated (1) that no person who should thereafter come into possession of the crown should go outside the dominions of England, Scotland, or Ireland without consent of Parliament, and (2) that in the event that the crown should devolve upon any person not a native of England, the nation should not be obliged to engage in any war for the defense of any dominions or territories not belonging to the crown of England, without consent of Parliament.

Bill of Rights debarred Catholics, and, this being taken into account, she stood first. Sophia narrowly missed becoming queen, because Anne outlived her by a year. But her son mounted the throne, in 1714, as George I, and the dynasty thus installed has reigned uninterruptedly to our own day. The present monarch, George V, is the eighth in the line. For a century and a quarter the sovereign of Great Britain was also the ruler of Hanover. At the accession of Queen Victoria in 1837, however, the union ended, because the law of Hanover forbade a woman to ascend the throne of that country.[7] The term "Hanoverian" which long clung to the dynasty came, therefore, to have only an historical significance; and in 1917 wartime sensibilities led to the adoption of the unimpeachably English name, House of Windsor.[8] Parliament would, of course, be entirely competent to repeal that part of the Act of Settlement which governs the succession and place a different family on the throne, or, for that matter, of course, to abolish kingship altogether.

A good deal of interesting history is connected with the sovereign's "style and titles." The royal title as it stands today is (in English translation of the official Latin): "George V by the Grace of God of Great Britain, Ireland, and the British Dominions beyond the Seas King, Defender of the Faith, Emperor of India." The title "Defender of the Faith" dates from the days of Henry VIII; that of "Emperor of India" from a royal proclamation of 1876; and the phrase "British Dominions beyond the Seas" from a proclamation of 1901. From 1801 to 1927 the general title included the words "of the United Kingdom of Great Britain and Ireland King," etc. At the last-mentioned date, however, a royal proclamation, issued in pursuance of an act of Parliament, dropped out the term "United Kingdom" and placed Ireland in the title coördinately

[7] A. W. Ward, *Great Britain and Hanover; Some Aspects of the Personal Union* (Oxford, 1899).

[8] It may be added that the war period saw the dynasty further Anglicized in that whereas previously no prince and few princesses had ever been permitted to marry any except royal blood—which, for Britain, meant foreign blood—no objection was thenceforth raised to intermarriages between royalty and the British aristocracy. Two of the present sovereign's children have married in this way since 1922.

with Great Britain and with the overseas dominions. This change was made in deference, of course, to the fact that, even though the Act of Union of 1800 stood (as it still stands) unrepealed, the constitutional changes in Ireland incident to the creation of the Free State had brought the United Kingdom, on its former basis, to an end.[9]

Within the reigning family, the throne descends according to the same principle of primogeniture that formerly governed in the inheritance of land.[10] When a sovereign dies, the eldest son—who is by birth Duke of Cornwall and is created Prince of Wales [11] and Earl of Chester—inherits; if he is not living, his eldest son succeeds. If no male heir is available in this branch of the family, the deceased sovereign's second son inherits, and so on, elder sons being always preferred to younger, and male heirs to female. The husband of a queen *regnant,* i.e., one reigning in her own right, and the wife of a king regularly bear the designation of "consort." If a situation should arise in which there should be no one, within the stipulated degrees of relationship, to succeed, Parliament would be called upon to install a new dynasty. In any event, the reign of the new monarch, as has been pointed out, begins the moment that of the former one closes; there is no interregnum.[12] A picturesque

[9] See pp. 708 ff. below. Cf. M. O. Hudson, "The Style and Titles of His Britannic Majesty," *Amer. Jour. Internat. Law,* Jan., 1928.

[10] Certain changes in the law of property, made in 1925, do not affect kingship or other hereditary titles.

[11] This title was created by Edward I in 1301. It involves no governmental duties; but in the rôle of traveller in outlying parts of the Empire and visitor to foreign lands various bearers of it, e.g., Edward VII before his accession and Edward Albert, son of George V, have unofficially rendered services of a social and ceremonial nature similar to those rendered by the sovereign himself. The sovereign may, of course, associate the crown prince with himself in the discharge of his governmental duties in so far as he likes. Edward VII, resenting his own total exclusion during his mother's prolonged reign, gave his son, the present George V, liberal opportunities of the sort.

[12] The Representation of the People Act of 1867 made the duration of Parliament independent of the "demise of the crown," and the Demise of the Crown Act of 1903 put tenure of office under the crown on the same basis. It is still required by law that upon demise of the crown, Parliament, if it be not already in session, shall meet immediately, without summons. There being a new sovereign, the members take the oath of allegiance afresh.

coronation ceremony is held, but usually not until some months after the accession, and though rich in historic associations, it is a mere formality, adding nothing to the new sovereign's rights and powers.[13]

The heir to the throne may, of course, be a mere child, in which case he cannot exercise regal prerogatives until he is eighteen. Or, a sovereign may be, or become, physically or mentally incapacitated. The constitutions of most monarchical states make definite provision for a regency in such circumstances. In Britain, a Regency Act of 1811, passed in view of the mental incapacity of George III, defines the limits of a regent's powers and sets up safeguards in the interest of both sovereign and nation,[14] but beyond this the matter is left to be dealt with afresh if and when occasion arises. Only Parliament can decide that a regency shall be created, and can name the regent, who is likely to be an elder relative of the minor or incapacitated sovereign. Precautionary steps may be taken to provide in advance for the possible need of a regency. Thus, soon after the accession of George V in 1910 a statute was passed providing that if any of his children should succeed to the throne while under eighteen, Queen Mary should, until the child reached that age, but not longer, have full power and authority in the name of such child "to perform all the prerogatives, authorities, and acts of government that belong to the sovereign of the realm with the style and title of regent." This act remained in force until Edward Albert attained his eighteenth birthday in 1912, when it lapsed. Similar arrangements were in effect during Queen Victoria's minority, and also Edward VII's.[15]

[13] The ceremony takes place in Westminster Abbey, where the coronation chair or throne, so constructed as to enclose the "stone of Scone," reputed to have been brought from Scotland to England by Edward I in 1297—and, further, to be the very stone which the patriarch Jacob used for a pillow at Bethel (Gen. xxviii, 18-19)—is viewed by thousands of visitors every year, at sixpence apiece.

[14] The text of this measure will be found in C. G. Robertson, *Statutes, Cases, and Documents,* 171-182. There is an excellent survey of the subject in T. E. May and F. Holland, *Constitutional History of England,* I, Chap. iii. Cf. W. R. Anson, *Law and Custom of the Constitution* (3rd ed.), II, Pt. i, 245-250.

[15] When the sovereign is to be absent from the country for some weeks or months Parliament may put the crown "in commission," i.e., appoint a

No Catholic may inherit, nor any one marrying a Catholic. This is by virtue of the Bill of Rights; and the Act of Settlement goes on to prescribe that the sovereign shall in all cases "join in communion with the Church of England as by law established." If after his accession he should join in communion with the Church of Rome, profess the Catholic religion, or marry a Catholic, his subjects would be absolved from their allegiance, and the next in line who was a Protestant would succeed. It is required, furthermore, that the sovereign shall at his coronation take an oath specifically abjuring the tenets of Catholicism. Until 1910, the phraseology of this oath, formulated in days when ecclesiastical animosities were still fervid, was offensive not only to Catholics but to temperate-minded men of all faiths.[16] An act of Parliament, passed in anticipation of the coronation of George V, made it, however, less objectionable. The new sovereign is now required merely to declare "that he is a faithful Protestant and that he will, according to the true intent of the enactments which secure the Protestant succession to the throne of the Realm, uphold and maintain the said enactments to the best of his power according to law."

The Royal Finances

The sovereign enjoys large personal immunities and privileges. He cannot be called to account for his private conduct in any court of law or by any legal process. He cannot be arrested, his goods cannot be distrained, and as long as a palace remains a royal residence no sort of judicial proceeding against him can be executed in it. He may own land and other prop-

commission of councillors of state to act in the sovereign's behalf during his absence and to sign papers that will not admit of delay. Such commissioners in no sense, however, constitute a regency. A "council" of this nature was set up in 1925 during a prolonged absence of George V from the country. Similarly, a council may be appointed to act as proxy during an illness incapacitating the sovereign. A recent illustration is the appointment of a council of six (including the queen, the Prince of Wales, the prime minister, and the archbishop of Canterbury) on December 4, 1928, because of the critical illness of George V.

[16] The words to be employed were originally prescribed in the Act for Establishing the Coronation Oath, passed in the first year of William and Mary. For the text, see C. G. Robertson, *Statutes, Cases, and Documents*, 65-68. Cf. A. Bailey, *The Succession to the English Crown* (London, 1879).

erty, and may manage and dispose of it precisely as any private citizen. Finally, he is entitled to a generous allowance out of the public treasury for the support of the royal establishment.

The present arrangements for keeping the king's purse filled date mainly from 1689, and are grounded upon the strict separation of his income and expeditures as sovereign from those of the government in general. In earlier centuries, when to all intents and purposes the king was the government, all revenues were his, whether derived from his extensive landed estates, the contributions of his vassals, fines and other profits of jurisdiction, forced contributions of food and other supplies (at an appraised, but usually low, price) under the practice of purveyance, or, in times of emergency, special aids or other levies. Out of the sum realized from these sources he was expected to support the civil service, maintain the army and the courts, carry on war, and keep up the royal establishment. As expenses increased, Parliament began to be called upon at frequent intervals to help out with subsidies; and more and more it became necessary to rely upon this resource, especially after the nation progressed to the point where purveyance ceased to be permissible and many of the feudal dues stirred more complaint than they were worth. By and by, Parliament is found bargaining with the monarch, inducing him to give up this or that burdensome exaction, and even to surrender certain properties and rights, in return for regular votes of funds derived from "tonnage and poundage,"[17] excises, and other forms of taxation. Some subsidies were granted only for a year at a time, others for the whole of a reign.

Even yet, the king was in a position to dip into the general fund for his personal purposes as heavily as he liked; at all events, anything that he could save in the outlays upon the civil government and the military establishment went to gratify his personal appetites or to swell his private purse. There had long been plenty of complaint on this score, but nothing very effec-

[17] Tonnage was a tax at some stipulated rate per ton upon imports of wine; poundage was, similarly, a duty paid on either imports or exports (or both) of merchandise of other specified kinds. For a typical grant of such subsidies, see G. B. Adams and H. M. Stephens, *Documents of English Constitutional History,* 210-212.

tive was done about it until the days of the later Stuarts. Charles II, in particular, though suave and pliable, could never be trusted to make due use of the funds put under his control; and while his generosity and good humor saved him from ever incurring much dislike personally, the nation was no longer of a mind to endure the squandering of public moneys on the pleasures of a profligate court. It is not strange, therefore, that when the status of the monarch was being freshly defined in 1689 the opportunity was seized to put matters on a different basis. The readjustment was further promoted by the definite adoption in this same period of the plan of appropriating money for specific objects, rather than in lump sums for general purposes.[18]

The scheme adopted was that of allocating to the king a fixed amount per year out of the sum total of expected revenue, the remainder being placed beyond his reach. The amount voted to William and Mary jointly was £700,000. This generous sum, however, was not exclusively for personal and household uses. On the contrary, the joint sovereigns were expected to pay out of it the salaries of the ambassadors and judges, to maintain the civil service, and to take care of pensions. That is to say, the sovereign must still provide out of his allotment for certain stipulated expenses of a public character; and from the practice of enumerating the items thus chargeable on the king's funds arose the name Civil List, nowadays often applied directly to the subsidy itself. For a long period, too, the monarch clung to most of the royal estates, and to various other sources of personal revenue. But as time went on the principle involved in the arrangement of 1689 found completer application. On the one side, the king relinquished most of his lands and revenues: George III, for example, gave up much. On the other hand, and by way of compensation, civil expenses for which the king had been responsible were stricken off the Civil List, until finally at the accession of William IV, in 1830, everything was withdrawn except the maintenance of the royal family and the court. In

[18] This practice was started to some extent under Charles II. Not until after another hundred years, however, was the plan given up of appropriating to particular ends the proceeds of particular taxes. See p. 169 below.

the original meaning of the term, there ceased to be a Civil List at all. Apart from annuities payable to the children of the royal family,[19] the Civil List of Edward VII amounted to £470,000, of which £110,000 was appropriated to the privy purse of the king and queen, £125,000 to salaries and retiring allowances of the royal household, and £193,000 to household expenses. At the accession of George V, in 1910, the Civil List was continued in the sum of £470,000.[20] Accuracy requires it to be added that, in addition to the revenues of the Duchy of Lancaster (amounting in 1926 to £70,000), which have never been surrendered, the king still has considerable income of a purely personal nature.[21]

The King's Position in the Government

Viewed from a distance, British kingship is still imposing. The sovereign dwells in a splendid palace, sets the pace in rich and cultured social circles, occupies the center of the stage in solemn and magnificent ceremonies, makes and receives stately visits to and from foreign royalty,[22] and seems to have broad powers of appointment, administrative control, military command, lawmaking, justice, and finance. Examined more closely, however, the king's position is found to afford peculiarly good illustration of the contrast between theory and fact which runs so extensively through the English governmental system. On the social and ceremonial side, the king is fully as important as the casual observer might take him to be; indeed, one has to know England rather well to appreciate how great his influence is in at least the upper levels of society. But his positive control over public affairs—appointments, legislation, military policy, the church, finance, foreign relations—is almost *nil*. There was

[19] The revenues of the Duchy of Cornwall (£66,000 in 1926) are sufficient to keep the Prince of Wales well supplied with means; hence there are no separate annuities for him.

[20] On the history of the Civil List, see T. E. May and F. Holland, *Constitutional History of England,* I, 152-175. Cf. J. A. R. Marriott, *The Mechanism of the Modern State,* II, 20-24. There is much interesting information in *Const. Year Book* (1928), 27-30.

[21] A. Fitzroy, *Memoirs,* 2 vols. (London, 1926), is a gossipy but informing account of life and affairs at the British court. The author was for twenty-five years clerk of the Privy Council.

[22] Naturally, these are fewer now than before the World War.

a time when his power in these great fields was practically absolute. It was certainly so under the Tudors, in the sixteenth century. But the Civil War cut off large personal prerogatives, the Revolution of 1688-89 severed many more, the apathy and weakness of the early Hanoverians cost much, and the drift against royal control in government continued strong, even under the superior monarchs of the last hundred years—until the king now finds himself literally in the position of one who "reigns but does not govern." When we say that the crown appoints public officers we mean that ministers, who themselves are selected by the king only in form, make the appointments. When the king attends the opening of a parliament and reads the Speech from the Throne, the message is one which has been written by these same ministers. "Government" measures are indeed continually framed and executive acts performed in the name of the crown; but the king may personally know little about them, or even be strongly opposed to them. Two great principles, in short, underlie the entire system: (1) the king may not perform public acts involving the exercise of discretionary power, except on advice of the ministers, betokened by their countersignature, and (2) for every public act performed by or through them these ministers are singly and collectively responsible to Parliament. The king can "do no wrong," because the acts done by him or in his name are chargeable to a minister or to the ministry as a group. This tends, however, to mean that the king can do nothing; because ministers cannot be expected to shoulder responsibility for acts which they do not themselves originate or favor.[23]

It would be erroneous, however, to conclude that kingship in England is moribund and unimportant, or that the king has no real influence in the government. Americans are likely to wonder why an institution which seems so completely to have out-

[23] Already in the time of Charles II this situation was well enough understood to call out an oft-cited passage of wit. A courtier once wrote on the royal bedchamber:

Here lies our sovereign lord the King
Whose word no man relies on;
He never says a foolish thing
Nor never does a wise one.

"Very true," retorted the king, "because, while my words are my own, my acts are my ministers'."

lived its usefulness has not been abolished; and Englishmen are free to admit that if they did not actually have a royal house they would hardly set about establishing one. Nevertheless, the uses served by the monarch are considerable; his influence upon the course of public affairs may, indeed, be great.

In the first place, the king still personally performs certain definite acts, which in some cases are so indispensable that if kingship were to be abolished some other provision would have to be made for them. He receives foreign ambassadors, even if only as a matter of form and in the presence of a minister. He reads the Speech from the Throne, although the Lord Chancellor may substitute for him. He assents to the election of a speaker by the House of Commons, though this, too, may be done by proxy.[24] But two important things, at least, he, and he only, can do. One is calling upon a political leader to make up a ministry; the other is assenting to a dissolution of Parliament, entailing a general election. The process of making up a new ministry will be dealt with later, and it will suffice here merely to note that, while the party system has developed to a point where the sovereign is left little or no discretion in selecting a prime minister, he is not bound to act upon the advice tendered him in the matter and might conceivably find himself in a position to make a real choice.[25] In any case, no one else can commission a new premier in the form required by immemorial custom. The whole executive authority of the realm falls back temporarily into the king's hands when a ministry resigns. The situation with regard to dissolution is substantially the same. The decision to dissolve is invariably made by the cabinet, which, however, must obtain the king's consent before the plan can be proceeded with; and although consent has not actually been withheld since before the reign of Queen Victoria, it is commonly considered that in a very unusual situation it might be denied (as it sometimes is by the governor-general in the dominions),[26] and even that the sovereign could dismiss a ministry in order to force a dissolution—

[24] As assenting to bills passed by Parliament invariably is. See p. 421 below.

[25] See pp. 132-135 below.

[26] A. B. Keith, *Responsible Government in the Dominions* (2nd ed., Oxford, 1928), I, Pt. ii, Chap. iii.

although there has been no instance of the kind since 1784.[27]

The King as Adviser

But of far greater practical importance than acts of the kind just mentioned is the monarch's rôle as general adviser and friend. In the oft-quoted phrase of Bagehot, the sovereign has three rights—the right to be consulted, the right to encourage, and the right to warn. "A king of great sense and sagacity," it is added, "would want no others." [28] Despite the fact that during upwards of two hundred years the sovereign has not attended the meetings of the cabinet, and hence is deprived of opportunity to wield influence directly upon the deliberations of the ministers as a body, he keeps in close touch with the prime minister, and cabinet meetings at which important policies are to be formulated are frequently preceded by a conference in which the subject in hand is threshed out more or less completely by king and chief minister. Merely because the ancient relation has been reversed, so that now it is the king who advises and the ministry that arrives at decisions, it does not follow that the advisory function is an unimportant thing.

On numerous occasions Queen Victoria wielded decisive influence upon public policies and measures, especially in connection with the conduct of foreign relations. She mediated effec-

[27] The date formerly assigned was 1834; but it has now been shown that William IV's alleged dismissal of the Melbourne ministry in that year was in reality only the acceptance of a proffered resignation. A speech of Mr. Asquith, delivered at the National Liberal Club in London in December, 1923, precipitated much discussion of the sovereign's function in connection with dissolution. Asserting that the king is "not bound to take the advice of a particular ministry to put his subjects to the tumult and turmoil of a series of general elections so long as he can find other ministers who are prepared to give contrary advice," the ex-premier, in effect, argued that when the prospective Labor ministry of Mr. MacDonald should reach the end of its tether and the premier should advise the king to dissolve Parliament, the request ought to be refused and a Liberal leader ought to be invited, without an election, to form a government. Mr. MacDonald made a spirited reply, contending that the sovereign is bound to take the premier's advice; and it was generally considered that, in view of the precedents, he was right. See *Manchester Guardian* (weekly ed.), Dec. 28, 1923, p. 515, reprinted in E. M. Sait and D. P. Barrows, *British Politics in Transition* (Yonkers, 1925), 18-22.

[28] *English Constitution* (rev. ed.), 143.

tively between the ministers and the House of Lords on the disestablishment of the Irish church in 1869. She called Lord Palmerston sharply to account in 1850 because the Foreign Office was not showing her due regard. "The Queen requires, first,"—so ran the famous memorandum sent to her somewhat supercilious foreign secretary—"that Lord Palmerston will distinctly state what he proposes in a given case, in order that the Queen may know as distinctly to what she is giving her royal sanction. Secondly, having once given her sanction to such a measure, that it be not arbitrarily altered or modified by the minister. . . . She expects to be kept informed of what passes between him and the foreign ministers, before important decisions are taken based upon that intercourse; to receive the foreign dispatches in good time; and to have the drafts for her approval sent to her in sufficient time to make herself acquainted with the contents before they must be sent off." [29] During the troubled later years of Louis Philippe the Queen practically prevented war between Great Britain and France; and on the advice of the Prince Consort, she, in 1860, caused Lord John Russell's peremptory dispatch on the *Trent* affair to be softened, and thereby quite possibly averted war with the United States. She was more responsible than Palmerston for the dispatch of adequate reinforcements to India at the time of the Mutiny; and when, in 1884, the Conservative House of Lords and the Liberal House of Commons were at stalemate because they could not agree on whether Gladstone's Representation of the People Bill should provide for a redistribution of seats, she interposed suggestions which led to a sensible settlement.[30]

Edward VII, coming to the throne in 1901, when his country

[29] T. Martin, *Life of His Royal Highness, The Prince Consort* (London, 1875-80), II, 306. For a full account of the affair, see L. Strachey, *Queen Victoria* (London, 1921), Chap. V.

[30] The influence exerted by the successive sovereigns from George III to Victoria is described at length in T. E. May and F. Holland, *Constitutional History of England,* I, Chaps. i-ii. Queen Victoria's activities are reviewed in J. A. R. Marriott, *The Mechanism of the Modern State,* II, 38-48. Cf. *The Letters of Queen Victoria,* second series, especially Vol. III, covering the period 1879-1885 (London, 1928); C. Mallet, "Queen Victoria and Mr. Gladstone," *Contemp. Rev.,* Mar., 1928; and K. Martin, "The Victorian Monarchy," *Edinburgh Rev.,* Apr., 1926.

was suffering from unpopularity in Europe engendered by the South African war, contributed powerfully by his visits on the Continent, by his entertainment of foreign dignitaries, and by voluminous correspondence carried on directly with the heads of foreign states, to the turn of events which brought Britain into a close understanding with France in 1904 and with Russia three years later. Furthermore—while the extent of his influence on domestic affairs is less measurable—he is known to have approved and encouraged the Haldane army reforms, to have sought to dissuade the House of Lords from rejecting the Lloyd George budget of 1909, and not only to have felt deep concern about the reform of the House of Lords, but to have had a reform plan of his own.[31] In other words, while content as a constitutional monarch to remain in the background of political controversy, the king not only had opinions but did not hesitate to express them; and in the shaping and execution of public policy his advice was undoubtedly at times a factor of importance. Unlike Queen Victoria, who seldom saw the ministers, but trusted rather to correspondence, King Edward was always accessible to the ministers and enjoyed discussing public matters in a direct and informal way with them.[32]

The present sovereign, George V, has at times taken an active part, especially in relation to the Irish question and to various matters incidental to the World War. At a moment in 1914 when the situation in Ireland was especially critical, and when the party forces in Parliament seemed hopelessly deadlocked on the issue, he called a conference of British and Irish leaders to meet at Buckingham Palace and appealed in an opening speech for a peaceful settlement in the spirit of compromise; and although his "interference" called out loud protest in some

[31] S. Lee, *King Edward VII* (London, 1925-27), II, 695.

[32] The most satisfactory estimate of the political and governmental activities of Edward VII is contained in Sidney Lee's memoir of the king, printed in the *Dictionary of National Biography,* Second Supplement (London and New York, 1912), I, 546-610. The second volume of Mr. Lee's *King Edward VII,* cited in the preceding note, contains much interesting material. See an article by the same author entitled "Edward VII and the Entente," reproduced in *Living Age,* July 22, 1922; also J. G. S. MacNeill, "Foreign Policy and Royal Influence," *Fortnightly Rev.,* Dec., 1921, and Viscount Esher, *The Influence of King Edward, and Essays on Other Subjects* (London, 1915).

quarters, and did not eventuate in an immediate settlement, he must be regarded as having contributed something to the solution of an exceptionally baffling problem.[33]

It is, perhaps, superfluous to say that the king's suggestions and advice on matters of public policy need not be acted upon. Ministers will be slow, however, to disregard them. His exalted station alone would give them weight. But there is the further consideration that a sovereign who has been on the throne for some time is likely to have gained a broader knowledge of public affairs than that possessed by most of the ministers. After ten years, Peel once remarked, a king ought to know more about the government than any other man in the country. Even more important is the fact that the sovereign's personal fortunes are less affected by party politics than those of other people, and that accordingly he can usually be depended on to take a dispassionate and impartial view of matters that stir heated controversy in Parliament and press. He, if anyone, can think in terms of the best interests of the nation as a whole.

Other Uses of Kingship—Why It Survives

But the monarchy serves still other important uses. It furnishes a leadership for British society which, during the past century at all events, has had a generally good effect in matters of taste, manners, and morals. Furthermore, it provides a symbol of imperial unity which Englishmen almost unanimously agree is indispensable. For it must be remembered that the vast, sprawling British Empire is none too securely held together by governmental machinery. Ireland, Canada, Australia, South Africa, New Zealand—all have their own parliaments and cabinets, and laws made in London apply to them to only a very limited extent. India, the crown colonies, and the protectorates, although more closely tied to Britain by formal governmental control, contain multifold millions of

[33] For documentary and newspaper materials on the incident, see E. M. Sait and D. P. Barrows, *British Politics in Transition,* 1-16. Cf. S. Brooks, "The King and the War," in *Nineteenth Cent.,* May, 1918; *London Times Illus. Hist. and Encyc. of the War,* Pt. 225 (1918). J. A. Farrer, *The Monarchy in Politics* (New York, 1917), is an excellent study of the influence of monarchy on governmental policy in England. See also H. L. McBain and L. Rogers, *New Constitutions of Europe,* Chap. vii.

people who think of government in terms of personality and can much more easily summon up respect, and even attachment, for an emperor or king at London than for any less tangible or visible expression of political authority. Whether for Scotchman, Welshman, Canadian, Jamaican, Hindu, or Englishman, allegiance to the king is the one common manifestation of imperial unity and feeling. In the words of H. G. Wells, the British crown—"the golden link of empire"—stands as a symbol of unity in diversity as no other crown, unless that of Austria-Hungary before 1914, can be said to have done in modern times.[34] "It is doubtless," says another English writer, "almost impossible to exaggerate the importance of the personal element as a factor of cohesion within the Empire; the difficulty of preserving unity would be enormously increased if the United Kingdom were under a republican constitution." [35] So eminent a student of English government and law as Professor Dicey wrote as recently as 1914: "Any great change in the form of the constitution of England, e.g., the substitution of an English republic for a limited monarchy, might deeply affect the loyalty of all the British colonies. Can any one be certain that New Zealand or Canada would, at the bidding of the Parliament of the United Kingdom, transfer their loyalty from George V to a president chosen by the electorate of the United Kingdom, and this even though the revolution were carried out with every legal formality, including the assent of the king himself, and even though the king were elected the first president of the new Commonwealth? . . . The king is what the Imperial Parliament has never been, the typical representative of imperial unity throughout every part of the Empire." [36]

[34] "The Future of Monarchy," *New Republic*, May 19, 1917.

[35] A. B. Keith, *Constitution, Administration, and Laws of the Empire*, 13.

[36] *Law of the Constitution* (8th ed.), p. xci, note. "You cannot," declared General Smuts, speaking at London in 1917, "make a republic of the British Commonwealth of Nations." *War Time Speeches*, 34. To all of the considerations adduced above must be added the further important fact that since the Imperial Conference of 1926 recognized the full equality of the self-governing members of the British Commonwealth of Nations, the king—the king in person, not the king-in-council—has become the sole legal bond which ties Britain, the Irish Free State, and the dominions together. Cf. Chap. xxxi below; also *Great Britain and the Dominions* (Harris Foundation Lectures, Chicago, 1928), 51-59.

It is so important to get the British point of view in this matter of the uses of the king that still another English authority, Mr. Edward Jenks, may be quoted at some length. "In the first place," he writes, "the king supplies the vital element of personal interest to the proceedings of government. It is far easier for the average man to realize a person than an institution. Even in the United Kingdom, only the educated few have any real appreciation of such abstract things as Parliament, the cabinet, or even 'the crown.' But the vast mass of the people are deeply interested in the king as a person, as is proved by the crowds which collect whenever there is a chance of seeing him; and it is possible that the majority of the people, even of the United Kingdom, to say nothing of the millions of India, believe that the government of the Empire is carried on by the king personally. He therefore supplies the personal and picturesque element which catches the popular imagination far more readily than constitutional arrangements, which cannot be heard or seen; and a king or queen who knows how to play this part skillfully, by a display of tact, graciousness, and benevolence, is rendering priceless services to the cause of contentment and good government. . . . Very closely allied to this personal character of the king is the great unofficial and social influence which he wields, and not he alone, but the queen, and, in a lesser degree, the other members of the royal family. Their influence in matters of religion, morality, benevolence, fashion, and even in art and literature, is immense. . . . How much good was done in this way by the late Queen Victoria, is a matter of common knowledge; it was one of the striking triumphs of her long reign. And, be it remembered, in such matters the monarch is in no way bound to follow, or even to seek, the advice of his ministers; for such matters lie outside the domain of politics. . . . A king who is fully informed of affairs becomes, in course of time, if he is an able man, an unrivaled storehouse of political experience. Ministers come and go; they are swayed, it is to be feared, by the interests of their party as well as by those of the state; they may have had to make, in order to obtain support, bargains which tie their hands; they have ambitions for the future, which they are loath to jeopardize. Not so the king. He is permanent; he is above all parties; he does not bargain for places and honors; he has nothing in the way of ambition to satisfy, except the noble ambition of securing his country's welfare. So he can say to his ministers, with all the weight of his experience and position: 'Yes, I will, if you insist, do as you wish; but, I warn you, you are doing a rash thing. Do you remember so and so?' Only, the king must not give his warning in public; he must not *seem* to overrule his ministers. But a minister will, unless he is an exceptionally rash person, think many times before disregarding a warning from the king." [37]

To all of these considerations must be added certain final facts. 1. The continuance of kingship has been no bar to the progressive development of democratic government. If royalty had been found blocking the road to fuller control of public affairs by the people, it is inconceivable that all the forces of tradition could have pulled it through the past seventy-five or eighty years. 2. The royal establishment does not cost the nation much, considering the returns on the investment; in actual figures, the outlay is only about seven one-hundredths of one per cent of the total British budget. 3. The cabinet system, upon which the entire governmental order of Great Britain hinges, has nowhere been proved a workable plan without the presence of some titular head, some dignified and detached figure, whether a king or, as in France, a president with many of the attributes of kingship; [38] and nothing is clearer than that, if monarchy were to be abandoned in Britain, provision would have to be made for a president or other "chief executive," raising all sorts of troublesome questions about his powers and entailing serious possibilities for the cabinet system itself.

Thus it comes about that monarchy, although on its face a bald anachronism in a country like Britain, remains impregnably entrenched. At a low ebb in popular respect a hundred years ago, because of a succession of weak or otherwise un-

[37] *Government of the British Empire,* 37-40.

[38] Interesting experiments with cabinet government in the absence of any titular head of the state (except in the sense in which the "minister-president," or prime minister, serves as such) are being made in Prussia and other German *Länder;* but it is still too early to say how the arrangement will work. See F. F. Blachly and M. E. Oatman, *The Government and Administration of Germany* (Baltimore, 1928), Chap. ix.

worthy sovereigns, it has regained all that it had lost and is today indubitably popular.[39] Such republican talk as one could have heard even a generation or two ago has died down. Throughout the stormy years 1909-11, when the nation was stirred as it had not been in decades on issues of constitutional reform, every proposal and plan took it for granted that monarchy would remain an integral part of the governmental system. In the general bombardment to which the hereditary House of Lords was subjected, hereditary kingship entirely escaped. In the early years of the World War some criticism was directed at the royal family because of what proved an ill-founded suspicion that the court was the base of influences antagonistic to republican institutions in allied or other friendly states. But the misunderstanding passed, and the years of feverish republican experiment on the Continent following the war left kingship as solidly grounded in Britain as before. Of greatest significance is the fact that the Labor party, although long on record in favor of the abolition of the House of Lords,[40] has never, as a party, advocated the suppression of British kingship. Individual Laborites have declared themselves republicans in principle; and at a party conference in 1923 a motion was introduced asserting that the royal family is no longer necessary as a part of the British constitution. This motion, however, was defeated by a heavy majority; and most Labor men, equally with Conservatives and Liberals, consider that as long as the sovereign is content with the sort of position that he occupies today the country will, and should, continue, as now, a "crowned republic." [41]

[39] More so, even, than in Victoria's day. The Queen herself was, on one occasion, hooted in the streets, and the Prince Consort was openly criticized and denounced. Somewhat earlier, the Prince Regent's carriage was stoned. One cannot imagine such things happening in the reign of Edward VII and George V. It must, of course, be added that whereas Victoria was vehemently partisan on many occasions and clearly unconstitutional on some, her successors were tactful, impartial, and in every way strictly faithful to the obligations and limitations imposed by their constitutional position. For interesting comment, see *Manchester Guardian* (weekly ed.), Dec. 28, 1928, p. 502.

[40] See p. 333 below.

[41] This does not mean, of course, that criticism is never heard in Labor and socialist quarters. In 1926 H. G. Wells stirred considerable feeling by belittling royal personages through the medium of his novel, *William*

Clissold. George V, for example, was described as "the worthy, conscientious, entirely unmeaning and uninteresting son of plump old Edward VII"! Attacks on royalty are made occasionally by left-wing Laborites in the House of Commons. Thus, in 1925, when a supplementary grant to defray the expenses of a visit by the Prince of Wales to South Africa and South America was before the House, ninety Labor members, led by the "wild men of the Clyde," voted against the appropriation, and there was a similar demonstration in 1927 when an allowance for a trip by the Duke and Duchess of York was pending. In both instances, however, the party leaders voted for the grant, or at the most abstained. In their *Constitution for a Socialist Commonwealth of Great Britain* (p. 61)—which, although never officially endorsed by the Labor party, gives a very good clue to labor views on most subjects—Sidney and Beatrice Webb say: "If we pass from the constitutional theory of the textbooks to the facts as we see them today, what we have to note is that the particular function of the British monarch—his duty as king—is not the exercise of governmental powers in any of its aspects, but something quite different, namely, the performance of a whole series of rites and ceremonies which lend the charm of historic continuity to the political institutions of the British race, and which go far, under present conditions, to maintain the bond of union between the races and creeds of the Commonwealth of Nations that still styles itself the British Empire." The authors go on to say, however, that there are some present social disadvantages (tendency to snobbishness, etc.) in the existence of monarchy, and that unless they are removed, monarchy will become unpopular and perhaps "very quickly disappear" (p. 109, note). For the attitude of another prominent Labor leader, see J. H. Thomas, *When Labor Rules* (New York, 1920), 45-47.

Brief discussions of the position of the sovereign in the governmental system include A. L. Lowell, *Government of England,* I, Chap. i; J. A. R. Marriott, *English Political Institutions* (3rd ed.), Chap. iii; and S. Low, *Governance of England,* Chaps. xiv-xv. More extended treatment of the subject will be found in W. R. Anson, *Law and Custom of the Constitution* (3rd ed.), II, Pt. i, Chaps. i and iv; W. Bagehot, *English Constitution,* Chaps. ii-iii; J. A. R. Marriott, *The Mechanism of the Modern State,* II, Chaps. xxiii-xxiv; and M. MacDonagh, *The English King* (London, 1929).

CHAPTER VI

PRIVY COUNCIL, MINISTRY, AND CABINET

We have seen that the powers of the crown are very great, and are still growing. We have seen also that, with slight exceptions, they are no longer exercised by the sovereign in person. Who, then, wields them? In what ways? Under what conditions? With what results? These are big questions, answers to which will occupy us through several chapters of this book; even then, much will have to be left unsaid. Four main institutions, or authorities, will come into the picture. One of them is largely historic and formal, though still vital; the other three are working devices or agencies of the highest practical, day-to-day importance. The four are: (1) the Privy Council, (2) the ministry, (3) the cabinet, and (4) the permanent civil service. These parts of the governmental system once understood clearly, we shall be prepared to take up the great instrumentality of popular control through which, directly or indirectly, all are held within the bounds marked out for them and kept in touch with the nation, namely, Parliament.

The Privy Council

The Privy Council is one of the most venerable, as also nowadays one of the most curious and most misunderstood, parts of the constitutional system. How it arose has been pointed out in an earlier chapter,[1] and it is unnecessary to repeat the story, save to remind ourselves that its remotest ancestor was the Great Council of the Norman and Angevin kings; that, more immediately, it is derived from the smaller administrative and judicial body known as the Curia Regis, and still more immediately from that part of the Curia Regis

[1] See pp. 18-19 above.

(known as the Permanent Council) remaining after the King's Bench and other high courts were split off from it; and that, in substantially its present form, it emerges in the fifteenth century as an offshoot, in turn, of this Permanent Council. It was the final product of that oft-repeated process of subdivision and devolution by which the functions of advising the king and carrying on the government in his name were kept in the hands of a relatively small and workable body; and yet not the final product, in that, as we have seen, from the Privy Council itself sprang, in the seventeenth and eighteenth centuries, another selective, smaller group, i.e., the cabinet, which in practice, if not in legal theory, now advises and directs and governs.

The Privy Council as it stands today has some three hundred and forty members. The two archbishops and the bishop of London belong to it; also higher judges and retired judges, many eminent peers (especially such as have held high administrative posts at home and abroad), a few colonial statesmen, and varying numbers of men of distinction in literature, art, science, law, and other fields of endeavor, upon whom membership has been conferred as a mark of honor. The principal mode of recruitment, however, is the appointment as privy councillors of all members of every successive cabinet that is formed. Indeed, since the cabinet as such is wholly unknown to the law, it is only as a minister that a man can be legally placed in charge of a high government post and only as a privy councillor that he can be required to take the historic oath of secrecy which the advisory aspect of the cabinet's functions is considered to make essential. Once created a privy councillor, a man remains such for the rest of his life; [2] so that the body always consists principally of present and past cabinet officers. Inasmuch as every prime minister selects his colleagues in the cabinet with a free hand, it is really he, of course, and not the king, who confers the dignity, although the sovereign may personally have some influence, especially in selecting the occasional persons who are appointed as a token of honor

[2] The king may, however, remove a councillor by striking his name from the roll, as was done in the case of Cecil Rhodes after the Jameson raid into the Transvaal in 1895.

and with no intent that they shall become members of the cabinet. A mark of distinction of all privy councillors is the title of Right Honorable.

The rise of the cabinet system has left the Council in a position where—aside from committee work—its services are largely of a formal character. But this does not mean that they are unimportant, or even unessential. Except when a new sovereign is to be crowned, or some other solemn ceremony is to be performed, the general body of councillors is never called together. The majority either have never possessed governmental functions or have long since ceased to exercise them; rarely is any one invited to attend a Council meeting who is not an active cabinet member—at all events a minister—and in actual practice not more than four members are summoned for the purpose.[3] But meetings are held, with considerable frequency. Shortly before the war there were fourteen or fifteen meetings a year; during the war period the number rose to an average of about thirty; subsequently it has been twenty or slightly above.[4] These meetings are held commonly at Buckingham Palace, and—quite in contrast with cabinet meetings—with the king in attendance, although an order in council has made it possible for meetings to take place, if necessary, in the sovereign's absence. The Lord President of the Council is invariably present, and also the clerk of the Council, who issues the summons, and who since 1923 has served also as secretary of the cabinet.[5]

What is there for these meetings to do? A variety of important acts can be performed only in them. It is at a Council meeting that ministers take their oath of office. It is also there that sheriffs receive their formal appointment. By all odds the most important function, however, is the issuing of rules and orders under the name of "orders in council." As will appear later, increasing numbers of administrative rules and regulations are promulgated independently by individual executive

[3] Three are competent to transact business.

[4] J. A. Fairlie, *Administrative Procedure in Connection with Statutory Rules and Orders in Great Britain* (Urbana, 1927), 55.

[5] See p. 157 below. The Privy Council Office, with an administrative and secretarial staff (including the attachés of the committees) of some thirty-five persons, is quartered in the same building as the Treasury.

departments and other agencies.[6] But certain matters are dealt with only through the medium of orders in council, and, in general, the more important orders, on whatever subject, are cast in this form. Prominent examples are proclamations summoning, proroguing, and dissolving Parliament, orders relating to the government of the crown colonies, orders granting royal charters to municipal corporations and other bodies, orders affecting the permanent civil service, war-time orders concerning such matters as neutral trade and blockade, and a great variety of orders issued in pursuance of authority conferred in more or less general terms in acts of Parliament on such subjects as health and education. Of late, the total number of orders issued has been around six hundred a year; in time of war, it runs considerably higher. Many come from the various departments already fully drafted, and requiring merely the Council's formal approval; others are only in rough form and have to be put in shape by the drafting experts of the Privy Council Office.

Be it noted, however, that the Privy Council is no longer a deliberative or advisory body.[7] Its functions of this character have been absorbed to some extent by the departments, which have a good deal of leeway in determining not only what rules they shall severally promulgate but what ones they shall carry to the Council to be assented to and promulgated as orders. In a larger way, the Council's old deliberative functions have passed to the cabinet. Upon matters of moment the cabinet deliberates and frames policy. If parliamentary assent is required, it goes to Westminster for the requisite action. If, however—as is frequently the case—an order in council will suffice, it turns to the Council for the desired decree. The cabinet group decides that orders shall be given, or that the sovereign shall be advised to act in a certain manner. But it does not, as a cabinet, give orders; that is the function of the Council (more properly, the king-in-council), which is now—whatever may

[6] See pp. 200-203. This matter is discussed in illuminating fashion in J. A. Fairlie, *op. cit.*

[7] The last occasion on which the Council exercised deliberative as well as executive powers—thereby acting as a cabinet—appears to have been in 1714, immediately before the death of Queen Anne. See W. R. Anson, *Law and Custom of the Constitution* (3rd ed.), II, Pt. i, pp. 96-97.

have been true in the past—essentially an executive, rather than a deliberative and advisory, body.[8]

Further evidence that the Privy Council still has vitality is supplied by the existence of a number of active and important Council committees. Foremost among these is the Judicial Committee, created by statute in 1833, and serving as a great quasi-tribunal which renders final judgment (in the guise of advice to the crown—for the advisory function survives on the judicial side) on all appeals from ecclesiastical courts, admiralty courts, and courts in India, the dominions, and the colonies.[9] There is an ancient non-statutory committee on the affairs of the Channel Islands,[10] and statutory committees exist for the Scottish universities and the universities of Oxford and Cambridge. Several important administrative boards and commissions, furthermore—for example, the Board of Trade and the Ministry of Education—originated as Privy Council committees.[11]

The Ministry

It is manifest, however, that, whatever may have been true in earlier centuries, we must look beyond the Privy Council to discover the men and agencies that carry on the government at the present day; and the quest soon brings us to two outstanding groups or bodies, i.e., the ministry and the cabinet. The names of these two institutions are sometimes used interchangeably; but they denote parts of the government that are

[8] On the relation of present-day orders in council to the old royal power of legislating by proclamation, see A. V. Dicey, *Law of the Constitution* (8th ed.), 48-52.

[9] See pp. 755-760 below.

[10] The Channel Islands, Jersey and Guernsey, are not part of Great Britain and not subject to the British king as such, but to the duke of Normandy, who happens to occupy the British throne. This arises from the fact that they were part of the old duchy of Normandy which conquered England in 1066. Their people are England's "masters," and in 1925 they raised so much opposition to proposed taxation from Westminster that a special Privy Council commission had to be appointed to treat with them on the subject. The king has ceased to be duke of Normandy, but the Channel Islanders have not stopped regarding themselves as Normans.

[11] C. H. Tupper, "The Position of the Privy Council," *Jour. of Compar. Legis. and Internat. Law,* Oct., 1921; M. Fitzroy, *The History of the Privy Council,* as cited previously.

quite distinct from each other, and our first concern must be to see what the difference is. Broadly, the distinction is twofold, according as it has to do with (1) composition and (2) functions. The ministry comprises the whole number of crown officials who have seats in Parliament, are responsible to the House of Commons, and hold office subject to the approval of the working majority in that body. It is this relation to Parliament—in other words, the *political* nature of their offices—that distinguishes those crown officials who are to be regarded as ministers from the far greater number who have no such character, but form, rather, the permanent civil service, about which more will be said presently. Broadly, the ministers are those officers of the crown who have to do with the formulation of policy and the supreme direction of carrying it out. Yet this is not precisely true, because there are ministers who have very little to do with policy, and others who do not administer; which is tantamount to saying that the line which divides ministerial from non-ministerial offices has been drawn by usage, and even accident, not by logic. It is, furthermore, a shifting boundary, which leaves the number of ministerial posts, and hence of ministers, subject to continual fluctuation.

Looking over the list of ministers at any given time, one discovers four or five main groups or elements. The first is the heads, actual or nominal, of the principal government departments, e.g., the Secretary of State for Foreign Affairs, the First Lord of the Admiralty, the Chancellor of the Exchequer, the Minister of Health, and the President of the Board of Education. Second, there are other high officers of state, who, however, are not in charge of departments, e.g., the Lord Chancellor, the Lord President of the Council, and the Lord Privy Seal. Third, there are parliamentary under-secretaries. Not all under-secretaries in the departments and offices are parliamentary under-secretaries. There are permanent under-secretaries, who are not ministers, are non-political, and compose the topmost part of the permanent working staff, which is unaffected by the ups and downs of politics and the rise and fall of ministries.[12] The parliamentary under-secretaries (of whom

[12] See p. 207.

at least one will be found in every important department) are specially useful as spokesmen of their departments in the branch of Parliament in which the department head, in any particular case, does not have a seat.[13] A fourth small but important group of ministers consists of the government whips in the House of Commons. These are now four in number—a chief whip and three assistant whips. All serve as whips and draw salaries by virtue of holding certain other posts. But their actual work is chiefly as whips, and their salaries are justified mainly on the theory that by helping keep a quorum they enable supplies to be voted and the government to be kept running.[14] Finally, there are a few officers of the royal household, e.g., the Treasurer, the Comptroller, and the Vice-Chamberlain, who are still—despite changes made in 1924—regarded as having a political character.[15]

This makes up a considerable group of officials, which, indeed, tends to increase still further as governmental activities multiply and new machinery is called into play. To a certain extent, the present proportions of the ministry are traceable to the exigencies of the World War and its aftermath; although, compared with Continental ministries, the British ministry was already numerous when the war began—from fifty to sixty members, as compared with twelve each in France and Italy and eight in Germany[16]—and although, further, there had been, since the cabinet became a distinct group and the ministry as such ceased to be a policy-framing body, and even to hold meetings, no very determined effort to keep the number down. But during the war period new ministries were

[13] British usage, unlike that in Continental cabinet-government countries, permits a minister to speak only in the house to which he belongs. It is always desirable to have a spokesman also in the other house, and parliamentary under-secretaries are appointed with this in view.

[14] There are also opposition whips. But they are unpaid, and of course do not belong to the ministry.

[15] On the status of the officers of the household, see J. A. R. Marriott, *The Mechanism of the Modern State,* II, 200-202.

[16] It is to be noted, however, that the ministries of these countries consisted only of heads of departments, and that if under-secretaries and other officials corresponding to those of ministerial rank in England had been included, the number would have been—and would be today—much larger.

created, departments were divided and otherwise reconstructed, and the number of officials of ministerial rank (especially parliamentary under-secretaries) was increased with such freedom that the membership of the ministry was brought up, by June, 1918, to ninety-three. The principal ministries thus established after 1914 were: Munitions in 1915; Blockade, Labor, Pensions, Food Control, Shipping Control, and Air Service in 1916; National Service and Reconstruction in 1917; and Transport and Health in 1919.[17] Several of these were created for war purposes only and have now disappeared, e.g., Munitions, Blockade, Food Control, and Shipping Control; others, notably Reconstruction, were set up, while the war was still in progress, with a view to laying the foundations for post-war recovery; still others, e.g., Labor, Air Force, Pensions, and Transport, were intended to be permanent and still exist. The net result, taking into account all post-war reorganizations, is that at the date of writing (1929) the total number of officials of the government who are regarded as of ministerial rank is sixty-six.

The Cabinet

The cabinet is a different matter. It consists at any given time of such members of the ministry as the prime minister (who is head of ministry and cabinet alike) invites into the charmed circle. All cabinet members are ministers, but not all ministers are cabinet members. One should hasten to add that in deciding upon the composition of his immediate official family the prime minister has considerably less option than the foregoing statement might be taken to imply, because certain of the ministers occupy posts of such administrative or historical importance that they can never be left out. Such are the First Lord of the Treasury, the Chancellor of the Exchequer, the First Lord of the Admiralty, the seven "principal secretaries of state," [18] and (on grounds of prestige) the Lord

[17] A full account of the origins of the new ministries created before 1919 will be found in J. A. Fairlie, *British War Administration* (New York, 1919), Chaps. ix-xii.

[18] These head the Foreign Office, the Home Office, the War Office, the Dominions and Colonial Offices, the India Office, the Ministry for Air, and the Scottish Office.

President of the Council and the Lord Privy Seal.[19] In all, some twelve or fourteen positions invariably carry cabinet membership with them. Beyond this, however, the prime minister really decides, being influenced in some cases by the aptitudes or susceptibilities of the particular minister, the importance of the office in question at the moment, the best interests of the party, or even geographical distribution of the honors which it is in his power to bestow. In days before the World War the presidents of the Board of Trade, the Board of Education, and the Local Government Board were almost always included, together with the Lord Lieutenant or the Chief Secretary for Ireland.[20] The Secretary for Scotland and the Chancellor of the Duchy of Lancaster were usually brought in, the Postmaster-General and the President of the Board of Agriculture and Fisheries frequently, and the Attorney-General, the First Commissioner of Works, and the Lord Chancellor for Ireland occasionally. All of these officials were considered of cabinet rank, whether or not actually included all of the time. The readjustments of the war period upset the accustomed arrangements to some extent, the president of the abolished Local Government Board being superseded by the Minister of Health, the officials of Ireland dropping out, the new Minister of Labor, the Air Minister, and the Secretary of State for Scotland coming in, and other more or less permanent substitutions being made.

Like the ministry as a whole, the cabinet has never had a fixed number of members; and in both cases there has been a gradual increase, both in absolute numbers and in the proportion of the members drawn from the House of Commons. Eighteenth-century cabinets contained, as a rule, not above seven to nine persons. In the first half of the nineteenth century the number ran up to thirteen or fourteen; the second

[19] The duties of the last-mentioned official are purely nominal, but when, in 1870, Sir Charles Dilke moved to abolish the office as useless, Gladstone urged the desirability of having in the cabinet at least one man who is not burdened with the management of a department, and the motion was lost.

[20] In theory, the powers of the executive were exercised in Ireland by the Lord Lieutenant, but in practice they devolved upon the nominally inferior Chief Secretary. See p. 693 below.

cabinet presided over by Lord Salisbury, at its fall in 1892, numbered seventeen; and most of the time from 1900 to the outbreak of the World War there were twenty members. The causes of this increase included pressure from ambitious statesmen for admission, the growing necessity of giving representation to varied elements and interests within the dominant party, the multiplication of state activities which called for organization under new and important departments, and the desire to give every major branch of the administrative system at least one representative. An inevitable effect was to make the cabinet a somewhat unwieldy body, and for some years before the war there was not only a steadily growing use of sub-committees but a tendency toward the emergence of a small inner circle bearing somewhat the same relation to the whole cabinet that the early cabinet had itself borne to the overgrown royal council. This trend was viewed with apprehension by some people who feared that the concentration of power in the hands of an "inner cabinet" would not be accompanied by a corresponding concentration of responsibility. British and foreign observers, however, agreed that the cabinet had come to be too large for the most effective handling of business.[21]

The stress of the World War brought the country to an experiment with a small selective cabinet such as very likely would never have been made under normal, peace-time conditions. The first step taken was, however, in the opposite direction; for the coalition cabinet organized by Mr. Asquith in the spring of 1915 was the largest in the country's history, namely, twenty-three. Experience soon showed that a cabinet of such proportions was totally unadapted to make the prompt decisions demanded by the emergency, and in December, 1916,

[21] A. L. Lowell, *Government of England,* I, 59; W. R. Anson, *Law and Custom of the Constitution* (3rd ed.), I, Pt. i, 211. Speaking of the unwieldiness of the cabinet in pre-war days, Lord Lansdowne said in the House of Lords in 1918: "The trouble really arose from the increase in the number of the members of the cabinet . . . If only a few of them took part, the cabinet ceased to be representative. If many of them took part, the proceedings tended to become prolix and interminable, and it is a matter of common knowledge that reasons of that kind led to the practice of transacting a good deal of the more important work of the government through the agency of an informal inner cabinet." *House of Lords Official Report,* June 20, 1918.

when Mr. Asquith yielded leadership to Mr. Lloyd George, a new "war cabinet" was called into being, consisting of only five persons—one Liberal, one Labor member, and three Conservatives. Only one of the five was burdened with an administrative office, i.e., the chancellorship of the exchequer. The other four, including the prime minister, were left free to devote all of their time to the supreme direction of the war and related affairs.[22] As would be surmised, this quite upset the customary relations of the cabinet with the other ministers and with Parliament. But the plan served the immediate purpose, and, with membership increased in 1917 to six (with an occasional seventh), and in 1919 again reduced to five, the new style cabinet continued at the head of the government throughout the remainder of the conflict and for almost a year after the armistice. Furthermore, in 1917 the prime ministers of the dominions, together with representatives of India, were invited to attend a series of special meetings of the body, held in conjunction with a new Imperial Conference; and thus arose a novel and interesting "imperial war cabinet," which held two subsequent series of meetings in the summer and autumn of 1918.[23]

These reconstructions were accomplished by entirely informal and extra-legal means. [Cabinet government in England rests on convention, and can be modified, and even revolution-

[22] For Lloyd George's defense of the plan, see E. M. Sait and D. P. Barrows, *British Politics in Transition,* 39-40. From as far back as 1904 there had been a cabinet committee on imperial defense—itself an outgrowth of a committee on national defense dating from 1895—and in 1915-16 this body, renamed the "war committee," was several times reorganized. It rendered valuable service, and its recommendations were practically certain to be adopted by the cabinet. But, starting with five or six members, it grew to be almost as large as the cabinet itself; and the action taken in December, 1916, was intended to restore deliberation upon military policy to a small, workable group. It was intended also to vest this critically important function in a body which should have the power to act upon its own decisions, and withal upon a body composed of men who should not be obliged to formulate great policies amidst the distractions of administrative and parliamentary duties. Cf. H. E. Egerton, "The Committee of Imperial Defense," *Polit. Quar.,* Feb., 1915.

[23] *Report of the War Cabinet for 1917,* 5-10. On the Imperial Conference, see *Extracts from Minutes of Proceedings and Papers laid before the Conference* [of 1917]. Cmd. 8566 (1917). Documentary materials relating to the sessions of 1918 are presented in Cmd. 9177 (1918).

ized, without changes in the law. Hence no act of Parliament was passed, and no proclamation or order in council was issued, establishing, or even announcing, the new machinery. General Smuts, representing the South African Union, sat as a member of the smaller British war cabinet from the summer of 1917 to the end of 1918, although he was, of course, neither a minister nor a member of Parliament. But again no law was violated; for it is only custom—even though nowadays adhered to rigidly enough under ordinary conditions—that requires cabinet officers to be members of Parliament.

So long as hostilities continued, the war cabinet wielded the powers of an autocrat. It acknowledged responsibility to the House of Commons in a general way, but was practically independent, and nothing short of a national convulsion could have overthrown it. Already shorn of real initiative, and heavily depleted by war service, Parliament became little more than a machine for registering executive edicts. The bulk of the ministers practically stopped attending the sittings, partly because they were unusually pressed with administrative work and partly because of the perfunctory character of the proceedings; many ministers, indeed, were not even members. After the armistice, however, the situation changed. Criticism of the war cabinet as an arbitrary "junto," long repressed, broke forth; and the new parliament elected in December, 1918, although containing a huge government majority, showed much independence of spirit. Men began not only to predict the end of the war cabinet but to demand it; and the premier himself intimated that such a change was not unlikely to come. After the Peace Conference convened at Paris, in January, 1919, only three members of the governing group were left in England; and Mr. Law, who in the absence of Mr. Lloyd George acted as a sort of deputy prime minister, began to call ministerial conferences bringing together twenty or thirty persons, and hence bearing a strong resemblance to the cabinet of pre-war days. Upon resuming the reins in Downing Street in midsummer, Mr. Lloyd George made it known that the war cabinet was soon to be superseded; and for some weeks the details of the impending reorganization absorbed much of his thought.

The cabinet in its new form had served a useful purpose. But it was not conspicuously successful in coördinating the work of the different departments, and it virtually abrogated the principle of the collective responsibility of the ministers for the acts of the government. Its early abandonment, in its present form at all events, was desired in almost every quarter.

The proposed reconstruction raised, however, several questions, some of them decidedly difficult. How large should the reorganized cabinet group be made? Should certain innovations in procedure, notably in regard to records and reports, be perpetuated? [24] Was the principle of coalition to be continued, or should there be a return to the plan of party homogeneity? Especially baffling was the question of size. Even if only the ministers who were heads of departments were brought in, there would now be at least thirty members. But pre-war cabinets had never contained more than twenty-two members; that number had usually been considered too large; the experiences of 1914-16 had vividly demonstrated the disadvantages of a large cabinet; and the machinery of government committee of the Ministry of Reconstruction was urging that for the proper performance of its functions the cabinet should consist of not more than twelve—indeed, preferably ten—members. Mr. Lloyd George's own idea was that only twelve of the most important department heads should be admitted, which would mean a cabinet of the same size as that over which Disraeli presided in 1874-80. He found it impracticable to adhere to this plan, however, and as the new cabinet gradually took form in October, 1919, it steadily approached the proportions of pre-war days and finally attained a membership of twenty. Partly as a result of provisions of the Government of Ireland Act (1920) converting the Lord Lieutenant into a viceroy and abolishing the office of Chief Secretary, Mr. Bonar Law was able to keep his cabinet, organized in November, 1922, down to sixteen. But when Mr. Baldwin succeeded to the premiership, in May, 1923, the number was brought up again to nineteen, and it has never since fallen below that figure. Accordingly, the cabinet is again of substantially the same size

[24] See p. 157 below.

as before the war, and the problems raised by its unwieldiness are yet to be solved.[25]

In personnel, as we have seen, ministry and cabinet differ in that the latter is an inner circle of the former, comprising, in these days, something like a third of the larger group. Functionally, they differ in that whereas ministers as such have duties only as individual officers of administration, each in his particular portfolio or less important station, cabinet members have collective obligations, i.e., to hold meetings, to deliberate, to decide upon policy, and in general to "head up" the government. They also play the most important part in the leadership of their party. Of course, all cabinet members are also ministers—"cabinet ministers," they are sometimes called; and as such they (or most of them), like the rest, have departments to administer or other ministerial work to do. But the ministry as such never meets; it never deliberates on matters of policy; it is, indeed, misleading to speak of it as a "body" at all. In sum, the cabinet officer deliberates and advises; the privy councillor decrees; and the minister executes. The three activities are no less legally distinct because it frequently happens that cabinet officer, privy councillor, and minister are one and the same person.

The Process of Forming a New Ministry and Cabinet

Before going farther, however, into functions and methods of work it will be well to take some account of the way in which matters are arranged when a cabinet retires and a new one is to be installed in its stead. At the outset, be it noted that at such a juncture the ministry also resigns. Ministry and cabinet stand or fall together, even though the non-cabinet ministers may personally have had no part in creating the situation which made a change necessary. This is not illogical, because as a rule the shift comes on account of the cabinet losing the confidence of the House of Commons, and the min-

[25] The number of members at the opening of 1929 was twenty. On the war cabinet, see especially J. A. Fairlie, *British War Administration,* 31-58 (also in *Mich. Law Rev.,* May, 1918); R. Schuyler, "The British War Cabinet," *Polit. Sci. Quar.,* Sept., 1918, and "The British Cabinet, 1916-1919," *ibid.,* Mar., 1920.

isters, after all, belong to the party the leaders of which are yielding control. They are "political" officers, and they accepted their posts in full knowledge that their fortunes would be bound up with those of their more important colleagues. Even if a change of party control is not involved, however, the rule applies; although in such a case the greater part of the ministers, of all grades, will promptly be put back in their old positions. To ask how a new cabinet is made up is therefore tantamount to inquiring how a new ministry is brought into existence.

The first step is the selection of the prime minister; for he is the head equally of both groups. And this brings us to the official who is by all odds the most powerful and important in the entire government—the only one who is worthy of being compared in these respects with the president in our American system. For some time after the cabinet took its place as an accepted part of the machinery of government, its members recognized no superior except the sovereign, who supplied all of the leadership that was needed.[26] But when, after 1714, the king stopped attending meetings and ceased in other respects to have much to do with the government, the group found itself leaderless, with the result that a sort of presidency naturally developed in one of its own number. In time, what was hardly more than a chairmanship grew into a thoroughgoing leadership—in short, into the prime minister's office as we behold it today. It is commonly considered that the first person who discharged the functions of prime minister in the modern sense was Sir Robert Walpole, first lord of the treasury from 1715 to 1717 and from 1721 to 1742. The term "prime minister" was not yet in common use; Walpole disliked the title and refused to allow himself to be called by it. But that the realities of the office existed is indicated by a motion made in the House of Commons attacking the clever leader on the ground that he had "grasped in his own hands every branch of government; had attained the sole direction of affairs; had monopolized all the powers of the crown; had compassed the disposal

[26] Under Charles II there was some tendency to recognize a "first," "chief," or "principal" minister. But under William III and Anne there was hardly any trace of anything of the kind.

of all places, pensions, titles, and rewards"—almost precisely, as one writer puts it, what the present prime minister is doing and is expected to do." [27] By the time of the establishment of the ministry of the younger Pitt, in 1783, the ascendancy of the prime minister among his colleagues was an established fact and was recognized as both inevitable and legitimate. The essentials of his position may be regarded as substantially complete when, during the later years of George III, the rule became fixed that in making up a new ministry the king should simply receive and endorse the list of nominees prepared and presented by the premier.[28]

We have already said that one of the few public acts which the king can still perform without the advice of a responsible minister is the naming of the prime minister; and, truly enough, when a premier goes to Buckingham Palace and places his resignation (along with that of his colleagues) in the king's hands, the sovereign sends out a summons to the statesman deemed best fitted to head a new ministry, and the latter reports at the Palace and is formally commissioned to prepare the ministerial list; that is to say, he is appointed prime minister. In earlier days, the sovereign was likely to have some real choice in the matter; he could select as well as appoint. The person designated must, of course, be a party leader who presumably could make up a ministry that would command a parliamentary majority. He must, as Gladstone put it, be chosen "with the aid drawn from authentic manifestations of public opinion." But there might be two or three, or even half a dozen, eligibles; and the king could make his selection among them. The crystallization of the two-party system, however, coupled with the growth of party machinery, brought it about that each party almost always had a chosen and accepted leader, with the result that when one party went out and the other came in, the sovereign could not do otherwise than call upon the leader of the incoming party, however much his personal preferences might run in a different direction. On certain occasions

[27] T. F. Moran, *Theory and Practice of the English Government,* 99.

[28] On the rise of the prime-ministership, see J. A. R. Marriott, *The Mechanism of the Modern State,* II, 71-76. Curiously, no systematic history of the office has ever been written.

—notably in 1852 and 1859—Queen Victoria determined by her personal choice which of two or more prominent members of the dominant party should be placed at the head of a new ministry. But she failed in 1880 to prevent Gladstone from becoming premier, although she strongly preferred Lord Hartington or Lord Granville; and never in the past sixty years has the sovereign been in a position to make a real choice. The emergence of Labor as a major party has, indeed, created a situation suggesting interesting possibilities. Two occasions have already arisen (in 1923 and 1929) on which no one party had a majority in the House of Commons, and it is conceivable that in such a situation the sovereign might have a chance to decide which of at least two party leaders should be entrusted with the premiership. Few things are better assured, however, than that even under these extraordinary conditions advice would reach the king which would mark out the proper path for him to take, and that no monarch in twentieth-century Britain would risk rocking the throne to its foundations by insisting upon a choice of his own as against one that could be made for him.

Who, then, actually selects the prime minister? The answer is two-fold: the House of Commons, or the country at a general election, brings the party into power; the party has the man in readiness—a man, be it noted, who has been chosen party leader, not by the rank and file of the party throughout the country, but by the party members in the House of Commons (along with usually a few other men of prominence in the party) in caucus assembled. If by any chance the party does not have the man in readiness when the call comes, it takes prompt steps to single him out. Thus, when, in 1894, Gladstone somewhat precipitately retired from office on account of physical infirmity, the Liberal parliamentarians canvassed the question whether the successor should be Sir William Vernon Harcourt or Lord Rosebery. They chose the latter, and he was forthwith appointed by the queen. He happened to be her personal preference, but that was not the deciding factor. Again, in 1922, when the Lloyd George coalition ministry resigned, Mr. Bonar Law accepted the premiership only tentatively until he should have been elected Conservative leader in succession to Mr. Austen Chamberlain, who had refused to break with Mr. Lloyd George.[29]

The premier, duly commissioned, proceeds to draw up a list of ministers, deciding what post each shall occupy, and, in cases where there is room for doubt, whether this man or that shall be invited into the cabinet. Theoretically, he has a free hand. In no direct way does Parliament control either his selection of men or his assignment of them to places;[30] and he can be sure that whatever list he carries to Buckingham Palace will receive the formal—though indispensable—assent of the king. Practically, however, he works under the restraint of numerous precedents and usages, to say nothing of the conditions imposed by the immediate party and public situation. He cannot be guided solely by his personal likes and dislikes; on the contrary, he must consult with this ambitious (perhaps unpleasantly aggressive) party leader, sound out that man for whom no place can be found except of a minor and perhaps otherwise undesirable sort, and plead with A. to come in and explain to B. why he must stay out, and so at last arrive at a list which will have the requisite qualities of prestige and coherence, even though a product, from first to last, of compromise. It is rarely as difficult to make up a ministry in Britain as it is in France and other Continental states, where ministries are always coalitions, and where not only the ministerial group itself but also the party *bloc* which is to support it has to be built up out of more or less jealous and discordant elements.[31] In Britain, too, the statesman who is called upon to organize a ministry is apt to have ample time in which to lay his plans, not only because a change of ministries can usually be foreseen with reasonable certainty a good while in advance, but also because the premier-to-be has known all along that whenever the change comes it will be he, and no one else, who will have to handle the situation. Consequently, the making up of the new ministry is, as a rule, a matter of only a few hours. Even so, it is a task of much delicacy—"a work," as Disraeli

[29] See p. 501.

[30] For comment on this fact, see S. and B. Webb, *A Constitution for the Socialist Commonwealth of Great Britain*, 65.

[31] J. W. Garner, "Cabinet Government in France," *Amer. Polit. Sci. Rev.*, Aug., 1914, pp. 366-367.

once said, "of great time, great labor, and great responsibility." The prime minister is fortunate who accomplishes it without incurring personal or party embarrassment.

Considerations Affecting the Selection of Ministers

What are some of the rules, traditions, and practical considerations that the makers of ministries find it necessary to take into account? The first is that all ministers must have seats in one or the other of the two houses of Parliament. This does not mean literally that every man [32] appointed to a ministerial post must at the time be actually in Parliament.[33] If there is strong desire to include a person who does not belong to either house—and the reasons may arise either from party expediency or from general public advantage—he may be named, and may enter provisionally upon the discharge of his duties. But unless he can qualify himself with a seat, either by election to the House of Commons or (in cases of special urgency) by being created a peer, he must give way in a brief time.[34] With rare exceptions, therefore, the prime minister selects his men from the existing membership of the two houses. We have seen that Parliament once unwisely undertook, in the Act of Settlement

[32] Or woman; because nowadays there are occasionally female ministers. Miss Margaret Bondfield was the first such, in the capacity of parliamentary secretary to the Ministry of Labor in the MacDonald government of 1924. The Duchess of Athol became parliamentary secretary to the Board of Education when the Baldwin ministry of 1924 was formed. In the second MacDonald government, formed in 1929, Miss Bondfield was assigned the post of minister of labor, thus becoming the first woman to sit in a British cabinet.

[33] Sir William Harcourt, for example, was not a member of Parliament when appointed Secretary of State for the Home Department in 1880; and there have been other cases of the kind.

[34] The matter is usually handled through an arrangement, engineered by the prime minister, by which a loyal party member gives up his seat, thus opening the way for a by-election at which the provisional minister is voted into Parliament by his adopted constituents. The retiring member may be rewarded for his sacrifice by appointment to an office not requiring membership in Parliament, or even by a peerage. The last case (aside from World War days) of a minister holding office for a considerable time without having a seat in Parliament was that of Gladstone as colonial secretary in 1845-46. Some of the self-governing colonies have formal constitutional provisions on the subject. Thus, in both Australia and South Africa a minister is not allowed to hold office longer than three months unless he is, or becomes, a member of parliament.

of 1701, to make it impossible for ministers, as well as other officers under the crown, to sit in the House of Commons. But we have seen also that before the time came for the restriction to take effect the legislation was so modified, by the Security and Place Acts of 1705-07, as not to put any serious impediment in the way of ministers sitting in the popular chamber.[35]

The substitute plan adopted was that while members of the House of Commons might accept appointment by the crown to "older" ministerial posts, i.e., those that existed in 1705, they should remain members only if they vacated their seats, submitted themselves to their constituents for reëlection, and were duly returned.[36] The theory behind this provision was that the voters should have an opportunity to say whether they were willing to be represented in Parliament by a man who held an office under the crown, and who therefore might be divided in his allegiance. And though the continued growth of parliamentary at the expense of royal power eventually robbed this consideration of all practical importance, the rule survived intact until a short time ago. The restriction applied only, be it noted, to ministerial posts antedating 1705; in the case of such positions—by far the greater number—created after that date, it became usual to make special statutory provision permitting the holder to sit in the House without submitting himself for reëlection. Like many other rules, the requirement of reëlection as applied to the older offices was suspended (three different times, in fact) during the World War; in 1919 a Reëlection of Ministers Act so far rescinded it as to relieve members from vacating their seats if they accepted ministerial office "within nine months after the issue of a proclamation summoning a new parliament;" and finally, in 1926, an amending measure on the subject brought the old requirement completely to an end. The arguments which eventually prevailed were not only that the rule had become an anomaly, but that it was positively objectionable, in that the financial burden of seeking reëlection was unfair to poorer men, and also in that a prime minister was sometimes prevented from making a desirable selection by

[35] See p. 50 above.

[36] It was not essential, of course, that the minister be returned from the same constituency which he previously represented.

uncertainty as to whether the man in mind could succeed in being reëlected.

Every ministry since the early eighteenth century has contained members of both the House of Commons and the House of Lords; even Mr. MacDonald found places for four peers in his Labor ministry of 1924. Indeed, a law which forbids more than six of the seven "principal secretaries of state" to sit in either house at the same time in effect necessitates distribution between the two; and inflexible custom requires the Chancellor of the Exchequer to be a member of the House of Commons and the Lord Privy Seal, the Lord Chancellor, and the Lord President of the Council to belong to the House of Lords. Beyond this, there is no positive requirement, in either law or custom; although there is a feeling that the Home Secretary should be in the House of Commons, and also an idea that the Foreign Secretary may most appropriately be in the House of Lords, where he will be less disturbed with embarrassing questions than in the popular chamber. To fill the various posts the premier must bring together the best men he can secure—not necessarily the ablest, but those who will work together most effectively—with only secondary regard to whether they belong at one end of Westminster Palace or at the other. An important department whose chief sits in the House of Commons is certain to be represented in the House of Lords by a parliamentary under-secretary, and vice versa. In France and other Continental countries executive departments are, as a rule, represented in Parliament by their presiding official only. But this official is permitted, as English ministers are not, to appear and speak on the floor of both chambers.

Since the days of Walpole, who was himself a commoner, the premiership has been held approximately half of the time by commoners and half of the time by peers. Lord Rosebery (1894-95) and Lord Salisbury (1895-1905) were, however, the last premiers who sat in the upper house, and it is felt more strongly today than ever before that enforced absence from the House of Commons, the principal theater of legislative and other activity, imposes an almost fatal handicap. Peerages for retired premiers are deemed fitting; witness the titles conferred on Mr. Balfour and Mr. Asquith. But possession of a peerage militates against attaining the premiership; witness Lord Curzon, who, in part at least on this account, was passed over in 1923 in favor of Mr. Baldwin.[37] Distribution of other ministers between the two houses has varied greatly, with, however, a steady tendency since the early nineteenth century to an increased proportion of commoners. Within the cabinet, as distinguished from the ministry as a whole, members of the two houses were usually about equally numerous at the middle of the century; but of late commoners have preponderated, although not decisively (except in Labor cabinets). Peers have usually been more numerous in Conservative than in Liberal cabinets.[38]

A second general rule or principle which the incoming prime minister must observe in making up both a ministry and a cabinet is that of party solidarity. William III set out to govern with a cabinet in which Whigs and Tories were deliberately intermingled. The plan did not work well, and during his reign and that of Queen Anne it was gradually abandoned in favor of cabinets made up with a view to party homogeneity. George I naturally placed his confidence in the party that had brought about his accession. Under him, "there was no question of playing off one party against another, or selecting the best men from both sides. The ministry of George I was necessarily Whig." [39] Eighteenth-century cabinets, after the days of Walpole, still sometimes included men of divers political affiliations —for example, the famous "coalition" of Fox and North in 1783. But gradually the conviction took root that in the interest of unity and efficiency the political solidarity of the cabinet group is indispensable. The last occasion (prior to the World War) upon which it was proposed to make up a cabinet from utterly diverse political elements was in 1812. The scheme was abandoned, and from that day to 1915 cabinets were regularly composed, not always exclusively of men identified with a single political party, but at all events of men who were in substantial agreement upon the larger questions of policy, and

[37] See p. 152 below.

[38] For an interesting analysis of the social and other backgrounds of cabinet ministers, see H. J. Laski, "The Personnel of the English Cabinet, 1801-1924," *Amer. Polit. Sci. Rev.*, Feb., 1928.

[39] W. R. Anson, *Law and Custom of the Constitution* (3rd ed.), II, Pt. i, 97.

who expressed willingness to coöperate in carrying out a given program. From 1915 to 1922 the country experimented with coalition governments; and under war-time conditions they were useful if not essential. The experience, however, left the majority of Englishmen hating the principle of coalition, and nowadays, as before, it is taken for granted that a new premier will draw his ministerial timber from the resources of his own party.

In selecting his co-laborers the prime minister works under still other practical limitations. One of them is the well-established principle that surviving members of past ministries of the party, in so far as they are in active public life and desirous of appointment, shall be given preferential consideration. There are always a good many of these veterans of the Front Opposition Bench, and as a rule they want to get back into office. At all events, they would be offended if not given an opportunity to do so when their party returns to power. Then there are the young men of the party who have made reputations for themselves in Parliament, and consequently have claims to recognition. A certain number of them must be taken care of. After all, the party will need leaders in years to come—men who have had long experience in official life—and its ministerial personnel must be continuously recruited from the ranks. Regard must be had also for geographical considerations; there must be ministers not only from England but from Scotland, Ireland, and Wales. Different wings of the party must be given representation; disaffected elements must be placated. Even social, economic, and religious groupings throughout the nation must be borne in mind.

By no means the smallest difficulty is that of assigning the ministers to individual posts in a reasonably appropriate way and so that all will be at least moderately satisfied. The first question is as to the post which the prime minister himself shall occupy. He has, of course, his choice; he is first in the field. He is not, indeed, obliged to take a post at all—save for one consideration, namely, that he will draw no salary as premier, but only as holder of one of the legally recognized salaried positions.[40] This being the case, his object—in view of the

[40] The salaries of ministers range from £2,000 to £5,000 a year. Posts of the grade which the prime minister regularly occupies pay £5,000. Minis-

arduous character of the duties which will fall to him simply as chief minister—is usually to find a position which has dignity and prestige but does not entail much administrative work. Such a post was long ago discovered in the first lordship of the treasury. As will be pointed out later, it is specially appropriate for the actual head of the government to occupy a Treasury position;[41] and with few exceptions, the prime ministers of the past half-century have done so. One of the exceptions was Lord Salisbury, whose keen interest in international affairs led him to take upon himself the heavy burden of the Foreign Office. Another was Mr. MacDonald, who occupied the same post in 1924, partly because of the supreme importance of international problems at that juncture, and partly because Mr. MacDonald had a wider acquaintance abroad and was better versed in diplomatic matters than any of his colleagues. Still another case was that of Mr. Baldwin who, as prime minister, held simultaneously for a few months in 1923 the portfolios of First Lord of the Treasury and Chancellor of the Exchequer, though only because he was waiting—vainly, as it proved—for Sir Reginald McKenna to make up his mind to accept the latter post.[42]

The prime minister's problem is not so much, however, the selection of his own post—usually that is no problem at all—as the placing of the other ministers, and especially the cabinet members. Two or more of them may want, and have equally

terial salaries are not included in the Civil List (see p. 105), and, being voted by Parliament every year, are subject to change whenever desired. In addition to their salaries, the Attorney-General and a few other ministers receive certain fees.

[41] See p. 166.

[42] Gladstone, on two occasions, combined the chancellorship of the exchequer with the prime-ministership. Pitt and Canning, in their respective days, held the same two posts simultaneously. Inasmuch as the cabinet is an inner circle—almost, one may say, a committee—of the Privy Council, it would simplify matters, as Low points out (*Governance of England,* 155), if the Lord President of the Council were also the prime minister; and in 1894 Lord Rosebery, upon assuming the premiership, took for himself the Lord President's titular position. Usage, however, has not developed on these lines; and a practical obstacle is the tradition, amounting to a requirement, that the Lord President shall be a member of the upper house. In Continental countries and in the British self-governing colonies the prime minister is officially president of the council of ministers.

good claim to, the same position; some may insist upon having posts for which they are not best fitted; some, on the other hand, may be reluctant to take places of specially arduous or hazardous character for which they have been singled out; some, when offered the only thing that is left for them, will refuse in language that will leave the harassed premier, as Gladstone once remarked, "stunned and out of breath." In the expressive simile of Lowell, the prime minister's task is apt to be "like that of constructing a figure out of blocks which are too numerous for the purpose, and which are not of shapes to fit perfectly together." [43] He will have to display much patience and tact, often finally subordinating his own wishes to the inclinations and susceptibilities of his future colleagues.

The list finally completed, or at least substantially so, the prime minister submits it to the king, by whom, in law, the final appointments are made; and an announcement forthwith appears in the official publicity organ of the government, the *London Gazette*, to the effect that the persons listed have been chosen by the crown to occupy the posts with which their names are bracketed. There is no mention of the cabinet; for the cabinet is unknown to the law, and nobody is ever officially named to it, as such. The logic of the political situation is, however, usually so plain that enterprising gentlemen of the press have pretty well guessed in advance who the members of the cabinet will be and in what particular office this statesman and that will find his chance to serve the country.[44]

[43] *Government of England,* I, 57. Cf. M. MacDonagh, *Book of Parliament,* 148-183. On the ministers as amateurs, see pp. 209-212 below.

[44] The process of making up a ministry and cabinet is commented on from various angles in A. L. Lowell, *Government of England,* I, Chap. iii; W. R. Anson, *Law and Custom of the Constitution* (3rd ed.), II, Pt. i, Chap. ii, *passim;* and M. MacDonagh, *The Pageant of Parliament,* I, Chap. xii. Much interesting information will be found in C. Bigham, *The Prime Ministers of Britain, 1721-1921* (London, 1922). A complete list of prime ministers since 1721 is printed in *Const. Year Book* (1928), 75, and of ministries since 1824, with the principal members of each, in *ibid.,* 76-78.

CHAPTER VII

THE CABINET AT WORK

WRITERS on the British constitution have vied with one another in devising phrases by which to indicate the importance of the cabinet. Bagehot terms it "the hyphen that joins, the buckle that binds, the executive and legislative departments together;" Lowell calls it "the keystone of the political arch;" Sir John Marriott refers to it as "the pivot round which the whole political machinery revolves." It is true that Gladstone found the center of the British system, "the solar orb round which the other bodies revolve," in the House of Commons; that Sidney Low reminds us that "from the legal point of view, the cabinet is only a committee of the Privy Council, and its members merely 'His Majesty's servants';" and that Sidney and Beatrice Webb, in their illuminating comments on the working constitution, assert that "the government of Great Britain is in fact carried on, not by the cabinet, nor even by the individual ministers, but by the civil service." Nevertheless, as we shall see, the cabinet has grown steadily in power at the expense of the House of Commons since Gladstone wrote; [1] and neither the cabinet's lack of independent legal status nor the indispensable rôle played by the civil servants in carrying forward the work of government day by day makes it any less true that, from whatever angle approached, the cabinet looms as the central figure in the picture.

On the one hand, the cabinet is the working executive. Its decisions and the advice tendered the crown in pursuance of them set in motion the departments of government concerned; and if we be reminded that the commands which lead to action emanate from the king-in-council, we have only to recall that "king-in-council"—however distinct in the eye of the law—

[1] See pp. 451-454 below.

means, to all intents and purposes, the cabinet. It is within the cabinet circle that executive and administrative policies are decided upon, and it is the cabinet ministers, aided by their colleagues and subordinates in the several departments, that carry these policies, and the laws of the land generally, into effect. The cabinet is as truly the executive in Britain as is the president in the United States.

A hundred years ago the cabinet, indeed, drew its importance mainly from its executive functions. Since 1832, however, it has come to have so much to do with legislation that a careful observer has been moved to remark, without a great deal of exaggeration, that it is the cabinet that legislates with the advice and consent of Parliament. The fact that cabinet members have seats in one or the other of the two houses is, of itself, the least important aspect of the matter. The main consideration is that—as will be explained more fully when we come to deal with the processes of legislation—the cabinet ministers guide and control the work of Parliament, in both branches, in a fashion with which there is nothing to compare in the United States, and in a measure unparalleled even in France, Germany, and other cabinet-government countries.[2] They prepare the Speech from the Throne in which the state of the country is reviewed and a program of legislation set forth at the opening of every parliamentary session; they formulate, introduce, explain, and urge the adoption of legislative measures upon all manner of subjects; and although bills may be presented in both houses by non-ministerial members, measures of a controversial nature, or of importance for any other reason, rarely receive serious attention unless they have originated with, or at all events have the active support of, the cabinet. For weeks at a stretch the cabinet demands, and is allowed, practically all of the time of the House of Commons for the consideration of the measures in which it is interested. In short, the cabinet ministers formulate the policy of the nation on every great question that arises, and ask of Parliament only that it take whatever action is requisite to enable this policy to be carried out. So necessary to the system is it that the ministers shall have their way that any check or rebuff at the hand

[2] See Chaps. xvii, xix below.

of the House of Commons considered by them to be serious precipitates a political crisis—a change of ministry, or even a general election.

The cabinet has sometimes been described as a committee of Parliament—a committee chosen, as Bagehot bluntly puts it, to rule the nation. It is, of course, not a committee in any ordinary sense. Parliament does not appoint it; and, far from having bills referred to it like a committee of the usual sort, it is itself the originator of practically all bills that assume much public importance. Nevertheless, its members are drawn from the membership of Parliament, and they constitute a sort of parliamentary inner group or circle recognized and accepted as an agency of leadership—endowed, it is true, with large initiative, but yet drawing its power primarily from its parliamentary setting or connection. Allowing for exceptional intervals such as the eclipse of the bi-party system has lately produced, the basic feature of the system is rule by party majority; and within the party majority the power that governs—in party matters and in public affairs alike—is the cabinet. As Lowell phrases it, the governmental machinery "is one of wheels within wheels; the outside ring consisting of the party that has a majority in the House of Commons; the next ring being the ministry, which contains the men who are most active within that party; and the smallest of all being the cabinet, containing the real leaders or chiefs. By this means is secured that unity of party action which depends upon placing the directing power in the hands of a body small enough to agree, and influential enough to control." [3]

[3] *Government of England,* I, 56. The place of the cabinet in the governmental system as a whole, and especially the causes and results of the cabinet's greatly increased powers in recent times, will be described more fully in Chap. xix. An observation by Gladstone is worth quoting. "The cabinet," he once wrote, "is the threefold hinge that connects together for action the British constitution of king or queen, Lords, and Commons. . . . Like a stout buffer-spring, it receives all shocks, and within it their opposing elements neutralize one another. It is perhaps the most curious formation in the political world of modern times, not for its dignity, but for its subtlety, its elasticity, and its many-sided diversity of power. . . . It lives and acts simply by understanding, without a single line of written law or constitution to determine its relations to the monarch, or to the Parliament, or to the nation; or the relations of its members to one another, or to their head." *Gleanings from Past Years,* I, 224.

Ministerial Responsibility and Its Enforcement

Under what conditions, and by what methods, does the cabinet perform its multifarious tasks? First of all, it is limited and guided at all times by the inescapable rule of ministerial responsibility. This responsibility is of two kinds, which may be termed legal and political. Legal responsibility is that which arises from the principle that every act of the crown must be countersigned by at least one minister, who can be held liable in a court of law if the thing done can be shown to be illegal. This principle is a part of the law of the constitution—unwritten, indeed, but nevertheless law.[4] The other, or political, form of responsibility is that which lies in the direction of the House of Commons. This responsibility is the essence of the cabinet, or parliamentary, system, which, in turn, is Britain's principal contribution to modern political practice. What does such responsibility mean? Simply that every minister—whether or not in the cabinet—is answerable individually to the popular branch of Parliament for all of his public acts, and that the ministry—in effect, the cabinet—can be held to account collectively not only for its policies and actions as a group but for any word spoken or any act performed by any one of its members in his public capacity. Being "answerable" and "held to account" is no mere form or gesture; it means that one or all of the ministers can at any time be forced out of office by a displeased or censorious House. This is not a matter of law, written or unwritten. A minister or a cabinet might cling to office in supreme indifference to a hostile House of Commons, and the courts would take no cognizance of the fact. But custom almost two hundred years old is behind the principle that cabinets and individual ministers alike shall remain in power only so long as they enjoy the confidence of the country; and no convention of the constitution is more freely accepted and cheerfully obeyed.[5]

In remoter centuries—before the cabinet system arose—the only means by which ministers could be made really answerable to Parliament was impeachment. This, however, was a clumsy

[4] This form of responsibility is described succinctly in A. V. Dicey, *The Law of the Constitution* (8th ed.), 321-324.

[5] See, however, p. 460 below.

and uncertain device, not often called into play, and usually entailing tumultuous proceedings and other disagreeable consequences. After 1689 the altered relation between king and Parliament threw greatly increased powers into the hands of the ministers, and at the same time left them more exposed to parliamentary criticism. The situation no longer called for mere occasional proceedings to oust a minister because of some peculiarly offensive act or policy on his part; rather, it presumed a continuous relationship of responsibility, grounded upon a sort of "gentleman's agreement" to the effect that if the minister (no longer the *king's* minister, except in name) could not keep the respect and support of a House of Commons majority, he should have the good sense and common decency to resign. In the eighteenth century, this principle fully established itself, and as a result impeachment as applied to ministers fell completely into disuse.[6] For a time, responsibility continued to be purely, or at least mainly, a personal, or individual, matter. A minister—even a cabinet member—might be forced out without affecting the tenure of his colleagues. The first cabinet, indeed, to bow as a body before a hostile House of Commons was that of Lord North, in 1782. Eventually, however, the cabinet developed such a degree of unity and solidarity that the rule came to be, as it now is, that members of the cabinet circle—and, of course, of the ministry as a whole—should stand or fall together; and not since 1866 has a cabinet officer retired singly as a result of a hostile parliamentary vote. If an individual minister falls into serious disfavor, one of two things almost inevitably happens. Either he is persuaded by his colleagues to change his course or to resign before formal parliamentary censure shall have been visited upon him, or the cabinet as a whole rallies to his support and stands or falls with him.

[6] The earliest recorded instance of impeachment was in 1376. After being dormant from the reign of Edward IV to the end of the sixteenth century, the practice was revived, and between 1620 and 1688 there were about forty cases, including the famous ones involving Lord Bacon (1620), the Duke of Buckingham (1626), the Earl of Strafford (1640), and the Earl of Danby (1679). The last cases were those of Warren Hastings (1788-95) and Lord Melville (1805). On the impeachment process, see T. E. May, *Treatise on the Law, Privileges, Proceedings, and Usage of Parliament* (13th ed., London, 1924), Chap. xxv.

There are at least four ways in which a ruling majority in the House of Commons may manifest its displeasure with a cabinet, and thus bring to a head the question of its continuance in office. It may pass a simple vote of "want of confidence," thereby expressing disapproval of general policy. It may pass a vote of censure, criticizing the cabinet, or some member thereof, for some specific act. It may defeat a measure which the cabinet has sponsored and refuses to abandon. Or it may pass a measure but amend it in ways that the ministers are unwilling to accept. The cabinet is not obliged to pay any attention to a hostile vote in the House of Lords; but when any one of the four forms of action enumerated is taken in the popular chamber, the prime minister and his colleagues must normally do one of two things: resign or appeal to the country. If it is clear that the cabinet has lost the support, not only of Parliament, but also of the electorate, the only honorable course for the ministers is to resign. If, on the other hand, there is doubt as to whether the parliamentary majority really represents the country upon the matter at issue, the ministers may very properly "advise," i.e., request, the sovereign to dissolve Parliament, which, of course, brings on a general election. In such a situation the ministers tentatively continue in office. If the election yields a majority prepared to support them, the cabinet is given a new lease of life. If, on the other hand, the new parliamentary majority is hostile, no course is open to the ministry save to retire, either immediately or upon suffering an actual defeat (generally on the reply to the Speech from the Throne) when the new parliament begins work. It is usual in such cases for the ministers to hand over their seals of office as soon after the polling as they can put business in shape to do so. As has been indicated in another connection, the Conservative government of Mr. Baldwin, however, defeated in the elections of 1923, patriotically tided over the exceptionally unsettled interval while the victors were deciding upon their course of action and allowed itself to be ousted by a technical defeat after Parliament met.

It is hardly necessary to say that a cabinet may save itself by abandoning a bill the defeat or emasculation of which is in certain prospect, or by accepting amendments offered from the floor; also that some ministries are more "thick-skinned" than others, i.e., more disposed to bear up under rebuffs without making them grounds for resignation or a dissolution—a characteristic displayed notably by the Lloyd George coalition government during the two or three years preceding its collapse in 1922. Indeed, a survey of the political history of recent decades would show that cabinets rarely resign without giving themselves the benefit of the chance that goes with a national election. They like to think that the country is behind them even though the House of Commons is not; and sometimes the outcome shows that they were right. A different twist is given the situation when a cabinet that has the confidence of the House brings about a dissolution in order to take a sort of referendum on a policy or measure on which it wants a clear mandate from the people. This is not often done; and the experience of Mr. Baldwin's government in 1923 shows that to take such a step may mean to court disaster.[7]

Leadership of the Prime Minister

Turning to the way in which the cabinet carries on its work, three main features appear, i.e., the leadership of the prime minister, the use of committees, and the activities of the secretariat. How the prime minister comes by his office and how he selects his colleagues have been described above. Something further, however, may be said about his duties, and especially his relations with the other ministers, the sovereign, and Parliament.

The prime minister, in relation to the ministers generally, is often described by the phrase *primus inter pares,* the intention being to emphasize that, notwithstanding greater importance and unique functions, he is, after all, not a different order of political being, like the German chancellor (under both empire and republic),[8] but only one of a group, fundamentally

[7] See pp. 505-508 below.

[8] On the German chancellorship and ministry under the Empire, see F. K. Krüger, *Government and Politics of the German Empire* (Yonkers, 1915), Chap. viii. For the situation today, see the national constitution, Arts. 52-59; R. Brunet, *The New German Constitution* (New York, 1922), 172-177; and F. F. Blachly and M. E. Oatman, *The Government and Administration of Germany,* Chaps. v-vi. Formerly, the chancellor was,

on a footing with the others. Strictly, there is no *office* of prime minister at all; certainly there is no salary for such a dignitary, the incumbent receiving pay from the state only by virtue of the secretaryship or similar post which he holds. Not until 1878 did the term "prime minister" make its appearance in any public document, and then only in the opening clause of the treaty of Berlin, in which Lord Beaconsfield was referred to as "First Lord of Her Majesty's Treasury, Prime Minister of England." [9] For social purposes, the prime minister was indeed given a definite and exalted rank by an act of 1906 fixing the order of precedence in state ceremonials; in this very first statute to take note of his existence he was made the fourth subject of the realm.[10] But even here he is preceded by the Lord Chancellor, one of his "subordinates" in the cabinet, who socially is second only to the archbishop of Canterbury. As a minister, the premier has statutory duties and a salary; as *prime* minister, he has neither, being merely accepted and recognized for what he is, after two centuries of hazardous historical development.[11]

"First among equals" he undoubtedly is. Rather better is Sir William Vernon Harcourt's phrase, *inter stellas luna minores.* For, within ministry and cabinet alike, the premier is the key man, even if not always the outstanding personality. He has put the other ministers where they are. He exercises a general surveillance and coördinating influence over their work. He presides at cabinet meetings, and counsels continually with individual members, encouraging, admonishing, advising, and instructing. He irons out difficulties arising between ministers

in effect, the only minister; the so-called ministers were in the strictest sense his subordinates. Nowadays the gap is not so wide; but even yet the ministers are primarily only administrators of departments, and the general course of cabinet policy is determined by the chancellor alone.

[9] "This was, no doubt, a concession to the ignorance of foreigners, who might not have understood the real position of the British plenipotentiary if he had been merely given his official title." S. Low, *The Governance of England* (rev. ed.), 156.

[10] For the full order of precedence, see *Whitaker's Almanack* (1928), 141.

[11] "Nowhere in the wide world," says Gladstone, "does so great a substance cast so small a shadow; nowhere is there a man who has so much power, with so little to show for it in the way of formal title or prerogative." *Gleanings of Past Years* (New York, 1889), I, 244. This was written, of course, before the statutory recognition of 1906.

or departments. If necessary, he can require of his colleagues that they accept his views, with the alternative of his resignation or theirs; for it is tactically essential that the cabinet, however divided in its opinions when behind closed doors, shall present a solid front to Parliament and the world.[12] Indeed, he can, and occasionally does, request and secure from the sovereign the removal of a minister for insubordination or other offense.[13] He is, and is expected to be, the leader of the ministerial group; as its chief spokesman, he will have to bear the brunt of attacks made upon it; and it is logical enough that his authority shall be disciplinary as well as merely moral. It goes without saying, however, that in all this he must not be overbearing, or harsh, or unfair, or tactless. His government will at best have enough obstacles to overcome; its solidarity must not be imperilled or its morale lowered by grudges or injured feelings within its ranks.[14]

The prime minister is the active medium of intercourse between the cabinet and the sovereign. Any minister who is in charge of a department has, indeed, a legal right of access to the sovereign; but with rare exceptions this right is not exercised for official purposes, being waived in favor of the

[12] There have been cases in which a cabinet member has resigned rather than accept a policy supported by the prime minister. One of the most notable was the resignation of Lord Randolph Churchill as Chancellor of the Exchequer in 1887, as a protest against expenditure on armaments requested by the Admiralty and War Office and assented to by the premier. Lord Palmerston, when prime minister, once said that his desk was full of Mr. Gladstone's resignations, though as a matter of fact the difficulties were always ironed out.

[13] A good illustration is the dismissal of E. S. Montagu as Secretary of State for India in 1922, on the ground that he had given publicity to an important state paper (a communication from the government of India) without consulting his colleagues. *Annual Register* (1922), 33-34.

[14] The question of the extent to which the prime minister may impose his personal will upon his colleagues as a group is more or less an open one, although the general principle that he shall not override their wishes is clear. There have been instances, for example, in which the prime minister publicly announced an intention to ask for a dissolution of Parliament when the cabinet was not agreed upon the plan. The most recent was Mr. Baldwin's historic announcement at Plymouth in 1923. Most precedents indicate, however, that such a decision must be reached by the cabinet as a whole and not by the premier alone. On two occasions Gladstone, when prime minister, wanted a dissolution, but the cabinet was opposed, and no dissolution took place.

premier, to the end that he may be able to put government affairs before the sovereign in a coherent and systematic manner. Frequent conferences at Buckingham Palace and elsewhere give the prime minister opportunity to report on the progress of discussion in the cabinet and of debate in Parliament; and in busy periods these conversations are supplemented by daily letters.

In the branch of Parliament of which he is a member, the prime minister also represents the cabinet as a whole in a sense which is not true of any of his colleagues. He is looked to for the most authoritative statements and explanations of the government's policy; he speaks on most important bills; and at crucial stages he commonly bears the brunt of debate from the government benches. A prime minister who belongs to the House of Commons is, of course, more advantageously situated than one who sits in the House of Lords. The latter must trust a lieutenant to represent him and carry out his instructions in the place where the great legislative battles are fought; and this lieutenant, the government leader in the House, tends strongly to draw into his own hands a part of the authority belonging to the cabinet's nominal head. During Lord Salisbury's last premiership this difficulty was largely obviated by the fact that the government leader in the lower chamber was the prime minister's own nephew, Mr. Balfour. But, as Gladstone once wrote, "the overweight of the House of Commons is apt, other things being equal, to bring its leader inconveniently near in power to a prime minister who is a peer." [15] Upon the resignation of Mr. Law as prime minister in 1923, Lord Curzon's strong claims to the succession were passed over in favor of Mr. Baldwin largely—although there were additional reasons—because it was considered almost imperative that the head of the government be a member of the popular branch.

It goes without saying that, even when the prime minister takes a portfolio, such as the first lordship of the treasury, which involves no heavy labor, he is hard-worked and always pressed for time. He must go through innumerable papers, supervise endless correspondence, receive a steady stream of

[15] *Gleanings of Past Years,* I, 242.

callers on more or less important public business, confer with individual ministers, visit and submit reports to the sovereign, hold cabinet meetings, and—as if that were not enough—spend much of almost every day when Parliament is in session either on the Treasury bench (if he is a member of the House of Commons) or in his private room behind the speaker's chair, ever ready to answer questions, to plunge into debate in defense of the government's policy, to decide points of tactical procedure put up to him by his lieutenants. Social demands have to be met also; and groups of constituents will occasionally expect to be taken to the public galleries or entertained to tea on the Terrace overlooking the Thames.[16] Small wonder that in 1924 the broad shoulders of Ramsay MacDonald drooped under the double load of the premiership and the secretaryship for foreign affairs; or that Gladstone was moved to remark, more than forty years ago, that these two offices cannot be combined successfully.

Few, if any, positions in the world carry with them greater power than the British prime-ministership. This does not mean, however, that all British prime ministers have been, in practice, equally powerful; on the contrary, like presidents of the United States, the premiers have differed widely in both power and (what comes to pretty much the same thing) influence. In the first place, some have been strong, dominating personalities—men of the type of the Pitts, Peel, Disraeli, Gladstone, Lloyd George—while others have been mediocrities, such as North, Newcastle, Liverpool, and Campbell-Bannerman. In the second place, those who, like Salisbury and MacDonald, have tried to carry the premiership along with another important office have been unable to realize the possibilities of either post to the full. Furthermore, the growth of the number of departments and ministerial offices—the sheer spreading out of the field covered by the government—has so augmented the task of supervision as to make it increasingly difficult for the prime minister to wield the control of earlier and simpler days. A prime minister in the House of Lords is, as has been pointed out, at a great disadvantage. And, as Palmerston once lamented, the premier's

[16] See F. Dilnot, *Biographical Sketch of Lloyd George* (New York, 1923), 104-107.

relative power in his government inevitably tends to be diminished when the principal offices are filled by conspicuously energetic and able men.[17]

Cabinet Committees and Cabinet Meetings

Like most bodies of even twenty to twenty-five people, the cabinet finds use for committees. There is no fixed and regular committee system; but special committees are set up from time to time as need arises, and at least two committees—one on home affairs and another on finance—are referred to as "permanent." Whatever their composition or tenure, committees regularly have as their function the preparation of business for consideration by the cabinet as a whole. They have no power of final action, but only to report and recommend; and their sittings, particularly in the case of the home affairs committee, may be attended by ministers who are not in the cabinet. The Committee of Imperial Defense, of which one frequently hears, is not technically a committee of the cabinet, but in reality it falls not far short of being such. It consists of the prime minister as chairman, the political and technical heads of the defense services (War Office, Air Ministry, and Admiralty), the Chancellor of the Exchequer, and the secretaries of state for foreign affairs, the colonies, and India, and also representatives of the dominions, as occasion requires. It and its sub-committees investigate, report, and recommend on all defense questions, but it has no executive power. Cabinet committees have been used rather more freely since the World War than before.

When Parliament is in session, regular cabinet meetings are held once or twice a week, during morning and early afternoon hours so as not to conflict with the sittings of the houses. Special meetings may be called by the prime minister; indeed, in tense periods meetings are likely to be held almost daily.

[17] E. Ashley, *Life and Correspondence of Henry John Temple, Viscount Palmerston,* II, 257. For an interesting brief summary of the characteristics of the thirty-seven British prime ministers from Walpole to Bonar Law, see W. B. Munro, *Governments of Europe,* 66-68; and for the best full treatment of the subject, C. Bigham, *The Prime Ministers of Britain, 1721-1921* (London, 1922). Cf. S. Herbert, "The Premiership and the Presidency," *Economica,* June, 1926.

When, however, Parliament has been prorogued, meetings are only occasional, at the prime minister's discretion.[18] In earlier days there was no regular meeting place. "I see them [the cabinet ministers]," wrote Algernon West, "meeting everywhere." [19] Nowadays, the meetings are pretty generally held at the prime minister's official residence, No. 10 Downing Street, although sometimes in the prime minister's room back of the speaker's chair in the House of Commons, and occasionally at the Foreign Office or any other convenient place. The proceedings are decidedly informal. The prime minister presides, and of course he guides the deliberations, even to determining when they shall be brought to a close. But there are no rules of order; there is no fixed quorum; and speeches give way to discussion of a conversational nature in which everybody has a chance to participate. Attempt is made to get decisions, not by formal votes, but by the give-and-take of debate which results in unanimous conclusions.[20]

[18] In 1920 there were eighty-two cabinet meetings, and in 1921, ninety-three. The number was somewhat smaller in succeeding years, e.g., in the year ended March 31, 1925, when it was sixty-two. In addition, there were in the last-mentioned period 159 meetings of cabinet committees and 154 meetings of the Committee of Imperial Defense and its sub-committees.

[19] "No. 10, Downing Street," *Cornhill Magazine,* Jan., 1904.

[20] Although a thing of the past, the war cabinet is still of interest—if for no other reason, because it contributed some lasting features to cabinet organization and procedure. Its methods of work are quite fully described, not only in its published reports, but in certain speeches of its members on the floor of Parliament (notably one by Lord Curzon in the House of Lords on June 19, 1918, *Parliamentary Debates, 5th series* [*Lords*], xxx, 263 ff.). The body met every day, often two or three times a day, and hence, for all practical purposes, was in session continuously. Part of the time was given to hearing reports, including a daily summary of the military situation. Part was given to discussion of military policy and of public questions, participated in by the members alone and behind closed doors. But most of the sittings were taken up largely with hearings and discussions, attended and participated in by ministers, military and naval experts, and persons of many sorts and connections who were invited to appear. Thus, if the agenda of the day called for a consideration of diplomatic questions, the Secretary of State for Foreign Affairs, accompanied perhaps by one or more of his under-secretaries or other aids and subordinates, would be likely to be present. "The majority of the sessions of the war cabinet," says the *Report* for 1917, "consist, therefore, of a series of meetings between members of the war cabinet and those responsible for executive action at which questions of policy concerning those departments are discussed and settled. Questions of overlapping or conflict between depart-

Nobody has better reason than a group of cabinet ministers to know that in unity there is strength. At all events, they are well enough aware that, exposed as they are to a steady flow of inquiry and criticism in the House of Commons, any lack of harmony, or even the appearance of it, will soon rise to plague them. Two main features or devices help the group to present a solid front. One—already considered—is the leadership and disciplinary authority of the prime minister. The other is the secrecy of proceedings. No one needs to be told that a group of men brought together to agree upon and carry out a common policy in behalf of a large and varied constituency will be more likely to succeed if their inevitable clashes of opinion are not published to the world. It was on this account mainly that the old German Bundesrath always transacted business behind closed doors. For the same reason, the public was excluded from the sittings of the convention which framed the present constitution of the United States. It would not be expected that such a body as the English cabinet would deliberate in public; no group of men charged with duties of similarly delicate and solemn character does so. But not only are reporters and other outsiders (except secretarial employees) entirely excluded; the subjects discussed, the opinions voiced, and the conclusions arrived at are divulged only in so far, and at such time, as is deemed expedient. In other words, the cabinet not only deliberates privately, but it throws a veil of secrecy over its proceedings. Following a cabinet meeting, the prime minister—or, in rare instances, some other authorized

ments are determined and the general lines of policy throughout every branch of the administration coördinated so as to form part of a consistent war plan. Ministers have full discretion to bring with them any experts, either from their own departments or from outside, whose advice they consider would be useful." Cmd. 9005 (1918), p. 2. In pursuance of this work of coördination, scores of special committees were set up, consisting usually of the heads of the departments most concerned, under the chairmanship of a member of the war cabinet. Finally, it is to be observed that all of the principal ministers were occasionally convoked in a "plenum of the cabinet" for the consideration of great public questions such as the Irish situation and the Representation of the People Bill, although even on these matters the final choice of policy lay with the war cabinet. Cf. R. L. Schuyler, "The British Cabinet, 1916-1919," *Polit. Sci. Quar.*, Mar., 1920 (reprinted in part in E. M. Sait and D. P. Barrows, *British Politics in Transition*, 31-36).

spokesman—may give the press some indication of what has happened, or may make statements in Parliament from which a good deal can be deduced. Indeed, much may be told freely. But on the other hand the veil may not be lifted at all; and in any event remarks and situations that would tend to reveal serious differences of opinion will always be withheld. One is obliged to add, however, that some cabinet ministers are less discreet than others, and that, in one way or another, enterprising reporters usually contrive to know pretty well what is going on.[21]

Cabinet Records—the Secretariat

There is, too, the matter of cabinet records—which brings us to an important piece of governmental machinery that has made its appearance only recently. In the early nineteenth century it was not uncommon for brief memoranda, or minutes, of cabinet proceedings to be written out and placed at least temporarily on file. The practice, however, died out, and for decades no clerk was allowed to be present in the meetings and no records were kept, even for the use of members. For knowledge of what had been done the ministers had to rely upon their own or their colleagues' memories, supplemented at

[21] E. M. Sait and D. P. Barrows, *British Politics in Transition,* 51-52. In 1925 it was announced that members of the cabinet had agreed not to write for publication, during their stay in office, anything of a controversial nature. Later in the year Lord Birkenhead, then Secretary of State for India, raised somewhat of a storm by publishing in a woman's journal an article in which he said, among other things, that the incursion of women into industry and politics "has failed, is failing, and must of necessity fail." A great deal of information about what has taken place in cabinet meetings eventually becomes available through autobiographies and memoirs published by former cabinet members, often, however, impaired in value by the haziness or untrustworthiness of the reminiscences upon which the writer relies. Noteworthy examples are Gladstone's *Gleanings of Past Years,* Lord Oxford and Asquith's *Fifty Years of British Parliament,* 2 vols. (London, 1926), and his *Memoirs and Reflections* (London, 1928), and Lord Morley's *Recollections* (London, 1917). See, in this connection, a war-time memorandum by Lord Morley published in the *New Republic,* Oct. 10, 1928. With material of this sort may be compared, on the American side, such works as *Diary of Gideon Welles, Secretary of the Navy under Lincoln and Johnson* (Boston, 1911); D. F. Houston, *Eight Years with Wilson's Cabinet, 1913 to 1920,* 2 vols. (Garden City, 1926); W. C. Redfield, *With Congress and Cabinet* (Garden City, 1924); and *T. Roosevelt; an Autobiography* (New York, 1913).

times by privately kept notes. It was, indeed,—so Mr. Asquith stated in the House of Commons in 1916—"the inflexible, unwritten rule of the cabinet that no member should take any note or record of the proceedings except the prime minister;" and he went on to explain that the prime minister did so only "for the purpose . . . of sending his letter to the king." [22]

Mr. Asquith's statement was by way of interpolation in a speech of his recent successor in the prime ministership, Mr. Lloyd George; and what Mr. Lloyd George was divulging was that, along with the creation of the war cabinet, it had been decided to introduce arrangements for keeping a complete official record of all cabinet decisions. The need for something of the sort had been felt before. "The cabinet," declared Lord Curzon retrospectively in 1918, "often had the very haziest notion as to what its decisions were . . . cases frequently arose when the matter was left so much in doubt that a minister went away and acted upon what he thought was a decision which subsequently turned out to be no decision at all, or was repudiated by his colleagues." The creation of the war cabinet made the need even greater; only half a dozen ministers were included, and not all of them could attend regularly, and practically everything that was done had to be communicated to the greater number outside. Taking over a device already in use in the war committee of the Asquith coalition—which, in turn, had developed from the secretariat of the Committee of Imperial Defense—the cabinet therefore provided itself with a secretary who was to keep minutes and see to it that every decision arrived at was transmitted not only to all of the cabinet members but also to all other officials or departments affected.

The arrangement was supposed to be for only so long as war conditions should last. But it proved so useful that in 1919 steps were taken to continue it indefinitely; and nowadays the cabinet secretariat is apparently to be regarded as a permanent feature of the government. The innovation did not go without challenge, especially when Parliament's attention was called, in 1922, to the fact that the secretarial staff established at Whitehall Gardens had grown to include 137 persons of all grades and the annual cost of it to £36,800. It was charged that a

[22] *Parliamentary Debates* [*Commons*], Vol. LXXXVIII (1916), col. 1343.

new "department" was in effect being thrust in between the cabinet and the "administration," and that it was an appropriate adjunct of the new system of personal government which Mr. Lloyd George was accused of seeking to build up. It was argued, too, that all proper purposes would be served by substituting for it a modest enlargement of the prime minister's personal secretariat at Downing Street. Coming in as prime minister in 1922, when feeling on the subject was strong, Mr. Bonar Law brought about a gradual reduction of personnel to thirty-eight and of cost to approximately £15,000 a year; and thenceforth the secretariat has functioned on substantially this scale. It is now to be regarded as a permanent part of the nation's governmental machinery.

Already by 1922 Lord Robert Cecil could remark that the secretariat did "a great deal more than merely record the decisions of the cabinet;" and among the additional things which it still does—not by virtue of any statute (if the statutes do not know the existence of the cabinet itself, it is natural that they should not take cognizance of the cabinet secretariat), but only at the behest of the cabinet—are to arrange the agenda of cabinet meetings, to collect data and perform general secretarial work for both the cabinet itself and all cabinet committees, including the Committee of Imperial Defense, and similarly for various conferences, international and otherwise, with which the cabinet is concerned, to communicate cabinet decisions to all officials and departments that have need to know them, and, indeed, to do whatever else the cabinet requires of it. There are certain duties, too, in connection with the League of Nations. In 1917 and 1918 volumes were published containing reports of cabinet proceedings for the year. This was, however, only as a contribution to keeping up the morale of a war-wracked nation, and in point of fact the published reports were of a very general character, rarely or never taking one behind the scenes.[23] After the war, publication was discontinued, and nowadays cabinet proceedings remain no less confidential, and even secret, than before. Instead of being treasured

[23] These reports were printed as parliamentary papers: *Report of the War Cabinet for Year 1917* (Cmd. 9005, 1918), and *Report of the War Cabinet for 1918* (Cmd. 325, 1919).

only in members' minds, however—or, at best, in fragmentary notes—they are preserved in systematic minutes, from which they may some day be drawn by the historian for the enlightenment of an interested world.[24]

[24] J. R. Starr, "The English Cabinet Secretariat," *Amer. Polit. Sci. Rev.*, May, 1928; H. Craik, "The Cabinet Secretariat," *Nineteenth Cent.*, June, 1922; C. Jones, "The War Cabinet Secretariat," *Empire Rev.*, Dec., 1923, and Jan., 1924. It will be recalled that no formal record is kept of proceedings of the president's cabinet in the United States.

The workings of the cabinet in general are described in S. Low, *Governance of England* (rev. ed.), Chaps. ii, iv; W. R. Anson, *Law and Custom of the Constitution* (3rd. ed.), II, Pt. i, Chap. ii; and J. A. R. Marriott, *Mechanism of the Modern State,* II, Chap. xxv. W. Bagehot, *The English Constitution,* Chaps. i, vi-ix, is decidedly worth reading. H. J. Laski, "The Personnel of the English Cabinet, 1801-1924," *Amer. Polit. Sci. Rev.,* Feb., 1928, is a study of the social antecedents, professional connections, education, and other characteristics of all cabinet officers between the dates indicated. Much that is interesting and significant will be found in biographies and memoirs of British statesmen, as, for example, Lord Rosebery, *Robert Peel* (London, 1889); J. Morley, *Life of William Ewart Gladstone,* 3 vols. (London, 1903); W. F. Monypenny and G. E. Buckle, *Life of Benjamin Disraeli,* 6 vols. (London, 1910-20); W. S. Churchill, *Lord Randolph Churchill,* 2 vols. (New York, 1906); Lord Oxford and Asquith, *Fifty Years of British Parliament,* 2 vols. (London, 1926); *ibid., Memories and Reflections* (London, 1928); Lord Morley, *Recollections* (London, 1917); Earl of Ronaldshay, *The Life of Lord Curzon,* 3 vols. (London, 1928). A classic comparison of the English cabinet system and the American presidential system is Woodrow Wilson, *Congressional Government* (Boston, 1885). A suggestive recent discussion is H. L. McBain, *The Living Constitution* (New York, 1927), Chap. iv.

CHAPTER VIII

EXECUTIVE DEPARTMENTS AND OFFICES

As in other governments, the laws are enforced and the multifold work of administration is carried on mainly through a number of executive departments; and most of the ministers—although with some very important exceptions—are in charge of, or otherwise attached to, these departments. In the United States, the ten executive departments of the national government stand on a common footing and bear much resemblance to one another. All have been created by act of Congress; all are presided over by single heads, known as secretaries except in the cases of the Post Office Department and the Department of Justice; all stand in substantially the same relation to the president and to Congress.[1] The executive departments in most Continental countries, notably France and Germany, likewise give the appearance of having been set up with due regard for considerations of logic and symmetry.[2] The English departments, however, are very heterogenous. To begin with, there is no uniformity of terminology. Some are offices of secretaries of state, some are boards, and some are ministries; and the differences of title often conform to no fixed principle. From the point of view of origins, some, notably the Treasury and the Admiralty, represent survivals of great offices of state of earlier times; eight, i.e., Foreign Affairs, Home Affairs,

[1] A brief description of these departments will be found in F. A. Ogg and P. O. Ray, *Introduction to American Government* (3rd ed., New York, 1928), Chaps. xix-xx. For a fuller historical account, see L. M. Short, *The Development of National Administrative Organization in the United States* (Baltimore, 1922).

[2] On the French executive departments, see E. M. Sait, *Government and Politics of France* (Yonkers, 1920), Chaps. iii-iv; on the German, F. F. Blachly and M. E. Oatman, *The Government and Administration of Germany* (Baltimore, 1928), Chap. vi.

War, Colonies, Dominions, India, Scotland, and Air, are offshoots of the ancient "secretariat of state";[3] others, as the Board of Trade and the Board of Education, have sprung from committees of the Privy Council; still others are ministries, boards, or commissions established outright by statute in recent decades, such as the Board of Works and the Board (now Ministry) of Agriculture and Fisheries, organized a generation ago, and the Ministry of Labor and the Ministry of Health, created in the period of the World War.

Again, viewed functionally, the departments present at least three main types: first, purely "political" departments, e.g., the Foreign Office, the War Office, the Admiralty, and the Home Office, exercising the oldest and most fundamental functions of government; second, the "economic" departments, such as the ministries of Labor and Agriculture and Fisheries, and the Board of Trade; and third, the departments having to do with matters of a broadly social character, i.e., the Ministry of Health and the Board of Education. Furthermore, there is hardly less diversity of organization than of origins and functions. In practically all cases, it is true, the departments are presided over by a single responsible minister, assisted by a parliamentary under-secretary, two or three, or more, permanent under-secretaries, and a greater or lesser body of secretaries, counsellors, legal advisers, chiefs and assistants, and other non-political officials, who, under direction, carry on the detailed administration and other work, and whose tenure is not affected by the political fortunes of their chiefs. Beyond these larger aspects, however, there are more differences than similarities.

Manifestly, the departments, taken as a group, are not susceptible of description in general terms.[4] Accordingly, we turn

[3] See p. 172 below.

[4] A convenient outline of the general scheme of ministries, boards, and other agencies as it existed before the World War is contained in R. H. Gretton, *The King's Government; a Study of the Growth of the Central Administration* (London, 1913), and a similar sketch of arrangements shortly after the war is C. D. Burns, *Whitehall* (London, 1921). A still more recent, though meager, survey is J. J. Clarke, *Outlines of Central Government* (2nd ed., London, 1925). Cf. H. H. Ellis, "The Relations Between the State Departments and the Nation," *Public Administration,* IV, 95-106 (1926).

to a brief account of the more important of them, viewed one by one. Afterwards, a few observations upon certain tendencies and developments affecting most or all of them will be in order; and following these, a more detailed description of the far-flung civil service establishment by means of which the departments carry on their work both in the central offices at London and throughout the realm.

The Treasury

The oldest department, the only one that exercises substantial control over the others, and therefore in many respects the central and most important one of them all, is the Treasury. This is true whether one is thinking simply of the consultative, policy-framing, and supervising establishment presided over by the Chancellor of the Exchequer, or, in a broader way, of the whole body of related, but more or less independent, agencies that are provided for by the same vote as the Treasury proper or are under the direct control of Treasury officials. No branch of the government better illustrates the curious intermingling of institutions and practices that have been carried down to the present day by the drift of history and other agencies and usages that have been scientifically planned and systematically provided for by statute.

The origins of the Treasury are bound up with the development of the Exchequer, or revenue office, of the Norman-Angevin kings. The Exchequer was the place to which the sheriffs twice a year, at Easter and at Michaelmas, brought their accounts and the money which they had collected. The funds were received and acknowledged in the presence of the Court of Exchequer, consisting of the great officers of state—Chancellor, Justiciar, Constable, Chamberlains, etc.—and they were stored in chests, each having three locks opened with keys carried by the Teller, who deposited the money, the Clerk of the Pells, who recorded on a pell, or parchment, all receipts and disbursements, and the Auditor, who saw that no money was paid out except on proper authority.[5] For a long time,

[5] The name Exchequer arose from the chequered table at which the work of accounting was performed. This table was about ten feet in length and five in breadth and was covered with black cloth divided by white lines into squares three or four inches in breadth. Coins were used as counters,

wherever the king went the treasure-chests, i.e., the Treasury, went also. But at length London became the permanent location; although the elaborate ritual of triple-locked chests and wooden tallies was discarded only in 1834.[6]

In the twelfth and thirteenth centuries the supervisory Court of Exchequer underwent changes which brought into prominence two fiscal officials of great importance in later days, namely, the Treasurer and the Chancellor of the Exchequer. Originally the Treasurer was hardly more than a clerk. But the separation of the Chancery from the Exchequer in the reign of Richard I and the suspension of the justiciarship in the reign of Henry III gave room for the Treasurer to become the principal fiscal officer of the realm; and under the Tudors, bearing the more impressive title of Lord High Treasurer, he superseded even the Chancellor as the first minister of the crown. The Chancellor was, among other things, custodian ex-officio of the Great Seal, and his withdrawal from participation in the work of the Exchequer made necessary some other arrangement for giving decisions the stamp of legality.[7] What happened was that the Chancellor's clerk, acting at first merely as his substitute, became, in the thirteenth century, under the name of Chancellor of the Exchequer, a regular official of the department. He had charge of the special seal of the Exchequer, and he gradually added to his purely formal duties functions which made him an influential person.

The next important development was the placing of the Lord High Treasurer's office "in commission," together with the rise of the Chancellor of the Exchequer to a position of chief control in the fiscal organization. In 1612 James I tried the

and these, together with the wooden "tallies," i.e., notched sticks, which served as the sheriff's receipts, were moved about over the table, giving the process of calculation the appearance of a game of chess. The workings of the early Exchequer are described in the *Dialogus Scaccario* ("Dialogue of the Exchequer"), written by Bishop Richard of London in the twelfth century. There is an edition of this treatise by A. Hughes, C. G. Crump, and C. Johnson (Oxford, 1902). The standard history is T. Madox, *History and Antiquities of the Exchequer* (London, 1711). For a brief account, see T. L. Heath, *The Treasury* (London, 1927), Chap. ii.

[6] Under terms of the Exchequer Act. See p. 168.

[7] The Chancellor continued to be an official of major importance, but in fields other than finance. See p. 184 below.

experiment of bestowing the lord high treasurership, not upon an individual, but upon a board of Lords Commissioners of His Majesty's Treasury, with, however, a certain primacy in the "First Lord." The office was conceived of as remaining undivided; but its duties were to be shared by a number of persons. Later in the century individuals were still occasionally given sole tenure of the treasurership, but the last such appointment was made by Queen Anne in 1714. The office was then almost immediately vacated because of the death of the Queen,[8] and never from that day to this has a Lord High Treasurer been appointed. Instead, the duties connected with the office have devolved continuously upon a Treasury Board of five members, and even the title of Lord High Treasurer has become extinct. For a time the sovereign attended meetings of the Board; but George III abandoned the practice (just as his great-grandfather had given up attending cabinet meetings), and control passed into the hands of the First Lord, who even now was usually also the prime minister. The nineteenth century brought still further important developments. After 1825 the Board gradually ceased to transact business in a collective capacity, and in 1849 an act of Parliament provided that documents, including requisitions for money, issuing from the Treasury should be regarded as valid if signed by any two of the five Lords.

Today, therefore, the situation, so far as the Treasury in the narrow and proper sense is concerned, is substantially this. The Treasury Board, which legally has charge,[9] never meets except to transact one or two minor sorts of formal business, and substantially all of the work is done by the members individually. Indeed, practically all of it except signing papers and some other incidental duties, is performed by one member alone, with his staff, i.e., the Chancellor of the Exchequer. The First Lord, the nominal head, is, as a rule, the prime minister. As we have seen, a new premier is not obliged to take this post for himself; but with only three or four exceptions all have

[8] The rule at that time was that upon the death of the sovereign the ministry should resign. See p. 278.

[9] The statutory designation continues to be "Commissioners of His Majesty's Treasury."

done so for more than a hundred years. While largely relieving the incumbent from administrative routine, it fits in with the functions of general fiscal supervision of the entire governmental system which the prime ministership, by its very nature, involves.[10] Three other members of the Board, known as the Junior Lords, have certain minor tasks in connection with the Treasury, but their really important work is performed in the capacity of assistants to the Parliamentary Secretary to the Treasury, who is chief government whip in the House of Commons; in other words, they are themselves government whips.

The fifth member of the group is the only one who gives his attention primarily to Treasury business. He is the "Second Lord," otherwise known as the Chancellor of the Exchequer. The Chancellor is very definitely the finance minister of the kingdom, and as such he is (in the words of a recent English writer) "answerable to Parliament for the due collection of the public revenue, the means by which it is raised, the loans by which it is supplemented, the taxes imposed, the remissions and exemptions allowed, the custody of the public balances, the broad outlines of the public expenditure, and the preservation of equilibrium between that expenditure and the revenue. He is responsible also for all government measures affecting currency and banking, local loans, and financial matters generally." [11] As the working member of the Treasury Board, he counsels with the spending departments and officers on the appropriations they will ask, prepares the annual budget, embodying a statement of the proposed expenditures of the year and a program of taxation calculated to produce the requisite income,[12] pilots financial measures through Parliament, acts as master of the mint, and supervises the collection of the revenues. It is hardly necessary to add that the nature of his

[10] The First Lord exercises a certain amount of supervision over a number of outlying departments which have no political chiefs of their own, notably the office of the Parliamentary Counsel to the Treasury, which drafts all the bills introduced by the ministers (see p. 414 below), and His Majesty's Stationery Office, which does all the government printing. He also recommends for Civil List pensions.

[11] T. L. Heath, *The Treasury,* 65-66.

[12] On the preparation of the estimates and of the budget, see Chap. xviii below.

duties makes it essential that he be a member of the House of Commons, where finance bills make their first appearance, and where, in fact, their fate is completely determined. Indeed, the Chancellor is usually government leader in that house if the prime minister is in the House of Lords or for any other reason finds it necessary to delegate the responsibility to one of his colleagues. In any case, it goes without saying that he is one of the busiest men in the government, and one of the most important.

In his dealings with Parliament the Chancellor is assisted by the Parliamentary, or Patronage, Secretary (who, technically, is the subordinate to the First Lord), by the three Junior Lords, acting as assistant whips, and particularly by another secretary (technically, the Chancellor's own subordinate), i.e., the Financial Secretary, who is the Chancellor's immediate spokesman in the House of Commons—"the workaday political chief of the Treasury." There is also the Permanent Secretary—the permanent head of the establishment in charge of three main sections into which the Treasury, since 1919, has been divided, i.e., (1) the department of establishments, which deals with the staffs of government departments and related matters, (2) the department of supply services, which has to do with other financial business of the departments, and (3) the department of finance, which administers the fiscal business of the Treasury. The first two secretaries named are ministers, i.e., political officers; the third is a non-political civil servant, and is indeed himself, since 1919, the officially designated head of the civil service. Each of the three "departments" named is in immediate charge of a comptroller. Assistant secretaries, principals, etc., make up a total higher, or administrative, staff of seventy-six—a smaller number, it may be observed, than in some other main branches of the government.[13]

Contrary to what might be expected, the Chancellor of the Exchequer is not in charge of the Exchequer. Indeed, he has no direct connection with it. His title arises from a past con-

[13] This machinery is described in detail in T. L. Heath, *op. cit.,* Chaps. v-vi. The figure given does not include the staff members of various agencies, e.g., the cabinet secretariat, which are subordinate to the Treasury.

nection, but nowadays the Treasury and the Exchequer—although both included in the Treasury in the broader sense—are quite distinct establishments. Speaking broadly, the function of the Treasury is to find out how much money each of the spending services must have and to see that the requisite amounts are raised and made available. In other words, the Treasury is responsible for balancing receipts and disbursements, and for carrying through whatever financial legislation is necessary for that purpose. The function of the Exchequer is, rather, to see that the money is disbursed according to law. With a view to promoting the latter end, an Exchequer Act of 1834 consolidated and reconstructed existing machinery in a non-political Exchequer Department, under a single Comptroller-General; and, this arrangement showing certain defects, an Exchequer and Audit Departments Act of 1866 merged the Exchequer's functions with those of the pre-existing Audit Department under the direction of a Comptroller and Auditor-General. This official is not a minister; and to protect his purely non-political status his salary is charged, like the salaries of judges, on the Consolidated Fund (explained below), and hence is not subject to annual vote. As Comptroller-General of the Exchequer, he and his staff scrutinize the requests for "credits" that come from the Treasury on behalf of the spending departments, see that the necessary parliamentary authority has been given (whether by a permanent statutory charge on the Consolidated Fund or by an annual vote), and authorize the money to be transferred from the account of the Exchequer at the Bank of England (or other bank) to the proper disbursing officer. As Auditor-General of the Public Accounts, he makes "appropriation" audits, to determine on behalf of Parliament whether each disbursement from a parliamentary vote does or does not come within the purposes of the vote; also audits on behalf of the government, to determine whether the expenditure included in an appropriation account is supported in every part by authority of the Treasury. Full annual reports are transmitted by him to the House of Commons.

The revenues are collected through three great offices, i.e., the Post Office, Customs, and Inland Revenue, and a minor one known as Woods, Forests, and Lands. All have separate organizations with distinct staffs, but are nevertheless within the Treasury and subject to such control as it may care to exercise. The Post Office, which has charge of communication by telegraph (since 1870) and telephone (since 1911) as well as by post, is presided over by a responsible minister, the Postmaster-General, who is usually included in the cabinet. Being regarded primarily as a revenue-producing service, it is, under the British scheme of organization, an integral part of the Treasury. In its day-to-day operations it is, however, largely autonomous.[14] The other three departments are in the hands of statutory boards of commissioners, the members of which belong to the permanent civil service and are represented in the ministry and in Parliament only by the Chancellor of the Exchequer and his deputy, the Financial Secretary to the Treasury.[15]

Formerly, the proceeds of various taxes were paid into separate accounts at the Exchequer, and Parliament charged particular outlays upon each. This system was wasteful and otherwise unsatisfactory; one fund might be inadequate to meet the drafts upon it while another had a large balance. An act of 1787 introduced a new and better plan. Under it, all revenues (with slight exceptions), including the proceeds of borrowing, are payable into a single Consolidated Fund at the Banks of England and Ireland and a designated bank in Scotland, to the account of the Exchequer; [16] and practically all disbursements on the national account are made out of this fund.[17] Most of the taxes are imposed by "permanent" statutes, which stand

[14] C. F. D. Marshall, *The British Post Office from its Beginning to the End of 1925* (London, 1927); E. Murray, *The Post Office* (London, 1927), in the Whitehall Series.

[15] For a brief account of the collection of the national revenue (eighty-six per cent of which came from taxation in 1924), see W. J. Hills, *The Finance of Government* (London, 1925), Chap. iv. Of the British people's annual income of about four billion pounds, something like one-fifth passes every year through the hands of the state.

[16] The banks have a right to make use of the money as in the case of any other deposits. In Scotland the custodianship is passed around from year to year among six banks.

[17] Under strict parliamentary control, the War Office, the Admiralty, the Air Ministry, and a few other departments are allowed to use certain minor revenues which they enjoy, and which therefore are neither paid into nor paid out of the Consolidated Fund.

unchanged for considerable periods of time; but some are laid afresh each year, or at all events are subject to an annual revision of rates. Similarly, some expenditures are regulated by standing laws and others by annual appropriations. Most disbursements fall in the latter category; only those which it is particularly desirable to keep out of politics, i.e., the Civil List, the salaries of judges, the interest on the national debt, and other outlays aggregating, before the World War, something less than one-fourth of the total expenditure, are "Consolidated Fund charges," paid directly out of the Fund without annual authorization.[18] Expenditures which are voted from year to year are said to be for the "supply services," because the appropriations are made by the House of Commons in Committee of Supply, which is a form of committee of the whole.

Payments of Consolidated Fund charges, e.g., salaries of judges, are made through the cashier of the Bank of England, on authorization from the Comptroller and Auditor-General, who, on requisition of the Treasury, grants quarterly credits at the Bank for the amounts prescribed by statute. Payments for supply services are made by the Paymaster-General,[19] directly or through subordinates known as sub-accountants, with money withdrawn from the banks in virtue of an order by the Comptroller and Auditor-General granting the requisite credits. Payments of Consolidated Fund charges do not require countersignature of the order by two Treasury Lords, but payments for supply services can be made only if so validated.

Even after money is got out of the Consolidated Fund and turned over to the disbursing officials, Treasury control does not entirely cease. The Treasury, and it alone, can transfer a surplus from one vote to meet a deficit in another (although

[18] The proportion is now far larger, because more than half of all that is raised by taxation today is paid out as interest on or amortization of the huge post-war national debt.

[19] Originally there were separate paymasters for various services, but by stages the duties were consolidated at the middle of the nineteenth century in the hands of a single paymaster-general, assisted by the permanent staff of the Pay Office. The paymaster-generalship is a political—and therefore a ministerial—office. T. L. Heath, *The Treasury*, 192-195.

only in the army and navy); a statute may specifically authorize the Treasury to fix certain salaries paid in other departments, or to supervise certain expenditures; and many contracts cannot be let without Treasury sanction. In short, Treasury control extends not only to the departmental estimates prepared for consideration by Parliament, but to varying, and in the aggregate large, operations of expenditure and related administration.[20]

The Defense Services

A second historic office which survives only in commission is that of Lord High Admiral. The navy is the oldest of the present fighting forces of the realm of a professional character, and the Lord High Admiral's office originated as early as the fourteenth century. By the seventeenth century the holder of this position was a man of great power, and Charles I agreed with the parliamentary party that it would be wise to put the office in commission. The arrangement was regularized in 1690, and it has been in effect continuously since 1708.[21]

[20] The best systematic accounts of the Treasury are R. G. Hawtrey, *The Exchequer and the Control of Expenditure* (London, 1921), and T. L. Heath, *The Treasury* (London, 1927), already cited. The latter is a volume in the Whitehall Series, edited by J. Marchant, and bearing considerable resemblance to the "Service Monographs of the United States" published by the Johns Hopkins Press under the auspices of the Institute for Government Research. See also A. L. Lowell, *Government of England,* I, 115-130; W. R. Anson, *Law and Custom of the Constitution* (3rd ed.), II, Pt. I, 173-190; and A. V. Dicey, *Law of the Constitution* (8th ed.), Chap. x. W. F. Willoughby, W. W. Willoughby, and S. M. Lindsay, *Financial Administration of Great Britain* (New York, 1917), is a scholarly treatise; and the financial system in general is treated in H. Higgs, *Financial System of the United Kingdom* (London, 1914); E. Young, *System of National Finance* (London, 1915); and J. W. Hills, *The Finance of Government* (London, 1925). Numerous articles dealing with specific aspects of financial machinery will be found in the *Journal of Public Administration* (later, *Public Administration*), issued by the (British) Institute of Public Administration (1923 ff). The subject of Treasury control is commented upon interestingly in an article on the subject by H. Higgs in the periodical mentioned, II, 122-130. Treasury organization and activities in the United States may be compared by consulting L. M. Short, *op. cit.,* Chap. xii; W. F. Willoughby, *The National Budget System* (Baltimore, 1927); sundry volumes in the Service Monographs series; and the annual reports of the Secretary of the Treasury.

[21] Except in 1827-28, when the Duke of Clarence, later William IV, was Lord High Admiral.

Since 1823 naval administration, formerly shared by many boards and other agencies, has been wholly in the hands of the "Lords Commissioners for executing the office of Lord High Admiral," otherwise known as the Admiralty Board.

The Admiralty Board now consists of a First Lord, four or more Sea Lords (naval officers of high rank), a Civil Lord, a parliamentary and financial secretary, and a permanent secretary. The First Lord, the Civil Lord, and the parliamentary and financial secretary are always members of Parliament, and the First Lord invariably has a seat in the cabinet. The Sea Lords are eligible to Parliament, but usually are not members. The permanent secretary, is, of course, ineligible. Unlike the Treasury Board, which never meets, the Admiralty Board holds regular and frequent sessions. Legally, all members are on a common footing and the First Lord is only a chairman. Actually, the First Lord has enjoyed a substantial primacy since 1832, and under orders in council of 1869 and 1872 he bears sole responsibility before Parliament for all business transacted. This being the case, his word governs. If his colleagues are unwilling to accept his decisions, they have the option of resigning; or the First Lord may himself resign, which automatically dissolves the Board. Practically, therefore, the First Lord has become a minister of marine assisted by an advisory council. The Sea Lords, being naval officers, usually of high rank, give most of their time to the administrative services of the department, and certain branches are assigned also to the Civil Lord and the secretaries.[22]

Eight of the great departments today are the product of a curious evolution of the ancient office of king's secretary, first heard of in the reign of Henry III. Originally there was but a single official known as king's secretary, or "secretary of state;" but, after sundry transmutations, a second was added in the eighteenth century, although no new *office* was created for him. At the close of the century a third was provided for, during the Crimean War a fourth, after the Indian mutiny of 1857 a fifth, during the World War a sixth, in 1925 a

[22] O. Murray, "The Administration of a Fighting Service," *Jour. of Pub. Admin.*, I, 205-219 (1923); G. Aston, *The Navy Today* (London, 1927).

seventh, and in 1926 an eighth. In theory, the incumbents of all of these eight "principal secretaryships of state" hold the same office, and except as limited by a few statutory restrictions each is legally competent to exercise the functions of any or all of the others. Acts of Parliament confer powers, not on one of the secretaries specifically, but simply on "a secretary of state," the distribution of functions being a matter of understanding and practice. In actual usage, each of the seven secretaries holds strictly to his own domain.[23] The group comprises: (1) the Secretary of State for Foreign Affairs, (2) the Secretary of State for the Dominions and Colonies, (3) the Secretary of State for War, (4) the Secretary of State for India, (5) the Secretary of State for the Home Department, (6) the Secretary of State for Air, and (7) the Secretary of State for Scotland.[24]

The organization of the War Office has never been as satisfactory as that of the Admiralty, and in the half-century preceding the World War it was the theme of numerous inquiries, criticisms, and reports. The subject is too extensive and technical to be entered into here, but a few salient facts may be mentioned.[25] In the first place, as Lowell has aptly observed, like other countries with a popular form of government, England has found it hard to reconcile military command and civil control. A great amount of English political history centers around the efforts of Parliament, from the fourteenth century onwards, to hedge about with effective, yet not entirely prohibitive, restrictions the power of the crown to raise, pay,

[23] Except that when one is absent from the country another acts in his place. Seven secretaries, rather than eight, for the reason that the secretaryship for the Dominions is as yet held by the same minister who presides at the Colonial Office. See p. 182 below.

[24] The last-mentioned office, dating in its present form from 1926, represents an expansion of the office of Secretary for Scotland, created in 1885. It is possible to view it as not historically an offshoot of the secretariat of state; but at all events it has been assimilated to the position occupied by the other branches or departments named. F. G. Evans, *The Principal Secretary of State* (London, 1924), is a scholarly monograph.

[25] E. Jenks, *Government of the British Empire,* 171-195, is an adequate fuller discussion. Cf. C. E. Callwell, "The War Office in War Time," *Blackwood's Mag.,* Jan., 1919. A comprehensive history of the War Office up to a decade and a half ago is O. Wheeler, *The War Office, Past and Present* (London, 1914).

and use armed forces. This end was partially achieved in the Bill of Rights, which to this day makes it unlawful for the crown to raise or keep a standing army within the kingdom, in time of peace, "unless it be with the consent of Parliament." Operating to the same effect was the annual Mutiny Act, which from 1689 onwards suspended for one year various provisions of the Petition of Right and the Bill of Rights that stood in the way of the maintenance of an army, and which from 1712 also fixed definitely the number of soldiers that the crown might lawfully raise.[26] Full parliamentary supremacy came only, however, after the Crimean War, when the War and Colonial offices were separated and the Secretary of State for War (dating from 1794) was vested with control of the army conjointly with a commander-in-chief, and with full responsibility, as a cabinet officer, to Parliament.

In 1870 the War Office was divided into three departments—military, ordnance, and finance—and in 1888 it was split into military and civil sections, the Commander-in-Chief as the head of the military side advising the Secretary for War on all military matters, while the latter remained responsible for the conduct of the whole. The unsatisfactory experiences of the South African war led to some changes in 1901, and three years later, as the result of a report by Lord Esher's War Office Reconstitution Committee, the office of commander-in-chief, which naturally had been an obstacle to unified control by the Secretary for War, was abolished. The administration of military affairs was vested in a new body, the Army Council, consisting of three ministers in the War Office and four military officials of high rank, and unity of control and the complete supremacy of Parliament were, in effect, secured by provisions making the Secretary for War president of the Council and giving the latter a function which, in the final

[26] In 1881 the great mass of military law representing the by-product of upwards of two hundred Mutiny Acts was consolidated in the Army Act; and it is this Army Act that nowadays is reënacted or revived every year, in lieu of the original Mutiny Act of William III. The measure continues to be referred to commonly, however, as the Mutiny Act. Cf. the clause of the Constitution of the United States (Art. 1, § 8) which forbids Congress to appropriate money, if designed for the raising and supporting of armies, "for a longer term than two years."

analysis, was only advisory, and therefore like that of the First Lord's colleagues in the Admiralty. Under the supreme test of the World War, the system yielded satisfactory results, and it stands today practically unchanged. Those portions of the department that have to do with parliamentary business, preparation of estimates, auditing accounts, making payments, and keeping records are manned mainly with civilians. The offices of the Chief of Imperial General Staff, Adjutant-General, Quartermaster-General, and Master-General of Ordnance are manned largely with members of the army.

The rapid development of aërial warfare during the World War led to the establishment of a third government department having charge of a defense service, namely, the Ministry of Air. Both the army and the navy had aircraft services when the war began, and there was a Joint Air Committee, composed of members of the War Office and the Admiralty. In 1916 this committee was superseded by an Air Board, with increased control over matters of policy, but without executive functions; and in December of the same year the Board was reorganized under a president ranking as a minister. As yet, the life of the Board was limited to the duration of the war. But in 1917 an Air Forces Act provided for a permanent Air Ministry under an Air Council headed by a sixth secretary of state. In its organization the Air Ministry is based on the same principles as the Admiralty and the War Office, although the amount of civilian work to be done is decidedly less and the departmental staff is far smaller.[27]

The creation of a separate air ministry naturally increased the dangers not only of wasteful and otherwise undesirable duplication, but of interdepartmental and inter-service jealousies; and considerable difficulty at these points has been experienced, arising especially out of the desire of the Admiralty to have control over an air force of its own. After studying the situation, a parliamentary committee on national expenditure reported in 1922 in favor of creating a coördinating ministry

[27] For an official account of the creation of the Air Ministry, see *Report of the War Cabinet for 1918* (Cmd. 325, 1919), Chap. vii. Cf. J. A. Fairlie, *British War Administration* (New York, 1919), 116-119. A separate air ministry was created in France in 1928.

of defense, which should see "that each force plays its part and is allotted appropriate responsibility for carrying out various functions." [28] But, on recommendation of the National and Imperial Defense Committee, the cabinet decided, in 1923, that it "was undesirable and impracticable to supersede the ministerial heads of the three fighting services by making them subordinates of a minister of defense;" also that an alternative plan for an amalgamation of the three fighting-service departments in a single department was equally impracticable. At the same time, it was conceded that more coördination was needed. The plan finally adopted was to define and strengthen the coördinating functions of an agency already existing, namely, the Committee of Imperial Defense.[29] This committee, in its present form, dates from 1904 and consists of the prime minister as president, with such other members as he, having regard to the nature of the subject to be considered, may from time to time summon to assist him.[30] Under the decision of 1923, the committee discusses general problems of defense, considers questions referred to it by the cabinet relating to coördination of expenditure for defense, and seeks to promote generally helpful interchange of information and opinion among the three departments concerned.[31]

Closely related to the defense services in origin and function, although not in organization, is the Ministry of Pensions. Formerly the Admiralty and the War Office included bureaus

[28] *First Interim Report of Committee on National Expenditure* (Cmd. 1581, 1922), 8-9, 86-102.

[29] *Recommendations of the National and Imperial Defense Committee . . . upon the Coördination of the Defense Services* (Cd. 1938, 1923), 13-15.

[30] In pursuance of a decision by the prime minister in 1923, the Committee put it on record that the members should regularly include, in addition to the secretaries of state, the Chancellor of the Exchequer (or the Financial Secretary), the Permanent Secretary of the Treasury, the chiefs of staffs of the three fighting services, and a chairman to act as deputy to the prime minister.

[31] It is of interest to note that the Irish Free State has substituted a ministry of defense for the conventional war ministry; that in 1928 the Kingdom of the Netherlands abolished its ministries of war and marine (until then under a single administrative head) and established in their place a ministry of defense; and that proposals for a similar change in the United States have often been made, e.g., by Nicholas Murray Butler in his *A Program of Peace* (New York, 1928).

which distributed pensions for death and disability out of the funds of the state; and during the World War sundry parliamentary commissions reported plans for increasing the sums available and for administering them more effectively. The upshot of a number of more or less unsatisfactory experiments in 1915-16 was an act of December, 1916, unifying in a Ministry of Pensions most of the powers and duties of pre-existing pension authorities. This ministry has to do only with military and naval pensions; old age pensions and civil service pensions are administered by entirely different authorities. Even so, it is responsible for a larger expenditure of public money than any other department. The central office of the ministry at London is concerned chiefly with supervising the awards and payments made through regional offices scattered throughout the kingdom; and each of these offices is advised, in turn, by local pensions committees, representative of various interests. In 1926 about two million men, women, and children received pensions through these channels.[32]

Foreign and Imperial Relations

Another important group of ministries consists of those that have to do with foreign and imperial relations. The Foreign Office conducts the country's dealings with other independent states; the Dominions, Colonial, and India Offices manage relations with the overseas dominions and dependencies. Historically, all four are offshoots of the ancient secretaryship of state, and legally all are only branches or phases of a single office or service. Except, however, for the fact that as yet the Dominions and Colonial Offices have a common head, the four are in practice quite separate, each being presided over by a secretary of state who is both a minister and a cabinet officer. A moment's reflection upon Britain's position in the world—the complexity of her foreign interests, the number and extent of her colonial possessions, and the critical character of her relationship with India—will suggest that every one of these

[32] On the creation of the Ministry of Pensions, see J. A. Fairlie, *British War Administration,* 157-164. Cf., on American military pensions, G. A. Weber, "The Bureau of Pensions," *Service Monographs of the U. S.,* No. 24 (Baltimore, 1923).

ministries is of more than average importance; and one will not be surprised to find that, especially in the case of the Foreign Office, the presiding minister is appointed with more regard for prestige and experience than is usual in other departments.

Under the general direction of the Secretary of State for Foreign Affairs, the work of the Foreign Office—which, incidentally, does not include "home" activities such as are assigned to our State Department in the United States—is carried on by an elaborate organization in Whitehall consisting of eight political and eight non-political "departments." The former have a geographical basis—American and African, Central, Eastern, Far Eastern, Egyptian, Northern, Western, and Dominions—and are charged with keeping informed concerning the international problems of the regions assigned to them and with making recommendations thereon. The latter are rather more administrative in character, and include a department of communications which codes and decodes telegrams and delivers dispatches by messenger where necessary; a news department, which gives information to the press; a passport office, which really has to do chiefly with immigration; a treaty department, which attends to procedural matters involved in treaty-making; a legal advisers' office; an office of the librarian and keeper of the papers; a chief clerk's office; and a consular department. Until 1921, the Foreign Service, both diplomatic and consular, although supervised by the Foreign Office, was a distinct organization, precisely as the Foreign Service of the United States, in relation to the State Department, is to this day. A statute of the year mentioned, however, amalgamated the two services, with results generally regarded as satisfactory. All members of the combined establishment are liable for service both at home and abroad, and recruits are regularly sent into the field for a period before being assigned definitely to the Foreign Office or to the Diplomatic Service for a career. Admission to the combined service comes only after several high hurdles have been surmounted. Candidates must first appear before and be approved by an ex-officio Board of Selection. After that, they must pass a searching oral examination. Finally, they take a written examination given by the Civil

Service Commission and similar to other civil service examinations except for the greater emphasis upon language. The candidate who stands highest must in every case be appointed when a vacancy arises.

The work of the Foreign Office is to only a limited extent administrative in the proper sense of the term. Rather, it consists chiefly in gathering and organizing information, corresponding with foreign governments, preparing instructions for representatives abroad, negotiating treaties and conventions, and formulating policy. These are difficult, delicate, and sometimes hazardous tasks, and it goes without saying that this branch of the government knows many things and does many things which the well-being of the country forbids to be made public, at all events until long after the event. From this it follows, first, that the proportion of higher officials in the Foreign Office is somewhat larger than in other departments; second, that a far greater proportion of decisions and actions emanate from, or at all events are expressly approved by, the head of the department than in departments whose work is more largely administrative; and, third, that the department is more detached, and even more immune, from parliamentary control than any of the others. All of the threads are gathered tightly in the Foreign Secretary's hands.[33] Parliament can promote or thwart foreign policies by granting or withholding funds; a foreign minister whose acts or policies are disapproved can be got rid of by sustained opposition in the House of Commons; and the ministers are expected to keep

[33] At all events, as nearly so as the increasing arduousness of that official's duties permit. The establishment of the League of Nations and the necessity of consulting more constantly than formerly with the governments of the overseas dominions have added much to the burdens of an already overworked department head. A special minister has, indeed, been provided to assist with League business, and in particular to represent the Foreign Secretary at meetings of the Assembly and Council when that official cannot himself go to Geneva. This minister is disguised under the historic title of Chancellor of the Duchy of Lancaster. But he works with the Foreign Secretary on all League matters, and on one recent occasion became Acting Secretary for Foreign Affairs when his chief was incapacitated by illness. The instance referred to was Lord Cushenden's rather calamitous substitution for Sir Austen Chamberlain in 1928. For the daily routine of a Foreign Secretary, see Viscount Grey, *Twenty-five Years,* II, Chap. XXX. Cf. *London Times,* Nov. 28, 1928.

both houses informed, at least in a general way, on foreign affairs. Furthermore, a greater proportion of treaties than formerly are now submitted for parliamentary ratification, either because their terms directly or indirectly require such procedure or because of a somewhat increased recognition of the general propriety of it. Most of the time, however, the Foreign Office functions without much relation to Parliament.[34] On the other hand, every successful foreign minister keeps his chief, the prime minister, fully informed, and important questions that arise within his domain are certain to be made the subject of cabinet discussion.[35] The sovereign, too, is consulted freely, and he more frequently wields influence here than in any other phase or branch of the government's activity.

The consular service is in a somewhat curious position. Its administrative affairs are looked after by the Consular Department in the Foreign Office. But its commercial work is directed by a different organization, the so-called Department of Overseas Trade, established in 1917 to do away with conflicts which had arisen between the commercial attachés and the consuls, and also to enable better use to be made of commercial information collected by the consular officials. Charged with promoting both trade within the Empire and British trade with foreign countries, the Overseas Trade Department is controlled jointly by the Foreign Office and the Board of Trade and presided over by a person who functions as a parliamentary under-secretary in both of these establishments. The arrangement means added machinery and expense, and on that ground

[34] Interesting data for comparison are presented in "Methods Adopted for Dealing with International Questions: Reports from H.M. Representatives Abroad" (Cmd. 2282, 1922). Cf. D. P. Myers, "Legislatures and Foreign Relations," *Amer. Polit. Sci. Rev.*, Nov., 1917; A. J. Herbertson and O. J. R. Howarth, *Oxford Survey of the British Empire* (Oxford, 1914), VI, Chap. ii; and A. Cecil, *British Foreign Secretaries, 1806-1926; Studies in Personality and Policy* (London, 1927). As is pointed out elsewhere, the program of the Labor party calls for the submission of "all international engagements to the House of Commons."

[35] "A considerable amount of fault has been found with what some people think is and what they call my foreign policy, but which, of course, ought not to be called my foreign policy, because it is quite impossible for any individual foreign minister to carry out a policy which is not also, in its main lines, the policy of the cabinet of which he is a member." Sir Edward Grey, quoted in *London Times* (weekly ed.), Jan. 26, 1912, p. 71.

it has been strongly opposed. It seems, however, to have yielded useful results.[36]

In the later eighteenth century colonial affairs were supervised by one of the two secretaries of state then existing; from him the function passed, as the century closed, to the War Office; and when the Crimean war broke out, in 1854, this department was relieved of the burden by the creation of a separate secretaryship for the colonies. Already various parts of the Empire occupied widely different positions politically, and from the outset the work of the Colonial Office had to be conducted in such a way as to be directive where the dependencies had few or no rights of self-government, but only consultative, or even merely informative, where, as in Canada and Australia, full self-government had been, or was being, arrived at. From 1907 to 1921 the ministry was organized in two main sections, the colonies and protectorates division and the dominions division, and in 1921 a third section, known as the Middle East department, was added, with administrative control over the mandated territories in the Near East. On the other hand, in 1925 the dominions division was erected into a separate and coördinate ministry, the Dominions Office. Like the Foreign Office, the Colonial Office is organized primarily on a geographical basis, i.e., the Middle East division and nine other departments having to do, respectively, with the West Indies, the Far Eastern settlements, East Africa, and other major portions of the Empire. In these various quarters the Colonial Office wields real and continuous administrative control, exercised principally through instructions to the governors, scrutiny and disallowance of ordinances, and regulation of finance.[37]

[36] A Cecil, *The British Foreign Service* (London, 1927); J. P. Bagge, "The British Consular Service," *Public Admin.*, Jan., 1929.

Comparisons with the American Department of State and Foreign Service may be made by consulting F. A. Ogg and P. O. Ray, *Introduction to American Government* (3rd ed.), 303-312; W. T. Stone, "The Administration of the Department of State; its Organization and Needs," *Foreign Policy Assoc. Information Service, Special Supp. No. 3* (Feb., 1929); G. Hunt, *The Department of State of the United States* (New Haven, 1914); and T. Lay, *The Foreign Service of the United States* (New York, 1925).

[37] G. V. Fiddes, *The Dominions and Colonial Offices* (London, 1926), Chaps. i-x, in the Whitehall Series.

The establishment of the Dominions Office as a separate ministry in 1925, like the creation of the Dominions Division eighteen years earlier, came by way of recognition of the growing importance of dominion affairs and of the increasing delicacy of problems arising from them. The object was to give fuller recognition to the "profound difference between the work of communication and consultation with the self-governing partner nations of the British Commonwealth and the administrative work of controlling and developing the colonies and protectorates." To the present day the Dominions Office has continued to be housed in the Colonial Office, and the two secretaryships of state are still combined in the same individual. There is nothing, however, to preclude the appointment of different heads for the two ministries, and already each has its own parliamentary and permanent under-secretaries and a substantially independent subordinate staff. The ministry is organized in three departments, partly but not wholly on a geographical basis; and to one of these is committed (among other things) responsibility for matters relating to the Irish Free State.[38]

Down to 1858 the government of British India was carried on by the East India Company, subject to supervision by a Board of Control representing the crown. The Mutiny further embarrassed the already discredited Company, which soon lost its charter, and the British government took over full and direct management of Indian affairs. Control of administration was assigned to a new ministry presided over by an added secretary of state and known as the India Office; and to advise the department a Council of India was created, consisting of from ten to fifteen members (at least nine of whom must have served or resided in India for ten years) appointed by the secretary of state for a term of seven years.[39] India continues to be governed, in the main, by the English in India rather than at London; and the Government of India Act of 1919, in addition to making some advance in the direction of self-government by the native populations, transferred the "agency"

[38] G. V. Fiddes, *op. cit.*, Chaps. xi-xix.

[39] At the present day the Council consists of from eight to twelve members, at least half of whom must have the qualification mentioned.

business of the India Office[40] to a High Commissioner for India, and also provided for progressive discontinuance by the Secretary for India of some of his duties. Nevertheless, the India Office—organized in sections having to do with (a) finance, (b) military affairs, (c) political matters, (d) judicial and public affairs, (e) revenue and statistics, and (f) public works—forms now, as before, an important and necessary link between the governing agencies in India and the policy-making authorities at London.[41]

The Home Office

The Home Office is, in the expressive phrase of Lowell, a "residuary legatee;" that is to say, it represents the most direct survival of the original secretariat, and as such retains whatever functions of that historic office have not been outgrown or assigned elsewhere. In addition, however, it has many functions that have come to it later; indeed, a British writer observes that its complex and multifarious duties are, "in largest part, due to the feverish legislative activity of the nineteenth century."[42] Save that its jurisdiction reaches so far beyond the water's edge as to include the Channel Islands and the Isle of Man, the Home Office has to do entirely with domestic affairs. It is not much like the Department of the Interior in the United States, for the reason that several of its functions belong in our system to the states, while others have no counterparts here. At the same time, it is even less like a Continental ministry of the interior; because although it controls the police establishment of London, inspects the police elsewhere throughout England, Wales, and Northern Ireland, and sees to the nation-wide enforcement of the factory acts and of much other welfare and remedial legislation, it does not supervise and direct the work of local government in any such comprehensive way as is done in France, Italy, and elsewhere. Its relation

[40] E.g., the purchase of supplies and the engagement of persons for service in India.

[41] M. C. C. Seton, *The India Office* (London, 1926), in the Whitehall Series. The government of India under the act of 1919 is described briefly in A. B. Keith, *Constitution, Administration, and Laws of the Empire,* 247-264. Cf. p. 749 below.

[42] J. A. R. Marriott, *English Political Institutions* (1910 ed.), 110.

to police is, however, exceedingly important, because under the British system the national government bears half of the cost of the police establishment in all counties and boroughs in which the constabulary meets the standards which the Home Office fixes, and because it is the Home Office that makes the inspections and issues the necessary certificates.[43] The Home Office receives and transmits petitions to the crown, prepares and countersigns the warrants, or orders, to which the sovereign affixes his "sign-manual," or personal signature, and advises upon the exercise of the pardoning power. It sees to the registration of voters and supervision of elections, although the writs for parliamentary elections issue from the office of the Lord Chancellor; and it supervises the naturalization of aliens. Finally—without taking account of numerous minor activities—it approves the arrangements for the "assizes," or circuits, of the judges; it selects the Director of Public Prosecutions;[44] and it supervises the management of prisons, both national and local. Altogether, as the conserver of "law and order," the Home Office must be assigned a high degree of importance.[45]

The Lord Chancellor and the Law Officers

There is in England no unified department of justice corresponding to a Continental ministry of justice or the Department of Justice organized in the United States in 1870.[46] Work of the same kind is performed, of course, but it is divided among three main departments and officers, i.e., the Home Office (as already indicated), the Lord Chancellor, and the Attorney-General. Far the most important is the Lord Chancellor. "The greatest dignitary," says Lowell, "in the British government, the one endowed by law with the most exalted and most diverse functions, the only great officer of state who has re-

[43] On the police establishment of the country, see *Report of the Committee on the Police Service of England, Wales, and Scotland* (Cmd. 253, 1919).

[44] See p. 186 below.

[45] E. Troup, *The Home Office* (London, 1925), in the Whitehall Series. A briefer account by the same author is "The Functions and Organization of the Home Office," *Public Administration,* IV, 127-140 (1926).

[46] Mr. (later Lord) Bryce once sketched a plan for such a department. See his article, "The Organization of a Legal Department," *Fort. Rev.,* Mar., 1873.

tained his ancient rights, the man who defies the doctrine of the separation of powers more than any other personage on earth, is the Lord Chancellor." [47] Here again we come upon an office of great antiquity. Originally—as far back as the eleventh century—the Lord High Chancellor was merely the king's chief scribe; the name is said to be derived from the *cancelli,* or screen, in the king's chapel behind which the scribes carried on their work. In time, however, he became a trusted adviser, especially in matters touching the exercise of the royal "grace," i.e., the redress of grievances for which the common law—often "a roguish thing," so Selden declared—made no provision; and by the sixteenth century, when Sir Thomas More appears as the first lay holder of the office, he was an imposing figure as the dispenser of "equity" in the Court of Chancery. As custodian of the royal seal, it fell to him to affix the stamp of authenticity to all royal proclamations. His primacy in the Court of Chancery, furthermore, brought him large judicial patronage; and when the judicial reforms of 1873-76 fused the organization of the common law and equity courts,[48] control over appointments to practically all important judicial positions passed into his hands. Meanwhile he gathered still other weighty functions and became a leading member of the cabinet.

Nowadays, therefore, the work of this remarkable dignitary runs somewhat as follows: he is the chief judge in the High Court of Justice and in the Court of Appeal; he is the principal legal member of the cabinet and adviser to the ministers generally on legal matters; he recommends for appointment to higher judicial positions, and in fact, although not in form, appoints and removes the county court judges and most of the justices of the peace; he presides in the House of Lords and—if a peer, as he now invariably is—participates freely in its debates; [49] he approves the regulations relating to public prosecutions; and he, of course, sits as a member of the cabinet and participates in the deliberative and advisory work of

[47] *Government of England,* I, 131.

[48] See p. 610 below.

[49] See p. 393 below. If a Lord Chancellor is appointed who is not a peer, he is promptly made one.

that body. He does not, properly, administer a department. But his activity and influence continually touch every branch of government at some vital point. There is really more than any one man can do, as is suggested in the half-humorous remark of a former Lord Chancellor, Lord Lyndhurst, that the work falls into three parts: "first, the business that is worth the labor done; second, that which does itself; and third, that which is not done at all." [50]

To be mentioned in close conjunction with the Lord Chancellor are the "law officers of the crown," i.e., the Attorney-General and his colleague and substitute, the Solicitor-General. Both belong to the ministry, the former usually also to the cabinet; and both are important and well-paid officials, being selected from among the most eminent barristers belonging to the party in power. Their duties are two-fold: first, to assist the Lord Chancellor in giving legal advice to the cabinet and the several departments (although, as in the United States, most of the latter now have legal advisers on their own staffs whose opinions suffice upon all except the most weighty matters), and, second, to represent the crown in legal proceedings, especially in important criminal and political trials. Their functions in this latter connection are still of major importance, although they have been made less burdensome by the development of the office of Director of Public Prosecutions under legislation of 1879 and 1884. Subject to control by the Attorney-General, checked in turn by the Lord Chancellor and the Home Secretary, the Director of Public Prosecutions now prosecutes in all sorts of capital cases, in offenses against the coinage, in cases of fraudulent bankruptcy, and in other cases where directed by the Attorney-General or Home Secretary or where prosecution seems to him necessary in the public interest. This does not mean, however, that cases have ceased to be prose-

[50] H. C. Robinson, *Diary,* III, 453. For much interesting information on the Lord Chancellor's office, see H. Graham, *Mother of Parliaments* (London, 1910), Chap. vi. M. MacDonagh, *The Pageant of Parliament,* II, Chap. vi, deals with the office in its relation to the House of Lords. In the Labor party there has grown up a good deal of feeling that the Lord Chancellor, as head of the judicial system of the country, ought to be appointed from among the higher judges on purely legal grounds and ought not to be regarded as a political official or have a seat in the cabinet.

cuted, as of old, under private direction; the great majority are, indeed, still conducted in this way.[51]

[51] A. H. Dennis, "The Legal Departments of the Crown," *Public Administration,* IV, 141-155 (1926). Cf. A. Langeluttig, *The Department of Justice of the United States* (Baltimore, 1927).

CHAPTER IX

OTHER DEPARTMENTS—SOME GENERAL PROBLEMS AND TENDENCIES

FINANCE, defense, foreign relations, justice—these, and perhaps certain other activities that have been mentioned, are the primary, fundamental functions of government. But the past two hundred years have added many other important functions, especially such as have to do with the control of economic relationships and the improvement of social conditions; and naturally it is on this side that new governmental machinery has been brought into play most extensively, in Britain as in other countries. Four executive departments at London which are concerned with economic affairs, and two which have to do with social matters, call for some attention. Three of the six owe their present form to legislation dating no farther back than thirteen years ago.

"Economic" Departments

The Board of Trade is traceable to the councils for trade and foreign plantations established in 1660 and the Board of Trade and Plantations which existed from 1695 to 1781. After 1782 there was a committee of the Privy Council on commercial matters; and in 1862 the Board of Trade was reconstituted in its present form and put on a statutory basis—even though, technically, it is still a Privy Council committee. Like other regulative boards already encountered, the Board of Trade is composed of the "principal secretaries of state," with, in this instance, the addition of the First Lord of the Treasury, the Chancellor of the Exchequer, the speaker of the House of Commons, and the archbishop of Canterbury. But this membership is only nominal. The Board never meets, and its work is carried on under the sole direction of the President of the Board and his staff. It is, in the words of Lowell, a "phantom" board, providing imaginary colleagues for a single responsible minister. Until three quarters of a century ago, the work of the Board consisted mainly in compiling commercial statistics and advising other departments on commercial matters. Practically all functions relating to the promotion of trade abroad have now been delegated to the Department of Overseas Trade, mentioned above. But for many decades the duties of the Board have been progressively expanded in other directions, and although subject to frequent shifts they are still numerous and varied. In addition to gathering and publishing statistics and other information on labor, wages, and other industrial subjects, the Board maintains a register of British ships, makes and executes regulations for the safety of merchant vessels, provides and keeps up lighthouses, controls harbors, registers and supervises joint stock companies, registers patents and trademarks, maintains standards of weights and measures, administers the law of bankruptcy, and grants provisional orders empowering borough councils to undertake the ownership or operation of tramways, gas plants, waterworks, and other public utilities.[1]

The Ministry of Transport was created in 1919 with a view to assembling in a single establishment various transportation functions exercised previously by a number of different departments. At that time the railroads were still operated by the government, as they had been during the war; and it was intended that the new ministry should occupy itself largely with railway affairs. The railway department transferred from the Board of Trade became the nucleus of the organization set up. Two years later, however, the railroads were returned to private management, and at once the proposal began to be heard that the Transport Ministry, thus deprived of its main reason for existence, be abolished. Action of the sort has not been taken, but the department continues to have an uncertain lease on life. In the not wholly improbable event of the adoption of the Labor party's program of railway nationalization, something like it would undoubtedly be required. Meanwhile one of the sections into which the ministry is divided today has to

[1] H. L. Smith, *The Board of Trade* (London, 1928), in the Whitehall Series.

do with the improvement and expansion of such facilities as light railways, docks, harbors, canals, and roads; another—the finance department—with fares, rates, and charges; and a third, with public safety.

In 1889 a Board of Agriculture was created to take over the duties previously discharged by a committee of the Privy Council in connection with diseases of animals, together with the duties of former land commissioners pertaining to inclosures, allotments, and the drainage and improvement of land; and in 1903 supervision of fisheries was transferred from the Board of Trade to the renamed Board of Agriculture and Fisheries. Like the Board of Trade, this board was a phantom; for although it consisted legally of a dozen of the highest officers of state, only one of its members, i.e., the president, gave time or thought to its work. During and after the World War much legislation was enacted aiming at the reorganization of British agriculture,[2] and in 1919 the Board became the Ministry of Agriculture and Fisheries, to be aided thenceforth, in agricultural matters, by a professional Agricultural Advisory Committee, based on a system of local agricultural councils. Financial stringency, however, compelled abandonment of most of the activities projected, and in 1921 various newly conferred powers were withdrawn. The principal sections into which the department is divided today are: (a) finance, having to do with expenses for agricultural education and research; (b) land and supplies, dealing with small holdings, copyholds, commons, and the supply of fertilizers and seeds; (c) intelligence, furnishing information on, and taking measures to curb, the dreaded foot-and-mouth disease and other diseases of animals; and (d) fisheries, collecting statistics, issuing orders, and in other ways promoting the interests of the fishing industry.[3] All told, the activities of the department are exceedingly varied and its regulatory power, in the interest of the well-being of both man and beast, exceptionally extensive.[4]

[2] F. A. Ogg and W. R. Sharp, *Economic Development of Modern Europe* (rev. ed., New York, 1926), 592-594.

[3] *Encyclopædia Britannica* (12th ed.), xxx, 75-78.

[4] F. Floud, *The Ministry of Agriculture and Fisheries* (London, 1927), in the Whitehall Series. The United States Department of Agriculture may

The Ministry of Agriculture and Fisheries, and to a considerable extent the Board of Trade, performs functions in connection with particular industries or occupations. The Ministry of Labor, on the other hand, has to do with industries and occupations of many different kinds. This department was created immediately after the Lloyd George ministry was formed in 1916, and to it was entrusted the administration of a long list of acts pertaining to employment which until then had been under the care of the Board of Trade; although certain labor problems continued throughout the war period to be dealt with by other departments. The present range of activities of the ministry can be indicated sufficiently by mention of the principal statutes which it is expected to execute, namely, (1) the Labor Exchanges Act of 1909, providing for a nation-wide system of offices at which workers can ascertain where employment is to be had and employees can find where labor is available; (2) the National (Unemployment) Insurance Acts of 1911 [5] and 1920, under which most workers except those in agriculture and domestic service are insured against unemployment; (3) the Trade Boards Acts of 1909 and 1918, providing for mixed boards to fix minimum rates of wages and curb "sweating;" and (4) the Industrial Courts Act of 1919, under which the state offers to workers and employers courts of inquiry and determination in industrial disputes.[6] In all of these fields the general policy of the government has been to promote and supplement the activities of trade unions, employers' associations, and other voluntary groups; and the function of the Ministry of Labor is, in the main, not to exercise positive control, but to coöperate with non-governmental groups and agencies in better organizing the relations between employers and workers. The report of the Liberal Industrial Inquiry in 1928 recommends that the Ministry of Labor be

be compared by consulting L. M. Short, *op. cit.*, Chap. xvii, and the annual reports of the Secretary of Agriculture.

[5] Part ii of this Act only. Part i, relating to health, is administered by the Ministry of Health.

[6] The ministry was also given the task in 1917 of encouraging the formation and use of the non-governmental joint industrial councils recommended by the Whitley Committee, of which there were, in 1922, some seventy in existence. See p. 234 below.

reconstructed under the name of Ministry of Industry, taking over the powers of the Home Office under the Factory Acts and Compensation Acts, the Mines Department of the Board of Trade, and such other functions as may be necessary to bring within the purview of a single ministry all the relations between the state and the organized bodies of employers and workpeople.[7]

"Social" Departments

The last two departments to be mentioned have to do with vast tasks of social conservation and betterment. One is the Ministry of Health; the other is the Board of Education.

The Ministry of Health dates from 1919 and is, in its present form, distinctly a product of war-time experiences. Medical examinations in connection with recruiting brought to light grave facts concerning the physical fitness of the people, especially the industrial classes, and forced the conclusion that the state must in the future concern itself far more with matters of public health than in times past. Before and during the war, public health functions were distributed loosely among a number of administrative agencies, with much resulting friction, confusion, and inefficiency, and it became clear that if the work of the government in this field was to be performed properly, control must be gathered in a single department clothed with adequate powers. The Ministry of Health, created by act of Parliament approved June 3, 1919, was intended to be such a department; although it is to be observed that the act applies only to England and Wales. Even Wales has a separate Board of Health, although responsible to the new ministry; and there is an entirely separate Scottish Board of Health, under the chairmanship of the Secretary for Scotland.

The establishment of the new ministry for England and Wales entailed an unusually extensive redistribution of supervisory and administrative functions; indeed practically every major function that the ministry possesses came to it by trans-

[7] *Britain's Industrial Future,* 471. Cf. C. D. Burns, *Whitehall,* 44-49; J. A. Fairlie, *British War Administration,* 248-252. On the United States Department of Labor, see L. M. Short, *op. cit.,* Chap. xix; various issues in the Service Monographs series; and the annual reports of the Secretary of Labor.

fer from some preëxisting authority. Thus it took over the powers of the Board of Education relating to the health of mothers and young children and to the medical inspection and treatment of school children, the powers of the Home Office pertaining to infant life protection and to lunacy and other mental deficiency, and the duties of the Ministry of Pensions with respect to the health of disabled officers and men after they have left the service. To it passed, also, the adminstration of those portions of the National Insurance Act of 1911 pertaining to health, previously in charge of a board of insurance commissioners. Finally, a large group of duties came to it as a result of the abolition of the Local Government Board and the transfer of its functions to the Health Ministry almost *en bloc*.

Although now extinct, the Local Government Board had, for upwards of fifty years, a rôle of such importance in the governmental system that it merits a word of comment. Legally, the Board dated from 1871. But its history really went back to 1834, when the Poor Law Amendment Act set up a Poor Law Commission charged with the supervision of the administration of public charity by the local authorities. In 1847 this body was converted into a Poor Law Board, with representation in the ministry, and in 1871 the functions of an earlier Board of Public Health and of the local government subdepartment of the Home Office were added and the name was broadened to Local Government Board. As will be pointed out in another place, centralizing legislation of the past hundred years has wrought a remarkable transformation in the English system of local government, and it is not too much to say that for several decades the Local Government Board was the principal means or medium employed in this readjustment; save in relation to police, education, and the regulation of public utilities, substantially all administrative and supervisory control wielded from London over the authorities of county, borough, urban and rural district, and parish was, until 1919, gathered in its hands. It had few powers of direct administration; but it exercised strong regulative influence in relation to poor relief, public health, sanitation, local borrowing and expenditure, old age pension administration, and half a score of other matters. It inspected, criticized, and advised; within the limits of powers conferred by Parliament, it made and executed regulations with the force of law; it approved, amended, and vetoed local legislation; it audited local accounts; in a few cases it appointed and removed officials. The president of the Board was not only a responsible minister but usually a leading member of the cabinet.

Many of the functions of the Local Government Board were patently inappropriate to a ministry of health, and the act of 1919 provided that such functions might be transferred elsewhere at any time by order in council. Several such transfers have been made, e.g., (1) the control of public libraries and museums, now assigned to the Board of Education, (2) sundry powers in regard to municipal electrical transportation, assigned to the Board of Trade, and (3) the supervision of registration and elections, transferred to the Home Office. Still other transfers will probably take place. But in any event the new ministry may be expected to carry forward permanently a great amount of the work which the Board used to perform, notably the coördination of local sanitary authorities, the repression of infectious diseases and of tuberculosis, the regulation of the sale of food and drugs and of the places where food is prepared, watching over the poor law authorities,[8] supervision of local taxation, audit of local expenditure, and many other things. To this list must be added the administration of housing acts; and the ministry's functions in this respect far exceed those of the former Local Government Board. Town-planning acts come also within its purview, and a special section has been created to deal with each of these important subjects.[9]

The second great department specially concerned with social

[8] W. Chance, *The Ministry of Health and the Poor Law* (London, 1922).

[9] The development of public health administration to date is best described in B. G. Bannington, *English Public Health Administration* (new ed., London, 1928). On the Ministry of Health, see I. G. Gibbon, "The Ministry of Health," *Public Administration,* IV, 243-266 (1926), and especially A. Newsholme, *The Ministry of Health* (London, 1925), in the Whitehall Series. The correlation or integration of the numerous and widely scattered public health agencies of the national government of the United States is a current problem of much interest and importance. See R. D. Leigh, *Federal Health Administration in the United States* (New York, 1927), and J. A. Tobey, *The National Government and Public Health* (Baltimore, 1926).

development is the Board of Education. Prior to the nineteenth century, facilities for elementary instruction were left to be provided, in England as elsewhere, by the church and by private philanthropy; not until 1833 did Parliament begin to appropriate money for the aid of local authorities in the maintenance of schools. In 1839 the amount of the annual grant was increased, and on the general principle that grants in aid should carry with them some rights of superintendence, an order in council created a committee of the Privy Council on education, whose vice-president became, in 1856, a member of the ministry. An Education Act of 1870 made no attempt to set up a nation-wide system of publicly supported schools, but it required all communities that were not adequately served by either grant-aided or denominational schools to see that the deficiency was supplied, and it provided for the election of local school boards to undertake the work of educational administration. During the next three decades the number of grant-aided schools increased, and in 1899 the Privy Council committee on education was converted by statute into the present Board of Education, composed of the President, the Lord President of the Council, the principal secretaries of state, the First Lord of the Treasury, and the Chancellor of the Exchequer. This again is a phantom board, the President being the effective single head of the department. The jurisdiction of the Board does not extend to universities, university colleges, or university education, or to certain other educational institutions and types of institutions; it extends in only a limited way to schools which do not receive financial aid from the national government. But outside of these limits it applies generally to elementary, secondary, technical, and collegiate instruction. The Board does not provide or administer school systems; it does not construct buildings, engage or control teachers, prescribe or supply text-books, regulate curricula (except in general terms), or control methods of teaching. Rather, its business is that of supervising and coördinating educational administration as carried on under the immediate direction of the local authorities, inspecting all grant-aided schools (and others on request), carrying on educational investigations, and publishing bulletins and reports. An Education Act of 1902 abolished the school boards and transferred the work of local administration to the county and borough councils, each of which is required to maintain a special committee on the subject; so that nowadays the supervisory contact of the central Board is principally with these committees. The administrative officers of the Board, numbering some sixty-five, are grouped in two sections, one having to do with England and the other with Wales.[10] A comprehensive Education Act of 1918 undertook to promote more fruitful partnership between the central and local authorities, in pursuance of newer ideals of public education inspired by war-time experiences; but it made no important changes in the machinery of supervision and administration.[11]

Such, in bare outline, are the principal departments and offices through which that great portion of the work of government which we think of broadly as executive and administrative is carried on. The organization and characteristics of the army of men and women who to a large extent actually do the work, namely, the permanent civil service, will be considered in two chapters that follow. But first, three or four further facts about the departments as a group call for mention.

Administrative Reorganization

One of these is that the scheme of departments as it now stands is in no sense final. Students of government do not need to be told that in these days of huge executive establishments

[10] Scotland's educational system is organized separately under acts of 1908 and 1918. Until 1918, a system of local school boards was employed, similar to that existing in England between 1870 and 1902. But the act of 1918 abolished the hundreds of boards and transferred their functions to elective county committees, whose administration of school affairs is supervised by a Scottish Department of Education, it, in turn, being advised by a representative National Council for Education.

[11] The best brief survey of the British educational system in its governmental aspects is A. L. Lowell, *Government of England,* II, Chaps. xlvii-l. The work of the Board of Education is described at length in L. A. Selby-Bigge, *The Board of Education* (London, 1927), in the Whitehall Series. For comparison with the United States, D. H. Smith, "The Bureau of Education," *Service Monographs of the U. S.,* No. 14 (Baltimore, 1923), may be used. On the proposal to establish a federal department of education in the United States, see J. E. Johnsen, *A Federal Department of Education* (New York, 1927).

and complicated administrative problems reconstruction of executive and administrative machinery with a view to greater efficiency or less expense, or both, is a perennial topic of discussion. This is true in our American states, some of which have carried out notable reorganizations in the past decade;[12] it is equally true in connection with the national administrative system of the United States, which still awaits sorely needed reconstruction, notwithstanding much effort in recent years to bring it about.[13] In Great Britain, the demands made upon all executive and administrative machinery by the World War and its aftermath entailed unusually rapid and extensive reorganization. New ministries were set up; new branches were added to existing ministries; agencies and functions were tacked on, transferred, remodelled, abolished, reëstablished. Many of the war-time accretions have now been dispensed with, but by no means all; and not one of the more important pre-war departments will ever again be precisely what it was in the old days. It is by no means solely, however, a matter of changes precipitated by the exigencies of war. Whether in war or in peace, the mechanism of government requires ever renewed adaptation to altered conditions and needs. Even if an administrative system were to attain perfection—which no one ever will—expanding governmental activities, new legislation, and development of improved techniques would necessitate readjustment from year to year, and almost from day to day. Important changes are sometimes dictated, too, by considerations of economy.

A glance at the present British administrative set-up as sketched above will reveal many surviving instances of overlapping, possible confusion, and probable waste. To American, and to some English, observers, the position of the Post Office as a revenue department seems anomalous. The linking up of fisheries with agriculture in a single department might be, and indeed is said to be, disadvantageous to the fishing

[12] E.g., New York, Pennsylvania, and Illinois.

[13] F. A. Ogg and P. O. Ray, *Introduction to American Government* (3rd ed.), 341-346. See especially G. A. Weber, *Organized Efforts for the Improvement of Methods of Administration in the United States* (New York, 1919), and W. F. Willoughby, *Reorganization of the Administrative Branch of the National Government* (Baltimore, 1923).

industry. Factory inspection remains a function of the Home Office, although it would seem to belong in the Ministry of Labor, or even the Ministry of Health. The Ministry of Labor as now constituted has little or nothing to do with labor in agriculture, in mines, or in ships on the high seas. The Ministry of Air has uncertain and unsatisfactory relations with the other defense departments.

As time goes on and activities multiply, the natural tendency is to set off preëxisting boards, committees, or other branches as separate departments, as, for example, in the case of the recently created Dominions Office. Sometimes there is distinct gain in doing this; sometimes the creation of the new ministry means only the bringing together in a single establishment of more or less similar activities formerly carried on in a number of scattered departments.[14] The best thought on the subject looks rather, however, to integration than to dispersion. While advocating the creation of at least one entirely new department, i.e., a department of research and information, the most important official report thus far made on the subject urges a drastic reduction of the number of departments and a coördination of those that remain, on the general plan of the ten federal departments in the United States.[15] Except in some relatively unimportant particulars, the recommendations thus made have not been carried out, and there is no present prospect that they will be. As the experience of our own country abundantly shows, administrative reorganization on broad lines of preconceived principle is an exceedingly difficult thing to bring about. Even piecemeal reconstruction, however, often entails new departures of more than ordinary significance.

[14] The Ministry of Pensions affords a good illustration. See p. 176 above.

[15] Report of the Machinery of Government Committee of the Ministry of Reconstruction. Cmd. 9230 (1918). The committee was of the opinion that the government's business should be organized in ten main divisions, as follows: finance, national defense, foreign affairs, research and information, production, employment, supplies, education, health, and justice. It did not say that there should be only ten ministries. It suggested, for example, that the division of production might very properly be organized in three ministries, i.e., commerce and industry, agriculture and forestry, and fisheries. But if its proposals were to be carried out the ministries would be considerably fewer, as well as more nearly coördinate. For fuller comment on the report, see F. A. Ogg, "Proposed Administrative Reorganization in Great Britain," *Amer. Polit. Sci. Rev.*, May, 1919.

An interesting and relatively new development in connection with the executive and administrative work of the government is the creation of standing advisory committees. Such committees may be intended to serve the cabinet as a whole, and through it, of course, Parliament as well; or they may function simply in relation to a particular department or office. The best illustration of the former type is the Committee of Imperial Defense (dating from 1904), which, as has been pointed out, is not a cabinet committee, but rather a body consisting in part of cabinet officers, but also in part of non-cabinet officials, including representatives of the dominions, and charged with investigating, reporting, and recommending on all questions of military organization and strategy. The Labor party advocates a similar National Economic Committee, to serve as "the prime minister's eyes and ears" on economic questions, and it returned to office in 1929 pledged to create such an instrumentality. The Liberal party, too, has a proposal for an Economic General Staff, to work in close touch with the cabinet.[16]

Equally important, however, is the rise of advisory committees attached to particular departments. There has never been anything to prevent department heads and other officers from conferring informally with individuals or groups outside of the public service, and consultations of the kind must often have taken place. As long ago as 1899, provision for departmental advisory committees began to be made by statute—first in an act of the year mentioned creating the present Board of Education, and later in the Trade Boards Act of 1909, the National Insurance Act of 1911, and one or two other measures. During the war years, large numbers of such committees were provided for by executive orders, without express statutory authority; and beginning again with acts of 1919 relating to the ministries of Transport, Health, and Agriculture and Fisheries, extensive statutory authorizations were made. Thus the Ministry of Transport Act provides for an advisory committee on rates and another on roads, and also a panel from which other similar committees may be appointed; and—as an illustration of the fashion in which committees of the kind are usually made up—the committee on rates, to which all proposed

[16] See p. 556 below.

changes of rates and fares must be submitted for advice, is composed of five persons: one, trained in law, named by the Lord Chancellor; two representing trade and agriculture, and named by the Board of Trade in consultation with the central chambers of commerce and agriculture; one representing transportation interests, and designated by the Minister of Transport; and one representing labor, named by the Minister of Labor, in consultation with the principal interests concerned. The Machinery of Government Committee, already mentioned, warmly endorsed the advisory committee plan, "so long as the advisory bodies are not permitted to impair the responsibility of ministers to Parliament;" and the general testimony seems to be that the committees are rendering good service, not only in bringing to the departments helpful information and advice, but in inspiring in the public a greater degree of confidence in the administrative authorities. It goes without saying that the committees have no power to direct or control administrative work, or to dictate policy. Their business is solely to discuss and advise.[17]

Newer Functional Developments in the Departments

Turning from structural to functional aspects of the departments, we note two developments that have lately attracted a great deal of attention, some of it unfavorable. One, i.e., the delegation of extensive legislative power to administrative authorities, has to do with the relations between the executive establishments and Parliament, or, as English writers often put it, between "Whitehall and Westminster;" the other, i.e., the placing of a large and increasing number of judicial functions in the hands of the departments, or under the jurisdiction of tribunals which the departments control and sometimes even appoint, materially affects the relation between the executive establishments and the courts.

In earlier centuries Parliament, as we have seen, slowly gathered to itself full powers of legislation, and the day came when

[17] J. A. Fairlie, "Advisory Committees in British Administration," *Amer. Polit. Sci. Rev.*, Nov., 1926. Cf. H. J. Laski, *A Grammar of Politics* (New Haven, 1925), 376-383. Committees of the sort are employed most extensively at present in the Board of Trade.

it was claimed that no law could be made except with parliamentary sanction. At no time did this mean that all laws were actually and literally made by Parliament; for the crown clung resolutely to its ancient law-making authority, and Parliament was always obliged, or at all events found it expedient, to tolerate, and even to recognize, that authority within certain bounds. As late as the seventeenth century the crown issued proclamations and enforced them as law, on the sole basis of prerogative; and, as every student of the period knows, the practice became one of the principal points of contention between the Stuart kings on the one side and Parliament and the judges on the other. So far as independent and autocratic royal legislation was concerned, the matter was settled by the triumph of the parliamentary cause; from 1689 onwards it was a fixed principle of the constitution that laws could be made only by, or on the express authority of, Parliament.

Even before this turning point was reached, however, it was found both convenient and necessary for Parliament to delegate the actual exercise of certain law-making powers to the crown, and almost at once after the Revolution the issuance of orders in council in pursuance of authority conferred at Westminster —"statutory orders," that is to say, in contrast with the former prerogative orders—became a familiar, even if not a very frequent, event. Through the eighteenth century, and well into the nineteenth, Parliament granted such authority sparingly, preferring to legislate directly even upon detailed matters of an essentially administrative character. But after 1832, when great fields of governmental regulation and administration—poor relief, public health, factory inspection, transportation, education—were freshly entered or subjected to new forms of control, acts delegating powers to make rules having the force and character of law multiplied rapidly; and by 1893, when a Rules Publication Act undertook to regulate certain features of the procedure involved, the volume of such rules had come to be truly impressive. Since the date mentioned, the development has continued on even larger lines, notably during the period of the World War. In a single year (1919) no fewer than sixty out of 102 public acts passed by Parliament delegated legislative power to some subordinate authority; in bulk, at least, orders and rules now contribute almost as much to the annual output of legislation as do statutes themselves.

No one doubts that delegation of power in this fashion is a practical necessity. Even if Parliament had the time, it would not have the skill, to frame all of the multifarious rules of a statutory nature which good administration requires. On many subjects it must perforce content itself with making regulations of a general character, leaving it to the king-in-council or an appropriate department to supplement them with orders. The National Insurance Act of 1911 was rendered almost unworkable by the attempt to meet every exceptional and every hard case in the statute itself. The phenomenal growth of the practice of delegation in recent times has, however, aroused misgivings. Parliament, it is said, is deliberately or unconsciously abdicating its proper functions. Few members, it is alleged, have any real appreciation of the lengths to which the device has surreptitiously been carried. Public bills originate, as a rule, with the government, i.e., with the ministers, who have a definite interest in increasing the freedom of the executive authorities to legislate independently, and there is a growing tendency for them to slip into bills clauses, frequently unnoticed by any one else, conferring the desired powers. As a consequence, the liberties of the citizen may be endangered. To all this there is, of course, the reply that the executive cannot override by orders the will of the legislature. There is, declares a recent judicial decision, "no prerogative to make regulations." [18] "All rules," reads another decision, "derive their validity from the statute which creates the power to make them, and not from the executive body by which they are made." [19] Furthermore, certain procedural changes have been introduced since the war which, at least in form, provide a greater measure of parliamentary control; more rules and orders than formerly—though still by no means the majority—require confirmation by resolution passed by both houses of Parliament. Finally, it is to be observed that orders and rules enjoy no such immunity from judicial veto as do statutes. No court will hold any act of Parliament *ultra vires*; but any

[18] Attorney-General v. De Keyser's Hotel (1920).
[19] The Zamora (1916).

judge, high or low, before whom any order or rule is brought for enforcement may pronounce it *ultra vires,* i.e., not authorized by statute, prerogative, or other alleged warrant, and refuse to apply it to the case before him. Even war-time orders in council issued under the broad authority conferred by the Defense of the Realm Acts fell to the ground in this way. There is, therefore, the added safeguard that the executive and administrative authorities, in the exercise of their growing legislative powers, are subject to the check of judicial review.[20]

Hardly less interesting than the growth of administrative legislation is the development of what may, by analogy, be termed administrative justice. It is true that there never has been, and never will be, any clear line of demarcation between administrative functions and judicial functions; long before our own day, administrators judged and judges administered. But the point is that, largely as a result of the social legislation of the past fifty years, the judicial activities of administrative authorities in, or under the control of, the executive departments have enormously increased, not by accident, but by de-

[20] An episode early in 1929 showed that Parliament is, at least occasionally, on its guard against encroachments of the executive through the channel indicated. A clause of the pending Local Government Bill undertook to give the Minister of Health power, in respect of any difficulties which might arise in the application of the act, "to remove the difficulty by order, or do anything necessary to bring the provisions into operation." Government and opposition members joined in attacking this as an unwarrantable grant of power; and although the minister in charge of the bill urged that the same grant had been made in six acts since 1888, without complaint of abuse, the government was obliged to agree that the provision should be altered before the measure's passage. *Manchester Guardian* (weekly ed.), Feb. 1, 1929, p. 85.

The best discussions of the general subject are C. T. Carr, *Delegated Legislation* (Cambridge, 1921), and J. A. Fairlie, *Administrative Procedure in Connection with Statutory Rules and Orders in Great Britain* (Urbana, 1927). Cf. J. Stamp, "Recent Tendencies Towards the Devolution of Legislative Functions to the Administration," *Jour. of Public Admin.,* II (1924), 23-28; I. G. Gibbon, M. L. Gwyer, and P. Anderson, "The Powers of Public Departments to Make Rules Having the Force of Law," *Public Admin.,* Oct., 1927; and H. Potter, "Legislative Powers of Public Administrative Authorities," *ibid.,* Jan., 1928. For full comparison of similar developments in the United States, see J. Hart, *The Ordinance-Making Powers of the President of the United States* (Baltimore, 1925), and especially J. P. Comer, *Legislative Functions of National Administrative Authorities* (New York, 1927).

liberate provision made in parliamentary statutes. For example, the housing acts make the Ministry of Health the appellate body in regard to a great series of important matters closely affecting the rights of owners of slum property and workmen's dwelling houses; and, the department having laid down requisite rules on the subject, appeals are decided by its officials in accordance with them and can be carried to no court of law. Again, the Board of Education hears and gives final decision upon appeals turning upon essentially judicial questions arising between local educational authorities and the managers of "non-provided," i.e., denominational, schools. The Ministry of Transport similarly disposes of appeals in regard to the granting of various kinds of licenses and in respect to the supplying of electrical power; and the Home Office exercises numerous functions of a judicial nature, involving intricate questions of law and fact, "ranging from the decision as to whether a man is or is not an alien, and if an alien, of what nationality, to the commutation of the death penalty in capital offenses." [21] Hardly any important department—indeed, hardly any major branch of a department—fails in these days to have a wide range of judicial powers which it exercises under statutory authority and in complete independence of the courts of law; and although the matter is too technical to be pursued at length here, the fact must never be overlooked in appraising the rôle which the departments and their auxiliary agencies play.

Like the growing delegation of legislative power, this development is viewed in certain quarters as unfortunate and unwarranted. The rights of the individual, to protect which the courts are supposed to exist, are felt by some to have been placed far too largely at the mercy of the executive; [22] administrative tribunals, it is charged, take advantage of loosely-drafted statutes and apply them in defiance of laws which courts of justice under the circumstances are unable to enforce; the bureaucracy, it is said, is getting the whip-hand over the judiciary. On the other hand, it is argued that, historically, the separation of judicature from administration has never been

[21] W. A. Robson, *Justice and Administrative Law* (London, 1928), 24.

[22] See J. H. Morgan's introduction to G. Robinson, *Public Authorities and Legal Liability* (London, 1925).

complete; that the swift expansion of social legislation in the past half-century has made the growth of judicial functions in the hands of administrative authorities inevitable; and that the administrative tribunals have accomplished, and are accomplishing, socially desirable ends which are beyond the competence of the courts of law as at present constituted. At all events, the phenomenon is one of exceptional interest for the student of comparative administration and jurisprudence.[23]

[23] The whole subject is treated fully and clearly in W. A. Robson, *op. cit.* See especially Chaps. i, iii, vi. Cf. R. Muir, *Peers and Bureaucrats,* 1-94.

CHAPTER X

THE PERMANENT CIVIL SERVICE

THE work of the government would never be done if there were only the secretaries of state and other heads of departments, presidents of boards, parliamentary under-secretaries, junior lords, and civil lords—in other words, the ministers—to do it. These people cannot collect customs, audit accounts, inspect factories, take censuses, to say nothing of keeping books, delivering mail, and carrying messages. Such manifold tasks (many of them purely clerical, but many others not at all so) fall, rather, to the body of officials and employees known broadly as the permanent civil service. The ministers number, as we have seen, around sixty-five; the permanent civil service numbered more than 364,000 in 1921, and, notwithstanding post-war reductions and economies (including the transfer of many thousands of civil servants to the payrolls of the Irish Free State in 1922), it is not far from 300,000 at the present day.[1] It is this great body of men and women—for a large percentage in the clerical grades are females—that translates law into action from one end of the country to the other and brings the national government into its daily contacts with the rank and file of the citizenry. It is likewise this reservoir of expert knowledge that furnishes Parliament with the exact information required in shaping and enacting policies on a multitude of subjects, being itself entrusted in ever-increasing degree with the completion of loosely woven statutes by means of department-made rules applying them to particular circum-

[1] These figures are for the civil service in the widest sense of the term, from under-secretaries of state down to letter sorters and charwomen. Speaking strictly, not all of the persons counted are "permanent;" and not all are "civil servants" in the narrower meaning frequently given the term. The present chapter and the following one, however, are designed to give an account of the service as a whole.

stances beyond the ken of the legislators at Westminster. The permanent civil service is a less conspicuous part of the government than the ministry, but it certainly is not a whit less essential.

Ministers and Permanent Civil Servants Contrasted

Certain sharp distinctions between ministers and permanent civil servants at once challenge attention and serve to bring out the character of the system as a whole. The first turns on the fact that the minister is a *political* official while the civil servant is not. So far as the minister is concerned, perhaps enough has already been said on this score.[2] He is openly identified with a political party, and, if a member of the House of Commons, has been elected as a party man; he has been made a minister with due, if not primary, regard for his party connections and prominence; he remains a party man—even a party leader—while minister, and if he is in the cabinet he helps frame party policy and secure its enactment into law; he remains in office only so long as his party stays in power. He is, of course, expected to serve the large and permanent interests of his country, not only diligently, but broadmindedly and impartially. While doing so he, however, quite frankly bears—and is expected to bear—a party label.

The position of the permanent civil servant is entirely different. He is what he is primarily because he is non-political. How he became so makes a long story. Custom has played some part. Regulations laid down by the Civil Service Commission have helped. Orders in council have done much. But back of all stand statutory restrictions imposed by Parliament. It is by statute chiefly that the great bulk of office-holders under the crown have been debarred from sitting in the House of Commons; and it is in a similar way, in the main, that such office-holders have been cut off from all other forms of active participation in party or partisan affairs. Membership in the elective branch of Parliament cannot be otherwise than political: one must go into politics in order to be elected, and, once seated, one cannot escape voting and acting on political lines. Beginning with the Security and Place Acts passed during

[2] See Chap. vi above.

the reign of Queen Anne,[3] a long line of statutes imposed restrictions, and finally unconditional prohibitions, upon office-holding by members of the House of Commons, until nowadays it is possible for only a few officers under the crown to sit in that body—none at all except the ministers and certain other specified officials having a frankly political character. Indeed, under a Treasury rule dating from 1884,[4] if a non-political office-holder desires today even to become a candidate for a seat in the House of Commons, he must resign his office as soon as he issues his address to the electors or in any other manner announces his candidacy.

But there are many forms of political activity in which a civil servant might engage without occupying, or even aspiring to, a seat in Parliament; and numerous statutes have been enacted, and civil service rules promulgated, with a view to making abstention complete. As long ago as 1710 a statute made liable to fine and dismissal any post-office official who should "by word, message, or writing, or in any other manner whatsoever, endeavor to persuade any elector to give, or dissuade any elector from giving, his vote for the choice of any person to sit in Parliament;" and in later times other groups were similarly placed under restraint, until at the present day no non-political official or employee may seek to wield personal or partisan influence in any way whatsoever except by quietly casting his vote at the polls. If he does so, he runs grave risk of being disciplined, and even removed. He may not make a political speech, write a partisan tract, edit or publish a party newspaper, canvass for a parliamentary candidate, or serve on a party committee. There was a time, indeed, when some groups of office-holders were even forbidden to vote. This was true of revenue collectors and postal employees from 1782 to 1868; although it should be added that this disfranchisement was originally at the officials' own request, in order that they might be relieved from the importunities of rival candidates. Police officers, too, were disfranchised by measures finally repealed only in 1887. Nowadays no civil service officials are excluded

[3] In 1705 and 1707 (see p. 137 above). G. B. Adams and H. M. Stephens, *Select Documents of English Constitutional History*, 483-485.

[4] Embodied in an order in council in 1910.

from voting;[5] but the rights of all such as party members or sympathizers begin and end with casting their ballots.

It goes without saying that there is complaint of this deprivation. Ought not civil servants, it is asked, to take as keen an interest and as active a part in party politics as other citizens? The theory underlying the arrangement, however, is that such employees of the state, having to do, not with the control of policy, but only with executing the laws, ought to be in a position to serve the government of the day with complete loyalty, consistency, and sincerity, regardless of what party is in power, and that they could not do this if they were to take an active and public part in favor of one party and its candidates as against another. An investigating commission of 1910-14 looked carefully into the question of whether any relaxation of the existing rules was desirable and decided that it was not; and a Treasury committee of 1925, after going over the same ground, came to a similar conclusion.[6] No change, therefore, is to be anticipated, although doubtless the matter will continue to stir discussion.

The Ministers as Amateurs

There is another way in which the ministers and subordinate civil servants differ. The former are, in the main, amateurs,

[5] The "returning officers," chiefly sheriffs and mayors, who have charge of parliamentary elections in the constituencies are not permitted to vote at the elections at which they serve; but they are not members of the national civil service.

[6] "The question," said the latter committee, "from the point of view of the state, becomes one not of 'civil rights,' but one of administrative efficiency. . . . The constantly extending disposition of Parliament to entrust the exercise of quasi-judicial duties to the executive departments without providing any of the established safeguards operative against judicial excess . . . as well as the sharper alignment of political parties in these days, unite to make the high reputation for political impartiality hitherto enjoyed by the public service a more valuable national possession than ever before." Cmd. 2408 (1925). Interesting testimony going to show that the reputation referred to is deserved comes from Mr. Sidney Webb, a member of the Labor government of 1924. "I and my colleagues in the House of Commons," he says, "have had the experience of coming as new people to offices which might legitimately have presumptions and traditions against us, and I am sure I am speaking for all my colleagues when I say that we have nothing to complain of in regard to the loyalty, fidelity, and zeal with which we found ourselves assisted during our short period of office." H. Finer, *The British Civil Service* (London, 1927), 69.

while the latter are, or are in process of becoming, experts. Anyone who has read what has already been said about the ministers will understand why they are, and with rare exceptions must be, amateurs. They are appointed with some regard, of course, for their personal aptitudes, but often, if not usually, for reasons that have little connection with the nature of the work to be performed in their particular departments; frequently they have had little or no experience with governmental administration in any form. While in office they—at all events the more important ones—must devote so much of their time to cabinet, parliamentary, party, social, and other activities outside of the fields specially assigned them that they can learn little about their departments except in their larger aspects. They are occasionally shifted from one post to another, and in any case have only the precarious, and usually rather brief, tenure which the political character of their positions entails. When the formation of a Labor ministry became imminent early in 1924 there was much apprehensive comment to the effect that it would be impossible for the leader of a party that had never been in power to assemble a group of ministers having the requisite acquaintance with the business of the government, to say nothing of the necessary experience in handling it. There was, of course, some ground for this feeling, because in the nature of the case there were not experienced Labor men, as there would have been experienced Conservatives and Liberals, to be drawn upon. In point of fact, however, a ministry of any party at all will, as already suggested, contain a good many men for whom the connections and responsibilities assigned are a novelty—men who know next to nothing about the branch of government of which they suddenly find themselves in charge. By way of random illustration: in the Baldwin ministry which was in office when these lines were written (1928) the foreign secretary (Austen Chamberlain) was not an experienced diplomat, but a politician and administrator; the Chancellor of the Exchequer (Mr. Churchill) was not a financial magnate, but a politician and soldier; the First Lord of the Admiralty (Mr. Bridgeman) was not an admiral but an administrator and general man of affairs; even the Postmaster General (Mr. Thompson) had never had any connection with the postal establishment before he took office, beyond having his mail transported and delivered by its employees. Merchants, lawyers, country squires, professional politicians, with an occasional journalist and university professor—these, rather than permanent under-secretaries, assistant under-secretaries, and bureau chiefs who have risen from the ranks, are the materials of which ministries are made. Ministers are generally laymen, and make no pretense of being anything else.[7]

To some people this has seemed an unfortunate state of things. The apparent incongruity of it has been commented on, for example, by a first-rate English writer who complains: "We require some acquaintance with the technicalities of their work from the subordinate officials, but none from the responsible chiefs. A youth must pass an examination in arithmetic before he can hold a second-class clerkship in the Treasury; but a Chancellor of the Exchequer may be a middle-aged man of the world, who has forgotten what little he ever learnt about figures at Eton or Oxford, and is innocently anxious to know the meaning of 'those little dots,' when first confronted with Treasury accounts worked out in decimals. A young officer will be refused his promotion to captain's ranks if he cannot show some acquaintance with tactics and with military history; but the Minister for War may be a man of peace—we have had such—who regards all soldiering with dislike, and has sedulously abstained from getting to know anything about it." [8] In France and other Continental states it has been not uncommon to put military and naval men in charge of the war

[7] Disraeli, forming a ministry, offered the Board of Trade to a man who wanted instead the Local Government Board, as he was better acquainted with the municipal affairs of the country than with its commerce. "It doesn't matter," said Disraeli; "I suppose you know as much about trade as ——, the First Lord of the Admiralty, knows about ships." "Well, I'll take the Colonies myself," Lord Palmerston once remarked to an assistant when he was having trouble finding a suitable colonial secretary; "just come upstairs with me for half an hour and show me where these places are on the map." "I am Chancellor of the Exchequer," wrote Robert Lowe to his brother in 1868, "with everything to learn." When Sir Edward Carson was made First Lord of the Admiralty in 1917 he declared that his only qualification for the post was that he was "absolutely at sea."

[8] S. Low, *Governance of England* (rev. ed., 1914), 201-202.

and marine ministries; and even in the United States there has been a growing demand that the men whom the President places at the head of at least a few of the executive departments, e.g., Agriculture, shall have had professional experience definitely related to the work which they will be expected to supervise.[9]

There is no gainsaying that, other things being equal, the department head who is well informed on the work to be carried on under his direction is to be preferred. But this does not mean that he can, or should, be expected to qualify as an expert or technician. Dozens of more or less related, but different, activities are to go on simultaneously in the department, each requiring a high order of technical proficiency. Neither the minister in charge nor any other man can be a master of all; and so far as the minister is concerned it is unnecessary that he be a master of any, because—and it cannot be too strongly emphasized—his business is not to do the work of the department but only to help frame general policies and see that they are carried out by the staff employed for the purpose. Indeed, there are strong reasons why it is better for him to be a layman, brought in from the outside. He must be able to see the department as a whole and in its relations to other departments and branches of the government. He must have a sense of proportion and values requisite to guide him in keeping the department within its proper sphere. He must serve as the intermediary between the department and the House of Commons, keeping the one in touch with public opinion and the other informed on administrative needs and problems. Though war minister, he must have the interests of more than the military men at heart; though minister of agriculture, he must serve others besides the landowners. These larger things he would be less adapted to do if he had grown up in the department and had only a departmental point of view. On general principles, too, it is often a good thing to have the work of experts supervised by laymen. If the supervision is at all tactful and sympathetic, less friction is likely to result than where experts are set to supervise experts.[10]

[9] W. B. Munro, *Governments of Europe,* 85.

[10] To quote Ramsay MacDonald: "The apparent incongruity of a minister being at the Education Office one year and the Admiralty the next

Relations of Ministers with their Subordinates

A salient, though by no means unique, feature of the British government is, therefore, the setting over against each other, in the executive and administrative service, of (1) the amateur, lay, political, non-permanent element and (2) the expert, professional, non-political, permanent element. Naturally, each reacts upon the other in a variety of ways, depending upon the personalities involved and the particular conditions existing. As spokesman in the department for the cabinet and Parliament, the minister directs and instructs; to a degree, he independently determines policy and imposes it upon his subordinates. On the other hand, as head of an administrative staff which is expert in matters of which he knows little or nothing, he is the beneficiary of advice, and even guidance. How largely he will be controlled by what comes to him from his subordinates will depend, as has been suggested, upon a variety of circumstances. In the nature of things, he will accept much of the advice that is offered him, especially on purely technical matters; and the contribution of the permanent staff—particularly,

disappears when examined at close quarters. The cabinet is not a collection of experts on any one subject. Were that so, its corporate responsibility for government would be unreal. It is a committee of men of good common sense and intelligence, of business ability, of practical capacity, in touch with public opinion, on the one hand, and by reason of that, carrying out a certain policy, and, on the other, it is the controller of a staff of experts who know the details of departmental work. . . . The cabinet is the bridge linking up the people with the expert, joining principle to practice. Its function is to transform the messages sent along sensory nerves into commands sent through motor nerves. It does not keep the departments going; it keeps them going in certain directions." *Socialism and Government* (London, 1909), II, 34-35. "There is a large class of skilled work," said Lord Haldane, "some of it requiring long training and even initiative, which is done better by competent, permanent officials than by statesmen even of a high order. But when we come to the highest order of work it is different. There is a common cry that this, too, should be left to the expert. There is no more complete misinterpretation of a situation. The mere expert, if he were charged with the devising and execution of high aims and policy, would be at sea among a multitude of apparently conflicting considerations. What is the relation of a particular plan to a great national policy and to far-reaching principles and ends? Questions like these must always be for the true leader and not for the specialist." Cf. S. and B. Webb, *A Constitution for the Socialist Commonwealth of Great Britain*, 66-68, and G. U. Stirling-Taylor, "Government by Amateurs," *Nineteenth Cent.*, May, 1928.

of course, the permanent under-secretaries[11]—to the shaping of departmental, and even general national, policy will be considerable. No minister, however, ever acknowledges any obligation to accept and act upon the views of his subordinates, however urgently pressed. It is he, not they, that will have to justify to the cabinet whatever decisions are made, and also bear responsibility for them on the floor of an inquiring, and perhaps censorious, House of Commons; and the last thing he would surrender would be the right to make the decisions himself. If things go well, he gets the credit; if ill, he shoulders the blame. So far as responsibility goes, it has been aptly remarked, the minister is the department.[12]

The Merit System—Conditions Before Its Adoption

Certain main characteristics of the permanent service, considered as a whole, have already appeared. It is non-political. It is expert, i.e., professional. And it does not change when a ministry goes out of office. Another thing to be noted about it is that it is operated from top to bottom in accordance with what we are wont to call in the United States the "merit" principle. That is to say, the service is recruited almost exclusively on the basis of tested capacity, and promotions and increases of pay are determined mainly by the quality of work performed. In

[11] "The permanent under-secretaries have usually had perhaps more than twenty years of very varied official experience before they attain their position; and it is very rare for any to have served in only one department." H. Finer, *The British Civil Service,* 69. These officials are the ministers' chief advisers, the chairmen of the departmental councils (see p. 235 below), and the principal points of contact with other departments for inter-departmental affairs.

[12] Cf. Viscount Milner's remarks: "The minister comes in, very often, knowing nothing at all about the business [of his department]. He has his policy, he has his ideas, but when he comes into contact with the practical difficulties, with the new facts, with the vast amount of accumulated knowledge and experience, which the permanent officials can bring to bear upon the subject, those ideas almost invariably undergo considerable modification. Indeed, one of the chief duties of civil servants of the upper ranks is to give shape and substance to the vague aspirations, the misty ideas, of the politician, and as long as that duty is loyally performed, with the honest desire not to defeat the minister's policy, but to produce something workable, the civil servant does in a perfectly legitimate way exercise an important influence on the course of politics." *Jour. of Pub. Admin.,* I, 88-89 (1923).

our own country, the merit principle was definitely adopted as a basis of recruitment in the national service only in 1883,[13] and even then was applied to only a few thousand members of the service, leaving the great majority subject to appointment and removal for political reasons; and although the line separating such politically selected office-holders from merit appointees has been gradually pushed upwards, until in 1927 it took in a total of 423,000, this is only about seventy-five per cent of the whole number, and large groups of relatively unimportant non-policy-determining officials, e.g., immigration commissioners, collectors of customs and of internal revenue, and field officers of the Department of Justice, remain on a political basis.[14] Under the British system, on the other hand, the officials having a political character form only a very limited group at the top—chiefly, as we have seen, the ministers. Such as they are, practically all have to do with policy-framing as well as administration, and hence are quite justifiably kept on a political basis.

This matter of appointment and promotion on grounds of merit calls for further comment. The British did not always have it. On the contrary, like ourselves, they attained it only after a long fight for "civil service reform." They came to it, however, a generation earlier than we, and the victory of the cause in their country did much to promote the substantial triumphs it has won on this side of the Atlantic. In Britain, as with us, the fight had to be made against various flagrant and insidious forms of what is commonly known as "patronage." All government in the Britain of the eighteenth and earlier nine-

[13] In the so-called Pendleton Act. It is interesting to note that this triumph of the long developing civil service reform movement was considerably promoted by the publication in 1880 of a book entitled *The Civil Service in Great Britain,* by Dorman B. Eaton, an ardent reformer whom President Hayes commissioned to study the advances made in Great Britain up to that point.

[14] F. A. Ogg and P. O. Ray, *Introduction to American Government* (3rd ed.), 295-297. Cf. J. A. McIlhenny, "The Merit System and the Higher Offices," *Amer. Polit. Sci. Rev.,* Aug., 1917, and A. W. Macmahon, "Bureau Chiefs in the National Administration of the United States," *ibid.,* Aug. and Nov., 1926. The principal historical account of the American civil service is C. R. Fish, *The Civil Service and the Patronage* (New York, 1904).

teenth centuries was—as there will be occasion to emphasize repeatedly in this book—decidedly aristocratic. Legislation at Westminster was a privileged affair of the leading members of a few governing families; justice and local government were largely in the hands of the propertied justices of the peace; and the national administration was entrusted mainly to persons who got their places by some sort of favoritism rather than in recognition of any particular capacity or competence. Many appointees to administrative posts had no claims other than that they were importunate constituents of influential members of Parliament—perchance useful aids at election time. Many were younger sons of powerful landholders or politicians. Many more were needy relatives or other more or less unpromising members of a magnate's entourage. "Admission into the civil service," said an official report of 1853 (to be mentioned again presently), "is indeed eagerly sought after, but it is for the unambitious and the indolent or incapable that it is chiefly desired. Those whose abilities do not warrant an expectation that they will succeed in the open professions, where they must encounter the competition of their contemporaries, and those whom indolence of temperament or physical infirmities unfit for active exertions, are placed in the civil service, where they may obtain an honorable livelihood with little labor and with no risk." [15]

"Clean sweeps," of the sort that came to be the fashion in the worst days of American politics, were never indulged in. The Englishman thought of a man, once in a public office, as having somewhat of a vested right in it. There was no such fear of entrenched office-holders as found frequent expression in America, especially in Jacksonian days; besides, under a cabinet system, with a change of government possible at almost any moment, the principle of rotation, if extensively applied,

[15] John Bright once referred to the civil service of his day as "the outdoor relief department of the British aristocracy." "Every appointment to the regular civil service," writes Graham Wallas, "was initiated by members of Parliament according to a system by which each member of Parliament voting with the Government had a certain section of the public patronage handed over to him, and the more inefficient his nominee, the more grateful were the relations of his nominee." *Public Admin.*, Jan., 1928, p. 4. Cf. E. Porritt, *The Unreformed House of Commons* (Cambridge, 1903), I, Chap. xv.

would, as any sane man could see, keep the whole governmental system constantly on the verge of chaos. Nevertheless, there were some removals on partisan or personal grounds. And when desirable places fell vacant, or new ones were created, the appointments almost invariably went to sons of the aristocracy or other place-hunters selected for reasons having little or no bearing upon competence. Promotions, too, were largely a matter of political or personal influence.[16]

The History of Civil Service Reform

High-minded heads of departments protested against a system which swamped the services with inefficient and lazy employees, and critics like Carlyle poured out the vials of their wrath upon the situation.[17] At only one point, however, did the national awakening which produced the parliamentary reform of 1832, and a long series of accompanying political and social improvements, have any immediate effect upon the civil service. That was in relation to India. Popular dislike of the East India Company's monopolistic rights and practices had long been growing, and in 1833, when the directors came up for a renewal of their charter, they were compelled to accept an arrangement under which four candidates were to be nominated for each vacancy in the Company's training school at Haileybury, and final selection for admission was to be made on the basis of competitive examination.[18] On its face, this

[16] The general state of the service at the middle of the century, as revealed in the report quoted above, is reviewed in R. Moses, *The Civil Service of Great Britain* (New York, 1914), Chap. i. The situation is portrayed half-humorously in Anthony Trollope's novel, *The Three Clerks*; and devotees of Dickens will have no difficulty in recalling the "circumlocution office" of *Little Dorrit*. One who wishes to read on the lighter side of the subject will be interested in H. Wolfe, "Some Public Servants in Fiction," *Jour. of Public Admin.*, II, 39-57 (1924).

[17] Carlyle's castigations were contained in a series of essays published in 1839 in the *Edinburgh Review*, and later issued (along with other papers) in book form under the title of *Latter-day Pamphlets* (1850). In a group of papers published in book form in 1830, under the title *Official Aptitude Maximized, Expense Minimized*, Jeremy Bentham developed the bases on which a reform ought to proceed. He advocated recruitment by open competition.

[18] The Haileybury school was established in 1813 and soon became noted for the rigorous training which it gave young men who had been selected for beginners' positions in the Company's service.

was a small matter. Only the India service was affected; and the change was not such as to interfere perceptibly with the monopoly in that service long enjoyed by scions of the old Anglo-Indian families. Nevertheless, the step was significant. Indeed, in view of the manifestations of public interest which attended it, it is hardly going too far to say that in the very period when, under Andrew Jackson's leadership, the United States was openly surrendering to the spoils conception of public office, Great Britain was definitely, even if somewhat slowly and grudgingly, setting her face in the opposite direction.

The rule of 1833, such as it was, was soon suspended. But in the next twenty years the civil service reform movement found in the historian Macaulay, Sir Charles Trevelyan (Macaulay's brother-in-law), and other men the same sort of aggressive and persevering leadership that the American movement of a generation later found in George William Curtis, Carl Schurz, and Dorman B. Eaton; and in 1853, when the East India Company was again receiving a renewal of its charter—destined to be the last—Parliament took away entirely its right to appoint to governmental positions in India and substituted a general scheme of selection by open competitive examination. A year later a commission headed by Macaulay worked out a detailed plan for the operation of the new system, which was forthwith installed.[19] If, however, a civil service recruited by competitive examination was desirable for India, why would it not be a good thing for England—particularly considering that improvements in the home service were now widely desired, and that the Treasury Board had already authorized an investigation designed to show what could be done. The logic of the situation struck home; and when, within the space of the same year, the Treasury's commission brought in an extensive report recommending that the main features of Macaulay's plan for India be adopted for the home service, occasion seemed ripe for action. The report was

[19] R. Moses, *The Civil Service of Great Britain,* Chap. ii. Cf. A. L. Lowell and H. M. Stephens, *Colonial Civil Service; the Selection and Training of Colonial Officers in England, Holland, and France* (New York, 1900).

the work of Trevelyan,[20] assisted by Sir Stafford Northcote, and it laid down the principles on which the entire civil service system of Britain rests today.[21] Stated briefly, these principles were: (1) that as an indispensable means of attracting able young men into the service, admission should be placed on a basis of competitive examination, open to all and administered by an independent central board; (2) that a sharp distinction should be drawn between routine work on the one hand and work calling for intellectual effort on the other, with separate types of examination for the two; and (3) that in relation to all posts of the latter sort the tests employed should be of a broadly intellectual, rather than an immediately practical, nature. The concrete plan which the commissioners deduced from these principles was pronounced by John Stuart Mill "one of the greatest improvements in public affairs ever proposed by a government."[22]

The country did not go over to the proposed arrangement immediately, or by a single leap. But in 1855 an order in council created a civil service commission of three members charged with administering examinations to candidates in junior positions in all departments; the pass examinations originally employed presently began to give way to competitive tests; and a superannuation act of 1859 supplied a powerful sanction by providing that thereafter no person (with certain exceptions) should be regarded as entitled to a retirement pension unless he should have been admitted to the service with a certificate from the commissioners. Finally, in 1870, an epoch-marking order in council completed the edifice by making open competitive examinations obligatory practically

[20] A graduate of Haileybury and a former official in India, but at this time permanent secretary of the Treasury.

[21] It is interesting to observe that the term "civil service," as applied to the home departments, made its first appearance in this document.

[22] On the report and its reception by different elements in the country, see R. Moses, *op. cit.*, Chap. iii. The report proper was issued late in 1853; with comments by various eminent people, it was presented to Parliament in 1854 under the title of *Report and Papers Relating to the Reorganization of the Civil Service*. Macaulay tells us that, when first published, it was laughed at in the clubs and had little support in the House of Commons. It is, nevertheless, the foundation of Britain's excellent civil service system today.

throughout the service. The commissioners, it is true, might waive examination in the case of offices of a strictly professional character if they so desired; but only a small number of distinctly superior places remained capable of being filled without certification.

Every step in the reform was stoutly resisted by politicians and others who had something to lose by a change, and during its first twenty years the Civil Service Commission was the object of almost continuous criticism and attack. There never was really serious danger, however, of a reversion to the earlier scheme of things; and from 1870 onwards it was a matter merely of studying and experimenting with modes of bringing the system up to the desired efficiency and keeping it abreast of the times. To this end, searching inquiries were made by successive commissions, notably in 1875, in 1884-90, in 1910-14, and in 1918;[23] and large numbers of orders in council were issued, e.g., one of 1910 repealing previous orders and consolidating those remaining, and another of 1920 largely superseding the measure of ten years before. In the whole process, Parliament played a distinctly minor rôle; indeed, the fashion in which the two houses kept their hands off the problem and allowed the entire present-day merit system to be built up upon the basis of executive investigations, plans, and orders has already been cited as an illustration of that legislative abstention from direct control of administration which so sharply differentiates methods at Westminster from those at Washington. The executive authorities, standing closer to the realities of the problem, really outran parliamentary, if not also popular, sentiment on the subject, and, almost before the country was aware of what was happening, gave it the first truly expert and professional civil service known to the western world.[24]

[23] The Playfair Commission, the Ridley Commission, the Macdonnell Commission, and the Gladstone Committee, respectively. It is not feasible to describe here the work of these various bodies. That of the first three is covered in some detail in R. Moses, *op. cit.*, Chaps. vi-vii.

[24] J. A. R. Marriott, *The Mechanism of the Modern State,* II, Chap. xxvii, is a serviceable account of the developments described in this chapter, and G. Wallas, "Government," *Public Admin.,* Jan., 1928, pp. 3-15, is an interesting piece of pertinent reading.

CHAPTER XI

CIVIL SERVICE METHODS AND PROBLEMS

Number and Classification of Civil Servants

THE broadening and deepening of the range of government activities in the last hundred years is strikingly reflected in the creation of new executive departments and offices, as outlined in earlier chapters.[1] It is similarly evidenced by the growth of the civil service. In 1832 the total number of civil servants —counting all members of administrative and clerical staffs, including postal officials, but excluding laborers (for whom there are no figures)—was 21,305.[2] By 1851 the figure had risen to 39,147, and by 1891, to 79,241; in 1914, on the eve of the World War, it was 280,900; in 1922, after a considerable decline from the peak reached during the war, it was 317,721; at the present day it fluctuates around 300,000.[3] Of this latest total, upwards of two-thirds are employed in carrying on the varied operations of the Post Office; of the remaining third, approximately half are engaged in work in and about Whitehall, the focal center of the administrative system, and the other half are in service elsewhere throughout the country and in foreign lands.

In earlier days little or no attempt was made to group the members of the civil service into definite classes. After 1870, however, it became necessary to distinguish between the higher posts, involving discretionary powers and requiring a thorough education, and inferior positions involving only work of a

[1] Chaps. viii-ix.

[2] To avert possible confusion, the reader may be reminded that only the national civil service is under discussion here. On the "municipal service," as Englishmen commonly term the employees of counties and boroughs, see pp. 659, 669 below.

[3] These figures are only approximate, but they serve for purposes of comparison. Laborers would add about 125,000 to the present-day figures. They, however, do not belong to the civil service proper.

clerical nature; and gradually a scheme of classification into first or higher division clerks, second division clerks, assistant clerks, boy clerks, and women clerks was worked out, although promotion from one class to another was rare and the articulation of the different parts of the system was generally unsatisfactory. A reorganization which was definitely in prospect at the time when the World War broke out was naturally delayed; but it was actively undertaken in 1918, and by 1922 it had been carried out in most of the important departments. A description of the classification now prevailing would be excessively technical for our purposes. Suffice it to say that the present classes are: (1) an administrative class, corresponding to the old first division, open alike to men and women, and recruited both by competitive examination and by promotion; (2) an executive class, doing the work of the supply and accounting departments and of other executive or specialized branches of the service, and recruited normally by promotion; (3) a clerical class, covering the lower range of the old second class, with the addition of the assistant clerks and the boy clerks, and subdivided into (a) the higher clerical class and (b) the clerical class proper; (4) a writing assistant class, recruited only from women, and engaged in copying, filing, addressing, counting, and other simple and largely mechanical work; and (5) a class of typists and shorthand typists, also recruited exclusively from women and girls.[4] Each class has a prescribed salary scale and definite standards for pay increase and promotion.

"The present organization of the civil service," writes the leading English authority on the subject, "is marked by three outstanding characteristics: Treasury control to unify and coördinate the work and organization of the departments; the Civil Service Commissioners as the creators and custodians of standards of efficiency; and the attempted connection between the ages at which the various grades of the service are recruited and the educational system of the country."[5] At least two of these phases or factors call for a few words of comment.

[4] There are certain other special groups, but the above is the regular classification.

[5] H. Finer, *The British Civil Service*, 26.

Treasury Control

The Treasury, as we have seen, exercises a thoroughgoing control over all of the executive departments in the matter of expenditure of money. This alone would enable it to reach down into the departments and wield substantial influence over their organization, activities, and relations. As if this were not enough, however, the consolidating order in council of 1920 authorizes this "purse-holding *pater familias*" of the governmental system to "make regulations for controlling the conduct of His Majesty's civil establishments, and providing for the classification, remuneration, and other conditions of service of all persons employed therein, whether permanently or temporarily," even to the extent of approving the conditions of admission to the service as laid down by the Civil Service Commissioners. The upshot is that practically every phase of civil service organization and activity is subject to whatever and as much control as the Treasury cares to exert, save only the matter of discipline, which is left to the departments. The Permanent Secretary of the Treasury is, indeed, known as the "head of the civil service." Technically, this is a misnomer; for in earlier times each of several Treasury divisions supervised a number of the departments, and since 1919 the work has been centralized in a new so-called establishment department, headed by a comptroller and deputy-comptroller of establishments. Whatever the immediate arrangement for the exercise of it, Treasury control is a very real and effective thing. Until a few years ago there was nothing in the United States to compare with it. Nowadays, however, the Bureau of the Budget—loosely attached to the Treasury Department—wields considerable authority of a similar character.[6]

[6] H. Finer, *The British Civil Service*, 26-32. It should be added that under the present form of organization in Britain each department has special "establishment" officers who look after its civil service conditions and needs and, when any change involving expenditure is contemplated, take up the matter with the Establishment officers of the Treasury. The control of the Treasury over the civil service is described at some length in T. L. Heath, *The Treasury*, Chap. x. On the relation of the American national budget bureau to appropriations, see H. P. Seidemann, "The Preparation of the National Budget," *Annals of Amer. Acad. of Polit. and Soc. Sci.*, May, 1924.

The Civil Service Commission

The pioneer order in council of 1855 created a central board of examiners of three members, and to this day the authority which makes and executes rules for entry into the service has been His Majesty's Civil Service Commissioners, commonly referred to simply as "the Commissioners," or the Civil Service Commission. The commissioners still number three, and are usually persons of long practical experience in the service. Appointed by the crown—which in practice means by order in council after the cabinet has duly consulted with the higher Treasury officials—they hold office "during His Majesty's pleasure;" and so strong is the desire that they shall be free from political interference that they are not made subordinate or answerable to any minister or department. This does not mean that in the performance of its work the Commission is completely exempt from outside influence. On the contrary, as was indicated above, the Treasury shares the rule-making power; indeed, it has the last word in case of dispute. In practice, however, the Treasury's function—so far as recruitment is concerned—is one of coöperation rather than compulsion, and the Commission's acts and decisions are never questioned or overruled. These acts and decisions are indeed subject to review by judicial process, on the ground, principally, of reasonableness. But there is neither partisan dictation nor administrative control.

The most recent official definition of the duties of the Commission is contained in the order in council of 1920 already cited.[7] In summary, they are: (1) to "approve" the qualifications of "all persons [8] proposed to be appointed, whether permanently or temporarily, to any situation or employment in any of His Majesty's civil establishments," (2) to make regulations prescribing the manner in which persons are to be admitted to the civil establishments and the conditions on which the commissioners may issue certificates of qualification; and (3) to publish in the *London Gazette* notice of all appointments and promotions with respect to which certificates of qualifications are issued. On the strength of these grants of

[7] Especially §§ 2-5.

[8] With certain stipulated exceptions.

power (and earlier ones which they incorporated) the Commission has built up, and administers from day to day, an elaborate and marvellously effective system of civil service examinations and of rules for promotion. Although it is only an examining agency, the volume of its work is impressively large. During the calendar year 1927 it dealt with some 50,000 candidates (of whom almost 43,000 were given formal examinations), and 16,540 positions were filled with persons certified by it.[9]

Recruitment—Civil Service Examinations

It must not be supposed that a single method of recruitment is employed for all branches and grades of the service. Quite the contrary. In the first place, tests may be applied (1) by written examination, in which, however, there may be an oral element, (2) by interview, the candidate conversing with a board of examiners, or (3) by a composite or mixed method under which personality is judged by means of interview and knowledge by written examination. In the second place, the competition may be held under regulations made by the Civil Service Commission and be open to all candidates who possess the qualifications laid down in the regulations; or it may be held under conditions prescribed by a department and restricted to candidates selected in advance by the department. In the third place, the candidates may be seeking initial entrance into the service; or they may be already serving in an established capacity, and merely in quest of promotion. To describe, one by one, the modes and processes employed in handling all of the types of cases arising from these various situations would lead us into an excess of technicality and detail, and it must

[9] *Report of His Majesty's Civil Service Commissioners on the Year 1927* (London, 1928), 3, 27-29. By way of comparison, it may be noted that in the fiscal year ending June 30, 1927, the United States Civil Service Commission examined 267,340 persons, and 46,534 received appointment. The United States commission, like most of the state civil service commissions, has a good deal to do with general personnel administration. The tendency seems to be, however, toward transferring all functions except those connected with examination from the Civil Service Commission to the agency of fiscal control. This would mean an arrangement broadly similar to the English. In Massachusetts the civil service commission has already become, as in Britain, merely an examining agency.

suffice to call attention principally to certain general characteristics of the examination system, especially as applied in those parts of the service in which recruitment is most fully under the Commission's control.

Great changes have taken place in English civil service examinations since the time when Anthony Trollope was admitted to the secretariat of the Post Office on the basis of a test which consisted in copying out a leading article from a newspaper, in the course of which he misspelled several words and finally dropped a blot on the manuscript. Furthermore, the English method of examining for admission to the service is very different from the American. In this country, candidates are tested almost exclusively to find out how well they are qualified to perform the duties of the particular position or type of position which they seek. There is one examination for people who are interested in becoming letter-carriers, another for those who would like a job at bookkeeping, and so on all the way round. The examinations are concrete, practical, non-academic; and to the average American it seems entirely natural and proper that they should be so. The English examinations, however, aim, not at finding out how well an applicant could presumably discharge the duties of a given post if he were appointed to it tomorrow, but at measuring his intellectual equipment and general ability. Thus, candidates for higher clerkships are given the same examination, whether they propose to seek employment in the Treasury, in the Foreign Office, or in the Admiralty. The subjects in which they are examined are distinctly academic—including, in varying combinations, history, mathematics, ancient and modern languages, philosophy, economics, political science, natural science, and others—and are drawn almost entirely from the realm of the liberal, as opposed to the technical, studies. And the questions are of a sort which ordinarily can be answered only by an upper-group university graduate; indeed, most of them are furnished by Oxford, Cambridge, and other university professors.[10] It is true that there are examinations for lower grades of the service which are easy enough to be passed by persons with a good secondary-school education; yet even they

[10] Specimen sets of questions are given in R. Moses, *op. cit.,* 294-305.

are of an academic rather than a "practical" nature.[11] A thorough university training which will ripen natural ability and develop administrative aptitudes is regarded as almost indispensable for members of the upper ranks of the service.

The English view of the matter is that it is desirable to get into the service people who, although they may at the moment know little or nothing about the duties of any particular position, nevertheless have education and capacity that will enable them to rise from lower to higher positions and to become increasingly useful servants of the state. Such people can be trusted to pick up in a very short time a sufficient knowledge of the special work with which they are to start. The main concern is that they be the sort that will prove capable of going on, some of them up to the under-secretaryships and other important offices which the British permanent service includes.[12] From this it follows that much emphasis is placed upon the civil service as a career. Rarely is it entered today except by persons who have decided to make it a life work, who have accordingly subjected themselves to the arduous discipline involved in carrying out the necessary preparations, and who come to the service as young men (they must be not more than twenty-four years of age [13]) who have looked to this alone, and

[11] For example, in a recent examination for the post of "female telegraphist," the candidates were asked to give an account of the reign of Alfred the Great, to compare the times of Elizabeth and Victoria, to discourse on ocean currents, and to compute algebraically the area of the face of a penny.

[12] "It would no doubt be possible to construct a scheme of examination comprising only subjects directly useful in the Home Office, another such for the India Civil Service, another for the Foreign Office, and so forth. But . . . the examination should continue to be a test of general rather than specialized ability and education. . . . We consider that the best qualification for a civil servant is a good natural capacity trained by a rational and consistent education from childhood to maturity. . . . We do not wish candidates to adapt their education to the examination; on the contrary, the examination should be adapted to the chief forms of general education." *Report of the Committee Appointed by the Lords Commissioners of His Majesty's Treasury,* Cmd. 8657 (1917). See E. M. Sait and D. P. Barrows, *British Politics in Transition,* 64-65.

[13] The age required for admission to the administrative class is twenty-two to twenty-four, and to the minor classes, variously from fifteen to twenty.

not as middle-aged persons who have tried a number of other things and failed.

There is something to be said, of course, for both the American and British systems. The American is more democratic; it exacts little of the beginner in the way of knowledge, and it affords a haven for men and women of all ages who are attracted by its pecuniary rewards, modest though they are. This, however, is about all that can be said for it. The British system is less democratic. But it attracts to the public service men and women who, on the average, not only are younger and more energetic than American appointees but far better fitted by education, and probably native capacity as well, to become progressively able, useful, and responsible officials. The American service is crowded with people who are perhaps adequately qualified for the clerical work that they do—and which they will keep on doing to the end of their days—but lamentably barren of material suitable for such higher posts as bureau chief and assistant secretary. It is a rare thing here for a university graduate to take a civil service examination.[14]

Promotion, Tenure, Pay, Pensions

A corollary of the principle that new appointees to the service shall be persons of demonstrated capacity for growth is the consideration that the way must be kept open for them to mount in the scale as experience fits them for more important duties. This means a scheme of promotions conceived in the best interests of efficiency and morale. Under the English system, promotion is not by examination, and (except in a few cases in which recertification of the promoted officer or endorsement of his existing certificate is required) the Civil Service Commission has nothing to do with the matter. In the higher grade of the administrative class, including all posts paying over £900 a year, promotion is at the discretion of the head of the department. Elsewhere it is controlled mainly by a departmental promotion board, consisting normally of the chief establishment officer or his deputy, the head of the sub-department in which the vacancy occurs, and one or more other

[14] Except as candidates for a relatively small number of technical positions.

departmental officers of standing and experience designated by the department head.[15] In connection with all posts falling in groups lower than the one mentioned, the staff itself, through the agency of the departmental Whitley council,[16] has the right to "make representations."

As is suggested by the term "permanent civil service," non-political officers and employees, once appointed, remain in the public employ until they die, resign, are removed for misbehavior, or are retired. Legally, it is true, tenure is precarious. Every member of the service is employed only "during the king's pleasure;" so far as the law goes, any official or employee can be dismissed at any time with no reasons assigned, or, so far as that goes, for very frankly admitted reasons of personal animosity or partisan disfavor; and, once discharged, a civil servant has no case in the courts for wrongful dismissal and damages. As was pointed out in the preceding chapter, however, promiscuous removals never became the fashion, even when the abuse of patronage was at its height; and the custom which protects an official nowadays in the right to be kept in the service during good behavior is as scrupulously observed as any law on the subject could possibly be. Nothing would sooner discredit a ministry than any manifestation of a disposition to tamper with the securities and immunities of the permanent service.

A difficult but fundamental problem in any civil service system is that of pay. What shall be the relation between the rate of pay for civil servants and for persons engaged in comparable work in private employ? How shall a scale be arrived at which will be fair as between class and class within the service, and fair also to the taxpayers who must carry the burden? There was a time when the bulk of the state's work was done by persons who secured their positions through patronage, who were frequently incompetent and negligent, and who—however they actually fared in particular cases—could hardly be regarded as having a claim to compensation on a basis fixed by market demand. Nowadays, however, the state seeks out the best talent available, competing for it with the professions and

[15] H. Finer, *The British Civil Service,* 59.
[16] See p. 235 below.

with private employers, and must expect to pay in strict accordance with the value of the work done or services rendered.

Mere acceptance of this situation does not solve the problem. On the one hand, civil servants are virtually assured of permanent employment; they have ample opportunities for promotion; they have a dignified connection and are shielded from certain of the casualties of private employment. On the other hand, they are subject to special rules of decorum; they are denied some of the privileges enjoyed by other citizens, chiefly in the direction of political activity; they have no chance to acquire riches at an early age, or indeed at all; once in the service, they cannot leave it without sacrifice of their superannuation rights, or, having left it, return to it except under the most unusual circumstances. The principle which controls in the shaping of British policy on the subject is, in brief, that the state—like any other employer—must "pay whatever is necessary to recruit and to retain an efficient staff." [17] This means that, on the average, the pay must be a little better than in the general run of employments outside the service, and that it must be continuously adjustable to changing economic conditions. Since 1920, indeed, the whole system of pay has been a pre-war base rate, to which is added a bonus rising or falling with the cost of living. In this manner the scale has been kept reasonably close to that prevailing in private industry. As a model employer, the state, said the committee quoted above, "offers security, a pension, a dignified service, and a moderate wage in exchange for the excitement and possibilities of private employment." [18]

Retirement and retirement allowances, or pensions, are regulated on larger lines by acts of Parliament, but in all details by the Treasury, and the system is administered by Treasury commissioners.[19] The normal retirement age is sixty; retirement on pension can take place before that age only upon

[17] These are the words of a special committee on pay in the civil service, reporting in 1923.

[18] Available material on the government's practice in regulating scales of pay is assembled and discussed in E. C. Shepherd, *The Fixing of Wages in Government Employment* (London, 1923).

[19] The principal statutes date from 1834, 1859, and 1909. See *Civil Service: Digest of Pension Law and Regulations* (1924).

presentation of a certificate of physical or mental unfitness; at that age any one may retire who desires to do so; at sixty-five, relinquishment of one's post is compulsory unless the Treasury allows an extension up to a maximum of five years. The pension system has had a checkered history since the earliest general provisions on the subject were made in 1810. During two lengthy periods pensions were contributory; that is to say, the prospective pensioner was required to contribute some fixed proportion of his salary toward the expense of the system, as are employees of the national government of the United States today.[20] At present, the contributory principle, so far as the law goes, does not enter into the plan, though employees have long contended that in effect it does so inasmuch as (so they quite correctly allege) salaries are lower than they would be if no pension rights existed. No one is entitled to a retirement allowance unless admitted to the service with a Civil Service Commission certificate, or holding an office specially exempted; no pension is due until after ten years' service;[21] and the right to a pension is in all cases subject to Treasury decision and is never enforceable in the courts.[22]

Organization of Public Employees

It is not surprising to find that in these days when organization and coöperative effort count for so much in industry, business, and politics those who have the interests of the civil servants specially at heart are doing all that they can to win for the service a definitely professional status and to empower it, through voluntary organization, to protect itself against parsimony and arbitrariness on the part of its employer, even though that employer be the state. The task is really two-fold, according as it relates to the higher and the lower grades of the

[20] Under a retirement act passed by Congress in 1920 and amended in 1926, three and one-half per cent of the employee's salary is deducted each month and added to the "civil service retirement and disability fund."

[21] Under certain circumstances, a "gratuity" may, however, be allowed.

[22] A serviceable treatment of the general subject will be found in a report by H. D. Brown entitled *Civil Service Retirement in Great Britain,* 61st Cong., 2nd Sess., Sen. Doc. No. 290. The standard work on government pensions is L. Meriam, *Principles Governing the Retirement of Government Employees* (New York, 1918).

service. Members of the former are relatively well paid and are interested broadly in promoting the cause of good administration and in advancing themselves to the level of dignity and prestige enjoyed by the learned professions. They are concerned about the scientific study of administration as an art and have had much to do with promoting the study of sociology, economics, statistics, and other subjects germane to the work of administration in its loftier reaches, and with founding and carrying on such organizations as the Institute of Public Administration.[23] Members of the more purely clerical and manipulative grades of the service, on the other hand, are concerned primarily about matters of salaries, hours, and general working conditions. Their outlook is not necessarily in all cases narrower than that of the others, but by and large they have the labor, as distinguished from the professional, point of view.

The spirit of organization has spread to all ranks, and nowadays considerably more than half of the whole body of civil servants are to be found in one or another of four major associations, as follows: the Civil Service Confederation, with 60,000 members; the Union of Postal Workers, with 90,000; the Institution of Professional Civil Servants, with 10,000; and the Joint Consultative Council, with about the same number. With the exception of the third, these associations are federations of societies whose interests are cognate, the first two comprising the principal organizations of middle and lower grade employees. The right of civil servants to form associations is fully recognized, and until 1927 the right of such associations to affiliate with bodies outside the service was similarly admitted. Until the date mentioned, this latter right was of more than theoretical importance, because the bulk of the civil servants' unions and federations had become affiliated with

[23] This Institute was established in 1923 by a group of civil servants and is open to all persons who have performed responsible governmental work of an executive or administrative character for as much as three years, in Britain or elsewhere in the Empire. It holds conferences, provides lectures, encourages research, and publishes the important quarterly, *Public Administration* (formerly the *Journal of Public Administration*), already cited. See H. G. Comer, "The Aims of the Institute of Public Administration," *Jour. of Public Admin.*, I, 49-55 (1923).

both the Labor party and the Trades Union Congress. For such organizations as the Union of Postal Workers, for instance, such a relationship was altogether natural. Pay and working conditions in the service are governed very largely by the standards prevailing in private employment, and it is to the interest of the government workers to coöperate in any effort of private employees to raise wage levels and improve conditions.

Such alliances, however, raise problems—in particular, that of the right to engage in strikes. The unionizing of government workers has been going on the world over, and the strike question never fails to come up. Various ways of handling it have been adopted. In the United States an act of Congress dating from 1912 recognizes the right of civil service organizations to affiliate with labor unions outside of the service, so long as such relationship does not entail any purpose or obligation to strike. In Germany full rights of association and affiliation are recognized in the national constitution,[24] but again stopping short of the right to strike—even though some strikes have actually taken place. In Britain the general strike of 1926 brought the issue dramatically to the fore, and a great deal of argument, pro and con, took place. The Civil Service Clerical Association—the largest constituent association of the Civil Service Confederation—sounded out its membership by a referendum and elicited a majority opinion that, so far as that organization was concerned, its officers had no power to call out the members on strike and its policy of affiliation could not be construed to involve any obligation to support a strike. Strong demand arose in governmental circles, however, that affiliation of civil servants' organizations with economic groups which accept the principle of the sympathetic strike and the "solidarity of labor" be definitely banned; and the drastic Trade Disputes and Trade Unions Act of 1927 (clause 5) not only prohibited civil servants from being members of any trade union unless the body is confined to persons employed under the crown and is independent of any outside trade union or federation of trade unions, but forbade any civil servant

[24] Art. 130. Cf. Art. 159. See F. F. Blachly and M. E. Oatman, "German Public Officers and the Right to Strike," *Amer. Polit. Sci. Rev.*, Feb., 1928.

organization to be associated, directly or indirectly, with any political party. The measure was strongly opposed by the civil service organizations, and by labor interests generally, as an unnecessarily sweeping action induced by sheer panic. Nevertheless, it prevailed, and all organic relations of the associations with both the Trades Union Congress and the Labor party came to an end. The solution can hardly be regarded as final; at all events, there will be plenty of further discussion of the subject.[25]

Whitley Councils in the Civil Service

A grievance of civil servants often voiced in earlier days was that they had no opportunity to participate in making the rules and determining the conditions under which they worked. They could, it is true, present memorials and petitions, which presumably received respectful attention from department heads and from the Treasury. But there was no provision for systematic discussion of and coöperative action upon civil service matters in joint committees or other agencies representing both officials and staff. This situation has now been remedied by the interesting device of "Whitley councils." In the autumn of 1916, when war-time industry was menaced by exceptionally serious unrest among the workers, a Ministry of Reconstruction committee, with J. H. Whitley (afterwards speaker of the House of Commons) as chairman, was set the task of working out ways of improving the relations of employers and employed; and in the following year a report submitted by this agency was adopted by the cabinet and urged upon employers and work-people alike as embodying a promising plan for the reorganization of industry.[26] The essence of the scheme was a system of national, district, and works councils or committees, to include equal numbers of representatives

[25] See pp. 516-519 below; also H. Finer, *The British Civil Service*, 77-82. The Trades Union Congress, meeting at Edinburgh later in the year, unanimously adopted a resolution vigorously denouncing the new legislation; and Ramsay MacDonald, speaking as leader of the Labor party, pledged the next Labor government to repeal it. On the general subject of civil servants' organizations, see L. D. White, *Introduction to the Study of Public Administration* (New York, 1926), Chap. xvii.

[26] There were, in point of fact, several reports, but the one referred to—commonly termed the Whitley Report—was the most important.

of capital and of labor,[27] and to be charged with "discussion about and adjustment of" industrial conditions, subject to the superior authority of the trade unions and employers' associations. No legislation made the formation of such councils mandatory; the government merely recommended the plan and left operators and workers to adopt it as far as they liked. Speaking generally, the larger industries, such as mining and shipbuilding, did not respond. But "Whitley councils" were set up in numerous lesser ones, such as furniture-making, pottery, and electrical supply.[28]

In the domain of private industry for which it was devised, the system did not work out altogether satisfactorily, and "Whitleyism" now stands somewhat discredited. In the civil service, however,—to which there was originally no intention to apply it—it has taken root and has worked considerable improvement. Impelled by the rising cost of living, and stirred by the plans of the Treasury to substitute an eight-hour for a seven-hour day, the civil servants demanded that they, equally with employees in private industry, be admitted to the benefits of the arrangement; and in 1919, after the committee had made a supplementary report and the cabinet had given its approval, the Whitley system was introduced rather generally throughout the service.[29] The machinery as it now stands consists principally of (1) departmental councils, varying somewhat in character from department to department, but each containing equal numbers of official and staff representatives, and (2) a national council, of fifty-four members, half appointed by the government to form the official side and half by the civil service associations grouped in certain ways.[30] Practically all civil servants are nowadays represented in both

[27] By agreement, representatives of the government also.

[28] S. and B. Webb, *History of Trade Unionism* (2nd ed., London, 1920), 490, 646, etc.

[29] The plan as applied in the civil service was worked out by a National Provisional Joint Committee composed of fifteen members from the official side and fifteen from the staff side. Cmd. 198 (1919).

[30] The official side must contain at least one representative of the Treasury and one of the Ministry of Labor. Provision was made in the plan also for district and office (or works) committees, to operate locally in a government office or establishment, e.g., a munitions factory, and many such have been formed.

departmental and national councils; and in most of the departments, as well as more broadly upon national lines, much useful work has been done. It is the business of the councils to consider matters relating to recruitment, hours, promotion, tenure, discipline, and remuneration; to devise ways of better utilizing the training and experience of the staff; to encourage the further education of staff members; and to propose remedial legislation. Many decisions arrived at can be put into effect by simple council agreement, although naturally some, by their nature, require action by the department head, by the Treasury, or even by Parliament. It is often charged that the official side enjoys the greater power—even that, in some cases, it is arbitrary and despotic. It has the unquestionable advantage of knowing that upon any matter upon which agreement cannot be reached its views will prevail; and, as a recent writer has warned, the employee side, speaking generally, must not expect too much. Ten years of experience with the system has, however, gone far toward substituting for the relationship of master and servant that of copartnership, and has, accordingly, helped greatly to bring the service into a more contented frame of mind.[31]

Defects and Merits of the Civil Service

Students of that increasingly challenging subject, comparative administration, concur in giving the British civil service system an exceptionally high rating. This does not mean that it is perfect; and if evidence were required that Englishmen themselves do not regard it as such, it could readily be found in the repeated official investigations of the system that have been made in the past thirty or forty years.[32] Evidences sometimes

[31] H. Finer, *The British Civil Service,* 83-87; J. H. Macrae-Gibson, *The Whitley System in the Civil Service* (London, 1922); G. H. S. Bunning, "Whitley Councils in the Civil Service," *Jour. of Pub. Admin.,* II, 172-183 (1924). A Civil Service Arbitration Board, which dealt with controversies arising out of claims for increased remuneration made by classes of government employees, was abolished in 1922. But in 1925 arbitration authority of a similar nature was conferred on an Industrial Court established under the Industrial Courts Act of 1919. T. L. Heath, *The Treasury,* 184-185.

[32] Documents embodying the results of the most recent inquiries are: *Fourth Report of the Royal Commission on Civil Service,* Cmd. 7338 (1914); *Report of the Committee Appointed by the Lords Commissioners*

appear that the evils of patronage have not been so completely eradicated as is fondly supposed. The nature and content of the examinations give rise to many protests—some on the ground that there is too much dependence on written tests; some on the charge that by over-stressing the classics and underrating natural science too much advantage is given the graduates of Oxford and Cambridge as against those of Manchester, Leeds, Birmingham, or Liverpool; some on the score that, in spite of systematic effort in that direction, the Civil Service Commission has not succeeded sufficiently in correlating its examinations with corresponding stages in the educational system of the country. There are even those who argue that the disadvantages of the examination system more than counterbalance anything that can be said in its favor.[33] There is the inevitable outcry against "red-tape"—although most people overlook the fact that this term is only the ruddy equivalent of the rule "one man, one job" which long ago gained general, and doubtless proper, acceptance in the world of private industry, and that the constant necessity which rests upon the departments to be prepared, at almost a moment's notice, to furnish their spokesmen in Parliament with the minutest and most exact information on the most inconsequential matters upon which questions may be asked necessarily renders the work of department employees more meticulous, and therefore slower, than it otherwise would be.[34] There is apprehension, too, lest the civil servants, as they become more and more organized and group-conscious, will be increasingly tempted to make use of their power, as unionized employees and as voters, to force unjustifiable legislation concerning pay, hours, pensions, and other matters of interest to them as a class.

Over against these real or fancied deficiencies are to be set many praiseworthy features. Several have been pointed out in

of His Majesty's Treasury, Cmd. 8657 (1917); and *Final Report of the Treasury Committee on Reconstruction of the Civil Service,* Cmd. 164 (1919).

[33] S. Demetriadi, *Inside a Government Office* (London, 1921), Chap. i. For a balanced discussion of the subject, see W. A. Robson, *From Patronage to Proficiency in the Public Service* (London, 1922), 17-27.

[34] M. Murby, "Routine and the Civil Servant," in M. Cary, *et al., The Development of the Civil Service* (London, 1922), 129-163.

preceding paragraphs and do not require to be mentioned again. Three of somewhat more general character may, however, be referred to in closing. The first is the almost uniformly high quality of the men and women attracted to the service. Some are impelled by a sense of civic duty; some are drawn by the prospect of a career in a field in which the way is open for talent and industry, irrespective of family connections; some, no doubt, are appealed to by a profession which promises a steady assured income, without much risk, instead of the worry and competition, the glittering prizes or possible failures, common to the outside world.[35] At all events, it is the universal testimony that the service attracts and holds a splendid body of workers. A second feature, closely related, is the excellent morale which the service displays, and, in particular, the interest in and sense of responsibility for its own improvement which it evidences. The Institute of Public Administration,[36] open to all grades of the service, and aimed at maintaining the high ideals and traditions of which civil servants are justly proud, is but one of the many indications of this spirit.

Finally may be mentioned the fact that the service does not constitute, and is not thought of by Englishmen as constituting, a bureaucracy. In pre-war Germany, the civil servants, while exceptionally efficient, formed, to all intents and purposes, a caste, separated from the rest of the people, acting according to procedures which they themselves created, and obnoxious to liberal elements generally by reason of their arbitrariness, haughtiness, and exclusiveness. Even in republican France, the numerous, highly integrated, and ceremonious administrative servants of the state form somewhat of a class apart and often offend democratic susceptibilities. In this Continental sense of the term, Britain has no bureaucracy. It is true that one can hear complaint on the score that a bureaucracy is, at all events, in the making; within recent times a Lord Chief Justice,[37] moved by the tendencies of the administrative authorities to encroach—by making and applying their

[35] H. Finer, *op. cit.,* 64.
[36] See p. 232, note 23, above.
[37] Lord Hewart.

own interpretations of the laws, as well as by issuing orders—upon the functions of the courts and of Parliament, has announced that he is writing a book upon the bureaucratic sapping of the Englishman's historic liberties. The fact remains, however, that the rank and file of the British civil service are like other men and women: they are recruited from no special classes or cliques; they have the same social and political background, to a steadily increasing degree; they are educated in the same schools and universities. There may be some sacrifice of efficiency. But, as the Englishman sees it, any possible loss at this point is more than offset by the fact that civil servants, of whatever station, are simply "ingredients in a political system in which the calm assurance was long ago planted that the citizen is the master of the Executive." [38]

[38] Finer, *op. cit.*, 10. For a lengthy discussion of the subject, see R. Muir, *Peers and Bureaucrats* (London, 1910), 1-94.

There is no adequate history of the British civil service, but there is much historical material in D. B. Eaton, *Civil Service in Great Britain* (New York, 1880), already cited. R. Moses, *The Civil Service of Great Britain* (New York, 1914), is also largely historical. The best brief description of the present-day system is a Fabian Society publication, i.e., H. Finer, *The British Civil Service* (London, 1927); but A. L. Lowell, *The Government of England,* I, Chap. vii, is by no means wholly obsolete. Another Fabian pamphlet of value is W. A. Robson, *From Patronage to Proficiency in the Public Service* (London, 1922). W. Beveridge, *The Public Service in War and Peace* (London, 1920), can be read with profit. M. Cary *et al.*, *The Development of the Civil Service* (London, 1922), contains a dozen suggestive lectures delivered before the Society of Civil Servants. F. G. Heath, *The British Civil Service; Colonial, Indian, and Diplomatic* (White Plains, 1917), is a popular account by a former civil servant; and an important book on a single phase of the subject is A. L. Lowell and H. M. Stephens, *Colonial Civil Service; the Selection and Training of Colonial Officers in England, Holland, and France* (New York, 1900). *The Journal of Public Administration,* published monthly by the Institute of Public Administration, is the best medium through which to keep abreast of current discussion. The annual reports of the Civil Service Commissioners are brief but informing.

The national civil service of the United States is described briefly in F. A. Ogg and P. O. Ray, *Introduction to American Government* (3rd ed.), Chap. xviii. Among extended works, mention may be made of L. Mayers, *The Federal Service* (New York, 1921); C. R. Fish, *The Civil Service and the Patronage* (New York, 1904); S. Spero, *The Labor Movement in a Government Industry; a Study of Employee Organization in the Postal Service* (New York, 1924); and, for a general treatment of administration, W. F. Willoughby, *Principles of Public Administration* (Baltimore, 1927).

CHAPTER XII

THE HOUSE OF COMMONS—CONSTITUENCIES AND VOTERS

On the left bank of the Thames, midway between Chelsea Bridge and the Tower, stands the largest and most impressive Gothic structure in the world, the Palace of Westminster; and within its massive walls sits, appropriately enough, the oldest, largest, most powerful, and most interesting of modern legislatures. Not only is the British Parliament [1] the principal instrumentality of popular government in one of the most democratic of states; it is, in a very real sense, the "mother of parliaments," whose progeny has spread into every civilized quarter of the globe. Much has been written in these last fifteen or twenty years about the decline in prestige and efficiency which this parliamentary assemblage, in common with legislative bodies elsewhere, is alleged to have undergone; [2] and critics propose all manner of changes in it, ranging from mere amendment of the rules of procedure to drastic reorganizations in structure and powers—changes aimed at a better adaptation of the body to the new conditions of a twentieth-century world.[3] Probably there has been a falling-off in effectiveness since the simpler days of Gladstone and Disraeli, and unquestionably there has been loss of prestige. Nevertheless, it is a habit of men, Englishmen included, to find fault with governmental institutions which they in reality cherish, and no balanced observer would for a moment be deluded into thinking

[1] Formerly, the "Parliament of the United Kingdom of Great Britain and Ireland," but nowadays, under enactment of April 12, 1927, the "Parliament of Great Britain and Northern Ireland." For corresponding change of the style and title of the sovereign, see p. 100 above.

[2] See Chap. xix below.

[3] F. A. Ogg, "New Tests of Representative Government," *University of Chicago Record,* XI, 270-279 (Oct., 1925).

of the parliament that sits at Westminster as a mere outworn relic of the past, or as in any absolute sense in decay or eclipse. No legislature will better repay the attention devoted to it by the student of political science, and this by reason of what it now is quite as much as on account of what it has been.

How Parliament originated and developed into its present form has been explained in earlier chapters: how its antecedents reach back deep into the Middle Ages;[4] how it became bicameral in the fourteenth century and gained substantial control of finance and legislation in the fifteenth; how it wrested supreme authority over the country's affairs from the king in the days of Hampden, Cromwell, and John Locke; how it ripened in the eighteenth century, and, in what came to be its more important branch, was reconstructed to meet changed conditions and ideas in the nineteenth. We turn now to a somewhat extended study of the remarkable institution as it stands today—first, to the composition of the two houses and the bases on which they rest, with such allusion as is necessary to the way in which present conditions came to be, and especially to structural and functional problems still awaiting solution; afterwards, to matters of organization and procedure, especially in the more active and important House of Commons; and, finally, to the interrelations and balance of forces, whether entirely within Parliament or partly outside, that go to make the working governmental system what it is—together with some of the larger questions about parliamentary government which Englishmen looking out upon the next fifty or seventy-five years are earnestly discussing. We begin with the House of Commons, not only because of the primacy which that body now enjoys in the constitutional order, but because the position, functions, and problems of the House of Lords cannot be understood until the nature of the popular chamber has been brought fully into view.

"When," once wrote Spencer Walpole, "a minister consults Parliament he consults the House of Commons; when the

[4] It is only fair to recall that the Hungarian Table (later Chamber) of Magnates had a continuous history from the sixteenth century to the collapse of the Austro-Hungarian political system in 1918, and that the Swedish Riksdag celebrated its five-hundredth anniversary in 1926.

Queen dissolves Parliament she dissolves the House of Commons. A new Parliament is simply a new House of Commons." [5] This is merely an epigrammatic way of saying that the leadership, power, and prestige of the House of Commons are such that for many purposes—though assuredly not for all—Parliament and the House of Commons are one and the same thing. It is the development of the House of Commons that has given Britain political democracy; and it is for the reason that—since the stripping of veto powers from the House of Lords by the Parliament Act of 1911—any measure, financial or otherwise (with very slight exceptions) can be made law by the unilateral action of the House of Commons, the people have it in their power, through their elected representatives, to accomplish any reform or other result of which legislation is capable, including any conceivable amendment of the constitution itself. We have said that, so far as legal restrictions are concerned, Parliament is omnipotent. Slight violence will be done to the truth if instead of "Parliament" we write "House of Commons." There were once reasons for calling the Commons the "lower house." Needless to say, it is such no longer, except in the relatively unimportant sense that its members are likely to be inferior in the social scale to the members of the so-called "upper" chamber. It is hardly necessary, too, to suggest that the tremendous influence exerted by English parliamentary institutions throughout the world has flowed almost exclusively from the House of Commons, or at all events from the relations of that body to other parts of the governmental system.

Parliamentary Constituencies

The outstanding fact about the House of Commons, considered structurally, is that all of its 615 members are elected, and all but twelve are chosen by voters grouped in constituencies arranged on a geographical basis. Representation on functional (as contrasted with geographical) lines, though existing in a very real sense in the House of Lords and strongly advocated by guild socialists and others for the House of Commons, finds legal recognition only in the election of a dozen "univer-

[5] *The Electorate and the Legislature* (London, 1892), 48.

sity members" by degree-holders of certain institutions of higher learning. More than six hundred members sit for definite territorial areas, just as do American congressmen.

These constituencies, or districts,[6] are in all cases counties, boroughs, or subdivisions thereof. Long before Parliament arose, counties and boroughs were the accepted community units for judicial, fiscal, and administrative purposes, and it was natural enough that they should become the areas for national, parliamentary representation. Until late in the nineteenth century, they were employed for the purpose practically without subdivision, each county and borough, as a whole, returning a stipulated quota of members—which in the great majority of cases (in England proper, at all events), and regardless of size or population, was two. Attempts to apportion representation to population in a more exact manner have led within the past fifty or sixty years to the cutting up of almost all counties and of a considerable number of boroughs into smaller electoral areas, laid out with a good deal of regard for historical boundaries, administrative divisions, and physical features, yet necessarily more or less arbitrary and artificial, and comprising groups of people combined for electoral purposes only. Just as congressional districts in the United States never cut across state boundaries, so British parliamentary districts are commonly contained wholly within a single county or borough.[7] Whereas, however, our congressional districts in any given state are known merely by number, every British constituency has a distinct name, e.g., the borough of Bradford, the Central Division of Portsmouth, or the East Grinstead Division of Sussex.[8]

[6] Speaking strictly, a "constituency" is a body of people represented, while a "district" is a territorial unit. The former term is commonly employed in Britain, the latter in America. For practical purposes the two may be used interchangeably.

[7] Exceptions arise when, for example, a municipal borough takes in new territory or otherwise alters its boundaries, because such changes have no effect upon the boundaries of "parliamentary" boroughs.

[8] It should be noted that the counties that figure in connection with parliamentary elections are the old historic counties, not the new administrative counties created in 1888. See pp. 651 ff. below. A map of parliamentary county divisions will be found in G. Philip, *Handy Administrative Atlas of England and Wales* (London, 1928), Plate 5. Plate 6 in the same book shows

A main reason for this partitioning was the triumph of the principle of single-member districts. When the first reform act was passed, in 1832, Welsh counties and boroughs were returning one member each, and Scottish boroughs were arranged in groups which, with few exceptions, also returned one member apiece. But, aside from five boroughs with one member each, and the county of Yorkshire and the City of London [9] with four each, all counties and boroughs of England proper had two. The act mentioned increased the number of single-member constituencies in England by taking away one seat from each of thirty-one less populous boroughs; and although the Reform Act of 1867 moved somewhat in the opposite direction by giving thirteen constituencies three members each, the Redistribution Act of 1885 definitely adopted the single-member plan, breaking all of the counties, and all of the multiple-member boroughs except twenty-three, into areas returning one member only. Today the only remaining multiple-member districts are twelve boroughs and the City of London, all with two members each.[10] Many present-day schemes of electoral reform look to a nation-wide revival of multiple-member constituencies; any system of proportional representation would, of course, require such a change. But the single-member plan is still in general use.

The one distinctly irregular feature in the present make-up of the House is the representation of the universities. This device dates from 1603, when, in answer to prolonged demand, Oxford and Cambridge were given the privilege of returning two members each, on the theory that they were affected by so many parliamentary enactments that they deserved to have special means of making themselves heard. Dublin was at the same time given a representative in the Irish House of Commons, this representative being transferred to Westminster when the Union went into operation (1801), and another being

the location of parliamentary boroughs. There are also volumes for Scotland and Ireland in the Philip series. On the disadvantages of the plan of division, see Ramsay MacDonald, *Socialism; Critical and Constructive,* 253.

[9] See p. 674 below.

[10] Four of the seven university constituencies, however, also return more than one member. See p. 245, note 13, below. There are, in all, 595 constituencies.

added in 1832.[11] The Reform Act of 1867 gave one seat to London University, one to Glasgow and Aberdeen combined, and one similarly to Edinburgh and St. Andrews. Finally, in 1918 a total of fifteen seats were distributed among university constituencies—although the setting up of the Irish Free State in 1922 led to the abolition of three,[12] leaving the number at the present figure, i.e., twelve.[13] University members are chosen, under a scheme of proportional representation, by registered degree-holders.[14]

Number and Distribution of Members

The Parliament that sits at Westminster is, of course, more than merely an English parliament in the narrower sense of the term; it is the Parliament of Great Britain and Northern Ireland. It became, indeed, the Parliament of the United Kingdom through the bringing in of representatives of the Welsh counties in the reign of Henry VIII, the abandonment of a separate Scottish parliament in favor of representation of the north country at Westminster in 1707, and a similar step taken for Ireland at the end of the eighteenth century. While still upon that basis, its membership, which had stood at 670 since 1885, was raised in 1918 to 707. Upon the establishment of the Irish Free State in 1922, however, all Irish representation ceased except in the case of the half-dozen northern counties which retained their close affiliation with Great Britain; and this change—reducing the Irish quota at a stroke from 105 to thirteen—brought the total number of members down to the present level, i.e., 615, of whom 492 sit for English constituencies, 36 for Welsh,[15] 74 for Scottish, and 13, as has been said, for Irish. Even so, the body is still the most numerous popular chamber in the world. Until the dropping out of the ninety-two Irish members, most of whom represented rural districts,

[11] On early university representation, see E. Porritt, *The Unreformed House of Commons* (2nd ed., Cambridge, 1909), I, Chap. v.

[12] Dublin's two and the National University's one.

[13] The list is as follows: Oxford, 2; Cambridge, 2; London, 1; combined English provincial universities, 2; Wales, 1; combined Scottish universities, 3; Queen's (Belfast), 1.

[14] See p. 274 below.

[15] Strictly, for Wales and Monmouthshire.

county representatives preponderated; since that time there has been an almost exact balance between county and borough members, i.e., 300 of the one and 303 of the other. The ancient legal distinction between "knights of the shire" and "burgesses of the borough" was, however, abolished by the Ballot Act of 1872, and so-called "rural" and "urban" constituencies are in so many cases practically indistinguishable in populational conditions and other respects that the classification is of slight significance. Officially, all representatives are now known simply as "members of the House of Commons." All except the university members are chosen at the same time, in the same way, and (since 1918) by the same suffrage. All have the same rights, privileges, and powers, except that the Scottish members always have places on that standing committee of the House to which measures specially affecting their portion of the realm are referred.[16]

The constitution of the United States requires a reapportionment of seats in the House of Representatives after every decennial census; in France there is such a redistribution every five years; most countries, indeed,—including the British dominions—have definite rules of the kind. The object, of course, is to keep electoral units (in terms of the number of voters) substantially equal, so that a vote will count for as much in one place as in another; and such equality—at least a reasonable approximation of it—seems to a good many people a rather indispensable condition of true democracy. Curiously, there has never been a law on the subject in Britain, nor does custom impose any definite requirements; and history shows that redistributions have taken place at very irregular intervals, as hardly more than incidents of widely separated suffrage extensions and other electoral reforms. The only reapportionments in

[16] See p. 390 below. The present membership of the House classifies as follows:

	County Members	Borough Members	University Members	Total
England	230	255 *	7	492
Wales and Monmouthshire	24	11	1	36
Scotland	38	33	3	74
North Ireland	8	4	1	13
Total	300	303	12	615

* Including 2 for the City of London, which is not technically a borough.

three hundred years that aimed at even approximately uniform constituencies were those of 1885 and 1918, described below, and they were made only after conditions had become shockingly bad, and with no anticipatory provision to prevent an equally unsatisfactory situation from arising again with the lapse of time. Infrequent redistributions reduce the opportunity for what is known in America as gerrymandering. But experience shows that the English habit of fair play can usually be depended upon to hold this abuse in check, and the long periods between reapportionments leave the constituencies much of the time decidedly unequal and, besides, tend to raise every apportionment, of even the simplest sort, to the level of a constitutional issue freshly to be threshed out, with much effort and delay, by the politicians and voters.[17]

The House of Commons as an Elective Body

The matters thus far spoken of are important to an understanding of the sort of body the House of Commons is, yet they are more or less incidental to the main topic of this and the succeeding chapter, i.e., the nomination and election of members. For the fundamental fact about the chamber is that it is a representative body, and its character is determined mainly by the people who choose its members—who and how many they are, and how they go about the task. What, then, of the suffrage? How do men and women become candidates? What qualifications must they have? How do they and their friends appeal to the voters? What form do the elections take, and how are the people's votes cast, counted, and recorded? To what extent does the House merit the description of "popular," and to what degree does the prevailing system satisfy various shades of political opinion? A vast amount of political and constitutional history is wrapped up in these questions, for Englishmen have been electing members of Parliament for more than six hundred years—to take no account of still earlier

[17] A definite arrangement for periodic redistribution has, of course, been advocated, e.g., by J. King, in *Electoral Reform* (London, 1908), 31-33. The failure of the Congress of the United States to make a reapportionment on the basis of the census of 1920 may be cited to show that periodic redistribution, even under constitutional provision, does not always actually work.

electoral activities of other sorts—and suffrage, nominations, canvassing, polling, electoral expenditures, contested seats, and other processes and practices have all of this time been developing on the devious lines that have brought them to their present status. The story of this development has been told in full elsewhere [18] and cannot be repeated here. A few of its more recent aspects must, however, be recalled as we go along, if we are to see how present arrangements and usages came to be what they are.

Electoral Conditions Before 1832

Aside from the university constituencies (which may for the moment be left out of account), the rules determining who may vote for members of the House of Commons are now the same in all parts of the land. That is, a man or woman must meet identical requirements, whether in England or Scotland, in town or in country. This was not always true. Indeed, it has been true only since 1918. Until this very recent date, there were county franchises and borough franchises, i.e., one set of requirements in one class of constituencies and another set in another, so that whether or not a man could vote might depend entirely on where he lived. In fact, in the boroughs there were, until 1832, almost as many different suffrage systems as places in which members were voted for. This state of things arose out of the fact that in medieval and early modern times shire, or county, representation was regarded as one thing and borough representation as quite another, coupled with the further fact that the boroughs were more or less the playthings of the crown, a borough being now admitted to representation and now debarred from it, and subjected to electoral regulations or not as circumstances determined in the particular case.[19]

It appears that originally the "knights of the shire," i.e., the representatives of the counties, were chosen by the freeholders assembled in the county court, and that—the election being by

[18] Notably in E. Porritt, *Unreformed House of Commons,* Vol. I for England, Vol. II for Scotland and Ireland.

[19] The creation of parliamentary boroughs by royal writ—always one of the most dangerous prerogatives of the crown—came to an end in the reign of Charles II. Newark, which attained the dignity of a parliamentary borough in 1677, was the last instance of the kind.

acclamation rather than a count of votes—few men who sought to participate were ever challenged. This state of things, however, did not last long, for in 1430, in the reign of Henry VI, a statute was passed restricting the county franchise to such male residents as possessed "free land or tenement" which would rent for as much as forty shillings a year above all charges. The object was said to be to prevent riotous and disorderly elections. However that may be, the effect was greatly to narrow the county electorate; for although forty shillings does not sound like a large sum today, in early modern times it represented a present purchasing value of perhaps forty pounds. Even in the fifteenth and sixteenth centuries the number of forty-shilling freeholders was not large. With the concentration of land in fewer hands, resulting from the agrarian revolution of the eighteenth and early nineteenth centuries,[20] it bore a steadily decreasing ratio to the total county population, being by 1832, when the county electorate in all England and Wales numbered hardly a quarter of a million, rather less than one to thirty-five.

If the definition of the qualifying freehold in the counties kept the lawyers busy (no fewer than 570 different kinds of freeholders were finally discovered!), the medley of franchises that grew up in the boroughs defied all analysis or classification. At the outset the theory was, as in the counties, that every freeman had a right to vote. But here also restrictions were set up which caused the actually existing arrangements to grow steadily less democratic; and whereas in respect to the counties there was at least a general statute, however susceptible of unexpected interpretations, very nearly every borough was a law unto itself, its suffrage arrangements being determined by the provisions of its charter, or by parliamentary enactment, or by local legislation, or merely by custom. We hear, indeed, of certain categories or types, e.g., "scot and lot" boroughs, "potwalloper" boroughs, burgage boroughs, corporation or "close" boroughs, and "freeman" boroughs. But the classification was not exact, and definitions would be wearisome. In some boroughs the suffrage was still reasonably democratic

[20] F. A. Ogg and W. R. Sharp, *Economic Development of Modern Europe* (rev. ed., 1926), Chap. vi.

when the nineteenth century dawned; in others it was tending to become so. But in the great majority it was confined to certain kinds of property-holders or taxpayers, to members of the municipal corporation, or even to members of a favored guild or industrial organization; and although there are no trustworthy statistics on the subject, it is fair to assume that on the average fewer people could vote in the boroughs than in the counties.[21]

Another extraordinary feature of the electoral system when the nineteenth century opened was the ill-adjustment of representation to population. We have seen that Britain has never had any rule requiring periodic redistribution of seats, and in point of fact, except for the addition of the Scottish and Irish members in 1707 and 1801 respectively, there were very few changes of apportionment from the time of Charles II to 1832—none at all of a general, nation-wide character. Regardless of population, every county continued to have its two members (in Wales, one), and likewise almost every represented borough. In earlier days nobody even thought of equal electoral districts. Parliament had little power, and representation was not highly valued, especially in the boroughs. By the middle of the seventeenth century, however, the control of votes in the House of Commons was coming to be a treasured privilege, and men began to take note of the grossly disproportionate legislative and financial power wielded by some counties and boroughs in comparison with others.

Instead of any relief being applied, the situation went from bad to worse for almost two hundred years. Some counties gained in population, others stood stationary, still others declined. Boroughs, as is natural with urban communities, showed even greater variation. Some decayed and became, as Burke said, "the merest villages whose streets can only be

[21] The exercise of the borough franchise was attended by many quaint practices, not to say subterfuges. Thus the potwalloper, or "pot-boiler," who qualified as being a man who had premises in which food could be cooked, might sometimes, as late as the eighteenth century, be seen on the eve of an election dining on a table set in the street in front of his house as a means of showing that he was self-sustaining and entitled to vote. If his house burned down, he could at least keep the chimney standing and at a suitable time build a fire in it for the same purpose. E. Porritt, *Unreformed House of Commons,* I, 31-32.

traced by the color of their corn;" others more favorably situated grew into large towns and even populous cities. This would have happened to some extent even without any exceptional changes in the social and economic condition of the realm. But such changes there were—a phenomenal overturn, indeed, which we commonly call the Industrial Revolution—one of whose principal features was a shifting of population between 1750 and 1825 quite beyond anything recorded in the history of any other old and settled nation. Until this time the great mass of English people lived in the south and east; and there, naturally, were to be found most of the boroughs which sent members to Parliament. Liverpool was only an insignificant town, Manchester a village, Birmingham a sand hill. The north and northwest, however, contained England's huge deposits of coal and iron, and it was to those regions that the invention of machinery and the rise of the factory type of manufacturing caused the center of industry to be shifted, leading, naturally, to an extensive shift of population in the same direction. The hitherto almost uninhabited valleys of Lancashire and Yorkshire were presently studded with thriving factory towns and cities.

All of this took place without any new arrangements for parliamentary representation. In 1831, when the total population of England and Wales had grown to fourteen millions, ten southernmost counties numbered 3,260,000 people and had 235 members in the House of Commons.[22] At the same date the six northernmost counties numbered 3,594,000, and had only sixty-eight members. Cornwall, with 300,000 inhabitants, had forty-two representatives; Lancashire, with 1,330,000, had fourteen. Among towns, Birmingham and Manchester, each with upwards of 100,000 people, and Leeds and Sheffield, each with 50,000, had no representation whatever except through the knights of the shires, or counties, in which they were respectively situated. On the other hand, boroughs which had ridiculously small populations, or even no settled population at all, were entitled to separate representation. Thirty-

[22] That is to say, the quota of members mentioned was returned by the counties as such, together with the boroughs contained geographically within them.

six, in England and Wales alone, contained fewer than twenty-five people apiece. Bosseney, in Cornwall, was a hamlet of three cottages, eight of whose nine electors belonged to a single family. But Bosseney sent two members to the House of Commons. Worse than that, Gatton, in Surrey, was a park; Old Sarum, in Wiltshire, was a deserted hill; and the remains of what once was Dunwich, in Essex, were under the waves of the North Sea. Yet, by virtue of one historic right or another, every one returned its two members.

The picture grows still darker when we inquire into the way by which the members for these atrophied constituencies won their seats. In many of the larger boroughs and most of the counties, there were bona fide elections, even though attended by plenty of what we should consider shocking irregularities; because, of course, voting was public and oral, and none of the corrupt and illegal practices laws of which Britain today is justly proud had as yet been enacted. The principal abuse in these cases was bribery and intimidation of the voters by the candidates or other persons seeking to control the results. It was, however, in the lesser boroughs that the electoral system rose to the full heights—or, better, fell to the lowest depths—of absurdity. Scores of these, with only a handful of qualified voters, passed into the legal possession, or at all events under the complete control, of wealthy and ambitious men, who valued them for the power and pleasure to be had from manipulating their representation in Parliament. The owner or dictator became the patron; the borough seats became his "patronage" to bestow as he saw fit—a situation out of which arose the sinister term which blackens many a page of political history in all English-speaking lands.[23] Sometimes the patron bestowed the seats—the form of election being, of course, duly gone through—upon members of his family, or upon friends; quite as often he put them up for sale, precisely as, and no less publicly than, he might put up a country-house or shares in a joint-stock company. Such seats were freely advertised in the public prints; and if a man did not want to buy he could "rent" for a term of years. Thrifty "boroughmongers" compiled lists of available seats, set politically ambitious men to

[23] W. B. Munro, *Governments of Europe,* 128.

bidding for them, and drove a business profitable to patrons and themselves alike. Sales at £3,000 were not uncommon, and at £5,000, or even more, not unheard-of. The most prodigal purchasers were likely to be "nabobs" returning to England after making their fortunes in the India service and desirous of securing social position by admittance into "the best club in the world," as the eighteenth-century House of Commons was familiarly called. Many of the patrons were members of the House of Lords, who often controlled from six to a dozen seats in the lower chamber; some were themselves members of the House of Commons; others were people outside of Parliament; and in plenty of instances ministers and other public officials did not scorn to take a hand in the game. Altogether, it is estimated that less than half of the borough members in 1832 were elected freely by their nominal constituents. The remainder sat for "rotten" or "pocket" boroughs of one description or another.[24]

Gladstone once eulogized "nomination" boroughs as a means of bringing young men of promise into the House; and it cannot be denied that in this way youths of ability got seats who might not have been successful in a popular election. The younger Pitt started his parliamentary career in this fashion. So did Charles James Fox. So, for that matter, did many of the men who made history in the rôle of reformers in the early nineteenth century. Something might also be said, however, of the uncounted dunderheads, or worse, who went in by the same gateway.[25]

The upshot of all this is that the Britain of the early nineteenth century was a decidedly aristocratic country, no less in its government than in its social structure and habits. One branch of Parliament consisted entirely of clerical and hereditary members; the other contained only a few members chosen by any considerable number of electors; administrators and judges owed their positions to men who acknowledged little

[24] In the whole of Cornwall there were not above one thousand voters. Of the forty-two seats to which that section of the country was entitled, twenty were controlled by seven peers, twenty-one were similarly controlled by eleven commoners, and only one was filled by free election.

[25] The patronage system is described and appraised in illuminating fashion in E. Porritt, *Unreformed House of Commons,* I, Chap. xvi.

or no responsibility to the people, and were themselves invariably of the "governing class;" local government in the counties, and very frequently in the boroughs, was in the hands of petty oligarchies; the true governing powers were the crown, the church, and the aristocracy.[26]

Some people—many indeed—were satisfied with things as they were. Blackstone in 1765 wrote complacently of the beneficent system of lawmaking by "gentlemen of the kingdom delegated by their country to Parliament";[27] Burke in 1790 proclaimed the system "perfectly adequate to all the purposes for which a representation of the people can be desired or devised."[28] Already, however, John Locke, far back in 1690, had denounced the absurdities of the existing allocation of electoral power.[29] And in 1783, the younger Pitt, speaking on the floor of the Commons, admitted bluntly that "this house is

[26] The monumental treatise on the House of Commons before 1832, covering every significant aspect of the subject, is E. Porritt, *The Unreformed House of Commons; Parliamentary Representation before 1832*, 2 vols. (2nd ed., Cambridge, 1909), already cited. Another extensive and excellent work, covering the subject less comprehensively, but presenting a vast amount of illuminating material, especially on the actual methods and results of parliamentary elections in counties and boroughs, is L. B. Namier, *The Structure of Politics at the Accession of George III*, 2 vols. (London, 1929). These volumes are to be followed by others dealing with the same subjects in later periods. A good briefer account of electoral conditions before the Reform Act of 1832 is C. Seymour and D. P. Frary, *How the World Votes* (Springfield, Mass., 1918), I, Chap. iv. The aristocratic tone of the entire political system in the eighteenth and early nineteenth centuries is depicted strikingly in J. Redlich and F. W. Hirst, *Local Government in England* (London, 1903), I, Bk. I, Chap. iii. Cf. O. F. Christie, *The Transition from Aristocracy, 1832-1867* (London, 1927). Mention should be made also of G. S. Veitch, *The Genesis of Parliamentary Reform* (London, 1913), Chap. i.

[27] *Commentaries*, Bk. IV.

[28] It is only fair to remember that when Burke voiced this opinion he had been forced far from his accustomed line of liberal thinking by the events in France.

[29] *Two Treatises of Government*, ed. by W. S. Carpenter (London and New York, 1924), 197. "To what gross absurdities," said Locke, "the following of custom, when reason has left it, may lead, we may be satisfied when we see the bare name of a town of which there remains not so much as the ruins, where scarce so much housing as a sheepcote, or more inhabitants than a shepherd is to be found, send as many representatives to the grand assembly of lawmakers as a whole county numerous in people and powerful in riches. This strangers stand amazed at, and every one must confess needs a remedy; though most think it hard to find one. . . ."

not the representative of the people of Great Britain; it is the representative of nominal boroughs, of ruined and exterminated towns, of noble families, of wealthy individuals, of foreign potentates."

The Reform Movement

By the time when Pitt delivered himself of these views there were many to applaud his words. Already the populational changes incident to the Industrial Revolution were far advanced, and already, stimulated by these developments and by the steadily increasing value placed upon representation, demands for reform were beginning to be heard on many sides. In 1780 a group of public-spirited men established a Society for Constitutional Information which in the next decade carried on an active campaign for parliamentary reconstruction; and at a meeting in 1781 under the auspices of this organization, and presided over by Fox, a program was drawn up calling not only for equal electoral districts, abolition of property qualifications for members, payment of members, and voting by secret ballot, but for universal manhood suffrage. These were indeed radical proposals—reading almost exactly like the demands of the Chartists half a century later [30] —and the few bills on the subject that made their appearance in Parliament went by no means so far.

Something might, however, have been done, had not the French Revolution struck terror into the hearts of many good Englishmen, causing them for a long time to look decidedly askance at everything that savored of political innovation. Apprehension was still keen when the country entered upon its fifteen-year contest with Napoleon; and of course that period was no time for reforms. Even after peace was restored, it proved difficult to get anything done. Victory found the Tory party in control, which it kept for a decade and a half, and the men of power in the party not only ran the government but lost no opportunity to proclaim it the best government—in exactly the form in which it had come down to them—that the world had seen. For evidence they cited the imitation of sundry of its features by France and other Continental states.

[30] See p. 259.

And in this attitude the government leaders were naturally backed up by every wielder of patronage, every political manipulator—in short, every vested interest—likely to lose by any shift of power to the people. Weighing heavily on their side, too, was the conservative temper of the English people generally.[31]

These were times, however, of economic and social distress, even more serious in some respects than that experienced by the country in the decade following the recent World War. Industry was deranged, agriculture depressed, food dear, unemployment widespread. Hard-worked, ill-fed, badly-housed populations in the newer manufacturing cities stood in urgent need of relief. Sanitation, education, regulation of the labor of women and children—all pressed for attention as newer but necessary functions of the state. Of course the men who governed the nation were not wholly blind to these conditions. But they were obsessed by the desire to serve the interests of their class and wedded to the notion that the best way to do this was to leave industry, and economic life in general, free from regulation. Most reform proposals that found their way to the floor of Parliament accordingly met short shrift, or, if adopted, were first whittled down until deemed harmless.[32]

And yet, Parliament held the key to the situation; for not much could be accomplished without some stiff legislation. And since it was fairly obvious to the leaders of liberal thought that there was little chance of getting what they wanted from Parliament as it was then constituted, they naturally turned to the idea that the first thing to do was to procure the reform of Parliament itself. There was talk of doing something with the House of Lords. That, however, seemed a less promising line of attack than liberalizing the House of Commons, and hence it was to this end that the new reform movement was eventually directed, even as the old one had been in the days of Pitt and Fox. Once more, peers and patrons did all they

[31] The eighteenth-century liberal movement and the restraining effects of the French Revolution are discussed at length in J. S. Penman, *The Irresistible Movement of Democracy* (New York, 1923), Bk. III, Chaps. ii-iv, and G. S. Veitch, *The Genesis of Parliamentary Reform,* Chaps. ii-xiii.

[32] J. Redlich and F. W. Hirst, *Local Government in England,* I, 58-79.

could to obstruct, and for years there was no assurance of victory. The walls of opposition began perceptibly to crumble in 1830, when the Tories fell from power and the Whig ministry of Earl Grey came in. Many of the Whigs were aristocratic enough; but the party as a whole was prepared to endorse, and the new ministry to push, a reform conceived on moderate lines. Even now there were not immediate results. A reform bill passed by the House of Commons in 1831 was thrown out by the upper chamber; and it was only after a parliamentary election, a second passage of the bill by the Commons, and agreement by William IV to create enough new peers to swamp the opposition that the Lords gave way, in 1832, and permitted the Great Reform Bill to be placed on the statute book.[33]

The Nineteenth-Century Reform Acts

This measure has been characterized as one of the most important in British legislative history, and justly, since it started a long series of notable electoral laws and gave the electoral system a slant or bent in the direction of political democracy which has been followed uninterruptedly to the present day.[34] In its immediate provisions, however, the act

[33] The reform movement up to 1832 is sketched in J. Redlich and F. W. Hirst, *op. cit.*, I, Bk. II, Chap. i; J. H. Rose, *The Rise and Growth of Democracy in Great Britain* (London, 1897), Chap. i; G. L. Dickinson, *Development of Parliament during the Nineteenth Century* (London, 1895), Chap. i; and J. S. Penman, *The Irresistible Movement of Democracy,* Bk. III, Chaps. v-vi. Special treatises of importance are G. S. Veitch, *The Genesis of Parliamentary Reform,* as cited; J. R. M. Butler, *The Passing of the Great Reform Bill* (New York, 1914); and G. M. Trevelyan, *Lord Grey of the Reform Bill* (London, 1920). A useful monograph is P. A. Gibbons, *Ideas of Political Representation in Parliament, 1651-1832* (Oxford, 1914). Mention should be made also of C. B. R. Kent, *The English Radicals* (London, 1899), and W. P. Hall, *British Radicalism, 1791-1797* (New York, 1912).

[34] This it did, not merely by increasing the number of voters at the moment, but by basing the suffrage for the first time, in counties and boroughs alike, upon a single type or style of qualification, i.e., property. This form of qualification involved specifying arbitrary figures expressing rental values, etc., and, as Lady Gwendolyn Cecil has pointed out in her *Life of Robert, Marquis of Salisbury* (I, Chap. vi), it became inevitable that every fresh agitation on the subject should center in a demand for the lowering of the property qualification, until, the vanishing point having been reached, "democracy" should finally be arrived at.

was far from revolutionary. It undertook to do two things, i.e., redistribute seats and broaden the suffrage, but both within moderate limits. It might conceivably have carried out a general redistribution of seats, meticulously adjusting representation to the number of voters in each district. But it did nothing of the sort. What it did [35] was to cut off separate representation from fifty-six boroughs (nearly all of them of the "rotten" or "pocket" variety) with fewer than 2,000 people, reduce thirty boroughs with populations between 2,000 and 4,000 from two members to one, cut the City of London from four members to two, and reassign the 143 seats thus liberated in such a way that twenty-two populous boroughs not hitherto represented got two members apiece, twenty-two were given one member apiece, sixty-five seats were divided among county constituencies in England, and the remainder were given to Scotland and Ireland.[36] The net effect was to transfer a good deal of political power from the south to the populous industrial sections of the north and west, although by no means all that an exact proportioning would have required.

Redistribution had been the chief bone of contention, but the act also widened the parliamentary suffrage. In the counties the forty-shilling freehold franchise was allowed to stand; but the voting privilege was extended to all leaseholders and copyholders of land rated as of a rental value of as much as £10 a year, and to tenants-at-will holding an estate rated at £50 a year.[37] In the boroughs all of the old complicated franchises, or qualifications, except that of "freemen," were abolished and a simple uniform franchise was substituted, defined as the "occupation," by a rate-payer, of a house worth £10

[35] Accuracy requires it to be pointed out that the act first passed applied only to England and Wales. Supplementary acts, on similar lines, were passed in the same year for Scotland and Ireland. The description given should be understood as applying to the series, rather than to a single statute, and the same is true with regard to the later reform acts described in the pages that follow.

[36] The number of Scottish members was increased from 45 to 54; the Irish quota was raised from 100 to 105; the members for England and Wales were reduced from 513 to 499. The total number remained the same, i.e., 658.

[37] In Great Britain local taxes, or "rates," are regularly levied upon the occupant, not the owner, of premises, and on the basis of the assessed rental value, not on the selling value as in the United States.

a year. The total number of persons newly enfranchised in England and Wales was 217,386, and in the whole of the United Kingdom, approximately 455,000. By basing the suffrage almost exclusively upon the ownership or occupancy of property of considerable value, the reform fell decidedly short of admitting to political power the great mass of factory employees and of agricultural laborers,[38] and for this reason the reform was not at all satisfactory to the more radical elements. If, however, the privilege of voting had not been extended to the masses, it had been brought appreciably nearer them; and —what was almost equally important—it had for the first time been made substantially uniform, for each of the two recognized types of constituencies, throughout the realm. It was this measure, too, that first required qualified persons to be registered in order to vote.[39]

Those who were responsible for passing the act of 1832 considered that it went quite far enough, but other people felt differently, and in the next few years the discussion passed into a new stage in which a group of radical and militant reformers known as Chartists [40] carried on a spectacular campaign for their "six points," i.e., universal manhood suffrage, equal electoral districts, voting by secret ballot, annual parliamentary elections, abolition of the property qualification for members, and payment of salaries to members out of the public treasury. Chartism as a movement did not survive to see its program realized, but by keeping its various issues before the nation for twenty years it contributed not only to the abolition of property qualifications for members in 1858 but to the enactment of the second major reform bill, in 1867, carrying the country another long step in the direction of the electoral democracy of the present day. This measure, also—which, it is interesting to note, was, by a curious turn of circumstances,

[38] It, indeed, took away franchises enjoyed by the common people in some of the boroughs.

[39] See p. 293 below.

[40] Because they formulated their program—which was in the main social rather than political—in a document termed the People's Charter. J. H. Rose, *Rise and Growth of Democracy,* Chaps. vi-viii; J. S. Penman, *The Irresistible Movement of Democracy,* Bk. III, Chap. vii. There are many books on the Chartists, e.g., by Gammage, Hovell, Rosenblatt, Faulkern, Slosson, and West.

the handiwork of a Tory, or Conservative, government—took away a batch of seats from over-represented boroughs and bestowed them where population most demanded.[41] But its most significant contribution was to the widening of the electorate. In county constituencies there was relatively little change; the forty-shilling freehold franchise was maintained, although copyholders and leaseholders might now vote with half of their former qualification, and a new £12 franchise made conditions easier for the tenants-at-will. In the boroughs, however, there were drastic readjustments, not only striking off the £10 requirement for householders, but admitting all "lodgers" who occupied, for as much as a year, rooms of an annual rental value, unfurnished, of £10 or over. The act of 1832 had enfranchised chiefly the urban middle class; that of 1867 brought in the bulk of the urban working class, increasing the electorate, in all, by almost a million.[42]

The main groups of people still outside the pale were the agricultural laborers and the miners, both belonging principally to county constituencies, and it was inevitable that sooner or later they should be made the subject of similar legislation. The ice had been broken, the old electoral system was gone in any case,[43] and it was an occasion for no surprise when in 1884 Gladstone redeemed a campaign pledge by introducing a bill extending to the counties the same electoral regulations that had been given the boroughs seventeen years before. After once rejecting the measure as it came up from the Commons, the House of Lords assented to it on the understanding that it would be followed by a bill making a further redistribution of seats; and this second bill duly became law in 1885.

What the Representation of the People Act of 1884 (and the accompanying acts for Scotland and Ireland) mainly did was to extend the existing borough franchises to the counties. Former county qualifications were not abrogated, nor were

[41] Fifty-two seats, in all, were transferred. England and Wales lost six, which Scotland gained, the total number still remaining unchanged.

[42] Again it should be pointed out that this was the combined effect of the act of 1867 for England and Wales and two acts of 1868 making similar, although not identical, provisions for Scotland and Ireland.

[43] The Ballot Act of 1872 and the Corrupt and Illegal Practices Act of 1883, dealt with below (p. 296), helped relegate it to the past.

any new franchises created, in either counties or boroughs. But the changes made were sufficient to multiply the county electors in England and Wales by almost three, and to add to the lists, in the United Kingdom as a whole, twice as many new voters as were created by the act of 1867. In 1886 the number of registered electors stood at approximately four millions.

The Redistribution Act of 1885 marks the first attempt in English history to apportion representation, the country over, in accordance with a fixed standard, and not by the hit-and-miss method of simply taking seats from a flagrantly over-represented county or borough here and there and by log-rolling methods bestowing them on more deserving ones elsewhere. Boroughs containing fewer than 15,000 inhabitants were disfranchised as boroughs, becoming for electoral purposes mere portions of the counties in which they were situated; boroughs of between 15,000 and 50,000 inhabitants were allowed to retain, or if previously unrepresented were given, one member each; those of between 50,000 and 165,000 were given two members, and those of more than 165,000 three, with one further for every additional 50,000 people, and similar arrangements were made in the counties. This statement, however, would give an erroneous impression unless it were recalled that it was this law that deliberately adopted the single-member-district principle, leaving only twenty-seven constituencies (including three university constituencies) with two members, and none with more than two. For example, the city of Liverpool, which prior to 1885 sent three members to Parliament, was cut into nine single-member constituencies, and the great northern county of Lancashire, which since 1867 had been divided into four portions, each returning two members, fell into twenty-three divisions with one member apiece. Still there was by no means mathematical equality of districts: a borough with 15,000 people was entitled to one member; one with 49,000 was entitled also to but one; one with 51,000 (unless divided) was entitled to two.[44]

[44] As has been indicated, the whole number of members was raised at this time to 670 (England and Wales, 495; Scotland, 72; Ireland, 103).

The parliamentary reforms of the period 1832-85 are dealt with briefly

Electoral Questions, 1885-1918

The electoral system as it was left by the acts of 1884 and 1885 stood practically unchanged until 1918. During all of these years almost any Englishman, if challenged on the subject, would have argued that his government was democratic, and certainly it was so regarded by the world generally. There were, however, some rather serious limitations, arising not only from the aristocratic character of the House of Lords, but from various aspects of the House of Commons; and the period—particularly the second half of it—saw a great deal of discussion of further reforms calculated to make at least the elective branch more truly representative of the nation.

In the first place, the suffrage was still defined entirely in terms of relation to property. A man voted, not as a person or citizen, but as an owner, occupier, or user of houses, lands, or business premises. The voter did not have to *own* property; and occupational requirements were, as we have seen, comparatively easy to meet. But there were many men—two millions or more by 1910, in fact—who were not "occupiers," nor yet "lodgers" or anything else that came within the limits of the law. Besides, the law itself was so complicated that nobody but lawyers even professed to understand it. "The present condition of the franchise," wrote Lowell in 1909, "is, indeed, historical rather than rational. It is complicated, uncertain, expensive in the machinery required, and excludes a certain number of people whom there is no reason for excluding; while it admits many people who ought not to be admitted if

in J. S. Penman, *The Irresistible Movement of Democracy,* Bk. III, Chap. viii; G. L. Dickinson, *Development of Parliament,* Chap. ii; J. H. Rose, *Rise and Growth of Democracy,* Chaps. ii, x-xiii; and T. E. May and F. Holland, *Constitutional History of England,* I, Chap. vi, and III, Chap. i. The act of 1832 is treated fully in the works of Butler and Trevelyan mentioned above (p. 257), and that of 1867 in J. H. Park, *The English Reform Bill of 1867* (New York, 1920); and the best treatise on the entire subject is C. Seymour, *Electoral Reform in England and Wales, 1832-1885* (New Haven, 1915). Important contemporary discussions of electoral matters include John Stuart Mill, *Considerations on Representative Government* (London, 1861); T. Hare, *The Election of Representatives, Parliamentary and Municipal* (3rd ed., London, 1865); and the preface written by Walter Bagehot for the second edition (1872) of his *English Constitution.* On Mill as a philosophic sponsor of reform movements in the third quarter of the nineteenth century, see J. Redlich and F. W. Hirst, *op. cit.,* I, 177-185.

any one is to be debarred."[45] The first demand of electoral reformers was, accordingly, for a law that would simplify the existing system and at the same time make provision substantially for manhood suffrage.

Then there was the matter of plural voting. In the British dominions and in almost all other countries, even before the World War, a person, if entitled to vote at all, had only one vote; any arrangement other than this seemed to most people to violate the principle of civic equality fundamental to popular government.[46] In a country, however, in which the suffrage was tied up as closely with property, historically and practically, as it was in Britain, it was at least comprehensible that an elector should, under certain safeguards, be permitted to vote in any and every constituency in which he could show qualification. This, indeed, had long been the British practice. A man might vote only once, at a given election, in any one division of a borough. But if he slept in Kensington, had an office in the City of London, and maintained a country place in Surrey, he was entitled to vote in all three places. He might own freehold in twenty counties and claim to vote in all of them. Until 1918, a general election was spread over a period of approximately two weeks, giving the plural voter ample opportunity, even before the day of the motor-car, to get from one constituency to another and thus to vote anywhere from two or three to a dozen or more times. And since there were more than half a million plural voters in the kingdom, one will not be surprised to learn that the results were often affected appreciably—or that, since the benefits of the system accrued almost entirely to the landholding Conservatives, the Liberal party early made "one man one vote" its slogan and set out to accomplish the total suppression of the practice.[47]

[45] *Government of England,* I, 213.

[46] The most notable exception was Belgium, where, under a constitutional amendment of 1893, qualified persons were entitled to as many as three votes. See T. H. Reed, *Government and Politics of Belgium* (Yonkers, 1924), 39-41, and for a fuller account, L. Dupriez, *L'organisation du suffrage universel en Belgique* (Paris, 1901). Plural voting in Belgium was abolished in 1921.

[47] A bill that would have suppressed plural voting was passed by the House of Commons, under Liberal leadership, in 1906, but was defeated in the House of Lords. See H. L. Morris, *Parliamentary Franchise Reform in England from 1885 to 1918* (New York, 1921), Chap. ii.

Another suffrage question which thrust itself into the forefront of public discussion soon after the opening of the present century was the enfranchisement of women. It was, however, not entirely unheard of before that time. A pamphlet dating from 1847 argued that as long as both sexes were not "given a just representation" good government was impossible, and in 1867 John Stuart Mill tried hard to get a clause into Disraeli's reform act enfranchising women taxpayers.[48] A national society to promote the cause was organized in the last-mentioned year; and in 1869 an act of Parliament went so far as to confer the suffrage in municipal elections upon all female taxpayers of England, Wales, and Scotland. From time to time for twenty years thereafter bills on the subject appeared in the House of Commons, though with hardly any possibility of success. A new chapter in the history of the movement was opened in 1903 by the organization of the Woman's Social and Political Union, under the auspices of which a spectacular campaign was carried on in the next decade, primarily with a view to inducing or compelling the cabinet to introduce a suffrage bill. It was plain enough that no private member's bill on so controversial a subject would ever stand a chance of becoming law.

The object sought was not attained until 1918. But meanwhile the cause was advertised, organized, and broadened until it gave promise of bringing the country to a genuine crisis. How the program grew is illustrated by the fact that whereas originally the demand was merely for the removal of the disqualification of women *as women*—in other words, for the enfranchisement of women upon the same terms, in respect to age, residence, and independent ownership or occupancy of property, as men—from about 1909 it was urged that substantially all adult women in the United Kingdom should be made voters. The first plan would have meant the enfranchisement of about two million women; the second, of ten million. A "conciliation" scheme, incorporated in a comprehensive electoral bill in 1910, provided as a first step for bestowing the suffrage in parliamentary elections upon such women as were

[48] The subject was indeed broached as early as 1792 by Mary Wollstonecraft in a book entitled *Vindication of the Rights of Women.*

already permitted to vote in local elections—approximately one and one-fourth millions. Proposals of every sort were blocked, however, during the pre-war years of the Liberal ministry of Mr. Asquith by the inflexible opposition of the prime minister and several of his colleagues, and by the resulting impossibility of getting before Parliament any government measure on the subject.[49]

Finally—to mention only the major electoral issues that drew attention between 1885 and 1918—there was the perennial question of redistribution. Markedly unequal, as we have seen, even when the arrangements of 1885 were fresh, the constituencies grew still farther apart numerically as time elapsed. In 1912 the most populous one (the Romford division of the county of Essex) had more than fifteen times as many people as the least populous one (the Irish borough of Kilkenny), and the disparity in the number of voters was even greater. The populations of the hundreds of county and borough constituencies throughout the United Kingdom fell at all points between these two extremes. Again, as in 1832, it was the rural and agricultural districts, like Oxfordshire, Hereford, and Devon, that were over-represented, as compared with the ever-growing industrial and mining centers. In particular, Ireland was excessively represented, because of the decline of the island's population by upwards of half since shortly before the middle of the nineteenth century.[50] If it was

[49] The history of the militant suffragist movement is told vividly in a book by the principal leader, i.e., Emmeline Pankhurst, *My Own Story* (London, 1916), and in a different form by the daughter of the foregoing, i.e., E. Sylvia Pankhurst, in *The Suffragette; the History of the Woman's Militant Suffrage Movement, 1905-1910* (London, 1911). A book of similar scope is A. E. Metcalfe, *Woman's Effort* (Oxford, 1917), and a sympathetic but trustworthy general treatise is [Mrs.] R. Strachey, *The Cause; a Short History of the Women's Movement in Great Britain* (London, 1928). A full account by the leader of the non-militants (organized in the National Union of Women's Suffrage Societies) is M. G. Fawcett, *Woman Suffrage; a Short History of the Great Movement* (London, 1912), and its supplement, *The Women's Victory—and After* (London, 1920). For a convenient outline, see H. L. Morris, *op. cit.*, Chaps. iii, iv. vi.

[50] Total population in 1841, 8,175,124; in 1911, 4,390,219. There had been no significant changes in the quota of Irish seats at any time since 1801, because the Act of Union guaranteed the country a minimum of one hundred, and so long as home rule was denied, Irish sentiment was unalterably opposed to any reduction of voting strength at Westminster.

the Liberals who clamored for an end of plural voting, it was the Conservatives who urged redistribution—in both cases for the good and sufficient reason that existing arrangements worked to the benefit of the opponents.[51] A redistribution bill brought forward by Mr. Balfour's government in 1905, however, failed to reach debate; and, although the Liberals, as the party in power, sponsored several electoral measures during the next ten years, they did not have enough interest in redistribution to lead them to do more than make indefinite promises on the subject.

Frustrated by the Conservative House of Lords in their effort in 1906 to do away with plural voting, the Liberals bent their efforts in the next few years to cutting away the veto power from the second chamber, the result being the historic Parliament Act of 1911;[52] and with the way thus cleared, they returned to electoral matters in 1912 by bringing forward the most ambitious bill on the subject that had appeared in Parliament since 1884-85. As has been indicated, nothing was to be done about a redistribution of seats. That a new apportionment was desirable was indeed conceded; but the position was taken that other reforms ought to come first. There was also nothing on woman suffrage—a subject on which the ministers were quite unable to agree. Three electoral changes of major importance were, however, provided for: (1) replacement of the existing medley of complicated, overlapping, and sometimes contradictory, franchises by a simple, uniform, residential or occupational franchise for men; (2) abolition of plural voting; and (3) simplification of the existing system of electoral registration. The universities were also to cease to be represented as such.[53]

The bill would have enfranchised more than two million men—quite as many as were reached by the great act of 1884. But it did not become law. Indeed, it did not even pass the

[51] The Conservatives suffered from the over-representation of Ireland for the reason that the great bulk of members from that part of the realm belonged to the Nationalist party, which was allied with the Liberals, especially in the movement for Irish home rule. See p. 697 below.

[52] See pp. 342-347 below.

[53] This was a natural provision of a Liberal bill, since practically all university representatives were Conservatives.

House of Commons. After the ministry had reluctantly agreed to accept a woman suffrage amendment if voted by the House, the speaker ruled that in case such an amendment were adopted it would utterly change the character of the bill, so that a new measure would have to be prepared and passed through all the required stages. This was an unpleasant prospect. In addition, many Liberals were lukewarm toward the measure; and the growing seriousness of the situation in Ireland,[54] besides other pressing business, left the government little time for following up the matter. The upshot was that early in 1913 the bill was withdrawn and the project dropped.[55] In the next eighteen months a less ambitious measure, prohibiting plural voting at general elections (although allowing it at by-elections) was twice passed by the lower, though twice rejected by the upper, chamber; and by August, 1914, this part of the Liberal program—thanks to the Parliament Act of three years before—was on the point of being realized. The outbreak of war, however, caused the plural voting bill, along with other pending measures of a controversial nature, to be abandoned, and the great opportunity seemed to have been lost.[56]

Representation of the People Act of 1918—Redistribution of Seats

As events proved, the war only paved the way for a more comprehensive, and decidedly less partisan, reconstruction of the electoral system than anybody had dreamed of in the old days; and, still more unexpectedly, the reform was accomplished —by the passage of the Representation of the People Act of February 6, 1918,—while the struggle was actually going on. It was, of course, not by choice that the government turned its attention to electoral questions while the nation was still fighting for its life within hearing of the Channel ports. Rather, it was compelled to do so by the sheer breakdown of the electoral system, caused by wholesale enlistments in the army and by the further dislocation of population arising from the development of war industries. The situation was bad enough in

[54] See p. 700.
[55] H. L. Morris, *op. cit.,* Chap. v.
[56] *Ibid.,* Chap. vii.

county, municipal, and parish elections. But a parliamentary election under the new conditions would have been a farce. By successive special acts, and with general consent, the life of the parliament chosen in December, 1910, was prolonged, in order to defer, and perhaps to avoid altogether, a war-time election. A general election, however, there must eventually be; and whether before or after the cessation of hostilities, it admittedly would demand, in all justice, a radically altered system of registration and voting, if not new franchises and other important changes. At the request of the cabinet, Parliament therefore took up the matter in the summer of 1916, the first step being to set up a special commission to study the subject and suggest the outlines of a bill. The thirty-six members of this exceptionally capable group were selected by the speaker of the House of Commons, with a view to fair representation not only of the different political parties but of all important bodies of thought on electoral matters, e.g., the believers in proportional representation, the friends of the alternative vote, the advocates and the opponents of woman suffrage, etc.; and the speaker himself took time from his other duties to serve as chairman. A well-matured report was submitted after five months, and the enactment of the law of 1918 followed in due course.[57]

The provisions of this great piece of legislation[58] that attracted most attention were those that swept away all surviving restrictions upon manhood suffrage, conferred the ballot upon eight and one-half million women, and thus raised

[57] The "Speaker's Conference," as the commission was aptly called, began its work October 10, 1916. Its report was presented to the House of Commons in the following March, and the bill based on its recommendations was introduced on May 5. Debate proceeded intermittently until December 7, when the measure, considerably enlarged, was passed and sent up to the House of Lords. Here, seventeen days were devoted to it, and on January 30, 1918, it was returned to the House of Commons with eighty-seven pages of amendments. Pressure of time made for compromise, and on February 6 the houses came to agreement upon a completed bill, which forthwith received the king's assent. J. King, "The Speaker's Conference on Electoral Reform," *Contemp. Rev.*, Mar., 1917; *Report of the Speaker to the Prime Minister,* Cmd. 8463 (1917); W. H. Dickinson, *The Reform Act of 1918* (London, 1918), reprinted in part in E. M. Sait and D. P. Barrows, *British Politics in Transition,* 83-93.

[58] Together with an accompanying act applying to Ireland.

a total electorate of some eight and one-half millions to one of slightly more than twenty-one millions. Upon the basis of this vastly augmented electorate, however, the act went on to erect an electoral system, by no means entirely new, to be sure, yet showing novel features at almost every turn; and the measure will be entirely misunderstood if thought of as only a suffrage law like the act of 1884, or even as a suffrage-reapportionment measure like the acts of 1832 and 1867. Slightly amended from time to time in certain respects, the system for which provision was made served the purposes of the general elections of 1918, 1922, 1923, and 1924; amended more drastically by an act of 1928 extending the suffrage to an additional five million women, it found its latest application in the election of 1929. In closing the present chapter we may take some notice of what the act of 1918, and legislation supplementary to it, did for constituencies and voters. In the following chapter we shall see how it affected electoral registration, campaign and election expenditures, the conduct of elections, and sundry other matters.

The circumstances being as they were, there was never any doubt that the new legislation would make a sweeping redistribution of seats. Taking as a standard one member for every 70,000 people in Great Britain,[59] and one for every 43,000 in Ireland, it merged forty-four old boroughs in the county constituencies surrounding them, took five seats from sparsely populated agricultural regions, bestowed representation on thirty-one new boroughs, and in other ways so rearranged the constituencies as to bring up the whole number of members of the House of Commons—already the largest legislative assemblage in the world—from 670 to 707. England, with 492 seats, gained 31; Wales with 36, Scotland with 74, and

[59] Under the reapportionment of 1911, based on the 1910 census, the nominal quota for each congressional district in the United States is approximately 250,000. Up to 1929, Congress failed to agree upon any reapportionment on the basis of the 1920 census, and during these eighteen years the population of the congressional districts became, on the average, far larger. A reapportionment measure, passed while this book was in press, fixed the number of representatives—following the census of 1930—at the existing figure (435), and hence looks to still more populous districts.

Ireland with 105, gained two each.[60] The arrangement for Ireland was admittedly provisional, because while the Home Rule Act of 1914 was still on the statute book, it was not in actual operation, and the general understanding was that the measure would not be put into effect—if ever—until it should have been amended. In point of fact, two years later the Government of Ireland Act gave the greater part of Ireland the status of a self-governing dominion without representation at Westminster and assigned the small northern section of the country which remained a quota of thirteen seats, thereby reducing the total membership of the House of Commons, as we have seen, from 707 to 615. The act of 1918 further reduced the number of constituencies returning more than one member.[61] But, as we have noted above, it failed to make provision for any future redistributions of seats, periodic or otherwise.

The Parliamentary Suffrage Since 1918

Effort to adapt electoral machinery to the conditions created by the war early convinced the Speaker's Conference that the old practice of defining franchises wholly in terms of relationship to property ought to be given up, and that in lieu of it the principle should be adopted that the suffrage is a personal privilege, to be enjoyed by the individual simply as a citizen. The two houses accepted this view, and hence the act swept away the entire mass of existing intricate parliamentary franchises, assimilated the county and borough franchises for the first time in a single uniform system, enfranchised several million men who were unable to meet the old tests, enfranchised also about eight and one-half million women on the basis of qualifications possessed either by themselves or by their husbands, and created a special, supplementary military and naval

[60] The distribution, in full, was as follows:

	Counties	Boroughs	Universities	Total
England and Wales	254	266	8	528
Scotland	38	33	3	74
Ireland	80	21	4	105
Total	372	320	15	707

The distribution as it stands today is shown on p. 246 above.

[61] See p. 244 above.

franchise for the benefit of service members not likely otherwise to be reached.

In their zeal for uniformity, the framers of the measure stopped short, however, of giving men and women the ballot on identical terms; and until fresh legislation on the subject was enacted in 1928 there continued to be one set of requirements for the sterner sex and another for the gentler. The qualifications required of male electors at last became relatively simple. Any man who is a British subject, twenty-one years of age or over, and not subject to any legal incapacity, is entitled to have his name on the voters' list in the constituency in which he resides, provided he has been a resident of that constituency for at least three months when the list is compiled, or even if he has lived for part of the qualifying period in some other constituency in the same or a contiguous county or borough. Furthermore, he is entitled to be on the voters' list in one other constituency (but only one) anywhere in the country on the basis of occupying, for business purposes, land or premises of a yearly rental value of not less than £10.[62] There are, of course, disqualifications. Peers cannot vote in parliamentary elections, on the theory that as members of the upper house they are already endowed with a sufficient amount of political power.[63] Lunatics and idiots are naturally debarred, and likewise persons convicted of treason or felony as long as the sentence has not been served or pardon granted. Soldiers and sailors in active service are, however, not excluded, as in some countries; and persons receiving aid out of the public funds for poor relief, while disqualified up to 1918, are no longer so.

The outbreak of the war in 1914 seemed to end all hope of early legislation on woman suffrage. The ultimate effect was, however, quite the opposite. Within two years and a half the conflict brought the suffragists an advantage which no amount of agitation had ever won for them, i.e., the active backing of the government; and a few months more carried their cause

[62] Occupancy must be for three months, under the same conditions that apply to the residential qualification.

[63] Irish peers sitting in the House of Commons are excepted. See p. 321 below.

to a victorious conclusion which might not have been reached in a full decade of peace. Now that men were to have the suffrage *as persons,* rather than simply as owners or occupiers of property, it was more than ever difficult to withhold it from women. Indeed, in the present juncture—in the face of woman's superb services to the nation during the war—to withhold it was quite impossible. Powerful opposition, of course, was raised. All of the old anti-suffrage arguments were heard again, and in addition it was contended, with a certain amount of plausibility, that a woman's enfranchisement act ought not to be put on the statute book without a referendum, or by a parliament which had overrun its time by two full years, or while three million men, including more than one-fifth of the members of the House of Commons, were absent in military service. There was the awkward situation, too, that the war had so depleted the man-power of the nation that if women were given the suffrage on the same terms as men there would be a heavy preponderance of female voters, even after the soldiers should have returned from overseas. And when it was proposed that the masculinity of the electorate be safeguarded by giving qualified women the ballot only at the age of thirty, it was objected, on the one side, that this was an arbitrary, illogical, and unfair disposition of the matter (especially as more than three-fourths of the women employed in the munition plants were under that age), and, on the other, that even if it were done the disparity, as a matter of practical policy, could not long be maintained.[64]

There was, at the time, however, no clear alternative, and accordingly the act as passed conferred the parliamentary suffrage on every female British subject thirty years of age, or

[64] Still other objections raised were: (1) that millions of inexperienced women voters ought not to be added to the electorate at precisely the time when the problems of war, peace, and reconstruction were about to make the largest demands upon the electoral capacities of the nation; (2) that, in the words of Mrs. Humphry Ward, the proposed measure would "cripple disastrously the indispensable conservative forces of the country at a time when there is a most imperative need of a due balance between conservative and liberal principles and influences;" and (3) that the wholesale enfranchisement of women was dictated largely by the Labor party, which expected to turn the new stream of electoral power to its own advantage.

over, who was herself, or whose husband was, entitled to be registered as a local government elector by virtue of the occupation of a dwelling-house, without regard to value, or of land or other premises (not being a dwelling-house) of the yearly rental value of £5. This sounds more complicated than it really is. The cardinal points are that the suffrage for women of requisite age, unlike that for men, was to be determined in relation to local, i.e., county or borough, government status; that a woman who was entitled to vote in local elections by reason of either of the specified property relationships might vote, if duly registered, for a member of Parliament; and that, even though she was not a local government elector, she could still vote in a parliamentary election if her husband was a local elector on either specified basis. The disqualifications laid down for men were to hold good also for women in so far as applicable, except that peeresses in their own right [65] were not to be debarred.

This legislation marked a long step in the direction of equal suffrage for men and women, but nevertheless deliberately stopped short of establishing it. Unlike men, women could not qualify independently, as simple residents (indeed there was no residential qualification for women at all); and there was a differential of ten years in favor of men in the age requirement. Everybody understood that this discrimination in the matter of age was designed primarily to meet an abnormal situation created by the war, and from the first it was fair to assume that after the male population should have regained something like its customary numerical proportion the law would be changed. Hardly was the measure on the statute book, however, before those who had been responsible for the triumph set about bringing their work to its logical conclusion. The National Union of Women Suffrage Societies reorganized itself under the name of the National Union of Societies for Equal Citizenship and adopted a program which stressed equal suffrage for the sexes; the Liberal and Labor parties were induced to put planks on the subject in their respective platforms; Conservative sentiment was roused to a point which led the Baldwin ministry of 1924 to enter office pledged to the

[65] See p. 319 below.

establishment of equal voting rights during the life of the existing parliament; a bill passed its second reading in the House of Commons in 1924, but was sidetracked; and finally, in 1928, a measure meeting substantially all demands—the Representation of the People (Equal Franchise) Bill—became law. Notwithstanding much heated opposition to the so-called "vote for flappers," the voting age for women was reduced to twenty-one, and all other provisions of the 1918 law which subjected women to different tests from those applied to men were repealed. The result was to add more than five million women to the electorate, bringing up the total of female voters to something like 14,500,000, as compared with 12,500,000 men.

Far from abolishing university representation, as the government bill of 1912 proposed to do, the act of 1918 increased the number of institutions entitled to be represented, the number of university members, and the number of holders of degrees qualified to take part in the election of university representatives.[66] In general, holders of all degrees (except honorary ones) may now participate, whereas formerly the privilege was restricted to recipients of the older arts degrees. This applies to women equally with men; and in the case of Oxford, which does not yet give degrees to women, a female may be enrolled as a voter if she can show that she has fulfilled the conditions that would entitle a man to a degree.

We have noted that soldiers and sailors are not debarred. On the contrary, special provision was made for them in the act of 1918—and not only for soldiers and sailors in the strict sense, but for persons (including women, e.g., nurses) occupied with subsidiary or analogous duties. All such are voters, provided they can show that, but for the service in which they are engaged, they could qualify under the ordinary residential or occupational provisions.[67]

[66] It was practically necessary either to abolish the system or to extend it, because if it was to be continued at all, the claims of certain of the younger universities, and of certain groups of degree-holders of older and younger ones alike, could not very well be denied.

[67] The clause of the act permitting young men who had enlisted with the colors while under age to vote at nineteen has, of course, become obsolete with the lapse of time.

Electoral reform under the auspices of a government of which Mr. Lloyd George was head might have been expected to bring plural voting absolutely to an end; and if the mass of Liberals could have had their way, it would have done so. The Conservatives, however,—and not merely the members of the party of that name but other people of conservative bent—insisted upon retaining it, for the same reason that they urged adoption of a plan of proportional representation,[68] i.e., to help save the more educated and wealthy part of the electorate from being submerged by the flood of laboring-class votes. The Liberal leaders pressed their point only to the extent of securing a restriction of the number of votes that any one elector may cast to two, as compared with five, or ten, or in fact any number whatever, under the old system. As matters now stand (since the supplementary legislation of 1928), an elector—man or woman—may vote in one constituency as a resident and in another as an occupier of business premises; or an elector may have a second vote as holder of a university degree. But in no case may a person have more than two votes, or indeed more than one in any single constituency.

The Present Electorate

The effect of the legislation of the decade reviewed was to bring the parliamentary electorate to rather more than three times its former proportions. Far more people were made new voters by the act of 1918 alone than by all the reform measures of the nineteenth century combined. The act of 1832 created half a million new electors, raising the proportion of electors to the total population to one in twenty-four; the act of 1867 created a million electors, raising the proportion to one in twelve; the act of 1884 added two million electors, making the proportion one in seven; the act of 1918 added over twelve millions, bringing up the proportion to one in three; the act of 1928 added over five millions, creating the interesting situation that decidedly more than half of the country's entire population are voters. In a total present electorate of over twenty-seven millions, women predominate, as has been pointed out, by about two millions; in not far from ninety per cent

[68] See p. 309 below.

of the constituencies, male voters are outnumbered by females.

So far as the composition of the electorate is concerned, few questions now remain to be settled. There are plenty of problems relating to the electoral system generally,[69] but the make-up of the electorate has pretty well passed out of the realm of controversy. It has been suggested that the voting age for both men and women be raised to twenty-five, but there is no interest in the matter. It will continue to be proposed that the separate representation of the universities be terminated, which would mean to abolish the university electorate; and something may be done on this score, even though, as we have seen, the act of 1918 moved rather in the opposite direction. Somewhat related is the question of plural voting. Except as it survives in Britain in the attenuated form of "dual voting" described above, plural voting has become practically obsolete throughout the world. In Britain it still obstructs the fullest realization of equalitarian democracy, and its total suppression is likely to continue to be an issue of some importance. On its present basis, however, it is naturally of less political significance than formerly, and little has been said about it in these last nine or ten years. Since nobody would suggest that degree-holders be restricted to voting for university members, plural voting will doubtless survive as long as the universities continue to be represented separately. Even so, it would, of course, be possible to cut off at any time the privilege of two votes on the separate bases of residence and occupation; and while there seems to be no strong interest in the matter at present, one may venture the guess that this will be the next point at which statutory change in the composition of the electorate will be made.[70]

[69] Some of these are reviewed in the following chapter.

[70] The act of 1918 and the suffrage system for which it provided are described satisfactorily in W. R. Anson, *Law and Custom of the Constitution* (5th ed.), I, 105-132, and are given full treatment in H. L. Morris, *op. cit.*, Chap. ix; J. L. Seager, *Parliamentary Elections Under the Reform Act of 1918 as Amended by Later Legislation* (London, 1921); and H. Fraser, *The Representation of the People Acts, 1918 to 1921* (2nd ed., London, 1921). Some important documents in relation to woman suffrage are presented in E. M. Sait and D. P. Barrows, *British Politics in Transition*, 102-122; and an interesting survey of the effects of the enfranchisement of

women is Helen Fraser, "What Came of Votes for Women," *Century Mag.*, May, 1926. Cf. H. Cox, "Franchise Reform," *Edinburgh Rev.*, July, 1927; F. Balfour, "The New Women's Franchise Bill," *Fortnightly Rev.*, July, 1927; and A. Comstock, "Women Members of European Parliaments," *Amer. Polit. Sci. Rev.*, May, 1926.

CHAPTER XIII

PARLIAMENTARY ELECTIONS

UNDER our American system of government, elections take place at regular intervals, regardless of whether they are really needed or whether the people want them when the time comes round. The president is placed in office for four years, no more and no less, and he must be reëlected or some one else elected to succeed him when that period is about to expire. In Britain, local elections take place at regular intervals,[1] but national—or, as the British say, general—elections do not. The only officers ever chosen at national elections are the members of the House of Commons; and they are elected under a rule which prescribes nothing more than that the maximum life of a parliament shall be five years. Even this rule is not insurmountable, as is evidenced by the fact that the parliament in existence when the World War broke out prolonged its own life, by special acts, three full years beyond the maximum fixed by law. That it had an undisputed right to do this, under emergency conditions at all events, affords some indication of the difference between its constitutional status and that of the Congress of the United States and most other national legislatures.

Dissolution and Writs of Election

Prior to 1688, a parliament could be terminated in only two ways, i.e., by decree of the sovereign or by his death. The second mode no longer exists; in keeping with the newer principle that a parliament is "the king's" only in name, the reform act of 1867 made the duration of a parliament entirely independent of the "demise of the crown," so that, for instance, upon the passing of Queen Victoria in 1901 her last parliament immediately became Edward VII's first. The other mode of

[1] See pp. 655, 665 below.

bringing a parliament to an end, and thus precipitating a general election, remains, but subject to two important limitations: first, the decision to dissolve is no longer made by the sovereign; and second, ever since 1693 the maximum duration, i.e., the life, of a parliament has been a subject of statutory regulation. From the date mentioned to 1716 the period was three years; thenceforth to 1911 it was seven years; since 1911 it has been five years. In point of fact, no parliament in all this time has been allowed to run its full term, and so "die a natural death." [2] Many have been cut short by a defeat of the ministry in the House of Commons, leading the premier and his colleagues to decide upon an appeal to the country, or, similarly, by the desire of a newly installed ministry to seek an endorsement and mandate from the people. Many have been terminated merely because at some stage in the course of the seven-year (later five-year) period the ministers judged the situation favorable for an electoral triumph conferring a new lease of official life. Three or four years may pass without an election; on the other hand, there may be two elections in a single year, as in 1910, or one in each of three successive years, as in 1922-24. Except in so far as their hands are forced by failure of support in the House of Commons, the matter lies entirely with the prime minister and his associates in the cabinet; and it goes without saying that this gives them and their party a considerable tactical advantage. They can nurse the country along until the situation is ripe for their purposes, and then announce a dissolution; indeed, they may deliberately "spring an election" so timed as to catch their opponents unprepared, although the trick is familiar and all parties try to be constantly in readiness. Of course the ministers will not make their decision lightly, for their fellow-partisans do not enjoy being put to the trouble and expense of seeking reëlection any more than do other people, and besides there is always the possibility of falling victim to miscalculation.[3] Speaking

[2] As has been observed, the war-time parliament of 1910–18 overran its regular term; but even it did not expire automatically by limitation of time.

[3] A notable instance of misjudgment of the sort is afforded by the dissolution of 1923, decided upon rather doubtfully by a cabinet that apparently had a long lease of life, in deference to Prime Minister Baldwin's

broadly, the parliamentary system ensures that an election will take place only when there are genuine issues to be settled; and to the extent to which matters work out in this way, elections tend to turn, not on vague generalities, but on definite and concrete proposals. Under the American plan, parties and candidates are sometimes hard put to it to find issues when election time inexorably comes round. Even in Britain, however, elections are sometimes called, not because a clash on some outstanding issue has set the nation by the ears, but only because of an arbitrary decision by the cabinet in its own interest, or, as in 1929, because of the approaching expiration of the existing parliament's five-year mandate.[4]

When an appeal to the country has been decided upon, a royal proclamation is issued which not only dissolves the two houses but indicates "the desire of the king to have the advice of his people in Parliament," instructs the Lord Chancellor to issue the necessary writs, and fixes the days for the nomination and polling. Writs of *summons* are sent to the members of the House of Lords (except the Scottish representative peers) individually; writs of *election* are dispatched to sheriffs of counties, mayors of boroughs, and chairmen of urban district councils, requiring them, as "returning officers," to make proper arrangements for the selection of members of the lower house.[5] Thus is set in motion the electoral machinery, which does not stop until the new House of Commons is chosen and in session.

Nomination of Candidates

British elections proceed with alacrity, and on the eighth day after the proclamation (Sundays and other holidays excluded)

desire to go to the country with a program of tariff reform. See p. 505 below.

[4] On the general subject of dissolutions, see M. MacDonagh, *The Pageant of Parliament,* II, Chap. xix. A list of parliaments, with dates of first meeting and dissolution, will be found in *Const. Year Book* (London, 1928), 107.

[5] For the form of the writs, see W. R. Anson, *Law and Custom of the Constitution* (5th ed.), I, 55-56. In the comparatively few instances in which a constituency includes more than one administrative area, the returning officer is such sheriff, mayor, or chairman as the Home Secretary may designate. In all cases the actual duties are performed by the regis-

all nominations must be made. On paper, at all events, the nominating process is exceedingly simple. There is neither convention nor primary, and all that is required by law is that a person who aspires to be a candidate shall, on the prescribed day, file with the returning officer a paper setting forth his name, residence, and business or profession, together with the names and addresses of two registered voters of the constituency who propose and second him and of eight others who "assent"—this, and one other thing, namely, a deposit of £150, to be forfeited unless the candidate proves to be unopposed or receives more than one-eighth of the total vote cast in his constituency on polling day. The latter unusual provision is intended, of course, to discourage frivolous and useless candidacies; and that it is decidedly effective is indicated by the fact that in the elections of 1922 and 1923, only about twenty-five candidates in the entire country were compelled to pay the forfeit.[6]

Of course, there is more to the matter of nominations than the hit-and-miss procedure suggested by the preceding paragraph. There are local party leaders and committees to be taken into the reckoning; also national party organizations at London which may take a hand, even to the extent of furnishing a candidate if none of satisfactory character can be found locally; and as a rule candidates are sufficiently agreed on, and even announced, in advance to avert uncertainty and delay if a dissolution takes place unexpectedly.[7] Contrary to what one

tration officer (normally the clerk), who may appoint deputies. See p. 297 below.

[6] Since 1882 parliamentary candidates in Canada have been required to deposit with the returning officer the sum of $200, which is returned only in case the candidate is successful or obtains a number of votes at least equal to half the number polled by the candidate elected. In Japan, under an electoral law of 1925, candidates must deposit the sum of 2,000 yen ($1,000), to be forfeited unless they obtain one-tenth as many votes as the quotient obtained by dividing the number of voters in the district by the number of seats. For arrangements on these lines in the Irish Free State, see p. 721 below.

[7] Lists of prospective candidates are not only kept by the central party office, but sometimes published. See *Liberal Year Book for 1928*, pp. 78-119. On March 1, 1929,—long before even the date of the 1929 general election had been fixed—more than four hundred accepted Liberal candidates were convened at London and addressed by Mr. Lloyd George on the party's policies in the coming campaign.

might expect, in the great majority of single-member constituencies only two or three candidates enter the lists—more frequently three, now that there is that number of important parties. And one will not be surprised to learn that while ten signatures suffice to meet the requirements of the law, candidates frequently deposit several papers containing scores, and even hundreds, of names of voters of various classes and sections in the constituency, in order to give an impression of popularity. The truth is that the matter is so completely under the control of the party organizations that there is practically no room for candidacies except such as these organizations endorse. The man—especially the beginner—who aspires to be a candidate must either wait until the organization (local or national) invites him or look about for a constituency in which he may hope, by taking the initiative, to be accepted. It is sometimes felt to be hardly less difficult to win acceptance or adoption as a candidate than to be returned as a member. Especially is this true in the Conservative party, where, as an ex-Commoner (a Liberal, but of Conservative antecedents) testifies, such acid tests are applied as: "Can you subscribe £500 a year to the local organization? Can you pay your election expenses? Can you keep up the dignity of the local traditions of the party by subscribing liberally to all local enterprises . . . ?" The same witness, however, goes on to say that perhaps, after all, an even severer test is applied by the other parties, i.e., "Have you sufficient ability to persuade *other people* to find your expenses?" [8]

Qualifications, Legal and Otherwise

Who is eligible to be nominated? Or, to put it differently, what qualifications must a person have in order to be elected and seated at Westminster? A history of the laws that have at one time or another governed qualifications for membership in the House of Commons would fill a volume, but regulations on the subject nowadays are liberal and relatively simple. Measures passed in the fifteenth century required residence

[8] F. Gray, *The Confessions of a Candidate* (London, 1925), 6. Cf. Chap. ii of this same book on "the choice of a constituency and selection as a candidate."

in the county or borough represented. These soon fell into disuse; but religious tests set up severe restrictions, and in the eighteenth century property requirements were added.[9] The last obsolete residential requirement was repealed in 1774;[10] property qualifications, which had proved easy to evade through fictitious conveyances of land,[11] were swept away in 1858; and the last survival of religious tests is to be seen in the present rule disqualifying clergymen of the Church of England,[12] ministers of the Church of Scotland, and Roman Catholic priests. Nowadays the only requirements of a positive character are that the member be of age,[13] a British subject (by birth or naturalization), and willing to take a very simple oath or affirmation of allegiance compatible with any shade of religious belief or disbelief. Negatively, certain other requirements are

[9] By an act of 1711, requiring (with a few exceptions) that county members have an income from land of £600 a year and borough members half that amount. The measure was designed to perpetuate the ascendancy of the "country," or Tory party, as against the rich manufacturers and traders, who were largely Whigs. Swift described it as "the greatest security that was ever contrived for preserving the constitution, which otherwise might in a little time be wholly at the mercy of the monied interest." Only in 1838 were general property or professional incomes allowed to be counted toward meeting the qualification.

[10] For interesting comment on the advantages of a system which not only permits, but encourages, constituencies to take from any place in the national jurisdiction any one they desire for service as their representative, see H. J. Ford, *Representative Government,* 165-170. Under American practice, members of Congress must be residents of the state, but not necessarily of the district, from which they are elected. Except in a few instances in the largest cities, however, congressmen are—by usage as old as Congress itself—almost invariably residents of their districts, and it is not worth while for an outsider to seek election. See J. Bryce, *The American Commonwealth* (4th ed), I, 191-195, and H. W. Horwill, *The Usages of the American Constitution,* Chap. ix. A list of "parliamentary migrations" would include most of the great names in modern British politics. Thus, Gladstone sat successively for Newark, Oxford University, South Lancashire, Greenwich, and Midlothian; Balfour for Hertford, East Manchester, and the City of London; Asquith for East Fife and Paisley; Bonar Law for Blackfriars (Glasgow), Dulwich, Bootle, and Central Glasgow.

[11] Pitt, Burke, Fox, and Sheridan are only a few of the members who were beneficiaries of this practice.

[12] Since the disestablishment of the Anglican Church in Wales in 1920 Anglican clergymen in that part of the realm are eligible.

[13] The presence of members under age was winked at until within the past hundred years. Fox, Lord John Russell, and other noted members were elected and seated before they were twenty-one.

imposed by the debarment not only of clergymen of the three historic churches named but of peers (except that Irish peers may sit for any but Irish constituencies), persons holding contracts from the government, convicts, lunatics and idiots, pensioners of the state (except as former civil servants or diplomats), and holders of office under the crown except such as are regarded as of a political nature.[14] From a very remote day the sheriffs of counties and the mayors of boroughs, as being officials in charge of parliamentary elections, have been excluded; and persons who as candidates for seats have violated the corrupt and illegal practices laws, or have condoned such violation in their behalf, are debarred for seven years, and indeed permanently so far as the constituency in which the offense occurred is concerned.[15]

Women first became eligible to sit in the House of Commons as a result of legislation supplementary to the Representation of the People Act of February 6, 1918, described above. No sooner was the latter measure, which enfranchised over eight and a half million women, on the statute book than the question arose whether its effect was to make women eligible for election. The law officers of the crown took a negative view. Women, however, began to announce their intention to be candidates; the Labor party declared in favor of female eligibility; and the House of Commons went on record by a decisive vote in favor of prompt enactment of a law on the subject. Opposition was half-hearted, and such serious discussion as took place centered around the question of amending the hurriedly introduced bill so as to abolish a wide variety of legal disqualifications against women as such.[16] In the House of Lords it was suggested that the measure be made to include authorization of peeresses in their own right to sit and vote in

[14] See p. 137 above.

[15] If the violation was without the candidate's knowledge or approval the penalty does not extend beyond debarment for seven years in the constituency concerned. For a list of statutes pertaining to disqualifications of the several kinds, see W. R. Anson, *Law and Custom of the Constitution* (5th ed.), I, 101-104. The earlier history of parliamentary qualifications is related at length in E. Porritt, *Unreformed House of Commons,* I, Chaps. vii-xi.

[16] This proposal did not prevail, but in the main it was realized in the Sex Disqualification Removal Act of the following year.

the second chamber; but it was successfully argued that this subject ought to be left for separate legislation, and in November, 1918, the Parliament (Qualification of Women) Act as it came from the House of Commons was carried through its final stages. At the elections of the following month, one woman candidate was successful, although, being a Sinn Feiner, she did not take her seat.[17] The first woman who actually served as a member of Parliament was Lady Astor, the American-born wife of Viscount Astor. After a spirited campaign, she, as a Unionist candidate, defeated her Liberal and Labor rivals in a by-election on November 15, 1919. The legislation of 1918 fixes no age limit for election to the chamber, which of course means that women are eligible at the same age as men.[18]

What sorts of people become candidates for seats in Parliament, and win them? The answer is more literally, "All kinds," than it would be in relation to perhaps any other important legislative assemblage in the world, and far more so in relation to the British Parliament today than before the rise of the Labor party to its present importance. On the green benches sit great landowners, sons of peers, bank directors, coal and iron magnates, along with teachers, journalists, farmers, and manual laborers. Hardly a business, a social class, a profession, or an interest is without representation. There are lawyers; but a conspicuous and significant contrast with American legislatures, both national and state, is the relatively small number of them and the less important rôle which they play. In 1925, when there were 262 members of the legal profession in the House of Representatives at Washington there were only ninety in the much more numerous House of Commons at Westminster. There is never a Congress in the one country in which lawyers do not preponderate; there is never a House of Commons in the other in which they constitute more than a fifth to a sixth of the membership. Mainly, in-

[17] See p. 705 below.

[18] A. Comstock, "Women Members of European Parliaments," *Amer. Polit. Sci. Rev.*, May, 1926, 379-384. In all, twenty-one different women were elected to the House of Commons from 1919 up to, and including, the general election of 1929. It may be noted that a Qualification of Women Act of 1907 made unmarried women eligible to membership in borough and county councils and in boards of poor-law guardians.

deed, because its membership is not disproportionately filled with lawyers, as well as because of the presence of increasing numbers of workingmen, the House of Commons, as an English observer has remarked, is a considerably more perfect mirror of the national life in Britain than is the House of Representatives in America.[19]

Electoral Campaigns

Electoral campaigns in the United States are long-drawn-out, and often rather tedious, affairs. In Britain they are at least never long-drawn-out. There is a sense, of course, in which they may be said to be going on most of the time. The parties are continually sparring for advantage. By-elections to fill vacant seats keep up the spirit of contest. Men who propose to go in for a parliamentary career address public gatherings, subscribe to civic and philanthropic causes, and in a dozen other ways keep themselves before and ingratiate themselves with the people of the constituency to which they are pinning their hopes. Members who want to continue their public careers systematically "nurse" their constituencies in similar fashion.[20] And of course when a dissolution looms in the offing party

[19] H. W. Horwill, *The Usages of the American Constitution* (Oxford, 1925), 171. See J. A. Thomas, "The House of Commons, 1832-1867; a Functional Analysis," *Economica*, Mar., 1925; and for a description of the social and economic structure of the House of Commons twenty years or more ago, J. Redlich, *Procedure of the House of Commons,* II, 115-130. A similar analysis of the situation in days before the reform acts will be found in E. Porritt, *The Unreformed House of Commons,* I, Chap. xxvi, and about 1760, in L. B. Namier, *The Structure of Politics at the Accession of George III,* I, Chap. i. A full tabulation of the professional connections or interests of the members of the House of Commons in 1928, classified also by parties, is presented in *Const. Year Book* (1928), 217. "Of the 194 Labor members in the present House of Commons [1925], roughly 136 are connected with manual working occupations, and fifty-eight with what it is customary to describe as the liberal professions. In the former, by far the largest single group is the miners, who number forty-six. The latter are extremely miscellaneous, including fourteen journalists, twelve business men, twelve teachers, five lawyers, three doctors, and a miscellaneous group ranging from peers to the humblest of God's creatures, such as university lecturers." R. H. Tawney, *The British Labor Movement* (New Haven, 1925), 40.

[20] On the methods—and the humors—of nursing a constituency, see F. Gray, *The Confessions of a Candidate,* Chaps. iv-v, and M. MacDonagh, *The Pageant of Parliament,* I, Chap. v.

committees and candidates set actively to work without awaiting the moment when it will actually befall.[21] The "campaign," however, in the stricter sense of the word is limited to less than three weeks. Nominations are made eight days after dissolution, and the people go to the polls nine days after that, Sundays and other holidays excluded. In these eighteen or nineteen days, all told, the battle of the ballots must be fought.[22]

Brevity is not the only respect in which the British campaign differs from the American. There is no political platform in quite the sense in which we have it in this country. It is true that the national conferences, or congresses, held by all of the parties at least once a year regularly adopt resolutions which embody party principles and policies; also that at the opening of a campaign a general statement of the issues to be pressed in that contest is likely to come from the prime minister (in behalf of the party in power), from the opposition leader or leaders, and especially from the central office of the Labor party at London.[23] Every candidate—even a Labor candidate—is, however, entitled to issue his own address or manifesto to the people of his constituency, and on this address—which may differ markedly from any general statement issued by his party and from the addresses of other candidates bearing the same party label—he makes his fight. Authorized by law to send one circular post-free to every voter in his constituency, the candidate can broadcast his manifesto without other expense than for printing; and in this way, as a rule, his campaign is formally launched. Too much stress should not, however, be placed upon the platform as an element of contrast between British and American elections. Any British party—particularly Labor—has, at any given election, a substantially agreed program which is to all intents and purposes a platform, even if not drawn up and promulgated for the particular occasion by a representative convention or other

[21] Thus the party manœuvering leading up to the general election of 1929 started at least with the conferences of the three principal parties held in September and October, 1928.

[22] Electoral campaigns are relatively brief in all cabinet-government countries. In France and Germany they seldom exceed three or four weeks.

[23] See Chap. xxiv below, and observe how (p. 587, note 20) Labor's program intended for use in the 1929 campaign was prepared.

body on the American plan. Furthermore, formally adopted platforms frequently play a less important rôle in American elections than the pronouncements of individual candidates, as notably in the case of the presidential election of 1928.

The country is more wrought up at some elections than at others, and contests are keener in some constituencies than in others.[24] But even in the most one-sided fight, in the most apathetic election, the appeal to the voters is more or less of the whirlwind variety. In the course of it, every reputable means known to politicians the world over is employed—and of course, occasionally expedients less unexceptionable. Meetings are held in halls and parks, and on street corners; advertisements are placed in newspapers, and some literature, although less than in America, is sent to the voters through the mails; billboards are plastered with cartoons, slogans, and appeals, and "sandwich-men" are employed by the day to trudge along crowded streets bearing placards soliciting votes; above all, house to house canvassing is carried on by volunteer friends and supporters of the candidate (hired canvassers are forbidden by law) with a thoroughness rarely encountered in similar efforts in the United States.[25] About the only campaigning device which as yet is employed rather less in Britain than in America is radio broadcasting.[26]

[24] As will be pointed out presently, there are always some constituencies in which, for lack of competition, there is no contest at all.

[25] "Canvassing," we read in a handbook issued to Liberal party workers in 1922, "is the most important part of the election campaign. If you do even a very little, you are rendering a valuable service; and if you can put in two or three hours every day for a fortnight, you will take front rank as an electioneering force. Remember that this is the work that really matters."

[26] For interesting comment on the way in which extensive use of the radio has transformed American national elections, see W. B. Munro, "The Campaign in Retrospect," *Yale Rev.*, Dec., 1928. The feature of the British campaign that would be most likely to interest, and indeed amaze, the American observer is the "heckling" of the candidates and other speakers by their audiences. Speakers at political meetings in America are occasionally interrupted by having questions shot at them from the floor or gallery, but incidents of the kind are so rare as to stir comment. In Britain the quizzing proceeds so mercilessly that many campaign addresses become little more than a series of questions, replies, interjections, retorts, thrusts, and parries. It is of no use for the speaker to grow impatient or lose his temper; heckling is part of the game, and he may as well make up his mind to meet

In it all, the candidate is naturally the leading figure, although much of the planning and actual work are done, of course, by the local party committee, the candidate's official agent, and other persons who are actuated by friendship for the candidate, interest in the "cause," or merely love of the game. There is only a relatively small area to be covered—even though the number of voters to be reached is now, on the average, almost three times as large as before 1918—and the task is carried out with a regard for detail that is rivalled in the United States only perhaps by the management of a Tammany campaign in New York. There is not much place in British political usage of today for the notion of John Stuart Mill, shared by Macaulay, that making a personal appeal to the voters is an undignified and improper procedure in a system under which men are supposed to be sent to Parliament to serve the public.

Campaign Expenditures

As has been indicated, the campaign is run to some extent with the aid of voluntary, unpaid workers. But there are many things to be settled for—halls when used for meetings, newspaper advertisements, postage, printing, billboard space, the services of sandwich-men—and without some pretty stringent regulation the wooing of the electors would be likely to prove a decidedly costly performance. It was such, indeed, in the old days, not only because no statutory limits were placed upon expenditures which were inherently defensible, but because of the very general practice of buying votes, with money or something equivalent. Within the memory of men still liv-

it and turn it to his own profit as best he can. If he is sufficiently quick-witted, tactful, and well-informed to be able to stand up impressively under the barrage, he may easily command more sympathy and win more votes than by the most smooth-flowing and masterful formal speech he could expect to deliver. He may be sure, however, that his hearers are not easily deceived. "You have not asked me many questions; now's your chance," a candidate once said to his audience in closing an address. From the back of the hall came the instant rejoinder: "Ain't no good asking you questions. If we ask you a question you answer seven that ain't been asked." Women speakers are no more spared than are men. But, after all, the spirit of fairness is usually present, and indeed that is what keeps the practice from becoming an intolerable abuse.

ing, British parliamentary elections were, speaking generally, shameless affairs. Great numbers of the voters looked upon their franchise primarily as a pecuniary asset, on which they expected to realize to the utmost whenever an election came round. In many constituencies a candidate could not hope to get anywhere at all unless he showered food, drink, money, and other tangible favors upon the people; and after the voters had pocketed their bribes and eaten and drunk and smoked and rollicked and had their bills paid at a candidate's expense they were considered men of conscience indeed if they did not end by going over to a still more free-handed competitor. The notorious "spendthrift election" of 1768 at Northampton, in the course of which a body of voters numbering under a thousand were recipients of hospitalities from the backers of three candidates which aggregated upwards of a million pounds, was, of course, exceptional; but countless other cases differed from it only in the amounts laid out. In the borough of Shoreham the electors actually formed a joint-stock company for the purpose of obtaining top prices for their votes.[27]

Today an altogether different state of things obtains. From having been one of the most corrupt, Britain has become one of the most exemplary of nations in all that pertains to electoral procedure. There was, it is only fair to recognize, no lack of legislation aimed at securing purity of elections, even when conditions were at their worst. A law of 1696 defined bribery

[27] "Oh, sir," one of Sheridan's constituents once complained to him, "things cannot go on this way; there must be a reform. We poor electors are not paid properly at all." At one election in the Irish borough of Cashel a candidate, anxious to win the seat honestly, got the parish priest to preach a sermon at mass, on the Sunday before polling, against the immorality of trafficking in the franchise. "The good man, indeed, went so far in the course of his impressive sermon as to declare that those who betrayed a public trust by selling their votes would go to hell. Next day the candidate met one of the electors and asked what was the effect of Sunday's sermon. 'Your honor,' said he, 'votes have risen. We always got £20 for a vote before we knew it was a sin to sell it; but as his reverence tells us that we will be damned for selling our votes, we can't for the future afford to take less than £40.'" M. MacDonagh, *The Pageant of Parliament,* I, 27. Good accounts of electoral corruption in the eighteenth and early nineteenth centuries will be found in C. Seymour, *Electoral Reform in England and Wales, 1832-1885,* Chaps. vii-viii, and C. Seymour and D. P. Frary, *How the World Votes,* I, Chap. v.

and fixed penalties for it, and acts of 1726 and 1809 added new precautions. The first measure to have very much effect, however, was a corrupt practices act of 1854, which was considerably strengthened by corrupt practices clauses of the Ballot Act of 1872; and at length, in 1883, a consolidating Corrupt and Illegal Practices Prevention Act was placed upon the statute book, which has proved so effective that it has never since been necessary to do more than readjust its provisions in certain more or less important particulars.

It is this great statute, with later amendments, that regulates the whole matter of campaign expenditures—and, indeed, electoral manners generally—today. This it does, first, by defining and penalizing *corrupt* practices, e.g., bribery, treating, intimidation, personation, and falsifying the count, all of which are acts involving moral turpitude; second, by defining and more lightly penalizing *illegal* practices, i.e., acts which, while not immoral, are deemed contrary to good electoral practice, such as the hiring of canvassers, paying for conveyances used in getting voters to the polls, or voting or attempting to vote in more constituencies than the law allows;[28] and, third, by rigorously regulating the amount, and to some extent restricting the mode, of expenditure by candidates or in their behalf. In the matter of the amount, it was recognized that it would be unfair to fix a flat maximum sum; obviously it would cost more to carry on an equally intensive campaign in a county constituency, with people living farther apart, than in a borough constituency, and, besides, constituencies of the same type differ widely, as we have seen, in population. Hence a sliding scale was adopted in terms of numbers of voters. In boroughs containing not more than 2,000 registered voters the maximum amount was put at £350, with an additional £30 for every thousand voters above that number. In rural constituencies, the sum of £650 was allowed when the number of registered electors was under 2,000, with £60 for each additional thousand. Beyond this, the candidate was permitted an outlay of £100 for expenses of a purely personal character.

In later years it was felt that these amounts were too large,

[28] For a convenient summary of election offenses, see *Liberal Year Book* (1928), 169-170.

and the Representation of the People Act of 1918 set up a new and reduced scale, defined in still more exact relation to the number of voters. As modified slightly by the Representation of the People (Equal Franchise) Act of 1928, the maximum expenditure in county constituencies is now (aside from a small agent's fee) 6*d.* (12 cents) per elector, and in borough constituencies 5*d.* (10 cents); though of course, it must not be overlooked that the enormous increase of the electorate by the suffrage sections of the two acts mentioned largely offsets the effect of the reduction as figured on a per capita basis.[29] There is also the important fact that, whereas formerly the candidates in a constituency were required to pay jointly the costs of the election itself—polling-stations, printing, clerk hire, fees and travelling expenses of returning officers, etc.—the act of 1918 made these a charge upon the national treasury.[30] With a view to unified and complete reports of the outlays of candidates, every one is required to have a single authorized agent charged with the disbursement of all moneys (except certain specified "personal" expenditures, e.g., for living quarters during the campaign, not exceeding £100) in his behalf, and with the duty of submitting to the returning officer within thirty-five days after the election a sworn statement covering all receipts and disbursements.[31]

The range of expenditure still permitted by law is, of course, considerable, and the records of election cases brought into the courts demonstrate that in practice its limits are often exceeded. Nevertheless, the effect of the legislation of the past fifty

[29] Japan regulates expenditures in parliamentary elections after the same method as Great Britain, permitting an outlay equivalent to 40 sen (20 cents) per elector.

[30] In 1919 they were given the status of Consolidated Fund charges. In France and other Continental countries various electoral expenses, e.g., the cost of ballots, are still borne by the candidates.

[31] On the functions and influences of these agents, see A. L. Lowell, *Government of England,* I, 481-484. It may be noted that the statutory restrictions as to amount of expenditure do not apply to merely prospective, as distinguished from "adopted," candidates. Even though a person has been fully agreed upon in a constituency as the man or woman whom the party will put up when an election comes round, he and his supporters may spend money in any sum, with no accounting, until, the election being at hand, the local party organization formally "adopts" him. Thereupon his outlays begin to count under the law.

years has unquestionably been to restrain the outpouring of money by candidates and their backers, and therefore to purify politics, and at the same time to enable men of moderate means to stand for election who otherwise would be at grave disadvantage as against wealthier and more lavish competitors.[32]

Registration of Voters

When the campaign has run its course and polling day arrives, who is entitled to vote? Manifestly, only persons who come within the bounds of the suffrage laws, chiefly the acts of 1918 and 1928. There is, however, a further very important requirement; such persons may vote only if their names are on the registration list of the constituency. A permanent system of listing the names of qualified voters was introduced for the first time by the reform act of 1832, and thenceforth a main concern of party leaders and workers was to get the names of actual or potential supporters on the lists and keep them there from election to election. Indeed, we shall see that this form of activity had much to do with the earliest development of local party machinery on lines something like the present ones.[33] Much red tape was involved, and in spite of the efforts of the party canvassers, large numbers of men failed to register. But the system stood practically unchanged until the present century; and, as we have seen, the proposals of the electoral bill

[32] The history of corrupt and illegal practice legislation through 1885 is well told in C. Seymour, *Electoral Reform in England and Wales, 1832-1885,* Chaps. xiii-xiv. In 1900 a total of 1,103 candidates for 670 seats reported an expenditure of £777,429 in getting 3,579,345 votes; in January, 1910, 1,311 candidates for the same number of seats reported £1,296,382 and polled 6,667,394 votes; in 1924, 1,428 candidates for 615 seats reported £921,165 spent in getting 16,384,629 votes. In all cases expenditure on uncontested seats was, of course, negligible. The regulation of campaign expenditures in the United States may be compared by reading J. K. Pollock, Jr., *Party Campaign Funds* (New York, 1926), Chaps. vii-viii. Cf. E. M. Sait, *American Parties and Elections* (New York, 1927), Chap. xix. On American corrupt practices acts, see *ibid.*, Chap. xx; E. R. Sikes, *State and Federal Corrupt Practices Legislation* (Durham, 1928); and H. M. Rocca, *Corrupt Practices Legislation* (Washington, 1928). The fundamentals of the problem as it still exists in the United States are set forth in Sait, "Campaign Expenditures," *Amer. Polit. Sci. Rev.*, Feb., 1929.

[33] See p. 573 below.

of 1912 on this subject failed along with the remainder of that measure.

The present simple and effective system of registration came in with the act of 1918, as modified by the Representation of the People (Economy Provisions) Act of 1926. Parties have by no means lost interest in the matter, which is no less vital for them now than in the old days. But the new law is based on the principle that it is the business of the state to see that every qualified person, man or woman, is put on the register in the proper constituency (or constituencies), despite all obstacles that may be set up by over-zealous party watchers or the ignorance or apathy of the voters themselves; and while the lists are, of course, not infallibly accurate, they are made and kept up to date with a painstaking care hardly known in any other country. Practically no burden at all is placed upon the electors. In every county and borough there is a registration officer—regularly the clerk of the council, elected by the council itself—whose business it is to compile and revise the list of parliamentary, as well as that of local, electors;[34] and this he does by sending canvassers from house to house in July of each year with copies of the last previous list on which are to be entered all changes that are discovered.[35] The results—embodied in three lists, (1) the register then in force, (2) the new voters proposed to be added, and (3) the names proposed to be stricken off—are assembled and printed, and copies are placed on exhibit in the town or county hall, at post-offices and libraries, and even at the doors of churches and chapels, so that anybody who has been missed can discover and report the fact, and any other error can be detected and corrected.[36] A final list

[34] These lists are, of course, not identical. In the case of university constituencies the governing body of the university prepares and revises the register.

[35] Under the act of 1918 the lists were revised twice a year, and the canvass was made both in January and in June. Under the act of 1926 revision takes place only once a year, as was the case prior to 1918.

[36] The definitive lists must be thus published by July 15 in England and Wales and by August 8 in Scotland. For the complete registration calendar as it now stands, see *Constitutional Year Book* (London, 1928), I. It is to be noted, however, that in order to enable the new voters created by the equal franchise legislation of 1928 to be absorbed promptly into the effective electorate, a new register was prepared on a special schedule and put into operation on May 1, 1929.

is then prepared, the registration officer using his best judgment in doubtful cases, with the additional safeguard of appeal to the county court and thence, on a point of law, to the Court of Appeals. The elector is expected to take the initiative under only one circumstance, i.e., if he wants to be put on the special list of "absent" voters. Having once been prepared in this scrupulous manner, the list stands for the twelve months beginning October 15;[37] and no one whose name does not appear may be admitted to vote within the period, even though there is some difference of practice in respect to permitting persons to vote who are discovered to have got on the list through obvious error.[38]

Election Day and Polling Day

Formerly, when the sheriffs and mayors, as returning officers, received writs of election they exercised their discretion, within limits set by law, in fixing the election day, and also the polling day if one was necessary. As a result, from a week to upwards of two weeks elapsed from the time the first results were known until the last ones were declared, and it was often possible for the constituencies voting late to see in advance how the contest was coming out and to swing their votes accordingly if any motive appeared for doing so. In any event, the country was kept in electoral turmoil for many days, suffering some of the inconveniences that are entailed in the United States by an excessively prolonged pre-election campaign. The act of 1918, however, changed all this. As has been explained, the eighth day after the proclamation goes forth is now election day for all constituencies, and the polling takes place nine days thereafter, the only exception being the university constituencies, whose voting is principally by mail and is spread

[37] From 1918 to 1926, for six months, beginning April 15 and October 15.

[38] Since registration is carried on simultaneously and by the same authorities for both national and local elections, the expense is shared equally between the borough or county and the national treasury. The earlier development of the registration system is described in C. Seymour, *op. cit.*, Chaps. v, vi, xii. On the actual method of registration in boroughs, see A. S. Wright and E. H. Singleton, *Organization and Administration of the Town Clerk's Department and the Justices' Clerk's Department* (London, 1925), Chap. iv.

over some five days. Election day is really "election" day literally in only those constituencies in which there is no contest. In such cases, the single candidate is formally nominated, the returning officer declares his election, and the transaction completes itself without any voting at all. The number of such uncontested elections is not as large as it used to be when Ireland still had her hundred-odd seats and most of them were filled with Nationalists against whom it was useless to make a fight. But there are always cases of the sort—sometimes many of them—in other parts of the kingdom.[39] Where there is a contest, election day, so-called, is merely the day on which the nominations are made, the election itself being adjourned to the ninth succeeding day in order that a "poll," or count of votes, may be held to decide which candidate shall have the seat.

Until about half a century ago, voting was by show of hands at a public meeting of the electors, and, in view of what has already been said about electoral manners, it is hardly necessary to add that polling days were tumultuous occasions. Rivers of beer were set flowing; bribes were openly offered and accepted; organized bands of "bludgeon-men" went about intimidating and coercing electors; non-voters thrust themselves joyously into the fray; political convictions were expressed in terms of rotten apples and dead cats; heads were broken and a generally riotous time was had by all. From 1832 onwards, there was incessant demand on the part of reformers for voting by secret ballot.[40] The Chartists made the reform one of their "six points," and for nine years the historian Grote annually moved a resolution in its favor. Forty years of agitation, however, leading up to a challenging report by a special committee of the House of Commons, were necessary to bring Parliament to the point of action, and even then action was taken over the protest of no less enlightened a student of gov-

[39] In 1922 there were fifty-seven; in 1923, fifty; in 1924, thirty-two; in 1929, only seven. It is hardly necessary to point out that, on account of these constituencies in which the electors are not brought to the polls the popular vote of the country as actually recorded does not indicate the total popular support enjoyed by the various parties.

[40] James Harrington made perhaps the earliest argument for the secret ballot, in his *Commonwealth of Oceana,* published in 1656.

ernment than John Stuart Mill.[41] The Parliamentary and Municipal Elections Act, commonly known as the Ballot Act, finally passed in 1872, was for eight years only, and from the end of that period until 1918 it was kept alive simply by being included in the annual Expiring Laws Continuance Act. In the last-mentioned year, however, it was at last converted from an annual into a permanent statute; and certainly no feature of British political methodology is now to be regarded as more securely established.

When, therefore, the properly qualified and registered elector presents himself at the voting-place today, it is not as a member of a disorderly mass-meeting but as a peaceful and responsible citizen about to discharge a solemn duty in a manner befitting the occasion. Arrangements for the poll are made by the returning officer in accordance with minute statutory regulation: polling places in sufficient numbers are designated in each constituency;[42] ballot-papers are printed at the expense of the state and got in shape for distribution; a deputy returning officer is appointed to preside at each polling place, and poll clerks are named, at the rate of one for every five hundred voters or fraction thereof; the ballot-boxes are brought forth, inspected, and sent to the polling places, along with lists of the eligible voters, bundles of blank ballots, an official stamp which every ballot must bear in order to be counted, pencils, pens, sealing wax, and other necessary equipment; deputies and

[41] Mill's argument was that, the suffrage being a public trust, confided to a limited number of the community, the general public, for whose benefit it was exercised, were entitled to see how it was used, openly and in the light of day. *Representative Government,* Chap. x, "On the Mode of Voting" (ed. by A. D. Lindsay, pp. 298-312). Meanwhile Victoria had introduced the system in 1856 and other Australian dependencies were following the example. In Continental Europe the ballot was introduced in Piedmont in 1848 and extended throughout the kingdom of Italy in 1861, and it was provided for in the German electoral law of 1869. In the United States voting by ballot was common from the Revolutionary period, although the "Australian" system, effectually securing secrecy, did not prevail until late in the nineteenth century. The first complete law on the subject was enacted by Massachusetts in 1888. See E. C. Evans, *A History of the Australian Ballot System in the United States* (New York, 1921).

[42] The rooms of any school which receives aid from parliamentary grants, or of any building maintained out of the local rates, may be used without charge. Failing these, other places may be hired, in inns or other privately owned houses, or even in churches or chapels.

clerks are instructed in their duties and reminded that dereliction on their part will lay them liable to fine and imprisonment. On the morning of polling day, the presiding officer first of all displays the ballot box—which is made of steel, enameled in black, and with a slot in the lid—in such a way as to show those present that there is nothing in it; then he locks it, seals it so that it cannot again be opened without breaking the seal, and, on the stroke of eight, announces that polling will begin.[43]

What happens when Mr. X, green-grocer of Putney, or Mrs. Y, housewife of Cheltenham, steps into the polling place prepared to do his or her part to save the nation from disaster? First of all, a poll clerk asks the name and address. These obtained, the information is checked against the registry; and if there is no discrepancy, the elector is handed a ballot. It would be a novel and disconcerting experience for any elector in Britain to find in his hands a "blanket" ballot, or a sheaf of half a dozen separate ballots, of the sort with which the American is ordinarily expected to wrestle.[44] For, in national elections regularly, and in local elections usually, he is called upon to express his choice among only two or three candidates, for but a single position. Consequently, the ballot which he receives at a parliamentary election is a very simple affair—a bit of white paper hardly larger than an ordinary envelope, numbered on the back and bearing the official stamp on back and front, but devoid of party names and emblems, and indeed containing nothing but the names, addresses, and vocations of the candidates. These ballots are put up in the style of check-books, each paper having a counterfoil or stub; and as the poll clerk detaches a paper and gives it to an elector he writes on the stub the elector's number on the register, which of course makes it possible to trace the vote of any elector should occasion arise. Taking his paper to a screened compartment, the voter makes a cross in the space to the right of the name of the candidate of his choice; and then, folding the ballot so as to conceal the marking, but leaving the stamp exposed, he drops it in the ballot box and goes his way. If a voter is incapacitated from marking

[43] The regular polling hours are 8 A.M. to 8 P.M., but on request of the candidates they may be changed in any constituency to 7 A.M. to 9 P.M.

[44] E. M. Sait, *op. cit.*, 531-540.

the ballot himself, the presiding officer may mark it for him, in the presence of the candidates' agents.

Every candidate, it may be noted, has a right to have an agent present throughout the polling, for the purpose of checking off the names of those who vote, watching for attempts at fraud, and challenging persons who are suspected of trying to vote under false names. Challenges are, in point of fact, not very numerous, and are sustained or overruled by the presiding officer, with no appeal from his decision. Agents as well as officials are bound by oath not to divulge who have voted, and are forbidden to seek to induce any one to tell how he is going to vote or has voted, or, indeed, to interfere with the voter's freedom in any way, save only to establish his identity in case there is question.[45]

When the closing hour arrives, the presiding officer announces the fact and, in the presence of the agents, closes the slot of the ballot box and seals it, makes sure that the box is locked, binds red tape around it and seals that also, and then takes or sends the box to the returning officer, accompanied with (1) a written statement showing the total number of ballot papers supplied to the polling station and the number used, unused, and spoiled, (2) the unused ballots, (3) the counterfoils or stubs, (4) the marked copies of the register of voters, and (5) the list of "tendered" votes, i.e., votes cast by presumably authenticated persons who find on arrival at the polling place that—despite the precautions—somebody has been permitted to vote under their name. It will be observed that, contrary to American practice, the count is not made at the several polling places. Instead, it is made at some central point in the constituency—usually the town hall or county hall

[45] As a rule, British electors are much less remiss about going to the polls and voting than are Americans. For example, in the parliamentary election of 1924 16,384,629 votes were polled in an electorate of 21,729,385, amounting to almost 75.5 per cent, as compared with 29,138,935 in an electorate of 56,941,584 in the presidential election in the United States in the same year, amounting to only 49.1 per cent; and this takes no account of the large number of British voters not called to the polls because of the lack of a contest in their constituencies. Nevertheless, the reported success of compulsory voting in the Commonwealth of Australia at its first trial on a national scale in 1925 has led to proposals that the plan be adopted in the mother country.

—and by the returning officer or one of his assistants, in the presence of the candidates' agents.[46] Furthermore, before it is made all of the ballots turned in for the constituency are mixed together, so that the result is never published for polling places, or precincts, separately, but only for the constituency as a whole. When the outcome is determined, the writ which served as the returning officer's authority is endorsed with a certificate of election, and, together with all of the ballot papers, is transmitted to the clerk of the crown in chancery, an official in the Lord Chancellor's office, by whom the writ was originally sent out. This official copies into a book the names of all the persons certified as elected and delivers it to the clerk of the House of Commons to be used in making up the roll when the new parliament assembles.[47]

The act of 1918 introduced two interesting novelties in the manner of voting at elections, i.e., voting by post and voting by proxy. The main immediate purpose of the statute was, indeed, to bring back into the effective electorate the millions of men whose absence from the country in military or naval service to all intents and purposes disfranchised them for the time being. Accordingly, electors were authorized to receive and return their ballot-papers by post, provided they were registered on the absent voters' list; and a supplementary act of 1920 continues the arrangement, subject only to the added qualification that the voter must have an address in the United Kingdom. Even under normal, peace-time conditions, this device liberates from practical disfranchisement many thousands of persons—merchant seamen, commercial travellers, fishermen, and others, as well as soldiers and sailors—whose pursuits keep them away from their homes. The act of 1918 permitted proxy voting only to soldiers and sailors serving abroad (in places specified by orders in council) and to seamen. But the measure of 1920 opens the privilege to any elector who is on the absent voter's list and who satisfies the registration official that he will probably be, at the time of the next parliamentary elec-

[46] Central counting is not entirely unknown in the United States. It is in use in San Francisco and under a California law of 1921 may be extended to any city or city-and-county in the state.

[47] The conduct of elections in the United States may be compared by reading E. M. Sait, *American Parties and Elections,* Chap. xx.

tion, at sea or otherwise out of the country. Such a voter gives to a proxy whom he chooses a proxy paper which, unless cancelled, holds good as long as the elector continues to be registered in respect of the same qualification and to be on the absent voters list. The proxy must be either a relative (wife, husband, parent, brother, or sister) or a person registered as an elector for a constituency in which the elector for whom he acts as proxy is himself registered; and, except as a relative, no person may serve as a proxy for more than two absent voters in a constituency. In view of the great numbers of British subjects who spend their time chiefly at sea or in sojourns in the colonies or other distant lands, proxy voting is of larger practical use than it would be in most other countries.

Certification of the successful candidate by the returning officer of the constituency is not necessarily the last stage or step in the electoral process. For if a defeated candidate—or, for that matter, any voter—believes that there has been a miscount, or that the victor or his agents have been guilty of corrupt or illegal practices, or that the victor is ineligible, he can petition to have the election invalidated. If the question is merely one of legal eligibility, the House itself settles it. But if it relates to any electoral irregularity, it goes, not to the House, but to two judges of the King's Bench division of the High Court of Justice,[48] selected for each case by the whole body of judges in that division. They take evidence and certify a report to the House, in accordance with which the member in question keeps his seat or loses it. In the United States the House of Representatives is judge of the qualifications of its members in the full sense that disputed elections are decided by investigation and vote of the House itself,[49] and prior to 1868 the same plan prevailed in Great Britain.[50] Partisan handling of

[48] In cases relating to England and Wales; the Court of Session, in cases relating to Scotland; and the High Court of Justice, in those relating to Northern Ireland.

[49] D. S. Alexander, *History and Procedure of the House of Representatives* (Boston, 1916), Chap. xvi.

[50] On the early fight of the House of Commons to obtain jurisdiction over disputed elections, and the difficulties experienced after such control had been won, see C. Wittke, *The History of English Parliamentary Privilege* (Columbus, 1921), Chap. iii.

electoral contests in that country led, however, in 1868, to adoption of the present highly preferable system. Protests are not numerous nowadays, and the actual voiding of an election is a rare event.[51]

Voluntary Vacating of Seats

"I begin to wonder," wrote Macaulay to his sister in 1833, after a few years of experience in the House of Commons, "what the fascination is which attracts men, who could sit over their tea and their book in their own cool, quiet room, to breathe bad air, hear bad speeches, lounge up and down the long gallery, and doze uneasily on the green benches till three in the morning." By and large, men are found to be perfectly willing to undergo these and other hardships for the honor and influence that go with service in the House.[52] Still, it sometimes happens that a member grows weary and wants to retire. His

[51] Brief general accounts of the electoral system as it stood before the act of 1918 will be found in A. L. Lowell, *Government of England,* I, Chap. x, and M. Ostrogorski, *Democracy and the Organization of Political Parties,* trans. by F. Clarke (London, 1902), I, 442-501. Formal treatises include H. Fraser, *Law of Parliamentary Elections and Election Petitions* (2nd ed., London, 1910), and a monumental work is M. Powell (ed.), *Rogers on Elections,* 3 vols. (16th ed., London, 1897). Electoral procedure nowadays is described in popular fashion in M. MacDonagh, *The Pageant of Parliament,* I, Chaps. i-iv, and more thoroughly in J. R. Seager, *Parliamentary Elections under the Reform Act of 1918, as Amended in Later Legislation* (London, 1921). On the mode of conducting "by-elections" to fill vacancies arising between general elections, see T. E. May, *op. cit.,* Chap. xxiv, *passim.*

[52] *Some* men, but not all. An ex-member, already quoted, recently wrote: "Mr. Reginald McKenna and Sir Robert Horne probably have it within their power to make the greatest contribution of all our public men to political life today, yet both seek solace in business, and are prepared to sacrifice the greater glamour of life which the political world can give. I am not surprised. I have seen Sir Robert rise to the despatch box in the Commons as the star turn speaker of the Conservatives in a full-dress debate—a man worthy to occupy that position for any party—and yet during the progress of his carefully prepared speech I have seen him twitted and checked by Mr. George Buchanan and Mr. Daniel Kirkwood of the Clydeside, and tittered at from other benches, for here all are, equal, and this a man whose presence at a Board meeting would silence in awe the giants of our commercial world. Probably he submits to greater indignities in his constituency. It is sad that men prefer the City, the bank, and the counting house, to the laurels and rewards of public life, but it is intelligible." F. Gray, *The Confessions of a Candidate,* 2-3.

health may have failed; he may want to engage in some private undertaking that will absorb all his time and energy. Here, however, a curious fact presents itself, namely, that under a rule dating from 1623 a member cannot resign his seat, just as, indeed, he cannot refuse to take it even if nominated and elected against his will.[53] He may be dropped because he has gone into bankruptcy or become a lunatic; he may be expelled for any reason deemed sufficient by the House, e.g., conviction on charges of treason or felony; [54] he may be translated, willingly or unwillingly, to the House of Lords; but he cannot resign outright. This does not mean, however, that there is no way by which he can voluntarily sever connection. There is a roundabout way, which consists in procuring appointment to some public office which under the statutes is incompatible with membership. There are, of course, many such offices. But the one usually sought for the purpose is the stewardship of His Majesty's three Chiltern Hundreds of Stoke, Desborough, and Burnham, in Buckinghamshire. Centuries ago, this officer was appointed by the crown to have the custody of certain forests frequented by brigands. The brigands are long since dead, and the forests themselves have been converted into parks and pasture lands, but the stewardship remains. The member who wishes to give up his seat applies to the Chancellor of the Exchequer for this, or for some other old office with nominal duties and emoluments,[55] receives it, "with all wages, fees, allowances," etc., and thereby disqualifies himself, and afterwards retains it only until such time as the appointment is revoked to make way for another man. On at least four occasions since 1850 the stewardship of the Chiltern Hundreds has been granted twice, and resigned as often, on the same day.

[53] The rule is, of course, a curious reminder of the days before Parliament gained much power, when country gentlemen frequently had to be dragooned into taking upon themselves the duties and responsibilities of representatives. Cf. C. Seymour and D. P. Frary, *How the World Votes,* I, 66-67.

[54] Expulsion does not disqualify for immediate reëlection, by either the same constituency or a different one. Walpole, Wilkes, and Bradlaugh are among members who have been expelled but promptly sent back. See T. E. May, *op. cit.* (13th ed.), 66-69.

[55] The stewardship of the Manor of Northstead sometimes figures in this way.

Applications have, however, been known to be refused.[56] No way, it may be added, has ever been devised by which a constituency, on its part, can rid itself of a duly elected representative before the dissolution of the parliament to which he has been chosen, no matter how grossly he may neglect his duties or otherwise abuse the confidence of the voters.

Electoral Questions of the Future

Electoral systems never attain perfection. On the contrary, they are always, at best, rather hazardous devices, serving their purpose in a rough sort of way, but open to criticism alike from disinterested observers and from parties and groups which fare badly under their operation. Growth of population and changes in its distribution require frequent readjustments, in addition to such as may arise from new conceptions and ideals of the electoral process, and even of representative government generally. In some countries, e.g., France and Italy, the machinery of elections is among the most unstable parts of the political system. As a result of a full century of agitation and experiment, Britain has achieved electoral arrangements which, so far as any absolute standard can be recognized, rank with the best in the world. From many points of view, however, the system still has shortcomings; many Englishmen are profoundly dissatisfied with it; and as time goes on plenty of further changes will have to be made. So far as any major question is concerned, the parliamentary suffrage is presumably settled. The removal of age and other discriminations against women in 1928 leaves room for only relatively unimportant changes.[57] Plural voting, though much attenuated, survives and no doubt will yield further discussion. University

[56] *Report from the Select Committee on House of Commons* (*Vacating of Seats*), 1894. For an excellent account of this curious office, see M. MacDonagh, *The Pageant of Parliament,* II, Chap. xviii. Cf. E. Porritt, *Unreformed House of Commons,* I, 242-250. When Mr. (later Lord) Bryce was named as ambassador to the United States in 1907, he was obliged to accept appointment to the stewardship of the Chiltern Hundreds in order to be enabled to relinquish his seat in the House of Commons; for, although an office of profit under the crown, a ministership or ambassadorship to a foreign state does not disqualify for membership in the House.

[57] The suffrage in local elections (with which we are not concerned here) offers some further questions.

representation, with which, as we have seen, plural voting is at present tied up, will continue to stir opposition; and indeed the whole problem of "functional," as opposed to geographical, representation promises to be a leading theme of debate, if not a practical issue of party politics.[58] Adoption of something like the Australian scheme of compulsory voting has been proposed, though not discussed seriously.[59] The need for a general redistribution of seats will reappear and grow more urgent as time passes; already a period of years has elapsed, since the existing distribution was made, equal to that which the American constitution fixes as the interval between reapportionments. One other change—as fundamental as any except a general substitution of functional for geographical representation—is well within the bounds of possibility, namely, the introduction of some form of that now very familiar feature of Continental electoral systems, proportional representation—or, at all events, of some device for securing systematic representation of minorities; and inasmuch as such a departure promises to become an increasingly important issue in years that lie ahead, leading to drastic electoral reorganization in the event that a plan is adopted, something may well be said upon the subject.

The Problem of Representation of Minorities

Interest in electoral arrangements calculated to give minorities some representation in the House of Commons arose simultaneously with the movement for a broader suffrage and gained in intensity as the electorate progressively expanded and minorities, as well as majorities, grew larger and more articulate. The first device hit upon by reformers was that known as the "limited vote" and consisted of a scheme under which, in constituencies returning three or more members, the electors were to vote only for two candidates, or at all events for some number less than the full quota of seats to be filled.

[58] For a brief discussion of functional, or occupational, representation in general, see J. W. Garner, *Political Science and Government,* 655-664; and cf. p. 359 below.

[59] Compulsory voting was adopted by Queensland in 1915, and by the Australian Commonwealth in 1925. The percentage of qualified electors who go to the polls is, however, higher in Great Britain than it was in Australia or is in the United States.

The idea was that the majority elements in the constituency would concentrate their votes upon certain candidates of their preference, leaving the remaining choices to be made by the minority. This plan was suggested when the reform bill of 1832 was before Parliament; [60] it appeared in an abortive parliamentary representation bill of 1854; and the Representation of the People Act of 1867 undertook to make trial of it in thirteen multiple-member constituencies, including the City of London and the important northern towns of Glasgow, Liverpool, Manchester, Birmingham, and Leeds. The results were interesting, but the nation was not won over to the "fancy franchise," and in 1884-85, when the single-member-district plan came into general use, the scheme was abandoned.[61] Gladstone argued that the single-member-district system would itself go a long way toward providing the minority representation "which many gentlemen have much at heart."

Another scheme brought forward in the same mid-century period was that of "cumulative voting," under which the elector has as many votes as there are seats to be filled and is permitted to distribute them among an equivalent number of candidates or to concentrate them upon a lesser number, or even to bestow all of them upon one, at his discretion. By cumulating votes upon a minority candidate, a small but well organized political element may be able to push him over the line. An effort was made to get a provision of this kind into the act of 1867, but without avail; and the only use of the system that has ever been made in Britain was in connection with school-board elections from 1870 to 1902.[62]

[60] Especially by Mackworth Praed, who may be regarded as the father of the minority-representation movement. J. H. Humphries, *Proportional Representation* (London, 1911), 63-64.

[61] See p. 575 below for the ingenious way in which the Liberals at Birmingham contrived to defeat the purposes of the legislation. On the important part played by this experiment in the development of English party machinery, see, further, A. L. Lowell, *Government of England,* I, 469-478, and M. Ostrogorski, *Democracy and the Organization of Political Parties* (New York, 1902), I, 161 ff.

[62] The legislative council of Cape Colony was elected according to this plan until the establishment of the South African Union in 1910, and the members of the lower house of the legislature of Illinois have long been both nominated and elected under it.

Meanwhile still another plan had been devised. In 1857 Thomas Hare published a pamphlet entitled *The Machinery of Representation* (elaborated in a *Treatise on the Election of Representatives, Parliamentary and Municipal* in 1859) expounding a system under which, in order to be elected, a candidate in a multiple-member constituency need not obtain a majority of the votes polled, but only a certain number (known as the "quota"), so fixed that it could be obtained by a number of candidates equal to the number of seats to be filled, but by no more. The elector might indicate on his ballot paper not only his first choice, but also his second, third, and other choices. At the first count first choices only were to be included, and any candidates receiving the quota (or more) on this basis would be declared elected. If all seats were not thus filled, the unused votes of those candidates who had a surplus would be transferred according to the second choices indicated and added on at the proper places. If this still left seats vacant, the lowest candidate would be eliminated and his votes transferred according to the next preferences, and so on until all the seats were filled. This "single transferable vote" plan was ardently endorsed by John Stuart Mill, who tried hard to get it into the Reform Act of 1867, and who, in his classic treatise, *Representative Government,* published in 1861, pronounced it "among the very greatest improvements yet made in the theory and practice of government." [63] As Mill also pointed out, the plan was not merely theoretical, because a system of almost exactly the same character had been put into operation in Denmark two years before Hare first wrote. Hare and Mill wished to treat the entire country as a single constituency. Those who took up their ideas, however, came to feel that this would be impracticable, and the plan as it developed became, rather, to apply the transferable vote to smaller constituencies returning anywhere from three to a dozen or more members. Thus arose, with many additions and modifications, the characteristic English scheme of proportional representation—the scheme of the single transferable vote—as opposed to the "list" system preferred in Continental Europe, under which the voter casts his

[63] In Chap. vii, "Of True and False Democracy" (Everyman's Library ed., p. 263).

ballot for a particular party ticket and the seats are divided among the parties in proportion to the number of votes which their lists have polled.[64]

The Movement for Proportional Representation

Ever since Hare and Mill wrote, proportional representation—grounded upon the single transferable vote, but with no end of differing details of application—has been before the nation as a possible mode of solving the minority-representation problem. The efforts of Leonard Courtney [65] and others to get the device into the Representation of the People Act of 1884 failed; and in 1885, as we have seen, a single-member-district plan was adopted which was incompatible with it. A Proportional Representation Society, however, was organized in 1884; [66] literature was published; and each new adoption of the proportional principle abroad—in the Swiss cantons in 1891 and after, in Belgium in 1899, in Sweden in 1907, and especially in Tasmania in 1907 and South Africa (for senatorial elections) in 1909—was made an occasion for bringing the cause afresh to Englishmen's attention. A royal commission appointed in 1908 to study electoral systems the world over and to recommend improvements in the British system, reported in 1910 that the proportional principle was not adapted to existing British conditions.[67] Friends of the plan refused, however, to consider this judgment final.

One will not be surprised to learn that the subject came into fresh prominence when the electoral system was being overhauled at the close of the World War. The Speaker's Conference which prepared the plan for the act of 1918 unanimously recommended a nation-wide scheme under which proportional representation (based on the single transferable vote) was to be employed in all multiple-member constituencies that might result from the impending redistribution; and the House of

[64] The list system is described and compared with the single transferable vote in J. H. Humphreys, *Proportional Representation,* Chaps. vii-ix.

[65] Subsequently Lord Courtney of Penwith.

[66] The organization later grew inactive but was revived in 1905 and has ever since been vigorous. It maintains offices at 82 Victoria St., London, and publishes *Representation* and other literature.

[67] Cmd. 5163. The report was a conservative document, advocating few changes.

Lords, looking forward apprehensively to the day when wealth and education would probably be in an even more decided minority than they were at present, held out resolutely for the proposal. No question raised by the bill proved more thorny.[68] Five successive times the House of Commons rejected the plan, in one form or another, and for weeks the deadlock threatened the whole bill and even the life of the ministry. In the end the popular chamber won, although not until it had agreed to an optional provision for the appointment of a commission to prepare a plan for the election of approximately one hundred members by proportional representation in specially formed constituencies returning from three to seven members each. The experiment was actually to be undertaken only if definitely arranged for at a later time by parliamentary act; and such a measure has never been passed, or even seriously considered. Proportional representation failed under the legislation of 1918;[69] but it at least was raised to the dignity of a great national issue.

Throughout its history the proportional plan has been supported in Britain from two main directions, i.e., by professional and more or less disinterested students of government like Hare and Mill, Sir John Lubbock (founder of the Proportional Representation Society), and Lord Courtney, and second, by political elements and forces which considered that their position would be improved if the system were adopted. In 1918 it was the Conservative House of Lords, backed especially by the agricultural interests, that was most appealed to by the practical aspects of the matter. Even then, however, most of the Conservatives in the lower house were voting against the plan, and the Liberals for it; and in after years it was the Liberals, suffering eclipse as a great party and feverishly seeking ways and means of rehabilitation, that chiefly saw practical advantages in the scheme. In 1924, with a Labor government in office but dependent upon Liberal support, the time

[68] On the rôle played by proportional representation in the debates on the bill, see H. C. Morris, *Parliamentary Franchise Reform in England from 1885 to 1918,* Chap. ix.

[69] The failure was not quite complete, in that university members (in the case of multiple-member constituencies) were henceforth to be chosen according to the proportional plan.

seemed ripe for action. A private member's bill providing for a general system of proportional representation was introduced, with the official endorsement of the party. Labor, however, although on record since 1918 in favor of electoral reform that would ensure "every minority . . . its proportionate and no more than its proportionate representation," had come into a position such that the proposed plan would not clearly help it win seats,[70] and hence the cabinet decided to leave the matter to a "free vote." As a result, the bill was defeated.[71]

Several years have elapsed since the decisions of 1918 and 1924, and there is nothing to indicate that they will soon be reversed. The issue, however, is far from dead. With the rise of Labor to the rank of a major party, the number of "three-cornered" contests, and consequently the number of instances in which the representative of a district wins on a decided minority of the votes cast, has greatly increased.[72] Under this situation, the argument that the present single-member, plu-

[70] At the 1923 election it had won a majority of all contested seats on a minority of the votes in both Scotland and Wales.

[71] The vote was as follows:

Party	For the Bill	Against the Bill
Conservative	8	149
Labor	28	90
Liberal	107	1
Independent	3	1
Total	146	240

[72] The publications of the Proportional Representation Society abound in "horrible examples." To cite merely two or three random instances, drawn from the election of 1922: (1) in Dewsbury the Labor candidate won with 9,921 votes as against 8,065 and 6,744 for the Liberal and Conservative candidates, respectively; (2) in Huddersfield a Liberal triumphed with 15,879 votes, as against 15,673 and 15,212 for the Labor and National Liberal candidates, respectively; (3) in Central Portsmouth, 7,666 votes sufficed to give a Conservative candidate victory, as against 7,659 votes for a National Liberal, 7,129 for a Liberal, and 6,126 for a Laborite.

The relation of votes polled to seats obtained at the election of 1924 is shown in the following table:

Party	Votes Polled	Seats Obtained by Votes	Average Number of Seats per Vote
Conservative	7,854,523	399	19,686
Labor	5,489,077	143	38,383
Liberal	2,928,747	36	81,354
Others	367,932	5	73,586
Totals	16,640,279	583	(Average) 28,543

rality-election system provides, by and large, for the representation of minorities has been perceptibly weakened. Since the war, the proportional plan has made great conquests, not only in Continental Europe (Germany, Austria, Poland, Czechoslovakia, Jugoslavia, Holland, Finland, and many other states), but also within the British Commonwealth—in various Canadian provinces, in India, in Northern Ireland and the Irish Free State, in Malta, and in mandated Southwest Africa. For the time being, at all events, the world-trend is clearly favorable to the proportional system.[73] On the other hand, Britain cannot fall into line without sweeping away the entire existing system of single-member constituencies and redividing the country into districts returning three or more members—a proceeding which, even though it would involve merely a revival of the historic multiple-member type of constituency which was the usual thing up to a bare half-century ago, would require a deal of argument. There is apprehension lest so exact a representation of the varying shades of political opinion as the proportional plan contemplates would result in the destruction of the traditional type of party government and the substitution of the unstable multiple-group system of France and other Continental countries. And it is argued that any proportional plan would be too complicated to be understood by the people, or to be administered effectively. Nothing is likely to happen, remarked an English authority some years ago, until one of the great parties adopts the principle as a part of its program.[74] Ostensibly, the Labor party embraced the proportional idea in 1918, and the Liberal party soon thereafter. In a matter of this nature, however, these or any other parties are likely to be guided by purely opportunist considerations: when proportional representation promises more seats, they will be for it; when it is likely to work to the advantage of their rivals, they will be against it, or at least indifferent. Under these conditions, progress is slow and prophecy futile.[75]

[73] Since 1918, too, it has been in use in electing school authorities in Scotland.

[74] M. L. Gwyer, in W. R. Anson, *Law and Custom of the Constitution* (5th ed.), I, 150.

[75] The fact that at the general election of 1929 the Liberals increased their popular vote by upwards of two and one-half millions, but obtained only

The Second Ballot and the Alternative Vote

In conclusion, it may be noted that it is not necessary to adopt the proportional plan in order to prevent the election of members by mere minorities. In the districts as they now exist a second balloting could be held whenever no one candidate receives a clear majority at the first balloting, such second balloting being used to determine the voters' preference as between the two candidates standing highest. This plan was employed rather successfully in the German Empire, and has often been advocated in Britain. The main objection is the expense and effort involved in bringing the voters to the polls a second time [76]—as would, under present British conditions, be necessary in a large number of constituencies at every general election. With a view to obviating this difficulty, an "alternative vote" plan has been proposed under which the voters would be expected to indicate first, second, and third preferences among the candidates, such preferences being used for the same purpose as the second ballot, thus saving the electors the trouble of going to the polls a second time. The alternative vote was recommended in the electoral commission report of 1910, and it played a large part in the discussions of 1918. Neither it nor the simple second ballot, however, definitely guarantees any representation for minorities; and since such representation is the really vital issue in present-day British electoral discussion, there is no reason to expect that either will be adopted.[77]

twelve additional seats caused leaders of that party, following the electoral count, to set up a strong demand for a proportional system. Labor, however, had largely lost interest in the matter, and it was difficult to see what the Liberals, with only a handful of members, could do about it.

[76] It is objected also that the result does not necessarily reflect the real opinion of the electorate, but only what is practicable.

[77] On proportional representation in general, see W. W. Willoughby and L. Rogers, *Introduction to the Problem of Government* (New York, 1921), Chap. xv; H. L. McBain and L. Rogers, *The New Constitutions of Europe*, Chap. v; J. R. Commons, *Proportional Representation* (New York, 1912); and J. H. Humphreys, *Proportional Representation*, already cited. Mr. Humphreys is secretary of the British Proportional Representation Society and an ardent, though fair-minded, advocate of the system. The plan is advocated for Britain in Humphreys, *Practical Aspects of Electoral Reform; a Study of the General Election of 1922* (London, 1923); J. F.

Williams, *Proportional Representation and British Politics* (London, 1914), revised and republished as *The Reform of Political Representation* (London, 1918); and many other books and articles, including, of course, the files of *Representation* and other publications of the Proportional Representation Society. It is opposed notably in G. Horwill, *Proportional Representation; its Dangers and Defects* (London, 1925); H. Finer, *The Case Against Proportional Representation* (Fabian Society Tract, 1924); and J. M. Robertson, "Proportional Representation," *Edinburgh Rev.*, July, 1917. A useful survey of the spread of the system, by J. F. Williams, will be found in the *Jour. of Compar. Legis. and Internat. Law,* Jan., 1921, and a complete list of countries and other areas in which it was in effect in May, 1929, in *The Electoral Gamble* (published by the Proportional Representation Society in 1929), pp. 24-26.

CHAPTER XIV

THE HOUSE OF LORDS

THE British government of our day is pivoted upon the House of Commons—more particularly, upon the relations between that branch of Parliament and the cabinet. This, however, was not always true; hardly two hundred years ago the House of Lords was, all things considered, the more conspicuous and powerful of the two bodies. Even now, although correctly termed a second, and even a secondary, chamber, that much-discussed and oft-maligned assemblage is a weighty part of the constitutional system, besides being the oldest, the largest, the most strictly hereditary, and in several respects the most interesting, "upper house" in the world. The Labor party would abolish it; men of other parties would reform it; and one can hardly doubt that it will see important changes in the coming, as it has seen them in the past, generation. On no account, however, can it be left out of the picture of British government as it is, or is likely to be.

How the House of Lords came into existence as a separate branch of Parliament has been explained sufficiently elsewhere,[1] and it is necessary only to recall, as a means of understanding its composition and character today, that it is descended from the Great Council of the Norman-Angevin kings, representing and continuing substantially that part of the Council which remained after the lesser clergy had dropped out and the minor barons had cast in their lot with the knights and burgesses in the House of Commons. That is to say, it was

[1] See p. 24 above. The best detailed histories of the chamber are two books by L. O. Pike, namely, *Constitutional History of the House of Lords* (London, 1894), and *Political History of the House of Lords* (London, 1901). Another ambitious and important historical work is A. S. Turberville, *The House of Lords in the Reign of William III* (Oxford, 1913), and *ibid., The House of Lords in the Eighteenth Century* (Oxford, 1927).

the higher clergy and greater lay magnates who made the upper chamber what it was five centuries ago, even as it is their successors that give it the tone and form which we recognize in it in our own time. With insignificant exceptions, every one of the more than seven hundred members on the present roll are either peers or clergymen.

Groups of Members—the Hereditary Peers

Analyzed a little more closely, the members nowadays are found to fall into not fewer than six distinct categories or groups, namely, princes of the royal blood, hereditary peers, representative peers of Scotland, representative peers of Ireland, lords of appeal (or "law lords"), and lords spiritual. The first group need not detain us. It consists simply of such male members of the royal family as are of age and within specified degrees of relationship—rarely more than two or three at a given time—and it has little practical importance because so far has Britain traveled from the days of royal control over Parliament that the princes of the blood do not, except on rare occasions, so much as attend sittings of the upper chamber, and never do they take any active part in the proceedings.[2]

By far the most important group numerically is the hereditary peers. Indeed, substantially nine-tenths of the members belong in this category; and on this account, as well as because the peerage is a complicated and much misunderstood institution, something must be said concerning it. The term "peer," of course, means "equal;" and its earliest use in English constitutional terminology was to denote the feudal tenants-in-chief of the crown, all of whom were, literally, the peers one of another. As the separation of greater barons from lesser ones progressed, the term became restricted to the greater ones, who, as we have seen, formed an important element in the developing House of Lords, and before the end of the fourteenth century it was being used to denote exclusively those members of the baronage who were accustomed to receive a personal writ of summons when a parliament was to be held.

[2] For an account of the induction of Edward Albert, Prince of Wales, as a member of the House of Lords in 1918, see London *Times* (weekly ed.), Feb. 22, 1918, p. 159.

It does not appear that the kings had it in mind to create a peerage whose members should have an inalienable right to be called to Parliament, much less to endow such a peerage with an hereditary character. Nevertheless, by stages too numerous and complicated to be described here, precisely such a peerage came into existence. Not only was the principle established that a baron who once received a writ of summons was entitled to receive a writ on all future occasions when a new parliament was to meet, but also the principle that the receipt of such a writ, even a single time, operated to confer a hereditary right. In the course of time the House of Lords definitely ruled that proof of the receipt of a writ of summons, followed by an actual appearance of the person in a sitting of Parliament in virtue thereof, operated to confer an hereditary peerage, even though no proof was forthcoming that any subsequent writ was ever addressed to the person or to his descendants. And this is the law today.

Peerages descend under the same rule of primogeniture that long governed the inheritance of land, and the heir must accept the inheritance, whether or not he desires to do so.[3] It sometimes happens that when a peerage falls vacant the heir is a member of the House of Commons, and more than once such a person, objecting to involuntary transfer to the less powerful chamber, has sought to evade the obligation. But no one has, in modern times, been permitted to escape it. In 1895 Mr. William W. Palmer, later Lord Selborne, inheriting a peerage but wishing to remain somewhat longer in the House of Commons, put the rule to a test by neglecting to apply for a writ of summons as a peer. The decision of the Commons, however, was that he was obligated to accept membership in the upper chamber, and that the West Edinburgh seat which he had held in the lower house had been automatically vacated. In 1919 Viscount Astor sought to rid himself of his newly acquired title with a view to continuing in the House of Commons, but could find

[3] This does not mean, however, that a man who is offered a peerage not previously existing is obliged to accept it. Gladstone, for example, repeatedly declined peerages that were tendered him. In 1928 a retiring speaker of the House of Commons (Mr. J. H. Whitley) declined a viscountcy, thereby interrupting the long-established practice of elevating retiring speakers to the peerage.

no way to do it; a bill which would have made it possible was defeated in the lower house by a vote of 169 to 56. Indeed, as far back as 1640 it was settled that a peerage cannot be surrendered, extinguished, transferred, or otherwise got rid of, unless the blood be corrupted, e.g., by conviction for felony or treason; and possession of a peerage carries with it a seat in the House of Lords, whether wanted or not.[4] Possession of a peerage is a purely personal matter. It gives the possessor himself certain privileges, mainly a title and a seat in the House of Lords. But his children, including the heir to the title as long as he is merely heir, remain commoners.[5] The peerage is, therefore, quite unlike the nobility of Continental countries in earlier times, which invested families, and not merely individuals, with special status; properly, it should not be referred to as a nobility. Furthermore, the distinction of five different ranks, or grades, of peers—designated by the titles duke, marquis, earl, viscount, and baron, and all dating back several centuries—while of considerable social significance, is of no political import.

The oldest existing peerages (not very numerous) date from before 1707, and their holders are therefore peers of England only; others, created after the union with Scotland, but before that with Ireland, are peerages of Great Britain; and very many others, created since the union with Ireland, are peerages of the United Kingdom. This distinction, too, is of little or no practical consequence. There are also peers of Ireland and peers of Scotland, who, however, sit in the House of Lords at Westminster only by representation.[6]

Technically, peers are created by the sovereign; but in practice the matter is controlled by the cabinet (mainly by the

[4] Inheritance of a peerage sometimes calls home a man who has become rather firmly rooted in a distant part of the world. Thus in 1925 an Englishman who was a rancher in Wyoming, a past member of the state legislature, an Elk, and in sundry other respects a "good American" became, by the death of an elder brother, eighth earl of Portsmouth and found it necessary to resume residence in England.

[5] Custom permits eldest sons to bear "courtesy" titles, which sometimes cause bewilderment among the uninitiated; but they are none the less commoners. See W. B. Munro, *Governments of Europe,* 101, note 2, and for a list of existing courtesy titles, *Whitaker's Almanack* (1928), 129.

[6] See p. 320 below.

premier); and the object may be to honor men of distinction in law, letters, science, art, statecraft, or business,[7] or to win the favor and support—perchance, contributions to party funds—of a man of influence or wealth, or to change the political complexion of the house sufficiently to enable a controverted measure to be passed,[8] or even merely to keep in Parliament a man who has proved an exceptionally useful member.[9] There is no limit upon the number that may be created, or upon the kind, except that, under existing law, the crown cannot create a peer of Scotland or direct the devolution of a dignity otherwise than in accordance with limitations applying in the case of grants of real estate.[10] But certain classes of persons are ineligible—speaking strictly, ineligible to sit in the House of Lords, which is tantamount to the same thing. These classes are (1) persons under twenty-one years of age, (2) aliens, (3) bankrupts, (4) persons serving a sentence on conviction of felony or treason, and (5) women.

Under the terms of the patents in which they were bestowed, some of the older peerages are capable of being inherited and

[7] The first peerage bestowed purely in recognition of literary achievement was awarded Tennyson in 1884; the peerages conferred upon Macaulay and Bulwer Lytton arose partly from political considerations. The first professional artist to be honored with a peerage was Lord Leighton, in 1896. Lord Kelvin and Lord Lister are among well-known men of science who have been thus honored. Lord Goschen's viscountcy was conferred, with universal approval, as the fitting reward of a great business career. The earldom of General Roberts and viscountcies of Generals Wolseley and Kitchener were bestowed in recognition of military distinction. The viscountcy of Lord Bryce came as a fitting reward for a long life of scholarly achievement and public service. With some aptness the House of Lords has been called "the Westminster Abbey of living celebrities."

[8] Thus in 1711 Queen Anne and her ministers created twelve new peers in a batch so as to obtain a majority for the treaty of Utrecht. More often the mere threat to create peers on a large scale has sufficed to overcome the opposition, as in 1832 when the Reform Bill was pending and in 1911 when the Parliament Bill was under debate.

[9] Thus when the archbishop of Canterbury, Dr. Davidson, retired from office in 1928 he was made a viscount in order that his active and valued career in the House of Lords might not be terminated.

[10] Prior to 1914, the crown could not create an Irish peer except under conditions stipulated in the Act of Union of 1800. The settlement under which the Irish Free State was finally established in 1922 contains nothing on the subject, and the future of the Irish peerage is in doubt. See p. 321, note 18.

transmitted by women;[11] but no woman has ever been summoned to, or permitted to sit in, the House of Lords. When the Sex Disqualification (Removal) Act of 1919 was before Parliament, an amendment which would have authorized English peeresses in their own right, of whom there were at that time twenty,[12] to take seats in the House of Lords (and Scottish and Irish peeresses, of whom there were five, to participate in the election of Scottish and Irish members) was carried in the House of Commons. But the House of Lords rejected it;[13] and when in 1922, a vivacious English business woman, the Viscountess Rhondda, peeress in her own right, nevertheless laid claim to a writ of summons, her request was denied by the Committee of Privileges by a vote of twenty to four. That women will one day sit and vote in the upper chamber seemed to be foreshadowed in 1925, when a private bill on the subject, introduced by Lord Astor, was rejected by the Lords by the exceedingly slender margin of eighty votes to seventy-eight. Lord Birkenhead, government leader in the upper house, confessed himself on that occasion an unrepentant opponent of woman suffrage as practiced in parliamentary elections, but significantly based his opposition to Lord Astor's proposal on the consideration that if women were to be admitted to the House of Lords the thing ought to be done only by virtue of a government bill and as a part of the general reconstruction of the chamber which everybody admitted to be long overdue, and which, indeed, Lord Birkenhead affirmed could hardly fail to be carried out during the lifetime of the parliament then sitting. Another attempt by Lord Astor failed in 1926, this time by a vote of 125 to 80. A government bill would have had a far better chance; but it was disclosed that the ministers were hopelessly divided on the question.[14]

[11] In general, peerages "by writ," which date from the seventeenth century and before, as distinguished from peerages by letters patent, created concurrently with peerages by writ from 1375 and exclusively from about 1660.

[12] There are now (1929) twenty-two. See complete list in *Const. Year Book* (London, 1928), 162-165.

[13] 174 Commons' Journal, 330, 376; 151 Lords' Journal, 431.

[14] As might be expected, discussion of the subject was rich in humorous observations. Lord Banbury urged that males be left one place in the country where they can live in peace. Lord Cecil, answering the contention that women lack the physical strength to become legislators, said that it would

Other Groups of Members

A third group of members consists of the representative peers of Scotland. The Act of Union of 1707 made no provision for the creation of Scottish peers, and as a result the number of such peers has dwindled from 154 to thirty-two. Peerages have, of course, become extinct through the failure of heirs; and in numerous instances a peer of Scotland has been honored with a peerage of Great Britain or (since 1800) of the United Kingdom. The recipient, in the latter case, ceases to be reckoned as a member of the Scottish peerage in the narrow sense, and of course acquires a seat in the House of Lords in his own right. Of the surviving thirty-two purely Scottish peers, not all have seats in Westminster, but only sixteen of their number chosen at the beginning of each parliament by the entire group meeting as an electoral body in Holyrood Palace at Edinburgh.[15]

A fourth group of members is the Irish representative peers. When the Act of Union of 1800 was passed, the Irish peerage was a large body, and the measure provided, first, that thereafter the crown should create only one such peerage for every

be a very weak woman who could not withstand the physical demands made upon members of the House of Lords. And a woman trade unionist, speaking at a national conference of women unionists, averred that it did not matter much what happened to "the august upper chamber of Parliament," but that women should have the right to sit there if for no other reason than to cool the fevered brows of some of the noble lords when the hour came for drastic reform of their house.

On the development and status of the peerage, see W. R. Anson, *Law and Custom of the Constitution* (5th ed.), I, 200-241, and D. J. Medley, *Manual of English Constitutional History* (6th ed.), 137-149, 157-163. A complete classified list of peers as it stands today will be found in *Whitaker's Almanack* (1928), 111-128; A. P. Burke's *Genealogical and Heraldic History of the Peerage and Baronetage* (London, 1915) gives full information about all holders of titles; and the complicated legal phases of the subject are treated in J. H. Round, *Peerage and Pedigree: Studies in Peerage Law and Family History*, 2 vols. (London, 1910), and F. B. Palmer, *Peerage Law in England* (London, 1907). On the mode of receiving new peers in the House of Lords, see *Standing Orders of the House of Lords* (London, 1924), 13-14.

[15] For the process of election, see W. R. Anson, *Law and Custom of the Constitution* (5th ed.), I, 230-232. The day will come, of course, when the number of available peers will be no greater than that of places to be filled.

three that became extinct,[16] and, second, that the Irish peerage should be represented in the House of Lords by twenty-eight of their number, elected for life by the peerage itself. The total number of Irish peerages still extant is approximately 150. As in the case of Scotland, however, something like half of the persons holding such titles have received peerages of Great Britain or the United Kingdom, and have seats at Westminster by reason of that fact. It is those of the number who are still only Irish peers that choose the group which sits in a representative capacity. Fifty-four such peers at the present time are not "peers of Parliament." Unlike the Scottish peers, Irish peers, if not elected to the House of Lords, may stand for election to the House of Commons, although they cannot represent Irish constituencies.[17] While members of the lower house, however, they are ineligible for election to the upper one, nor can they participate in the choice of representative peers.[18]

A fifth group of members is made up of the lords of appeal in ordinary, who differ from other peers in that their seats are not hereditary. One of the functions of the House of Lords is to serve as a final court of appeal from the lower courts in England, Scotland, and Northern Ireland.[19] It is, therefore, desirable that the body shall contain at least a few able jurists

[16] Until the number of persons holding Irish peerages only should be brought down to 100; thereafter new Irish peerages might be created without restraint so long as the total number of such persons was not raised beyond the figure indicated. G. B. Adams and H. M. Stephens, *Select Documents of English Constitutional History,* 500.

[17] Lord Palmerston, for example, was an Irish peer, but sat in the House of Commons.

[18] The Irish settlement of 1922 made no provision for the election of Irish representative peers, and the death in 1924 of one of the twenty-eight then sitting (the Earl of Bandon) raised the question whether Irish representation in the Lords was destined to be reduced as members of the existing group died, and finally to cease altogether. The matter has not been settled officially; but no Irish representative peers have been chosen since the date mentioned, and at the beginning of 1928 there were only twenty-two such peers in service, with six vacancies. As matters stand, no election can take place, for the reason that the office of lord chancellor of Ireland has been abolished, and there is no one to whom, under provision of the Act of Union (1800), a writ for the election of a representative peer can legally be addressed.

[19] See pp. 620-622 below.

who will actually give their time to the work of the house, and, further, that business of a judicial nature shall be transacted largely by this corps of experts. In 1856 the desire to strengthen the judicial element of the chamber precipitated a memorable controversy over the power of the crown to create life peerages. On the advice of her ministers, Queen Victoria conferred upon a distinguished judge, Sir James Parke, a patent as Baron Wensleydale for life. There were some precedents, but none later than the reign of Henry VI; and the House of Lords, maintaining that the right had lapsed and that the peerage had become entirely hereditary, refused to admit Baron Wensleydale until his patent was so modified as to put his peerage upon that basis. Twenty years later, however, an Appellate Jurisdiction Act authorized the appointment of two (afterwards increased to four, and in 1913 to six) "lords of appeal in ordinary" with the title of baron; and by legislation of 1887 the tenure of these members, previously conditioned upon their continued exercise of judicial functions, was made perpetual for life. The "law lords," in the broader sense, include, in addition to the six who are specially appointed,[20] the Lord Chancellor and such other members of the House as have held high judicial office; and although any member of the chamber whatsoever has a full legal right to participate when judicial, quite as much as when legislative, business is in hand, in practice only the judicial members so act. Among these judicial members it is naturally the six lords of appeal in ordinary who attend most assiduously to judicial business. But a judicial decision may be rendered in the name of the House by any three of the larger group. The six alone receive a salary by virtue of being members of the chamber.

Finally, there are the ecclesiastical members—not peers, but "lords spiritual." In the fifteenth century the lords spiritual outnumbered the lords temporal. Upon the dissolution of the monasteries, however, in the reign of Henry VIII, the abbots dropped out, and the spiritual contingent fell into a minority. Nowadays it is numerically insignificant, being restricted, as a

[20] In November, 1928, the prime minister announced to the Conservative party conference that Parliament would be asked to pass a bill authorizing one additional lord of appeal in ordinary.

result of a variety of statutes, to twenty-six. Scotland, whose established church is Presbyterian, has no ecclesiastical members. Under the Act of Union of 1800 Ireland had four, but since the disestablishment of the Anglican Church in that island in 1869 it has had none. From the date mentioned to 1920, England and Wales shared the twenty-six clerical seats. Upon the disestablishment of the Anglican Church in Wales and Monmouthshire at the time mentioned, however, the four bishops from that section who were then sitting were withdrawn, leaving the ecclesiastical quota purely English; and such it remains today. By statute, the archbishops of Canterbury and York and three of the bishops, namely, those of London, Durham, and Winchester, are always entitled to writs of summons. This leaves twenty-one seats for the remaining twenty-eight bishops, who receive writs of summons in the order of the length of time they have been in charge of sees. When a sitting bishop dies or resigns, the one next on the list, in the order of seniority, becomes entitled to a writ, and the others advance a step nearer the goal. Once in possession of a seat, a bishop or archbishop retains it as long as he holds a see. But of course he does not transmit it to his heirs, nor (save in the case of the five mentioned above) to his successor in office. Normally, bishops and archbishops are elected by the dean and chapter of the diocese. When, however, a vacancy arises the sovereign transmits a *congé d'élire,* together with a "letter missive" containing the name of the person to be elected; so that, to all intents and purposes, appointment is made by the prime minister acting in the name of the king. Bishoprics are created by act of Parliament.[21]

The Question of Numbers—the "Honors" Investigation

The total membership of the House of Lords now fluctuates around 740, which makes it by far the largest second chamber

[21] On the composition of the House of Lords, in general, see A. L. Lowell, *Government of England,* I, Chap. xxi; W. R. Anson, *Law and Custom of the Constitution* (5th ed.), I, Chap. v; A. F. Pollard, *Evolution of Parliament,* Chap. xv; T. E. May and F. Holland, *Constitutional History of England,* I, Chap. v; S. Low, *Governance of England,* Chap. xii. The subject is treated in greater detail in L. O. Pike, *Constitutional History of the House of Lords,* especially Chap. xv.

in the world.[22] Formerly the body was decidedly smaller; indeed its most notable growth has taken place within the past hundred and fifty years. During the reign of Henry VII there were never more than eighty members, of whom the majority were ecclesiastics. At the death of William III the roll bore 192 names. At the death of Queen Anne the number was 209; and if an effort made by the Whigs in 1719 to introduce the principle that the number of new peerages created should not exceed the number of old ones becoming extinct had succeeded, the membership might have become stationary at about that point. Lord Sunderland's bill, however, was thrown out by the Commons on the very proper ground that it would tend to convert the House of Lords into a clan oligarchy, and the margin between the number of newly created peerages and peerages coming to an end steadily widened. By 1760 the House numbered 339; by 1820, 369; and by 1837 (the accession of Queen Victoria), 456. Since the last-mentioned date—less than a hundred years ago—there has been a net increase of about 270 members, or almost sixty per cent.[23]

This growth has come about almost entirely, of course, through the creation of new peerages, and in recent times it has proceeded so fast, and under such circumstances, as to arouse serious misgivings. During Mr. Asquith's premiership (1908-16) new peerages were created at a rate averaging almost ten a year, and during the six years covered by the Lloyd George coalition government, at a rate averaging fifteen a year.[24] In 1922 protest came to a head, especially on the ground that honors of all kinds, including peerages, were being bestowed, not only in recognition of party services, but with a view to party contributions—indeed, that not infrequently they

[22] On January 1, 1928, there were 3 peers of the royal blood, 2 archbishops, 24 bishops, 23 dukes, 28 marquises, 131 earls, 73 viscounts, 417 barons, 16 Scottish representative peers, 22 Irish representative peers, and 6 lords of appeal in ordinary—a total of 745. Of this number, some 20, however, were minors, and therefore not strictly members except by anticipation.

[23] More than half of the peerages of today date from within the past seventy years, and of the remainder only an insignificant portion can be termed ancient.

[24] This does not include the seventeen peers who were advanced in rank during the Asquith ministry and the twenty-five who were so advanced during the Lloyd George ministry. For a complete list of peerages created between 1905 and 1928, see *Const. Year Book* (1928), 167-169.

were practically sold for cash. The matter was investigated by a royal commission on honors, and although the report submitted to Parliament contained no very damaging evidence,[25] it recommended that as a safeguard the prime minister, before asking the sovereign to confer peerages or other honors, should submit his proposals to a specially constituted Privy Council committee which should investigate and report upon each nominee. If despite an adverse report a nomination was persisted in, the sovereign was at least to be put in possession of the committee's findings. No fault was found with the bestowal of peerages for political reasons; indeed, it was declared highly desirable to keep open the constitutional prerogative to create peers in any number with a view to overcoming a political crisis. But everything that savors of a traffic in honors was properly reprobated. The commission's plan was not put into operation as reported, but in 1925 an Honors (Prevention of Abuses) Act made it a misdemeanor to "give or offer, take or ask, any gift, money, or valuable consideration as an inducement to procure the grant of any dignity or title of honor;" and it is fair to assume that greater care will be exercised in the future to avoid lavish honors lists and to frustrate the efforts of honors "brokers." At one time it was supposed that if a Labor cabinet ever came into office the creation of new peerages would, for the time being, come to an end. Experience in 1924 showed that this was a mistake, although the power was used sparingly; three peerages, in all, were created during the first MacDonald premiership. In point of fact, it ought never to have been overlooked that a Labor government, like any other, would be obliged by law to have at least one of the principal secretaries of state and one under-secretary in the upper chamber. At the date of writing (1929) the newly installed second MacDonald government had just procured the elevation of two of its members to the peerage, and was reported to be considering the creation of fifteen or twenty more peers who would "accept the labor whip." [26]

[25] Cmd. 1780 (1922). The Labor member of the commission, Mr. Arthur Henderson, dissented from the report, charging that the investigation had been insufficiently thorough and that the proposed plan of reform was inadequate.

[26] The party continues to make such political capital as it can out of the "sale of honors." See *Labour Year Book* (1928), 224-241.

The House of Lords and the Second Chamber Problem

No one can look over the membership list of the House of Lords in our day without being impressed with the widely ramifying rootage of the institution in British (and Irish) history and life. In the peerage are represented all that the great landholding and industrial interests of the country have been and are, to say nothing of statecraft, military genius, naval achievement, literature, learning, and art. The little group of black-gowned bishops and archbishops personifies the mighty Established Church. The law lords suggest the glories of British jurisprudence. The Scottish and Irish representative groups bring to mind lengthy and dramatic chapters of military and political history. It is not altogether the sort of a second chamber that Englishmen would construct today if they were faced with the necessity of making one *de novo*. But it is so woven into the fabric of social traditions and economic interest, and so buttressed by age-long habits of thought, that a British government without it would be almost unthinkable. In no part of the nation's political system are changes made more grudgingly.

Nevertheless, very great changes have taken place. We have already noted the loss of paramountcy in the eighteenth century to the House of Commons; [27] and the progressive eclipse of the upper chamber in the succeeding hundred years is often, and justly, cited as a major illustration of the progressive readaptation of the British constitution. Moreover, the position of the body is by no means stabilized today. On the one hand, forces are beating upon it that threaten to crowd it still farther toward the edge of the picture, if not, indeed, to blot it out altogether; on the other hand, strong efforts are in the making to restore it to at least some of the prestige and power that it has lost. The public prints are filled with discussions of the subject; hardly a session of Parliament fails to yield plans and bills pertaining to it. Passing by, for the moment, such matters as how the upper chamber is organized for work and how it handles its business (which can best be touched upon when we come to speak of these same aspects of the great assembly sitting in the opposite wing of Westminster Palace), we may here look some-

[27] See p. 53 above.

what into this persistent problem of "second chamber reform." The membership of the body as outlined above is involved, because there are many proposals to change it. But the chamber's functions and powers are at least equally at issue, being, indeed, at the very center of the controversy.

The subject is the more deserving of attention for the reason that many states besides Britain have second chamber problems: whether there shall be a second chamber at all, and if so, how it shall be composed, what shall be its powers, and how it shall be geared up with the other parts of the government. The British example has undoubtedly had much to do with the prevalence of the bicameral form of parliamentary organization throughout the world. But it is equally certain that British experience has something to do with the practically unanimous decision of the peoples of Continental Europe to write into their post-war constitutions provisions which make of their upper houses not merely second, but also secondary, chambers, endowed with a cautiously devised "checking," or revising, power, but rarely capable of blocking any action or policy strongly supported by the popular branch; and one of the many things to be watched with interest in these states in the next twenty years will be the rôle which these subordinated upper houses play and the tendencies they show.[28] Hungary and Japan have lately reconstructed their second chambers; Italy and Spain have practically abandoned theirs; the Canadian Senate is under attack, on lines strongly reminiscent of the movement in the home country since 1909;[29] France, Australia, and other states find their upper houses provocative of reform proposals; the Irish Free State is experimenting; even the United States is not without its problems relating to the Senate and senatorial procedure.[30]

Historically, the British House of Lords has been at the same time a council, a court of law, and a legislature.[31] Its func-

[28] H. L. McBain and L. Rogers, *The New Constitutions of Europe* (Garden City, 1922), Chap. iii.

[29] R. A. Mackay, *The Unreformed Senate of Canada* (Oxford, 1926), especially Chap. xi.

[30] These are discussed at length in L. Rogers, *The American Senate* (New York, 1926).

[31] A. F. Pollard, *Evolution of Parliament*, 3.

tions as a council long ago became attenuated, having passed over in the main to the Privy Council and the cabinet. The other two functions, however, have survived to the present day and now constitute the chamber's sole reasons for existence.[32] A hundred years or more ago, the body began to be regarded by many people as unfit to exercise even these remaining prerogatives. The difficulty on the judicial side was the absence of any guarantee that the house would always contain an adequate number of juristically-trained members who would undertake to hear and decide the cases that came up on appeal. How this difficulty was overcome has already been pointed out.[33] At one stage (in 1873) the drastic action was taken of withdrawing the chamber's judicial powers altogether. Parliament, however, soon thought better of the matter and in 1876 wisely substituted the safeguard of specially appointed "law lords;" and this arrangement has worked so well that one seldom hears complaint nowadays—from disinterested sources, at all events—of the judicial work of the chamber, or, indeed, discussion of its judicial function in any connection except speculation as to where it would be assigned if the House of Lords were to be abolished.[34]

Grounds of Dissatisfaction with the House of Lords as a Legislative Body

Dissatisfaction with the chamber as a legislature was not to be so easily removed. It arose from deep-seated, complex, and highly provocative causes; and notwithstanding decades of heated discussion, punctuated by at least one sweeping piece of reform legislation, it cannot be said to have abated. After all, of course, the chamber is primarily a legislature, and it is as such that its future place in the constitutional system must be

[32] Even the once important function of sitting in judgment in impeachment cases brought by the House of Commons has disappeared, by reason of the fact that, as is explained above (p. 51), impeachment has become an unnecessary and obsolete process. Executive and administrative officers can be forced out without going to the trouble of impeaching them, and judges are removable, not by impeachment procedure, but by address or resolution of both houses.

[33] See p. 322 above.

[34] The House of Lords as a court is dealt with in Chap. xxvi, devoted to the judiciary.

determined. Hence it becomes important to see what have been the sources of complaint, what steps have been taken to bring the problem to a solution, what the present state of affairs is, and what are the major lines on which a settlement is proposed.

What, then, are the features of the House of Lords that have brought down upon it the criticisms and attacks of three generations of political writers, agitators, and leaders? First of all, the predominantly hereditary character of its membership; ninety per cent of the members sit exclusively by hereditary right. Second, the scant attendance at sittings, coupled with the meager and often perfunctory consideration given public measures.[35] Third, the fact that a great part of the members are at least accused of being more concerned about the interests of certain groups, e.g., the landowners and the Established Church, than those of the people generally. And, fourth, the undeniable circumstance that the house as a whole is irrevocably wedded to the principles and policies of a single political party, i.e., Conservative, although this party commands the allegiance of only a minority of the electorate.[36] Of course many other grounds of dissatisfaction exist—for example, the representation of the Established Church but of no other churches, which naturally does not appeal to Nonconformists. But the weightiest and most general complaints proceed from the four considerations mentioned.

[35] During the average session upwards of one-third of the members never attend, and another third attend fewer than ten sittings. Many peers so seldom show their faces in the gilded chamber that the attendants do not know them. When the great rally of the House of Lords was made in order to defeat Gladstone's second home rule bill, one member was stopped by the doorkeeper, who asked him if he was really a peer. The answer was: "Do you think if I weren't I would come to this blankety blank hole?" But see p. 356 below.

[36] "Its decisions are vitiated by its composition—it is the worst representative assembly ever created, in that it contains absolutely no members of the manual working class; none of the great classes of shopkeepers, clerks, and teachers; none of the half of all the citizens who are of the female sex; and practically none of religious nonconformity, of art, science, or literature." S. and B. Webb, *A Constitution for the Socialist Commonwealth of Great Britain*, 63. This statement by two scholarly and influential socialists represents a view widely prevalent outside government and business circles. A witty though unfair remark of a former Liberal leader (Augustine Birrell) was: "The House of Lords represents nobody but itself, and it enjoys the full confidence of its constituents."

Why are these matters any more a source of criticism, dispute, and protest today than in the times of Walpole and the Pitts? The answer is two-fold: first, that to some extent they represent conditions that had not arisen at this earlier period (for example, the monopoly of control enjoyed by a single party), and, second, that in these hundred years or more the country has undergone drastic changes of political opinion and organization without any corresponding shift of base on the part of the upper chamber.

Consider what has happened. A century ago the government of the realm could only by courtesy be called popular; certainly it was not democratic under any present-day definition of the term. The House of Commons was, of course, the most "popular" part of it. Yet, as we have seen, that body was hardly more representative of the general mass of the people than was the House of Lords itself. The two houses alike were largely in the hands of the landed aristocracy, and as a rule found little difficulty in working together harmoniously.[37] The Reform Act of 1832, however, broadened the basis of the lower house by admitting important middle-class elements to representation, and the Representation of the People Acts of 1867 and 1884 gave the parliamentary suffrage to the great majority of male inhabitants in both town and country. At the same time, the fuller ripening of the cabinet system brought the working executive within the range of effective public control, through the intermediary of the democratized lower chamber. But the House of Lords underwent no such transformation. On the contrary, it remained, as it still is, an inherently and necessarily conservative body, in the main representing, in a direct and effective way, the interests of landed property, instinctively hostile to changes which seemed to menace property and the established order, and identified with all of the forces that tended to perpetuate the aristocracy and the Anglican Church as pillars of

[37] Parliament, cabinet, the church, justice, local government—all were in the hands of a single class; the government was one of lords and squires. "There was no friction, because the whole machinery of the constitution was now controlled and guided by one and the same class in one and the same interest." J. Redlich and F. W. Hirst, *Local Government in England,* I, 54. On the relations of the two houses of Parliament prior to 1832, see E. Porritt, *The Unreformed House of Commons,* I, Chap. xxviii.

the state. By simply standing still while other branches of the government were undergoing progressive popularization, the second chamber became, more and more, a political anachronism—an assembly of men who were lawmakers by the accident of birth, "lifting its ancient towers and battlements high and dry above the ever rising and roaring tide of democracy." [38]

This was a change that took place outside the walls of the historic chamber. But another almost equally important readjustment, toward the close of the century, occurred inside. This was the conversion of what had been a bi-partisan body into a body composed, to all intents and purposes, of men of a single party. If any particular date is to be mentioned in connection with this development, it would be 1886, the year in which the Liberal party split asunder on Gladstone's first home rule bill; [39] for the result of that schism was the secession from the Liberal party of almost all of the members of rank and position, naturally including most of those who sat in the hereditary chamber. Down to that time both of the leading parties had been well represented in the chamber's membership. The Conservatives had been more numerous as a rule, but not greatly so. When a Conservative ministry was in office it naturally found no difficulty in obtaining the assent of the Lords for its measures; and when the Liberals were in power they could usually shape their program in such a way as to achieve their major purposes. But after 1886 the upper house is found overwhelmingly Conservative; and, so powerful did Conservative influences, interests, traditions, and prestige become in that quarter that the Liberals were never able to regain their strength, even though when Liberal governments were in power men of Liberal antecedents and connections were created peers by the score. In a total membership, in 1905, of over six hundred, there were exactly forty-five Liberals; even in 1914, after almost a decade of Liberal rule, there were only 116. The irony of the Liberal situation had come to be that, no matter how many peerages might be bestowed by Liberal governments upon men who were themselves Liberals, these men, or

[38] M. MacDonagh, *Pageant of Parliament,* II, 56. Cf. G. L. Dickinson, *Development of Parliament during the Nineteenth Century,* Chap. iii.

[39] See p. 490 below.

at all events their sons, were practically certain to yield to the subtle influences of the upper chamber and become Conservatives. Thus the process of recruiting the Liberal quota was continually frustrated, and the chamber remained a bulwark of Conservatism.

This was the really critical aspect of the problem of the House of Lords as it presented itself after 1886. The source of difficulty was not so much the antiquated structure of the chamber, nor its lack of touch with the people, nor even its disposition to resist change, as rather the fact that it was dominated absolutely and all of the time by one of the two great parties which alternately bore responsibility for governing the nation. When the Conservatives, or Unionists, were in power—as they were during most of the period 1886-1906—there was substantial harmony between the two houses of Parliament, and of course between Parliament and the ministry. But when the Liberals were in office they had to reckon with an almost solidly hostile House of Lords and were fortunate indeed if any considerable proportion of the measures in which they were chiefly interested found their way to the statute book.[40]

[40] It goes without saying that if, as the election of 1929 seems to assure, Labor is permanently to supersede Liberalism as the great party opposed to Conservatism, the situation described takes on an even greater seriousness; for, whereas the Liberals always had an appreciable quota of members in the second chamber, Labor has, and doubtless will continue to have, hardly any. A Labor government is consequently in an even more difficult position in relation to that body than is a Liberal government.

CHAPTER XV

SECOND CHAMBER REFORM, 1909-1929

THE question of second chamber reform is not new in our day; proposals on the subject were heard fully a hundred years ago. The problem became one of major importance, however, only after the developments described in the preceding chapter had worked their full effects, i.e., in and after the decades 1867-87; and even then it was in the foreground only, or chiefly, in periods when the Liberals were in power and were finding themselves baffled by a hostile upper house. Reform proposals have been of four main sorts: first, to abolish the chamber altogether and either set up a wholly different one in its place or, more likely, fall back upon a unicameral system such as did, in fact, prevail for a few years after the execution of Charles I in 1649; second, to change the composition of the chamber, there being, of course, many possible ways of doing so; third, to lessen the chamber's powers, making it legally as well as actually subordinate to the elected branch; and fourth, to readjust both membership and powers, simultaneously, or at least as part of an integrated reform program.

The Uses of a Second Chamber

The most fundamental question of all is, of course, whether to have a second chamber at all. This would seem a curious issue for Britain, the mother of bicameral parliaments, to raise; and, in point of fact, from the time when Englishmen found in Cromwell's day that, after all, notwithstanding an impetuous decision to the contrary, they wanted a parliament of two houses,[1] it was not often raised until the Labor party came by the idea, some twenty years ago, that the House of Lords is so

[1] This interesting experience is described in G. B. Roberts, *The Functions of a Second Chamber* (London, 1926), Chap. i, and J. A. R. Marriott, *Second Chambers* (new ed., Oxford, 1927), Chap. iii.

utterly out of keeping with democratic government that it ought to be suppressed root and branch.[2] A resolution moved in the House of Commons by the Labor representatives in 1907 reads: "That the upper house, being an irresponsible part of the Legislature and of necessity representative only of interests opposed to the general well-being, is a hindrance to national progress, and ought to be abolished;" and since 1918 the party has been officially on record as opposed not only to the continuance of the House of Lords as we know it but to the maintenance of any second chamber at all, even an elective one. In their challenging *Constitution for the Socialist Commonwealth of Great Britain,* the Webbs say categorically: "There is, of course, in the Socialist Commonwealth, no place for the House of Lords, which will simply cease to exist as a part of the Legislature." [3] Not infrequently in Labor discussion one hears quoted the historic asseveration of the Abbé Siéyès, "If a second chamber dissents from the first it is mischievous; if it agrees with it, it is superfluous." Indeed, in many books and articles coming from non-Labor and non-socialist sources one finds the uses of a second chamber heavily discounted and the abolition of the House of Lords viewed as perhaps im-

[2] The principal earlier English opponent of the bicameral plan was Jeremy Bentham. See L. Rockow, "Bentham on the Theory of Second Chambers," *Amer. Polit. Sci. Rev.,* Aug., 1928. Thomas Paine, English by birth, was also an advocate of unicameralism, as were his contemporaries, Samuel Adams in America and Turgot, Siéyès, and Condorcet in France. When, in 1922, the Australian state of Queensland abolished its second chamber, the Judicial Committee of the Privy Council was inclined to advise the crown to disallow the act as being contrary to the principles of the British constitution, but in the end did not do so. In point of fact, second chambers have almost disappeared from among provincial legislatures in the British dominions. Such a chamber was abolished in Nova Scotia in 1928, and since that time all Canadian provinces have had unicameral legislatures except Quebec.

[3] P. 110. Cf. pp. 62-63. The Webb volume is not an official statement of the Labor creed. The position taken on the House of Lords (as on most other matters) is, however, quite definitely that of the party; although it may be noted that in the latest officially adopted program of the party, *Labour and the Nation* (1928), the House of Lords is not mentioned and it is asserted merely that the party stands for "the maintenance of the unquestioned supremacy of the House of Commons," and that it is prepared to offer "uncompromising resistance to the establishment of a second chamber with authority over finance and power to hamper the House of Commons and defeat democratic decisions."

practicable—at all events until after some intermediate experiment has been tried and has failed—but neither revolutionary nor alarming if it were actually to be carried out.[4]

The general body of British opinion is, nevertheless, undoubtedly favorable to a second chamber, and—what is more—to a reformed House of Lords as constituting such a chamber. Labor itself, indeed, is divided on the subject, as one will see by reading the arguments for an elected upper house presented in *When Labor Rules,* by J. H. Thomas, Lord Privy Seal and leader of the House of Commons under the Labor ministry of 1924, and also in Fabian Tract No. 183, reprinted from the socialist weekly, *The New Statesman.*[5] The Bryce Conference of 1917-18, whose plan of reform will be mentioned presently, was unanimously of the opinion that a reconstructed House of Lords is a highly desirable part of the constitutional system, seeing in it four great uses which may be cited as expressing the best opinion of Englishmen on the subject today:

> 1. The examination and revision of bills brought from the House of Commons, a function which has become more needed since, on many occasions, during the last thirty years, the House of Commons has been obliged to act under special rules limiting debate.
>
> 2. The initiation of bills dealing with subjects of a practically non-controversial character which may have an easier passage through the House of Commons if they have been fully discussed and put into a well-considered shape before being submitted to it.
>
> 3. The interposition of so much delay (and no more) in the passing of a bill into a law as may be needed to enable the opinion of the nation to be adequately expressed upon it. This would be especially needed as regards bills which affect the fundamentals of the constitution or introduce new principles of legislation, or raise issues whereon the opinion of the country may appear to be almost equally divided.
>
> 4. Full and free discussion of large and important questions, such as those of foreign policy, at moments

[4] Note the tone of Sidney Low's comments in his *Governance of England* (new ed.), xv-xvii, and cf. H. B. Lees-Smith, *Second Chambers in Theory and Practice,* Chap. ii. The latter represents a moderate Labor view.

[5] See E. M. Sait and D. P. Barrows, *British Politics in Transition,* 166-173.

when the House of Commons may happen to be so much occupied that it cannot find sufficient time for them. Such discussions may often be all the more useful if conducted in an assembly whose debates and divisions do not involve the fate of the executive government."[6]

All of these functions are real and important, even though, as Sidney Low suggests at the conclusion of a list of his own making, some of them could conceivably be discharged by other agencies;[7] and it is interesting to note that the Webbs, while providing no place for the House of Lords in their carefully thought out scheme, seek to make some provision for the function of revision and for temporary suspension of hastily enacted legislation. Indeed, on the ground that Britain has none of the safeguards afforded by a rigid constitution, by referendum procedure like that of Switzerland, or by judicial review like that in the United States, it is sometimes contended that she, beyond most other states, has need of a second chamber with full deliberative and revisory powers.[8]

Earlier Proposals to Change Membership

Today as in the past, therefore, the really practical and urgent questions to which the House of Lords gives rise concern,

[6] *Report of the Conference on the Reform of the Second Chamber,* 4. Cf. J. A. R. Marriott, "The Problem of a Second Chamber," *Edinburgh Rev.,* July, 1917, reprinted in part in Sait and Barrows, *op. cit.,* 163-166. Classic discussions of the uses of a second chamber include J. S. Mill, *Representative Government* (London, 1860), Chap. xiii, entitled "Of a Second Chamber," and John Adams, *Defence of the Constitutions of Government of the United States of America* (Boston, 1787). The latter work will be found in C. F. Adams (ed.), *Works of John Adams* (Boston, 1851), IV, 270-588. The relative advantages of the unicameral and bicameral systems are set forth succinctly in J. W. Garner, *Political Science and Government,* 600-613. Cf. J. Bryce, *Modern Democracies,* II, Chap. lxiv; H. J. Laski, *A Grammar of Politics,* 328-335; and W. R. Sharp, *Le problème de la seconde chambre et la démocratie moderne* (Bordeaux, 1922). The subject is discussed with special reference to Britain in H. J. Laski, *The Problem of a Second Chamber* (Fabian Tract No. 213, London, 1925), and G. B. Roberts, *op. cit.,* Chap. ii. In the one case the conclusion is unfavorable, and in the other favorable, to a second chamber.

[7] *Governance of England* (new ed.), p. xvi.

[8] J. A. R. Marriott, "The Problem of a Second Chamber," *Fortnightly Rev.,* Mar., 1925, p. 354. G. B. Roberts, *The Functions of an English Second Chamber,* Chaps. ii, iv, is devoted to a lengthy commentary, with illustrations, upon the four uses assigned by the Bryce Report.

not the continued existence of the chamber, but its membership, powers, and relations to other parts of the governmental system, particularly the House of Commons. Down to 1909, such definite reform proposals as one encounters related almost exclusively to the matter of membership; by usage, powers were actually undergoing great changes, but hardly anybody was as yet so bold as to suggest formal legislation on the subject. The proposals most frequently made were that the number of members be reduced, that the ecclesiastical members be dropped out, and that members designated by some special process be substituted for a greater or lesser number of those sitting by hereditary right. In 1869 a bill of Lord John Russell providing for the gradual infiltration of life peers was defeated, and in the same year a project of Earl Grey, and in 1874 proposals of Lord Rosebery and Lord Inchiquin, came to naught. The rejection by the Lords of measures supported by Gladstone's government in 1881-83 brought the chamber afresh into considerable disfavor, and in 1888 the second Salisbury ministry—a Conservative ministry, be it noted—introduced two reform bills, one providing for the gradual creation of fifty life peerages, to be conferred upon men of attainment in law, diplomacy, and administrative service, and the other (popularly known as the "Black Sheep Bill") providing for the discontinuance of writs of summons to undesirable members of the peerage. The measures, however, were withdrawn after their second reading, and an attempt in 1889 to revive the second of them failed. Under the final Gladstone government of 1892-94 the second home rule bill, after passing the lower house, was defeated by the Lords, and several other Liberal measures were killed or emasculated; but, although the Liberal leaders urged that the popular will had been thwarted, and Gladstone declared that the relation between the two houses had created a state of things that could not continue, proposals for immediate second chamber reforms failed to strike fire. During ten years of unbroken Conservative rule (1895-1905) the issue was in abeyance. Looking back over the events of the past quarter-century, one is impressed with the amount of controversy and trouble that might have been averted if the question of the upper chamber had been taken in hand in that comparatively favorable period and brought to a reasonable solution. But the opportunity was missed.

The Liberals and the Lords, 1905-1910

The decade beginning in 1905, however, brought matters to a crisis, and out of one of the warmest constitutional controversies that modern Britain has witnessed emerged a great piece of legislation—the only legislation on the subject enacted to this day, in point of fact—designed to bring the problem to at least a partial solution. This was the Parliament Act of 1911, the antecedents and effects of which must briefly engage our attention. The situation was now ripe for a real fight. The Liberal party, entrenched in power early in 1906 by the most sweeping electoral victory that any British party had ever won,[9] could fairly claim to have the nation behind it; and it had no lack of large plans for social and economic legislation and political reform. On the other hand, the House of Lords, encouraged by its success in frustrating Gladstone on home rule, and on other matters too, and, furthermore, revitalized by the amalgamation of the Liberal seceders with the Conservatives, was more spirited, and even daring, than in half a century. Accordingly, trouble soon arose. Many, indeed most, of the Liberals' measures were, it is true, got through the upper chamber. But naturally they were the bills of least partisan and disputed character, and one after another of the government's big projects—abolishing plural voting, introducing a new scheme of land values for purposes of taxation, reconstructing the administration of public education, imposing heavier fees upon the liquor trade—were mowed down. Even before the end of 1907, the heavily Liberal House of Commons reached the point of passing a resolution asserting that, in order to give effect to the will of the people as expressed by their elected representatives, "the power of the House of Lords to alter or reject bills should be so restrained by law as to secure that within the limits of a single parliament the final decision of the Commons shall prevail." This was, of course, tantamount to saying that the upper house should no longer be,

[9] A Liberal ministry was formed in December, 1905, but its mandate from the nation came with the general election of January, 1906.

even in theory, a coördinate branch of Parliament; and the stand taken betokened the line upon which the Liberal assault was chiefly to proceed in later years.[10] Clearly placed on the defensive, and determined at all hazards to hold to such of their historic powers as remained, the peers, on their part, gave indication of their future tactics when, in 1908, a committee of the chamber, presided over by Lord Rosebery (a Liberal), reported a plan of reform under which (1) possession of a peerage should not of itself entitle the holder to a seat in the chamber; (2) the whole body of hereditary peers, including those of Scotland and Ireland, should elect for each parliament two hundred of their number to sit in the upper house; (3) hereditary peers who had occupied certain posts of eminence in the government and the army and navy should be entitled to sit without election; (4) the bishops should elect eight representatives, while the archbishops should sit as of right; and (5) the crown should be empowered to summon four life peers annually, so long as the total should not exceed forty.[11] The proposal was ingenious and suggestive, but the Liberal leaders in the lower house did not care at the moment to take it up.

In the autumn of 1909 the issue was reopened in a sensational manner by the unexpected decision of the House of Lords not to approve the government's Finance Bill (embodying the proposals of the Chancellor of the Exchequer, Mr. Lloyd George, for a reassessment of land values, taxation of unearned increment, and, in general, heavier impositions upon wealth) until the people should have had an opportunity to pass judgment upon the new departures at a national election. Nobody could allege that any law of the realm was violated by this performance; the upper chamber was accustomed to reject non-financial bills, and it had never been party to any formal agreement or pledge restraining it from doing the same thing for money measures. A tradition of long standing, however, to the effect that absolute and final authority in both the raising and spending of money

[10] Interest in the subject led the government in 1907 to publish a comprehensive document entitled *Reports from His Majesty's Representatives Abroad Respecting the Composition and Functions of the Second or Upper Chamber in Foreign States.* Cmd. 3428.

[11] *Report from the Select Committee on the House of Lords, together with the Proceedings of the Committee and Appendix* (London, 1908).

lay with the House of Commons was unmistakably shattered; and although the majority members in the Lords contended that they were not finally rejecting a finance bill but only suspending it until its principles could be referred to the high court of public opinion, and were doing so only because they considered it confiscatory of property in land, as well as practically unenforceable, most Liberals were prepared to argue that what the upper chamber had done was both unjustifiable and revolutionary.[12]

[12] So far as the impracticability of the new taxes was concerned, the House of Lords was proved by experience to have been entirely right. In 1919 the land value duties, which formed the special bone of contention, were—with Mr. Lloyd George's own consent—repealed as "in their present form unworkable." From year to year the costs involved had been from three to four times the sums received. From the point of view of political expediency, the course taken by the Lords on the budget proposals was, however, more open to question. In support of their contention that the second chamber was obligated to accept the government's bill embodying the proposals, or *any* finance bill sent up from the House of Commons, the Liberals could cite a good deal of interesting history. As early as 1407, Henry IV accepted the principle that money grants should be initiated in the Commons, assented to by the Lords, and thereupon reported to the crown. This procedure was not always observed, but after the two houses resumed their normal functions following the Restoration in 1660 the right of the commoners to take precedence in fiscal business, on the theory that taxation and representation should go together, was firmly and continuously asserted. In 1671 the Commons resolved "that in all aids given to the king by the Commons, the rate or tax ought not to be altered by the Lords;" and a resolution of 1678—following an historic contest between the houses—reaffirmed that all bills for the granting of supplies "ought to begin with the Commons," and that it was the "undoubted and sole right of the Commons to direct, limit, and appoint in such bills the ends, purposes, considerations, conditions, limitations, and qualifications for such grants, which ought not to be changed or altered by the House of Lords." These principles were construed to mean not only that the Lords should not initiate any bill or part of a bill laying a money charge on the people or regulating the administration or application of money raised by such a charge, but also that the chamber should not reject, or even amend, any such bill coming up to it from the House of Commons; and from the observance of them it resulted in later times (1) that the upper chamber was never consulted about the annual estimates, about the amounts of money to be raised, or about the purposes to which these amounts should be appropriated; (2) that proposals of taxation came before it only in matured form and under circumstances which discouraged criticism; and (3) that, since the policy of the executive is controlled largely through the medium of the power of the purse, the upper house practically lost the means of exercising such control. At no time, it must be observed, did the House of Lords formally accept the limitations laid down by the other chamber in its resolves and

Relations between the two houses were thus brought to a crisis. Backed by a resolution of the Commons pronouncing the action of the upper chamber "a breach of the constitution" and "a usurpation of the privileges of the House of Commons," and seeing in the upper chamber no disposition to retract, the ministry decided upon an appeal to the country, and at the general election of January, 1910, got a mandate to go on, even though with a much reduced majority; and when the Finance Bill again made its appearance, the upper chamber proved as good as its word and permitted it to become law. This, however, was not enough to satisfy. Liberal sentiment demanded that steps be taken to avert such difficulties in the future; and even Conservatives were rather generally prepared to concede that something would have to be done.

The question of *what* to do was, of course, crucial; and the two parties were totally unable to see eye to eye upon it. As in 1906, the Conservatives thought by a radical reconstruction of the membership of the upper chamber, so as to make it more representative, to stave off any impairment of its legal parity of power. But the Liberals, urged on by their Irish Nationalist and Labor allies, considered that while changes of membership were desirable enough, the first thing to do was to obtain legislation definitely assuring the paramountcy of the popular branch in general legislation and its "undivided authority" over finance. Hence, while Lord Rosebery was offering in the House of Lords resolutions declaring (1) that a strong and efficient

practices; on the contrary, it long resisted them, and never were they enacted into law. But the Commons found ways of enforcing them, and by 1909 it was a fair question whether they were not to be considered as embodied in the customary or conventional part of the constitution. Back in 1860 the Lords had, indeed, made bold to reject a bill for the repeal of the duties on paper. But the Commons rose to the defense of its asserted rights; the next year the repeal of the paper duties was written into the annual budget and forced through; and thenceforth it became the practice to include all proposals relating to taxation in the one great Finance Bill passed each year, with the result, of course, of cutting off the Lords from any opportunity to defeat a proposal of the kind except by rejecting the whole of a measure which was vital to the carrying on of the government. Down to 1909 it was hardly dreamed that the chamber would incur responsibility for so drastic a step as this. On the general subject, see A. Wartner, *The Lords: their History and Powers, with Special Reference to Money Bills* (London, 1910).

second chamber is not merely a part of the British constitution, but is necessary to the well-being of the state and the balance of Parliament; (2) that such a chamber may best be obtained by the reform and reconstitution of the House of Lords; and (3) that a necessary preliminary to such reform and reconstruction is the acceptance of the principle that the possession of a peerage shall no longer of itself confer the right to sit and vote in the House, Premier Asquith was introducing in the lower house another set of resolutions to the effect (1) that the House of Lords should be disabled by law from rejecting or amending a money bill; (2) that the power of the chamber to veto other bills should be so restricted by law that the will of the House of Commons might prevail within the period of a single parliament; and (3) that the duration of a parliament should be limited to a maximum period of five years. The first two of Rosebery's resolutions were accepted in the upper chamber without division, and the third was carried by a large majority. But, similarly, the government's resolutions were enthusiastically agreed to in the lower house, cast into the form of a bill, and started on the road to enactment. There was never much chance that the Rosebery bill—or another on somewhat similar lines introduced by Lord Lansdowne (Conservative leader in the upper house), and allowed to progress through second reading without division—would be taken up by the government and pressed through the House of Commons. The question was, rather, whether the government measure could be got through a bitterly hostile House of Lords.

The Parliament Act

The thing was done, but not until the country had seen some exciting times. A bi-partisan Constitutional Conference, composed of eight leading representatives of the two houses, wrestled vainly with the problem through the summer of 1910; another general election, in December, turned almost exclusively on the second chamber issue, leaving the relative strength of the parties in the popular branch practically unchanged; and after the government's Parliament Bill had been reintroduced and successfully passed in the popular house, the king, at the ministry's solicitation, let it be known that he was prepared to create enough new peers to ensure a majority for the measure in the upper chamber.[13] Confronted with the prospect of wholesale "swamping," the opposition fell back upon the policy of abstention; and although a considerable number of last-ditchers held out to the end for amendments which would have exempted constitutional and other matters of "great gravity" from the operation of the bill, a group of Conservatives sufficient to carry the measure joined the handful of government supporters, August 10, 1911, in a vote not to insist upon the alterations—which meant, in effect, to approve the bill as it had passed the lower house. The royal assent—a matter of form, of course—was given eight days later.

The triumphant Liberals had by no means thrown overboard the idea of reconstructing the upper chamber on more democratic lines, and in its preamble the Parliament Act promised supplementary legislation to this end. The present measure, however, dealt rather with the matter of powers, its general object being to provide ways by which finance bills could quickly, and other bills more slowly, be made law whether the House of Lords concurred in them or not. These arrangements might or might not be perpetuated after the chamber should have been reconstituted; but until then, at all events, they were to make impossible the recurrence of anything like the happenings of 1909. The great provisions in this connection were three in number. In the first place, "if a money bill, having been passed by the House of Commons, and sent up to the House of Lords at least one month before the end of the session, is not passed by the House of Lords without amendment within one month after it is sent up to that house, the bill shall, unless the House of Commons direct to the contrary, be presented to His Majesty and become an act of Parliament on the royal assent being signified, notwithstanding that the House of Lords have not assented to the bill." While, however, in

[13] During the controversy Edward VII died (May 6, 1910) and was succeeded by George V. On the difficult position in which the new sovereign was placed, and the constitutional significance of the crisis generally, see J. A. R. Marriott, *Second Chambers* (new ed.), 182-191. Sir Sidney Lee's *Edward VII; a Biography*, II, 695, shows that Edward was deeply concerned about the reform of the Lords and indeed had a scheme of his own.

many cases there could be no doubt as to whether a given bill was to be regarded as a money bill, in other instances there would certainly be differences of opinion. Hence the act went on in its second main provision to define a money bill as "a public bill which, in the judgment of the speaker of the House of Commons, contains only provisions dealing with all or any of the following subjects, namely, the imposition, repeal, remission, alteration, or regulation of taxation; the imposition for the payment of debt or other financial purposes of charges on the Consolidated Fund, or on money provided by Parliament, or the variation or repeal of any such charges; supply; the appropriation, receipt, custody, issue or audit of accounts of public money; the raising or guarantee of any loan or the repayment thereof; or subordinate matters incidental to those subjects or any of them." Every money bill presented to the House of Lords must be certified to be such by the speaker, whose decision is conclusive for all purposes and cannot be questioned in a court of law.[14]

This was as far as the events of 1909-10 alone would have required the authors of the measure to go. But the reformers had hardly less prominently in mind the defeat of the home rule bill of 1893, of the plural voting and licensing bills of 1906, and of other largely or wholly non-financial measures; and accordingly the third major provision became this: that any other public bill (except a bill to confirm a provisional order or to extend the maximum duration of Parliament beyond the period fixed by law) which is passed by the House of Commons in three successive sessions, whether or not of the same parliament, and which, having been sent up to the House of Lords at least one month, in each case, before the close of the session,

[14] An incidental effect of the act is to exalt the power and importance of the speaker, although it should be observed that the speaker had long been accustomed to state at the introduction of a public bill whether in his judgment the rights or privileges claimed by the House of Commons in respect to finance had been infringed. If he were of the opinion that there had been an infringement, it remained for the House to determine whether it would insist upon or waive its privilege. C. Ilbert, *Parliament,* 207. Since 1911 the speaker has on several occasions withheld his certificate from measures alleged to be finance bills, which, therefore, went up to the House of Lords as ordinary bills. On later proposals to take the function in question from the speaker and place it in a committee, see pp. 351 ff. below.

is rejected by that chamber in each of those sessions, shall, unless the House of Commons direct to the contrary, become an act of Parliament on the royal assent being signified thereto, notwithstanding the fact that the House of Lords has not consented to the bill.[15] It is required that at least two years shall have elapsed between the date of the second reading of such a bill (i.e., the first real opportunity for its discussion) in the first of these sessions of the House of Commons and the final passage of the bill in the third of the sessions. To come within the provisions of the act the measure, furthermore, must be, at its initial and its final appearances, the "same bill;" that is, it must contain no alterations save such as are made necessary by the lapse of time. In the case of either a money bill or a non-money bill, the measure is to be construed as "rejected" by the House of Lords if it is not passed, or if it is passed with amendments which the lower house is unwilling to accept, or which the House of Commons (in the case of a non-money bill) does not itself suggest to the House of Lords at the second or third passage of the bill.

Incorporated in the act was one important provision not directly connected with the subject in hand, but germane in the sense that it was aimed at bringing Parliament and its work into closer relation with public opinion, namely, that the maximum life of a parliament should thenceforth be five years, instead of seven as for almost two hundred years previously.[16]

By bringing to an end the parity of power which, in theory and in law if not in practice, the House of Lords had enjoyed through the centuries, the Parliament Act introduced one of the greatest changes in the British constitution ever deliberately made, incidentally affording at the same time a striking illus-

[15] It is interesting to observe that early in the nineteenth century James Mill (father of the better known John Stuart Mill) propounded, in an article for the *Encyclopedia Britannica,* a plan almost identical with this. "Let it be enacted," he wrote, "that if a bill which has been passed by the House of Commons, and thrown out by the House of Lords, is renewed in the House of Commons in the next session of Parliament, and passed, but again thrown out by the House of Lords, it shall, if passed a third time in the House of Commons, be law, without again being sent to the Lords."

[16] On this feature of the act, see J. G. Randall, "Frequency and Duration of Parliaments," in *Amer. Polit. Sci. Rev.,* Nov., 1916, especially pp. 674-679.

tration of the tendency to enlargement of the written, at the expense of the unwritten and conventional, parts of that great plan of government. As for the upper chamber, it has, of course, never been the same since. Its judicial powers are untouched; and in the domain of legislation it still enjoys much influence, and even power. No project of financial or other legislation can be put on the statute book without being submitted to it, and there is nothing except custom and convenience to prevent even the most important of non-financial measures from making their appearance first upon its calendar. A single, bare presentation, however, of any money bill fulfills all legal requirements and ensures that such a measure will become law; for such a bill will not be presented until it has been passed by the House of Commons, and, emanating from the cabinet, it will not be introduced in that chamber until the assent of the crown is assured. The upper house is allowed one month in which to approve or reject; but, so far as the future of the bill is concerned, the result is the same whatever it does.

In respect to non-financial bills, the second chamber still has a veto. This check, however, is only suspensive, not absolute. The terms required for placing such measures on the statute book without the Lords' assent are admittedly not easy to meet; and it is interesting to observe that in all the eighteen years from the passage of the act to the date of writing, not a single measure—financial or otherwise—has become effective without the upper chamber's consent. One should hasten to add, however, that apparently only the intervention of the World War prevented the thing from happening a number of times. The procedure contemplated in the act was invoked in the case of the Irish home rule bill of 1913, a plural voting bill of the same year, and a bill disestablishing and disendowing the Anglican Church in Wales in 1914; and while it is true that the first of these measures, though placed on the statute book, never went into operation,[17] that the second did not become law, and that the third was, in substance, finally assented to by the Lords after the war, the history of the bills shows that the procedure laid down in the legislation of 1911 is by no means to be regarded as unworkable. By repeatedly rejecting a prof-

[17] See pp. 700-702 below.

fered measure, the Lords may indeed rouse public sentiment against it or otherwise so influence the attitude of members of the popular branch as to cause the project either to be given up or to be defeated at a later test; and this is the more possible since a minimum period of two years is required to elapse before a non-financial measure can be carried over the Lords' veto. All possible allowance being made, however, on these scores, it is not only legally but actually possible for legislation of all kinds to be enacted without the Lords' assent. Reenforced by all manner of practical circumstances steadily operating in the chamber's favor, the preponderance assigned the House of Commons by the act of 1911 gives that body a control over law-making which, to all intents and purposes, is absolute.[18]

The Conference of 1917-18 and the "Bryce Report"

The Parliament Act definitely announced the intention of its authors to "substitute for the House of Lords as it at present exists a second chamber constituted on a popular instead of an hereditary basis." During the three years that elapsed before the outbreak of the World War the Liberal ministry was so preoccupied with the Irish question and other urgent issues that it did not get round to the resumption of its program; and of course the war period, at least in its earlier stages, was not a time in which the subject could be pressed. To this day, indeed, no further changes have been made. Discussion, however, was actively resumed, even before the war was over, and during the past decade many ingenious plans have been put forward, both in Parliament and outside. Conspicuous among these is the

[18] Cf. A. V. Dicey, *Introduction to the Law of the Constitution* (8th ed.), p. xxiv. The political history lying immediately back of the Parliament Act is well presented in A. L. P. Dennis, "Impressions of British Party Politics, 1909-1911," *Amer. Polit. Sci. Rev.*, Nov., 1911, and good analyses of the measure and its significance are to be found in T. E. May and F. Holland, *Constitutional History of England,* III, 343-384; A. L. Lowell, *Government of England* (rev. ed., New York, 1912), I, Chap. xxiiia; G. B. Adams, *Constitutional History of England,* Chap. xx; and A. L. P. Dennis, "The Parliament Act of 1911," *Amer. Polit. Sci. Rev.,* May, Aug., 1912. R. Muir, *Peers and Bureaucrats* (London, 1910), and H. Jones, *Liberalism and the House of Lords* (London, 1912), are historical surveys from a distinctly Liberal point of view.

scheme of reorganization formulated by a Conference on the Reform of the Second Chamber, appointed by the prime minister in August, 1917, at a time when, as we have seen, the prompt democratization of the House of Commons had been decided upon, and when it was rather keenly felt that if Britain was to make her political institutions square with her professions in a war of democracy against autocracy she must contrive to popularize the House of Lords. Presided over by Lord Bryce, and composed of thirty persons chosen to represent all shades of opinion on second chamber problems, this conference[19] spent some six months probing the question both of membership and powers in all of their ramifications and in the spring of 1918 submitted its findings, not, indeed, in the shape of a formal report, because upon most matters there was no general agreement, but rather through the medium of a letter from the chairman to the prime minister embodying the views of the majority and accompanied by a list of specific recommendations.[20]

The document begins by emphasizing the difficulties of the problem, especially of adapting an ancient institution to new ideas and new needs, of finding a basis for a second chamber that would be different in structure and viewpoint from the House of Commons, and of adjusting the powers and functions of the two bodies. It expressed the opinion that, in so far as possible, continuity ought to be preserved between the historic House of Lords and the future second chamber, which obviously would mean that a certain portion of the existing peerage should be included in the new body. At the same time, it agreed

[19] It was, in effect, a parliamentary joint committee, and its members were drawn equally from the membership of the two houses.

[20] *Report of the Conference on the Reform of the Second Chamber.* Cmd. 9038 (1918), reprinted in H. L. McBain and L. Rogers, *New Constitutions of Europe,* 576-601, and in part in E. M. Sait and D. P. Barrows, *op. cit.,* 175-185. On the work of the Conference, see H. B. Lees-Smith, *Second Chambers in Theory and Practice* (London, 1923), Chap. xi. G. B. Roberts, *The Functions of an English Second Chamber,* is largely a discussion of the Conference's conclusions, particularly as to the uses which a second chamber, under British conditions, ought to serve. It may be added that eleven of the members of the Conference (including the chairman) were Liberals, eighteen were Unionists (Conservatives), and one was a member of the Labor party. Fifteen of the thirty were hereditary peers (nine Unionists and six Liberals).

that "three important requisites" would be found "in its [the new chamber's] having popular authority behind it, in its opening to the whole of His Majesty's subjects free and equal access to the chamber, and in its being made responsive to the thoughts and sentiments of the people"—considerations which dictated that a large majority of the members should be "so chosen as to enjoy that popular authority."[21] And it was added (1) that all possible precautions ought to be taken to secure that in the reformed second chamber no one set of political opinions should be likely to have "a marked and permanent predominance;" (2) that the body should be so made up that it would aim at ascertaining the mind and views of the nation as a whole and should recognize its responsibility to the people as a whole; and (3) that certain elements ought especially to have a place in it, i.e., persons of experience in various forms of public work, persons who, while likely to serve efficiently, have not the physical vigor requisite for a career in the House of Commons, and persons who are not strong partisans.

Various modes of making up a second chamber which would meet these requirements were duly considered. Nomination by the sovereign, acting through the ministers, was rejected because "it did not provide any guarantees for the fitness of the persons who might be nominated, and because it would be liable to be frequently employed as a reward for political party services." Direct election by the same voters as those who choose the House of Commons was discarded because it would yield a second chamber which would be little more than a duplicate of the House of Commons, yet would be likely to become an undesirable rival of that body, and even to claim to "make and unmake administrations." Election by county and borough councils or other local authorities, grouped in areas of suitable size, had something to be said for it, but was open to the objection that it would tend to inject party politics into local elections hitherto conducted largely on non-partisan lines. Selection by a joint standing committee of the two houses found favor, yet was thought by the majority not to furnish a sufficiently broad basis of choice. Finally, election by the House of Commons, either by the body as a whole on some plan of pro-

[21] *Report,* 5.

portional representation or by groups into which the membership might be divided, was strongly supported, yet was felt to have disadvantages.

The plan finally recommended partook of features of the last two of these schemes. In the first place—leaving representation of Ireland out of account—the total membership of the chamber was to be reduced by half, i.e., to 327. Of this number, practically three-fourths, i.e., 246, were to be elected, by secret ballot and proportional representation, by the members of the House of Commons grouped according to thirteen regional divisions,[22] the commoners from each division electing the quota in the upper chamber to which their area, on a basis of population, was entitled. Thus the thirty-six members of the House of Commons from the South Eastern area (comprising Surrey, Kent, and Sussex) were to elect fifteen members of the second chamber, and the sixty-six commoners from the area of Lancashire were to elect twenty-seven. Not more than one-third of the portion of the chamber thus chosen should be elected by the members of any single House of Commons (i.e., in any one parliament); hence special arrangements were to be made for putting the system into operation by degrees. Except at one or two points, the qualifications for election to the House of Lords were to be the same as those for election to the House of Commons; and no sitting member of the latter body was to be eligible.

With a view to preserving the desired continuity of the reformed second chamber with the old one, the remaining eighty-one members were to be chosen from the whole body of peers by a joint standing committee of the two houses,[23] although after the first election persons not peers might be elected to this quota (in the same manner), so long as the number of peers so selected sitting in the second chamber should not fall below thirty. After the scheme should have come into full operation, all members of both groups were to be elected for

[22] Scotland was to form one and Wales and Monmouthshire another, the remaining eleven being in England. This plan was taken over largely from a bill introduced by Lord Lansdowne as an alternative to the Parliament Bill in 1911. The main principles were suggested by Lord Rosebery as early as 1888.

[23] Five members representing the Lords and five representing the Commons.

twelve-year terms, and in each group one-third of the members were to retire quadrennially.

As to functions, the committee was agreed that the reconstituted second chamber ought not to have equal powers with the House of Commons, nor aim at becoming a rival of that body, and that, in particular, it ought not to have the power of making and overturning ministries or of vetoing money bills. Nevertheless, some betterment of the legislative position assigned to it in 1911 was provided for by (1) a proposal that when there should be doubt whether a measure was to be regarded as a money bill the question should be settled, not by the speaker of the House of Commons, as now, but by a joint committee on financial bills, consisting of seven members elected by each house for the duration of a parliament,[24] and (2) a plan for reference of a bill on which the houses could not agree to a "free conference," sitting privately, and consisting of (a) twenty members of each house appointed at the beginning of a parliament by the Committee of Selection of each house and (b) ten members of each house added by the Committee of Selection on the occasion of the reference of any particular bill. This last plan was adopted as against joint sessions of the two houses, or popular referenda. A bill on which the two houses could not agree was to be brought before the free conference at the request of either chamber; and the method prescribed for handling it was such as to give the conference very great power in determining whether it should finally pass, and in what form.[25]

[24] The Labor party has steadily opposed this oft-suggested change, chiefly on the ground that the proposed committee would always have a majority of Conservatives on it, with the result (as Mr. Snowden once put it) that "a Labor government would be tied hand and foot in finding the money to carry out any schemes of social reform." It is doubtful whether the objection would be removed by reconstruction of the House of Lords on any of the lines at present proposed, because even then Labor could hardly hope to be the dominating force in the chamber.

[25] For criticism of this feature, see Lees-Smith, *op. cit.*, 231-235. The proposal looked to something in the nature of the familiar American "conference committee." See F. A. Ogg and P. O. Ray, *Introduction to American Government* (3rd ed., New York, 1928), 413-415, and for fuller treatment, A. C. McCown, *The Congressional Conference Committee* (New York, 1927). Cf. p. 419 below.

Proposals Since 1918

The scheme thus outlined has never been voted. The coalition government of Mr. Lloyd George did, indeed, get so far in 1922 as to present to the House of Lords five resolutions prepared by a cabinet committee and embodying several features of the Bryce plan, with one or two notable additions.[26] In summary, these proposals provided for (1) a House of Lords of some 350 members, (2) continuance of the peers of the royal blood, the lords spiritual, and the law lords as members ex-officio, (3) election of some other members and appointment of still others (numbers not specified) for a term of years to be fixed by statute, (4) transfer of the power to determine whether a given measure is a money bill from the speaker to a joint standing committee of the two houses, and (5) exemption of all bills altering the constitution or powers of the House of Lords from those provisions of the Parliament Act enabling bills to be passed into law without the consent of the second chamber during the life of a single parliament.[27] Both the House of Lords and the critics outside received these resolutions coldly;[28] and when the coalition government resigned some three months later they were left without official sponsorship. Members of the second chamber who were sincerely interested in the subject felt that the proposals were so indefinite on the composition of the reformed house as to be largely valueless, and were specially disappointed because the resolutions almost totally ignored what was felt to be the major issue in the problem, i.e., the question of powers; while at the same time the privileged position that the second chamber was to enjoy under the fifth proposal, as compared with every other part of the government, was regarded by people less friendly toward the chamber as highly objectionable.

The resolutions of 1922, never debated adequately, perished with the Lloyd George coalition.[29] The short-lived Conservative

[26] Cmd. 1715 (1922).

[27] Sait and Barrows, *op. cit.,* 185-187.

[28] H. B. Lees-Smith, *op. cit.,* Chap. xii.

[29] For such discussion as there was, see *Parliamentary Debates (Lords)*, 5th Series, Vol. LI, cols. 524-572, 642-682, 783-815, 963-996; Vol. LII, cols. 261-288.

government of 1922-24 marked time on the question, and the Labor government of Mr. MacDonald, in 1924, dared not, in its precarious position, take up the subject, even if the pressure of more urgent matters had permitted. When, however, the Conservatives returned to office at the end of 1924 with a large parliamentary majority, and with every prospect of a lengthy tenure, the time seemed to have come for something concrete to be done. That something *ought* to be done was as freely conceded by Conservatives as by Laborites; and equally clear was it, from the Conservative point of view, that whatever was done ought to be done while the friends of the second chamber were in a position to control the course of events. The fact that there had actually been a Labor government, coupled with the probability that some day there would be another one more favorably situated for carrying out its ideas, suggested that the Lords could not too soon be rehabilitated and brought into greater favor with the nation. There was plenty of feeling in the Conservative ranks that, quite apart from all considerations of party and class advantage, the membership of the chamber ought to be overhauled, reduced in number, and made more representative. There was also, however, a deep-seated desire to restore enough power to the body, or at all events to place the House of Commons under sufficient restraint, to make it impossible for a future Labor government to carry out a program of socialistic legislation by simple unchecked action of the popular branch alone. This might eventually mean the repeal of the Parliament Act. Indeed, to many adherents of the party in power, that is precisely what it did mean. Any lingering doubt about the ultimate objective was removed by a resolution adopted at a party conference at Newcastle, in anticipation of the general election of November, 1924, declaring it to be "urgently necessary" that the *powers and composition* of the second chamber be so modified as to ensure that no far-reaching change in the law or constitution of the country can be made by the House of Commons alone without the expressed consent of the electorate." To compel reference of a proposed change to the electorate would be the function of a House of Lords reconstructed and reëndowed with the veto powers withdrawn in 1911.

Matters, however, moved slowly. The Baldwin ministry did, indeed, publicly pledge itself to a reform of the chamber during the life of the parliament elected in 1924. But the prime minister was not personally keenly interested in the matter; other things seemed to him more imperative; he rightly considered that the man in the street was not at the moment greatly concerned; and it is the natural impulse of any premier to postpone the performance of a peculiarly difficult and delicate task unless and until he is assured of overwhelming support, not only from the party leaders and the representatives in Parliament, but from the rank and file in the constituencies. In 1925 there was discussion of a plan brought to the House of Lords by the government leader, Lord Birkenhead, but nothing resulted. Again in the summer of 1927 the House debated and adopted a resolution declaring that it would welcome "a reasonable measure limiting and defining the membership and dealing with defects inherent in the Parliament Act;" and a scheme of reconstruction, of the same general tenor as the resolutions of 1922, was presented on behalf of the government. Notwithstanding unusual attendance of interested members, and exceptional warmth of discussion, the occasion also passed without action—although it was rather widely believed that a government bill would in due time make its appearance.[30] During the ensuing twelvemonth the ministry concentrated its legislative efforts upon other subjects, and at the end of 1928 it became apparent that, with a general election in the offing, the subject would have to go over; it was not even mentioned in the Speech from the Throne at the opening of the last session of the then existing

[30] The annual conference of the Labor party, in session at Blackpool in October, roundly denounced the government's proposals "for the so-called 'reform' of the House of Lords," on the ground that if carried out they would deprive the democratically elected House of Commons of its complete control over finance and taxation, frustrate in the future the fulfillment of the declared will of the people regarding any change in the status of the upper house without the approval of the House of Lords itself, and would perpetuate the upper house "as the instrument of the Tory party." *Labour Year Book* (1928), 15. Cf. *ibid.*, 214-224. A manifesto of the Liberal members of the House of Commons took substantially the same position. On the other hand, a resolution of the Conservative party conference held at Cardiff in October declared the party's intention to support "those measures necessary to assure that the will of the people shall be safeguarded by an effective second chamber."

parliament. Throughout the 1927 discussions the crux of the problem was the question—manifestly involving the future of the Parliament Act—whether the House of Lords should be endowed with power to force a referendum on any proposal to change the fundamental law, and power also to prevent social legislation from being carried through, over its protest, under the guise of financial measures. Involved with this was the question of whether it should be made impossible to abolish or alter the second chamber without its own consent. Conservatives were generally favorable to the setting up of such a guarantee; Laborites and Liberals were strongly opposed.[31]

The Second Chamber Problem as It Stands Today

Of late, the problem has been in abeyance.[32] But it is always in the background of the political scene and liable to thrust itself into renewed prominence, or even preëminence. John Bright's observation that "a hereditary House of Lords is not and cannot be perpetual in a free country" is plausible,[33] and one would hardly be accused of rashness if he predicted significant changes

[31] The government's retreat from its proclaimed, and doubtless honest, intention to press for action was dictated in part by defection among its younger adherents in the House of Commons. The dissentients considered the ministry's plans too drastic. For the discussion in the two houses, see *Parliamentary Debates* (*Lords*), 5th Series, Vol. LXVII, cols. 755-802 862-950, 952-1006; Vol. LXVIII, cols. 664-667; and *Parliamentary Debates* (*Commons*), 5th Series, Vol. CCVIII, cols. 1285-1406.

[32] Near the end of 1928 a non-ministerial member of the House of Lords, the Earl of Clarendon, stirred some discussion in the chamber by proposing a plan under which the matter of powers was left to one side but the membership of the body was to be changed to include (in addition to princes of the blood and law lords) 150 peers to be elected by means of proportional representation by the whole body of peers, 150 other persons to be nominated by the crown in proportion to the state of parties in the House of Commons and to sit for life, and a limited number of life peers to be nominated in each parliament by the crown. The government refused to support the project; Labor declared it objectionable; and the matter ended with the adoption of only a general resolution to the effect that "it is desirable that early steps be taken to reduce the number of members of the House of Lords, and to make suitable provision for an elective representation of the peerage and for such other representation or nomination as would insure to each political party a fair position in the House."

[33] One is reminded also of Benjamin Franklin's remark that there is no more reason for hereditary legislators than for hereditary professors of mathematics.

within a measureable future. Save for the complicating question of powers, the membership problem would almost certainly have been settled before now. Speaking broadly, all Englishmen agree that some modifications are desirable, even though at the date of writing few people are excited about the matter. The question is, What modifications? Again speaking broadly, Labor says: "Abolish the second chamber altogether; *any* second chamber would be a reactionary body, and what is needed is merely improvement of the House of Commons by 'bringing it more closely in touch with the people.'"[34] Liberalism (what remains of it) says: "Reform the membership, but keep the chamber weak, chiefly by continuing the restrictions placed by the Parliament Act on its power of veto."[35] Conservatism says: "Reform the membership if you please, but give back the powers taken away in 1911."[36]

Fair-minded people recognize, of course, that there is much to be said for the House of Lords even as it now stands. Its roll is, indeed, crowded with the names of members who lack both ability and interest. But neither the House of Commons nor any other legislative body is composed entirely, or perhaps even mainly, of men who are all that could be desired; and in the case of the House of Lords the unfit rarely darken the doors of the chamber, or, if present, take any active part. The work of the house is done very largely by men who have genuine ability, interest, and experience; and of these there are, fortunately, many. Not all the members of achievement do, or can, participate regularly. Some of them, after appointment to or inheritance of a peerage, very naturally and properly go on with their professional, scholarly, or business careers. After all, it must be remembered that for most of them membership is a wholly involuntary matter, which cannot always be accepted

[34] *Labour Speakers' Handbook* (London, 1923), 122.

[35] Resolution passed by the executive committee of the National Liberal Federation, July 6, 1922. E. M. Sait and D. P. Barrows, *op. cit.*, 187.

[36] As Lord Lansdowne put it in 1925, "What really matters is (1) that we should be given a second chamber not unwieldy in numbers, representative of moderate and well-informed opinion in the country, and free from the suspicion which attaches to a purely hereditary chamber, and (2) that this chamber should have real powers of revision, and of appealing when necessary against the caprice of the country to its sober and deliberate judgment."

as transcending other obligations already incurred. But it is doubtful whether, by and large, the actual working House of Lords is surpassed in its resources of intelligence, integrity, and public spirit by even the House of Commons. Industry, finance, agriculture, science, literature, religion—all are represented there. Spiritual and intellectual, as well as material, forces find expression. The country is served from the red leather benches by men who have built up its prosperity, administered its great dependencies, risen to its highest positions in law, diplomacy, war, statecraft, and learning. The fact is not to be overlooked, furthermore, that many of the more active members have in their earlier days had the advantage of long service in the House of Commons—that, indeed, the popular branch is in a very real sense a nursery of the House of Lords.[37]

All this being true, one will not be surprised to learn that upon a good many occasions the upper house has interpreted the will of the nation, or the actualities of a political situation, more correctly than the popular branch, and that more than once it has saved the country from hasty and ill-considered legislation.[38] If it is not representative of the nation in any exact and calculated way, it at least represents broadly the best things for

[37] About one-fourth of the present members of the House of Lords have at some time had seats in the other house. A member of the House of Commons recorded in 1857 the fact, "not unimportant to constitutional history," as he well says, that, going over to the Lords from the Commons one evening, he observed that every one of the thirty peers then present had sat with him in the popular chamber.

According tc the *Constitutional Year Book* (1928), p. 166, members of the House of Lords, as the chamber stood at the end of 1927, had rendered public service as follows:

In the House of Commons	152
In offices of state	111
In war service	297
In naval service	27
In the regular army	316
In the air force	6
In Yeomanry, Militia, and Territorials	259
As judges and eminent lawyers	29
As colonial governors and ministers	42
As lords lieutenant and deputy lieutenants	53
As mayors and county councillors	100

[38] It may do this by a veto, which even under the Parliament Act may, to all intents and purposes, be final. Or it may put the ministry in a position where the natural thing to do is to take the measure to the country at a general election, in which case the chamber is practically calling into play the principle of referendum, as it so clearly did in 1909. Lord Salisbury used to say that the power to refer questions of importance to the elec-

which British life and culture stand. Nevertheless, when all this is said, the story is not completely told. There are shortcomings, some of them grievous and fundamental. There is no need to enlarge upon the allusions to them already made. All center in the system which undertakes to make legislators of men who do not want to be legislators, and in the conditions that cause the chamber to be filled with men who, broadly, are of a single class and a single political party. And the problem will never be solved until these aspects of the situation are changed, however serious the sacrifices that such changes may involve.

So far as membership goes, the most reasonable program of reform would seem to be, not the replacing of the present body by one constructed *de novo* and wholly on a "popular" basis, but (1) the adoption of the Rosebery principle that the possession of a peerage shall not of itself entitle the possessor to sit,[39] (2) the admission to membership of a considerable number of persons representative of, and selected by, the whole number of hereditary peers, and (3) the introduction of a substantial quota of life or fixed-term members, appointed or elected for their legal attainments, political experience, and other qualities of fitness and eminence. A body so constituted would still incline to conservatism; probably it would contain a Conservative majority, in the party sense, a good deal of the time. But a Liberal, Labor, or other non-Conservative government would hardly again find itself in the helpless position of Liberalism in pre-war days. The chief difficulty would be to hit upon a satisfactory way of selecting the life or fixed-term members. In a country organized, as is the United States, on a federal basis, it is easy to make up a second chamber that will not be a duplicate of the first; the people in small local groups can be represented directly in the lower house and the larger federated units or areas, as such, in the upper. Britain is not a federal state; at all events, so far as England is concerned, no obvious areas for upper chamber representation exist. Still, as was the opinion of the Bryce commission, it is not inconceivable that they

torate is the primary *raison d'être* of the House of Lords; and both in the discussions of 1909-11 and in those of later days much was made of this idea by Conservative defenders of the chamber.

[39] This principle already operates in connection with the Scottish and Irish peers. It ought not to be impossible to extend it to the entire peerage.

might be created; indeed, that body considered that the old historic counties, or combinations of them, could be made to serve. Great advantages would arise, also, from a system under which a considerable number of members should be chosen to represent important special groups or interests, including the great professions. The universities, the bankers, the medical profession, and even the trade unions, come readily to mind in this connection.[40]

A second chamber made up on the lines thus indicated would undoubtedly be respectable, capable, and vigorous; and this raises a further question, of which students of the subject have not been unmindful. Would not such an upper chamber justly claim equality of rights and powers with the popular house? Could it be kept on the subordinate plane to which the legislation of 1911 has lowered the House of Lords? In other words, would not the application of the representative principle to the chamber lead to an embarrassing revival of the authority of that body at the expense of the House of Commons? Some years ago Mr. Balfour, in a notable address, warned the lower chamber that this was what would happen; the Bryce commission evidently feared it; and other voices have been raised, in all of the great parties, to the same effect.

The apprehension, while natural, seems, however, groundless. In the first place, no legal alteration of the composition or status of the second chamber can take place save by an act of Parliament; and it is almost inconceivable that the House of Commons would ever approve a measure which restricted its ultimate control in, at all events, the two great fields of finance and administration. It is true, as has been pointed out, that there is much sentiment in the Conservative party, and among conservative-minded people generally, in favor of a repeal, or at

[40] On "functional" representation in general, see H. L. McBain and L. Rogers, *New Constitutions of Europe,* Chap. vi. It may be noted that during the discussions of 1910 Lord Wemyss proposed that the representative character of the chamber be given emphasis by the admission of three members designated by each of some twenty-one commercial, professional, and educational societies of the kingdom, such as the Royal Academy of Arts, the Society of Engineers, the Shipping Federation, and the Royal Institute of British Architects. An interesting discussion of this form of representation will be found in P. H. Douglas, "Occupational vs. Proportional Representation," *Amer. Jour. of Sociology,* Sept., 1923.

all events a drastic revision, of the Parliament Act, with a view to making it impossible for a Labor, or other radical, government to carry out its program over the opposition of the House of Lords. And, as we have seen, the government proposals of 1922 and 1927 stipulated that the provision of the Parliament Act enabling measures to be passed into law during the life of a single parliament without the consent of the House of Lords should not apply to any bill altering or amending the constitution of that chamber. But, notwithstanding their continued vogue during the discussions of 1925 and 1927, these proposals seem unlikely to bear fruit in actual constitutional change. On the contrary, the preponderance of the House of Commons is likely to be further increased rather than diminished.

In the second place, experience shows that in the long run an upper chamber, no matter what its basis, cannot maintain a parity of power and influence with the lower chamber under a system of responsible, i.e., cabinet, government. The constitution of France purports to make the cabinet responsible to both the Senate and the Chamber of Deputies, and the Senate is an exceptionally capable and energetic body. Nevertheless the Chamber of Deputies enjoys a substantial preëminence in the actual control of national affairs. The framers of the Australian constitution deliberately provided for a popularly elected upper house, with a view to making it an effective counterpoise to the federal House of Representatives. But the idea failed. Today a Commonwealth government recognizes the supremacy of the lower chamber only, and the Senate can be fairly characterized as hardly more than a debating society.[41] In Canada, likewise, the Senate—composed of life-members appointed by the governor-general on advice of the ministers—is notoriously weak.[42] The outcome could hardly be otherwise in Britain. It will not do to say with a recent writer that the cabinet system "is fatal to a bicameral legislature." As is proved by France, there is a legitimate and useful place for a second chamber in a cabinet system of government; indeed, most of the arguments that support a

[41] A. B. Keith, *Responsible Government in the Dominions* (2nd ed., Oxford, 1928), I, 491-496.

[42] E. Porritt, *Evolution of the Dominion of Canada* (Yonkers, 1918), Chap. xi. Cf. R. A. MacKay, *The Unreformed Senate of Canada,* Chap. vi

bicameral legislature in the United States are equally applicable in Britain. But it cannot be denied that, as the same writer goes on to say, "whatever the mode of selection or however able its personnel, the upper chamber will continue to play but a subordinate position in political life so long as the principle of the responsibility of the ministry to the House of Commons endures." [43] As an English authority has said, "a House of Commons, with the majority of the electorate behind it, could not be bitted and bridled by the Peers. . . . The Lords cannot prevent reform, or even revolution, if the electorate is in earnest and has a ministry to its mind." [44]

A subordinate position may, however, be a useful position; and it stands to reason that if a second chamber is to be retained at all, it ought to be made up in such a manner as to give it the greatest possible amount of industriousness and intelligence. The uses of a second chamber are to interpose criticism and compel deliberation; to make it more difficult for a legislature to be swept off its feet by a wave of passion or excitement; "to serve as an organ of revision, a check upon democracy, an instrument by which conservatism in action may be had, and a means for securing a representation of interests that is not feasible in a single chamber composed of members elected directly by the people." [45] The object, however, is not mere obstruction, such as may arise from inertia, incapacity, or partisanship. It is, instead, serious-minded criticism, deliberation, and revision, with a view to the general welfare rather than to class interest or partisan expediency. Properly discharged, the function of revision is no less honorable, and hardly less important, than that of initiation, or that of final decision, as performed by the lower chamber. The House of Lords has served the British nation well in the past. If it is reconstructed wisely, its usefulness ought to increase rather than diminish in years that lie ahead.[46]

[43] C. D. Allin, "The Position of Parliament," *Amer. Polit. Sci. Rev.*, June, 1914.

[44] S. Low, *Governance of England* (rev. ed.), 223.

[45] W. F. Willoughby, *Government of Modern States,* 318.

[46] The literature of second chamber reform in Britain is voluminous. Important books called out by the controversy of 1909-11 include W. S. McKechnie, *The Reform of the House of Lords* (Glasgow, 1909); W. L.

Wilson, *The Case for the House of Lords* (London, 1910); and J. H. Morgan, *The House of Lords and the Constitution* (London, 1910). Features and problems of the British second chamber are considered in comparison with those of foreign second chambers in H. W. V. Temperley, *Senates and Upper Chambers* (Oxford, 1910); J. A. R. Marriott, *Second Chambers* (new ed., Oxford, 1917); G. B. Roberts, *The Functions of an English Second Chamber* (London, 1926); and H. B. Lees-Smith, *Second Chambers in Theory and Practice* (London, 1923). Among almost innumerable articles, one may mention J. A. R. Marriott, "The Problem of a Second Chamber," *Edinburgh Rev.*, July, 1917; a paper by the same author with the same title in *Fort Rev.*, Mar., 1925; J. Ross, "The Reform of the Second Chamber," *Jour. Comp. Legis. and Internat. Law*, Nov., 1925; and H. Cox, "The House of Lords," *Edinburgh Rev.*, Oct., 1927. H. L. McBain and L. Rogers, *New Constitutions of Europe*, Chap. iii, is suggestive, as are also various articles in "The Second Chamber Problem; What the Experience of Other Countries Has to Teach Us," *New Statesman*, Feb. 7, 1914 (Supplement).

CHAPTER XVI

PARLIAMENTARY MACHINERY AND PAGEANTRY

THERE was a time when the organization of the English Parliament could be described in few and simple words; indeed, if we go back far enough in parliamentary history we find hardly any organization at all. As centuries passed, however, and powers and functions multiplied, new and increasingly elaborate devices for guiding, regularizing, and expediting deliberation were brought into play, until nowadays equipment in the form of officers, clerks, committees, rules, calendars, records—to say nothing of unwritten habits and usages—make up one of the most complicated and delicate mechanisms of legislation to be found on the globe. Parliament is, indeed, a vast, vibrant machine which receives proposals, refers them to committees, debates them, and votes on them under forms and rules almost as exact and relentless as the laws that govern the succession of the seasons. Naturally enough, the constitutional lawyers who chiefly have written the treatises and text-books on British government have portrayed the great central institution at Westminster as mainly a thing of rules, principles, and theories. This is, however, unfortunate, because Parliament is not only a legislative mill but a complex of human personalities—not only a machine but also a pageant. In the brief account of its organization and procedure to be given in the present chapter and the two that follow, these more human aspects, it is hoped, will not fail to find their place in the picture.[1]

[1] Former Speaker Lowther (now Lord Ullswater) relates that when Sir William Anson, author of *The Law and Custom of the Constitution,* frequently cited in this book, was being escorted up the floor of the House of Commons to take the oath and his seat for the first time, a member, being told that the gentleman had written a great work on the House of Commons, remarked, "Well, he will find it a very different place from what he thought it was."

Physical Surroundings

From the beginning of parliamentary history the meeting place of the houses has commonly been Westminster, once a separate city on the left bank of the Thames, but now incorporated in Greater London. The last parliament to sit at any other spot was the third Oxford parliament of Charles II, in 1681. The House of Lords, from the first appearance of the bicameral system, sat in the Palace of Westminster, built by Edward the Confessor and embellished by the addition of the Great Hall (now known as Westminster Hall) by William Rufus. The House of Commons originally met in the chapter house of Westminster Abbey (dating from the reign of the last Saxon king), but in 1547 took up its abode in the Palace, in a small, cheerless room known as St. Stephen's Chapel. In 1834 a fire, started by the over-generous use of old wooden "tallies" in the stoves that heated the House of Lords, gutted the historic but rambling and not particularly attractive structure; and the enormous and pleasing Tudor Gothic building (still technically a royal residence) which nowadays is pointed out to the visitor, usually as "the Houses of Parliament," was erected in 1837-52 —except Westminster Hall and St. Stephen's Crypt, which, happily, the fire had left intact. Lords and Commons first occupied their present quarters in 1847 and 1850, respectively.

Covering an area of nine acres, the building contains more than twelve hundred halls and rooms, including a great central hall (approached by visitors through St. Stephen's Hall, occupying the site of the old St. Stephen's Chapel and marked with brass plates to show where the speaker's chair and the table stood in historic days), the halls in which the two houses meet, lobbies, committee rooms, rooms allotted to the ministers,[2] libraries, refreshment rooms, smoking rooms, and commodious living quarters for the speaker of the House of Commons and some other parliamentary officers, to say nothing of the splendid Terrace which extends the whole length of the front, i.e., on the side toward the Thames. At one end is the lofty and extraordinarily beautiful Clock Tower, which supports "Big

[2] Every minister is now given at least one room (situated off the corridors back of the speaker's chair) in which to carry on work and receive members and other visitors.

Ben," and on whose topmost reach burns "that mighty light which shows to a sleeping city that the faithful Commons remain vigilant and at work;" at the other end is the colossal Victoria Tower. The structure, as a whole, is a masterpiece of architecture worthy of the historic assemblies that deliberate within its walls.

From opposite sides of the central hall corridors lead to the rooms in which the sittings of the houses are held, these rooms being so placed—the Lords' toward the Victoria Tower and the Commons' toward the Clock Tower—that the king's throne at the south end of the one is visible from the speaker's chair at the north end of the other. The rectangular hall occupied by the Commons is far smaller than the visitor, knowing that there are 615 members to be accommodated, would expect, being, indeed, only seventy-five feet long and forty-five feet wide. There is, too, no external outlook, fresh air being supplied through the perforated ironwork floor from the cavernous cellars underneath, and light—which is very soft and pleasing—through a low-hung glass roof tempering the glare of a galaxy of gas jets. The room is bisected by a broad aisle leading from the main entrance, at the farther end being "the table," used by the clerks, and also as the resting place of the mace and of piles of books and papers, and beyond this the high canopied chair of the speaker. Facing the aisle on each side, five rows of high-backed benches, covered with dark green leather and running the length of the room, slope upward tier upon tier to the walls; and through them cuts, transversely from wall to wall, a narrow cross-passage known as the "gangway." A sliding brass rail which can be drawn across the main aisle near the entrance forms the "bar" of the House, at which offenders against the dignity and privileges of the chamber are sometimes required, and more favored persons sometimes invited, to appear. A deep gallery runs entirely round the room. The portion facing the speaker is set apart for visitors. At the opposite end, the front rows are assigned to the press, and the rows further back, somewhat obscured by a brass lattice screen, are reserved for the use of women. Of prevailingly brown color, rich but not ornate, the chamber is pleasing to the eye; it is comfortable, and—a thing of great importance in an assembly where no debater can ever face his entire audience—acoustics has not been sacrificed, as in the House of Lords, to architecture.[3]

Although the palace was designed to be a magnificent structure, and its cost rose to two and a half times the original expectation, the hall allotted to the House of Commons was made too small to seat more than approximately two-thirds of the existing members.[4] By crowding the benches and utilizing the side galleries (which are reserved for members, although because of their disadvantageous location they are rarely occupied), about 450 persons can be seated—which means some eight score less than the present somewhat reduced total membership. One should hasten to add that this is not as serious as it sounds, because it rarely or never happens that the entire membership wants to be in the chamber at the same time. In point of fact, except on unusual occasions, the visitor will not find more than one or two hundred on the benches, the more by reason of the fact that, there being no desks, the member who wants to write, or even to read or otherwise occupy himself, seeks the library or other rooms adjoining, whence he can readily come if summoned to a division. Various plans for enlarging the seating capacity of the chamber, or even enlarging the room itself, have been proposed, but interest in the matter seems to have been greater three-quarters of a century ago than it is today.[5]

How do the commoners bestow themselves within the restricted space at their disposal? There is no regular assignment of seats to individuals, as in the American Congress (even there, as any observer knows, members by no means always occupy their allotted places), and the only rule that governs is that a member, having found a place that he likes, can reserve it for his own use—only for a single sitting, however—by depositing his hat in it, or, under more recent informal agreement, his card. There are, however, some important prac-

[3] Acoustic properties were, indeed, found to be bad when the chamber was first occupied, but they were made notably excellent by the insertion of the glass ceiling now obscuring the nobly arched roof on which the original architect, Barry, lavished his tenderest care.

[4] The architect planned it on an ampler scale, but the commoners preferred to have it of the same dimensions as the hall to which they had been accustomed.

[5] H. Lucy, *Lords and Commoners* (London, 1921), Chap. vi.

tices with regard to the grouping of members. In the first place, the front bench at the upper end of the aisle, at the right of the speaker, is known as the Treasury, or Ministerial, Bench, and, by custom, is occupied exclusively by those members of the House who belong to the ministry, or, at all events, such of the more important ones as it can accommodate.[6] The corresponding bench at the speaker's left is similarly reserved for the leaders of the opposition (hence is known as the Front Opposition Bench); practically, those who occupy it do so because of having been invited by the official opposition leader to share it with him.[7] The great bulk of members, having no claim to front-bench positions, range themselves, so far as their numbers permit, in squads behind their leaders, with a tendency for the less experienced ones, and also any of loose party connections, to content themselves with places "below the gangway." Groups belonging to minor parties, e.g., the Irish Nationalists in earlier days, have also usually occupied seats in the same section. "It is a tradition of the House that the benches below the gangway can be counted upon to furnish trouble if a minister goes looking for it." [8]

Though relatively more commodious, because fewer members attend the sittings, the hall occupied by the Lords is even smaller than that of the Commons. It differs, too, in other ways. It is more richly adorned with historical and allegorical paintings and frescoes, bronze statues, and stained-glass windows through which falls a soft rich light lending the appearance of a church or chapel. The upholstery is red. There are three or four cross-benches. Instead of the speaker's chair there is a circular crim-

[6] By long-established custom, the two members for the City of London are entitled to sit on the Treasury Bench, regardless of whether they are ministers, and even of whether their party is in power. Nowadays, however, they content themselves with sitting there for a few moments on the first day of a new parliament, merely by way of keeping the right alive.

[7] The opposition consists of those members who are accustomed to act regularly together against the ministry of the day on all matters involving party policy. According to an old dictum, their duty is "never to propose, always to oppose, and to turn out the government;" and they are so far recognized as prepared to form an administration, in case their object is achieved, that they are often, and not inaptly, termed "His Majesty's Opposition."

[8] W. B. Munro, *Governments of Europe*, 206.

son ottoman or lounge—the "woolsack" [9]—on which (although it is technically outside of the Chamber) the Lord Chancellor sits when presiding, with the mace tucked away behind him. And back of this, at the end of the room opposite the entrance from the central hall, is the most conspicuous and distinctive piece of furniture of all, i.e., the canopied throne—finely carved and sparkling with precious stones—provided for the king's occupancy when he meets his faithful lords and commons at the opening of a parliament. Beside the throne is a chair for the royal consort, and another one, smaller and lower, for the Prince of Wales. Outside of these features, the general arrangements are as in the House of Commons, with rows of benches facing each other on the two longer sides, no desks, a table in front of the woolsack, a bar, and galleries all the way round, for the use of peeresses, the press, and miscellaneous visitors. The acoustic properties are bad, but the lords have been content to stick to their architectural endowments and let their speeches take their chances. Members who belong to the ministry occupy the front bench at the Lord Chancellor's right hand and leaders of the opposition the front bench at the left, while the remaining members sit wherever they like, though usually on the same side of the room as the leaders of their party. Some attention is paid to seating according to rank when the sovereign is present, but at other times the only group, aside from government and opposition leaders, that sits in a body in a fixed place is the ecclesiastical members, whose presence on the "episcopal bench" (really four benches to the right of the woolsack) is noticeable enough to the visitor by reason of their flowing black gowns and ample white lawn sleeves. For members disposed to hold aloof from party alignments the cross-benches afford a resource not available, and seldom needed, in the other house.[10]

Sessions

So much for physical surroundings—which not only are interesting to the sightseer but have large practical importance

[9] In the days of Elizabeth the presiding official sat upon a sack actually filled with wool; hence the present name.

[10] The Houses of Parliament and the rooms occupied by the two chambers

in helping make parliamentary methods and manners what they are.[11] How, in the next place, does Parliament meet and prepare itself for the work of a session? How, also, does it break up when a session comes to a close? The rules and practices which govern the frequency, length, and termination of sessions have been mentioned in other connections, and it is necessary here only to remind ourselves of a few major facts. The statute which regulates the frequency of sessions dates from 1694 and prescribes that writs for "calling, assembling, and holding" a parliament shall be issued at intervals not exceeding three years. A fourteenth-century statute, which in point of fact was repealed only in 1863, required annual sessions. Through a quibble over its interpretation, however, this law was never enforced literally; and in later times there has been no formal requirement of annual sessions whatsoever. For more than two hundred years, as we have seen, annual sessions have prevailed, not because the law required them, but partly because of the practical necessity entailed by the increasing volume of business, and partly because of the equally practical circumstance that unless the Army Act is renewed every year disciplinary powers over the armed forces lapse, and unless appropriations are made for the "supply services," e.g., the army, navy, and civil service, at intervals of no more than twelve months, the government is powerless to keep these services in operation. As a matter of fact, Parliament is in session considerably more than half of the time. It sits, with only brief adjournments over week-ends and holidays, from the first week in November until near Christmas, and from the end of January or the

are described in A. Wright and P. Smith, *Parliament, Past and Present* (London, 1902), I, Chaps. xi-xii, xviii-xix, and more briefly in J. Redlich, *The Procedure of the House of Commons* (London, 1908), II, 21-27; M. MacDonagh, *The Pageant of Parliament,* I, Chaps. vii, xx, II, Chap. v; and H. Graham, *Mother of Parliaments,* Chap. iv. The classic history of the old Palace of Westminster is E. W. Brayley and J. Britton, *History of the Ancient Palace and Late Houses of Parliament at Westminster* (London, 1836).

[11] "The accident," wrote an English master of parliamentary affairs half a generation ago, "that the House of Commons sits in a narrow room with benches facing each other, and not, like most Continental legislatures, in a semi-circular space, with seats arranged like those of a theater, makes for the two-party system and against groups shading into each other." C. Ilbert, *Parliament,* 124.

first part of February to late July or early August, of every year.[12]

A highly important matter in this connection is the promptness with which Parliament meets and begins work after a general election. There is no rule requiring the lapse of a definite length of time between the election of a new House of Commons and the assembling of Parliament, but it is the practice to make the interval as brief as possible, and it rarely exceeds two or two and one-half weeks. There is a very good reason for this. Under the British system, the ministers must at all times possess the confidence and support of a majority in the House of Commons. In order to determine whether they have this support it is necessary to call the House into session; any ministry continuing in office for a considerable length of time after election without summoning Parliament would be guilty of trying to rule without a mandate from the nation. The result is that a new House of Commons goes to work almost immediately after its election, and certainly reflects—in so far as it is possible for any body so chosen to reflect—the sentiments and desires of the people at the moment. In Germany, the Reichstag must assemble for its first meeting not later than thirty days after election; in France, Belgium, the British dominions, and other states, the interval is always short. Only in the United States, among principal countries of the world, is it possible for legislators to continue in office and to function for months after their successors have been chosen at the polls.[13]

Each house at Westminster may adjourn at any time it chooses, without reference to the other one; and neither can

[12] J. G. Randall, "The Frequency and Duration of Parliaments," *Amer. Polit. Sci. Rev.*, Nov., 1916. Cf. T. E. May, *Treatise on the Law, Privileges, Proceedings, and Usage of the House of Commons* (13th ed., London, 1924), 52-54.

[13] C. L. W. Meyer, "Interval Between Election and Meeting of Parliaments," *Jour. of Comp. Legis. and Internat. Law*, Nov., 1928. A joint resolution proposing an amendment to the United States Constitution which would fix the time of the assembling of Congress in such a way as to eliminate the present biennial "lame duck" session passed the Senate for the fifth time in 1929. In the House of Representatives, however, the proposal has never secured the two-thirds majority necessary for the submission of amendments. See M. A. Mussman, "Changing the Date for Congressional Sessions and Inauguration," *Amer. Polit. Sci. Rev.*, Feb., 1924.

be adjourned by action of the crown. To adjourn means merely to interrupt the course of business temporarily, matters which were pending being carried over without any change of status. When, however, a session is to be brought to a close, the crown, i.e., the sovereign acting on the advice of the ministers, must intervene. There must be a prorogation; and only the crown can prorogue. Prorogation both ends the session and terminates all pending business, so that a bill which has fallen short of enactment will have to start at the beginning again in the next session if it is to be kept alive. Both houses must be prorogued together, and to a definite date, although the opening of the new session may, in point of fact, be either postponed or advanced by later proclamation. Sometimes, too, a proclamation of dissolution is issued before the date arrives, which means that the old parliament will never meet again. Dissolution ends a parliament, but, as we have seen, also sets in motion the machinery for electing a new one. Until 1867, death of the sovereign (in legal phraseology, the demise of the crown) automatically produced a dissolution. This is no longer the case; on the contrary, if Parliament is not sitting when the demise occurs it must immediately convene.[14]

How Sessions Are Opened and Closed

The two houses must invariably be summoned to meet simultaneously, and at the opening of a session the members gather, first of all, in their respective chambers. Thereupon the Gentleman Usher of the Black Rod, official messenger of the Lords,[15] invites the commoners to present themselves at the bar of the upper house, where they (or such of them as can squeeze into the small enclosure) hear read the letters patent authorizing the session, followed by announcement by the Lord Chancellor, in the event that the session is the first one of a new parliament, that it is the desire of the crown that they proceed to choose "some proper person" to be their speaker. Headed by the clerk, the commoners withdraw to attend to this matter, and on the next day the newly elected official,

[14] See, however, W. R. Anson, *Law and Custom of the Constitution* (5th ed.), I, 75-77. Cf. T. E. May, *op. cit.* (13th ed.), 54.

[15] So-called because he carries an ebony rod tipped with gold.

accompanied by the members, presents himself at the bar of the Lords, announces his election, and, through the Lord Chancellor, receives, as a matter of form, the royal approbation. Having demanded and received a guarantee of the "ancient and undoubted rights and privileges of the Commons,"[16] the speaker and the members then retire to their own quarters, where each takes a simple oath (or makes an affirmation) of allegiance and personally signs the roll.[17] If, as is not unusual,

[16] The privileges specifically asserted and demanded are free speech, freedom from arrest, access to the crown, and having the most favorable construction put upon proceedings. There are, of course, other privileges, e.g., the right to regulate its own proceedings, which the House does not specifically demand on this occasion. For the form employed, see *Companion to the Standing Orders of the House of Lords on Public Business* (London, 1909), 6-7; also T. E. May, *op. cit.* (13th ed.), 70. Freedom from arrest is enjoyed by commoners throughout a session, and for forty days before and after, but it does not protect a member from the consequences of any indictable offense, nor, in civil actions, from any process save arrest. Freedom of speech, guaranteed by the Bill of Rights, means that a member may not be held to account by legal process outside of Parliament for anything he may have said in the course of the debates or proceedings of the chamber to which he belongs. The right of access to the sovereign belongs to the House of Commons collectively through the speaker, but to the members of the House of Lords individually. The growth of parliamentary government has reduced both this right and that of "favorable construction" to slight practical importance. Members are also exempt from jury duty, although not from court attendance as witnesses. The two houses alike are entitled to regulate their own procedure, decide whether any breach of privilege has been committed, punish persons guilty of contempt, and judge the qualifications of their own members—although, as we have seen, the adjudication of contested parliamentary elections has been handed over to members of the higher judiciary. On the privileges of the Commons, individually and collectively, see W. R. Anson, *Law and Custom of the Constitution* (5th ed.), I, 162-198; A. L. Lowell, *Government of England,* I, Chap. xi; and T. E. May, *op. cit.,* Chaps. iii-vi. A valuable monograph is C. Wittke, *The History of English Parliamentary Privilege* (Columbus, 1921). A number of judicial decisions involving questions relating to the privileges of Parliament are summarized in B. A. Bicknell, *Cases on the Law of the Constitution,* 34-56.

[17] In the Commons, members are sworn in in batches of five, and the roll is in the form of a leather-bound book opening at the bottom instead of the sides; in the Lords, members are sworn in one by one, and the signatures—"Birkenhead," "Morley," "Rosebery," etc.—are placed on a long sheet of paper which winds around a roller, i.e., literally, a roll. The oath in both houses is: "I, ——— ————, swear by Almighty God that I will be faithful and bear true allegiance to His Majesty King ———, his heirs and successors, according to law. So help me, God." M. MacDonagh, *Pageant of Parliament,* I, Chap. ix. Cf. T. E. May, *op. cit.* (13th

the king meets Parliament in person, he goes in state, probably the next day, to the House of Lords and takes his seat upon the throne, and the Lord Chamberlain is instructed to desire Black Rod to *command* the attendance once more of the Commons. If the sovereign does not attend, five robed lords commissioners, serving as his personal representatives, bid the usher to *desire* the Commons' presence. In any case, the commoners present themselves, and the king (or, in his absence, the Lord Chancellor)[18] reads the Speech from the Throne, in which the cabinet—for it is the real author of the speech—comments briefly on the state of the realm, touches on foreign relations, demands the annual supply for the public service and bespeaks a sympathetic hearing for the requests later to be made on that score, and says something about the great measures that are to be introduced during the session. Following the retirement of the sovereign, the commoners again withdraw, and the Throne Speech is reread and an address in reply voted in each house, giving an opportunity for general debate which brings out the policies of the various parties and sometimes extends over several days.[19] Thereupon, committees are set up, bills introduced, and motions made; in short, the houses enter upon their regular activities. In the event that a session is not the first one of a parliament, the election of a speaker and the administration of oaths are, of course, omitted.

Richard Cobden once spoke of the ceremonies connected with

ed.), 158-169, where a history of the famous Bradlaugh case of 1880 ff. is presented.

[18] The sovereign, though present, may request the Chancellor to read the Speech. Henry VIII, proud as he was of his personal accomplishments, always did this; Queen Victoria did the same thing on every occasion after 1866. May, *op. cit.*, 171. Victoria, indeed, rarely opened Parliament in person in the later part of her reign. Edward VII did so only intermittently. George V, on the other hand, has never failed to do so when at all possible. He has even once or twice addressed the members of the two houses informally in the great royal room in the House of Lords.

[19] In the House of Commons the "address" is moved and seconded by two private members on the ministerial side, designated by the prime minister. Sometimes it passes without debate. But since it invariably expresses not only renewed loyalty to the crown but commendation of the program announced in the "most gracious Speech," opposition members are tempted to offer amendments, and in this way discussion sometimes arises. On the Speech and the Address, see May, *op cit.*, 170-195, and MacDonagh, *op. cit.*, I, Chaps. xvii-xviii.

the opening of a session of Parliament as "attended by much barbaric pomp." Certainly they abound in the quaint and picturesque, with something of the naïve, and possibly a little of the ridiculous. No people less loyal to tradition than are the British could quite go through the entire performance with straight faces. One of the humors of the occasion is the search of the corridors, vaults, and cellars of Westminster Palace on the morning of the first day of the session to see that the building is safe for king, lords, and commoners to enter. The quest is primarily for explosives, and the custom harks back to the famous Gunpowder Plot, associated with the name of Guy Fawkes, in 1605 [20]—even though we now know that it did not actually arise until toward the close of that troubled century. The searching party consists chiefly of twelve lusty Yeomen of the Guard, who, in all their picturesque Tudor regalia, solemnly march over from the Tower of London for the purpose, and, accompanied by certain public officials, and bearing aloft lighted lanterns of the style in vogue when Elizabeth was on the throne, tramp up and down and back and forth through miles of corridors and lobbies (brilliantly lighted with electricity, by the way) and poke among gas fittings, steam pipes, and whatever else they may encounter, to make certain that no explosives have been secreted there. Of course none are ever found. But the thing has been done religiously, in precisely such a fashion, for these hundreds of years, and nobody even suggests that the ceremony be dispensed with. Nor does anybody begrudge the wearied "beefeaters" the repast of cakes and ale with which the search is terminated, capped by a toast to the king. At one point only has concession been made to change of time and circumstance. Whereas, upon the conclusion of the hunt, the Lord Great Chamberlain, as custodian of the building, used to despatch to the sovereign a mounted soldier with the message

[20] Fawkes was employed by a band of conspirators to blow up Westminster Palace when Parliament was in session and the king present. Rumors of what was going to happen got abroad, however, and the plot was thwarted, though not until preparations for the explosion had been completed in an excavation dug under the House of Lords from underneath an adjoining building. The hinged key to the place of destruction, found on Fawkes when he was apprehended, is exhibited in a glass case in the Members' Library. Guy Fawkes Day (November 5) was long a public holiday.

"All's well," he now communicates the assuring information by the prosaic telegraph or telephone.[21]

Other curious customs also survive. For example, when, in the absence of the sovereign, the Lord Chancellor reads the Speech from the Throne, he solemnly assures his hearers that what he is about to read is "His Majesty's own words," although everybody knows that the sovereign has had little or no part in formulating what is to be said.[22] Another turn is the practice in each house of giving a dummy bill a first reading *pro forma* before the Speech is reread by the presiding officer, simply to show that the house has a right to debate other matters than those mentioned in the Speech and to initiate measures of its own. This sacred right once vindicated, the measure is promptly put aside and forgotten.[23] Still another curious usage is that which requires the mover and seconder of the Commons' address in reply to the Speech to be in uniform, or full dress, although this is the only occasion on which any member of either house is permitted to appear in Parliament otherwise than in civilian clothes.[24]

[21] It may be noted that recurring threats of Communist demonstrations have in late years given some point to the precautions taken.

[22] He may, indeed, have a poor opinion of it. "Did I deliver the Speech well?" George III inquired of the Lord Chancellor on one occasion. "Very well, sire," was Lord Eldon's reply. "I am glad of it," answered the king, "for there was nothing in it."

[23] In point of fact, it is always, in each house, the same measure—in the Lords, a "select vestries bill" and in the Commons a "bill for the more effectual preventing of clandestine outlawries." The outlawries bill, at all events, is, in theatrical parlance, a "property" bill, the same document having been preserved for the purpose in the drawers of the table since the present chamber was first occupied in 1852.

[24] Full dress necessitates the wearing of swords, once a common practice of the members, but now confined strictly to the two, and the occasion, mentioned. To prevent armed encounters between excited debaters, a red line was long ago drawn down the center aisle about two feet distant from the front benches on either side, and members were forbidden, when addressing the House, to step across the barrier. This, however, did not keep them from fighting it out in the lobbies, and to discourage such clashes, or at all events to render them less bloody, the present rule was adopted forbidding members (with the exception mentioned), or even distinguished visitors, to enter the Houses of Parliament with swords or other weapons. The sergeant-at-arms wears a rapier, but he is not a member, and besides his chair is outside the sacred precincts of the chamber. H. Lucy, *Lords and Commoners,* 96-97.

The ceremonies that bring a session to a close are the same whether it is expected that the existing parliament will meet again or it is known that prorogation is merely preliminary to a dissolution to be duly announced in the *London Gazette* at a later date. In earlier days the king usually appeared in person, and, the commoners having been summoned to the bar of the Lords' chamber by Black Rod, read a Speech from the Throne announcing the prorogation. Nowadays, however, a session is customarily closed, just as it is sometimes opened, not by the king in person but by his commissioners. In such a case, these commissioners (five in number, the Lord Chancellor always being one), in scarlet robes trimmed with ermine, and wearing curious three-cornered hats, take their places on a bench in front of the throne in the House of Lords, Black Rod summons the Commons, the speaker and other members appear, a gowned clerk reads from a huge parchment the names of "our trusty and well-beloved cousins" who compose the commission, and the Lord Chancellor reads the speech of prorogation. This communication always congratulates "my lords and gentlemen" on the useful laws they have passed and thanks them for the supplies they have granted. But even if a dissolution is definitely intended, it scrupulously refrains from saying so, or even hinting at the fact. The ceremony over, the Lord Chancellor gathers up his long robes, and, attended by the purse-bearer and the mace-bearer, walks down to the bar of the Lords and disappears; so far as the upper chamber is concerned, the session is over. In the Commons, however, it remains for the speaker to return, to "inform" the members where he has been, and to read the speech; whereupon, walking backwards, bowing to his empty chair, and closely followed by the sergeant-at-arms bearing the mace, he too disappears. If a dissolution is contemplated, everybody knows it, even though there has been such remarkable official reticence about it. The prospect need not disturb the peers; they know that they will be summoned again to the red benches. But the commoners are situated differently. They must go back to the constituencies and make a fight for reëlection, with the outcome in many cases uncertain. Many of them will not come back; for, as a defeated member once sorrowfully remarked, it is much easier to go to the country than to return from it.[25]

Sittings of the Houses

Both houses of the American Congress regularly meet at noon, on all week-days of a session except as adjournments are taken for lengthier intervals. The British House of Commons, under its standing orders, meets on the first four working days of the week at 2:45 P.M., on Friday (reserved for private business, petitions, notices, and motions) at 11 A.M., and on Saturday not at all except by special arrangement. As at Washington, the earlier portions of the day are reserved for committee work. Except on Friday, when the rules require the speaker to adjourn the House at 4:30, "notwithstanding there may be business under discussion," sittings continue uninterruptedly throughout the afternoon and into the night, to 11:30 (the rules say) unless certain specified kinds of business are under consideration, in which event there is no limit except the endurance of the members.[26] All-night sittings are not unknown, and in 1881 a sitting lasted without a break from Monday afternoon to Wednesday morning. Under less pressure of work, and disinclined to lengthy debate, the House of Lords meets only on Monday to Thursday inclusive, and from 4:30 to 6:30 or thereabouts. "The first principle of debate in the House of Lords is that, except under direct pressure, discussion shall be concluded in time to dress for eight o'clock dinner."[27] The usual meeting-hour for judicial business is, in-

[25] On the ceremonies connected with the opening, adjournment, prorogation, and dissolution of a parliament, see *Companion to the Standing Orders of the House of Lords on Public Business* (London, 1909), 1-16; W. R. Anson, *Law and Custom of the Constitution* (5th ed.), I, 63-72; J. Redlich, *Procedure of the House of Commons*, II, 51-64; T. E. May, *op. cit.* (13th ed.), Chap. vii; M. MacDonagh, *Book of Parliament*, 96-114, 132-147, 184-203, and *Pageant of Parliament*, I, Chaps viii-ix; and H. Graham, *Mother of Parliaments* (Boston, 1911), 135-157. For an account of the actual opening of a parliament, see *London Times* (weekly ed.), Nov. 30, 1922, pp. 353-354.

[26] *Standing Orders of the House of Commons* (1927), pp. 4-6. On the sittings of the House of Commons in general, see J. Redlich, *op. cit.*, II, 68-77.

[27] H. Lucy, *Lords and Commoners*, 58.

deed, 10:30 in the morning; but of course this affects only a handful of the members.

A sitting is opened in the Commons by the stately march of the speaker, accompanied by chaplain, sergeant-at-arms, and mace-bearer, up the center aisle to the table; whereupon the chaplain reads a psalm (always the 67th) and three short prayers, the members facing the aisle during the former and, for some unknown reason, turning toward the wall during the latter. Visitors are not admitted to the galleries until prayers are over; and members of the ministry are conspicuous for their absence, not—as one writer facetiously suggests—because they are less in need of the benefits of prayer than are the private members, but because, unlike the latter, they are not under the necessity of being on hand to reserve their seats.[28] Prayers ended, the mace is placed upon the table, the speaker assures himself that a quorum (forty) is present,[29] the doorkeeper shouts "Mr. Speaker at the chair"—and the day's business begins. The ceremony in the House of Lords is approximately the same, the ecclesiastical members taking turns in reading prayers.

Equally with the lighted lanterns of the beefeaters, the cry that resounds through lobby and corridor when at the close of a sitting the speaker leaves the chair carries one back to the London of long ago. The principal doorkeeper starts it. Stepping a pace or two into the lobby, he shouts "Who goes home?" The policemen stationed in the lobby take up the cry, which is echoed by their fellows at the doors of the library and the smoking-room, and wherever else they are likely to be heard by the more or less scattered members. Two hundred years ago, going home at midnight through the ill-lighted and poorly policed streets leading from Westminster to residential London was a serious matter, and hence at intervals during the evening squads of yeomen from the Tower were sent over to act as escorts to members desiring to leave. "Who goes home?" was the call employed to round up the departing groups; and although London's streets are now practically as safe by night as by day

[28] M. MacDonagh, *The Pageant of Parliament,* I, 236.

[29] If the requisite number is not present, bells in the corridors and other parts of the building are rung as summons to the tardy.

and the services of the beefeaters have long since been dispensed with, "Who goes home?" still breaks upon the midnight air exactly as when Charles II or Queen Anne reigned. More than that, as the members gather up papers, and file out, the attendants still ply them with the admonition, "The usual time tomorrow, sir, the usual time tomorrow," precisely as if everyone did not know that if there was any doubt about the House resuming business at 2:45 tomorrow, every newspaper would find material in the fact for a front-page story. Verily, as Sir Courtenay Ilbert has remarked, "the parliament at Westminster is not only a busy workshop; it is a museum of antiquities." [30]

Officers of the House of Commons

Some of these quaint usages could be given up with no more serious effect than that of making Parliament less picturesque. But officers, committees, rules—to which we now turn—are indispensable. The most conspicuous and important officer in each house is, of course, the man who presides, i.e., in the House of Commons, the speaker, and in the House of Lords, the Lord Chancellor. There are, however, other officers of dignity and power. In the lower house these are, chiefly, the clerk and his two assistants, the sergeant-at-arms and his deputies, and the chairman and deputy chairman of ways and means (now more commonly known as the chairman and deputy chairman of committees); to which may be added, as an officer of ceremonial importance, the chaplain. The clerk and the sergeant-at-arms, together with their assistants, are appointed for life by the king on nomination of the prime minister; the chaplain is appointed by the speaker; the chairman and deputy chairman of committees are, like the speaker, elected by the House for the duration of a parliament, although, being (unlike all of the others) political officers, they retire when the ministry that has nominated them goes out of office. Little comment on the functions and duties of these officers is required, except in the case of the speaker. The chaplain appears at the opening of each sitting and reads the psalm and prayers.[31] The clerk,

[30] In preface to J. Redlich, *The Procedure of the House of Commons,* I, p. vi.

[31] Originally, prayers were read by the clerk or by the speaker himself,

whose place, with his aides, is at the table, signs all orders of the House, endorses bills sent or returned to the Lords, reads whatever is required to be read during the sittings, records the proceedings of the chamber, has custody of all records and other documents, and, in collaboration with the speaker, supervises the preparation of the Official Journal.[32] The sergeant-at-arms (usually a retired military or naval officer), picturesquely clad and regularly stationed at the bar of the House, attends the speaker, preserves decorum in the chamber and its precincts, directs the doorkeepers and messengers, enforces the House's orders, executes warrants issued by the speaker in its name, and presents at the bar persons qualified or ordered to appear there.[33] The chairman of committees (in his absence the deputy chairman) presides over the deliberations of the House when the body sits as committee of the whole, and at other times on request of the speaker,[34] and exercises general supervision over private bill legislation. Although political officials, the chairman and deputy chairman are expected to preserve

and the speaker still performs the function on the rare occasions when the chaplain is absent. Chaplains were first appointed, "to pray with the House daily," during the Long Parliament, in the seventeenth century. T. E. May, *op. cit.* (13th. ed.), 149, note.

[32] Sir Thomas Erskine May, whose monumental treatise on English parliamentary procedure is cited frequently in this chapter and succeeding ones, held the office of clerk for many years.

[33] M. MacDonagh, *The Pageant of Parliament,* I, Chap. xix. Most people, including probably some members, do not know that about half way up the Clock Tower are two suites of rooms for the imprisonment of either members or visitors committed by the House to the sergeant-at-arms' custody. The last involuntary occupant was Charles Bradlaugh, member for Northampton, who in 1880 was shut up for twenty-four hours as an incident of his contest with the House over his demand, as an atheist, to be allowed to assume his seat without taking an oath mentioning the Deity.

[34] This provision for a substitute for the speaker has existed only since 1855. Prior to that time, if the speaker was absent on account of illness or for any other reason, the only thing to be done was to adjourn the House or committee; and in a case of prolonged absence the only solution was to accept the speaker's resignation and elect a successor. A select committee which investigated the subject in 1853 found that in almost two hundred years the speaker had been absent (rarely more than an hour or two) only seventeen times. It was deemed desirable, however, to provide a substitute, which was done by a Deputy Speaker Act of 1855 conferring full powers on the chairman of committees as being a member reasonably certain to be conversant with the rules. The deputy chairman's office dates from 1902.

as strictly non-partisan an attitude when in the chair as if either were the speaker himself.

The Speaker

The speakership is an office of much dignity, honor, and power. No one can say precisely when it originated. Sir Thomas Hungerford, elected to the post in 1377, seems to have been the first to bear the title. But he is reported to have had predecessors, and it is likely that some such office existed from the very beginning of the House. In the early days, it will be remembered, the commoners had no direct part in legislation. All that they could do was to send to the "king in parliament," i.e., in the House of Lords, requests for new or amended laws or for redress of grievances; and the speaker was the man whom they commissioned to bear their petitions and urge them upon the sovereign's attention. He got his title from being the spokesman of the House in its dealings with the crown—from speaking *for,* not *to,* his fellow-members. He was never supposed to do much talking in the House, and nowadays he does none at all except strictly in the performance of his duties as moderator. But he remains the official spokesman of the chamber in its dealings with the crown, even though the rise of the prime-ministership (the prime minister being usually government leader in the House) has left him little occasion, except on certain formal occasions, for saying anything in this connection.

It was a triumph for the House of Commons when it gained the right to choose its own speaker. In earlier days the king appointed; and long after the office became nominally elective the usage was, as Coke testified in 1648, for the sovereign to "name a discreet and learned man" whom the Commons then proceeded to "elect." To this day, the choice of the House is subject to the approval of the crown. No speaker-elect, however, has been rejected since 1679, and the royal assent has become merely a matter of form. A speaker is elected at the opening of each parliament and serves as long as the parliament lasts. If the speaker of the preceding parliament is still a member of the House and is willing to be reëlected, he may count on receiving the honor; for, the speaker having long ago become a purely non-partisan official, the invariable custom for a hundred years has been to reëlect an incumbent as long as he is disposed, and able, to serve. Changes of party situation in the House since he was originally elected make no difference; as speaker he is supposed to have no party connections or prejudices.[35] If, however, a new man must be found, the selection is made—just as it is, under similar circumstances, in the American House of Representatives—before the House itself convenes. At Washington, the choice is made by the caucus of the majority party, and election by the House follows, the unsuccessful nominee of the minority party usually becoming minority floor leader.[36] At Westminster, the cabinet, but chiefly the prime minister, looks over the field and decides upon the right man, after making certain that the selection will be acceptable to the House. A Conservative cabinet will always choose a Conservative for the position; and, if there is a contest, he will be elected on the floor of the House by Conservative votes. But, as has been indicated, once in the office, he may expect to be reëlected indefinitely, and as a matter of course, whatever party is in power.[37]

When a former speaker is to be reëlected, the ceremony in the House is a sheer formality; everyone knows in advance what is going to happen. After the commoners have returned from their first excursion to the House of Lords, the clerk, who by curious custom is forbidden to utter a word during the pro-

[35] The last occasion on which a speaker was opposed for reëlection was in 1835. Similar action was threatened in 1895, but did not materialize. The Liberals had lately brought Mr. William C. Gully into the speakership. The Conservatives objected to the selection, on the ground that the new incumbent had never taken an active part in the work of the House or its committees and necessarily drew his knowledge of the rules and precedents from books rather than from observation and experience. They themselves had a first-rate candidate in mind, and it was commonly believed that they would put him in Gully's place as soon as opportunity arose. The Liberals soon fell from power, and the Conservatives came in. Mr. Gully, however, was continued in the speakership, even though his opponents took the unusual step of contesting (unsuccessfully) his seat, in the borough of Carlisle, at the 1895 elections. M. MacDonagh, *Pageant of Parliament,* I, 126-127.

[36] F. A. Ogg and P. O. Ray, *Introduction to American Government* (3rd ed.), 387.

[37] In connection with the election of a new incumbent, Captain E. A. Fitzroy, in 1928, Labor members voiced doubt about the desirability of perpetuating this tradition but gave no clear indication that they would actually resist it.

ceeding, takes his place at the table [38] and recognizes, by pointing, a member who, according to previous understanding, rises and moves that Mr. ——— "do take the chair of this House as speaker." Another member, also designated in advance, and usually not of the same party as the proposer, seconds the motion. The member named, i.e., the previous speaker, rises and expresses his appreciation of the confidence reposed in him; the members "call him to the chair" by acclamation; the proposer and seconder conduct him to his place—and the matter is ended, without nomination of any opposing candidates, and without any actual vote being taken. So far as the rank and file of the members are concerned, their rôle is merely to watch a bit of pantomime. When a new man is to be installed in the office, the "majority" candidate is proposed similarly, but the opposition also puts up a candidate, and after a debate in which the qualifications and claims of the two are discussed, the House votes, first on the motion in favor of the majority candidate, and afterwards, if it does not prevail, on that made in behalf of his rival.

We have it from a sixteenth-century parliamentarian that a speaker ought to be "a man big and comely, stately and well-spoken, his voice great, his carriage majestical, his nature haughty, and his purse plentiful." The plentiful purse is still a convenience, though the haughty nature can easily be overdone. But in any case the speaker must still be a man of parts—able, vigilant, imperturbable, tactful. All of these qualities, and more, he will require in the discharge of his onerous and delicate duties. Sitting in his high-canopied chair, in wig and gown, he presides almost constantly whenever the House is in session. He decides who shall have the floor—a matter not as often simplified by prearrangement as in the American House of Representatives, and especially in Continental legislatures—and all speeches and remarks are addressed to him, not to the House. He warns disorderly members and suspends them from sittings, and, with the aid of the sergeant-at-arms, preserves decorum suitable to a deliberative assembly, adjourning the House if the disorder becomes too serious to be dealt with by the force at the command of the sergeant-at-arms. He inter-

[38] He may not occupy the speaker's chair.

prets and applies the rules. He puts questions and announces the results of votes. He decides points of order, and for that purpose must be a thorough master of the technicalities of procedure. Hardly a situation can arise that has not arisen before, and if the speaker knows the precedents he cannot go far wrong. Knowing the precedents of the British House of Commons is, however, no child's play. In any event, the speaker's rulings are final; "the Chair, like the Pope," humorously replied Speaker Lowther when asked how errors that he made could be rectified, "is infallible." The only requisite is that the speaker shall make his rulings in such fashion that the members will have entire confidence that they represent, not the speaker's own will imposed upon the House, but rather the will of the House itself as embodied in its rules and precedents. Under the Parliament Act of 1911, it falls to the speaker to decide (if there is doubt) whether a bill is or is not a money bill—a decision which may, of course, go far toward determining the measure's fate.[39] Upon him, as an impartial, non-partisan, and well-informed dignitary, is occasionally devolved also the task of appointing the members of great conferences or commissions, such as the one which did the spade-work preliminary to the electoral reform act of 1918.[40] Finally, as has already been noted, the speaker is the official mouthpiece of the House in its relations, not only with the House of Lords and with the departments of state, but also with the king (or his representatives, the lords commissioners in the House of Lords), although this is not nowadays a function of much practical importance.

In all these activities the speaker refrains scrupulously from any display of personal sympathies or partisan leanings. He never takes the floor to engage in debate, even when the House

[39] It will be recalled that there have been proposals to transfer this function to a joint committee of the houses. No such change, however, has as yet been made, and the Labor party, now (1929) in power, is on record as opposed to it. See pp. 351 ff. above.

[40] Occasionally, too, he is required to preside over a "constitutional conference," as, for example, in the case of the Buckingham Palace conference on the Irish crisis called by George V in 1914. See p. 701 below. Speaker Lowther served also as chairman of the Speaker's Conference which in 1920 presented a report on devolution. See p. 473 below.

is sitting as committee of the whole.[41] He never votes except to break a tie, and in the rare instances in which this becomes necessary he, if possible, gives his casting vote in such a way as to avoid making the decision final, thereby extending the House another opportunity to consider the question.[42] The constituency which he represents is, of course, in effect disfranchised, but it has its reward in the distinction which he brings it and almost unfailingly reëlects him to his seat without opposition.[43] Outside, no less than inside, of the House, the speaker abstains from every appearance of partisanship. He never publicly discusses or voices an opinion on party issues; he never attends a party meeting; he has no connections with party newspapers; he never sets foot in a political club; he, of course, makes no campaign for his own reëlection. The speaker of the American House of Representatives is, quite frankly, a party man—with less power, it is true, that can be used for partisan purposes than before the reforms of 1910-11, but nevertheless an official who serves, and is expected to serve, the interests of party so far as it can be done without too flagrant unfairness to the opposition. The contrast with the speakership at Westminster is indeed striking. This is not to say that the American speakership is wholly bad. Traditions and circumstances differ in the two countries, and the history of the American, as of the English, office has, on the whole, been honorable. But, as would be expected, the deference paid the chair at Westminster is considerably greater than at Washington, having often been, as Sir Courtenay Ilbert remarks, "the theme of admiring comment by foreign observers." [44]

[41] In his speech from the chair on taking leave of the House in 1921 Mr. Lowther humorously remarked: "The House will excuse me if I show any shortcomings in addressing it. I have not for a quarter of a century had the opportunity of making a speech in the House."

[42] During his ten years in the office Speaker Gully was called upon to break a tie only once. On the general subject, see T. E. May, *op. cit.* (13th ed.), 361-364.

[43] The speaker's constituents cannot look to him to advocate their interests or procure benefits for them, and political organization is practically suspended in the district. For further comment on this situation (for which there is no analogy in America), see E. Porritt, *The Unreformed House of Commons,* I, 481.

[44] *Parliament,* 140-141. Cf. E. Lummis, *The Speaker's Chair* (London, 1900), 6-7, and J. Redlich, *The Procedure of the House of Commons,* II,

As is befitting so assiduous a servant of the state, the speaker has certain perquisites. He has a salary of £5,000 a year. Since 1857 he has had as his official residence a wing of the Palace of Westminster extending from the Clock Tower to the Thames; and there, being repressed politically but not socially, he gives numerous dinners and other entertainments. In the official order of precedence, as fixed by an order in council of 1919, he ranks next after the Lord President of the Council, which makes him the seventh subject of the realm. And when he finally chooses to retire, he is elevated to the peerage as a viscount and liberally pensioned.[45]

136-139. A motion to censure Speaker Whitley in 1925 on the ground that he had violated precedent by allowing closure to be applied in the early stages of debate on the annual Finance Bill was a most unusual proposal and was overwhelmingly rejected.

[45] Upon retiring from the speakership in 1928, Mr. John H. Whitley, however, broke with precedent of more than a hundred years by declining the offer of a peerage. He assigned "personal reasons" for his act. The history of the speakership is recorded conveniently in E. Porritt, *Unreformed House of Commons,* I, Chaps. xxi-xxii, and more fully, in a biographical fashion, in A. I. Dasent, *The Speakers of the House of Commons from the Earliest Times to the Present Day* (New York, 1911). There is a useful sketch in J. Redlich, *Procedure of the House of Commons,* II, 156-168. The best brief description and interpretation of the office is *ibid.,* 131-155. Much interesting and useful information can be gleaned from J. W. Lowther, *A Speaker's Commentaries,* 2 vols. (London, 1925). The author—the present Lord Ullswater—was speaker from 1905 to 1921. Reference may be made also to J. G. S. MacNeill, "The Growth of the Speakership," *Fortnightly Rev.,* Nov., 1920, and "The Completion of the Speakership," *ibid.,* Aug., 1921, and to A. I. Dasent, "Mr. Lowther and the Speaker's Office," *Nineteenth Cent.,* June, 1921. A complete list of speakers from 1584 to 1928 is printed in *Const. Year Book* (1928), 37. The present speaker, Captain Fitzroy, was chosen, without opposition, in June, 1928, and was similarly reëlected in 1929. He had long served as deputy chairman of committees.

M. P. Follett, *The Speaker of the House of Representatives* (New York, 1904), deals with the development and characteristics of the American speakership during the first century of its history. The nature of the office today is analyzed satisfactorily in Chang-Wei Chiu, *The Speaker of the House of Representatives since 1896* (New York, 1928). For other references, see Ogg and Ray, *op. cit.,* 395. The American conception of the speakership, in its partisan aspect, is very well expressed in Speaker Longworth's statement, upon his election to the office in 1925: "I believe it to be the duty of the speaker, standing squarely on the platform of his party, to assist in so far as he properly can the enactment of legislation in accordance with the declared principles and policies of his party, and by the same token to resist the enactment of legislation in violation thereof." *Cong. Record,* 69th Cong., 1st Sess., p. 382.

Committees in the House of Commons

Legislative bodies the world over save time and gain other desirable ends by delegating most of the preliminary work on bills to committees of one sort or another. The British House of Commons is no exception to the rule. As early as the reign of Elizabeth it was not an unusual thing to refer a bill, after its second reading, to what we should now call a select committee, i.e., a group of members specially designated to study the measure and report on it; and in the last fifty years—notably since 1919—the amount of service required from committees has been steadily increasing.[46]

The committees now made use of are of five main types: (1) the Committee of the Whole House, (2) select committees on public bills, (3) sessional committees on public bills, (4) standing committees on public bills, and (5) committees on private bills. The Committee of the Whole consists of the entire body of members, and is distinguishable from the House itself only in that (1) it is presided over, not by the speaker, but by the chairman of committees (or his deputy), who sits, not in the speaker's chair, but in the clerk's chair at the table, (2) the mace, which is the speaker's symbol of authority, is for the time being placed under the table, (3) a motion need not be seconded, (4) the "previous question"—aimed at cutting off debate—cannot be moved, and (5) members are allowed to speak any number of times on the same question. Procedure is thus much less formal and rigid than in the House as such, making for ease, if not always for speed, in the handling of vital and complicated matters. When its work is done the committee "rises," the House again comes into session with the speaker in the chair, and the chairman of the committee reports, for adoption by the House, whatever conclusions the committee has arrived at. The practice of referring bills to committees of the whole house arose in the reign of Charles I,[47] from which

[46] The historical development of the committee system of the House of Commons to 1905 is outlined conveniently in J. Redlich, *op. cit.*, II, 203-214.

[47] The speaker was still at that time practically appointed by the king, and the device of committee of the whole was brought into play primarily as a means of enabling the House to rid itself of him as occupant of the chair.

time until 1907 it underwent little change. Until the date mentioned, a public bill, after its second reading, went normally to committee of the whole. Since 1907, however, when provision was made for increased use of standing committees, fewer measures have been referred to the larger body, and none (except money bills and bills for confirming provisional orders)[48] now go there unless the House, on motion made directly after second reading, so designates. The most important matters regularly considered in committee of the whole are the estimates of expenditure and of revenue and the resolutions by which the committee prepares the way for the passage of the great appropriation and finance acts by the House. When the business in hand relates to appropriations, the committee is known, technically, as the Committee of the Whole on Supply, or simply the Committee of Supply; when to revenues, it is styled the Committee of Ways and Means.[49]

Select committees consist, as a rule, of fifteen members, and are created from time to time to investigate and report upon specific subjects on which legislation is pending or contemplated. It is through them that the House collects evidence, examines witnesses, and otherwise obtains information required for intelligent action. A select committee, however, has no power to require the attendance of persons or the production of papers or records unless the House expressly authorizes it to do so. After a select committee has fulfilled the immediate purpose for which it was set up, it passes out of existence. Each such committee chooses its chairman, and each keeps detailed records of its proceedings, which are included, along with its formal report, in the published parliamentary papers of the session. Formerly, the members were usually designated by the Committee of Selection, which itself consists of eleven members chosen by the House at the beginning of each session. But nowadays the names of the men who are to compose the

[48] A provisional order is an order issued by an executive officer or department of the government authorizing a project in behalf of which application has been made. It is "provisional" because it is not ultimately valid unless confirmed by Parliament. See p. 426 below.

[49] See pp. 432 ff. below. The House occasionally sits, however, as Committee of the Whole on Public Bills for consideration of exceptionally important measures of a non-financial nature.

committee are proposed in the motion of the member who moves the committee's appointment.[50] The number of select committees is, of course, variable, but rarely small; something like a score are usually provided for in the course of a session. As a rule, eight or ten are created for an entire session, and hence are known as sessional committees. Of these, the Committee of Selection is itself an example; others of the sort are the Committee on Standing Orders, the Committee on Public Accounts, and the Committee on Public Petitions.

Beginning in 1882, certain great standing committees have been created, to the end that the time of the House may be further economized. The first two such committees, set up quite experimentally, had to do with (1) law, courts of justice, and legal procedure, and (2) trade, agriculture, fisheries, shipping, and manufactures; although it soon became customary to refer to one or the other of them matters which were not directly related to any of these subjects. In 1907 the number of such committees was raised, by standing orders, from two to four, each consisting of from sixty to eighty members; and all bills except money bills, private bills,[51] and bills for confirming provisional orders—that is to say, substantially all public non-fiscal proposals—were thenceforth required to be referred, after their second reading, to one of these committees (the speaker determining which one) unless the House directed otherwise. In other words, reference to a standing committee became the general rule, and only by exception were measures handled differently—such measures being withheld for consideration in committee of the whole, or, in the case of private bills, committees of an extraordinary character set up by the Committee of Selection. With a view to expediting business still further, the number of standing committees was raised in 1919 to six;[52] and whereas before that date no standing committee could sit while the House was in session except in pursuance of a motion offered by the member in charge of the bill before the committee, the rules now permit this to be done

[50] Standing Order 57.

[51] A private bill is one which has in view the special interest of some locality, person, or group of persons, rather than the interests of the people generally.

[52] It has since (in 1925) been reduced to five. Standing Order 47 (§ 1).

without any restriction.[53] It is expected that measures referred to a standing committee will be so thoroughly scrutinized and evaluated by it that they will consume no great amount of the working time of the House as a whole. When the number of standing committees was increased in 1919, the size of each was reduced to from forty to sixty (later changed to from thirty to fifty),[54] with the provision that the Committee of Selection, which designates the members—after conference with the government and opposition leaders—might add not fewer than ten nor more than fifteen members (at present, from ten to thirty-five) to a committee in respect to any bill referred to it, such additional members to serve during the consideration of that bill only. These additional and temporary members are intended, of course, to be experts on the subject in hand. All standing committees are made up afresh at the opening of the first session of a new parliament, and last (although with considerable shifting of membership) until that parliament is prorogued. For convenience, they are known, respectively, as the A, B, C, D, and Scottish Committees.[55]

British and American Committee Systems Compared

The committee system thus outlined bears obvious resemblance to the systems to be found in American legislative bodies, and, for that matter, to systems employed by deliberative assemblies everywhere. But it also has its own distinctive features. Taking the committees of the House of Representatives at Washington as a basis for comparison, the principal

[53] On a division being called in the House, however, the chairman of a standing committee is required to suspend the proceedings of the committee for such time as will, in his judgment, enable members to vote in the division. Select committees also may sit while the House is sitting. Standing Order 47 (§ 1).

[54] This does not apply to that one of the standing committees, known as the Committee on Scottish Affairs, to which all public bills relating to Scotland are referred. Under Standing Order 47 (§ 2), it consists of all the Scottish members of the House (74), together with from ten to fifteen other members designated by the Committee of Selection. Twenty members constitute a quorum of any standing committee (Standing Order 46, § 1).

[55] Committees on private bills will be spoken of later (see p. 424). Many such (with four members each) are set up every session, the Committee of Selection designating their members and dividing the private bills among them for consideration and report.

differences shown by the British are as follows: (1) Standing committees at Westminster are far fewer than at Washington —five, as compared with forty-six. Of the American committees, however, only about twelve—at the most fifteen—have much importance; some have not met for years.[56] There are no useless, or phantom, committees in the British system. (2) The British standing committees have a larger membership than the American. The largest standing committee at Washington, that on appropriations, has thirty-five members. Standing committees at Westminster, as we have seen, number from thirty to fifty, without taking into account the ten to thirty-five extra members that may be added for the consideration of any particular bill. The British committees are unquestionably large for the kind of work they are expected to do, though the more purely investigative select committees are, of course, smaller. (3) The British committees have no such rigid rules determining the relative rank of members and the succession to the chairmanship as we have in the United States, where the principle of seniority in point of service almost invariably governs. Committee chairmen are not chosen in the same way in the two countries. At Washington, the chairman of each standing committee is named by the same agency of the majority caucus (described below) that prepares the list of majority members of the committee. At Westminster, the Committee of Selection names a "chairman's panel" for standing committees, and this group designates the chairman from its own number.[57] Seniority, which is so strictly adhered to in the American system as to leave little opportunity for personal qualifications to be taken into account, has small place in the British system, either in naming chairmen or in selecting the members generally.

(4) As thus suggested, the committees themselves are differ-

[56] Several of the most obviously useless House committees were abolished in 1927, reducing the total number from some sixty to the present forty-six. A few inactive ones, however, survive. "A score of the House committees do nine-tenths of the work." R. Luce, *Congress; an Explanation* (Cambridge, 1926), 6.

[57] Chairmen of select committees on private bills are, however, named by the Committee of Selection itself. Select committees on public bills, as has been indicated, choose their own chairmen.

ently chosen under the two systems. In Britain, as we have seen, the lists of assignments are drawn up by the Committee of Selection, without action by the House itself. In America, the majority and minority parties in the House prepare their separate "slates" or lists of representatives on each committee, and the lists are then put together and voted through, as a matter of form, by the House. Each party employs for the purpose a group of members which is, in effect, an agency of the party caucus—the Republicans using a committee on committees containing one member from each state having a Republican delegation in the House, and the Democrats employing the Democratic members of the ways and means committee.[58] (5) From all this it follows that committees are built much more definitely on party lines at Washington than at Westminster. Not that considerations of party are absent from the British system. The Committee of Selection, being made up after conference between government and opposition leaders, is always a bi-partisan body; and in designating the members of standing and select committees this agency will unfailingly see to it that the parties in the House are represented on each of them in some reasonable proportion to their numerical strength.[59] Party, however, is not the major consideration as it is in America. In the case of the standing committees, at all events, this subordination of party is the easier for the reason that such committees are not really committees on anything in particular, being simply committees set up to receive and consider bills of any sort and on any subject that may happen to be sent along to them.[60] American standing committees have

[58] In earlier days the speaker of the House of Representatives appointed all committees, but in the "revolution" of 1910-11 he was shorn of this power. Committees are still, as a rule, appointed by the presiding officer in state legislatures and city councils.

[59] The party complexion of the five standing committees in 1927 was as follows:

Committee	Total Membership	Conservatives	Laborites	Liberals	Others
A	40	28	11	1	0
B	40	26	11	2	1
C	40	29	9	1	1
D	50	34	13	2	1
Scottish	73 *	38	26	8	1

* One Scottish seat vacant.

[60] The committee which receives all bills relating to Scotland is, of course, to some extent an exception to this statement.

definite provinces—ways and means, appropriations, agriculture, interstate and foreign commerce, banking and currency—which are usually party battlegrounds, and each party knows in advance that the precise balance of forces in any such committee may spell success or failure in a session.[61]

Organization of the House of Lords

What of the forms of organization in the more aristocratic and leisurely assemblage at the opposite end of Westminster? Here, in contrast with the Commons, the officers are almost all appointive. The most conspicuous—though hardly the most powerful—is the severely judicial figure in big grey wig and black silk gown who occupies the woolsack, i.e., the Lord Chancellor. The duty of presiding at sittings of the House of Lords is, of course, only one of many that fall to this extraordinary dignitary.[62] Any man who reaches the lord chancellorship is pretty certain already to be a peer. If he is not, the defect can easily be, and invariably is, remedied. There is, however, no legal necessity that this be done, because the theory is that the woolsack is outside the precincts of the chamber, and the presiding official, *as such*, is not a member of the body. Mem-

[61] The committees of the House of Commons as they were before the changes of 1919 are described in A. L. Lowell, *Government of England,* I, Chap. xiii; C. Ilbert, *Parliament,* Chap. vi; J. Redlich, *Procedure of the House of Commons,* II, 180-214; and T. E. May, *op. cit.* (13th ed.), Chaps. xvi-xvii. The committee system of the American House of Representatives is discussed briefly in F. A. Ogg and P. O. Ray, *Introduction to American Government* (3rd ed.), 381-395, and more fully in S. W. McCall, *The Business of Congress* (New York, 1911), Chaps. iii, v; D. S. Alexander, *History and Procedure of the House of Representatives* (Boston, 1916), Chaps. xii-xiii; and R. Luce, *Congress; an Explanation* (Cambridge, 1926), Chap. i. The last-mentioned author's views on the superiority of the American committee system are interesting. The committee system of the French Chamber of Deputies is described in R. K. Gooch, "The French Parliamentary Committee System," *Economica,* June, 1928, and more fully in L. Rogers, "Parliamentary Commissions in France," *Polit. Sci. Quar.,* Sept. and Dec., 1923. In the second of the two articles last mentioned there is some account of the interest in the French system aroused in Britain, especially by war-time experiences, and some consideration of the relations of the committee system to the general workings of parliamentary institutions in the two countries.

[62] It will be recalled that he is a leading member of the cabinet, and therefore a party figure, which puts him in sharp contrast with the speaker of the House of Commons.

ber or not, the powers allowed the Chancellor fall far short of those commonly assigned a moderator.[63] For instance, if two or more members simultaneously attempt to address the chamber, the House itself, not the chair, decides which of them shall have the floor. Order in debate is enforced, not by the Chancellor, but by the House, and when the members speak they address, not the chair, but "My Lords." As a peer, the Chancellor may, and regularly does, speak and vote, on party lines, like any other member; but in no case does he have a casting vote. In a word, his rôle as presiding officer is almost entirely formal.

Other principal officers of the House of Lords who owe their positions to governmental appointment are the clerk of the parliaments, who keeps the records; the sergeant-at-arms, who personally attends the presiding officer and acts as custodian of the mace; and the Gentleman Usher of the Black Rod, a pompous dignitary—usually a retired military or naval officer—whose function it is, as we have seen, to summon the commoners when their attendance is required and to play a more or less useful part upon other ceremonial occasions. The one important official whom the House itself elects (at the beginning of each session) is the lord chairman of committees, to whom it falls to preside in committee of the whole, in all committees on private bills, and indeed in all other committees unless it is otherwise ordered.[64]

The committee system is broadly similar to that found in the House of Commons, and hence does not call for detailed description. Besides the Committee of the Whole, large use is made of sessional and select committees; and there is a standing committee for textual revision, made up, however, at the beginning of each session, to which every bill, after passing through the Committee of the Whole, is referred unless the House orders otherwise. Sessional committees are created for a session, and consist either of all members present during the session (being thus identical in personnel with the Committee of the Whole) or of smaller, and sometimes indefinite, numbers of

[63] *Standing Orders of the House of Lords,* No. xx (London, 1913), 15-16. On the Lord Chancellor as a presiding officer, see M. MacDonagh, *The Pageant of Parliament,* II, Chap. vi. Cf. T. E. May, *op. cit.,* 186-189.

[64] *Standing Orders of the House of Lords,* Nos. XL-LIII (pp. 28-33).

members. The most important such committees are (1) the Committee of Privileges, to which the House refers questions touching its orders, customs, and privileges, and also claims of peerage and precedence; (2) the Appeal Committee, which considers such petitions concerning judicial business before the House as are referred to it; (3) the Standing Orders Committee (consisting of the chairman of committees and forty other members), which has to do with the standing orders of the House relating to private bills; and (4) the Committee of selection (consisting of the chairman of committees and eight other members), which proposes names of persons to compose the standing committee and certain select committees. In addition, there is a sessional committee on the journals, and another on the offices, of the chamber. Select committees are named by the House itself, usually with the power to appoint their own chairmen; and proposals may be referred to them at any time between the second and third readings when additional information is desired. The standing committee is made up by the Committee of Selection, and more than one such committee may be appointed if thought desirable.[65]

[65] *Companion to the Standing Orders of the House of Lords on Public Business* (London, 1909), 48-50, 77-80.

CHAPTER XVII

PARLIAMENT AT WORK: LAW-MAKING

Such, in outline, is the internal organization to which long centuries of arduous experience have brought the two branches of Parliament. How does the machinery thus built up actually operate? What is the routine of an ordinary parliamentary working day? How are debates carried on, decisions arrived at, records preserved? How are laws made, taxes levied, expenditures voted? What, in short, of that sometimes dull, yet usually interesting, and occasionally exciting, thing which we call parliamentary procedure?

The first fact to be noted is that Parliament has, not a single procedure, but many. That is to say, it has a more or less distinct way of transacting each of its several forms or types of business. Indeed, each branch has procedures of its own. Thus the House of Lords, sitting as a court, has a procedure—a way of hearing and deciding appeals—which naturally has no counterpart in the purely non-judicial House of Commons. On the other hand, the House of Commons, to which ministers bear a responsibility not shared with the second chamber, has a somewhat unique procedure for questioning occupants of the Front Treasury Bench. Many different procedures exist, however, in each house which do not spring from functional dissimilarities between the two, e.g., a procedure on money bills, a procedure on non-financial public bills, a procedure on private bills, even a procedure for receiving and seating new members and another for presenting petitions.

Rules of Procedure

Whatever the business in hand, each branch of Parliament deals with it by definite and accepted methods, as prescribed by the rules of the house. One will not be surprised to be told that both houses have had established ways of carrying on their work almost from the beginning; or that at the opening of the nineteenth century the main lines of procedure were hardly different from what they were in the sixteenth. In earlier days the rules consisted almost entirely of unwritten custom. Even in the House of Commons, the order of business was not "laid down in systematic enactments, still less in a code of parliamentary procedure; it rested on living tradition, on concrete precedents found in the journals of the House, and on definite resolutions, which, as a rule, were of a declaratory, not enacting, character." [1] Even so, the right to control its own procedure was gained by the House only after extended conflict with the king; and although no longer specifically enumerated among the "ancient and undoubted rights and privileges" which the newly elected speaker, presenting himself at the bar of the Lords, claims and is pledged to at the opening of every parliament, this right is still understood by everybody to be included. In the leisurely eighteenth century—a golden age of parliamentary oratory, but an epoch of relatively little great legislation—the customary law of the House was elaborated into a vast, technical, mysterious, stereotyped system of procedural precedents and rules which may have served well enough at the time, but which, under the changed conditions after 1832, became increasingly cumbersome and impossible. The "keen wind of democracy" had begun to whistle through the palace of Westminster; the problems with which Parliament had to deal mounted to unprecedented proportions; popular demand for remedial and constructive legislation grew by what it fed on; more and more, law-making, instead of being left to private members, became a matter of governmental leadership and initiative. As a consequence, the House, floundering amid a welter of time-consuming technicalities, began to cut its way out—doing so, naturally, by deliberately adopting new or revised rules in the interest of economy of effort and of time. Gradually, the jungle was to some extent cleared and the chamber came into possession of a considerably simplified scheme of procedure, in which custom still played an important rôle, but with "orders," i.e., definitely adopted regulations, holding an in-

[1] J. Redlich, *Procedure of the House of Commons,* I, p. xxix.

creasingly prominent position. And this is the situation today. Custom and precedent make up a great part of the general body of rules; but adopted orders supplement, summarize, and clarify. The heavy demands upon the speaker in his capacity of moderator, already referred to, arise from the fact that he must know not only the formal and printed rules but also the customs and the precedents.[2]

The whole development was much like that by which the general body of English law, or indeed the English constitution itself, has come to be what it now is. The orders of each house stand in the same relation to its customary law as acts of Parliament bear to the common law of the country. Some of these orders remain effective through relatively long periods; others do not. There are numerous "standing orders," for both public and private business, which, once adopted, are not often changed. There are "sessional orders" (fewer in number), which apply only during the session for which they were adopted; although some of these, by being repeatedly renewed, become, to all intents and purposes, standing orders. Finally, there are "general orders," i.e., resolutions which are observed as permanent without being made standing orders.[3] All, of

[2] To a large extent, these customs and precedents have never been reduced to writing. Consequently there is no one place to which either the speaker or any one else can go to find the whole body of procedural regulations at present in operation. In Continental countries there are codes of this sort. It may be added that legislative procedure in all English-speaking lands, and to a considerable extent in non-English-speaking countries as well, is based fundamentally on the historic usages of the British Parliament. In every one of the British dominions the constitution stipulates that, in the absence of specific direction to the contrary, the procedure of the legislature shall be in accordance with parliamentary procedure at Westminster. The manual of procedure which Thomas Jefferson drew up when serving as president of the Senate, and which is still the kernel of the great body of procedural rules developed at Washington, was based squarely upon eighteenth-century practice of the British Parliament. A treatise on that practice, written by Dumont but inspired by Jeremy Bentham, became a major influence in the framing of the rules of procedure for the European parliaments which came into existence in the first half of the nineteenth century.

[3] Curiously, these are both numerous and important, and some date back several centuries. Examples are the rules which forbid the speaker to take the chair unless as many as forty members are present and which prevent a member from speaking twice on the same question.

course, are actually subject to change at any time, by simple resolution adopted by simple majority. Furthermore, either house may at will suspend any order (or the whole body of orders) with a view to emergency action, or to getting around an awkward situation, without prejudice to the order's continued validity. Taken in conjunction with accumulated customs and precedents still regarded as enforceable, the written rules make up too formidable a body of regulations and practices ever to be completely understood by any considerable proportion of the members who have to work under them. Lord Palmerston admitted that he never fully mastered them; Gladstone was on many occasions an inadvertent offender against them. There was something more than humor in Parnell's reply to the Irish member who asked how he could learn the rules. The reply was, "By breaking them." [4]

Daily Order of Business

It is in the rules (mainly the standing orders) that one will find laid down the sequence of ceremonies and actions that go to make up the routine of a parliamentary working day. Briefly, this order of business in the House of Commons is as follows. At the regular opening hour, which, as we have seen, is 2:45 P.M., the speaker's procession moves down the central aisle, the speaker in wig and gown, the chaplain in gown and stole, the sergeant-at-arms with his sword, and the mace-bearer with the mace. A psalm is read, followed by two or three prayers. Thereupon the speaker takes the chair and business begins. First comes consideration of such private bills as may be listed on the printed orders of the day, followed by the presenting of petitions. For reasons that will be explained later, the former takes little time.[5] The latter also makes no heavy de-

[4] For seventy-five years it has been customary for the House of Commons orders (of all three kinds) to be collected from time to time in a handbook, known as *The Manual of Procedure in the Public Business,* under the editorship of the clerk of the House. Since 1811 there has also been published, from time to time, *Standing Orders of the House of Commons.* Comparable with these are *Standing Orders of the House of Lords* and *Companion to the Standing Orders of the House of Lords on Public Business.* Cf. J. Redlich, *op. cit.,* II, 10-20. The standing orders of the House of Commons are reprinted in T. E. May, *op. cit.* (13th ed.), 879-897.

[5] See pp. 422-426 below.

mands; for petitions are not presented now in such numbers as formerly, and all that happens is that members having such documents to submit rise, announce the fact (often without so much as telling what the petition asks), and, walking up the aisle, drop the papers into the yawning mouth of a big black bag that hangs at the left of the speaker's chair.[6] The first stage of the sitting that draws much interest is "question time," when members may put queries to the ministers concerning administrative or other matters. As we shall see, this right of question is exercised freely, and it is hardly surprising that question time is often the most interesting portion of the day's proceedings. Then comes the introduction of new members, if there happen to be any, after which the speaker calls upon the clerk to read the orders of the day. The House is now ready to turn its attention to the public bills that are down on the "order paper" for consideration. The clerk reads the title of the first one, and debate begins. The benches, empty for the most part during the dinner period, fill up as the evening wears on, and frequently the interest rises until the climax is reached in a final burst of oratory as Big Ben overhead booms the midnight hour. Sometimes the sitting extends later—occasionally, at times of special stress, throughout the night. But ordinarily adjournment is taken by twelve o'clock, when the passer-by may still hear the time-honored call, "Who goes home?" and the attendants' ancient admonition, "The usual time tomorrow, sir; the usual time tomorrow."[7]

Debate

Etymologically, Parliament is a place of talk, or discussion; and while nowadays it does many important things without talking much about them—at all events in public—it is most com-

[6] Record of petitions presented is made in the journal of the House, and a committee on petitions looks them over to see that they are in the prescribed form. But rarely are they heard of again. "As far as practical purposes are concerned, petitions might as well be dropped over the Terrace into the Thames as into the mouth of the appointed sack." H. Lucy, *Lords and Commoners,* 106. For general discussion, see T. E. May, *op. cit.* (13th ed.), Chap. xxii.

[7] Under extraordinary conditions, sittings are now and then prolonged to as much as thirty, or even forty, hours. T. E. May, op. cit. (13th ed.), 181 note.

pletely itself, and most interesting to observers, when engaged in the give and take of debate. In the House of Lords, as we have seen, all speeches are addressed to "My Lords," and the chamber itself decides who shall have the floor if two or more members claim it at the same time. In the Commons, however, all remarks are addressed to "Mr. Speaker," who, assisted somewhat by lists put in his hands by the party whips, indicates the member who is to go on with the debate when another has left off speaking. In so far as possible, he will give both sides an equal opportunity for expression of opinion; and he will not permit a member to speak twice upon the same question, unless it be to explain a portion of his speech which has been misunderstood, or in case an amendment has been moved which constitutes a new question. In accordance with long established usage (now embodied in the rules), he will not allow a member to read a speech from manuscript; [8] and he not only may warn one who is straying from the subject, or is merely repeating things he has already said, but may require him, after the third unheeded admonition, to terminate his remarks and give way to a fresh debater.[9] Although it has seen many tumultuous occasions, especially at the hands of the Irish Nationalists, and, more recently, of the Clydeside Laborites, the House of Commons rates high on the score of decorum.[10] This does

[8] The use of notes is permissible.

[9] Standing Order 19.

[10] One who wishes, however, to see how far rowdyism is sometimes carried will find illuminating and entertaining dispatches in the newspapers, e.g., *New York Times,* of June 25 to July 15, 1926. It was necessary for the speaker to suspend the sitting of the House on the first date mentioned because of disorder which he could not control. Altercations between members and the speaker, in the course of the latter's efforts to enforce the rules and preserve decorum, are not infrequent. Rather amusing was the termination of such a colloquy, a few years ago, between Speaker Whitley and Lady Astor. The latter had been required by the speaker to withdraw certain remarks hurled at an interrupter during the course of a speech which she was making. "If the noble lady," observed the speaker, "would act on my advice, frequently given, and address herself to me, she would not entangle herself in this way." "I quite agree," said Lady Astor, "but I do not think any member speaks under greater provocation than I do." "I cannot agree that the noble lady is not herself sometimes provocative," added the speaker. "I agree with that, sir," admitted Lady Astor, who then resumed her speech. On one occasion in 1927 Prime Minister Baldwin, choosing not to reply in person to a motion censuring his government, desig-

not mean, however, that the members scattered through the green benches are always attentive to what is going on, or deferential toward those who are addressing them. Looking down from the visitors' gallery, one is apt, much of the time, to see members restlessly moving in and out of the chamber, others chatting and joking and occasionally breaking into loud laughter, a few sitting abstractedly with their hats tilted over their eyes, still fewer listening with some appearance of interest; while from the dark recesses of the speaker's chair sounds the reiterated "order, order," designed to keep the noise and inattentiveness within bounds not positively inimical to the dignity of the chamber.[11]

The House is not more attentive to debate because many, if not most, of the speeches are not worth listening to, and because even if they were, they would, as every member knows, have

nated a colleague to speak for him. This was not in accordance with practice, and when the substitute tried to speak he was greeted with a roar of protests from the Labor benches which kept up until the speaker was forced to suspend the sitting. On the general subject, see T. E. May, *op. cit.*, (13th ed.), 334-341.

[11] Members of the House are required by statute to attend unless granted leave of absence on account of ill health or other urgent circumstances. This means only, however, that they must remain in London and participate in parliamentary work with reasonable fidelity. Regularity of attendance was stimulated somewhat by provision, in 1911, of an annual salary of £400 for members not already in receipt of salaries as ministers, as officers of the House, or as attachés of the royal household. In remoter days county and borough representatives received, as a rule, some compensation from their constituents, including travelling expenses. By the seventeenth century such payments practically ceased (the latest known instance was in 1678), though in the eye of the law the constituencies remained liable. In the nineteenth century demand arose, not only that members be paid, but that they be paid out of national funds. The Chartists urged such an arrangement; favorable resolutions were passed repeatedly in the Commons, but thrown out by the Lords; after 1900 Labor advocated the plan as a means of enabling poor but capable men to become candidates, and in lieu of the meager subsidies which it undertook itself to provide for such of its necessitous supporters as found their way to the green benches. A ruling of the House of Lords (the Osborne Judgment) in 1909, to the effect that payment of parliamentary members as such from the dues collected by labor organizations was contrary to law, supplied fresh impetus, and two years later the present regular salary system was introduced. In addition to the £400, members are entitled to travelling expenses between London and their constituencies, and to a very limited franking privilege. On the early abuse of franking, see E. Porritt, *The Unreformed House of Commons,* I, Chap. xiv.

little or no effect on the fate of the measure in hand. More and more, the real work is done in committee, where discussion takes on a conversational tone—even, as a rule, in committee of the whole.[12] The truth is that the House no longer has either time or taste for the extensive debates of the old days. Business crowds upon it; rules designed to expedite work tighten up from decade to decade; impatient members puncture bubbles of mere grandiloquence with satirical thrusts that drive all except the most thick-skinned offenders from the floor.[13] That parliamentary oratory is not what it once was cannot be gainsaid. But whether the change is not for the better is another matter. Much of the eloquence that used to crowd the benches was mere emotionalism; much more was only stateliness and ponderousness of speech, with no corresponding originality or richness of thought. It may have been effective once; on more than one occasion in earlier days, the records tell us, the House of Commons was so stirred by impassioned speeches that adjournment was taken to give members time to recover from the overpowering effects of a flight of eloquence. But nowadays the member who wants what he says to be listened to will speak briefly and to the point. He may easily produce more of an impression in ten minutes than in two hours; indeed, the surest way to empty the benches, and to gain personal unpopularity besides, is to run beyond the twenty minutes in which, proverbially, converts to a cause, if won at all, are gathered in. Rare indeed is the parliamentary debater of today of whom it could be written, as Ben Jonson wrote of Bacon, "the fear of every man who heard him was lest he should make an end." [14]

[12] It must, of course, be remembered that the House may resolve itself into committee of the whole whenever it so desires, and that it sits and works in that guise during a large part of the time.

[13] "I am speaking to posterity," once grandly declared a boresome member. "Faith, if you go on at this rate," broke in a voice from the Irish quarter, "you will see your audience before you." Townsend, *House of Commons,* II, 394.

[14] Mr. Asquith, in his *Fifty Years of British Parliament* (London, 1926), I, 200, comments interestingly on the growing disuse of classical quotation, and cites G. M. Trevelyan's remark: "It is significant of much that in the 17th century members of Parliament quoted from the Bible, in the 18th and 19th centuries from the classics, and in the 20th from nothing at all." On

Closure

Early in the history of parliamentary assemblages it was found necessary to provide ways of bringing debate to a close, especially when filibustering minorities were bent on preventing action on a measure until their wishes on that or some other subject were met. The Senate of the United States, indeed, got on until recently without any devices for this purpose, and the British House of Lords still continues to do so. As early as 1604, however, the House of Commons adopted a rule under which a motion that "the previous question be now put," if carried, caused a vote on the main question to be taken forthwith; and a similar regulation found a place in the first set of rules adopted by the American House of Representatives in 1789. In both cases, the "previous question" rule has been found useful, but insufficient. Other rules have been adopted empowering the speaker to refuse to entertain a motion which he considers dilatory; the House of Commons forbids a member to speak more than once (except in committee) on a question, and the House of Representatives allows a member only one hour for a speech (with certain qualifications in both instances); and both bodies have brought into play certain special regulations or processes which pass under the general name of closure.

Closure in the House of Commons takes three principal forms, i.e., simple closure, the "guillotine" (in the modified

British parliamentary oratory in general, see H. Graham, *Mother of Parliaments,* Chap. xii; H. Lucy, *Lords and Commoners,* Chap. iv; and J. Johnston, *Westminster Voices; Studies in Parliamentary Speech* (London, 1928). It is generally agreed that the House of Lords sustains a higher level of debate than the House of Commons. There is more time; there is at least as much ability; and only the leaders participate. "In the Lords," remarks Sir Henry Lucy, "only the big men speak, and when they have had their say all is over." *Op. cit.,* 58. A suggestion of Prime Minister Baldwin in 1925 that the debates of the House of Commons be broadcast by radio met with an unfavorable response. It was felt that arguments would tend to be addressed to the listeners-in rather than to the House itself. The House of Lords has, however, so far yielded to modern invention as to install amplifiers for the benefit of its own members. On the general subject of debate in the House of Commons, see J. Redlich, *op. cit.,* III, 51-69, and T. E. May, *op. cit.* (13th ed.), Chap. xii.

The day of the old-style parliamentary orator has passed in the United States no less than in Britain. See R. Luce, *Congress, an Explanation,* 20.

form of closure by compartments), and the "kangaroo." The previous-question rule served reasonably well until toward the end of the nineteenth century. Then, however, it proved insufficient as a defense against peculiarly ingenious and persistent obstructionism indulged in by the Irish Nationalists, and in 1881 the House adopted a stronger device which in the following year found a place in the standing orders.[15] The Nationalists have disappeared from the scene. But the new "urgency" rule, recast in 1888, has been found too useful to be given up. "After a question has been proposed," it reads, "a member rising in his place may claim to move 'that the question be now put,' and unless it shall appear to the chair that such a motion is an abuse of the rules of the House, or an infringement of the rights of the minority, the question 'that the question be now put' shall be put forthwith and decided without amendment or debate." [16] Discussion may thus be cut off at any time—even while a member is speaking—and a vote precipitated. At least one hundred members must, however, have voted with the majority in support of the motion.[17]

Closure in this form worked very well when it was a matter merely of terminating debate upon a single question. But it, in its turn, proved inadequate when applied to large, complicated, and hotly contested measures. As early as 1887, when a highly controversial bill (the Crimes Act) relating to the administration of justice in Ireland was before the House, a more drastic procedure was brought into operation under which a motion might be made and carried that at a stipulated hour on a stipulated day the presiding officer should put any and all questions necessary to end debate on a bill, irrespective of whether every part of the measure had by that time been discussed. From the point of view of government leaders bent upon securing the passage of their bills, this was an effective and useful

[15] For instances of obstructive methods as far back as 1641, see J. Redlich, *op. cit.*, I, 138 note. The story of Irish obstructionism and its repression is told admirably in Pt. ii, Chap. ii, of the volume cited.

[16] Standing Order 26.

[17] In the House sitting as such, or in committee of the whole; twenty in a standing committee. The rule was extended to standing committees in 1907. For a specific illustration of the workings of this form of closure, see *Parliamentary Debates* (*Commons*), 1924, Vol. CLXIX, col. 674.

device; and whereas it had been invented purely as an extraordinary remedy for an extraordinary state of affairs, the tendency was to bring it into play with increasing frequency and as merely a normal means of speeding up the work of the House. Its drastic features, however, won for it the sobriquet "guillotine," and it could hardly have been expected to be popular with the rank and file of the members; besides, experience showed that it was likely to result in the earlier clauses of a bill being considered at length and the later ones not at all. When Gladstone's second home rule bill was before the House in 1893, therefore, a modified and considerably improved form was adopted, under which the House agreed in advance upon an allotment of time to the various parts of the measure, debate on each part being terminated when the appointed time arrived and a vote thereupon taken on that part. In this modified form of "closure by compartments," the guillotine became, during the quarter-century preceding the World War, a familiar feature of the ordinary procedure of the House, and was employed in connection with several great measures, e.g., the Education Bill of 1902 and the National Health Insurance Bill of 1911. Notwithstanding, however, that it at least had the merit of ensuring an opportunity for all major divisions of a bill to be debated, it showed various defects in practice [18] and never became really popular. During the war it was resorted to only once, and afterwards it fell into disuse for half a dozen years, being by some thought—though still standing in the rules—to have become obsolete. But in 1927 it was brought successfully into play in connection with the government's hotly opposed Trade Disputes and Trade Unions Bill; [19] in 1928-29

[18] One of them was that, owing to the fact that clauses continued to be forced through the House of Commons without examination or discussion, amendments frequently had to be inserted during the debates in the House of Lords.

[19] On the nature of this measure, see pp. 516-519 below. After debate on the bill had proceeded fruitlessly for a time, Mr. Baldwin declared that the government, even with its overwhelming majority, could not get the measure through the House in time to permit other necessary business to be transacted unless closure was resorted to. The time-table adopted for the purpose allowed twelve additional days for debate at the committee stage (each of the bill's eight clauses to be granted a given period of time, ending with a vote), three days more for report stage, and one day for third read-

it was employed in committee stage of the Derating and Local Government Bill;[20] and it is fair to assume that it will be resorted to now and then on future occasions. As a device for expediting the handling of complicated measures which are vigorously opposed, it is too useful to be given up, even though the parties and members hostile to a bill in behalf of which it is employed can usually be depended on to resist it to the bitter end. It is interesting to observe that debate is very frequently limited on somewhat similar lines in the American House of Representatives by advance agreements on the amount of time during which discussion shall be allowed to continue on a given bill or part thereof.

The third form of closure—that nicknamed the "kangaroo"—arose from occasional authorization of the speaker (and chairman of committees) by the House to pick out for discussion from the amendments proposed for any motion, schedule, or clause of a bill those which he deemed most appropriate for discussion; whereupon those particular amendments could be debated, and no others. The chair was thus supposed to hop, kangaroo fashion, from amendment to amendment. In 1919 kangaroo closure was regularized by a standing order (27A) making the selection of proposed amendments for debate a permanent, and no longer a specially granted, function of the chair. The device saves much time, although it imposes heavy responsibilities on the presiding officer.[21]

ing. The Labor members were so incensed that they marched out of the House in a body, returning, however, on the following day. Closure by compartment was also utilized in connection with an unemployment insurance bill in 1927.

[20] See p. 645 below. Thirteen days were allotted to committee stage—an altogether inadequate period of time, it was objected by the bill's opponents, seeing that the measure was equivalent in length, complexity, and importance to four or five ordinary bills of first-rate moment. For a trenchant criticism by an expert adviser on the bill, see *Manchester Guardian* (weekly ed.), Dec. 28, 1928, 517.

[21] On the general subject of closure in the British Parliament, see A. L. Lowell, *Government of England,* I, Chap. xv; W. R. Anson, *Law and Custom of the Constitution* (5th ed.), I, 275-280; T. E. May, *op. cit.* (13th ed.), Chap. xiii; J. Redlich, *op. cit.,* I, 133-212; and H. Graham, *Mother of Parliaments,* 158-172. For a brief explanation of closure procedure in the American Congress, see F. A. Ogg and P. O. Ray, *Introduction to American Government* (3rd ed.), 406-413, and for a fuller account, L. Rogers, *The American Senate* (New York, 1926), Chap. v.

Votes and Divisions

When debate upon the whole or a portion of a measure ends, a vote is taken. It may or may not involve what is technically known as a "division." The speaker (or chairman, in committee of the whole) puts the question to be voted on and calls for the ayes and noes. He announces the apparent result, and if his statement of it is not challenged, the vote is so recorded. If, however, there is objection, the order "clear the lobby" is given,[22] electric bells in every portion of the building are set ringing, policemen in the corridors cry "division," and members come pouring in from smoking room, library, and restaurant, the more leisurely ones being urged along by the whips of their party in order that when the prescribed two-minute period has elapsed the party will be able to muster its full strength. At the end of the interval the speaker or chairman puts the question a second time in the same form. If, as is practically certain to be the case, the announced result is again challenged, the chair orders the members to the "division lobbies." The ayes pass into a small room to the speaker's right and the noes into a similar one to his left, and all are counted and their votes recorded as they file back to their places in the chamber.[23] The

[22] This requires the emptying of the "strangers'" seats behind the bar, but does not affect the galleries.

[23] It should be added, however, that while still in the lobbies the members have filed before tables at which sit clerks with members' lists, arranged alphabetically, and they have been checked off as voting aye or no. These "division lists" appear in the minutes on the following day and of course go into the permanent records, so that it is always possible to ascertain how any member voted in any division.

One of the oddities of the House is the rule that, whereas ordinarily a member speaking must stand, with bared head, a member desiring to raise a point of order while a division is in progress must speak sitting and "covered," i.e., with hat on head. Laughable incidents occur when members who have left their own hats in the cloak-room are forced to borrow from their neighbors, often enough getting a headpiece that either balances precariously on the top of the head or comes down to the nose. A hard-pressed member has been known to keep within the rules by adorning himself with a cocked hat fashioned out of the "orders of the day." This bit of ritual, however, is probably on the point of disappearing. At all events, when in 1929 a Labor member asked whether a rule "so difficult, irksome, and practically impossible" might not be abandoned, particularly in view of the fact that women members find it a little difficult to borrow hats, the House cheered the suggestion and the speaker ventured the opinion that since the

counting is done by tellers, four in number, designated by the chair. If the government leaders construe the vote as one of "confidence," two government and two opposition whips will be named; otherwise, any members may be called upon. The result having been ascertained, the tellers advance to the table, bow to the chair in unison, and one of those representing the majority announces the outcome. Since 1907, a member may, if he likes, remain in the chamber and take no part in a division. One who expects to be out of reach for any length of time, however, is required by the whips of his party to be "paired" with a prospective absentee on the other side, such pairings being arranged from day to day either by the members involved or by the rival whips in conference.

This method of taking a division has undergone but little change since 1836. It is both fair and expeditious. The average time consumed is only ten minutes, which contrasts most favorably with the thirty to forty minutes required for a roll call in the American House of Representatives. Under Standing Order No. 30, adopted in 1888, and amended and strengthened in 1919, the speaker is empowered, in the event that he considers a demand for a division dilatory or irresponsible, to call upon the ayes and noes to rise in their places and be counted. But there is seldom need to resort to this variation from the established practice.

In the House of Lords, important questions are decided, as a rule, by division. When the question is put, the "contents," i.e., those members who desire to register an affirmative vote, repair to the lobby at the right of the throne, the "non-contents," i.e., those opposed to the proposal, take their places in the corresponding lobby at the left, and both groups are counted by tellers appointed by the presiding officer, two clerks also making a list of the contents and non-contents respectively as they reënter the room. A member may abstain from voting by taking his station on "the steps of the throne," technically considered outside the chamber; furthermore, he is entitled, if he wishes—as a member of the House of Commons is not—to

regulation requiring members to be hatless when they address the House had never been enforced in the case of women, he saw no reason why the rule that had been brought in question should be adhered to.

make a written statement of his dissent from any measure passed by the body and of his reasons for objecting. Until 1868, absent members were allowed to vote by proxy. That privilege, however,—obviously objectionable on many grounds—was then abolished by standing order, and it is not likely ever to be revived. No division can be taken unless as many as thirty members are present.[24]

Records

The earliest extant records of parliamentary proceedings are the "Rolls of Parliament," in six folio volumes, which consist of petitions for redress of grievances, notes on the replies, records of pleas held in the high court of Parliament, and other items, all belonging to the period 1278-1503. The journals of the House of Lords begin in 1509; those of the House of Commons in 1547, although the records for the last twenty-two years of the reign of Elizabeth have been lost. In earlier times the journals were encumbered—although often enlivened —by accounts of striking episodes and by notes on important speeches. In the seventeenth century, however, the clerks were restrained from reporting the debates, and the journals nowadays consist only of formal records of "votes and proceedings," i.e., of things done rather than things said. In earlier times reports and papers presented to the houses were included. But nowadays these are published separately and become part of the vast collection of parliamentary papers popularly known as "blue books."

Long after 1628, when the House of Commons forbade its clerks to take notes on speeches, no records of parliamentary debates were kept except such as were based on notes taken more or less surreptitiously and published in defiance or evasion of parliamentary orders. After a notable contest on the subject in 1771, the debates were reported with some regularity. But only after 1834 was provision made for the accommodation of reporters, and until somewhat after that date the records were fragmentary and inaccurate. Meanwhile, various compilations

[24] The methods of voting and taking divisions in the House of Commons are regulated in Standing Orders XXVIII-XXX, and in the House of Lords in Standing Orders XXIX-XXXVI. See T. E. May, *op. cit.* (13th ed.), Chap. xiv; J. Redlich, *op. cit.*, II, 233-239.

partially supplied the lack of systematic reports. The first was the "Parliamentary History," published in 1751, and carrying the record down to the Restoration in 1660. This was superseded and continued by William Cobbett's "Parliamentary History," which came down to 1803. This, in turn, was succeeded by Cobbett's "Parliamentary Debates," published as a running supplement to the *Weekly Political Register.* In 1809 both the *Register* and the "Debates" passed into the hands of the well-known printing firm of T. C. Hansard. The "Debates," in successive series, under different forms of management, and for years after the Hansard family had ceased to have any interest in the publication, continued until 1908; and the long succession of portly volumes is known to all students of English parliamentary history as "Hansard." Until 1877, the publication was a purely private enterprise, but at that time the government, with a view to greater fullness and accuracy, began to subsidize it. It, however, remained unofficial; and only in 1909 was the decision reached to replace it by an official publication—known as "Parliamentary Debates"—prepared by a staff of reporters in each house who were not connected with any newspaper or commercial publisher.[25] The records of each day's debates are now made up by these reporters, and, under the name of "Votes and Proceedings," are distributed in an unrevised form to members of the House of Commons by breakfast time of the succeeding day, although the more leisurely House of Lords does not permit its reports to be put into print until the members have had an opportunity to revise the proof sheets of their speeches. The journals of the two houses are made up from the Votes and Proceedings and are printed at the end of each session.[26]

[25] After somewhat similar preparatory experience, the Congress of the United States made provision for the official *Congressional Record* in 1873. See F. A. Ogg and P. O. Ray, *Introduction to American Government* (3rd ed.), 416-417.

[26] A sessional index is appended to the journal of each session, and a general index is published at intervals of about ten years. The general subject of publicity and publications is treated in J. Redlich, *op. cit.,* II, Chaps. ii-iii; C. Ilbert, *Parliament,* Chap. viii; H. Graham, *Mother of Parliaments,* Chap. xvi; and M. MacDonagh, *Pageant of Parliament,* II, Chap. ix. On the published collections of the statutes of the realm, see C. Ilbert, *Legislative Methods and Forms,* Chap. ii. P. W. Wilson, "Reporting Parliament and

Having thus seen something of the general manner in which Parliament carries on its work, we turn to examine a little more closely two of its major activities or functions, i.e., law-making and finance. The financial work of the two houses—levying taxes, authorizing loans, making appropriations—is often spoken of loosely as "legislative." It is not, however, strictly of that nature; and in any event it is carried on in a manner sufficiently different from the mode of general legislation to call for independent treatment. Accordingly we shall deal first, and separately, with the handling of public measures which are not money bills, and later (in the succeeding chapter) with the method of preparing and passing revenue and appropriation measures. Meanwhile, however, in the present chapter, something will also be said about the way in which the houses dispose of the scores of private bills that come before them every year.

Law-making Power and Procedure

It will be recalled that Parliament originally had no power to make laws. That power belonged exclusively to the king, and the most that either house, as such, could do was to petition the crown for laws of specified character or on stipulated subjects. The king complied or refused as he chose; and even when he nominally complied, the new law often turned out to be very unlike what had been asked for. This led to demand, especially by the House of Commons, for a share in the work of law-making; and gradually, as we have seen, the demand was met, until at last, by the fifteenth century, the two houses became (whatever else they were besides) full-fledged legislative bodies, formulating and introducing bills, giving these bills successive "readings," referring them to committees, voting on them, and finally sending them to the king, no longer in the guise of humble requests, but as completed measures to which

Congress," *N. Amer. Rev.*, Sept., 1921, is an informing article, and a readable history of the long battle between Parliament and the press is M. MacDonagh, *The Reporters' Gallery* (London, no date). The publications of the British government—issued through His Majesty's Stationery Office—are famous for their quantity and quality, and for their wide use in Britain and in other lands. They are easily obtainable in the United States through the British Library of Information, 5 East 45th St., New York City.

his full and prompt assent was respectfully requested.[27] Long ago it became true that any sort of measure upon any conceivable subject might be introduced, and, if a sufficient number of members of both houses were so minded, enacted into law. No measure might become law until it had been submitted to both houses; and this is still the case, even though under the terms of the Parliament Act it is now easy for money bills, and not impossible for most other kinds of bills, to be made law without the assent of the House of Lords.

Definite procedures for the handling of bills of various kinds grew up early, although always, of course, subject to modification as new conditions developed or needs arose. As matters now stand, a bill, in the ordinary course of things, is introduced in one house, put through three readings, sent to the other house, carried there through the same routine, deposited with the House of Lords to await the royal assent,[28] and, after having been approved, is given its place among the statutes of the realm. Bills, as a rule, may be introduced in either house, by a spokesman of the government or by a private, i.e., a non-ministerial, member. Certain classes of measures, however, may originate in one only of the two houses, e.g., money bills in the House of Commons and judicial bills in the House of Lords. Furthermore, as we shall see, the leadership and control of the ministers have come to be such that both the number and the importance of private members' bills have been reduced to insignificant proportions, while the chances that such bills will be passed, in case they deal with large or controversial matters, have almost completely vanished.[29] The procedure of the two chambers upon bills is broadly the same, although, as is illustrated by the fact that

[27] In theory, of course, it is still from the king that all legislation proceeds, as is illustrated by the enacting clause with which every non-financial parliamentary statute of a public character begins: "Be it enacted by the King's most Excellent Majesty, by and with the advice and consent of the Lords Spiritual and Temporal and Commons, in this present Parliament assembled, and by the authority of the same, as follows . . ." For the corresponding formula used in finance measures, see J. Redlich, *op. cit.,* II, 254 note.

[28] Except that money bills, after having their inning in the House of Lords, return to the custody of the House of Commons.

[29] See pp. 452 ff. below.

amendments may be introduced in the Lords at any stage but in the Commons at only stipulated stages, the methods of conducting business in the more leisurely upper house are more elastic than those prevailing in the over-worked popular branch.

The process of converting a public bill, whether introduced by the government or by a private member, into an act of Parliament is long and intricate; usually it is spread over several weeks, or even months—occasionally, indeed, years, although in the latter case the bill will have to be introduced afresh at least a time or two in order to be kept alive.[30] The numerous stages that must be gone through have been found to be useful or indispensable, either as devices of convenience or as safeguards against hasty and ill-considered action. Some of them, it is true, have become mere formalities, involving neither debate nor vote, and the process—especially since certain changes were made in 1919—is decidedly more expeditious than it once was. On the whole, the work of law-making is, however, still slow, and, as will be pointed out, much thought continues to be given to modes of speeding it up, or at all events relieving the House of Commons of the excessive pressure of business under which, as everyone agrees, it still labors.

Bill Drafting

The first step is, of course, the drawing up, or "drafting," of the bill itself. If it is a private member's measure, it is drafted by its sponsor, or by any one whom he may employ for the purpose. If it is a government bill, it is prepared by expert public draughtsmen in the office of the Parliamentary Counsel to the Treasury—lawyers expert in the quaint and often prolix legal verbiage which custom, disregardful of the patience and convenience of the man in the street, still requires to be employed.[31] Being, in this case, a measure on whose fate the fortunes of cabinet and of party may depend, all care will be

[30] By suspending the standing orders of both houses it is, however, possible, in grave emergency, to carry a measure through all of its stages within a single day. The Defense of the Realm Act of 1914 was enacted in this fashion.

[31] Parliamentary counsel for this purpose was first provided in connection with the Home Office in 1837. The present connection with the Treasury dates from 1869.

taken with not only its form but also its content. The minister in whose province it falls, or who for some other reason has been assigned the task, first prepares a rough outline, showing the main features of the project. Then the cabinet (which very likely has already discussed the general subject) scrutinizes the plan and makes such changes as it likes. Perhaps it sets up a committee of its members to ensure more thorough consideration. The crude sketch is elaborated into a fairly exact statement of points and principles. Then the official draughtsmen are called in to work up the measure in detail, using the written memoranda that have been handed them, but also conferring almost daily with the ministers. Finally the bill comes back into the hands of the cabinet in full array of numbered clauses, sections, and subsections, ready to be carried to the House and started on its hazardous journey. The expert service of the Parliamentary Counsel is, of course, designed to ensure that bills will be so drawn as to mean precisely what their sponsors want them to mean, and nothing else; and the end is so well attained that English statutes—in contrast with statutes generally in America, notwithstanding assistance rendered here by numerous bill-drafting bureaus—rank exceptionally high in orderliness and clearness. Despite all precautions, however, bills as they finally emerge from the rough and tumble of debate are frequently considerably less clear than when presented at the clerk's table. Much latitude is commonly left for judicial interpretation, and sometimes, e.g., in the case of the Education Act of 1902, it is discovered long after a statute has taken effect that it means something different from what had been supposed.[32]

[32] "Look at any act of Parliament; often it is a mass of unintelligible jargon. This may partly be the fault of the civil servant who drafted it, but it is more often the consequence of the way in which it has been hacked and cut about in its passage through the Legislature. . . . Even the best acts of Parliament leave room for, and indeed demand, the exercise of a considerable amount of discretion in their execution. Latitude of interpretation is necessarily very wide." Viscount Milner, in *Jour. of Public Admin.*, Apr., 1923, p. 88.

The drafting of public bills is described authoritatively in C. Ilbert, *Legislative Methods and Forms* (London, 1901), 77-79, and *The Mechanics of Law-Making* (New York, 1914), Chaps. i. iv-vi. The author of these books was for many years one of three officials in the Treasury who are

Stages in the Consideration of a Bill

The procedure of getting bills before the House of Commons is not as complicated as it used to be. Until 1902, it was necessary, in order to introduce a bill, to ask and obtain leave. Nowadays all that the member needs to do is to give notice of his intention to bring in a bill, which notice appears on the "orders of the day" (the daily printed agenda of proceedings in the House) and, when called upon by the speaker, to present his bill at the clerk's table without any ceremony.[33] The title of the bill is read aloud by the clerk—and the initial stage, i.e., "first reading," is over. The bill is then printed and placed on the calendar to await its turn to be called up. Occasionally, however, a minister, introducing an important measure, makes a brief explanation of it, one equally short speech in criticism being, in that event, allowed the other side. And once in a while a minister reverts to earlier usage by asking leave to introduce, thereby gaining an opportunity to make a long speech both explaining and defending the bill's contents. Considerable debate may follow; and of course the House must vote whether to grant or withhold the desired permission. The government majority can usually be depended upon to see that the request is granted, for refusal would mean a defeat for the ministry.

On a day fixed in advance by an order of the House, the introducer of the bill moves that it "be now read a second time;" and it is at this point that the battle between friends and foes of the measure really begins. The former explain and defend it in lengthy speeches; the latter criticize and attack it,

known respectively as the first, second, and third "parliamentary counsel." "The average number of bills prepared in the Parliamentary Counsel's office during the three years before 1925-1926 was 89, in addition to statutory rules and orders and amendments to private members' bills; and during the same period 20 consolidation bills were prepared. The number of statutory rules and orders prepared during the period was very considerable, including a large number of orders in council. . . ." T. L. Heath, *The Treasury*, 191-192. A. Russell, *Legislative and Other Forms* (2nd ed., London, 1928), is a handbook prepared primarily for use in the British colonies, but of much general interest.

[33] The paper deposited on the table may in fact be only a "dummy," i.e., a blank folded sheet of paper with merely the bill's title written on the outside. In such a case the bill itself is turned in afterwards at the Public Bill Office to be printed and circulated among the members.

usually ending by moving a hostile amendment. Sometimes the amendment states specific reasons why the second reading should not be proceeded with, but more frequently it runs simply, "that this bill be read a second time this day six months"—or some other time at which the House is expected not to be in session. The second form of amendment, equally with the first, has, of course, as its object the defeat of the bill. The debate on second reading is confined to the bill's aims, principles, and larger proposals. There is no point to discussing details until it appears whether the House is minded to enact any legislation of the kind at all, and any member who at this stage enters into the minutiæ of the measure further than is necessary to a consideration of its principles will be admonished or stopped by the chair. The debate ended, the motion is put. If the opposition prevails, the bill perishes; and while government bills almost always come through (failure to do so, being a government defeat, would be likely to upset the ministry), the mortality of private members' bills at this stage is very great. A bill which passes second reading is "committed," bringing it up against another and still higher hurdle.

Prior to 1907, the bill would normally have gone to Committee of the Whole. Nowadays it goes there if it is a money bill [34] or a bill confirming a provisional order, or if, on grounds of its exceptional importance or highly controversial nature, the House so directs; otherwise it goes to one of the five standing committees, the assignment being made, in accordance with certain principles, by the speaker. In any case, the opposition will have rushed in a number of amendments (which are set down in order on an "amendment paper") designed, if adopted, to make the measure something quite different from what was intended by its authors and to force them into a position where they will either have to accept a modified bill that they do not like or withdraw it from further consideration. Committee stage is, of course, the time for discussion of the bill in all its details, and one will not be surprised to learn that such discussion—interspersed, of course, with much business of

[34] In 1919 the rules were modified so as to permit money bills also to be considered by standing committees, although the change was made for one session only. See p. 445 below.

other kinds—frequently occupies weeks, or even months. After second reading a bill may, indeed, be referred to a select committee. This does not happen often, but when it does, a step is added to the process; for, after being returned by the select committee the measure goes, as it would have in any case, to the Committee of the Whole or to one of the standing committees. Eventually the bill—unless in the meantime withdrawn—is reported back to the House, amended or otherwise. If reported by a standing committee, or in amended form by the Committee of the Whole, it is considered by the House afresh and in some detail; otherwise the "report stage" is a mere formality. Nearly all bills require extended consideration at report stage; most of the big issues involved are again fought over, as they were at second reading and in committee, and alternative amendments may be offered of such character as to lead even to a recommittal.

Finally comes the "third reading." Although the fate of the bill has by now been pretty well settled and little can be said that has not been said before—perhaps a dozen times—the opposition is reluctant to give up, and a set debate ensues in which the principles of the bill are once more attacked and defended. No further changes, however, except of a purely verbal character, can be made;[35] the bill as it stands must either be adopted or rejected. The result, as we have indicated, is almost a foregone conclusion. The speaker puts the motion "that this bill be now read the third time;" the division is taken; and, the motion prevailing, the bill is considered to have passed, without any question of passage, as such, being put.[36]

The bill then goes to the House of Lords. Formerly, ministers or other members whose bills had passed the Commons carried them personally to the upper house, often at the head of a sort of triumphal procession of supporters. But since 1855 the method has been for the clerk of the one house to carry the measure to the bar of the other and there deliver it. What follows need not be related, because, as has been observed, procedure in the Lords is not markedly different from that in the

[35] If it is desired that any such be considered, the bill must go back to committee.

[36] J. Redlich, *op. cit.*, III, 85-99; T. E. May, *op. cit.* (13th ed.), Chap. XV.

Commons except in being simpler and, as a rule, speedier—mainly because the burden of responsibility for what is done rests more lightly upon the second chamber. Normally, measures of some importance, after being read twice, are considered in committee of the whole, referred to the standing committee for textual revision, reported back, and adopted or rejected. Many bills, however, are not actually referred to the revision committee. Select committees are occasionally brought into play. But ordinarily the Committee of the Whole, with or without help from the revision committee, serves all necessary purposes. Unlike the Commons, the Lords may amend a bill in its substance as well as its form at third reading; and further opportunity for debate is provided by a supplementary stage, dropped in the other chamber in 1856, i.e., the motion "that this bill do pass."

Adjustment of Differences Between the Houses

A bill which originated in the House of Commons is returned there from the House of Lords, and vice versa, whether or not it has been agreed to. If amendments have been added, the originating house may accept them, in which case the measure becomes law upon receiving the royal assent. But it may also, of course, reject them; and if both houses stand their ground, the bill fails. Two ways of overcoming disagreement have at times been resorted to with success. One is a conference between representatives of the two houses; the other is an exchange of written messages. A conference is a meeting of members, known as "managers," appointed by their respective houses—by "ancient rule," twice as many from the Commons as from the Lords. If it is designated a "free conference," the managers on behalf of the dissentient house present the reasons for their disagreement, and each group tries to bring the other around to its way of thinking, or, at all events, to hit upon a mode of getting the houses into agreement. If the conference is not "free," the statement of reasons is presented, but no argument is used or comment made. In any case, the proceedings are very formal; the representatives of the Lords sit, with hats on except when speaking; the Commoners stand, with heads bare.

Far, however, from establishing itself as an indispensable feature of parliamentary life, as has the somewhat similar conference committee in the procedure of the American Congress,[37] the British conference has practically become obsolete. There has not been a free conference since 1836; and as long ago as 1851 the houses, by resolution, decided to receive reasons for disagreement, or for insistence on amendments, in the form of messages, unless one house or the other should demand a conference.[38] So far as formal action goes, the method employed nowadays to bring the houses together is, therefore, the written message, drawn up by a committee of the house which sends it, and borne to the other house, as a rule, by the clerk; and messages may be exchanged *ad libitum.* Practically, however, any adjustments that are reached are likely to flow, not from this rather stilted procedure, but from informal discussion among the party leaders, sometimes itself involving conferences of an unofficial nature. The problem is one of considerable seriousness. Of course, under the Parliament Act it is no longer strictly necessary to bring the houses into agreement in order to accomplish legislation. As a matter of fact, however, it is only now and then, on subjects of exceptional importance, that law-making will take place without the assent of both houses; in the vast majority of cases the two must, in the nature of things, be brought to agree, or the bill fails. In view of this fact, and with the feeling that the existing methods are inadequate, the Conference on the Reform of the Second Chamber, presided over by Lord Bryce, recommended in its report, submitted in 1918, that the old method of the free conference be revived, the conference to consist of twenty members of each house appointed at the beginning of each parliament, with ten additional members of each house on the occasion of the reference of any particular bill.[39]

[37] A. C. McCown, *The Congressional Conference Committee* (New York, 1927).

[38] W. R. Anson, *Law and Custom of the Constitution* (5th ed.), I, 298. On the general subject, see T. E. May, *op. cit.* (13th ed.), Chap. xx.

[39] Cmd. 9038 (1918), p. 11. It may be noted that joint select committees are occasionally set up by the two houses for the investigation of a bill. A committee of this kind consists of the combined membership of select committees appointed by the respective houses, sitting usually under a chairman appointed from the Lords.

The Royal Assent

The houses having finally passed a bill in identical form, all that remains is the royal assent—indirectly and perfunctorily given, it is true, but still indispensable. The sovereign may, if he likes, extend it in person. But the thing is now actually done differently, in a manner which Sir Courtenay Ilbert describes vividly as follows: "The assent is given periodically to batches of bills, as they are passed, the largest batch being usually at the end of the session. The ceremonial observed dates from Plantagenet times, and takes place in the House of Lords. The king is represented by lords commissioners, who sit in front of the throne, on a row of armchairs, arrayed in scarlet robes and little cocked hats. . . . At the bar of the House stands the speaker of the House of Commons, who has been summoned from that House. Behind him stand such members of the House of Commons as have followed him through the lobbies. A clerk of the House of Lords reads out, in a sonorous voice, the commission which authorizes the assent to be given. The clerk of the crown at one side of the table reads out the title of each bill. The clerk of the parliaments on the other side, making profound obeisances, pronounces the Norman-French formula by which the king's assent is signified: 'Little Peddlington Electricity Supply Act. Le Roy le veult.' Between the two voices six centuries lie." [40]

Formerly, acts of Parliament were proclaimed by the sheriffs in the counties, but nowadays they are not announced to the public in any way whatsoever. Two copies of each measure are printed on special vellum, one to be preserved in the Rolls of Parliament, kept in the Victoria Tower, the other to be deposited in the Public Record Office.[41] The dutiful subject is presumed to know the law, and ignorance of it cannot be

[40] *Parliament,* 75-76. For a fuller account of the ceremony and its significance, see M. MacDonagh, *Pageant of Parliament,* II, Chap. iii. Cf. H. Lucy, *Lords and Commoners,* 62-63; J. Redlich, *op. cit.,* III, 106-109; T. E. May, *op. cit.* (13th ed.), 430-435.

[41] R. A. Roberts, "The Genesis of the Public Record Office," *Edinburgh Rev.,* Jan., 1927. The laws are, of course, eventually published officially, in the Statutes of the Realm, to which one or two stout volumes are added every year. Much of the bulkiest statutory output consists, however, not of new law, but of consolidation measures.

pleaded as an excuse for violation. But he is left to find out what it is as best he can.[42]

Private Bill Legislation

The foregoing account, be it emphasized, applies only to one general class of bills, i.e., public bills. For private bills there is—contrary to the situation in the American Congress—a different form of procedure. A public bill, as we have seen, is one which applies to the people generally, or at all events to a large proportion of them, as, for example, a measure introducing a system of old age pensions or one regulating the conditions of military service. A private bill, on the other hand, is (to quote the House of Commons *Manual of Procedure*) one whose object is "to alter the law relating to some particular locality, or to confer rights on or relieve from liability some particular person or body of persons." [43] The commonest source of private bills is the desire, perhaps of an individual, but more often of a municipality or a private corporation, to build or extend a railway, to construct a tramway, to provide a community with gas, electricity, or water, to erect a municipal

[42] The procedure of the House of Commons on public bills of a non-financial nature is described briefly in A. L. Lowell, *Government of England,* I, Chaps. xiii, xvii, xix; W. R. Anson, *Law and Custom of the Constitution* (5th ed.), I, 267-280; J. Redlich, *Procedure of the House of Commons,* III, 85-112; and T. E. May, *op. cit.* (13th ed.), Chap. xv. May's work, as periodically brought up to date in successive editions, is the standard detailed guide to the whole subject of British parliamentary procedure, but is lacking in the richly historical treatment to be found in Redlich. Annotated rules on public bill procedure are set forth in *Manual of Procedure of the House of Commons* (4th ed.), Chap. ix. C. Ilbert, *Legislative Methods and Forms* (London, 1901), and *The Mechanics of Law-Making* (New York, 1914), cover the subject fully and expertly. Procedure on public bills in a British dominion can be compared with procedure at Westminster by reading E. Porritt, *Evolution of the Dominion of Canada* (Yonkers, 1918), Chap. xiv. Procedure in the United States can be similarly compared by means of D. S. Alexander, *History and Procedure of the House of Representatives* (Boston, 1916). An illuminating historical and philosophical survey of English law-making is A. V. Dicey, *Lectures on the Relation between Law and Public Opinion in England during the Nineteenth Century* (London, 1905). On the general subject of English statutes, see P. H. Winfield, *The Chief Sources of English Legal History* (Cambridge, 1925), Chap. v.

[43] *Manual* (4th ed.), p. 139.

building, to lay out a cemetery, to dig a canal, to construct a system of sewerage, in short, to engage in undertakings which may or may not be for profit but which by their very nature involve limitation upon or interference with public or private (e.g., property) rights. Parliament alone can abrogate or abridge public or private rights; hence, when any of these, and many other, things are proposed, it is necessary to resort to that authority for the requisite permission. In the United States these matters—relating mainly, it will be observed, to franchises—are almost entirely in the control of the state legislatures or of subsidiary bodies like city councils. But in Britain, where there is nothing corresponding to our states, the national government has sole jurisdiction. A private bill can usually be recognized at a glance. Sometimes, however, there is room for doubt, in which case, under the British usage, it falls to the chair to decide how the bill shall be classified, and therefore how it shall be handled.

Every private bill must go through the same stages in the two houses as a public bill. That is to say, it must be presented in one house, read a first time, read a second time, referred to a committee, reported, read a third time, sent to the other house to be put through the same stages, and finally given the royal assent which transforms all bills into acts of Parliament. There are, however, certain special or additional features which do not apply in the case of public measures. In the first place, whereas a public bill can be presented in either house without any preliminary proceedings outside, a private bill cannot be presented until a petition for the given bill, together with a description of the proposed undertaking and an estimate of its cost, has been filed with (a) a bureau known as the Private Bill Office, and (b) the government department concerned with enterprises of the kind in hand (e.g., the Board of Trade in the case of a bill incorporating a gas company), and until, also, all persons affected (e.g., the owners or occupiers of any land that may be required for carrying out the proposed operation) have been duly notified. Each house has an official known as an examiner of petitions for private bills; and only after the examiner for a given house has certified that all these requirements have been complied with may the petition, with the bill attached, be introduced in that body.[44]

Once on the calendar, a private bill may slip through with little further attention. This, of course, depends on whether anybody is interested in opposing it. If objection does not arise, reference to a committee (of five members) on unopposed bills is a mere matter of form. If, however, some new principle is involved, a special committee may be called into play. And if there is opposition, the bill is referred to one of the rather numerous private bill committees set up in each house at every session—committees of four members each in the Commons and of five each in the Lords, named in each case by the Committee of Selection (which also distributes the bills) from lists prepared by the party whips. As a rule, each of these committees receives a considerable batch of bills; and no member of either house may serve on a committee to which it falls to consider any bill in which either he or his constituents have an interest.[45] Service on the committees is onerous, without giving much chance for distinction, and, by one means or another, many members contrive to evade it. Those unlucky enough to be drafted must, however, serve; for persistent neglect, the penalty may even be an involuntary sojourn in the clock tower.

Along a splendid up-stairs corridor in the palace of Westminster, paralleling and facing the Thames, is a series of nineteen numbered rooms for the use of private bill committees of the two houses. There on almost any day of the session, from noon until four o'clock, one may see several of the committees at work on their grist—the committee members sitting at a large table, barristers in wig and gown passing to and fro, witnesses being questioned or awaiting their turn, clerks and stenographers diligently keeping minutes, the walls covered with maps or plans designed to make more graphic the information

[44] Unless a sessional committee on standing orders, maintained by each house, recommends, in behalf of a particular bill, that certain of the technicalities be waived.

[45] It may be noted also that the private bills which are to be introduced at a given session are, in advance, divided into two approximately equal lots, one to go first to the House of Commons and the other to the House of Lords. The division is made in conference normally between the ways and means chairman of the Commons and the chairman of committees of the Lords.

or arguments being presented. The general aspect is that of a court-room; and indeed the proceedings, although aimed at legislation, are, in form and character, quasi-judicial; the committee members sit as judges; they hear evidence as presented by the promoters and opponents of the bill; they listen to speeches of rival counsel; and finally they adjudicate upon the merits of the undertaking. Occasionally the sittings are colorful. As a rule, however, they are pretty dull, being made so not only by the limited interest of the issues involved but by the prosiness of witnesses and the tediousness of counsel.

The first task is to decide, after evidence and argument, whether the object of the bill as set forth in the preamble is desirable. If the conclusion is negative, the hearing comes to an end and the bill is dropped. If it is affirmative, the measure is considered in detail; and at the end the committee reports it back to the House, favorably or unfavorably, and with or without amendments. If reported favorably, the bill's adoption by the House is practically assured; although if it encounters opposition in the other branch it will have to go through the same process there, and may even be brought to defeat.

It will have been surmised that the handling of private bills has little to do with party politics. That is as it should be. Whether the London and Northwestern Railway shall be permitted to build some new trackage or the borough of Bury St. Edmunds shall be empowered to operate a gas plant is not a proper matter on which to send Conservatives and Liberals into the division lobbies. The ministers bear no responsibility for private bill legislation; indeed, they rarely take any part in it. The British plan of handling all such business is based on the sensible idea that the thing to do is to secure careful, dispassionate, non-partisan examination of every project and to let the final decision be reached, in effect, by those who have heard the evidence and consulted with the experts. This is advantageous in another way besides promoting intelligent decisions. It vastly economizes the time of the two houses. In the American Congress, where private bills—"special bills," they are commonly termed with us—are introduced freely by any and all members and are dealt with under precisely the same forms of procedure as public bills, certain committees which receive the greatest volume of business are likely to be swamped. Consideration of important public bills is impeded, and the passage of some private measures and the pigeonholing of others becomes largely a matter of chance. The objection is raised against the English system that it is expensive; and it is true that in order to get a private bill through—or to defeat one—it is often necessary to hire highly-paid counsel,[46] to pay the travelling expenses of numerous witnesses, and to incur other costs, including a fee which is exacted whenever a private bill is introduced. It may usually be assumed, however, that the privilege sought is worth being paid for; otherwise it would not be sought. At all events, the advantages on other scores undoubtedly overbalance the defect, if it be one.

Confirming Provisional Orders

When, however, a municipality wants to extend a tramway system or erect a hospital it does not necessarily turn *directly* to Parliament for authorization. In many general statutes dealing with public health, transportation, poor relief, education, finance, and similar subjects Parliament has conferred upon the appropriate government department at London, or in some instances upon a suitable local authority, power to issue "orders" extending specified amounts and kinds of authority to both municipalities and private corporations. Not only that, but such departments and local authorities may anticipate future action of Parliament by issuing provisional orders, i.e., orders whose ultimate validity is contingent upon subsequent parliamentary confirmation. More and more use is, indeed, being made of such provisional orders. The petitioning individual or body gains by not being held up while awaiting parliamentary action, and Parliament gains, in time and labor, by placing the burden of investigation and tentative decision upon the government department. In such a case the two houses, as a rule, play only a perfunctory rôle. Provisional orders that have been issued by the departments are grouped each year into a series of "provisional orders confirmation bills," which commonly go through with no opposition, and therefore no debate, just as in the case

[46] Many able lawyers give most of their time to serving those who are seeking or opposing private bill legislation.

of unopposed private bills.[47] Should opposition develop, a bill to confirm must go to a special committee; and the houses may end by refusing assent to a grant which a department has provisionally made. Refusal, and even opposition, is, however, rare; and the increasing use made of the device of orders has, by appreciably lessening the number of private bills to be considered, contributed by so much to a solution of the urgent problem of saving the time, especially of the members of the House of Commons, for consideration of bills of public, nationwide interest.[48]

[47] It has been computed that in forty years less than one per cent of such orders have been disapproved by Parliament.

[48] Order-issuing powers have been conferred extensively in the United States upon such federal agencies as the Interstate Commerce Commission and the Federal Trade Commission, and upon such state agencies as public utility, industrial, health, and other commissions and boards. A system of provisional orders is, however, not practicable in this country because of the extreme uncertainty, under our form of government, whether the legislature will be sufficiently harmonious with the executive to ratify the actions which the latter has taken. See W. B. Munro, *Governments of Europe,* 186. The adoption of something like the British system of provisional orders is, however, advocated in R. Luce, *Congress; an Explanation,* 145-147, as a means of relieving Congress and other legislatures of a portion of their present burden of business.

On the general subject of private bill legislation and the system of orders, see *Standing Orders of the House of Commons* (London, 1927), 61-268; A. L. Lowell, *Government of England,* I, Chap. XX; C. Ilbert, *The Mechanics of Law-Making,* 132-149; T. E. May, *op. cit.* (13th ed.), Chaps. xxvi-xxix; M. MacDonagh, *Book of Parliament,* 398-420, and *The Pageant of Parliament,* II, Chap. xv. The standard treatise on the subject is F. Clifford, *A History of Private Bill Legislation,* 2 vols. (London, 1885-87). Provisional orders are specially treated in May, *op. cit.,* Chap. xxxi.

Mention may be appended of a volume issued so recently that the present writer has not had an opportunity to see it, i.e., G. F. M. Campion, *An Introduction to the Procedure of the House of Commons* (London, 1929).

CHAPTER XVIII

PARLIAMENT AT WORK: FINANCE

From the description of parliamentary procedure thus far given one main form or type of public bill has intentionally been omitted, i.e., the bill which has to do with the fiscal interests and operations of the government. For such "money bills" there is a special procedure, by no means entirely different from the procedure employed for other public measures, yet sufficiently distinctive to call for consideration apart. It was, as a recent writer has remarked, around taxation that the historic battle of securities for good government and the liberty of the subject was fought and won; and revenue and expenditure are still, by all odds, the most important matters with which the people's representatives at Westminster have to do.

Four tasks, in all, Parliament, as dual guardian of the national well-being and the taxpayers' interests, is called upon to perform: (1) to determine the sources from which, and the conditions under which, the national revenues shall be raised; (2) to grant the money estimated by the ministers to be necessary to carry on the government, and to appropriate these grants to specific purposes; (3) to criticise, in debate, the manner in which the funds are spent; and (4) to see that the accounts of the spending authorities are properly scrutinized and audited. No taxes may be laid without express parliamentary sanction, and no public money may be expended without similar authority, conferred either in annual or other formal appropriation acts or in permanent statutes. Furthermore, the ministers are constantly subject to interrogation on the floor of Parliament concerning the use of public money under their direction; and the accounts of the spending departments and officers are minutely audited—not only by the Comptroller and Auditor-General but by a parliamentary committee, i.e., the Committee on Public Accounts—to make certain that the money voted by Parliament for a particular service has been spent upon that service and upon no other.[1]

Such are the fundamental conditions under which the all-important power of the purse is now exercised, not only in Britain, but in all parts of the world in which English principles of representative government have taken root. The thing in which we are interested here is the way in which Parliament—mainly, of course, the House of Commons—goes about voting taxes and expenditures; that is, the methods of financial, as distinguished from other, legislation. This will best appear if we trace the order of procedure, step by step, first for appropriation bills and afterwards for bills designed to raise the requisite revenue.

The Estimates of Expenditure

We take expenditures first because that is what the government itself does; certainly it is not illogical to find out what is going to be spent before trying to decide how much money to raise or how to go about raising it. The first step, then, in making financial arrangements for a given fiscal year is to prepare the estimates of expenditure. Parliament, however, as we have seen, does not have to make fresh provision for all expenditures every twelve months. Outlays for support of the royal establishment, the salaries and pensions of judges, interest on the national debt, the public expense of conducting parliamentary elections (since 1918), and other Consolidated Fund services or charges, while initially authorized and at all times alterable by Parliament, go on from year to year until changed by new enactment;[2] and this takes care of a considerable, though minor, part of the annual national disbursement.[3] The estimates of which we are here speaking are, rather, for the "supply services"—principally the army, navy, air, and civil services—provision for which is made for but a single year at a

[1] We say "Parliament," be it noted; because, although the House of Commons long ago gained priority, and in 1911 an absolute control, in public finance, no money bill can even yet become law until the House of Lords has at least been given an opportunity to take action upon it.

[2] See p. 170 above.

[3] In 1925-26, a total of £398,149,777.

time. They apply to outlays which, in amount if not in general purpose, are matters of discretion, or policy, and hence are, and should be, subject to frequent readjustment. It is an inflexible rule that every request for an appropriation shall be submitted to Parliament in the form of an "estimate," i.e., a written statement showing precisely how much money is expected to be needed for a designated purpose, together with a request that the stipulated sum be granted for the purpose specified.

How are the estimates got ready for Parliament's attention? First of all, matters of general policy that might entail large changes of expenditure, e.g., a housing program, an increase of the army, a naval base at Singapore, are threshed out in conferences between the officers of the Treasury and representatives of the departments concerned, and also, in the case of matters as important as those mentioned, in cabinet discussions. The departments thus get a reasonably definite idea of how far the Treasury is willing to go in support of their projects, and of what outlays can be planned without risk of cabinet disapproval. On October 1 preceding the fiscal year for which the estimates are to be prepared (beginning the following April 1) the Treasury sends a circular letter to all officials responsible for estimates requesting them to make up and submit estimates of the expenses of their departments, offices, or services, in the coming year. All are asked to plan as economically as possible, and in particular are admonished not to adopt the easy method of simply taking the estimates of the past year as the starting point for those of the next. The responsible officers of the departments thereupon set their staffs to compiling and entering figures, using the forms sent out from the Treasury on which comparative data have already been entered. At all stages of the work close contact is maintained with the Chancellor of the Exchequer and other Treasury officials; the rules, indeed, require that, in so far as possible, additions, omissions, or other alterations of the existing arrangements shall be referred to the Treasury before the departmental proposals as a whole are formally presented. If the Treasury demurs, the department may appeal to the cabinet. But such appeals are rarely made unless the question is one of exceptional importance; and there is a strong presumption that the cabinet will back up the Treasury in any position that it takes. The result is, as one writer puts it, that the estimates, when finally submitted by the departments, "represent little more than the statement of proposals that have already been agreed upon between the various submitting departments and the Treasury."[4] The sum total of these estimates as finally approved by the Treasury, added to the provision required for Consolidated Fund services, gives the expenditure which will have to be met out of the revenue for the year if no deficit is to be incurred.

Ordinarily, all estimates of expenditure, in complete form, are in the Treasury's hands by January 15; whereupon the estimates clerk, making sure that there is nothing in them which the Treasury has not approved, has them printed in three huge quarto volumes. No estimate from a governmental source can by any chance reach Parliament unless it has the Treasury's endorsement. And this is as good a point as any at which to note the very important further fact that no request or proposal, from *any* source, looking to a charge upon the public revenue will be received or given attention in Parliament unless the outlay is asked or supported by the crown, which in effect means the Treasury. This rule, first adopted in 1706 as a defense against a flood of private members' petitions in behalf of persons claiming back pay as officers or making some similar demand, became a standing order in 1713 and was brought up to date in 1852 and 1860.[5] It totally prevents private members

[4] W. F. Willoughby *et al., Financial Administration of Great Britain* (New York, 1917), 61. It must not be inferred, however, that the Treasury's rôle is an easy one. A generation ago the burden of proof rested so clearly on the spending departments that the Treasury officials could refuse applications almost without giving reasons. Nowadays, however, the onus is rather on the Treasury to justify its refusal; "the hand of every man is against the Treasury." Well might a permanent secretary once aver that he "couldn't sleep o' nights for thinking of the defenseless condition of the British taxpayer!" The most convenient account of the preparation and submission of the estimates is Chap. iii of the volume mentioned above.

[5] Standing Order 66. The rule reads as follows: "This House will receive no petition for any sum relating to public service, or proceed upon any motion for a grant or charge upon the public revenue, whether payable out of the Consolidated Fund or out of money to be provided by Parliament, unless recommended from the crown." Prominent among the motives for adopting the principle originally was the desire to prevent the crown

from introducing appropriation bills or resolutions, i.e., from moving that a specific sum be granted for a specific purpose; although it is not construed to prohibit non-ministerial resolutions favoring or opposing some specified kind of expenditure on general principles; and it averts most of the evils which are associated in the United States with the idea of the congressional "pork-barrel." [6] The House of Commons can determine the amount of money that will be granted and the sources from which the money shall be drawn. But it has denied itself the privilege of deciding whether any money shall be granted at all, unless the proposal for a grant emanates from the crown.

Authorization of Expenditures by Parliament

Parliament opens a new session at the end of January or the beginning of February, and as a rule the estimates of expenditure, in accordance with formal announcement made in the Speech from the Throne, are presented during the first two weeks thereafter—the estimates for the civil service and revenue departments by the Financial Secretary to the Treasury, those for the army, the navy, and the air force by the Secretary of State for War, the First Lord of the Admiralty, and the Minister for Air, respectively. On an early day, agreed upon at the beginning of the session, the House resolves itself into Committee of Supply, which, as has been explained, is a committee of the whole, sitting under the presidency of the chairman of committees. From the reign of James I until 1912, the estimates of expenditure could be considered only in Committee of Supply; and although, as will be pointed out, provision was made in the year indicated for reference of some of them to a select committee, this arrangement was not very successful, and consideration in committee of the whole went on practically as before. Similarly, reference made experimentally to a standing committee in 1919 failed to establish itself as a regular practice. So that, nowadays, the estimates are once more handled exclusively in Committee of Supply; and after

from obtaining supplies surreptitiously, without incurring responsibility for either the requests made or the mode of expenditure. On the significance of this and other general principles underlying Parliament's handling of finance, see J. Redlich, *Procedure of the House of Commons,* III, 114-124.

[6] See p. 441 below.

the committee has engaged in a brief preliminary debate on "grievances"—which was once important, but is meaningless now that Parliament holds the remedy for grievances in its own hands—the estimates are taken up for such scrutiny as time permits, and with a view to the adoption of resolutions which can be reported back to the House as the basis for appropriation bills. Twenty days only are allowed for the purpose, scattered through the session; and under the present rules this business is made the first order of the day on Thursday of successive weeks.[7]

The estimates are considered in separate groups termed "votes"—some one hundred and fifty in all—corresponding as closely as possible to distinct services, and divided into subheads and items to facilitate rapid scrutiny and definite discussion.[8] Each "vote" becomes the basis of a "resolution of supply," which is adopted in committee and duly reported to the House. There is not time to consider all the votes before April 1; and yet the government must have authority by that date to spend something under practically every vote.[9] Accordingly, the first thing done is to pass resolutions giving the government provisional authority to spend a limited sum under every vote, without committing Parliament to grant, at the end, the total amount asked for. This provisional authority is known as a "vote on account." In the cases of the civil service and the army, sums are allowed under every vote which are calculated to be sufficient to carry the services along for four and a half or five months. In the cases of the navy and the air force, one or two of the larger votes are put through in full, which suffices for a time for the entire service, inasmuch as in each of these establishments money granted under one vote can be employed under any of the other votes—that is to say, can be used for the navy or air force as a whole as long as the sum holds out. In this way the government finds itself on April 1 armed with provisional authority to spend on the supply services sums sufficient to last until about the following August, when the session

[7] Standing Order 67.

[8] On the character and form of the estimates, see W. F. Willoughby *et al*, as cited, Chap. iv.

[9] Unused portions of grants for the previous year lapse on March 31.

will end. Legally, the authority is strictly provisional; no appropriations, in the proper sense of the word, have yet been made, and the resolutions that have been passed will have no validity beyond the end of the session.

This authority to spend does not of itself carry authority actually to draw the money from the Consolidated Fund. This particular authority comes by virtue of resolutions passed in another committee of the whole, known as the Committee of Ways and Means, whose function is two-fold: (1) to authorize issues from the Consolidated Fund, and (2) to consider proposals for raising money, whether by taxes or by loans. At an early stage of the session the House also begins to sit from time to time as Committee of Ways and Means; and by April 1, when the government must begin to draw upon the Exchequer for the expenses of the new fiscal year, the committee has reported to the House resolutions "granting ways and means" (including provisions for necessary temporary borrowing) which have been incorporated in a bill and passed as a Consolidated Fund (No. 1) Act. The "ways and means" thus granted regularly equal the total of the votes of supply thus far provisionally adopted.[10]

Accordingly, the government enters upon the fiscal year with (1) expenditures authorized in amounts adequate—barring the unexpected—to carry the services up to August, and (2) access to funds sufficient to last to the same approximate date. It remains to fill out the fiscal schedule, so to speak, and make it definitive for the entire year. And to this task the Committee of Supply, the Committee of Ways and Means, and finally the House proper devote themselves from time to time throughout the remainder of the session. In the case of the estimates of expenditure, it is simply a matter of continuing consideration of them with a view to fixing the final and exact amounts to be allowed. One or two further Consolidated Fund acts are likely to be passed, between April and August, giving the government further access to funds; and at the very end of the

[10] Together with any supplementary votes that may have become necessary for the expiring year and any excess votes for the previous year. See *Manual of Procedure in the Public Business of the House of Commons* (4th ed.), 178-183.

session, after ways and means for the year have been definitely determined, all such measures that have been enacted are gathered into a general Consolidated Fund (Appropriation) Act, commonly known simply as the Appropriation Act, which (1) prescribes the appropriation of all sums carried by the votes in supply, and (2) authorizes the issue of a sum from the Exchequer equal to the total of these votes and gives the Treasury temporary borrowing powers up to the whole of the amount. Standing Order 15 requires that consideration of the estimates of supply shall be completed not later than August 5. At no time while these estimates are under consideration can a private member move an increase in a vote, for to do so would violate the rule which requires all proposals for expenditure to emanate from the crown. Such a member may, however, move a reduction. The Committee of Supply can vote the grant asked of it in full, reduce it, or refuse it altogether. It cannot increase it, annex a condition, or alter its destination; although it may be able to induce the government to introduce a revised estimate. Since, as has been noted, the rules of the House allow only twenty days in all for the debates in Committee of Supply, it invariably happens that most of the time is consumed on a few "votes," not necessarily the most important ones, and that many are passed with only the most perfunctory scrutiny and with no discussion whatever.[11]

The Estimates of Revenue

All this, however, tells only a part of the story of how arrangements for a coming fiscal year are made. It is true that the first thing undertaken is to compile estimates of expenditure. But this work will not have been going on long before attention will be directed also to the matter of probable revenue;

[11] Three "allotted" days, however, may be added by vote of the House, with consent of the government. In times of emergency, such as war, actual or threatened, recourse may be had to a "vote of credit." In such a case the crown asks for a grant of money in general terms, it being impossible at the moment to furnish (as in an ordinary estimate) a detailed statement of the manner in which it will be spent; and Parliament, by acceding to the request, in effect places the money at the disposal of the executive to be spent at the discretion of the latter on any object within the terms of the vote. W. R. Anson, *Law and Custom of the Constitution* (5th ed.), I, 289.

and even before the estimates of outlay reach the Treasury in their matured form they are not unlikely to have been trimmed down because the word has been passed around that the funds in sight will not bear such charges as were originally contemplated. For the estimates of revenue the Treasury is responsible, even more directly and completely than for estimates of expenditure; from first to last they are the handiwork of Treasury officials. While the multifold and scattered spending offices are at work on their figures for the coming year, the revenue departments in the Treasury—chiefly customs and excise, inland revenue, and post-office—are making the best guesses that they can as to the amount that each source, e.g., land taxes, the income tax, stamp duties, death duties, the postal service, and what not, will yield, and the Chancellor of the Exchequer and his assistants are balancing off prospective outgo against prospective income and working out plans by which, if given parliamentary approval, ends can probably be made to meet. If, by happy chance, the revenues promise to exceed what will be required, the Chancellor (in consultation with the cabinet) may decide to recommend a lowering of the income tax, or of the tea duty, or even the remission of certain taxes altogether. But if, as is much more likely to be the case, the outgo promises to mount higher than the income, even after all feasible economies have been provided for, it becomes necessary to decide what existing taxes shall be pushed upward, and how far, and what new imposts, if any, shall be laid. In reaching these decisions the ministers may be actuated, of course, not solely by the desire to raise more money, but by the purpose to shift the tax burden in this direction or that, in the interest of social or economic changes which they have at heart. Indeed, the whole policy of a government may be wrapped up in the tax proposals that it carries to the House of Commons.[12]

[12] One recalls in this connection the tax proposals embodied in the historic Lloyd George budget of 1909. Other illustrations include the repeal of the corn laws, the revival of income taxes, and the general adoption of free trade during the period 1841-60. See F. A. Ogg and W. R. Sharp, *Economic Development of Modern Europe* (New York, 1926), 251-256. Had Premier Baldwin's protectionist proposals won at the general election of 1923, the scheme of taxation which they contemplated would presently

The Budget

Early in the session at which the estimates are to be considered comes one of the big occasions in the parliamentary history of the year, i.e., "budget night." [13] The House of Commons resolves itself into committee of the whole on ways and means; and, with a huge pile of carefully arranged typewritten documents before him—the benches being crowded with members and the galleries with spectators—the Chancellor of the Exchequer unfolds the government's proposals. He reviews the finances of the recent past, tells what outlays are to be provided for and what revenue is to be expected, touches on the condition of the national debt, and then, to an audience growing in eagerness (it already knew, at least in a general way, about these things, but it has hardly an inkling of what is now to come) discloses the increases or decreases of old taxes and the nature and extent of the new taxes provided for in the government's fiscal program. Small wonder that the "budget speech" is always interesting, sometimes surprising, and occasionally startling. Rarely in times past did the speech consume less than three hours; sometimes it ran to twice that length. "Spoke 5-9 without great exhaustion," recorded Gladstone in his diary following his budget speech of 1860, "aided by a large stock of egg and wine. Thank God! Home at 11. This was the most arduous operation I have ever had in Parliament." Inasmuch as the Great Commoner was called upon to introduce, or "open," at one time or another, thirteen different annual budgets, it was well for him, as for his hearers, that he had the knack, as some one once remarked, of "setting figures to music." [14]

Nowadays, the budget speech is likely to be shorter, because

have made its official appearance in connection with the government's estimates, i.e., in the annual budget.

It may be noted here that while this book was in press the Baldwin government took the extraordinary and unprecedented step of entirely remitting the duty on tea (April, 1929).

[13] Speaking of this "political high-water mark" of the session, Redlich says: "Pitt made it what it ever since has been, the most important scene in the drama of government." *Op. cit.*, III, 144-145.

[14] It was, indeed, his celebrated budget speech of 1853, lasting five hours, that first gave him a place in the foremost ranks of British statesmen. See S. Buxton, *Gladstone as Chancellor of the Exchequer* (London, 1901).

it has come to be only a general announcement, or explanation, preliminary to placing the budget itself, in printed form, in the hands of the members. Filling, as a rule, only a few printed pages, the document known technically as the budget does not look very formidable.[15] It is buttressed, however, by masses of statistical and other matter that challenge the industry of any person who would really comprehend it. The essence of a budgetary system is, of course, the careful consideration, at one and the same time, or at least in their relations to each other, of both sides of the national account, first by those whose business it is to initiate fiscal proposals, and afterwards by the legislature that votes them; and in the House of Commons the proposals relevant to revenue (including loans) are dealt with, not only by the same general procedure as those for expenditures, but throughout the same general period of time. The proposals are debated serially in committee of the whole (i.e., Committee of Ways and Means) and, after adoption—as originally proposed, or as amended—in the form of resolutions, are reported to the House and passed as bills. Private members may not move new taxation, although they may move to reduce taxes which the government has not planned to alter, or to repeal them altogether. A further interesting feature of the system is that, formerly by mere custom but since 1913 by law, increased or otherwise altered income, customs, and excise taxes proposed in the budget speech, and tentatively approved in ways and means resolutions passed immediately, become operative on the morning following the delivery of the speech. If the proposals are not definitely adopted within a period of four months, the money collected has, of course, to be returned to those who paid it. Only very rarely, however, does this situation arise. The practice is a striking illustration of the strong presumption that exists in favor of the actual carrying out of

[15] Historically and accurately, the term denotes only the Chancellor's exposition of the state of the finances and the measures rendered necessary thereby—in other words, the Chancellor's speech. In everyday parlance, however, it is often applied to the whole annual plan of finance. The word is derived from *budge,* an obsolete term for a small bag, and seems to have come into use in the early eighteenth century. A pamphlet of 1733 entitled *The Budget Opened* satirically pictures Robert Walpole, when explaining his financial program, as a quack doctor opening a bag filled with medicines and charms. "Opening the budget" is still a common phrase.

whatever proposals, especially in the domain of finance, the government carries to the floor of the Commons.

Appropriation Act and Finance Act

The results of the whole fiscal operation as described finally emerge in two great statutes, i.e., the Appropriation Act, already mentioned, and the Finance Act. The first of these, as we have seen, definitely authorizes all of the grants that have been made for the services to be paid out of the Consolidated Fund; and it is passed by the House on the basis of resolutions reported back to it partly from the Committee of Supply, and partly also from the Committee of Ways and Means. The Finance Act, based upon resolutions reported from the Committee of Ways and Means, reimposes existing taxes at the rates newly agreed upon, remits taxation if it has been so decided, and provides such new or additional revenues as the necessities of the situation require. As in the case of appropriations, taxes are not freshly authorized in full every year. Indeed, whereas most expenditures are thus authorized, most taxes are not, being based on permanent statutes which are always subject to repeal or alteration but do not need to be renewed annually.[16] Thus, death duties, stamp duties, most customs duties, and certain excises are imposed by continuing statutes. For many years the imposts that were regularly reserved for annual readjustment, with a view to balancing the budget, were the tea duty and the income tax—the one an indirect levy resting on the mass of the people and the other a direct tax regarded as levied upon property. In the early years of the present century, however, it became the usual thing to deal with the customs duties on tobacco, beer, and spirits, and with the corresponding excise taxes on beer and spirits, in the same fashion. In earlier times it was the habit to include in the Finance Act only the provisions for the annual and temporary taxes; the permanent taxes, and special arrangements regarding particular taxes,

[16] Something like sixty per cent of the total yield of taxes comes from imposts that are not levied annually. The nature and sources of the revenues in recent times are set forth fully in A. L. Bowley and J. Stamp, *The National Income, 1911-1924* (London, 1927). Cf. F. W. Hirst and J. E. Allen, *British War Budgets* (London, 1926), and H. F. Grady, *British War Finance, 1911-1919* (New York, 1927).

were provided for in separate acts. The death duties were incorporated in the general measure only in 1894,[17] the provisions for the Sinking Fund only in 1899. Nowadays, however, as we have seen, it is customary to include in the act all fiscal regulations for the year relating both to revenue and to the national debt.[18]

All finance proposals make their first appearance in the House of Commons. Those that are approved by that body, however, must invariably be submitted also to the House of Lords, which formerly must pass them, equally with the popular chamber, if they were to become law. Since 1911, the concurrence of the Lords has not been necessary. Any bill affirmed by the speaker of the House of Commons to be a money bill,[19] if sent to the Lords at least one month before the close of the session, is submitted for and duly receives the royal assent, and thereby becomes law, whether or not consented to—or even considered—by the upper chamber.

British and American Financial Legislation Compared

The British system of handling financial legislation has long been held up as a model throughout the world, and has been widely imitated. It undoubtedly has many excellent features. Most of all, it guarantees a financial program which has been prepared as a unit and for which full responsibility rests upon a single authority, the cabinet. Notwithstanding large advance in budgetary matters in recent years, the United States still lacks any such coherence and definiteness of responsibility. It is true that under the Budget and Accounting Act of 1921 the director of the budget at Washington receives all estimates of expenditure from the several departments, boards, and commissions and works them into a coördinated fiscal plan, to be presented

[17] Indeed the name Finance Act superseded the term Customs and Inland Revenue Act only at this date.

[18] Thus the title of the Finance Act approved August 3, 1928, reads: "An Act to grant certain Duties of Customs and Inland Revenue (including Excise), to alter other duties, to amend the law relating to Customs and Inland Revenue (including Excise) and the National Debt, and to make further provision in connection with Finance;" and the act is divided into three parts: 1. Customs and Excise; 2. Income Tax; and 3. Miscellaneous.

[19] The term "money bill" is defined minutely in the Parliament Act. It covers taxation, appropriations, loans, and audits. See p. 344 above.

to Congress on the sole responsibility of the president. But after the two branches have come into possession of the plan, each in its turn may introduce any changes that it desires, increasing appropriations here, reducing them there, and even inserting items altogether new; so that by the time when the appropriation bills finally emerge as enacted measures they may be far from what the executive intended, and responsibility for them quite impossible to fix. To make matters worse, proposals for raising revenue—which may originate with the executive, but may also be introduced by any member of the House on his own initiative—are still considered, in both branches, by committees entirely distinct from those that have to do with appropriations, often resulting in a working at cross-purposes which is totally foreign to the British House of Commons, where revenue and appropriation proposals are considered by committees (of the whole) which are indeed distinct in name but absolutely identical in personnel. Still further, whereas in Britain the ministers whose financial program is being submitted to Parliament may follow it there and, as members, explain and defend it on the floor, in the United States the executive, after having once transmitted the annual budget, has no opportunity to give it support except by messages, conferences, and other more or less indirect methods. There is considerable demand in America for a budgetary procedure that will come a good deal closer to the British than anything we as yet have—that will enable the executive to have spokesmen present in the financial sittings of the houses, and that will prevent Congress from appropriating money not asked for by the executive, or, at all events, will give the president power to veto separate items inserted in appropriation bills contrary to executive judgment.[20]

Criticisms of the British System

It would be a mistake to infer, however, that the British system is faultless, or that every Britisher is satisfied with it.

[20] F. A. Ogg and P. O. Ray, *Introduction to American Government* (3rd ed.), 501-509; W. F. Willoughby, *The Problem of a National Budget* (New York, 1918); C. G. Dawes, *The First Year of the Budget in the United States* (New York, 1923).

On the contrary, criticism is often heard, with discussion of possible improvements. The system may be said to have the defects of its merits. It is unified, concentrated, expeditious; but it is so because Parliament has largely abdicated, in favor of the cabinet, that full and direct control over taxation and expenditure which the legislature, under popular forms of government, is supposed to exercise. Analyzed a little more closely, the situation presents four main difficulties. The first is the antiquated character of the rules of procedure followed in handling fiscal matters. These rules originated largely in the seventeenth and early eighteenth centuries, when it was still considered the duty of all good members to delay, postpone, or obstruct the royal demands for money, and the rules were framed with this end in view. Few changes have been made, and roundabout processes prevail where direct ones would be preferable. Fictions lead to empty, and sometimes dilatory, ceremonies (e.g., the debate on "grievances"); much of the ritual, as one critic has remarked, is now no more useful than the annual search for gunpowder in the cellarage.

A second and more serious matter is that the House of Commons, sitting as committee of the whole, is ill-adapted to consider the estimates adequately. The body is altogether too large for the kind of work that needs to be done. It cannot examine witnesses; its time is limited; its deliberations must perforce take the form of slow and general debate; some "votes" receive due attention, but far the greater number go through with no discussion at all. A third disadvantage is the lack of intelligible financial information. On account of sundry features of the estimates and accounts as presented to Parliament, which are too technical and extensive to be explained here, both the quantity and the quality of the information at the disposal of the ordinary member are not such as to enable him, even if he had the requisite time and patience, to comprehend the fiscal plans of the government in all of their bearings and ramifications.

Most important of all is the fact that there is next to no discussion upon the merits of the financial proposals as such. These proposals have come from the government, and the government's supporters feel it incumbent upon them to accept and uphold them as necessary and proper; otherwise they will seem to be inviting embarrassment, and perhaps disaster, for the ministry and the party. On the other hand, the proposals are viewed by the opposition as furnishing just so many opportunities for ventilating general grievances and for bringing the political policy of the government under critical review. If, therefore, a vote is challenged or a reduction moved, the matter tends instantly to become one of confidence, and the debate proceeds accordingly. What should be free discussion simply of the desirability of holding to or altering the government's estimated figure becomes a debate, on party lines, of the whole sweep of government policy. Few economies, therefore, are introduced from the parliamentary side; no one expects much in this direction. Members of the party in power will not embarrass the government by urging them, and with rare exceptions, will feel duty bound to vote them down when advocated by the opposition. The latter will let most of the majority proposals go through without challenge, concentrating its fire on a few here and there which offer most inviting chances for publicly putting the ministers on the defensive. Of dispassionate, straightforward, constructive financial criticism there is very little.[21]

The result is that parliamentary control is, save on rare occasions, merely a matter of form. The House of Lords no longer has the power even to obstruct, much less to prevent, the adoption of money bills; the House of Commons, shorn by self-denying ordinances of the right either itself to originate proposals for expenditure or to increase the proposals submitted to it by the crown, normally assumes that the government knows best what is needed and accepts whatever proposals are offered; and while the popular branch has the right to reduce the amounts called for, or even to refuse to make any grant at all, the conditions that have been described leave it poorly equipped to exercise this power with much intelligence and impartiality. "It is not surprising," said a committee which investigated the subject in 1917-18, "that there has not been

[21] Even so, ministries have occasionally been wrecked by incidents occurring during the estimates debates. Lord Rosebery's cabinet was defeated in 1895 on a trifling item in the army estimates and immediately resigned.

a single instance in the last twenty-five years when the House of Commons by its own direct action has reduced, on financial grounds, any estimate submitted to it. . . . The debates in Committee of Supply are indispensable for the discussion of policy and administration. But so far as the direct effective control of proposals for expenditure is concerned, it would be true to say that if the estimates were never presented, and the Committee of Supply never set up, there would be no noticeable difference." [22] Responsibility for preventing extravagance, therefore, falls almost entirely upon the executive, rather than the legislative, part of the government—primarily, of course, upon the officials of the Treasury. Fortunately, the means provided for such protection are very efficient, and little extravagance results. The fact cannot be got round, however, that millions of pounds of public money are voted every year with only the scantest attention from the people's representatives at Westminster, and other millions with no attention from them whatever. To all intents and purposes, the power of the purse is in the cabinet.[23]

Experiments and Obstacles

Realization of this fact has long made members of Parliament (including no small number of cabinet officers themselves) uncomfortable. Forty years ago the House of Commons began setting up select committees to study the problem, but without avail. One such committee, appointed in 1902 to inquire whether any plan could be adopted for enabling the House "more effectively to make an examination, not involving criticisms of policy, into the details of national expenditure," recommended, among other changes, the creation of a select committee on estimates, which, without any power of direction or control, should each year make a detailed investigation of estimates, organization, methods, and activities of some one service or group of services (to be designated by the Public Accounts Committee), and report its findings to

[22] *Ninth Report of the Select Committee on National Expenditure,* 1918 (House of Commons), 121.

[23] On the extent of control over appropriations actually exercised by the House, see W. F. Willoughby *et al.,* as cited, p. 129 ff.

Parliament. No action was taken until 1912. In that year the House of Commons set up a select committee on estimates, charged with examining, each session, such of the estimates presented to the House as it should see fit to take up, and with reporting to the House any possible economies which it discovered. The new committee worked diligently and intelligently. In 1912 it dealt with some civil service votes, in 1913 with navy votes, and in 1914 it began on army votes. Its labors were, however, too slow, and too much cramped by the limitations imposed by the House, to be of much value.

The World War ran the nation's expenditures up to unprecedented figures, and parliamentary control became even more of a fiction than it had been before. Accordingly, in 1917 still another select committee was set up to study the problem. A year later this committee presented an interesting series of reports, recommending, chiefly, (1) more active financial supervision over the departments by the Treasury, (2) the appointment at the beginning of each session of Parliament of two committees on estimates, of fifteen members each, which should examine the estimates with a view to discovering and suggesting economies, and (3) parliamentary acceptance of the principle that a motion carried in Committee of Supply in pursuance of the recommendations of the estimates committees should not be taken to imply that the government of the day no longer enjoyed the confidence of the House. The committee's report attracted much attention, but thus far has borne little fruit. It is true that in 1919 the House adopted a rule, for a single session, which permitted the estimates (with certain exceptions) to be considered by a standing committee, rather than solely in committee of the whole. Strong objection, however, was raised on the ground that to deprive the House, in any degree whatsoever, of its hard-won right to criticize and control the executive through discussion of the estimates would rob it of its most valued and essential function; and since the only apparent result of the new plan, in practice, was to impede business without effecting many economies, the experiment was not repeated.[24] All estimates, both of expenditure and of revenue, continue to be considered only in committee of the whole,

[24] T. E. May, *op. cit.* (13th ed.), 458-459.

as described above; while as for the war-time committee's recommendations, none have been adopted.

The suggested agreement under which amendments offered by members, when the House is sitting in supply, should be regarded, not as expressions of want of confidence in the ministry, but merely as business proposals to be considered in a business-like rather than a partisan spirit, has much to commend it. Ministers, however, have no enthusiasm for it; for, obviously, if the principle were once admitted, the cabinet's present dominant position in financial matters would come to an end, or at all events be seriously impaired. The greatest single factor in the ascendancy of the cabinet in public affairs today is the almost positive assurance which it enjoys that its financial program, year in and year out, will ride through at Westminster substantially unaffected by criticism and amendments. Ministers are not always unwilling to accept alterations suggested, by friend or foe, in parliamentary committee; indeed, they habitually frame their proposals in accordance with what they understand to be the parliamentary and national temper. As a rule, they will not press an issue to the point of stirring up serious antagonism. But they would not relish a state of things under which their finance bills would be in danger of emerging from Parliament emasculated and unrecognizable, or such that their fellow partisans at Westminster would feel equally free with the opposition to offer and urge different plans from those which the Treasury had stamped with its approval. Hence, the problem remains. Cabinet government is generally conceded to be one of the crowning glories of the British constitution. Englishmen cannot, however, help wondering occasionally whether, in the domain of finance, it has not to some extent overreached itself.[25]

[25] Procedure on money bills is described in A. L. Lowell, *Government of England,* I, Chap. xiv; W. R. Anson, *Law and Custom of the Constitution* (5th ed.), I, 281-296; C. Ilbert, *Legislative Methods and Forms,* 284-298; J. Redlich, *Procedure of the House of Commons,* III, 113-158 (pp. 159-172 contain a very convenient history of financial procedure); and T. E. May, *op. cit.* (13th ed.), Chap. xviii. It must be noted that most of these works are somewhat out of date, though still trustworthy for the fundamentals. W. F. Willoughby, W. W. Willoughby, and S. M. Lindsay, *Financial Administration of Great Britain* (New York, 1917), Chaps. ii-vi, viii, afford a more recent, and a very good, analysis of the budgetary process. Chap.

xiv of this same work, summarizing the fundamental features of the British system and comparing them with the American system (before the adoption of a budget plan in this country), is well worth reading. R. Stourm, *The Budget,* ed. by W. F. McCaleb (New York, 1917), relates principally to French financial procedure, but nevertheless contains much that is helpful to an understanding of the British system. Other useful discussions include J. V. Durell, *Principles and Practice of the System of Parliamentary Grants* (London, 1917), and E. H. Davenport, *Parliament and the Taxpayer* (London, 1919), embodying a summary of the work of the commission of 1917.

CHAPTER XIX

PARLIAMENTARY TENDENCIES AND PROBLEMS

FOR four hundred years, commentators on the English constitution have reiterated, in varying phrases, the assertion of the Elizabethan court secretary, Thomas Smith, that "Parliament representeth and hath the power of the whole realm," and that "the consent of Parliament is taken to be every man's consent." [1] What Blackstone termed the "sovereign and uncontrollable authority" of the two houses includes, as we have seen, full power to make and repeal laws on any and all subjects, to levy taxes and vote expenditures, to question ministers and force them into a position where no course is open to them except to resign, and to go as far as they like in giving new form and character to the national constitution itself. Such, at all events, is the theory of the matter as the constitutional lawyers continue to declare it.[2] In point of actual fact, however, Parliament has never been, and is not now, omnipotent. Except in the realm of pure theory, its powers are relative, limited, and shifting—restricted, for working purposes, and as determined partly by precedent, partly by convenience and expediency, to those which either are or quite conceivably might be actually exercised. They tend to be steadily widened as new fields of government control, e.g., radio communication and aërial trans-

[1] *De Republica Anglorum* (ed. by Alston), 49. Sir Edward Coke's way of putting it, a generation later, was that the power of Parliament "is so transcendent and absolute, as it cannot be confined either for causes or persons within any bounds."

[2] "Parliamentary sovereignty is . . . an undoubted legal fact. It is complete both on its positive and on its negative side. . . . No one of the limitations alleged to be imposed by law on the absolute authority of Parliament has any real existence, or receives any countenance, either from the statute-book or from the practice of the courts." A. V. Dicey, *Law of the Constitution* (8th ed.), 66-68. "Parliament is not controlled in its discretion, and when it errs, its errors can only be corrected by itself." T. E. May, *op. cit.* (13th ed.), 51.

portation, are opened by scientific invention or by changing conceptions of the limits to which it is desirable for public regulation to be carried. But they also tend to be progressively narrowed as new restrictive forces and conditions of one kind or another come, by design or otherwise, into play.

It will surprise many people to be told that of late the balance has been inclining rather sharply against Parliament as the dominating, controlling agency in the state. Both in power and in prestige, the houses, taken together, have receded perceptibly from the high point at which they stood in the mid-Victorian era. True enough, it is hazardous to indulge in many assumptions as to what Parliament cannot—in any case will not—do. In the eighth and definitive edition of his *Law of the Constitution,* published in 1915, Mr. Dicey asserted that "Parliament would not at the present day prolong by law the duration of an existing House of Commons," although before the year was out that very thing was done (for war-time reasons, of course) without a word of protest in either house. Nevertheless, that there has been a positive curtailment of the practical, working powers of not only the House of Lords (e.g., by the Parliament Act of 1911) but also the House of Commons, there is no doubt in any observer's mind. It is not a question merely of the moral inhibitions which, to all intents and purposes, make it impossible for Parliament to enact, for example, a law subjecting civilians to trial by court-martial in time of peace. Such restraints there have always been. It is a matter, rather, of restrictions of more recent origin growing out of changing relations between Parliament and other authorities or agencies in the state.

Changed Relation to the Electorate

Let us see what has happened. In the first place, there has been a loss of power to the electorate. Inasmuch as under the modern theory of English government all authority resides ultimately in the electorate, and Parliament is only an agency through which the people's sovereignty actively functions, it seems a bit strange to say that Parliament has lost power to the electorate. Nevertheless, that is exactly what has occurred; or, if not power, at all events independence—which comes to the same thing. Several factors have contributed to strip the two houses of the freedom and immunity with which they used (e.g., in the eighteenth century) to carry on their work. One of them is the development of the means of quick and cheap dissemination of news and ideas. Time was when the houses, sitting at Westminster, were not much in the public eye. There were no telegraphs or telephones; newspaper service was slow and scant; people travelled but little; public opinion—outside of the capital, at all events—had small opportunity to form or function. Now, all is different. As Lowell remarks, "a debate, a vote, or a scene that occurs in Parliament late at night is brought home to the whole country at breakfast the next morning, and prominent constituents, clubs, committees, and the like, can praise or censure, encourage or admonish, their member for his vote before the next sitting of the House." [3] The inevitable result is that, under the steady gaze of his constituents (and of other interested people as well), the member is not such a free agent as he was a hundred years ago, when, upon going off to London to attend a session, he was largely lost to view. Parliament as a whole has to keep its ear to the ground, to have regard for the reactions of the man in the street, as was not formerly the case. By so much, it has lost in spontaneity and freedom of action.[4]

Changes in the electoral system have also played their part. The widening of the suffrage, and the consequent growth in the size of the electorate, has increased the expense of obtaining a seat, and accordingly has made members more sensitive to the threat of a dissolution and less disposed to support any measure or policy likely to start a back-fire in the constituencies. Still another factor is the increasing number of members who are representatives, not only of regular constituencies, but of special interests. Burke's memorable assertion in 1774 that "authoritative instructions, mandates issued, which the member is bound blindly and implicitly to obey, to vote, and to argue for . . . are things utterly unknown to the laws of this land," [5]

[3] *Government of England,* I, 425.

[4] Carlyle, even in his day, could refer to parliaments "with twenty-seven millions, mostly fools, listening to them." *Latter-day Pamphlets: the Stump Orator,* No. 5.

[5] Speech at Bristol defending the freedom of the M. P. to vote according

if broadly true when uttered, no longer holds good. Session by session, the number of members increases who are servants, agents, or officials of some organization—a trade union, a coöperative association, a temperance society, or what not—which represents a special interest. A recent estimate puts this number, in the House of Commons alone, at not less than one-third of the total.[6] In so far as such relationships exist, the houses are likely to be guided by extraneous influences rather than by their own judgment independently arrived at.[7] Finally, there is the matter of the national referendum, or mandate. As has appeared,[8] the notion that Parliament should not alter the fundamental law in any important way until after the nation shall have been given a chance, at a general election, to register its will on the proposal, although warmly advocated and widely supported in the past twenty years, is not to be regarded as having established itself in either the law or the custom of the constitution. Nevertheless, the idea already operates to some extent as a restraining force; and in so far as it may at any time deter Parliament from acting according to its own dictates, without waiting to secure express popular assent, it will to that extent have shifted the primary power of decision from Westminster to the constituencies.[9]

Loss of Power to the Cabinet

But Parliament—chiefly the House of Commons—has lost power not only to the electorate; it has yielded heavily to the cabinet. Indeed, the growing dominance of the cabinet represents probably the most important single development of the British constitution in the past fifty years. We know well

to his own convictions rather than as instructed by his constituents. *Works and Correspondence,* III, 236. For the circumstances, see M. MacDonagh, *Pageant of Parliament,* I, 11-14.

[6] H. Young, "The Authority of the House of Commons," *Contemp. Rev.,* July, 1925, p. 29.

[7] One recalls, of course, that in the days before the reform acts large numbers of members of the Commons represented only narrow local oligarchies or other special interests, or even the interests of a single "pocket borough" patron. The comparison here drawn is, rather, with a somewhat later period—especially the last quarter of the nineteenth century.

[8] See p. 74 above.

[9] J. A. R. Marriott, *The Mechanism of the Modern State,* I, 455-465. Cf. A. V. Dicey, *Law of the Constitution* (8th ed.), pp. xci-c.

enough what the theory of cabinet government is. The ministers are members of Parliament; they (in Britain, a limited group of the more important ones) formulate policy and introduce bills; they see to the carrying out of the measures agreed upon; singly and collectively, they are responsible for all executive and administrative acts; this responsibility is to the House of Commons, of which, to all intents and purposes, the cabinet is a working committee; the group is in no sense an independent authority, but only the servant of the House, charged with its high duties for only so long as it can hold the confidence and support of that body. It was on these lines that Bagehot, sixty years ago, skillfully analyzed the relations existing between the cabinet and its parliamentary master. The theory, as a theory, still holds. But for a good while the facts have been growing more difficult to reconcile with it.

Take first the matter of legislation. A hundred years ago the cabinet as such had relatively little to do with the processes of law-making. Even then, the ministers were, with few exceptions, members of Parliament. But their duties were chiefly executive, and they bore no disproportionate share in the legislative activities of the houses. Now, all is different. They write the Speech from the Throne which lays down the legislative program for a session; they decide what subjects shall occupy the attention of the houses, prepare the bills on these subjects, introduce them, explain and defend them, press for their passage, take full responsibility for them both before and after they are passed, and throw upon the House of Commons the onus of upsetting the government and very likely precipitating a general election if any of their important measures are emasculated or rejected. They demand, and obtain, most of the time of the houses—all of it in the House of Commons after a certain stage of the session is reached—for the consideration of the measures in which they are interested.[10] They crack the whip of party loyalty over the heads of their supporters on the benches and make it next to impossible for even the most spirited to call in question, much less to vote against, the proposals

[10] For the actual rules, see Standing Order No. 4. On the control of time in the American House of Representatives, see P. D. Hasbrouck, *Party Government in the House of Representatives* (New York, 1927), Chap. vi.

upon which Whitehall has resolved. In the broad field of finance their control is greater still, because, as we have seen, the House of Commons will give no consideration at all to any request for money that does not come from, or at all events with the express approval of, the crown, i.e., the cabinet. Indeed, its consideration of even these proposals is often a mere matter of form. Granting of supply has so far lost its earlier importance as a check of the legislature upon the executive that millions of pounds are voted every year with no debate whatever, even in committee of the whole. It is true that some of these restrictions arise from rules which the House of Commons has itself made, and that they could be terminated by simple amendment of the standing orders.[11] But the point is that even these regulations—including the whole body of rules relating to closure—have, in effect, been dictated by the government, which could be depended upon to resist, and successfully too, any effort to relax them.[12]

The upshot of it all is fairly obvious. "To say," remarks the American writer who has made the closest study of the subject, "that at present the cabinet legislates with the advice and consent of Parliament would hardly be an exaggeration; and it is only the right of private members to bring in a few motions and bills of their own, and to criticize government measures, or propose amendments to them, freely, that prevents legislation from being the work of a mere automatic majority. It does not follow that the action of the cabinet is arbitrary. . . . The cabinet has its finger always on the pulse of the House of Commons, and especially of its own majority there; and it is ever on the watch for expressions of public feeling outside. Its function is in large part to sum up and formulate the desires of its supporters, but the majority must accept its conclusions, and in carrying them out becomes well-nigh automatic." [13]

[11] E.g., the rule forbidding consideration of appropriations not asked for by the crown (Standing Order No. 66) and that automatically closing debate on the last day but one allotted to supply (Standing Order No. 15, § 7).

[12] The hostility of ministers—in any government and of any party—to changes that would give the House of Commons more actual control over appropriations was noted near the close of the preceding chapter.

[13] Lowell, *Government of England,* I, 326. For criticism of the alleged

What of Parliament's relation to the executive and administrative work of the government? Here, less startling changes are to be recorded, because at no time in the past has Parliament either actually or theoretically wielded such direct control as in the domain of legislation. Even in this field, however, the tendency has been in the same direction. Most cabinet members are principal officers in the great executive departments. As ministers, their business is to supervise the work carried on in and through these departments; and ever since the cabinet system assumed its matured form, their direct and full responsibility to Parliament (actually, the House of Commons) for all their executive actions has been accepted as axiomatic. The theory is that the ministers are responsible to the elected chamber for all that they do, singly in small or isolated matters, collectively in more important ones; that their acts are constantly subject to inquiry and criticism; and that the great powers which they wield can be stripped from them at any time by the simple withholding of support. There are, furthermore, several recognized methods by which this responsibility can be enforced; and some mention of them may well be made before comment is ventured upon the extent to which the ministers' executive work is actually controlled.

Methods of Enforcing Ministerial Responsibility

In the first place, at many different stages of a session there is opportunity for criticism of executive acts which may give rise to what is, to all intents and purposes, a vote of censure, entailing either resignation of the ministers or a dissolution. The debate on the address in reply to the Speech from the Throne is such an occasion; the debates on going into committee of the whole, whether Supply or Ways and Means, is another. The discussions in Committee of Supply, which, as we have seen, furnish a particularly favorable chance for attack upon the government's acts and policies, constitutes still another.

autocracy of the cabinet in legislation, see E. Clark, "Woman Suffrage in Parliament; a Test for Cabinet Autocracy," *Amer. Polit. Sci. Rev.*, May, 1917. Fundamentally, the development that has taken place is, however, not only inevitable but logical. See p. 460, note 27, below.

In the second place, there is the device of the "question." Subject to conditions, any member of the House may address a question to a minister, actually or ostensibly to obtain information. The principal conditions are (1) that every such question shall be addressed to that minister in whose province the subject-matter of the inquiry falls, (2) that notice shall be given at least one day in advance, (3) that the query shall contain no "argument, inference, imputation, epithet, or ironical expression," (4) that it must not have been disapproved by the speaker as improper, (5) that it must not relate to statements made by members outside the House, and (6) that no member may submit more than four questions on any one day.[14] Until three-quarters of a century ago, the right of questioning ministers was not much used,[15] but nowadays the number of questions put to them at every session runs into the thousands; and, as we have seen, "question time" is a regular, and usually an interesting, portion of every daily sitting. Sometimes the questions have, indeed, no object except to elicit information; and the questioner may be fully satisfied by what he hears. They may come from the minister's political friends no less than his foes. More often, however, they are intended to imply criticism, and to place the minister and his colleagues on the defensive. It is the minister's privilege to decline to answer if he likes; all he needs to say is that to reply would be contrary to the public interest. But arbitrary or too frequent refusal will, of course, tend to create an unfavorable impression. The process of answering questions, as Lowell remarks, gives to the Treasury Bench an air of omniscience not wholly deserved, because, the queries having been put on the "question paper" in advance, opportunity has been given for the minister's subordinates to look up the matter and supply him with the necessary data. In most cases all that the minister has to do with the replies is to read them to the House, although after he has finished members may aim "supplementary questions" at him from the floor, and it behooves him to have as much personal

[14] A further limitation is imposed by the rule that no question may be put which brings the name of the sovereign, or his actual or possible influence, directly before Parliament, or which casts reflection upon him.

[15] A special place in the Orders of the Day was first assigned to questions in 1849.

familiarity with the matter as he can muster. The average number of questions per day is in these times between 150 and 200. The answers to such of them as are not reached within the allotted hour—usually only forty-five minutes, i.e., 3.00 to 3.45 P.M.—and are not postponed at the request of the questioner, are printed, along with those given orally by the ministers, in the proceedings of the House.[16]

The question privilege is undoubtedly liable to abuse; the questioner is sometimes actuated by no very lofty motive, and a good deal of time is consumed on trivial matters. As an English authority testifies, however, "there is no more valuable safeguard against maladministration, no more effective method of bringing the searchlight of criticism to bear on the action or inaction of the executive government and its subordinates. A minister has to be constantly asking himself, not merely whether his proceedings and the proceedings of those for whom he is responsible are legally or technically defensible, but what kind of answer he can give if questioned about them in the House, and how that answer will be received." [17] The system helps greatly, as Lowell observes, not only to keep the administration of the country up to the mark, but to prevent the growth of that bureaucratic arrogance which is quite unknown in England.[18]

Although a means of calling ministers to account, questions do not, of themselves, involve a debate or a vote. Whether answered satisfactorily or not, they do not immediately en-

[16] "Civil servants," writes Sir William Beveridge, "are on the inside of one of the indispensable frauds of the British constitution, namely, the great illusion that a cabinet minister really runs his department and knows all about it and what it is doing. The main piece of machinery by which the illusion is fostered is the parliamentary question and answer, and the apparent omniscience that a cabinet minister then shows. Sometimes, of course, . . . the mask slips a little. There was a regrettable incident during the war, when, the official in charge, having supplied the answer, appended to it a note for the guidance of the minister, and the minister unfortunately read out both the answer and the note. It was something as follows: 'The answer to the first part of the question is in the negative; the remaining parts therefore do not arise. This member is being very tiresome; to give him any information only whets his appetite for more." M. Cary *et al.*, *The Development of the Civil Service*, 229.

[17] C. Ilbert, *Parliament*, 113-114.

[18] *Government of England*, I, 332. Cf. p. 238 above.

danger the tenure of the ministry—except in one contingency. If a member, seeking fuller information or bent upon testing the government's strength, moves "to adjourn for the purpose of discussing a definite matter of urgent importance," [19] and if as many as forty members support the motion, a debate takes place, nominally on the motion to adjourn, but really on the subject involved in the question and answer. The government opposes the motion, and if defeated must resign, or at least the minister directly affected must do so. This procedure, although furnishing a means by which any specific act or omission of the government can be made the basis of a vote of censure, is not often brought into play; and while bearing a certain resemblance to the French device of interpellation—which, indeed, was derived from it—it lends itself in no such fashion to the swift upsetting of ministries, often on mere pretext.[20]

Two further methods of bringing ministers to account require mention. The first is private members' motions censuring particular acts or policies. These may emanate from any member who can gain the floor for the purpose, and they may lead not only to embarrassing debates but to hostile votes. However, under the rules, there are only seventeen days in an entire session (all in the earlier part) on which any kind of private motion may be made; the time allowed for considering such motions is so limited that only a small proportion ever reach a vote; and many of those offered have objects entirely foreign to criticism of the government. There are ways by which, at the worst, the Treasury Bench can usually stave off a vote on a motion likely to prove disastrous; and even in the event of a vote, such a motion, as the statistics of the matter plainly show, is very unlikely to prevail. The criticism of individual members, directed at some particular act (often of secondary

[19] The rather intricate origins of this form of motion are explained in Lowell, *op. cit*, I, 333-336.

[20] E. M. Sait, *Government and Politics of France*, 235-242. It should be emphasized that the questions dealt with above are exclusively such as are addressed to ministers. Questions may be addressed also to unofficial members on a bill, motion, or other matter connected with the business of the house in which such members are concerned. A question to an ex-minister concerning transactions during his tenure of office has been ruled out of order. T. E. May, *op. cit.* (13th ed.), 241.

importance), has very much less effect than in France. The theory, and to a large extent the practice, of the English system is, rather, that the ministers shall stand or fall upon their general policy, upon their whole record, or if upon a particular matter, at all events only upon one of first-rate importance. They are, however, subject to challenge upon general policy; and this brings us to the second of the methods referred to, i.e., a vote of want of confidence in the government, moved by the leader of the opposition and directed, not at any specific act, but at the ministry's policy in general. This is, of course, an extreme procedure, but it is sometimes resorted to. Ordinarily the government will not dare attempt to prevent debate on such a motion; and defeat in the resulting division—which is squarely on the issue of turning out the ministry—must immediately be followed by resignation or a dissolution.

Actual Parliamentary Control, Today and Formerly

Such are the principal lines upon which, under the English cabinet system as it has developed down to the present day, the responsibility of ministers in their executive capacity is capable of enforcement.[21] This does not mean, however, that the House of Commons actually participates in, or even habitually interferes with, the ministers' administrative work. On the contrary, the British executive is more free from legislative control than is either the president of the United States or the ministry in France. Never, save when the Long Parliament, in the Cromwellian era, drew to itself the executive power and bestowed it upon committees which it appointed, has Parliament as a whole or the House of Commons in particular manifested a disposition to take part in any direct way in the exercise of that power. "It provides the money required for administrative purposes by authorizing taxation; it appropriates, with

[21] It should, perhaps, be added that executive acts and policies may be made the subject of inquiry or investigation by special committees, and that the reports of such committees may become the means of putting the government on the defensive, and even of forcing it from office. Such investigations are, however, not frequent, and they do not often have disastrous effects. On similar investigations in the United States, see M. E. Dimock, *Congressional Investigating Committees* (Baltimore, 1929), and E. J. Eberling, *Congressional Investigations* (New York, 1928).

more or less particularity, the purposes to which the money so provided is to be applied; it criticizes the mode in which money is spent and in which public affairs are administered; its support is indispensable to those who are responsible for administration; but it does not administer." [22] Nor does it often seek to regulate administration except in the most general way. It does not attempt to say how the departments shall be organized, how large their staffs shall be, what the civil servants shall be paid, or how reports shall be prepared. It does not expect any appointments of officials, high or low, to come before it for confirmation.[23] It keeps hands off the executive and administrative machinery in a fashion quite unknown to the American Congress, which, notwithstanding our supposed deference to separation of powers, insists on reaching over into the executive and administrative spheres and regulating even the matter of salaries down to the last detail.[24]

The thing that Parliament (that is to say, the House of Commons) is supposed to do is to furnish the inquiry and criticism that will keep the ministers and their subordinates up to the mark—not to issue orders in advance as to what they shall do, but to survey the things that they have already done and hold them to account therefor. "A strong executive government, tempered and controlled by constant, vigilant, and representative criticism," is the objective.[25] The point to be impressed, however, is that, on the executive side equally with the legislative, the tendency in later years has been toward a considerably less direct and effective responsibility of the ministers

[22] J. Redlich, *op. cit.,* I, p. vii. Parliament is thus quite unlike county, district, municipal, and parish councils, which conduct administration with the help of committees of their members to which large powers of an administrative nature are often delegated.

[23] It will be recalled that Parliament left the entire merit system in the civil service to be built up almost exclusively by means of orders in council, and that it rests mainly on that basis today.

[24] See W. F. Willoughby, *The Government of Modern States* (New York, 1919), 250-254, and J. A. Fairlie, "Congress and the National Administration," *Mich. Law Rev.,* Jan., 1928. Cf., however, the assertion of Representative Luce: "The allegation that Congress itself wilfully seeks to interfere with the executive branch and of its own initiative harries the various [administrative] offices by legislation, is quite contrary to the facts." *Congress, an Explanation,* 4.

[25] C. Ilbert, Parliament, 119.

than, for example, when Bagehot wrote. The war had something to do with it, but the change was going on earlier, and the causes are to be found to some extent in the same general shift of conditions that has rendered Parliament less independent of the electorate in the field of legislation. Here, too, the major fact is the closer contact between London and the provinces, produced by the railroad, the telegraph, the telephone, the newspaper, the motor-car, the aëroplane, and radio broadcasting, enabling the ministers to keep the country informed and to receive back the people's impressions and reactions in a fashion undreamt of even a generation ago. This means that the ministers now take their cue more largely from what seems to be public opinion, and that, so long as they feel that they have backing from this source, they are relatively indifferent to what is said or done at Westminster. Criticisms are taken lightly; rebuffs which formerly would have caused a political sensation, perhaps an immediate cabinet crisis, are ignored or explained away.[26] Other factors, however, enter in. The growing volume of business in the House of Commons (to be touched upon presently) makes it impossible to scrutinize the work of the government as closely as formerly—which, by so much, means more freedom of action in the great offices in Whitehall. Parliament, furthermore, has suffered a decline in prestige which has caused people to look more hopefully to the executive agencies, and this has tended still further to induce the ministers to tie up their political fortunes rather with public sentiment than with parliamentary debates and votes. The truth is that scarcely a ministry in fifty years has been turned out of office by a hostile Parliament because of its executive acts; and the chances of such a thing happening have of late been steadily diminishing.[27]

[26] The Labor government of Ramsay MacDonald was defeated in the House of Commons ten times between February 12 and August 7, 1924, without surrendering the seals of office. The Lloyd George coalition government was similarly thick-skinned. It has, however, come to be a definite principle of British parliamentary practice that a ministry need not—indeed, should not—resign unless it is clearly the well-considered desire of a majority of the Commons that it do so. Mere casual or momentary defeats do not ordinarily indicate such a desire.

[27] The fundamental change which time and experience have wrought in the interrelations of the different parts of the English government is ex-

Some Results of the Cabinet's Stronger Position

Some of the consequences of the developments described must already have suggested themselves. One of them is an exceptionally unified and continuous leadership in legislation, as compared with the leadership that exists in the American Congress or in Continental parliaments. For every session there is a program, not only of financial, but of all other, legislation —a program prepared by the cabinet, introduced and managed by cabinet members, and so favored by the rules of procedure (once a weapon to be used against crown and ministers, but nowadays a weapon or tool of the cabinet itself) that it cannot

cellently summed up in J. Redlich, *Procedure of the House of Commons,* I, 207-210. A few sentences deserve to be quoted. "In the British cabinet of today is concentrated all political power, all initiative in legislation and administration, and finally all public authority for carrying out the laws in kingdom and empire. In the sixteenth century and down to the middle of the seventeenth, this wealth of authority was united in the hands of the crown and its privy council; in the eighteenth century and first half of the nineteenth, Parliament was the dominant central organ from which proceeded the most powerful stimulus to action and all decisive acts of policy, legislation, and administration; the second half of the last century saw the gradual transfer from crown and Parliament into the hands of the cabinet of one after another of the elements of authority and political power. . . . The union of all political power in the hands of the House of Commons and the simultaneous transfer of this concentrated living force to a cabinet drawn exclusively from Parliament are the dominant features of the modern development of public law and politics in England. . . . The very completeness of its power, which, if we disregard technicalities, may be said to comprise the whole administration of domestic and foreign affairs, has compelled the House of Commons to abdicate the exercise of almost all its authority in favor of its executive committee, the ministry [i.e., cabinet]. This was inevitable for the reason, if there were no other, that 670 members [the passage was written a good many years ago] cannot initiate legislation, cannot even govern or administer. The evolution of the modern state has set before every nation the problem how the sovereignty of the people, realized in the form of representative constitutions, can be rendered operative for the current work and constructive activity of the state. . . . In . . . the United States of America, it has been solved by the careful division of political authority and legal power among several organs, each dependent on the popular will. In Great Britain, on the contrary, a solution has been found in the completest possible concentration of actual and legal power in one and the same organ, the cabinet, which is part and parcel of Parliament." On the general subject, see L. Rogers, "The Changing English Constitution," *North Amer. Rev.,* June, 1924, and the same author's review of *The Reform of Parliament; Two Reports Submitted to the Annual Conference of the Independent Labor Party* (1925), printed in *New York Times Book Review,* Sept. 27, 1925.

be shunted off the main line or seriously impeded by rival legislative proposals from non-ministerial sources. In the United States no member of the executive branch can introduce a bill, or appear in Congress to speak on one; and while there is often an "administration program" of legislation—in part, at least, set forth in the president's message at the opening of a session—such a program does not presume to cover all of the subjects likely to come up, it is got actually before Congress only as senators or representatives can be found to sponsor different parts of it, and there is no such likelihood that it will all go through as in the case of a government program introduced at Westminster. Many bills at Washington emanate from administrative sources. But they rarely hang together as concerted parts of an integrated legislative program, and it is significant that even major statutes bear, not the uniform label of the "government," as in Britain, but commonly only the names of the chairmen of committees which have decided upon, formulated, and introduced the bills, quite independently, and often without the approval, or even the full knowledge, of the White House or the departments.[28] There may be a question whether the centralization and unification of legislative leadership have not been carried too far in the British system—whether cabinet government has not overreached itself in this regard. Some Englishmen, as well as many foreign observers, think that it has done so. But in so far as such concentration and unity are useful, the British system certainly leaves nothing to be desired.

Another result is greater stability for the ministry than prevails in most cabinet-government countries. Political, i.e., party, homogeneity is, of course, one reason why cabinets, on the average, last considerably longer at Whitehall than in Paris or Berlin. But another reason is to be found in the power which the cabinet possesses to turn upon a rebellious parliament, procure its dissolution, and subject its members to the trouble and expense of recapturing their seats, if they can, at a general elec-

[28] For example, the Sherman Act, the Adamson Act, the Volstead Act, etc. On the devices that have grown up in the American Congress to supply the lack of cabinet (or other executive) leadership, see F. A. Ogg and P. O. Ray, *Introduction to American Government* (3rd ed.), 386-391.

tion. Even if a defeated cabinet merely resigns, the ruling party goes out of power. But if it chooses to precipitate a dissolution, it brings upon everybody the costs and hazards of an electoral campaign. Faced with these cold facts, a government majority can usually be depended upon to see that the ministers get what they ask, whether or not there is any real enthusiasm for their proposals. Armed with paramount rights of initiative, supported by procedural rules drawn in their favor, and holding the power of life and death over Parliament itself, the cabinet indicates what is to be done; and Parliament, on its part,—at all events the House of Commons (which chiefly counts in such a matter)—dreading the consequences of refusal, complies. In France, where the cabinet enjoys less ascendancy, and where, in particular, a dissolution of the Chamber of Deputies is almost an impossibility,[29] cabinets are notoriously short-lived. Under a multi-party system, they have less dependable support; the hope of sharing in a new ministry affords at least a mild incitement to putting the cabinet out; and in case of a defeat there is, in practice, nothing that the ministers can do but resign. The Chamber of Deputies therefore tends to play fast and loose with the government's bills, while helpless cabinets rise and fall in bewildering succession. Well might the Frenchman, observing his own ministries toppling and rebuilding every few months, envy the stability of Whitehall! On the other hand, contemplating the inevitable decline of free parliamentary life on the Thames-side, he might also feel that perhaps stability can be bought at too great a price.

For there are consequences of cabinet domination at Westminster that arouse misgivings. Everybody agrees that there has been not only a decline of parliamentary oratory but a falling off of interest on the part of members in the proceedings of the two houses. In the House of Commons, where the change is most marked, and also most significant, many factors—among them, the use of closure—have borne a share. But a main cause is the growing sense of the futility of

[29] Partly because the consent of the Senate must be obtained, but mainly because of the lingering effects of the discreditable circumstances under which the one dissolution of the Chamber during the entire existence of the Third Republic took place, i.e., in 1877. See E. M. Sait, *Government and Politics of France,* 274-276.

debate on measures the form and fate of which have already been largely determined before the House so much as saw them. Occupants of the Front Treasury Bench will, of course, explain and defend their bills. Occupants of the Front Opposition Bench will, from force of habit, if not from hope of rallying and capitalizing opposition strength, criticize and denounce. But for the "back-bencher" (and that means the great bulk of members, government and opposition) there is not much opportunity, either to influence decisions or to win prestige. He may, of course, gain a fleeting prominence at question time; he may propose amendments to government bills when in committee stage; he may introduce bills of his own on any except financial subjects; he may get the eye of the speaker and have some part in debate. But so far as any independent bills of his own are concerned, he may be pretty sure that unless they deal with unimportant, or at any rate non-controversial, matters they will never be advanced beyond second reading;[30] and as for debate, he may usually as well recognize before he starts that no argument that he can make will have any effect on the outcome, although, of course, if it shows ability it may serve to bring him to the notice of the powers that be and thereby improve his outlook for a career. It does not matter much whether he is a government or an opposition member. The former is not consulted any more than is the latter on measures which ministers propose to introduce.. "He sees them only when they come from the printers; and then he knows that, whether he likes them or not, he will be expected to support them by his vote in the lobbies."[31]

Students of legislation are aware that in all parliamentary

[30] On an average, about eighty-five per cent of the government bills introduced in a session become law, but only ten or twelve per cent of private members' bills. For statistics covering the period 1900-23, see W. H. Chiao, *Devolution in Great Britain* (New York, 1926), 115.

[31] S. Low, *Governance of England,* 79. "When the division bell rings, he [the average back-bencher] hurries to the House, and is told by his whip whether he is an 'Aye' or a 'No.' Sometimes he is told that party tellers have not been 'put on,' and that he can vote as he pleases. But open questions are not popular; they compel a member to think for himself, which is always troublesome. Not that a member is a mere pawn in the game, but the number of questions which even a member of Parliament has leisure and capacity to think out for himself is necessarily limited." C.

bodies there are some members who lead and others who follow. Hardly anywhere else, however, do the bulk of members so largely forego liberty of action as in the British House of Commons. There is considerably more chance for the private member to get important bills acted upon, to help turn the tide in debate, and to vote independently, in the French Chamber of Deputies and most other Continental legislatures; and the position of the ordinary congressman in the American House of Representatives is decidedly freer. The latter may not only introduce, but secure action on, bills of any character whatsoever, even including money bills; [32] he can take as much, and conceivably as effective, part in debate as anybody else; he can, and frequently does, oppose measures sponsored by the leaders of his party, including the president; he may even vote against such measures with impunity, at all events if—as is true of a large proportion of bills—they have not been made the subject of caucus action. Party lines weigh so much less heavily at Washington than at Westminster that, as compared with the British back-bencher, the "gentleman from New York," or "from Texas," is a free lance indeed. How largely this contrast arises from the dominating position of the cabinet in the one case and the absence of any corresponding executive leadership

Ilbert, in J. Redlich, *op. cit.*, p. xvii. As this passage suggests, the existing situation is not without advantages from the point of view of the average member. And of course it must be borne in mind that a member's activity and usefulness are not measured solely by his participation in debates and divisions. There is, for example, his work on committees (both on public and on private bills), on investigating commissions, etc.

[32] This does not mean that congressmen are, in any true sense, the authors of the bulk of the bills which they introduce. "For by far the greater part of the 15,000 and more of proposals laid before each Congress nowadays," writes an experienced member of the House of Representatives, "senators and representatives are merely conduits, the means of transmission, and for very many of them they are not even endorsers to the extent of guaranteeing more than perfunctory interest. The true source may usually be found in some administrative official, or in some organization, or with some constituent with a grievance, an ambition, or a hope. Congress is not to any material extent an originating body." R. Luce, *Congress; an Explanation*, 3. This, however, in no way invalidates what is said above about the freedom, prominence, and potential influence of the congressman as compared with the unofficial commoner. E. P. Herring, *Group Representation before Congress* (Baltimore, 1929), describes the rise of organizations and agencies at Washington which represent special groups in respect to legislation affecting their interests.

and command in the other must have become sufficiently apparent to require no comment.[33]

Dissatisfaction with Parliament

As the great bulwark of popular self-government, Parliament has traditionally stood high in the esteem of the nation. We have already noted, however, that of late—meaning in the last thirty or forty years—it has suffered a decline of repute, and is today the object of much criticism and solicitude. Some of those who find fault with it are radicals who consider all political methods futile and would like to see parliamentary machinery dispensed with completely. Others do not go so far as this, but nevertheless feel that parliaments (the British included) as constituted today are bankrupt and will have to be totally reconstructed and reoriented before they will function acceptably. Antiparliamentarism, in one form or another, has become a weighty factor in French and other Continental politics,[34] and it is to be reckoned with in Britain as well. Still other critics consider that Parliament as we have known it is by no means played out, but is merely the victim of circumstances that have come about naturally, perhaps inevitably, and that to a considerable extent can be overcome or alleviated. They see, with Lord Bryce, many causes that have been tending to reduce the prestige and authority of legislative bodies,[35] but believe,

[33] The changing relations of Parliament (especially the House of Commons) and the cabinet are discussed in A. L. Lowell, *Government of England,* I, Chaps. xvii-xviii; S. Low, *Governance of England,* Chap. v; C. D. Allin, "The Position of Parliament," *Polit. Sci. Quar.,* June, 1914; L. Rogers, "The Changing English Constitution," *N. Amer. Rev.,* June, 1924; and H. Young, "The Authority of the House of Commons," *Contemp. Rev.,* July, 1925.

[34] See R. K. Gooch, "The Antiparliamentary Movement in France," *Amer. Polit. Sci. Rev.,* Aug., 1927.

[35] *Modern Democracies,* II, Chap. LVIII, on "the decline of legislatures." Cf. F. A. Ogg, "New Tests of Representative Government," *University of Chicago Record,* XII, No. 4 (Oct., 1925). It should be emphasized that, contrary to rather general supposition, the phenomenon is not confined to the years since the World War. As long ago as 1907, Professor Redlich wrote of the "widespread increase of mistrust in parliamentary government." *The Procedure of the House of Commons,* I, p. xxvi. Indeed, almost a decade earlier than that, the American editor, E. L. Godkin, wrote trenchantly of "the decline of legislatures." *Unforeseen Tendencies of Democracy* (Boston, 1898), Chap. iv.

as he also did, that, with suitable readjustments and reforms, such bodies will remain effective instrumentalities of government. In particular, they lament the congestion of business which prevents the House of Commons from functioning as it once did as a deliberative assembly, the domination of the cabinet (which is largely an outgrowth of this pressure of business), the extinction of the private member except as an automatic voter, the appropriating of millions of pounds every year with no scrutiny whatever from Parliament, the delays and uncertainties encountered in bringing about legislation on matters of grave public import. They are more or less appreciative of the fact that the power of the cabinet, like that formerly enjoyed by the American speaker, has developed out of the necessity of giving direction and leadership to the zealous and often misdirected energy of the House; and they are fully aware that the complexities of modern life render it necessary for law-making to be increasingly the business of experts. They believe, however, that ways can be found of restoring the deliberative character of the House on something like the traditional lines; and to that end their practical proposals are mainly directed.

Disregarding the opinions of the very small number of Englishmen who would do away with political machinery and methods altogether, the current criticisms practically boil down to two: (1) Parliament has too much to do, and (2) even if this were not the case, it is not the proper agency to perform some of the tasks that are now entrusted to it. Upon the fact of overloading there is no difference of opinion. The statistics of measures passed at any average session bear impressive testimony. More significant, however, are the hurried consideration given most of these measures, the failure of numerous important government proposals so much as to get upon the calendar, the repeated instances in which parliamentary and royal commissions carry on extensive investigations and submit painstaking reports, only to see their work become useless as a basis of legislation because of the inability of Parliament to get round to the subject until after the data have become obsolete. A thing that is often overlooked is that the parliament that sits at Westminster is, in truth, a dozen or more parliaments rolled into one. It is called upon to make laws, control finance, scrutinize administration, and enforce executive responsibility, not only for England alone, but also for England and Wales, for Northern Ireland, for Scotland, for Great Britain, for the United Kingdom, for India, for the crown colonies (singly and collectively), for mandates and protectorates—even, to some extent, for the Empire at large; being, in these several capacities, "responsible, directly or indirectly, for the peace, order, and good government of a quarter of the population of the earth." Small wonder that, in these days of rapidly expanding governmental regulation, the burden has become intolerable! Small wonder that the men at Westminster cannot perform all of the multifarious functions involved without neglecting some, overrating others, and losing sight of the problem as a whole! [36]

Remedies, Actual and Proposed: Devolution

Such remedies as have thus far been applied have aimed principally at expediting the handling of business, once it is before the House. One of them is the use of committees—especially the newer standing committees—as described in an earlier chapter. Another is the introduction of the various forms of closure. Still another is, of course, the progressive modification of the rules, beginning as far back as 1811, so as to give precedence to government bills, together with the shortening of the time for considering the estimates of expenditure to twenty days. All of these procedural devices, while not without disadvantages, have made it possible to accomplish more in a session; and from time to time more or less successful efforts

[36] The difficulties and shortcomings of Parliament are discussed from various viewpoints in H. M. Hyndman, "Are We Constitutionally Governed?" "An Antiquated Assembly," *Nineteenth Cent.*, June, 1921; A. G. Gardiner, "The Twilight of Parliament," *Atlant. Monthly*, Aug., 1921; E. Barker, "The Origin and Future of Parliament," *Edinburgh Rev.*, July, 1921; C. Watney, "The Defects of Our Parliamentary System," *Fortnightly Rev.*, Feb., 1927; J. M. Kenworthy, "The Decay of Parliament," *ibid.*, July, 1927; H. A. L. Fisher, "The Adequacy of Parliaments," *Contemp. Rev.*, Feb., Mar., 1928; H. Cox, "The Decay of Parliament," *Eng. Rev.*, Jan., 1929; J. R. MacDonald, *Parliament and Revolution* (New York, 1920); and H. Belloc, *The House of Commons and Monarchy* (London, 1920). The last-mentioned book is interesting but unconvincing.

are made to find still other changes in the rules that will serve the same purpose. Another line of solution is the growing practice of delegating legislative power to the executive, to be exercised by order in council. Detailed regulations are required, for example, to fix the functions of a new administrative agency, or on such a subject as import licenses. Parliament has not time to attend to the matter. Accordingly it gives the king-in-council, or an executive department, or even a local authority, power to make laws about it, in the form of orders. It dislikes doing so; a proposal to leave a matter to be regulated by administrative orders is always unpopular in the House. But frequently there is no alternative. Regulative powers are delegated even to quasi-governmental bodies such as trade boards and canal commissions. Sixty years ago it was found desirable, on grounds quite apart from relieving parliamentary congestion, to abandon altogether a form of activity which had come to be somewhat exacting, i.e., the making and revising of the rules of court procedure.[37] But in the ordinary course of events relief does not often come in this fashion.

All this, however, leaves the problem largely unsolved. Business in hand is somewhat expedited, but the amount that piles up demanding attention seems no smaller than before. In this situation, the obvious proposal is to give relief by making some far more extensive, and perhaps essentially novel, provision for part of the work which now produces the overcrowding; and of late, suggestions to this end have called out a great amount of interesting discussion. The idea is to devolve Parliament's present powers and duties, on a new and grander scale, upon other authorities. How to go about it is, however, not so easy to determine. It might, of course, be done geographically; that is to say, certain powers might be transferred to substitute bodies, to be exercised throughout given sections of the kingdom. On the other hand, it might be done functionally, in which case control over certain subjects or interests would be relinquished, for the entire country, to suitable separate authorities. According as the one plan or the other were to be followed, the country would have territorial devolution or functional devolution.

[37] See p. 625 below.

Functional Devolution

Both plans have ardent advocates. In general, the functional scheme is favored by the more radical political elements, the territorial by the more conservative; although plenty of people are still disinclined to see either proceeded with to any great extent. The functional principle could, of course, be applied in connection with many different fields of governmental control, e.g., education and public health, for each of which might conceivably be set up a separate national body charged with either conditional or absolute legislative power. As a matter of fact, however, the idea is urged mainly in relation to what may broadly be termed industrial matters. Thus a large portion of the Labor party follows Sidney and Beatrice Webb in their proposal to draw a sharp line between political government and industrial government, to set over against the political parliament and the present political executive a social parliament with separate executive organs, and thereby to accomplish the double purpose of achieving industrial (equally with political) democracy and relieving the present political parliament of an appreciable share of the burden of work under which it staggers.[38] Guild socialists go farther, and, in pressing the doctrine of self-government in industry, narrow the field of the political state, and therefore of Parliament as we know it, to exceedingly limited bounds, looking forward, indeed,—although not all are agreed, and none are too clear in what they say—to the eventual extinction of the political state altogether.[39] A great industrial conference of 1919 went on record for a permanent national industrial council consisting of two hundred representative employers and an equal number of representatives of labor, and authorized to consider all questions of an industrial nature and submit its recommendations to Parliament, which would be expected to give them the form and sanction of law. Such a plan was provided for in the German republican constitution of the same year, and in later times has been realized to

[38] *A Constitution for the Socialist Commonwealth of Great Britain* (London, 1920), Pt. ii, Chap. 1.

[39] G. D. H. Cole, *Social Theory* (London, 1920), Chaps. v-vii. The guild socialist movement is in decline, but ideas for which the guild socialists have stood will undoubtedly persist.

a considerable extent in practice; a National Economic Council functions actively as a feature of the politico-economic system of the Reich. There has been a somewhat similar development in France, dating from the Socialist régime of M. Herriot in 1924, and Fascist Italy has been profoundly influenced by the idea.[40]

Plans of Territorial Devolution

There is a good deal to be said for the functional principle. Many students of the subject feel, however, that such devices as the German and French economic councils, while doubtless of value for advisory purposes, do not really point the way to a full solution—that, in any case, the rescue of parliaments from their present congested condition must be by means of organs clearly subordinate to them, not through independent or quasi-independent authorities.[41] Moreover, recent association of the functional idea with various forms of Continental radicalism, e.g., syndicalism and bolshevism, has cooled even such interest as the average Englishman's native conservatism had permitted him to develop. Certainly public feeling today is not, on the whole, favorable to the adoption of any definite functional plan. Territorial, or regional, devolution is, however, not only a much discussed, but a highly practical, question. The essential idea in it is that the congestion of business from which Parliament suffers might be relieved, and legitimate aspirations to regional self-government at the same time satisfied, by dividing the kingdom into certain great areas, each to be given a subordinate, yet reasonably powerful, parliament of its own. Under such an arrangement, a great deal of the business that now clutters up the calendars at Westminster would pass over en-

[40] See Art. 165 of the German national constitution; and for an account of the German National Economic Council, H. Finer, *Representative Government and a Parliament of Industry* (London, 1923). The establishment of the French National Economic Council is described by Miss E. C. Bramhall in *Amer. Polit. Sci. Rev.*, Aug., 1926. On Italian developments, see W. Y. Elliott, *The Pragmatic Revolt in Politics* (New York, 1928), Chap. xi. C. E. Coles, "Occupational Franchise," *Fortnightly Rev.*, Dec., 1923, proposes a reconstruction of the British House of Commons on the basis of an occupational franchise as a means of forestalling guild socialism.

[41] This view is voiced, for example, in H. Speyer, *La réforme de l'état en Belgique* (Brussels, 1927).

tirely to the regional assemblies; and although the latter would not be sovereign bodies in the same sense as the imperial parliament, most of their acts would not require even so much as review by that authority. Adoption of the plan, furthermore, would not necessitate cutting the country into new and arbitrary divisions; for although it is occasionally suggested that the areas for the purpose should be formed by combining counties in more or less artificial groups,[42] it is usually considered that both the natural and proper areas would be the great historic lands out of which the United Kingdom was built, i.e., England, Wales, Scotland, and Ireland. As things stand, much legislation has to be enacted at Westminster for each of these regions separately. In 1912, indeed, it was computed that 49.8 per cent of all the public laws passed by Parliament in the previous twenty years applied to some one only of the four constituent parts of the United Kingdom. More recently it has been computed that, even with the Irish Free State managing its own affairs, a full quarter of parliamentary time at Westminster goes to matters of a regional character. Let the bulk of this regional legislation, it is argued, be turned over to regional parliaments, so that the parliament at Westminster may be freer to give proper time and attention to the affairs of the realm in general, including those of England unless a subordinate parliament should be set up for that area also. The argument is strengthened not only by the circumstance that Scotland and Wales are actively agitating for parliaments of their own,[43] but by the fact that Northern Ireland, under the Government of Ireland Act of 1920, has been given a separate legislature and therefore affords a true example of devolution already in operation—to say nothing of Free-State Ireland with its full dominion status.[44]

[42] For example, by dividing England into three provinces. with legislatures meeting at London, Winchester, and York.

[43] See pp. 681-688 below.

[44] It is interesting to observe that the historic Irish home rule movement always looked to home rule not only for Ireland but for other parts of the United Kingdom, i.e., "home rule all round," and that the Irish home rule bills of 1912 and 1919 were put forward by the respective cabinets as parts of a general program of regional devolution. In the end, the greater part of Ireland got much more than "home rule," becoming, in effect, a self-governing dominion. But the northern counties are on a home rule basis,

At the close of the World War it was common opinion that Parliament had reached its lowest ebb, and it is not strange that at a juncture when constitutional readjustment was more than usually in the air, devolution should have become a leading subject of discussion—the more by reason of the fact that the Irish question was still awaiting settlement. The House of Commons itself took up the matter and after lively debate went on record, in 1919, by a decisive vote, in favor of "the creation of subordinate legislatures within the United Kingdom" and asked the government to appoint a parliamentary commission to prepare a plan. The result was a "speaker's conference," of thirty-three members, which in the spring of 1920 laid before Parliament, not a single plan—because agreement on all points was found impossible—but two alternative plans, one commonly referred to as the speaker's plan, the other as the plan of Mr. Murray Macdonald, one of the minority members.[45] The government having introduced a new bill on Ireland while the commission was deliberating, it was decided to leave that part of the realm out of account. But in England, Scotland, and Wales, it was felt by all members to be desirable that new subordinate legislatures should be created; and there were no wide differences of opinion upon the powers that might properly be transferred to them. In general, these powers embraced all regulation of trades and professions, police, public health, public charities, agriculture, law and minor judicial administration, education, ecclesiastical matters, housing, insurance, highways, and municipal government, together with control of a long list of sources of public revenue. The main difference between the two schemes related to the composition and form of the proposed regional legislatures. Under the speaker's plan, each area was to have a "grand council" consisting of (a) a council of commons, composed of all of the members of the national House of Commons sitting for constituencies within that area, and (b) a council of peers, consisting of members of the

almost exactly of the sort that present advocates of territorial devolution have in mind. See pp. 716-717 below.

[45] *Conference on Devolution: Letter to Mr. Speaker from the Prime Minister* (with appendices). Cmd. 692 (1920). In view of the subject-matter of the investigation, the speaker (Mr. J. W. Lowther) was the natural person to act as the commission's chairman.

House of Lords designated by the committee of selection of that body, and half as numerous as the members of the lower house. All members of the divisional parliaments would, therefore, be members also of the general parliament; and the meetings of the former were to be held in the autumn of each year so as to avoid conflict with the sessions of the latter.[46] The Macdonald plan, on the other hand, provided for divisional parliaments whose members were to be specially elected to them, without relation to membership in the national parliament. This would put them on an entirely separate basis and would enable them to sit when and as long as they pleased; and they were to be organized in one house or two as the government should later determine.[47]

Merits and Defects of Devolution

It was one thing to contemplate the beauties of devolution in the abstract, and quite another to take responsibility for the constitutional wrench that would be necessary to put it into effect. The commission's plans attracted much attention, both at Westminster and throughout the country. But the nation was not ready for the plunge, and to the present time nothing further has been done, beyond keeping up discussion of the general problem from all conceivable angles,[48] and, perhaps one should add, carrying out in 1929 certain decentralizing changes in the relations of national and local authorities in line with the devolution principle. The proposal in general and the plans of 1920 in particular have been criticized on many grounds. It is objected that to proceed on any of the suggested lines would mean to turn back the pages of history—to loosen bonds of union which, as Mr. Balfour has reminded his countrymen, two hundred years of constitutional development have consistently aimed to strengthen. The Irish settlement has, of

[46] This scheme might be viewed as, in essence, an extension of the existing committee system, except that (1) the regional bodies would be *joint* committees, (2) they would sit elsewhere than at Westminster, and (3) they would have power not merely to discuss and report but also to act.

[47] The work of the conference and the schemes proposed are described at length in W. H. Chiao, *Devolution in Great Britain* (New York, 1926), Chap. vi.

[48] The progress of opinion on the subject to 1926 is reviewed briefly in W. H. Chiao, *op. cit.*, Chap. viii.

course, shattered some of those bonds irreparably; the less reason, it is argued, for deliberately relaxing those that remain. By the same token, devolution would obscure the unitary character of the government and impart a decided slant toward federalism; it might even end in outright federalism. But no centralized state (so it is argued) has ever regarded a more loosely knit system of sovereignty as an object of deliberate policy; development has always led in the opposite direction. Federalism is on the decline throughout the world. Even in the United States, the activities and functions of the national government are steadily growing at the expense of the states.[49] Furthermore, it is contended, devolution, if tried, would prove a disappointment. Certainly in the form proposed in the majority scheme of 1920 it would not make life any easier for the men who would find themselves members of two parliaments instead of one. But in any case the effect would be to duplicate machinery, complicate tasks, and produce confusion and conflict of jurisdiction, to such extent that the wear and tear of present legislative life would be but slightly relieved, if at all. Particularly prolific of difficulties would be the allocation of control over revenues and the tendency to *ultra vires* legislation. In the homely English phrase, much of what was gained on the savings might easily be lost on the roundabouts.

Finally, it is pointed out that the time and effort of the House of Commons could be economized appreciably by changes less drastic than devolution, and entailing fewer disadvantages. One such would be the transfer of all private bill legislation to an entirely distinct body, of a frankly judicial character, and able to sit locally when, as in large numbers of cases, there would be gain in doing so. In reality, this would itself, of course, be a species of devolution, on functional lines; and it may be added that the increasing use of provisional orders, while not relieving Parliament of the necessary formalities of confirmation, has already appreciably reduced the number of private bills coming before the body, and therefore the labor

[49] Federalism as a possible solution of Britain's problem is discussed unfavorably in A. V. Dicey, *Law of the Constitution* (8th ed.), Chap. iii. The relations between federalism and devolution are discussed in W. H. Chiao, *op. cit.,* 28-36.

involved in handling them. Another mode of relief would be the granting of wider powers to county, borough, and other local authorities—a policy which some capable students of the problem believe would of itself yield all the saving of Parliament's time that could possibly be realized from any scheme of devolution. Of such decentralization—on lines of what in America would be termed "home rule"—there has already, of course, been a good deal. There will be more, in certain directions. If, however, we accept the common view that the trend of modern social and economic development is toward consolidation and compactness, requiring more uniform and concentrated legislative control, the gains to be looked for from this source are problematical. Certainly in the United States the tendency is toward the increase of the functions and activities of the national government at the expense of the states; [50] and one is moved to wonder how far a nation with a highly unitary government such as the English can expect to go in the direction of federalism in an age in which another kindred nation endowed with a thoroughgoing federal system is finding that system increasingly inadequate for its purposes.

At all events, how to reconcile the legitimate demands of the cabinet with the equally legitimate rights of parliamentary minorities; how to find time within parliamentary hours for disposing of the growing mass of public business; in what measure, and by what means, Parliament can hope to recover its lost prestige—these and other questions (plenty of them) challenge the British statesman at every turn. Solutions will have to be found. When attained, however, they will probably be discovered to have taken the characteristic English form, not of instant, drastic, carefully calculated, and systematic change, but of slow and piecemeal readjustment.[51]

[50] F. A. Ogg and P. O. Ray, *Introduction to American Government,* Chap. xxix; W. Thompson, *Federal Centralization* (New York, 1923).

[51] The case for devolution is strongly put in J. A. M. Macdonald and Lord Charnwood, *The Federal Solution* (London, 1914); J. R. MacDonald, *Parliament and Revolution* (New York, 1920), Chap. viii; and W. H. Chiao, *Devolution in Great Britain* (New York, 1926), Chaps. ii-iii. The last-mentioned book is a convenient general outline of the movement, but suffers somewhat from lack of intimate contact by its author with the realities of the problem. The objections are presented in Chiao, *op. cit.,* Chap. vii, and in G. B. Hurst, "Federal Devolution," *Contemp. Rev.,* Oct-

1919. See also criticism by H. J. Laski, in *A Grammar of Politics*, 309-311. Other discussions include J. A. R. Marriott, *The Mechanism of the Modern State*, II, Chap. xxxviii; A. V. Dicey, "Thoughts on the Parliament of Scotland," *Quar. Rev.*, Apr., 1916; J. A. MacDonald, "Devolution or Destruction," *Contemp. Rev.*, Aug., 1918; W. R. D. Adkins, "Home Rule for England," *ibid.*, Mar., 1920; Anon., "The Better Government of the United Kingdom," *Round Table*, Sept., 1918; J. S. Henderson and H. J. Laski, "A Note on Parliamentary Time and the Problem of Devolution," *Economica*, Mar., 1925; H. B. Lees-Smith, "The Time-Table of the House of Commons," *ibid.*, June, 1924.

France has a similar problem, except that there the emphasis is on administrative, rather than legislative, decentralization. On the "regionalist'" issue, see J. W. Garner, "Administrative Reform in France," *Amer. Polit. Sci. Rev.*, Feb., 1919; J. Hennessey, *La Réorganisation administrative de la France* (Paris, 1919). An interesting plan prepared by a parliamentary commission will be found in *Revue Générale d'Administration*, July-Aug., 1919.

CHAPTER XX

THE DEVELOPMENT OF POLITICAL PARTIES

POLITICAL parties are groups or bodies of people who, holding the same general views on some, if not all, public questions, seek by concerted action to gain control of the government as a means of ensuring that the policies in which they are interested will be carried into effect.[1] They are not peculiar to any age, or to any particular quarter of the world. Patricians and Plebeians in ancient Rome, Guelfs and Ghibellines in medieval Italian towns, Roundheads and Cavaliers in seventeenth-century England—these and many other fiercely contending groups display undeniable characteristics of parties, even though the term "faction" would undoubtedly fit them better. It is, however, where popular government prevails, rather than in lands under autocratic rule, that parties, in the truest sense, flourish chiefly.[2] There it falls to the people to decide upon public policies—or, more often, to select from among themselves the persons with whom the final decision will lie—a thing, however, which they can rarely or never do without developing wide differences of opinion and of purpose. Out of these differences political parties arise. Parties may be largely personal followings; they have been notoriously such in modern Italy and in Latin American countries. They may become barren of principles—bottles (to use a metaphor of Lord Bryce) bearing different labels, but empty. They may be sectional rather than national, ephemeral rather than durable. But they have, or have

[1] Burke's definition, occurring in a classic passage in his *Thoughts on the Causes of the Present Discontents* (1770), runs on slightly different lines. "Party," he says, "is a body of men united for promoting the national interest on some particular principle in which they are all agreed."

[2] This is no less true when autocracy takes the form of a presumably temporary dictatorship than when it is the rule of an absolute king or emperor. There is no free party life in Soviet Russia, Fascist Italy, Riverist Spain, or Horthyan Hungary.

once had, a program; they rally as many people to their standard as direct appeals and other means can be made to attract; and in so far as they are able they push public policy forward along the lines of their convictions, or their interests, or both.

It is common enough to hear political parties spoken of disparagingly. They exist, some one has cynically remarked, not because there are two sides to every question but because there are two sides to every office—an outside and an inside. Party organizations, party caucuses, party bosses, party finances, party campaigns, the spirit of party—all come in for reprobation; and rightly, considering how grievously the interests of good government often suffer at the hands of party managers and workers.[3] Nevertheless, to quote Lord Bryce again, "parties are inevitable. No free large country has been without them. No one has shown how representative government could be worked without them. They bring order out of the chaos of a multitude of voters. If parties cause some evils, they avert and mitigate others." [4] "The most gifted and freest nations politically, "remarks an American writer, "are those that have the most sharply defined parties. . . . Wherever political parties are non-existent, either one finds a passive indifference to all public concerns, born of ignorance and incapacity, or else one finds the presence of a tyrannical and despotic form of government, suppressing the common manifestations of opinion and aspiration on the part of the people. Organized, drilled, and disciplined parties are the only means we have yet discovered by which to secure responsible government, and thus to execute the will of the people." [5]

To be more specific, the uses of political parties in a popular government are at least five-fold. First, they enable men and women who think alike on public questions to unite in support of a common body of principles and policies and to work together to bring these principles and policies into actual operation. In the mass, and without organization, the people can formulate no principle, agree on no policy, carry through no

[3] While men may be willing to die for party, it has been wittily remarked, they seldom praise it. S. Low, *Governance of England* (new ed.), 119.

[4] *Modern Democracies,* I, 119.

[5] P. O. Ray, *Introduction to Political Parties and Practical Politics* (new ed., New York, 1917), 9-10.

project. Second, parties afford a convenient, and indeed indispensable means by which men who have the same objects in view may agree in advance upon the candidates whom they will support for office, and recommend them to the electorate. Third, they educate and organize public opinion and stimulate public interest by keeping the public informed upon the issues of the day through the press, platform, radio, and other agencies. Fourth, they furnish a certain social and political cement by which the more or less independent and scattered parts of the government (in so far, at all events, as they are in the hands of men belonging to the same party) are bound together in an effective working mechanism. Fifth, the party system tends to insure that the government at any given time will be subject to steady organized criticism, the effect of which will usually be wholesome. These are all important services, essential to well-ordered popular government.[6]

Connections Between the Party System and the Cabinet System in Britain

It was in English-speaking countries that party first became a force in free political life, and nowhere today does "government by party" hold completer sway than in the English motherland. We may leave to the historians the question of when English parties really began. Sir Thomas Erskine May thought of the Puritans of Elizabethan days as forming the earliest English party. Macaulay found nothing worthy of the name before 1641. Almost everybody agrees that, at all events, the Whigs and Tories of the later years of Charles II were true parties, the progenitors of the two great opposing political forces which thereafter, for almost two centuries and a half,

[6] Compare, however, the trenchant discussions in H. Belloc and G. Chesterton, *The Party System* (London, 1911), and R. Michels, *Les partis politiques; essai sur les tendances oligarchiques des démocraties* (Paris, 1914), trans. under the title *Political Parties: a Sociological Study of the Oligarchical Tendencies of Modern Democracy* (New York, 1915). On the nature and functions of parties, see also A. L. Lowell, *Public Opinion and Popular Government*, Chaps. v-viii; E. M. Sait, *American Parties and Elections* (New York, 1927), Chaps. vi-vii; C. E. Merriam, *The American Party System* (New York, 1922), Chap. xiii; and C. A. Beard, *The American Party Battle* (New York, 1928), Chap. i. J. Bryce, *Modern Democracies*, Chap. xi, is an exceptionally illuminating exposition of the subject.

divided the nation between them. This means that the generations which saw the ripening of responsible government—of the cabinet system—were the same that witnessed the rise of the party system. And the thing to be specially observed is the natural and necessary relation between the two developments—if, indeed, they can be spoken of as two rather than as one. The essence of the cabinet system is the control of the government at any given time by a group of persons who are in substantial agreement upon political principles and policies, and the continuance of these persons at the helm only so long as they have the active support of a working majority in the popular branch of the legislature. But, as William III discovered more than two centuries ago, the only way to get a group of ministers who can work together harmoniously is to take them all from the same political element, or *party;* while experience also taught that the only kind of a parliamentary majority having sufficient coherence and stability to make it at all dependable is a majority held together by the ties of party. Historically, the cabinet system arose out of the warfare of parties; in the absence of party alignments and rivalries, it is difficult to see how it could ever have arisen at all. Without parties, one or the other of two equally undesirable situations would exist. Either ministries would rise and fall with bewildering rapidity because there were no organized forces interested in keeping them in power, or they would go on ruling indefinitely after they had got entirely out of harmony with the popular chamber. There would be small point to the resignation of a ministry if an opposing party did not stand ready to furnish a ministry of a different sort and assume full power and responsibility.[7]

[7] "The 'noiseless revolution' which brought about the modern system began under William III between the years 1693 and 1696, and the system then initiated was developed under the Hanoverian dynasty by Walpole and his successors. The executive authority of the king was put in commission, and it was arranged that the commissioners should be members of the legislative body to whom they are responsible. The king has receded into the background. . . . The ministry must govern. How can the ministry control the body on whose favor their existence depends? How can they prevent the supreme executive council of the nation from being an unorganized, uncontrollable, irresponsible mob? The answer is by party machinery. It is this machinery that secures the necessary discipline. The cabinet system

In Britain, the cabinet system and the party system are, therefore, intimately bound up together, by historical growth and by present practical necessity; indeed, they are but different aspects of the same working mechanism. In the United States, parties stand almost wholly outside the formal governmental system; they are unknown to the Constitution, and until recently their activities were not even regulated by statute. Many of the chief party leaders and managers—for example, the chairmen of the national committees—are not public officials at all, and platforms are made by conventions whose members are drawn mainly from private life. In Britain, however, party works inside rather than outside the governmental system; to a considerable extent, the machinery of party and the machinery of government are one and the same thing. The ministers—at all events those who sit in the cabinet—are at the same time the working executive, the leaders in legislation, and the chiefs of the party in power. The majority in the House of Commons, which legislates, raises and appropriates money, holds the ministers accountable for the conduct of the executive departments, and by its support keeps them in power as long as it is able, is, to all intents and purposes, the party itself; while over against the ministry and its parliamentary majority stands the opposition, consisting of members who belong to a different party and whose leaders are prepared to take the helm whenever their rivals fall out of favor in the popular chamber. In former times, when there were only two major parties, this oscillation was simple, natural, almost automatic. With three great parties in the field, since the rise of Labor to undisputed parity with Conservatism and Liberalism, the system works by no means so smoothly. In 1924, and again at the moment when this book went to press (June, 1929), a ministry was in office representing a party, i.e., Labor, which had only a minority in the House of Commons.[8] Upon occasion, there may even be doubt, as for

presupposes the party system. . . ." C. Ilbert, in J. Redlich, *Procedure of the House of Commons,* I, p. xv.

[8] This was not an entirely unprecedented situation, in that minor groups, e.g., the Peelites near the middle of the nineteenth century and the Irish Nationalists in 1886, 1892-95, and 1910-14, had sometimes held the balance of power between the two great parties. Alliance with such groups, however, always gave the party in power a more effective working majority

example, at the assembling of the House of Commons elected in 1918, as to what group is entitled to be regarded as "the opposition." Government, nevertheless, as we shall see, is still government by party; notwithstanding novel and embarrassing contingencies that have risen, all of the foregoing observations hold true, fundamentally, as before.[9]

This matter of the number of parties is of prime importance. Not only does a responsible ministry postulate government by party; in order to work smoothly, such a ministerial system requires the existence of two great parties and no more—each, in the words of Bryce, "strong enough to restrain the violence of the other, yet one of them steadily preponderant in any given House of Commons."[10] Considerations of unity and responsibility demand that the party in power shall be strong enough to govern alone, or substantially so. Similarly, when it goes out of power, a party of equivalent strength ought to come in. Obviously, this must mean two great parties, practically dividing the electorate between them. Any considerable splitting up of the people beyond this point is likely to result in the inability of any single party to command a working majority, with the result that ministries will have to be based upon coalitions, and consequently will lack unity and responsibility, and will be liable to be toppled over by the first adverse wind that blows. This is precisely the situation in France, Germany, and practically all other Continental countries, which, having copied the outlines of the English cabinet system, are severely handicapped in operating the scheme by the multiplicity of parties and fac-

than the Labor party in 1924, supported only passively by the Liberals, could claim to possess. See pp. 508-510 below. In 1929 Labor entered office, not only without a parliamentary majority, but also without any alliance, even passive, with another party.

[9] For a fuller presentation of the relations of party and the cabinet system, see A. L. Lowell, *Government of England,* I, Chap. xxiv, and "The Influence of Party upon Legislation in England and America," *Annual Report of Amer. Hist. Assoc., 1901* (Washington, 1902), I, 325-335. There is, curiously, no convenient general history of English parties, nor indeed any systematic and up-to-date treatise on the English party system. Chapters xxiv-xxxvii of Lowell's *Government of England* treat the subject satisfactorily, except that they are out of date; and certain phases are covered exhaustively in M. Ostrogorski, *Democracy and the Organization of Political Parties,* trans. by F. Clarke (London, 1902), I.

[10] *American Commonwealth* (3rd edition), I, 287.

tional groups.[11] Despite the rise, fifty years ago, of the Irish Nationalist group, and later of the Labor party, it was still true in Great Britain at the outbreak of the World War, as it had been since political parties first made their appearance there, that nearly the entire population gave its allegiance to one or the other of two parties only. The defeat of one meant the triumph of the other, and either alone was normally able to govern independently if elevated to office. As has been explained, the war brought about the formation of a series of coalition ministries, lasting, all told, from 1915 to 1922. At the end of that time party government was resumed, with the Conservatives in power. In opposition now, however, were found, not one great party, as in former times, but three separate parties—National Liberal, Independent Liberal, and Labor. And although the two branches of Liberalism were reunited in 1923, Labor had meanwhile attained such strength that even yet there were three major parties rather than two. This remained the situation at the date of writing (1929); although there seemed still a chance that, in one way or another, the country would eventually find itself back on a bi-party basis.[12]

The seventeenth-century origins of English parties, the relations of Whigs and Tories after the Revolution of 1688-89, and the prolonged supremacy of the Whigs under the early Georges have been noted at an earlier point.[13] To tell the story of party development from these days of beginnings to the present moment would require far more space than is available here; besides, our main interest is not party history, but the composition, organization, methods, and outlook of parties to-day—in short, the workings of the party system in its relations with the governmental institutions that have been described in the foregoing chapters. Accordingly it must suffice to set

[11] See, for example, E. M. Sait, *Government and Politics of France,* Chap. x. Mr. MacDonald's Labor government of 1929, having no parliamentary majority, nor yet any alliance with another party, presented, of course, a different situation, but one which certainly gave no promise of stability.

[12] See p. 563 below. W. J. Shepard, "The Psychology of the Bi-Party System," *Social Forces,* June, 1926, is a suggestive discussion of the bi-party principle. Cf. G. M. Trevelyan, *The Two-Party System in English Political History* (Oxford, 1926).

[13] See pp. 56-58 above.

down a bare outline of party events leading up, by long stages, to the alignment of political forces which the observer meets in the Britain of the present date.[14]

Conservatives and Liberals in the Nineteenth Century

As the eighteenth century advanced, the cabinet system slowly took on its present characteristics, under the stimulus of unre-

[14] Developments of the past twelve or fifteen years will be sketched somewhat more fully than those of earlier times. As has been pointed out, there is no satisfactory history of English political parties from their origins to the present day. An old work, G. W. Cooke, *History of Party from the Rise of the Whig and Tory Factions in the Reign of Charles II to the Passing of the Reform Bill,* 3 vols. (London, 1836-37), covers the subject reasonably well to the end of the last unreformed parliament. Systematic histories of particular parties are also largely lacking—at all events, works covering the history of a party in its entirety. H. Fyfe, *The British Liberal Party; an Historical Sketch* (London, 1928), is a work of this kind, and for the Irish Nationalist and Labor parties the need is largely supplied by F. H. O'Donnell, *History of the Irish Parliamentary Party,* 2 vols. (London, 1910), and H. Tracey (ed.), *The Book of the Labour Party* (London, 1925), Vol. I. Period histories of the Tory (later Conservative) party include K. G. Feiling, *A History of the Tory Party, 1640-1714* (Oxford, 1924); M. H. Woods, *A History of the Tory Party in the Seventeenth and Eighteenth Centuries* (London, 1924); and T. E. Kebble, *A History of Toryism from the Accession of Mr. Pitt in 1783 to the Death of Lord Beaconsfield in 1881* (London, 1886). The first two are systematic and scholarly works; the third is hardly more than a series of sketches, chronologically arranged, of Tory prime ministers and other leaders. The value of Woods' volume is increased by the addition of a substantial chapter on the Tory party in the nineteenth and twentieth centuries. A general history of the Liberal party, less recent than Fyfe, is W. L. Blease, *A Short History of English Liberalism* (New York, 1913), although the main theme is rather the development of liberalism as a political philosophy and program than the growth of the Liberal party as a piece of political machinery. R. S. Watson, *The National Liberal Federation from its Commencement to the General Election of 1906* (London, 1907), is useful but not particularly informing. There is a certain amount of party history in such works as L. T. Hobhouse, *Liberalism* (London, 1911); H. Cecil, *Conservatism* (London, 1912); and G. G. Butler, *The Tory Tradition* (London, 1914). Various aspects of party history are brought out in W. Harris, *History of the Radical Party in Parliament* (London, 1885); J. B. Daly, *The Dawn of Radicalism* (London, 1892); and C. B. R. Kent, *The English Radicals* (London, 1899). It goes without saying that there is a great deal of party history in works of the nature of W. E. H. Lecky, *History of England in the Eighteenth Century,* 8 vols. (New York, 1878-90), and in innumerable biographies and memoirs. A complete list of ministries since 1824, indicating the holders of some of the principal offices, will be found in the *Const. Year Book* (1928), 76-78.

mitting rivalries of the Whig and Tory elements. The Tories, indeed, reconciled themselves to the Hanoverian succession with much difficulty, and only after the period of the American Revolution did they give up their Jacobite connections and become as loyal to the new dynasty as were their rivals. Only then, also, did they accept the single-party cabinet as a permanent feature of the governmental system. Throughout the era of the French Revolution and of Napoleon they were in power almost continuously, and in their efforts to protect the nation, not only against the Corsican but against the contagion of Continental revolution, they had the steady support of the great bulk of the governing classes. In 1815 their position seemed impregnable. The restoration of peace, however, brought new and weighty problems with which their strongly conservative bent fitted them but poorly to deal; the movement for political reform, held in check during the quarter-century of war, got out of hand, and, notwithstanding that the more liberal-minded leaders like Peel and Canning piloted several progressive measures through Parliament, the party failed to satisfy the nation in the new and restless mood that had come over it. With the resignation of the Duke of Wellington's ministry in 1830, a solid half-century of Tory rule came to an end.[15]

Except for two or three brief intervals, the Whigs held office from this date until 1874. At the outset they were hardly less aristocratic than the Tories. But they were reënforced and appreciably liberalized by the infusion of newly enfranchised middle-class townspeople after the legislation of 1832, and their first decade of power became a period of notable and long-awaited reform, in which, it should be added, they had the

[15] Beginning with 1815, the best work on English political history in the earlier nineteenth century is S. Walpole, *History of England from the Conclusion of the Great War in 1815*, 6 vols. (new ed., London, 1902). Good general accounts are presented in I. S. Leadam, *History of England from the Accession of Anne to the Death of George II* (London, 1909), and W. Hunt, *History of England from the Accession of George III to the Close of Pitt's First Administration* (London, 1905). The period 1783-1830 is treated briefly in T. E. May and F. Holland, *Constitutional History of England*, I, 409-440, and *Cambridge Modern History*, IX, Chap. XXII, and X, Chaps. XVIII-XX. A good political biography is A. Aspinwall, *Lord Brougham and the Whig Party* (Manchester, 1927).

support not only of various radical groups but of many discontented Tories as well. Now were passed (in addition to the Reform Act itself) the earliest measure making a parliamentary appropriation in aid of public education (1832), a law emancipating all slaves in the colonies (1833), a Factory Act (1833) which was long referred to as the "Great Charter" of labor, a Poor Law Amendment Act (1834) which, with relatively unimportant changes, regulated the administration of public charity until our own day, a Municipal Corporations Act (1835) liberalizing and otherwise putting on its present basis the government of the boroughs, and many other statutes of almost equal permanence and importance. This was the time, too, at which the more meaningful party nomenclature of later days came into use: the name "Whig" gave way to "Liberal;" the term "Tory," although often heard even in present-day Britain, yielded to the term "Conservative." [16]

In 1842 the Liberals were beaten decisively in a parliamentary election; and they might have remained out of power for a long time had not the Conservatives, attempting to carry out some reforms of their own, fallen into hopeless division on Sir Robert Peel's plan for doing away with the historic corn laws. The unpopular restrictions were abolished, and the country was planted firmly on the non-protectionist basis on which it has ever since rested. But the Conservative party was split wide open, and not only were the Liberals enabled to regain office in 1847 but the mid-century decades—roughly, the forties and fifties—became a period of political disintegration during which men crossed freely from one party to another and voting in Parliament frequently followed no clear party lines at all. Gladstone's acceptance of office under Palmerston in 1859 marked the final severance of the "Peelites," i.e., the free-trade element, from the Conservative party and foretokened their final absorption into the Liberal ranks during the ensuing decade.

The next fifteen years, i.e., to 1874, saw party lines once

[16] The name "Conservative" was employed by Canning as early as 1824. Its use was already becoming common when, in January, 1835, Peel, in his manifesto to the electors of Tamworth, undertook an exposition of the principles of what he declared should henceforth be known as the Conservative—not the Tory—party.

more sharply drawn, party voting in Parliament revived, and the two historic parties themselves reconstructed on patterns largely maintained down to the World War. The Liberals, in particular, were cast in a new mold. As long as Palmerston lived, the Liberals of the old school—men who abhorred radicalism and felt that the reforms of the thirties had gone quite far enough—had the upper hand. But after that imperious statesman's death, in 1865, new ideas and influences asserted themselves and a new Liberal party came rapidly to the fore. Curiously enough, the leader of this renovated party was a man of aristocratic birth, a graduate of Oxford, a Conservative by temperament and early allegiance—William E. Gladstone. Coming into the party, however, along with other Peelite seceders from Conservatism, he quickly became, and for almost forty years remained, its most conspicuous figure, serving it and his country at four different periods (in all, more than twelve years) as prime minister. Throwing overboard the laissez-faire ideas of the classical economists, and appropriating many of the principles and policies of a hitherto largely unattached group of Radicals, the party under its new leadership made "peace, retrenchment, and reform" its slogan and started out both to democratize the government by giving the parliamentary suffrage to the masses and to write on the statute book a new set of laws for the protection and general betterment of the common people.[17] It was not Liberalism alone, however, that reoriented itself in these days. Conservatism also acquired a new leader—the middle-class Jew, Benjamin Disraeli—who, reversing Gladstone's experience, started as a Radical but became a staunch Conservative. Conforming to the trend of the times, the Conservative party also interested itself in a wider parliamentary suffrage, becoming, by an unexpected turn of events, the actual sponsor of the Reform Act of 1867. It likewise sought to show that it believed in other types of reform, especially as affecting the conditions of industry. There could be no denying, however, that, in the main, it wanted to keep things as they were, and that its heart was not so much in

[17] On the passing of laissez-faire and the rise of the new Liberalism represented by Gladstone in the world of action and by John Stuart Mill in that of thought, see L. T. Hobhouse, *Liberalism,* Chaps. iv-vii.

the domestic readjustments demanded by the Liberals, as in a strong foreign policy and the upbuilding of the Empire. In a generation when the country was gradually recovering its earlier interest in foreign expansion and dominion, Disraeli was the great imperialist. Many of the sharpest clashes between him and Gladstone as leaders, and between the parties which they led, turned on the question of whether the nation should give itself primarily to tasks beyond seas or to others nearer home.

One of these questions nearer home was that of Ireland. For one reason or another, Ireland had always been a problem. Never since English rule was first planted in the island in the days of Henry II had things gone very smoothly, and at the juncture when Gladstone and Disraeli began moving in and out of Downing Street by turns the situation was rather less favorable than usual. The main difficulty now was that, whereas the Act of Union of 1800 left Ireland without a separate parliament and subjected her to numerous laws made at Westminster, throughout the center and south—the more truly Irish parts of the country—there was insistent demand for "home rule," involving, among other things, the restoration to Ireland of a parliament of her own. Seventy-five or more constituencies were regularly sending to Westminster representatives pledged to fight for such home rule; and in times when the balance between the two great parties was fairly close, these "Nationalists" not only could but did obstruct proceedings in the House of Commons and make life generally uncomfortable, especially for the government party.[18] Gladstone and his followers suffered as much inconvenience from this source as did their opponents; both the first and second ministries of the Great Commoner were driven on the rocks mainly by issues relating to Ireland—in the second instance, by hostile votes of the Nationalists themselves. Feeling, however, some real sympathy with the Irish position, and considering that it would be good strategy to attach the Nationalists to his own party, the Liberal leader now decided upon a bold course, namely, to make his party sponsor for a bill that would give the Irish what they

[18] As has appeared, it was the tactics of the Nationalists that first drove the House of Commons to adopt rules providing for closure of debate. See p. 405 above.

wanted. And when, in 1886, the Conservatives were in turn upset because of their unwillingness to meet the Nationalist demands, the opportunity was seized.

The first home rule bill was a momentous measure. Not that it became law; it did not even pass the House of Commons, and once again the Liberals fell from power on an Irish question. But the episode led to political realignments of first-rate importance. In the first place, the Nationalists, recognizing in the Liberal party their true—and only—friend, became in effect an affiliated political group, even though they were not very amenable to discipline and sometimes failed their allies at critical moments. Over against this accession of strength (such as it was) had, however, to be set severe losses suffered through the defection of large numbers of Liberals who were totally unwilling to go along with Gladstone in his new policy. More than a hundred Liberal members of the House of Commons voted with the Conservatives against the bill, thus ensuring its defeat, and then—it appearing that Gladstone and those who had stood by him had no intention of giving up the plan—drew off entirely from the party. For a time the dissenters, known as Liberal Unionists, followed an independent course. But most of them found that upon other matters besides Ireland they could rather easily fall into line with the Conservatives, with the result that they gravitated into the ranks of that party and eventually were absorbed into it. Speaking broadly, they represented the elements of wealth and station in the historic Liberal party; and they included many men of exceptional ability, as, for example, Joseph Chamberlain, destined to loom large in the councils of the party of his new allegiance. To Conservatism the recruits from this unexpected source brought fresh vigor, new issues, and even a new name, since in time the term "Conservative" almost completely gave way to the term "Unionist."[19] As for the Liberals, they could only console themselves with the thought that what they had lost in numbers, financial resources, and social connections they had perhaps gained in solidarity.

[19] After the settlement of the Irish problem in 1922 by the creation of the Free State, the term "Unionist" lost its erstwhile significance and "Conservative" came back into general use.

Returning to Downing Street in 1892 for his fourth and last premiership, Gladstone again tried to put a home rule bill on the statute-book. This time (1893) the measure passed the House of Commons. But the House of Lords rejected it, and little more was heard of the subject for ten or fifteen years. Aged and weary of parliamentary strife, Gladstone retired to private life in 1894, not, however, without a final arraignment of the House of Lords and a prophecy of the crisis which in 1911 led to the curtailment of the powers of that body. Lord Rosebery succeeded to the premiership. Already, however, the Liberal majority was dwindling, and a few months sufficed to bring the Conservatives, under Lord Salisbury, again to power. From this point (1895) dates a full decade of Conservative, or Unionist, rule, rounding out thirty years of office broken only by three intervals (two of them very brief) of Liberal supremacy. During the earlier portion of the decade the Liberals, rent by factional disputes and personal rivalries, offered no very serious opposition. The home rule question, as has been said, fell into abeyance; and although the Unionists carried a considerable amount of social and industrial legislation, the interest of the period centers largely in policies and achievements in the domain of foreign and colonial affairs. The most hotly contested issue was imperialism; the most commanding public figure was the colonial secretary, Joseph Chamberlain; the most notable enterprise undertaken was the war in South Africa.

Rare is the political party that, having piloted a nation through a war, is able to remain in control of affairs very long after peace is restored. The Unionists, after the Peace of Pretoria (1902), proved no exception to the rule. Taking advantage of the country's restlessness under increased taxation, of animosities roused by an education act of 1902, and especially of sharp division in the Unionist ranks precipitated by a proposal of Chamberlain for the introduction of a system of protective tariffs, the Liberals—although led by the rather colorless Sir Henry Campbell-Bannerman—pulled themselves together and put such obstacles in the ministry's pathway that near the end of 1905 Mr. Balfour [20] and his colleagues, al-

[20] Nephew of Lord Salisbury, and successor as prime minister upon his uncle's retirement to private life in 1902.

though still able to count a working majority in the House of Commons, decided to give up the fight. The Liberals, under Campbell-Bannerman, took office tentatively; and at a general election held early in 1906 they secured the most impressive parliamentary majority ever possessed by a British party since the cabinet system began.[21]

Liberal Rule in Pre-War Years

The Liberal ascendancy thus established lasted substantially a decade, i.e., until 1915, when war-time conditions forced party government to give way temporarily to the principle of coalition. Few periods of equal length in modern English history have been more crowded with action or more productive of significant constitutional change. Led at the outset by Campbell-Bannerman, and after 1908 by Asquith, the party in power addressed itself to an ambitious program of political reform and social legislation—abolishing plural voting, introducing new forms of social insurancc, providing machinery for the settlement of industrial disputes, undenominationalizing schools, tightening up the regulation of the liquor traffic, readjusting the burden of taxation—only to be brought up short in some of its most important ventures by the hostility of a heavily Conservative House of Lords. We have seen how the veto, in 1909, of the far-reaching tax proposals of the new Chancellor of the Exchequer, the vibrant Lloyd George, led, first, to a vindication of the project at a general election of early 1910, and, later, to an equally successful appeal on second chamber reform, culminating in the historic Parliament Act of 1911.

[21] The political history of the larger part of the period 1830-1905 is covered in S. Low and L. C. Sanders, *History of England during the Reign of Queen Victoria* (London, 1907). Briefer treatment will be found in T. E. May and F. Holland, *Constitutional History of England,* I, 440-468, III, 67-127, and *Cambridge Modern History,* XI, Chaps. i, xi, xii; and XII, Chap. iii. Indispensable biographies include J. Morley, *Life of William E. Gladstone,* 3 vols. (London, 1903); W. F. Monypenny and G. E. Buckle, *Life of Benjamin Disraeli, Earl of Beaconsfield,* 6 vols. (London, 1910-20); S. H. Jeyes, *Mr. Chamberlain, His Life and Public Career* (London, 1903); E. T. Raymond, *The Life of Lord Rosebery* (London, 1923); and L. Strachey, *Queen Victoria* (New York, 1921). The history of the Tory (Conservative) party in the nineteenth century is sketched in M. H. Woods, *History of the Tory Party,* Chap. xxi.

Possessed of the whip-hand as never before, the party now began putting one significant measure after another on the statute-book, even though, somewhat curiously, its deliberate bringing into play of the provisions of the Parliament Act on such great measures as the home rule bill of 1913, the plural voting bill of the same year, and a bill of 1914 disestablishing and disendowing the church in Wales did not result in any actual and effective legislation under the terms of that hard-won statute.[22] The growing problem of woman suffrage, on which the leaders were totally unable to agree, proved, however, increasingly harassing; and at the moment when the World War unexpectedly broke, the party faced the solemn probability that it would plunge all Ireland, perchance Britain herself, into civil war unless the resurrected home rule program, on which everything had been staked, was given up. Besides, a general election was in the offing, with victory decidedly uncertain.

War-Time Conditions and Coalition Government

War can usually be depended upon to force politics out of accustomed channels and to thrust parties into unanticipated situations. New or dormant issues are brought to the fore; men are driven into unfamiliar relations, which upset their habits and change their ways of thinking; and even if, as is usually the case, public sentiment is stirred, in the face of a sudden external danger, to demand a complete suspension of party contests—that is to say, a party truce—in the end there is likely to be an intensification, rather than otherwise, of party spirit and party activity. So it was in the United States after the Civil War; and so it has certainly been in Britain since 1914.

As soon as the die was cast for war, a truce was entered into by the leaders of all parties and groups, to be binding as long as the contest should last. The decision for war was supported by all elements except the Independent Labor group;[23] and all (even the element mentioned) eventually subscribed to the

[22] See p. 346 above. The home rule bill was carried, but was not put into operation.

[23] See p. 541 below.

truce. Divisive domestic questions, including the Irish crisis, were to be shelved; adherents of all parties were to work together in Parliament for the country's well-being in the emergency, without consideration for or prejudice to their party standing; no party was to try, at a by-election, to wrest a seat from a different party to which it "belonged." The war, it was supposed, would soon be over. All that was required was for domestic dissensions to be suspended while the supreme effort was being made. Afterwards, things could go on as before.

But of course the war was not soon over. On the contrary, it presently gave promise of lasting a long time, and in view of this, as well as because there was dissatisfaction with the way things were going, the idea arose that the government ought to be broadened out so as to be directly representative of all main political elements rather than merely of one. Conservatives and Laborites could not so far forget their past associations as to be willing to go on indefinitely taking orders from a government that was purely Liberal. Besides, many Liberals were willing enough, in a time of such exigency, to take their erstwhile rivals into a partnership of responsibility and labor. The upshot was the adoption, in May, 1915, of a plan of coalition, the Liberal prime minister remaining at the helm but surrounding himself with colleagues who were in about equal numbers Liberals and Conservatives, with also some representation for Labor. No one would have supposed that seven long years would pass before Britain should again have a ministry made up on the traditional party basis. Yet so it proved.

The novel arrangement did not always work smoothly. From time to time dissatisfied ministers threw up their positions, and more than once the entire scheme seemed to be going on the rocks. The Irish question flared up repeatedly, and it was difficult enough for men who held the most divergent views upon it to work together amicably.[24] A general reorganization late in 1916 brought Lloyd George into the premiership, introduced the war cabinet, and imparted fresh vigor to the prosecution of the conflict overseas. But it left the friends of the deposed Asquith disgruntled and marked the beginning of a rift in the Liberal ranks which, resting back upon the sharply

[24] See pp. 703 ff. below.

differing backgrounds, temperaments, and characters of the two leaders, eventuated in a complete split in the party and the emergence of the Asquith, or Independent, Liberals in the rôle of a small but troublesome parliamentary opposition. Furthermore, in the early summer of 1918 the Labor party, over the protest of its representatives in the ministry, openly repudiated its agreement of four years previously and began to work on independent lines toward the goal of a Labor government. Many months before military victory was assured, therefore, the truce of 1914 broke down; and by the date of the armistice (November 11, 1918) the country was again witnessing party strife almost as heated as before the war, even though the lines were drawn differently and the issues were considerably less clear.

Three days after hostilities were suspended on the western front the long-delayed dissolution of Parliament was announced; and in December the people went to the polls at the first general election that the country had known since 1910. War-time conditions joined with the recently enacted electoral law to give the contest many novel features. The electorate, including eight and a half million women, was twice as large as ever before; balloting, except by soldiers and other absentees, was confined to a single day; votes were allowed to be sent in by post, and even to be cast by proxy; the usual party contest was replaced by a trial of strength between a coalition government seeking a fresh lease of life and a number of groups whose physiognomy would hardly have been recognized by a pre-war observer.

The avowed object of the Coalition was to secure, in preparation for the anticipated peace conference, a House of Commons fully and freshly representative of the nation—a parliament that could be trusted to take up with unspent vigor the tasks of economic and social reconstruction. The joint election manifesto of the two leaders, Lloyd George and Bonar Law, stressed land reform, housing reform, reduetion of the war debt without fresh taxes on food and raw materials, reform of the House of Lords, solution of the Irish problem on the basis of self-government but without independence, and sundry other matters. Proclaiming their intention to go their own way and to work for a resuscitation of the historic Liberal party, the Independent Liberals, led by Asquith, pronounced the decision to hold an election at this juncture "a blunder and a calamity," took advanced ground on industry, agriculture, housing, capital and labor, and other social topics, and reaffirmed the conviction that free trade was vitally necessary to the welfare of the nation. The Labor party,[25] which waged a more vigorous campaign than any other group except those in Ireland, demanded "a peace of reconciliation and international coöperation," self-determination for all parts of the British Empire, the nationalization of land, mines, railroads, and electric power, a large program of improved housing at the public expense, heavily graduated direct taxation on capital to pay the war debt, a national minimum wage, universal right to work and maintenance, and complete adult suffrage. In the Catholic portions of Ireland the issue was drawn sharply between the Nationalists and the Sinn Feiners. The former wanted home rule made effective, under the law of 1914; the latter insisted upon full and immediate independence.[26]

The outcome was a complete triumph of the Coalition. There was hardly room for doubt before the poll that the combination would win. But no one expected its margin of success to be so wide. Polling about five-ninths of the popular vote,[27] it obtained 478 seats out of the new total of 707. The Asquith Liberals fared badly. The ex-premier was himself defeated in the constituency of East Fife which had returned him at every election since 1886, and the party captured only twenty-eight seats. Several ex-ministers suffered the humiliation of forfeiting their

[25] A systematic account of the origins and growth of this party is deferred to Chap. xxii. The party was reorganized on a broader basis early in 1918.

[26] See p. 703 below.

[27] The aggregate popular vote, in the United Kingdom as a whole, for Coalition candidates was 5,180,257, as compared with 5,608,430 for non-Coalition candidates, or approximately forty-eight per cent. Unionists contributed 3,471,968 of the Coalition total; Liberals, 1,501,837. The principal non-Coalition votes were: Independent Liberals, 1,320,345; Labor, 1,754,133. These records are, of course, only for constituencies in which there were contests. A total of 107 seats were uncontested. The estimated total Coalition strength in all constituencies was 7,346,286; non-Coalition, 6,527,289. For a complete table of the distribution of the vote, see *Const. Year Book* (London, 1928), 281.

electoral deposits because of failing to poll as many as one-eighth of the votes in their constituencies. Labor increased its representation, winning sixty-three seats. Yet this was by no means the showing that had been confidently predicted; and the three ablest leaders, J. Ramsay MacDonald, Philip Snowden, and Arthur Henderson, were defeated. Somewhat more than a score of non-Coalition Unionists were elected, and two or three minor groups won scattering victories—chiefly the Social Democrats, favorable to the Coalition, with eleven seats. Southern and central Ireland were swept by the Sinn Feiners, who won seventy-three seats, while the Nationalists came off with but seven. Before the election the Nationalists had seventy-eight seats and the Sinn Feiners six.[28] Of sixteen women candidates in the United Kingdom as a whole, one—the Sinn Fein Countess Markievicz—was elected; although, like the other Sinn Fein victors, she declined to take her seat.

Scrutiny of the results led to certain very definite conclusions. The first was that the nation endorsed the coalition government which had brought it successfully through the war, approved its peace terms as far as they had been announced, and wanted peace negotiated by the men then in office. A second was that the people as a whole had no sympathy with pacifism or bolshevism; a score of Labor and Liberal candidates whose names had become associated with the idea of a negotiated peace were defeated decisively. A third conclusion was that the era of Liberal rule begun in 1905 was at an end—that the nation, in other words, had "gone Unionist." Not only was the Coalition quota in the new parliament predominantly Unionist, but the House of Commons as a whole, even counting the non-participating Sinn Feiners, was Unionist by a margin of fifty-three seats. Finally, the result in Ireland proved (if anybody had doubted it) that the situation in that country was more critical than any faced by an English government in a hundred years.

Supported by his new and impressive mandate, the prime minister reconstructed the Coalition ministry, naturally giving most of the important posts to the Unionists; the war cabinet

[28] Ulster returned twenty-five Unionists, most of whom were favorable to the Coalition.

was continued; and attention was turned to the exceptionally difficult problems, both of pacification abroad and readjustment at home, brought to the fore by the cessation of war. Coalition supporters commonly assumed an air of confidence. But unbiased observers were doubtful whether this or any other ministry could expect to last long in such times without a further appeal to the electorate; and no great amount of time was required to show that, while the régime might go on for months, and even years, it would do so, not because of its inherent solidarity and strength, but only because the opposition forces were too divided to be capable of upsetting it. In point of fact, the ministry as refashioned in 1918 lasted, on this somewhat uninspiring basis, full four years.

CHAPTER XXI

PARTIES AND ELECTIONS SINCE 1918

THE political events of the later Coalition years cannot be detailed here. One particularly tortuous chapter, having to do with the handling of the Irish question, will be outlined in another place.[1] As for the rest, it must suffice to mention only three or four outstanding developments. One was the steady waning of the popularity of the ministry, almost from the first. Mr. Lloyd George and his colleagues had made large, not to say reckless, promises. Time showed that, in the main, these could not be kept; and the post-war years became, as everyone knows, a period of progressive disillusionment, with corresponding discontent and depression. Under these circumstances the prestige of the cabinet was worn down and the country was prepared for a reversion from coalitionism to straight party government on the traditional lines. From 1919 onwards, rebuffs were suffered in the House of Commons such as, under normal conditions, would have been regarded as defeats entailing resignation. Choosing, however, to consider itself exempt from the ordinary rules of party government, and maintaining that it had, fundamentally, the support of the country, the ministry clung resolutely to power.

A second main phase was the discussion of, and efforts toward, the rehabilitation of the old parties. Since 1915 the familiar party régime had been in abeyance. First the truce, and later the coalition, had put party activity under the ban; and although, as has been pointed out, the second half of the war saw the truce repudiated and the coalition abandoned by certain elements, and notwithstanding that no gift of prophecy was required to foresee a rapid and general revival of party life, there was still much uncertainty in 1919 whether party lines

[1] See Chap. xxx.

would be redrawn substantially as they were in 1914, or whether they would assume some widely different aspect. Two questions, mainly, presented themselves. First, would the old Liberal party, now so sharply divided between adherents and foes of the Coalition government, be reunited and generally brought back to its former position? Second, would the Coalition, dropping off reactionary Conservatives on the one side and radical Liberals on the other, consolidate its position and develop into a permanent center party? Labor's intentions were fairly well known, and its possibilities were not underestimated by well-informed observers. But the future of the older parties was far from clear.

Effort to bring Liberalism together and restore the party to its former place in the life of the nation began without delay; and, as we shall see, it was kept up, on one line or another, until it approximated the goal in the general election of 1923. It was, of course, the Independents that carried the cause along; and, although more than four years were required to crown their efforts with success, they had many powerful arguments on their side—among them the notorious subordination of the Liberal to the Unionist element in the Coalition, the Coalition's increasing unpopularity, and (by no means least important) the fact that the Independents were in possession of the old party machinery and party chest. Parallel with the efforts to restore unity among the Liberals went discussion, although no great amount of positive effort, looking to the conversion of the Coalition into a permanent party. The scheme failed, for a variety of reasons, but chiefly because it ran counter to deep-seated traditions, beliefs, habits, and loyalties, so that the rank and file of the two great parties simply would not have it.

A third important development of the period was the steady consolidation and growth of the reconstructed Labor party. Indeed, a main argument for the proposed center party was that the menace of Labor called for a firm and permanent union of the conservative elements of both of the older parties. For the first time in history, the Labor party had become the official opposition; [2] during the four years following the election

[2] There had been some uncertainty when the parliament elected in 1918 assembled as to the element, or elements, that should be regarded as the

which brought it into this position it won nine seats at by-elections and lost only two; and there was a manifest drift in its direction, not only in industrial districts, but in middle-class constituencies.

A dissolution of Parliament, oft impending and as oft postponed, came at last in October, 1922. Before it took place, however, the Coalition government was no more. Weary of being dominated by a prime minister who was, after all, not one of themselves, and yearning for a revival of their party on the earlier lines, the Unionist members of the House of Commons caucused on their future course and by a decisive vote agreed to go into the next campaign "as an independent party, with its own leaders and with its own program." Thus abandoned (although some leading Unionists opposed the decision), Lloyd George had no course save to resign; and the former Unionist leader, Bonar Law, having once more been elected leader of his party, accepted the king's commission to make up a ministry.[3] For the first time since 1915, Britain found herself, in October, 1922, possessed of a government constructed on the time-honored principle of party unity and responsibility.

The Election of 1922

Four parties, in addition to five relatively unimportant groups, went into the contest: the Conservatives,[4] the National

formal opposition. Having the largest number of seats, next to the government, Labor was clearly entitled, under all precedent, to occupy the Front Opposition Bench. The Independent Liberals, however, could not reconcile themselves to such an arrangement, and the outcome was a compromise under which Labor, led by William Adamson, was indeed recognized as technically the opposition, but the Independent Liberals shared the coveted strategic position on the benches. Though often coöperating, the two groups were not formally allied.

[3] Mr. Law had been succeeded as Conservative leader by Austen Chamberlain in 1921. Because of his refusal to desert Lloyd George, Chamberlain was, of course, not available for the premiership at the present juncture; hence the reëlection of Law, who, being a Canadian by birth, became the first dominion-born prime minister in Britain's history. Chamberlain clung for a time to the idea of a center party, but, in deference to the desires of the great majority of Unionists, he finally gave up hope of a new party and promised his support to Law.

[4] The Irish question having presumably been solved by the setting up of the Free State in this same year, the term "Conservative," as previously explained, now came back rapidly into use.

(or Coalition) Liberals, the Independent Liberals, and Labor. The Conservatives made it their policy to coöperate, whenever possible, with their late allies, the Coalition Liberals, with a view to opposing a united front to Labor and socialism; although agreements of this import within the constituencies were actually made only in cases where the Liberal candidate would promise, if elected, to give general adherence to the policies of Mr. Law and his colleagues. The point most stressed in the party's program was the purpose to relieve the country of the uncertainties, the abrupt decisions, and the tense situations that had alternately bewildered and frightened people during the Lloyd George régime; and the promise of tranquillity was accompanied by pledges of rigid economy, emergency measures on unemployment, assistance to agriculture, and maintenance of good relations abroad, coupled with curtailments of foreign obligations whenever feasible.

All proposals for a union of the two wings of Liberalism failed, and each group nominated its own candidates, announced its own program, and carried on its own campaign. Save for a significant reiteration of their traditional hostility to protective tariffs, the National Liberals presented a platform which differed but slightly from that of their former Conservative associates. The program of the Independents was dissimilar chiefly in placing greater stress on social and political reform, to the extent, indeed, of approximating the position of Labor on several important subjects.

Labor went into the campaign with perfected organization and confident of at least doubling its parliamentary quota, which at the time was seventy-six. A total of 412 candidates were put in the field;[5] and, notwithstanding that the borough council elections in London, occurring during the course of the national campaign, resulted in severe Labor reverses, expectation of considerably increased parliamentary strength proved well-founded. The party manifesto—termed "Labor's Call to the People"—declared for an "all-inclusive" League of Nations; revision of the peace treaties; "real independence" for Egypt; self-government for India; prompt acceptance of the

[5] As compared with 444 by the Conservatives, 339 by the Independent Liberals, 138 by the National Liberals, and 57 by minor groups.

pending constitution of the Irish Free State; a graduated capital levy, for war-debt redemption purposes, on fortunes exceeding £5,000; readjustment of the income tax; taxation of land values; remission of indirect imposts; nationalization of mines and railways; a national housing scheme; relief of unemployment; repeal or amendment of the Parliament Act; reform of parliamentary procedure; and removal of all disabilities affecting women as citizens, voters, and workers.

A main defense of the Coalition for continuing so long in office was that no single party could win a clear working majority over all other parties in the House of Commons. The outcome of the present election demonstrated this to be a fallacy. The Conservatives obtained 344 seats, or an absolute majority of thirty-six.[6] Equally manifest, however, was the fact that almost three and one-half million more people had voted against the government than for it, which meant that Bonar Law and his colleagues were to go on governing on the basis of the support of a decided minority of the nation.[7]

[6] This was the first general election in which the portions of Ireland now constituting the Free State did not participate, and the total number of members of the House of Commons had now been reduced to 615. Seats (both contested and uncontested) were won as follows:

	Conservative (Unionist)	National Liberal	Independent Liberal	Labor (and Socialist)	Independent	Nationalist	Sinn Fein	Total
England	312	39	38	95	7	1	0	492
Wales and Monmouthshire	6	1	9	18	2	0	0	36
Scotland	15	13	14	29	3	0	0	74
Northern Ireland	11	0	0	0	0	1	1	13
Total	344	53	61	142	12	2	1	615

The popular vote of the leading parties was as follows:

	Conservative (Unionist)	National Liberal	Independent Liberal	Labor
England	4,822,095	1,128,412	2,143,768	3,376,252
Wales and Monmouthshire	190,919	247,010	60,874	363,877
Scotland	379,396	297,818	311,645	501,254
Northern Ireland	107,972	....	....	....
Total	5,500,382	1,673,240	2,516,287	4,241,383

A complete table of the popular vote will be found in *Const. Year Book* (London, 1928), 283.

[7] How great was the disproportion between the Conservative popular vote and the Conservative quota in Parliament is indicated by the fact that whereas the Conservative members were elected (in contested constituencies),

This was a novel and disconcerting situation. In the old days of the straight two-party system it had, indeed, occasionally happened, as in 1886, that, through the vagaries of electoral mechanics, a party won a parliamentary majority by something less than a majority of the popular vote. But the discrepancy never approached that now brought to light. The fact was, of course, that—for the time-being, at all events—Britain had come to be a multiple-party country, like France and Germany, and, as in those lands, no one party could hope to poll an absolute majority of the total popular vote. Even a government fortunate enough, as Mr. Law's had been, to scrape together a parliamentary majority on this basis would have to labor under the psychological handicap of being a "minority" government. When a situation should arise in which no one of the parties could command *either* a popular majority or a parliamentary majority, there would be difficulty indeed. As we shall see, this is precisely the position in which the country found itself in 1923 and again in 1929.[8]

The next salient feature of the election of 1922 was the emergence of Labor in the undisputed rôle of the opposition. Both its popular vote and its parliamentary representation exceeded that of the two Liberal parties combined; the popular vote was raised from twenty-four per cent of the total in 1918 to twenty-nine per cent, and the parliamentary quota (brought up to 142) was almost doubled. Furthermore, practically all of the leaders whose pacifism had caused, or helped cause, their defeat in 1918 were now restored to public life, and Ramsay MacDonald, already the chairman of his party, became also opposition leader.

As for the Liberals, the National wing, led by Lloyd George, fared very badly, winning only fifty-three seats; and while the Independents won sixty-one seats, almost doubling their quota, this was by no means what had been hoped for. Nothing was clearer than that if the Liberals wanted to regain their old position they must bury their differences and once more become a

by an average of 17,900 votes apiece, each National Liberal member represented 29,100 votes, each Labor member 30,800 votes, and each Independent Liberal member 46,200 votes.

[8] See pp. 508, 525 below.

united party. Certain it was, too, that if Mr. Lloyd George was ever to regain the lost premiership it would have to be with the backing of reunited Liberalism. Nevertheless, the shock of another electoral campaign—one in which the historic Liberal policy of free trade was at stake—was required to accomplish the fusion, even externally; and for the present the two groups started off quite independently, each with its own leader, whips, and other instrumentalities of action.

The Baldwin Tariff Proposals and the Election of 1923

With the Conservative party freshly established in office, and commanding a parliamentary majority ample for all ordinary requirements, and with the opposition split into three more or less irreconcilable bodies, the political situation seemed to have attained greater stability than at any time since the earlier part of the war period. The ministry was not one of conspicuous capacity—"a government," it has been called, "of under-secretaries." But for the moment it had a great asset in the desire of the people for tranquillity, and if only the country's post-war troubles, foreign and domestic, had been of such a nature as to yield promptly to well-meant treatment it might have continued in office for a considerable time. As it was, the depression of industry and trade, the stupendous burden of unemployment, the pressure of an apparently insoluble housing problem, the recurrence of strikes, and disappointments in foreign affairs brought endless difficulty and threatened to upset the ministry at almost any moment. Mr. Law was much handicapped, too, by failing health, which eventually, in May, 1923, compelled him to resign. Succeeding to the dual rôle of party leader and prime minister, Stanley Baldwin introduced fresh blood in the ministry so as to give it a more definitely progressive character. But prestige was lost through failures in foreign policy, and the outstanding domestic problem, i.e., unemployment, proved equally baffling—until a supposed solution was hit upon which, indeed, turned out to be no solution at all, but only a mirage luring the ministry to disaster. This fancied solution was nothing less than the abandonment of the country's fiscal policy of the preceding seventy-five years and the adoption of a system of protective tariffs, the argument being that the proposed barriers against foreign goods would stimulate British agriculture, industry, and trade.[9] Announced suddenly in public addresses in October, 1923, this program—and the prime minister's declaration that he was prepared to go to the country with it and to stand or fall by the result—was hardly less sensational than the historic "tariff reform" pronouncement of Joseph Chamberlain twenty years earlier. Mr. Law had pledged the existing Conservative government not to touch the established fiscal policy, and Mr. Baldwin felt that the only honorable course that he could take was to get a new parliament and, in doing so, to appeal to the people quite specifically for a mandate on this subject. Accordingly, a dissolution took place in November, and a general election in the following month.

The election of 1923 turned more largely on a single issue than any since 1910, although before the ballots were cast that issue, i.e., protective tariffs, was found to have many unsuspected and bewildering ramifications. As developed during the campaign, the Conservative program embraced, chiefly, a general tariff on imported manufactures, no protective duties on foodstuffs, preferential rates for the colonies, and a bonus for proprietors of all land under cultivation; and on these policies the prime minister succeeded in winning the active support of sundry prominent Conservatives who had been at outs with the party ever since its desertion of Lloyd George in the previous year.

By far the most striking development of the campaign was the restoration of at least outward unity in the Liberal party, after seven weary years of schism. Confronted with an opportunity to fight side by side on a great and irresistible issue, i.e., free trade, the leaders of the two wings, Lloyd George and Asquith, agreed to make common cause, with the latter as formal leader; machinery and funds were consolidated; and notwithstanding occasional manifestations of jealousy and dis-

[9] A Safeguarding of Industries Act of 1921 had imposed protective duties for the benefit of certain "key" industries, and, in particular, had taxed imports from countries having a depreciated exchange. Although regarded with suspicion by free traders as a potential entering wedge of protectionism, the measure was too limited in its scope to serve the purposes which the prime minister had in view.

trust, the party forces worked together effectively.[10] Denouncing Labor's projected capital levy, the party platform [11] equally castigated the government's proposed fiscal changes, demanded strict maintenance of free trade, urged a great program of public improvements as an alternative remedy for unemployment, and offered a scheme of foreign policy designed to bring an end to the cabinet's alleged diplomatic failures and its sacrifice of British influence abroad. Although injured in morale and weakened financially by the prolonged economic depression, the Labor party welcomed the election as a test of public opinion on tariffs and other economic issues. The party program [12] ran on substantially the same lines as at the preceding election, except that now there was greater concentration on the uppermost problem of the day, i.e., relief of unemployment, together with the subsidiary issue of assistance to agriculture. In the large, the position taken on both of these subjects was practically identical with that of the Liberals. The capital levy was again insisted upon as a means of reducing the "dead-weight war debt;" nationalization of mines, railways, and other utilities, " in a practical spirit," was advocated; remedial labor legislation, adequate housing, and other social reforms were demanded; and a program of foreign policy was outlined looking to disarmament as its great objective.

The vigor of the canvass by reunited Liberalism, the drift toward Labor produced by economic depression, and the revolutionary nature of the Conservative fiscal proposals foreshadowed some shrinkage of the government's existing parliamentary majority. That this majority would be wiped out altogether, entailing the elevation of one of the opposition parties to office, was hardly expected in any quarter—still less that the minority party brought into power would be Labor. Yet this is exactly what happened. The total poll was only slightly larger than in 1922, and, speaking broadly, it was divided among the three contending forces—Conservative, Liberal, and Labor—in practically the same proportions. But it was so dis-

[10] Four hundred and forty-three candidates were put in the field, as compared with 500 by the Unionists, 420 by Labor, and 30 by minor groups.

[11] Embodied in a joint manifesto of Lloyd George and Asquith.

[12] Official manifesto of November 17, printed in the *London Observer* of November 18.

tributed in the constituencies as to yield surprisingly different results.[13] Whereas the total Conservative vote was somewhat larger in 1923 than in 1922, the number of seats won was only 258, as compared with 344. On the other hand, a Liberal vote less than 125,000 in excess of the combined votes of the two Liberal parties in 1922 yielded 159 seats, as compared with 114; and a Labor vote larger than in 1922 by not so much as two hundred thousand yielded 191 seats, as compared with 142.[14] Counting Liberalism and Labor for free trade, Mr. Baldwin's protectionist scheme was defeated by more than three million votes. Counting Liberalism and Conservatism as against the capital levy, that proposal was rejected by almost five and one-half millions.

The First Labor Government

No party had a majority in the House of Commons. The Conservatives had a decided plurality. But they had gone to the country with a program on which they had been roundly beaten, and if party government meant anything at all, they were now due to surrender the reins. Proposals were made, naturally, that a reconstructed Conservative ministry should attempt to retain power. But the prime minister and his colleagues did not

[13] Seats (both contested and uncontested) were won as follows:

	Conservative (Unionist)	Liberal	Labor	Independent	Total
England	227	124	138	3	492
Wales and Monmouthshire	4	12	19	1	36
Scotland	16	23	34	1	74
Northern Ireland	11	......	......	2	13
Total	258	159	191	7	615

The popular vote was as follows:

	Conservative (Unionist)	Liberal	Labor	Independent
England	4,775,024	3,575,809	3,550,886	56,552
Wales and Monmouthshire	178,113	312,343	355,172	1,037
Scotland	468,526	420,995	532,450	77,356
Northern Ireland	117,161	....	....	125,097
Total	5,538,824	4,311,147	4,438,508	260,042

[14] It must constantly be borne in mind, of course, that in all general elections some seats are won by the various parties without a contest, and hence without a polling. Proportions between popular vote and seats won are therefore not precisely comparable from election to election.

encourage them; the farthest that they deemed themselves warranted in going was to remain in office until the new parliament assembled. In this situation the alternatives were (1) a return to a coalition government, and (2) a ministry made up by one of the minority parties and passively supported by the other. The first plan was impracticable because of general dislike of the coalition principle, and because neither the Conservatives and Liberals nor the Liberals and Laborites were willing to enter into any arrangement of the sort. The question of a Liberal government supported by Labor or a Labor government supported by Liberals was answered shortly by the decision of the Labor leaders to form a government independently if and when invited to do so. Circumstances so shaped themselves that the expected invitation became unavoidable; and when, in January, 1924, the Baldwin ministry suffered its inevitable defeat in the new House of Commons, a Labor ministry took the helm. Making the best possible use of the material at his disposal (including a certain amount drawn from sympathetic Liberal sources), the incoming prime minister, Ramsay MacDonald, built Labor's long-awaited first cabinet in such a way as to secure not only appropriate representation of the various leading elements in his party, but also an unexpectedly large amount of talent and experience.[15]

The new ministry took office under conditions in some respects favorable and in others quite the reverse. On the one hand, the nation, having recovered from its initial nervousness, was disposed to give Mr. MacDonald and his associates a fair chance. Furthermore, neither of the older parties coveted the thankless task of handling the country's problems as they then stood. On the other hand, Labor was in power only by suffer-

[15] The question of whether Labor was "fit to govern" had been debated from as early as 1920. A public assertion by Winston Churchill in that year that Labor was "entirely unprepared" to assume the responsibilities of office called out spirited replies by Arthur Henderson and other Labor leaders to the effect that their party had at its disposal many men trained in public affairs and intellectually the equals of the best at the command of the other parties, and that, in any case, Labor ministers could not do worse than Unionist and Liberal ministers had done. The fitness of Labor to take over the administration of the great departments of state was discussed pointedly in Ramsay MacDonald, *A Policy for the Labour Party* (London, 1920), Chaps. vii-viii.

ance of the Liberals and could go on only so long as support from this source was forthcoming. This manifestly imposed restraints. In the second place, the Labor forces were not well enough united and disciplined to be secure against internal friction. The new ministry represented antecedents almost as diverse as any coalition; there was plenty of danger that, once the party was installed in office, the different elements composing it would find themselves unable to agree upon the policies to be pursued. In particular, there was likelihood—amounting almost to certainty—that exaggerated expectations in various quarters would fail to be realized, leading to discontent and defection. The prime minister repeatedly admonished the working classes not to look for the millennium. A generally critical social and economic situation, coupled with a peculiarly difficult juncture in international affairs, offered tasks which had baffled statesmen of far larger experience. Ironically enough, too, the new government was hardly in office before a series of extensive strikes—first the railwaymen, then the dockers, and afterwards the miners—brought it embarrassment and trouble from the very sources to which it might reasonably have looked for its chief encouragement.

It would not have been expected that the successes of a Labor government would be won chiefly in the domain of foreign relations. Yet so it happened in the present case, partly because the European situation had taken a slight turn for the better before the Baldwin ministry resigned, partly because a general election in France presently brought into office in that country a semi-socialist government (that of M. Herriot) with which it was easy for British Labor to do business, but largely because of the skillful handling of foreign relations by Mr. MacDonald, who himself, as has been mentioned at another point, occupied the post of foreign minister.[16] The outstanding achievement was the breaking of the seemingly hopeless deadlock between Great Britain and France, eventuating in an agreement of

[16] Like Lord Salisbury before him, MacDonald found the double load of the premiership and the foreign secretaryship exceedingly heavy, and the attempt to carry it undoubtedly had something to do with abbreviating his term of office. Unlike Lord Salisbury, he was also government leader in the House of Commons. Upon returning to the premiership in 1929, he did not resume the foreign secretaryship.

mid-summer, 1924, embodying the Dawes Plan and liquidating the French adventure in the Ruhr—the "first real treaty of peace since the war, inasmuch as it was made by agreement and not dictated by force." This was no mean accomplishment. Other developments of note were the decision to suspend operations on the Singapore naval base (which pleased the Liberals), the carrying out of the Baldwin cabinet's plan to lay down five new cruisers (which was made possible only by Conservative votes), and the firm rejection of Zaglul Pasha's demand that Great Britain relinquish the Anglo-Egyptian Sudan to Egypt (in which all parties significantly concurred). Russia, however, offered a stumbling block; and after the cabinet had reversed its predecessor's policy and had recognized the Soviet government, it became involved in prolonged and futile negotiations with Moscow which produced embarrassment and drew censure not only from the Conservatives but from Liberals as well. In domestic affairs the record was uneven, and on the whole disappointing. A budget was carried—with, of course, no mention of a capital levy—which won favor, especially with the Liberals. But two major problems for which Labor was supposed to have solutions, i.e., unemployment and housing, went entirely unsolved. The explanation given, e.g., by Miss Margaret Bondfield, who had the distinction of being the first woman minister in British history,[17] was that Labor's remedy was the nationalization of land, mines, and railroads, which could not be carried out until the party had obtained "power as well as office." This was perhaps plausible enough, but it did not satisfy. The real difficulty was that the majority of workers who were employed were unwilling to risk reduction of wages and dilution of labor for the sake of those who were idle.

Within nine months after the Labor experiment began, the ministry found it necessary to dissolve Parliament and make a fresh appeal to the country. The circumstances are too complicated to be described here; but the culminating event which put Mr. MacDonald and his colleagues in a position where they were forced to choose between resignation and dissolution was a vote of the House of Commons indirectly censuring the min-

[17] Her post was that of parliamentary under-secretary to the Ministry of Labor.

isters for abandoning the prosecution of a Communist editor charged with seditious utterances.[18] This turn of the wheel came partly by design, partly by accident. But if the "Campbell case" had not furnished the occasion, something else—probably the government's Russian policy or the Irish boundary issue—would undoubtedly have done so in a very short time. For the understanding between Labor and Liberalism was wearing thin, and the Conservatives were fast regaining confidence. A third dissolution within the space of two years, however, was rather more than the country was prepared to witness cheerfully.[19]

The Election of 1924

Placing the blame for the situation upon a "partisan combination of Liberals and Tories," the Labor campaign manifesto invited attention to the progress made under Labor leadership toward the establishment of genuine peace in Europe, took credit for sweeping away heavy taxes on food and for remedial housing legislation, alleged that other significant social and industrial betterments had been blocked only by Conservative and Liberal apathy and hostility, and appealed for the establishment of a "really socialist commonwealth." In short, the party expressed pride in what it had accomplished and asked a mandate to go on, freed from hampering dependence on the untrustworthy Liberals. The much-discussed capital levy was discreetly kept in the background. The principal Liberal statement, signed by both Asquith and Lloyd George, placed the responsibility for the election squarely on the government, declared that while the party had rejected Labor's crude

[18] Ross John Campbell, editor of the *Worker's Weekly*. See account in *Annual Register* (1924), 96. A Conservative motion of direct censure failed, but a Liberal motion calling for a parliamentary inquiry prevailed, and it was this that led immediately to the decision to dissolve.

[19] The ministry had previously been defeated in the House of Commons no fewer than a dozen times. But in line with a definite development of British parliamentary practice, Mr. MacDonald had refused to surrender the seals of office until it became clearly the well-considered desire of a Commons majority that he should do so. The immediate occasion of the dissolution was characterized by T. P. O'Connor, perhaps rightly, as a "tin pot issue." The real reason, of course, was the fundamental and inevitable dissonance between a socialist ministry and a non-socialist parliamentary majority.

schemes of nationalization it had supported every move for sound social reform, reiterated devotion to free trade, promised to restore agriculture by a policy that would "combine the advantages of ownership and tenancy without the disadvantages of either," and advocated electoral reforms calculated to "ensure a genuine correspondence between polling strength and parliamentary representation." The Conservative manifesto, issued by Premier Baldwin, severely criticized the government for entering into indefensible agreements with Soviet Russia, pronounced Labor's unemployment policy a total failure, urged imperial preference as an indispensable condition of industrial revival, promised a conference to inquire into the condition of agriculture, pledged protection of the employment and standard of living of the people in any efficient industry in which they were imperilled by unfair competition,[20] and appealed—as, in effect, the Liberals also did—for "a broad and stable government based on an independent majority in Parliament."

Conservatives and Liberals were interested most of all in preventing a victory for Labor. Accordingly, the Liberals put up candidates for hardly more than half of the seats, and in numerous constituencies "pacts" were entered into under which Liberals and Conservatives refrained from opposing each other, with a view to keeping Labor candidates from winning by mere pluralities in three-cornered contests, as they had done in some sixty constituencies in 1923. The campaign was even briefer than usual in Britain, but it lacked nothing in intensity. The most exciting incident was the publication by the Foreign Office of a letter purporting to be signed by Zinovieff, president of the central committee of the Third International, and calling upon English Communists to foment sedition among the military and naval forces and otherwise prepare the way for the proletarian revolution—a letter which was given out along with the text of a vigorous protest which had been forwarded to Moscow. Questioned sharply, the government was obliged to

[20] Only, however, by applying the principles of the mildly protectionist Safeguarding of Industries Act (see p. 506 above). The leaders were moved by the party catastrophe of the previous year to deny that a general tariff was any part of the immediate Conservative program.

admit that there was doubt about the authenticity of the letter, and that efforts to clear it up had failed. This precipitated a barrage of charges and counter-charges which undoubtedly cost the party many votes.[21]

The outcome was a decisive triumph for the Conservatives.[22] At all events, so it seemed on the face of the returns. With a popular vote of slightly more than five and one-half millions in 1923, the party had secured 258 seats; with a popular vote of slightly under eight millions in 1924, it won 412—not only a clear majority, but more than two-thirds of the total 615. So far as parliamentary numbers were concerned, the showing was indeed impressive. Scrutiny of the complete situation, however, revealed facts of a different color. The party's huge popular vote was, after all, only forty-seven per cent of the total, i.e., less than half. Furthermore, a great number of these so-called Conservative votes were really votes of Liberals.[23] And while Labor's quota of seats had been cut down from 193 (at the time of dissolution) to 151, the party's popular vote exceeded

[21] A committee of the later Conservative ministry investigated the affair and came to the conclusion that the letter was genuine, although Moscow officials continued to insist that it was a forgery. The matter is still involved in obscurity. See A. J. Toynbee, *Survey of International Affairs* (London, 1926), 246-250, 492-496.

[22] Seats (both contested and uncontested) were won as follows:

	Conservative	Liberal	Labor	Constitutional	Independent	Total
England	352	20	109	7	4	492
Wales and Monmouthshire	9	11	16	0	0	36
Scotland	38	9	26	0	1	74
Northern Ireland	13	0	0	0	0	13
Total	412	40	151	7	5	615

The popular vote was as follows:

	Conservative	Liberal	Labor	Constitutional	Independent	Communist
England	6,479,963	2,391,311	4,469,174	185,075	30,222	39,416
Wales and Monmouthshire	224,014	245,885	321,118	....	....	....
Scotland	699,268	291,551	698,785	....	29,193	15,930
Northern Ireland	451,278	....	....	....	21,639	46,457
Total	7,854,523	2,928,747	5,489,077	185,075	81,054	101,803

[23] The pacts had resulted in throwing many more Liberal votes to Conservative candidates than Conservative votes to Liberal candidates.

that of 1923 by considerably more than a million. Both Conservatives and Labor had profited decidedly—at least for the time being—at the expense of the Liberals. That party's popular vote fell off by more than a million and a quarter, and its representation in the House of Commons slumped from 158 (at the date of dissolution) to a pitiful forty. Striking, indeed, was the fact that with but forty-seven per cent of the popular votes, the Conservatives had secured sixty-seven per cent of the seats, while with fifty-three per cent of the votes the other two parties had obtained only thirty-three per cent of the seats. Broadly, the Conservative party got one seat for every 19,000 votes which it polled; the Labor party, one for every 36,000; the Liberal party, one for every 73,000. Small wonder that demand for electoral reform—especially for the adoption of some scheme of proportional representation—was heard afresh in every corner of the land!

The aspect that stirred most comment was the crushing defeat of the Liberals. After all allowances were made for the presumably temporary effects of the Conservative-Liberal understandings in the constituencies, the fact remained that Liberalism had fallen to an estate in the House of Commons decidedly lower than that of even the Irish Nationalists in the old days. Over and over, the outcome was interpreted as portending the disappearance of the party and the revival of a straight two-party system. Labor was particularly gratified. Notwithstanding that the election took place in a period of the most intense anti-radical feeling since the year following the armistice, the party's candidates polled more than a third of the total popular vote, and the increase over 1923 was accounted for not only by the contesting of new constituencies but by a gain of three-quarters of a million in the constituencies contested on the previous occasion. "The election results," commented the *Daily Herald* exultantly, "clear the air. Now we know where we are and what forces we have got to conquer. We have shaken off false friends. . . . The three-party system was a nuisance. The English mind could not understand it. It would have taken us a long time to destroy it by gradually beating the Liberals. Fortunately, they decided to save us this trouble; they have committed suicide. There is now no

Liberal party. There are only fragments which will rapidly be absorbed into either Toryism or Labor."

The Conservatives in Power, 1924-29

The Conservative government organized by Mr. Baldwin after the election proved long-lived, and the new parliament had the rare experience of surviving very nearly to the limit of its mandate, i.e., to the late spring of 1929. Throughout this lengthy period, the party was not merely in office but in power. The House of Lords, of course, stood solidly behind it; and its majority in the House of Commons never varied far from two hundred. This did not mean, however, a smooth road to travel. The international situation had been eased somewhat since the party's last tenure at Whitehall, but there were still plenty of difficulties; and the domestic situation—the prevalence of unemployment, the rising cost of living, the unsolved housing problem, the depression of trade and industry, together with recurring and almost unprecedented unrest in the labor world—promised little save anxious days and sleepless nights. The question which thinking people everywhere had been asking—Is England done?—still awaited answer.

Under these hard circumstances, the record achieved, up to the general election of 1929, was naturally an uneven one. Several things of importance were done. The country was put back on a gold basis in 1925; the Locarno treaties were ratified in the same year; an Imperial Conference in 1926 introduced important changes in the structure of the Empire and gave the great dominions a more comfortable position; a successful stand was taken against the so-called general strike of the same year, even though the failure of that dramatic effort was caused as much by unsympathetic public opinion as by governmental vigilance; a momentous Trade Disputes and Trade Unions Act was placed on the statute book in 1927; in the following year all discriminations between men and women as parliamentary voters were removed from the law and over five million females were added to the electorate; and in 1929 a bold program of local government and tax reform was successfully carried out. On the other hand, there were conspicuous failures. At the end of 1928, a million and a quarter work-people were still unemployed, i.e., practically as many as in 1924; the housing situation was improved but little; a system of long-term credits on farm mortgages as an aid to agriculture was projected but not realized; reform of the House of Lords, promised repeatedly as something to be accomplished during the life of the parliament elected in 1924, was attempted feebly and finally postponed. A proposed Anglo-French naval agreement of 1928 not only collapsed but laid the cabinet open to the charge of grave inepitude, if not insincerity. Much of the time the government gave an impression of merely beating the air, or of sheer inertia. "Has any King's Speech," pointedly asked Ramsay MacDonald at the opening of the first session in 1927, "ever intimated more plainly that His Majesty's advisers had nothing to advise His Majesty about?"

It is likely to be the opinion of historians that the outstanding development of the period was the government's sharp challenge to labor and socialism, and, by the same token, its contribution to a definite marshalling of the forces of conservatism and of radicalism for a grander combat than any yet known. That underneath the more superficial ebb and flow of party politics in recent decades a swelling current of industrial and political radicalism has been beating harder and harder against the bulwarks of the existing economic and social order, can hardly have escaped the notice of any one who follows English public affairs. Nor can the fact be missed that both sets of interests are completely aware of the developing situation—conscious of its trends and awake to their meaning for the future. As has been pointed out, the entire program of the Conservative party in respect to the House of Lords is dictated by apprehension as to what might follow if, with the powers of legislation allocated as they now are, labor and socialism, working through the Labor party, were to come into actual, as opposed to merely nominal, control at Westminster and Whitehall. The fast-ripening issue was brought dramatically into view by the general strike of May, 1926, and the resulting Trade Disputes and Trade Unions Act of 1927.[24]

[24] In the summer of 1925 the government staved off a long-threatened strike of the coal-miners by agreeing to subsidize the industry for a period

The strike collapsed speedily, but not before the power of the state to keep the public services in operation had been directly challenged; and whereas the government had even earlier given some thought to amending the Trade Union Act of 1913 in respect to trade unionists' contributions to political funds,[25] it now decided to take advantage of its huge parliamentary majorities to procure a far more comprehensive and drastic piece of repressive legislation. The act as passed made sympathetic strikes, or strikes designed to coerce the government, illegal;[26] introduced a new scheme of legal injunction against such strikes; stiffened the existing law on intimidation; rescinded the law of 1906 exempting trade union funds from attachment for damages in connection with strikes; undid the legislation of 1913 by forbidding unions to collect money for political uses except from members signing a form expressly indicating their desire to contribute for such purposes; and prohibited civil servants from belonging to trade unions unless such unions are confined to civil servants only and are independent of any outside union, and also are not affiliated with any political party. The measure provoked one of the stubbornest parliamentary battles in a decade, and, as has been mentioned elsewhere, it was only by calling into play the unpopular device of the guillotine that interminable debate was

of nine months. During the interval it adopted in principle the report of a Royal Coal Commission recommending national ownership of the coal mines, with private management and operation. At the expiration of the nine-month truce, a million miners struck; and a general strike was declared (by the General Council of the Trades Union Congress) in sympathy with them. A million and a half railway and other transport workers, dock and harbor laborers, iron and steel workers, and building and printing operators, i.e., certain key groups forming the "first line" of the labor forces, were called out. G. D. H. Cole, *Short History of the British Working Class Movement* (New York, 1927), III, 203-212; J. R. Hayden, "Great Britain's Labor Strife," *Curr. Hist.*, June, 1926. On the problem of the coal industry, see I. Lubin and H. Everett, *The British Coal Dilemma* (New York, 1927).

[25] As many as eleven private members' bills on the subject had previously made their appearance in Parliament, and the annual conference of the Conservative party in 1925 had called for a change of the existing law.

[26] In the language of the statute, a strike having "any object other than or in addition to the furtherance of a trade dispute within the trade or industry in which the strikers are engaged," or a strike "designed or calculated to coerce the government either directly or through inflicting hardship upon the country."

cut off and matters brought to a conclusion.[27] The Conservatives fought for the bill as a necessary legal bulwark against the threatened domination of the state by the laboring class through the instrumentality of the general strike—as, indeed, an indispensable defense for the whole existing British political and social order. Labor protested with all its might against a measure which it considered to be designed, not to save the state, but to destroy the unions, to impoverish the Labor party, and to strangle the labor movement generally. Most of the Liberals also were hostile. After the new law was on the statute book, regrettable bitterness remained. Labor organizations declared their intention to evade the measure and strive for its repeal; the political situation became more tense than at any time since the election of 1923.[28]

The prime minister stood pledged by campaign commitments of 1924 not to introduce a "general tariff." His party, and even the cabinet, was, however, divided sharply on the subject, and much pressure was brought to bear to lead him to violate his pledge. He stood firm, but as the election of 1929 approached the more aggressively protectionist wing of the party made no secret of its purpose to force the tariff as a major issue in the contest. Meanwhile the government's policy, officially, was to uphold and extend the principle of the Safeguarding of Industries Act of 1921, according to which all "substantial and efficient" British industries except those producing food were regarded as entitled to protection against exceptional competition arising from special conditions in foreign countries such as depreciated currency, subsidies, bounties, longer hours, and lower wages. Even this plan was strongly opposed by the Liberals and Laborites as a subterfuge imperiling the basic system of free trade.

At the Liberals' annual congress of 1925 Mr. Asquith, speaking as leader, declared that the party was "now again on

[27] See p. 406 above.

[28] S. Webb, "Britain's New Industrial and Political Crisis," *Curr. Hist.*, July, 1927; A. T. Mason, "The British Trade Disputes Act of 1927," *Amer. Polit. Sci. Rev.*, Feb., 1928; R. Muir, *Trade Unionism and the Trade Union Bill* (London, 1927); E. B. Ferguson, *The Trade Disputes and Trade Unions Act, 1927; Annotated with Introductory Chapters and Notes* (London, 1928).

its feet, revitalized and as loyal and effective as ever to the cause of the democratic principles which had always been the foundation of British character." That this was a truly optimistic view of the situation was shown again and again during the ensuing four years. Dislike of the government's protectionist leanings indeed afforded some rallying ground; and agreements of 1926-27 under which Lloyd George turned over for the use of the party the income and part of the principal of the famous political fund which he had somehow built up [29] brought larger means with which to prepare for and to fight the coming election. But when, in 1925, the indomitable Welshman launched a crusade for a land policy based upon eliminating the landlords, by state purchase, from the scheme of agricultural production and giving the existing farmers a tenure tantamount to ownership as long as the land was cultivated efficiently, sharp dissensions arose and one man of prominence after another broke away from the party.[30] The general strike of 1926 brought Asquith as leader of the party and Lloyd George as chairman of the Parliamentary Liberal party into open and dramatic warfare. Young and rising men the country over showed a disposition to align themselves either with Conservatism or with Labor, not with Liberalism, suggesting that the day might come when the latter could no longer claim the proud distinction of containing the best brains of the nation. Finally, the hard-won financial arrangements of 1926-27 admittedly rested upon a bargain under which the Lloyd George money was to be put at the disposal of the party only on condition that the Lloyd George policies should be pushed and the party machinery purged of people with whom the donor could not work. Such a reorganization of personnel, indeed, took place, and, Asquith having already retired from the post of leader (in 1926), Lloyd George came into as effective control as any one could expect to possess in a demoralized and discordant party. Early in 1928 an extensive report by a

[29] See p. 591 below.

[30] This plan was based on a report of a Liberal Land Committee which had carried on a two-year investigation of the agricultural situation. The report was published in two parts, one a rural report and the other an urban report, and entitled, respectively, *The Land and the Nation* and *Towns and the Land* (London, 1925). See p. 560 below.

Liberal Industrial Inquiry Committee, embodying the views of the progressive wing of the party, urged abandonment of the Liberals' traditional *laissez-faire* attitude and the adoption of a broad, constructive program of national economic rehabilitation.[31]

Labor came through the period with equally doubtful prospects. The trade union legislation of 1927 tended to close the ranks; municipal elections from year to year showed steady Labor gains; parliamentary by-elections yielded notable victories; unrelieved industrial depression—more and more perceived to be the result of no mere after-war crisis but the inevitable consequence of profound and permanent changes in Britain's industrial position in the world—raised doubts as to whether any social and economic policy less comprehensive and bold than that of Labor would ever bring relief. On the other hand, trade unionism (always the main resource of the party) was suffering an almost unprecedented slump; a million members were lost in the single year 1926. By the same token, the party was in a bad way financially. The falling off of trade union membership diminished receipts from that source; contributions from many unions were in arrears, and the restrictions imposed in the legislation of 1927 operated to reduce them still further. In addition, there were rifts in the party—traceable mainly to left-wing dislike of the leadership of moderates like MacDonald and Henderson—which came persistently to the surface and at intervals threatened to do irreparable damage.

The Election of 1929 and the Second Labor Government

Under the British parliamentary system the cabinet may frequently exercise a good deal of discretion in selecting the time at which it will appeal to the country for a fresh lease of power. It must, however, observe the rule which restricts the life of a parliament to five years, and consequently the Baldwin government was under the necessity of seeing that a general election was held at some date not later than the autumn of 1929. The dissolution of the existing parliament

[31] *Britain's Industrial Future* (London, 1928). Cf. H. Clay, "The Liberal Industrial Report," *Econ. Jour.*, June, 1928, and p. 555 below.

took place, in point of fact, on May 10 of that year, and the polling occurred twenty days later.

The contest was in many respects a notable one. To be sure, it was the quietest and most urbane in a generation. The explanation, however, was to be found not so much in popular apathy as in the moderation of the party programs, the tolerant tone of discussion, and the absence of issues and incidents calculated to stir the emotions. And there were conditions which lent a special interest. In the first place, the election resolved itself into a three-cornered contest on a wholly unprecedented scale. The Labor party placed more candidates in the field than ever before, and the supposedly rejuvenated Liberal party likewise had more candidates than at any time since 1910. Only seven seats went uncontested—a far smaller number than in any previous election—and three-cornered fights in the constituencies were the rule rather than the exception.[32] In the second place, this was the first general election held after the final extensions of the suffrage under terms of the Representation of the People (Equal Franchise) Act of 1928. In a total potential electorate of nearly twenty-eight millions, there were upwards of seven million new voters—over five millions of them women—and it goes without saying that an election at which a full quarter of the eligible voters have never voted before is bound to be surrounded with exceptional uncertainty.[33] Throughout the campaign much special appeal was directed to the mis-termed "flapper vote," and despite frequent argument that the millions of new women electors might be expected to vote very much as other people voted, party leaders were generally apprehensive about the havoc which might conceivably flow from this source.

To the Conservatives it fell to play the least challenging rôle in the campaign. That is usually the penalty of being in

[32] For the 607 contested seats there were candidates as follows: Conservative, 596; Labor, 571; Liberal, 514; Communist, 26; others, 21—a total of 1,728, or three hundred more than in 1924. Sixty-eight of the number were women—thirty Laborites, twenty-five Liberals, ten Conservatives, and three Communists. There were 470 three-cornered contests.

[33] It should be observed, however, that the number of voters actually on the registration lists was considerably smaller, i.e., 25,092,848, which was an increase of 3,361,543 over the registration in 1924. Of the registrants, 13,227,690 were women and 11,865,158 were men.

office and merely asking to be continued in office. In his election address, Premier Baldwin urged that his party alone could "provide that continuity of policy and stability of government which the country needs at the present time;" and throughout the contest the argument was pressed that the only alternatives to a Conservative victory were "a Socialist government with or without Liberal support, or a state of political chaos and uncertainty"—both "disastrous to the welfare of industry and the welfare of the nation as a whole." British trade was held to have made large progress as a result of safeguarding legislation, which was to be extended cautiously; the Liberal and Labor solutions for unemployment were pronounced objectionable and futile, and the milder devices which the government had been trying—especially transference of unemployed persons to places (including the dominions) where they could obtain work—were explained and defended; state assistance to railways to enable them to reorganize and modernize their equipment was promised. Slow and careful national recovery on the lines of present policy was the appeal; "safety first," the slogan.

In Mr. Lloyd George the Liberals had by all odds the most spirited and daring leader, and their campaign followed closely the course that he marked out. Scoffing at the notion that Liberalism was dead, and advancing from one sweeping claim to another, he made unemployment the paramount issue, promising that if the nation entrusted his party with the responsibilities of office it would be found ready with schemes of work which could be put immediately into operation, and of such magnitude and character that "the terrible figures of the workless" would within a single year be reduced to normal proportions, without adding "one penny" to national or local taxation. As the campaign advanced, stress was placed also on "the firm establishment of world peace by the substitution of arbitration for force and by the effective reduction of the menacing armaments which nations are maintaining today."

The most notable feature of Labor's campaign was its tone of careful moderation. The collective election address, based on the much fuller statement of policy contained in *Labour and the Nation,* published in the previous year, asserted emphatically that the party is "neither Bolshevik nor Communist," that it is "opposed to force, revolution, and confiscation as means of establishing the new social order," and that it "believes in ordered progress and democratic methods." Socialism was mentioned but once in the document. Furthermore, not many sweeping promises were ventured. Even if the party were to come into full control, the nationalization of industry, it appeared, would proceed slowly. The coal industry would be taken up first, and others not more rapidly than perhaps one in a parliament. Railways and transport would merely be "reorganized;" other industries would be made the subjects of inquiry by committees. The significant trend of Labor thought toward national control as an alternative to national ownership received abundant illustration. Even the trade union act of 1927 which had stirred so much feeling was, apparently, merely to be amended, not repealed outright. As in the case of the Liberals, the problem of unemployment was given chief prominence; and the policies propounded were very much on Liberal lines. A National Economic Committee, modelled on the Committee of Imperial Defense, and including representatives of both employers and employees, was to be set up, and with its aid a Labor government would determine upon and put into operation a comprehensive program of works and improvements, including road and bridge building, housing and slum clearance, land drainage and reclamation, afforestation, and electrification. In the domain of finance, the earlier proposal of a surtax on unearned incomes of over £500 a year was softened to a promise of mere increase of the existing differentiation between incomes that were earned and those that were not. Nothing, of course, was said about a capital levy.

Conservative leaders were frank to concede that their party would suffer a considerable net loss of seats. On the other hand, it was clear that Labor would have to make enormous gains if it were to capture control. Both parties, therefore, feared chiefly a parliamentary deadlock arising from the lack of any independent party majority in the House of Commons, and both appealed passionately for such a majority. Baldwin called it "a stable government," MacDonald "a fair chance;"

but both meant the same thing. The Liberals had no hope of attaining a majority, but they expected to win a hundred seats or more, and probably to hold the balance of power. The party strength at dissolution was: Conservative, 400; Labor, 162; Liberal, 46; Independent, 7. The Conservative majority over the two chief opposition parties was, therefore, 192. On the face of things, it seemed hardly possible that the government's losses would be such as to put it in a minority. Yet persons best acquainted with the situation were prepared to witness precisely such an outcome; and polling day showed that they were right.

The results can be summarized briefly.[34] Labor won 289 seats; the Conservatives, 269;[35] the Liberals, 58. In addition, minor parties won eight seats (Independents, four; Nationalists, three; and Prohibitionists, one). The popular vote polled by the three leading parties was: Conservative, 8,658,918; Labor, 8,384,461; and Liberal, 5,305,123. Certain major facts were obvious. In the first place, the thing that had been feared had happened; no party had secured an independent parliamentary majority. Labor had a substantial plurality, but (counting only the seats of the three main parties) it lacked thirty of having a majority. In the second place, the Conservatives, though suffering a net loss of 140 seats, and reduced to second place on the roll of the new House, had polled somewhat more popular votes than any other party. How largely the defection of former supporters, including the great number of Liberals who voted for Conservative candidates in 1924, had been offset by increments of strength from the newly enfranchised electorate, there were no means of knowing. But it was significant that, notwithstanding the increase of the registered electorate by nearly three and one-half millions since 1924, the Conservative popular vote was less than three-quarters of a million larger than in that year. The Labor vote, on the other hand, was upwards of three millions larger. In the third place, notwithstanding that they had the most brilliant leaders, the ablest general staff of economists and writers,

[34] In less detail, necessarily, than in the case of elections dealt with above, because full data were unobtainable when this volume went to press.

[35] Including a seat for the borough of Rugby, where polling was delayed until June 13 on account of the death of a candidate.

ample funds, and an energetic press (reinforced by several normally Conservative papers controlled by Lord Beaverbrook and Lord Rothermere), the Liberals had succeeded in raising their contingent in the House by exactly twelve seats. There was comfort in the fact that they had almost doubled their popular vote. Seemingly they had won back a good many deserters, and had also attracted many new voters. But only the relatively even balance between the other two parties saved them from facing the thankless parliamentary rôle of a disappointed faction.[36]

The results of the polling left no doubt that there would be another Labor government. The only question was whether the Baldwin ministry would resign at once or would wait, as in 1923, to be turned out after the new parliament met. The prime minister was advised both ways, but there were no such reasons for staying in office as on the earlier occasion, and he very properly decided upon immediate resignation. On June 4 the ministers surrendered their seals, and on the following day Mr. MacDonald was called to Windsor Castle, where the king was recovering from a serious illness, and asked to form a government. "The Right Honorable James Ramsay MacDonald, M. P.," laconically reported the evening's *Court Circular,* "accepted His Majesty's offer of the post of prime minister and kissed his hands upon his appointment."

So rapid has been the rise of the Labor party's fortunes that there has been comparatively little time for developing the talents of a technical character that are essential for the business of government, nor even for attracting in great numbers from the outside the ambitious men of capacity who always attach themselves to a prospering cause. Even at its first opportunity to take command in Whitehall in 1924, however, the party surprised and impressed the country with the sum total of admitted ability that it was able to muster, and

[36] SEATS CAPTURED FROM OTHER PARTIES

by

(from)	Labor	Conservatives	Liberals	Independents
Labor	......	1	2	0
Conservatives	110	..	29	3
Liberals	15	2	....	0
Communists	1	0	0	0
Independents	2	0	0	..

five years later its position was considerably stronger. It is true that it seemed advisable to assign a number of posts, e.g., the lord chancellorship and the secretaryship of state for India, to men who had but very recently identified themselves with the party, and that the attorney-generalship was bestowed on an eminent lawyer who had actually been elected to the new parliament as a Liberal. But with Henderson, Sankey, Snowden, Webb, Clynes, Trevelyan, Buxton, Greenwood, Thomas, and Miss Bondfield in leading places of responsibility, even the defeated Tories were bound to admit that the new government was an able one. Mr. MacDonald wisely took the traditional first lordship of the Treasury rather than the foreign secretaryship; and, as has been noted elsewhere, the government derived distinction from inclusion in the cabinet of the first woman to hold such a position, i.e., Miss Bondfield, as minister of labor.[37] Of particular significance was the fact that even after the full list of minor ministerial appointments was announced, there was hardly a trace of anything revolutionary or extremist about the group. The clamorous left wing of the party went practically unrepresented, and trade unionism, in general, did not loom large.[38]

Labor was again in office. Was it also in power? Obviously not, in the important sense of commanding the support of an independent parliamentary majority; and any government devoid of such a majority must necessarily be regarded as in a precarious position. Nevertheless, the situation was far better than in 1924. Instead of being heavily outnumbered in the House of Commons by the Conservatives, and completely at the mercy of nominal but not dependable Liberal allies, the new MacDonald government was secure against every contingency except a combination—rather improbable, at least for a time—of Conservative and Liberal votes. Its added experience and newly recruited ability were important assets. The

[37] Miss Susan Lawrence also became a minister (though not a cabinet member) as parliamentary secretary to the ministry of health.

[38] The minor appointments were not, however, devoid of interest. John Hayes, a former London policeman, became the vice-chamberlain of the royal household, and Ben Smith, who drove a horse-cab in London streets until automobiles came into fashion, found himself treasurer of the king's household, charged with supervising the royal expenditures generally.

moderation of its program commanded the confidence of the country and left little excuse for active Liberal opposition. Large parts of this program were capable of being achieved by administrative orders, involving no controversial legislation. The extravagant expectations cherished by the rank and file of the party, and by many outside sympathizers, in 1924 had been greatly toned down. Though no one could tell how long it would last, there was a general disposition to give the new government the fair chance which its leader so ardently coveted. The country did not want another election at an early date and responded sympathetically to the premier's promise that there would be none in the next two years if he could prevent it. The settlement of the troublesome reparations question, and the readiness of the Hoover administration in the United States to meet the British at least half way on the almost equally bothersome question of armaments, cleared the path for easier travelling in the domain of international relations.

Much, of course, would depend on the Liberals. Their parliamentary numbers were unimpressive, but, as Mr. Lloyd George was quick to point out, they held the balance of power. In 1924, when the Conservatives possessed many more seats than Labor, Mr. MacDonald sought and obtained a working agreement with the Liberal contingent which, unsatisfactory as it was, kept his government going for upwards of a year. In 1929, with the Conservatives outnumbered, the Labor policy was to refrain from alliances; neither Labor nor Liberals desired, or apparently made any effort to bring about, any agreement whatsoever. The Labor hope lay, rather, in pursuing a policy of such moderation—a policy, indeed, so harmonious with that of the Liberals on matters of prime importance like unemployment relief—that even if Mr. Lloyd George should attempt to make trouble he could not carry his followers with him. It was a bold course, but the only one possible under the circumstances.

When these pages were written, there was much to indicate that the Liberals were prepared to abstain, for some time to come, from placing Labor's tenure in jeopardy—only, however, for a price. The price was to be a new electoral law providing for proportional representation, or at least the alternative vote. On all sides, following the election, the scant fruits realized from a really impressive popular vote (almost a fourth of the total) was the subject of lively Liberal comment. "We have once more," observed Mr. Lloyd George, "been tripped up by the triangle," meaning, of course, the three-cornered contest. "We intend," he declared further, "to use all our power in the new parliament to obtain speedy redress of this glaring wrong." When a small and struggling party, Labor, as we have seen, itself espoused the proportional idea. In its day of prosperity—standing, as it now does, on the brink of independent control of the government—it is far less interested. It does not concede the permanence of the three-party system. No more do the Conservatives. Both cling to the conviction that the Liberal party will eventually disappear and the historic bi-party system reëstablish itself; both, as matters stand, would lose heavily by meeting the Liberal demand for a proportional system. Accordingly, notwithstanding that there are plenty of friends of proportional representation in the Labor ranks, as in other parties, the price proposed to be exacted for Liberal abstention is indeed high. If it is insisted upon, the resulting clash of interests and policies may not only wreck the second Labor government but precipitate a general election turning mainly, or solely, on electoral reform.[39]

[39] As these pages were closed for printing (June 25, 1929), the new parliament was assembling, the first Speech from the Throne that Labor ministers ever had an opportunity to prepare was about to be presented, and the nation was awaiting with interest the program of action with which Mr. MacDonald and his supporters proposed to start their new day in office.

CHAPTER XXII

PARTY STRUCTURE

FROM the foregoing outline of party history we turn, in this chapter and others that follow, to some significant aspects of parties as they exist at the present time: the elements of the population out of which they have been built up; the social and geographical distribution of their followings today; their similarities and differences as to principle and policy; the national and local machinery by means of which they recruit members, carry on campaigns, and keep up morale; their finances; and their connections with auxiliary organizations. Through these avenues of approach the true nature of parties and the party system can be brought to light as no amount of mere political history and of electoral statistics can reveal it.

At the outset, one is confronted with the fact—apparent enough from the narrative in the preceding chapters—that the period of the World War drew a bold line athwart the entire development of British party alignments and techniques. The suspension of party activities during the truce, seven years of coalition government, the disappearance of Irish Nationalism, the eclipse of Liberalism, the rise of Labor to major party rank—these and other phenomena of the decade starting in 1914 have converted the party scene of pre-war days into something of entirely different character, not merely as witnessed by the compiler of electoral returns or the observer of votes in the House of Commons, but as viewed by the student of party membership, organization, methods, and procedures. Approaching the matter first on the side of structure, or make-up, of the party groups, it will therefore be well to see something of what the situation was when the elder Chamberlain and Rosebery and Campbell-Bannerman walked the stage, and afterwards to bring into view some of the developments that have produced the reorientation of our own day.

Elements Composing the Unionist and Liberal Parties Before 1914

Leaving out of account the Irish Nationalists, localized in central and southern Ireland, and the Laborites, scattered thinly over the industrial districts, the politically active population of the United Kingdom in the earlier years of the century was divided rather evenly between the Unionist (or Conservative) and Liberal parties. This does not mean that all classes of the people were divided thus, because to a greater extent than in the United States and other English-speaking countries the lines of cleavage corresponded to distinctions of economic status, professional connection, and social position, running in that degree horizontally rather than perpendicularly.[1] All kinds of contradictory affiliations did indeed appear, and it was never safe to assume that a man was of a given party simply because he belonged to a certain profession, class, or group. In the Conservative ranks were found, however, decidedly the larger part of the people of title, wealth, and social position; almost all of the clergy of the Established Church, and some of the Nonconformists, especially Wesleyans; a majority of the graduates of the universities [2] and of members of the bar; most of the prosperous merchants, manufacturers, and financiers; a majority of clerks; approximately half of the tradesmen and shopkeepers; and a large proportion of the small landholders, and especially of the agricultural laborers. In the Liberal party were found, on the other hand, a goodly share of the professional and commercial elements, considerably more than half of what may be termed broadly the middle class, especially in the towns (but omitting clerks and other employees living on small fixed incomes), and at least half of the urban workingmen, although the latter were being drawn off in increasing numbers by Labor. The membership of the Established Church in England and Wales was preponderantly

[1] "My boy," once said an old and experienced English politician to a novice, "bring me a register of electors. Tell me the occupations and circumstances of each, and I will tell you what they are in politics." F. Gray, *The Confessions of a Candidate*, 9.

[2] From 1885 to 1918 not a Liberal member was returned by any of the universities.

Conservative, but the Nonconformists were everywhere heavily Liberal.[3]

Liberalism drew the support of only an insignificant portion of the rank and wealth of the kingdom. This had not always been the case. At the middle of the nineteenth century the party consisted, as has been noted elsewhere, of two main elements: (1) the aristocratic Whigs, of eighteenth-century antecedents, the limits of whose liberalism were rather quickly reached, and (2) middle-class people enfranchised in 1832, who confronted political questions with considerably less predisposition against change. The reform acts of 1867 and 1884 brought this second element large accessions of strength, and by drawing in the working people of the towns accentuated its liberal, and even radical, tendencies. The old-Whig and the more popular forces were, however, never really fused, and, beginning with the secession of the Liberal Unionists on Gladstone's first home rule bill in 1886, the elements representing title, wealth, and fashion migrated almost *en masse* into the ranks of the opposing party. This drew off most of the old Whigs. In addition, many of the great manufacturers and traders, representing new and socially ambitious families, chose to link up their fortunes with Conservatism. The immediate result was a decided weakening of the party, evidenced no less by the failure to govern impressively in 1892-95 than by the low estate to which it fell while in opposition during the succeeding decade. In the long run, however, there was a gain in unity, and the party was able to become more consistently liberal than would have been possible under previous conditions.[4]

The strength of Irish Nationalism lay, of course, almost wholly in Ireland, and that of the Labor party was confined largely to the industrial centers of England and Wales. The major parties, too, while less localized, were decidedly stronger in some portions of the country than in others. Scotland was

[3] A book of some interest in this connection is R. H. Gretton, *The English Middle Class* (London, 1917).

[4] The Liberal secession of 1886 and succeeding years is described and interpreted in M. Ostrogorski, *Democracy and the Organization of Political Parties,* I, Chap. ix. See also J. Morley, *Life of William Ewart Gladstone,* III, Bk. x; W. S. Churchill, *Lord Randolph Churchill,* II, Chaps. xi-xiii; and A. Mackintosh, *Joseph Chamberlain,* Chaps. xvi-xx.

overwhelmingly Liberal. Half of its counties and boroughs invariably returned Liberals to the House of Commons; a third more were predominantly Liberal; three or four counties were politically doubtful; not more than that number were predominantly Conservative. The situation in Wales was practically the same, except that the Liberal preponderance was even more marked. On the other hand, England presented the aspect of a predominantly Conservative, or at all events Conservative and doubtful, stretch of country, generously spotted over with Liberal areas. Five of these Liberal regions stood out with some distinctness: (1) the extreme northeast, especially Northumberland, Durham, and parts of Cumberland; (2) a great belt stretching westward from the Humber to Morecambe Bay, and including northern Lincoln, southern Yorkshire, and northern Lancashire; (3) Norfolk and the other lands bordering the Wash; (4) a midlands area containing parts of Leicester, Warwick, Northampton, and Bedford; and (5) Devon and Cornwall, in the far southwest. The Conservative strongholds lay farther to the south and east. From Chester and Nottingham to the English Channel, and from Wales to the North Sea—this was the greatest single area of Conservative strength, aside from a half-dozen Protestant counties in the Irish province of Ulster. From Oxford and Hertford southward past London to the Channel there was not a county in which the Conservatives were in danger of being outvoted. Perhaps the most strongly Conservative section of the entire country was the southeasternmost county of Kent.[5]

The existence of "two Britains," a northern and a southern, a Liberal and a Conservative, had long been a matter of comment among students of political and social phenomena. Disraeli gave it literary recognition in his novel *Sybil.* Leaving Wales out of account, the division line may be indicated roughly as the Trent River. North of the Trent, temperament, attitude, outlook were, and had been for a hundred years, predominantly Liberal; south of the Trent, they had been predominantly Con-

[5] See E. Krehbiel, "Geographic Influences in British Elections," *Geog. Rev.,* Dec., 1916. A map which accompanies this article shows in colors the distribution of party strength on the basis of composite returns for the eight parliamentary elections between 1885 and December, 1910.

servative. "The panics and perils of the Napoleonic wars," says an English writer, "had the sad result of driving out of the southern shires, where they once ran deep and strong, the traditions of Milton and Bunyan, of Pym and Hampden, each a southerner, and each a fearless apostle of liberty and democracy. Since 1800 the impulse to liberality of thought and action in politics has consistently come from the north and won its way against the steady resistance of the south. From the north came Wilberforce to banish slavery; from the north came Grey, Durham, Brougham, and the *Edinburgh Review* to give Britain parliamentary reform in 1832; from the north came Cobden and Bright to give her economic freedom and a true perspective of the American Civil War; from the north came Gladstone and his great Liberal majorities of 1868 and 1880; and in the northern by-elections after 1902 began the stern revolt of outraged democracy against the jingo imperialism of the Boer War period, which ended in Campbell-Bannerman's crushing victory of 1906. All progressive causes and Liberal administrations in Britain for the last century have drawn their electoral support and moral inspiration from the north, just as Tory imperialism and reaction have had their strong house of refuge in the south." [6]

This statement conveys a somewhat exaggerated impression; the south has been less uniformly illiberal than is here affirmed, and, whatever the differences between Liberalism and Conservatism in earlier times, Conservatives in later decades repeatedly proved themselves hardly less open-minded and progressive than their rivals.[7] Still, it cannot be denied that north and south have been, and even yet are, fundamentally unlike in political temper and attitude. There are several reasons why this should be so. The first is the predominantly industrial character of the north as compared with the south. It was, indeed, the Industrial Revolution that first created the two Britains—the one devoted

[6] "Hespericus," in *New York Nation,* Aug. 17, 1919, p. 166.

[7] In reading British political history one must always beware of taking the terms "Conservative" and "Liberal" too literally. Far apart as the parties often were on particular principles and policies, the gulf between them was rarely such as to prevent a flexible-minded man from crossing from one to the other. The record shows that neither had a monopoly of the qualities and points of view which we term conservative and liberal.

to manufacturing and mining, largely urban, meeting new problems, requiring novel legislation and drastic reforms, the other mainly landholding and agricultural, rural rather than urban, bound by immemorial custom, and hence by nature conservative. Trade unionism, the political activities of labor, the impulse toward higher standards of education created by the technical demands of industry—these and other forces long counted powerfully (in days before the Labor party grew to its present proportions) for liberalism in the general sense (and also Liberalism in the party sense) in the north.[8] On the other hand, the south has always been the chief seat of the great military and naval organizations, with their preconceptions of caste and their lack of touch with democratic influences. Furthermore, in the south dwell practically all of the very large number of retired and returned planters, merchants, sportsmen, concession-holders, and other magnates from the various parts of the overseas Empire—the successors of the Indian "nabobs" of a century ago, and, like them, too long accustomed to lording it over the undeveloped folk of the tropics to be likely to incline very strongly toward democracy at home. Finally may be mentioned the influence of the institutions of learning—not only the ancient universities but the great schools like Eton and Harrow—which in their general atmosphere, and often in their actual teaching, are strongly conservative. Three-fourths of these institutions are south of the Trent.

In general, down to 1914, those regions in which the people were engaged mainly in manufacturing and mining were Liberal, those in which they were engaged in agriculture were Conservative; and among agricultural districts, it was the most

[8] It is true that certain great northern cities—Liverpool, Birmingham, Manchester—usually returned more Conservatives than Liberals to the House of Commons. But in most instances an explanation can be found in certain special situations that reversed the natural tendencies. Thus, Liverpool went Conservative for the reason that the Conservatives, once in control of the municipal council, met the demands of the industrial population by surprisingly progressive legislation and thereby won, and kept, the support of the masses, in national as well as local politics. Birmingham's leanings to Conservatism were traceable to the influence of the city's most eminent statesman of the past generation, Joseph Chamberlain. Manchester, formerly Conservative, swung into the Liberal column in 1906 as a protest against "tariff reform."

fertile and best favored, such as Kent, that were most decidedly Conservative. Regions in which small landholders abounded were likely to be Liberal. Scotland was Liberal because of the traditional dislike of landlordism, the strong sense of independence and the sturdy democracy of the middle and working classes, the absence of the Church of England as an established church, and the weakness of the peerage in both numbers and influence. Wales was Liberal because of the predominance of industry and mining, the scarcity of great landed estates, the radical temperament bred by an austere mode of life, and the strength of Nonconformism.

The Labor Party: the Trade Unionist Contribution

Before turning to the realignment of Conservative and Liberal forces in more recent days, due account must be taken of a main factor in bringing about the shift, i.e., the rise of the Labor party to its post-war eminence. To the present point, this party, which in 1923-24, under the astonished gaze of a somewhat nervous world, stepped into the leading rôle in the political drama, has been mentioned only as the requirements of an historical narrative dictated. We must retrace our steps sufficiently to see from what sources the party sprang, of what elements it was built up, and what its structure has come to be in these days of full equality with its older rivals.

Speaking broadly, the Labor party is a product of two chief principles or forces playing upon the widened electorate created by the reform acts of 1867 and 1884. One of these is trade unionism; the other is socialism. The one has contributed, mainly, the funds and the votes; the other, the leadership, the energy, and the spirit. Trade unions are combinations of workers in particular crafts designed to promote collective bargaining and other forms of concerted action in dealing with employers. Appearing in England in the early stages of the Industrial Revolution—when, as one writer has remarked, the factory first made them possible and the conditions of the factory made them necessary [9]—they grew steadily in numbers in the nineteenth century, and by the close had a membership not far short of two millions. Their legal status was long a

[9] A. Shadwell, *Industrial Efficiency* (London, 1906), II, 307.

matter of controversy. The restraints imposed by the common law were largely abolished by legislation enacted between 1824 and 1876. But in 1901 grave discontent was stirred by a decision handed down by the House of Lords in the Taff Vale case recognizing the right of employers to collect damages from trade unions for injuries arising from strikes.[10] In 1906 the Liberals rewarded the labor elements for their support by passing a Trade Disputes Act practically exempting the unions from legal process.[11] Again, in the Osborne Judgment of 1909 the House of Lords made trouble for the unions by ruling that they could not legally collect compulsory contributions for the support of labor representatives in the House of Commons;[12] and once more the Liberals saved the day for their allies, first by the act of 1911 providing salaries for members of the popular branch of Parliament, and later by a new Trade Union Act of 1913 which permitted trade union funds to be used for political purposes in so far as they were derived from contributions made knowingly and voluntarily for such purposes.[13]

The period of the World War brought unprecedented growth, both in numbers and in influence. A membership which passed the two-million mark in 1900 and the four-million level in 1914 rose to six and a half millions in 1918, and to a top figure of eight and a third millions two years later. Then, however, came a sharp recession. Trade and industry, already suffering when the peak was attained, passed into an era of baffling depression; unemployment grew apace; unionists, unable to pay their dues, dropped off the rolls, and entire organizations disappeared. By 1925 membership had fallen to five and a half millions; two years later it was hardly four millions. Not only, furthermore, was there such shrinkage in numbers, but financial resources dwindled almost to the vanishing point. Coupled with the falling off of dues, the swollen demands of "out of work pay" for unemployed members bled the organizations white. Between 1920 and 1925 they paid out millions of pounds from their

[10] F. A. Ogg and W. R. Sharp, *Economic Development of Modern Europe*, 412-414; G. D. H. Cole, *A Short History of the British Working Class Movement* (New York, 1927), III, 28-33.

[11] F. A. Ogg and W. R. Sharp, *op. cit.*, 414-416.

[12] *Ibid.*, 416-417.

[13] *Ibid.*, 417-418.

accumulated funds for unemployment relief; in two more years half of the balance was gone, and practically all of the residue was earmarked for the liabilities of the various superannuation funds. The richest union of all, the National Union of Railwaymen, spent everything it had upon the general strike of 1926, and in fact incurred a bank overdraft of nearly a million pounds. The year 1926 was easily the most disastrous in the whole two centuries of trade union history; and after it came, in 1927, the body blow inflicted by the Trade Disputes and Trade Unions Act described in the preceding chapter, giving the legal status of unionism a wrench which left it decidedly less favorable than a quarter of a century earlier. Experience shows that trade unionism advances in waves, and that the peaks following the low points commonly bring the movement, as measured both by numbers and by resources, to a stronger position than before. Given time enough, history will probably repeat itself, despite even the sharp decline of the past few years. Remembering, however, that trade unionism is the backbone of the Labor party, it is clear that the interests of that party—on the financial side at least—must suffer for a good while to come.

Viewing the trade union situation broadly and without reference to the exceptional conditions just described, two or three main facts emerge. One of them is that unionism is invariably strongest in those industries in which the workers are congregated together; for example, a few years ago, when about seventy per cent of the coal miners were organized, hardly ten per cent of the agricultural laborers held trade union membership. To state it differently, the strength of unionism lies particularly in areas of localized industry, such as Lancashire, Yorkshire, the counties on the northeast coast, and south Wales. The movement is relatively weak among women workers, primarily because a great proportion of these marry and cease to be wage-earners at an early age. At no time have the unions enrolled more than twenty per cent of the country's female wage-earners. In the case of men, the maximum proportion has been about fifty per cent.

A second fact is that while the number of trade unionists has grown greatly in the last forty years, the number of unions has somewhat fallen off; there were nearly a hundred fewer in 1925 than in 1892.[14] The explanation, of course, is amalgamation. The bulk of trade union membership is, indeed, concentrated in a few large associations, of which the best examples are the National Union of Railwaymen, the Transport and General Workers' Union, and the Amalgamated Engineering Union. Furthermore, unions which are technically separate are extensively linked up in federations; in 1925 rather more than half of the whole number of unionists belonged to organizations which were thus affiliated. A good example is the Miners' Federation, embracing numerous separate miners' unions with an aggregate membership, in 1925, of eight hundred thousand, but acting in all important matters for the miners as a whole. Often it is difficult to distinguish for practical purposes between amalgamations and federations. To complicate matters further still, there are inter-occupational groupings, both local and national. Locally, these take the form of trades councils, consisting of the unions in different crafts in a community, and frequently, as we shall see, affiliated with the local Labor party in a constituency. In the national field, the oldest and most important such organization is the Trades Union Congress, in which, as a matter of fact, both unions in the strict sense and federations, such as that of the miners, are represented.[15]

[14] To be exact, 1,233 at the earlier, and 1,144 at the later, date.

[15] See p. 589 below. In 1927 the Congress embraced organizations having an aggregate membership of over four millions. A General Federation of Trade Unions, once a close rival of the Trades Union Congress, has become a mere strike insurance society, and a Triple Industrial Alliance, founded in 1914 and consisting of the Miners' Federation, the National Union of Railwaymen, and the Transport Workers' Federation, failed to function in any very effective way and eventually passed out of existence.

The standard treatise on English trade unionism is S. and B. Webb, *History of Trade Unionism* (new ed., London, 1920). The subject is dealt with adequately in various chapters of G. D. H. Cole, *Short History of the British Working Class Movement,* 3 vols. (New York, 1927). Other important books include *ibid., An Introduction to Trade Unionism* (London, 1918); S. and B. Webb, *Industrial Democracy* (new ed., London, 1920); and R. M. Rayner, *The Story of Trade Unionism* (London, 1928). The legal aspects (until recent years) are covered in H. Slesser, *The Law Relating to Trade Unions* (London, 1921), and more briefly in H. Tracey (ed.), *The Book of the Labour Party* (London, 1926), I, Chaps. ix-x. On the legislation of 1927, see A. T. Mason, "The British Trade Disputes Act of 1927," *Amer. Polit. Sci. Rev.,* Feb., 1928, and H. A. Millis, "The British

The Labor Party: the Socialist Contribution

Notwithstanding that the shift of industrial methods and conditions which underlies the modern socialist movement came first and was most extensive in England, socialism in that country is a comparatively recent development. The Englishman is not naturally a socialist. He values government, but he does not want an excessive amount of it, and as late as a generation or two ago it was commonly thought that socialism would never take any such hold in the "tight little island" as in Germany, France, and other Continental lands. In point of fact, however, Britain in the quarter-century preceding the World War was the scene of unremitting and decidedly effective socialist agitation. Vigorous socialist organizations came into being; the spirit and ideals of socialism were injected into parliamentary debate, and into national and local legislation, quite as extensively as in most states across the Channel; and in 1924 the country found itself with a party in control at Westminster the leadership and policy of which—even if not all of its friends and adherents—were frankly socialist. Besides many thousands of bona fide, avowed socialists, organized as such, there are numerous men and women who are thoroughgoing socialists, yet not members of any socialist party or society; also multitudes whose minds are saturated with socialist ideas, who, however, do not call themselves by the name.

Among the numerous more or less independent socialist organizations of recent decades, three specially deserve to be mentioned. The oldest is the Social Democratic Federation, with a checkered history beginning in 1880. Renamed in 1911 the British Socialist party, the "S. F. D." labored to win the British workingman to an intellectual acceptance of Karl Marx, with the result only that in 1916—when the organization became affiliated with the Labor party—there was a following of ten thousand. In protest against the party's anti-war attitude, a section including the party's founder, Henry M. Hyndman, seceded in 1916 and formed an independent organization

Trade Disputes and Trade Unions Act," *Jour. of Polit. Econ.*, June, 1928. A brief analysis of the legal status today will be found in H. B. Lees-Smith, *Encyclopedia of the Labour Movement* (London, 1928), III, 217-232.

which, after being known for a time as the National Socialist party, resumed, in 1920, the old name Social Democratic Federation. With a membership not much above two thousand, this society is, as we shall see, tied up with the Labor party. What remained of the British Socialist party was largely fused, in 1920, with a number of local communist organizations under the name of the Communist party, a bolshevist society, with ten thousand members in 1921, affiliated with the Third (or Moscow) International, but neither then nor since with the Labor party. The most widely known socialist organization is the Fabian Society, founded in 1884, and composed largely of scholars, writers, clergymen, and other intellectual leaders—such as Sidney and Beatrice Webb, Bernard Shaw, H. G. Wells, and Graham Wallas—on the right wing of the socialist movement. During their first quarter-century, the Fabians, through their books, tracts, and other propagandist efforts, exercised a powerful influence on the formation of socialist opinion.[16] Of late, many of the leaders have transferred their best effort to the cause of the Labor party, with which the society is affiliated, with the result that the organization, as such, has dropped into the background. There are about two thousand members.

The largest purely socialist organization is the Independent Labor party, organized, under the leadership of Keir Hardie, at a conference of labor delegates held at Bradford early in 1893, with the object of promoting the "collective ownership and control of the means of production, distribution, and exchange," and the election to Parliament of men pledged to carry out this policy. Not sufficiently radical to escape quarrels with the Social Democratic Federation, the "I.L.P." was nevertheless too pronouncedly socialist to make great headway among the laboring masses, and in 1914 its membership was only about sixty thousand. In 1927 the book membership was fifty thousand, the actual paid-up membership nearer thirty thousand. The organization, however, has supplied most of the leadership and driving power of the Labor party, within whose generous limits, as will appear, it still maintains its own identity.

[16] Several "Fabian Tracts" and other publications of the society are cited at various points in this book.

Its importance, therefore, is quite out of proportion to its numbers.[17]

Origins and Early Growth of the Labor Party

One can easily agree with Arthur Henderson when he says that "the organization, growth, and consolidation of the Labor party forms one of the most dramatic, instructive, and significant chapters in the history of democratic development in Great Britain;[18] and at this point the process by which the party was created and made a leading factor in the political situation may appropriately receive a word of comment. Trade unionism long existed, and organized socialism assumed considerable importance, before there was any attempt to weld workingmen together in a political party. Toward the close of the third quarter of the nineteenth century, however, various steps, not involving the formation of a distinct party, were taken to bring about the election of workingmen, as such, to the House of Commons. In the very year of the enfranchisement of the working classes in the towns (1867) a newly formed Workingmen's Association in London resolved "to procure a direct representation of labor interests by the return of workingmen to Parliament," and at the general election of the following year three candidates, put up by the Radical wing of the Liberal party, made their campaign, although in vain, as spokesmen of labor. A Labor Representation League, formed in 1869, was active for several years and at the election of 1874 saw the success of two of the dozen candidates whom it sponsored. Still there was no thought of a separate party, and for a decade and a half there were no further developments, except

[17] The standard work on socialism in Great Britain is Max Beer, *History of British Socialism,* 2 vols. (London, 1919-20), which is based largely on the author's *Geschichte des Sozialismus in England* (Stuttgart, 1912). Another work of almost equal value is G. D. H. Cole, *Short History of the British Working Class Movement,* as cited. The best account of the Fabian Society is E. R. Pease, *History of the Fabian Society* (2nd ed., London, 1925), and a full exposition of Fabian ideas on Britain's political and economic reorganization is contained in S. and B. Webb, *A Constitution for the Socialist Commonwealth of Great Britain,* previously cited. A weekly organ, known as *The New Statesman,* was founded in 1914 to advocate Fabian doctrines, and its files are indispensable for any study of the subject.

[18] H. Tracey (ed.), *The Book of the Labour Party,* I, 8.

that workingman candidates appeared at every election under the Liberal banner, especially in the mining districts, and that as a rule ten or a dozen of them won seats.

As the century drew toward a close, however, demand arose in labor circles for a separate party. In 1888, indeed, such a party was organized in Scotland; and in 1893, as has been indicated, the Independent Labor party was formed at a conference of labor and socialist bodies, with the object not only of propagating socialism but of giving labor a political alliance distinct from the existing parties. The new organization started off with the usual paraphernalia of political parties—an executive committee, an annual congress, a treasury, a platform—and in local elections it had considerable success. Nationally, its progress was slow; not until 1900 was it able to win a seat in the House of Commons,[19] and already its numbers were dwindling. The bulk of trade unionists were not ready for socialism. Accordingly, in 1899 the Trades Union Congress, meeting at Plymouth, projected a new, non-socialist organization which, at a conference of representatives of seventy trade union, coöperative, socialist, and other organizations held at London in 1900, took form as the Labor Representation Committee. The forces chiefly influential in the Committee were the politically-inclined but non-socialist trade unions (although the I.L.P. and certain other socialist organizations held membership); and its avowed object was the formation of a labor group in Parliament which, although ready to collaborate with any party showing friendliness toward labor interests, should have its own whips, methods, and policies.

Unheralded by the press, ignored by the great parties, and frowned upon by a powerful section of trade union leaders, the new organization represented a truly audacious effort to secure political power for the workers. Nevertheless it struck root, and within the space of twenty-four years the man who acted as secretary at the initial meeting found himself head of Britain's first Labor government. Winning twenty-nine seats in the House of Commons in 1906, the Committee—with a

[19] When Keir Hardie, defeated in 1895, was again elected. His first election antedated the establishment of the I.L.P. See E. Hughes (ed.), *Keir Hardie; His Writings and Speeches* (London, 1928).

popular following grown to almost a million—dropped its modest title, confidently assumed the name of "Labor party," and adopted a new constitution, which stood practically unchanged until 1918. In order to avoid alienating trade unionists who were not socialists, the party as such declined to declare itself a socialist organization. In 1907, the party congress, under I.L.P. leadership, did, indeed, adopt a resolution declaring for "the socialization of the means of production, distribution, and exchange, to be controlled in a democratic state in the interest of the entire community, and the complete emancipation of labor from the domination of capitalism and landlordism, with the establishment of social and economic equality between the sexes;" and resolutions of similar tenor were voted pretty regularly at the annual congresses thereafter. Such pronouncements were admittedly socialistic. They contained, however, no hint of class war or revolution, and the party's growth seems not to have been greatly impeded by them. The resulting closer identification of the I.L.P. with the main party became, rather, a source of added vitality.

In after years the party advocated, as practical and immediately obtainable reforms, medical inspection of school children and public provision of meals for those who were necessitous, the setting up of wage boards for sweated industries, a more generous administration of the fair-wages clause of government contracts, unemployment insurance and the establishment of labor exchanges, regulation of the liquor trade on the principle of local option, and taxation aimed at "securing for the communal benefit all unearned increment of wealth" and "preventing the retention of great fortunes in private hands." It aided in the enactment of minimum wage legislation and of old age pensions and miners' eight-hour laws, and it strenuously resisted the Conservative tariff proposals, especially on food. It urged salaries for members of the House of Commons, and in a challenging resolution introduced by its representatives in that body in 1907 it called for the abolition of the House of Lords, as being "a hindrance to national progress." [20]

[20] *Labour Year Book* (1916), 323.

Labor's Phenomenal Growth Since 1914

From 1910 to the beginning of the World War the representation of Labor in the House of Commons (counting a few so-called Liberal Laborites who went their own way on industrial matters but otherwise acted with the Liberal party) fluctuated around forty-five. The group, however, enjoyed power far beyond its numbers, for the reason that the Liberal government, having lost the huge parliamentary majority won in 1906, was in these days quite dependent upon the support of its allies, the Irish Nationalist and Labor members. Naturally, the Laborites turned the situation to good account in the promotion of industrial and social legislation. The proposal to abolish the House of Lords was kept alive, although, on the principle that half a loaf is better than none, the party finally gave its support to the program of second chamber reform which culminated in the Parliament Act of 1911. The National Insurance Bill and the bill for the payment of members were likewise carried with Labor aid in 1911; and Labor was to a great extent the author of the Minimum Wage Act of 1912 and of the Trade Union Act of 1913 reversing the Osborne Judgment.

The influence of the labor forces on legislation was thus considerable. Practical-minded labor leaders realized, however, that the situation from which they then drew so much power would not last and that, in the long run, labor could expect to be politically potent only in one of two ways, i.e., by using its votes under some consistent plan within the ranks of the older parties, or by building up a third party of sufficient strength to meet its rivals on something like even terms. The first mode was not promising, if for no other reason, because of the diffusion of labor support among the older parties and because of the difficulty of so harnessing labor strength within either the Liberal or the Conservative party as to make it effective in the control of party policy. The other alternative also, although not hopeless, was beset with serious obstacles. The elements from which a Labor party of major rank would have to be constructed were, and seemed likely to remain, fundamentally inharmonious, the principal source of friction being socialism. Furthermore, even if the tendencies to internal discord could be overcome, there would remain the fact that the bi-party system appeared to be solidly intrenched in the country and that no third party had ever been able to prevent the dissipation of its strength through the continuous reabsorption of its membership into the ranks of its older rivals.

What might have required decades to accomplish was, however, brought about within the space of less than ten years by the social and political reorientation produced by the World War and by the tasks of reconstruction which it imposed. In preceding chapters the salient aspects of Labor party history from 1914 to the election of 1929 have been mentioned. It will, therefore, suffice to recall here that upon the outbreak of the war Labor, with only a slight amount of dissent after the true situation was understood, subscribed to the party truce; that in the spring of 1915 it was given modest representation in the Asquith coalition government; that it was also represented in the first Lloyd George coalition government, and in the war cabinet; that in August, 1917, the executive committee of the party took in hand the preparation of a plan of party reorganization; that early in 1918 this plan, in the form of a new party constitution, was adopted by a party conference held at London;[21] that in June, 1918, the party decided, over the protest of some of its representatives in the ministry, to repudiate the truce and to begin to work on independent lines toward the goal of a Labor government; that at the general election of December, 1918, it polled 2,224,945 votes, elected fifty-seven members, and became the official opposition, although sharing the Front Opposition Bench with the Independent Liberals; that during the next four years (the period of the second Lloyd George coalition government) the party maintained a completely independent position, while the popular drift in its direction, not only in industrial districts, but in middle-class constituencies, was indicated by a gain of nine seats at by-elections and a loss of only two; that at the general election of 1922 the party's popular vote rose to four and one-fourth millions and its parliamentary strength to 142, exceeding the combined quotas of the as yet unreconciled wings of Liberalism; and that

[21] The new basis of the party and the machinery developed in accordance with it are described in the following chapter.

the country's rejection in 1923 of the tariff reform program with which the Conservative government went to the electorate opened the way for the first Labor government in British history at a date less than a quarter of a century removed from the real inception of the party in 1900. In the checkered history of third-party movements, the record is equalled only, perhaps, by the rise to power of the Republican party in the United States in 1850-60 and of the Labor party in Australia in 1892-1910.[22]

Changed Distribution of Party Strength Since the War

It goes without saying that the rise of a party of the magnitude of Labor, combined with the tortuous career and sharp decline of one of the two major parties of earlier days, i.e., the Liberal party, has given the political map of the country an aspect quite different from that which it bore in 1914; and it will be interesting to see something of the new situation that has come about. The first fact to be noted is that Conservatism still enjoys its great hold upon the rural sections of the country, especially in southern England. At the election of 1922 the Independent Liberals won some seats in the county constituencies, and in 1923 the United Liberals cut rather deeply into the rural vote, especially in the region westward from London to the Severn. In 1924, however, they captured hardly a rural constituency in the entire country, and in Scotland,

[22] The antecedents and growth of the Labor party are set forth sympathetically and at length in G. D. H. Cole, *Short History of the British Working Class Movement,* Vol. III; M. Beer, *History of British Socialism,* II, Chaps. xvi-xix; R. H. Tawney, *The British Labor Movement* (New Haven, 1925), Chap i; J. R. MacDonald, *A Policy for the Labour Party* (London, 1920), and H. Tracey (ed.), *The Book of the Labour Party,* Vol. I. The last-mentioned book contains chapters written by twelve or more Labor leaders. The earlier phases of the story are presented in A. L. Lowell, *Government of England,* II, Chap. xxxiii, and more fully in C. Noël, *The Labour Party: What It Is and What It Wants* (London, 1906), and A. W. Humphrey, *History of Labour Representation* (London, 1912). The best account of the labor movement during the war is P. U. Kellogg and A. Gleason, *British Labor and the War* (New York, 1918), with numerous important documents. Among source materials, the *Labour Year Book,* issued in 1916, 1919, and various later years, is useful. W. B. Catlin, *The Labor Problem in the United States and Great Britain* (New York, 1926), compares the labor movement in the two countries.

where they had made a strong showing in 1922 and a fair one in 1923, they also won no seats except in the extreme north. In 1929 they picked up some twenty-two rural seats in England and doubled their quota in Scotland. Until recently, Labor has never given the Conservatives more than a scattered and largely futile fight in the rural constituencies. The entrenchment of the great landowners in most rural sections, the weakness of trade unionism among the agricultural laborers, and the cost of campaigning for rural votes has left the party almost purely urban, and until within the past four or five years it made no attempt to formulate an intelligible agricultural policy. The farmers, constituting almost the only important group of British employers who cling to their ancient objections to trade unionism, look with disfavor upon the Labor party as the symbol of labor unrest, and except here and there the party, like trade unionism itself, has made no strong appeal to the agricultural laborers; it never captured a purely agricultural constituency until 1922. It should be pointed out, however, that the party organizers and propagandists have lately been extending their operations into the rural areas, and that a considerable number of local Labor parties have been organized in rural constituencies.[23] Recognition of the fact that Labor cannot hope to gain an independent working majority at Westminster, and so to come into actual power, until many rural seats can be won is supplying a strong stimulus to such effort.[24] The overwhelming Conservative victory in 1924 was, of course, not typical of what is to be expected in the future. As has been indicated, the Liberals regained some of their lost ground in 1929, and Labor began making serious inroads into the rural vote. For a long time to come, however, the Conservatives are likely to continue to be able to go into an election with at least fifty rural seats in their pocket, and with assurance that if they do not suffer downright disaster in the boroughs—as they did in 1929—they have nothing to fear as to the larger outcome.

In general, the same sections of society and the same vested

[23] *Labour Year Book* (1928), 24.

[24] It will be recalled that county constituencies and borough constituencies are practically equal in number, although, of course, many of the former have pronounced urban characteristics. See p. 246 above.

interests adhere to the Conservative party as previous to the political reorientation of the past fifteen years; and large accessions from Liberalism have been won, through the adhesion of people who gravitated over during the days of the coalition, of others who see no future for the Liberal party, and of still others who aspire to political careers and consider that their only chance lies with the Conservatives. Many of these recruits come from what may be called broadly the middle class, especially in the towns; even more, proportionally, have been drawn from such wealth, leisure, and fashion as Liberalism formerly boasted. On the other side, working-class, and also middle-class, Liberals have been strongly attracted to the reorganized and broadened Labor party; and the defections, chiefly of course in the towns, have been large—far larger than from the corresponding ranks of Conservatism. The upshot is that Liberalism has dwindled all along the line. One section or element, considered from the viewpoint of social status, economic interest, and professional connection, has suffered about as much as another. In its general structure the party, therefore, remains a good deal as before; it is simply a smaller-sized edition of its former self. Geographically, there have been significant changes. In 1922 Liberalism was represented on the election map by sizeable, though scattered, areas in all major parts of England except the southeast; in Wales, by practically the whole of the country except for Labor splotches in the northwest and extreme south; and in Scotland, by all except a fifth or sixth of the country, i.e., the region, in general, between the Firth of Forth and the Firth of Clyde, which was shared by Conservatism and Labor. In 1923 the Liberal areas were more numerous and larger in England (especially in the southwest); in Wales they included everything except the south, which was now predominantly Labor; in Scotland they receded markedly, being restricted to the farther north and parts of the east, while the great north central area was Conservative and the Firth of Forth to Firth of Clyde territory was almost solidly Labor. In 1924 they appeared as only three petty "islands" in England; in Wales they were more restricted than in 1923, because of losses in the southeast and southwest to Conservatism (losses which were shared also by Labor); and in Scotland—classic land of Liberalism though it has been—they were pushed back to a small section of the remotest north. A net gain of twelve seats at the election of 1929 produced no important changes.

Labor has vastly extended its constituency. Years ago, it was not incorrectly conceived of as merely the political organ of the class interests of a single section of society. Its social background was indubitably supplied by the drawing together of the working classes in trade union, coöperative, socialist, and similar movements; its appeal was at one time directed to manual laborers almost exclusively. Even before the World War, this ceased to be the case; and since the reorganization of 1918, bracketing brain workers with manual workers, and opening wide the party doors to men and women of every station who concur in the party's major aims, the ranks have come to be representative of every important element and section of the British people. Manual workers still preponderate heavily, as they must always do; and, as will be emphasized presently, the party is strongest where the two great types of manual laborers that thus far have been chiefly appealed to predominate, i.e., the factory workers and the miners. But there are physicians, lawyers, bankers, business-men, teachers, preachers, civil servants, scholars, writers, even capitalists and peers—as variegated and representative a lot of people as have ever been drawn together in any other British party. In respect to the geographical distribution of its strength, the party in the past decade has experienced fluctuations comparable with those of Liberalism, while yet far more nearly holding its own. Outside of the London area, its color, in England, was spread on the 1922 map in scattered regions on the Severn, in Norfolk, on the shores of the Wash, and especially in the great mining and industrial regions from Leicester northward deep into Lancashire and York, and on both the eastern and western coasts adjacent to the Scottish border; in Wales it dominated in the northwest and south, and in Scotland in the aforementioned region between the Firth of Forth and the Firth of Clyde. In 1923 ground was lost in northwest Wales, but the areas in England became more numerous and larger, notably on the shores of the North Sea; while in Scotland the hold upon the Clydeside was extended and consolidated. In 1924 the North Sea accessions were completely lost; nearly all other English areas were sharply curtailed; the territories in Wales remained practically as before; and much of the Firth of Forth to Firth of Clyde region was sacrificed, though compensated for in some degree by large gains at Conservative expense in the middle Highlands. The heavy gains of 1929 were spread rather generally over the country, but were most notable in Lancashire, Yorkshire, parts of the Midlands, London and its environs, and Wales. In general, and without regard to the ups and downs produced by particular elections, Labor's strength is in the coal fields, the manufacturing regions of southern Scotland, the North and Midlands of England, and South Wales.

CHAPTER XXIII

PARTY PRINCIPLES AND POLICIES

SUCH is the new social and geographical distribution of party followings as brought to light by the last four or five parliamentary elections. It is far from stabilized, as is true of the party situation generally; but at all events it reveals some of the currents that have been flowing in the past twelve or fifteen years. Turning to the matter of party principles and policies, one discovers also some outstanding differences as compared with a generation ago, or even half that length of time. In the first place, whereas the fundamental antithesis used to be simply between the positions of the Conservatives and the Liberals, it is now, speaking broadly, between the Conservatives on the one hand and the Liberals and Laborites on the other. It is true that on some matters, including a few of major importance, e.g., the perpetuation of the capitalist régime, Conservatives and Liberals stand on common ground and offer joint opposition to the Labor position. It is true also that the Liberals and Laborites find it considerably easier to agree on foreign and colonial policy than on most domestic problems. If, however, a single dividing line were to be drawn athwart the political arena, with reference to the positions taken on actual, present-day questions, one would find the "Tories," as the Conservatives are significantly termed by all their rivals, on one side and the rest of the nation on the other. A second new aspect of the party situation today is that at least one great issue on which the parties used to divide sharply has disappeared. This is the Irish question. The settlement of that outstanding problem would alone have been enough to produce a reorientation of party politics. It may be that the problem is not solved for all time. But every party now stands pledged to the arrangements worked out in 1920-22, and the subject has passed out of the field of party discussion.

In the third place, the range and character of party issues have been affected tremendously by the generally altered position in which the nation finds itself since the war. Old issues, though by no means extinct, have dropped into the background; new ones have forged to the front, or at any rate old ones in new guises. Seven or eight years of unprecedented industrial and trade depression, unemployment on a staggering scale, realization that the nation allowed its industrial successes in the nineteenth century to betray it into inexcusable, and perhaps fatal, neglect of agriculture, the partially irremediable collapse of the coal industry, the necessity of accepting altered relations with the overseas dominions—these and other developments have shifted the emphasis in practical workaday politics, by nobody's design, to points far removed from those on which it formerly was placed. One has only to read the campaign speeches and parliamentary utterances of Gladstone and Disraeli, and afterwards those of Baldwin, Lloyd George, and MacDonald, to realize how completely the scene has changed.

The questions on which the three major parties divide today fall into some half-dozen main groups, although it must not be supposed that any mechanical enumeration or classification of issues will give a complete picture of the situation. Differences are far oftener matters of tendency or bent, and especially of degree, than of sheer contrariness of view and policy. With this qualification in mind, six groups of issues may be passed rapidly in review.

Foreign and Imperial Policy

First, there are questions of foreign and imperial policy. Time was when there was an appreciable, even if rarely a fundamental, difference between the Conservative and Liberal parties on this score. In the days of Disraeli and the elder Chamberlain, the former was, as a rule, stiffer in its dealings with foreign powers, more imperialistic in its relations with backward peoples, more bent upon extending the bounds of the Empire. Under the changed conditions of the past fifteen years, this has probably ceased to be the case. There has been no opportunity in this period to see a Liberal government in action.

But while, of course, the Liberals severely criticize their opponents' handling of foreign and colonial affairs, their own proclaimed principles give no ground for supposing that there would be any marked shift of policy if they were to come into office. The case of the Labor party is different. That party, too, would maintain many of the historic lines of British policy. Even it cannot get away from the hard facts of Britain's insular location, her dependence upon foodstuffs from abroad, her tradition of sea power, her heritage of empire. But a Labor government—so we are told—would reduce armaments, by international agreement, to the minimum required for police purposes; require all international engagements to be submitted to the House of Commons; make larger use of the League of Nations as an instrumentality of international coöperation;[1] strengthen and extend the authority of the League's mandates commission; establish diplomatic and commercial relations with Russia; give India dominion status; contrive adequate safeguards against the exploitation of native peoples in the Empire, and prepare them for self-government "at the earliest practicable date." The "closest possible coöperation, on terms of complete equality, between Great Britain and the dominions" is advocated; although to that the other parties are perhaps equally committed.[2]

Industry and Trade

Then there are the problems of industry and trade. In the country's post-war position, these are basic, involving as they do the unemployment situation and the admitted breakdown of certain staple industries, and ramifying into the broad issues of fiscal policy, agricultural rehabilitation, and the development of social services. As the party in power during most of the depressed period, the Conservatives naturally have little to say

[1] All three of the parties profess willingness to support the League, but Labor gives most evidence of being genuinely interested in its success. The Conservatives find it difficult to show much enthusiasm for any instrumentality of internationalism, and the dealings of Mr. Baldwin's government with League affairs in 1924-29 was felt by friends of the League, both at home and abroad, to be essentially legalistic and negative.

[2] On Labor and international affairs, see R. H. Tawney, *The British Labor Movement,* Chap. iv; H. Tracey (ed.), *The Book of the Labour Party,* I, Chaps. iv-vi.

on the subject. Their leaders are under the influence of the old principle of *laissez-faire,* from which the deduction is that industry must solve its own problems. Furthermore, such inquiries and experiments as they undertook when in office failed to do more than reveal the deep-seated nature of the difficulty and the futility of any ordinary remedial measures. In the face of this situation, they stood largely helpless, except in so far as relief was afforded by "safeguarding" and by the derating provisions of the Local Government Act of 1929; and the only solution on large lines which they as yet have to offer is, as noted below, the full and frank adoption of a protectionist policy.

The Liberals, also, have long been devotees of *laissez-faire.* They seem, however, to be swinging over to a policy of government control which puts them almost on common ground with Labor.[3] At all events, this is the purport of a monumental report of the party's Industrial Inquiry Committee in 1928, prepared by a group of the ablest younger leaders and economists and given further weight by being financed and sponsored by Mr. Lloyd George, Sir Herbert Samuel, Sir John Simon, and other older leaders. In so far as this remarkable document charts the future course of the party, Liberalism will be found advocating, as means of restoring industrial health to the nation, (1) improvement in the management of present state-operated undertakings, e.g., railway transport; (2) the taking over by public authority of important enterprises not well adapted to private ownership, through lack of profit or through danger of monopoly; (3) nationalization of coal deposits and royalties, and the amalgamation of mining operations for greater efficiency; and (4) adoption of a nation-wide integrated policy for industry as a whole, embracing such features as (a) lessening unemployment by carrying out a program of national development in such matters as motor roads, housing, waterways, electric power, and land reclamation, (b) larger use of national savings in home developments of this character rather than in investments abroad, (c) im-

[3] Labor orators naturally contend that Liberalism's newer social-economic policies are mostly borrowed from Labor's program and that adoption of them is only the death-bed repentance of a doomed party.

provement of industrial relations, (d) rational minimum wage levels in the various industries, and maintenance of actual wages at the highest possible figures, (e) thorough publicity of accounts in all big businesses, and (f) checking of the exploitative power of monopoly over consumers. Fitted into this general program is the creation of important new investigative and advisory agencies, notably an Economic General Staff, to work in close touch with the cabinet, and a National Council of Industry, to function in the broad field of industrial relations.

To almost all of this, Labor could easily subscribe. It, too, looks upon large programs of internal improvements and public works, the nationalization of certain industries, the protection of the consumer against exploitation, and publicity with regard to costs and profits as indispensable to the new and improved industrial order; it also calls for a National Economic Committee to advise the government on economic policy. It says less about (although it is not necessarily less interested in) the betterment of managerial technique. But to coal, it would add transport, power, and insurance as industries to be nationalized. It would have industry relieved (as, indeed, has come about to some extent through the derating legislation of 1929) by the readjustment of relations between national and local finance. It wants the Trade Disputes and Trade Unions Act of 1927 repealed and former trade union rights restored, numerous existing pieces of industrial legislation strengthened, unemployed miners transferred, the reconstruction of the cotton industry studied, and the Bank of England placed under control of a public corporation; and it favors more active support of international agencies and standards of labor investigation and control. The Labor program as now actively pressed admittedly results from an abandonment, at least for the time being, of the bolder, more fully and frankly socialistic, principles of the left wing (represented chiefly by the I.L.P.) in favor of a more moderate and "safer" course of action placing stress on interim reforms, most of which can be set going without nationalization. The two programs—Labor and Liberal—differ, as a well-known Labor spokesman has said, rather in accent and appeal than in concrete plans. "The Liberal aim is to reorganize industry. The Labor party enumerates, rather, a long series of benefits for the workers." [4]

Fiscal Policy

The same general situation appears when one turns to the closely related subject of fiscal policy. The broad line of distinction is between the Conservatives on the one hand and the Liberals and Laborites on the other; in turn, the latter two differ on some questions of emphasis and method. Again speaking generally, the Conservative notion has been that national prosperity can be restored only by falling into line with practically all other nations of the world—indeed, with the British dominions themselves—and adopting a policy of protective tariffs, with appropriate preferential treatment for the colonies. Agitated by the elder Chamberlain a generation ago, the idea lay relatively dormant until the World War; and import duties imposed during the war years were regarded as only temporary measures. As has appeared, the critical industrial situation of the post-war period led the Baldwin cabinet in 1923, however, to revive the scheme as a matter of general, and perhaps permanent, policy. The attempt was unsuccessful; the government lost in its appeal to the country; and, aside from upholding the safeguarding-of-industries legislation (protectionist as far as it went) enacted shortly after the war, the Conservatives, when again in power in 1924-29, took no further steps. The idea has, however, by no means been given up. After floundering a while longer, the country—so most Conservatives believe—will eventually come round to it. Meanwhile, the principle of safeguarding should be maintained and extended.

Liberalism and Labor continue, on the whole, unshaken in

[4] H. N. Brailsford, in *Foreign Affairs,* Oct., 1928, p. 60. On Liberal policy relating to industry, see R. Muir, *Liberalism and Industry* (London, 1921), Chaps. v-vi, viii-xiii, and "Liberalism and Industry," *Contemp. Rev.,* May, 1928; S. Hodgson, *The Liberal Policy for Industry* (London, 1928); and H. Samuel, "The Liberal Industrial Report," *Contemp. Rev.,* Mar., 1928. A book by a Liberal who has lately become a Conservative is A. Mond, *Industry and Politics* (London, 1928). Labor's industrial policy is described at length in H. Tracey (ed.), *The Book of the Labour Party,* II, Chaps. i-viii. The nationalization of the coal industry is discussed from the Labor point of view in R. H. Tawney, *op. cit.,* Chap. iii.

their devotion to free trade.[5] Admitting that a thoroughgoing protectionist system would probably stimulate industry, reduce unemployment, and raise wages, they nevertheless feel that these gains would be offset by an increase in the cost of living which would leave the worker no better off than he is today. On larger lines, they maintain that, however strongly momentary conditions may point to an opposite conclusion, the cardinal principle of the international economic policy of a country so densely populated as Great Britain must always be "to encourage the utmost freedom of commerce between the nations." [6]

There are other important fiscal differences besides those in which the matter of tariffs is involved. In general, and apart from tariffs, the Conservatives would keep the tax system substantially as it is, with occasional readjustments such as the derating legislation of 1929 accomplished. They are inclined to be tender toward landed proprietors, the liquor trade, big business, and all interests of invested capital. The Liberals agree that the existing system of national taxation, taken generally, is "in the main well conceived," [7] although they would tax inheritances far more drastically as a means of distributing ownership. They have advocated a reform of the rating system (now in part achieved), and they talk a good deal about reduction of expenditure on armament as a mode of alleviating tax burdens.

A few years ago the central position in Labor's taxation program was occupied by the capital levy, and the idea has not yet been wholly abandoned. More than half of all the money that the nation raises by taxation every year is paid out as interest on or amortization of the post-war national debt, and Labor's proposal was that all considerable accumulations of capital be levied upon in such amounts as might be necessary

[5] The former more decidedly so, however, than the latter; for protectionist ideas have of late been making some progress in Labor ranks, mainly among the trade unions in the depressed trades. No Labor leader of the first rank, however, has wavered. Mr. MacDonald, Mr. Snowden, and others still avow themselves "unrepentent free-traders."

[6] *Britain's Industrial Future* (cited above), 47. Cf. R. A. Young, "Great Britain's Recent Trend toward Protection," *Annals of Amer. Acad. Polit. and Soc. Sci.*, Jan., 1928.

[7] *Britain's Industrial Future*, 432.

to put an end to this discouraging burden once for all, and as an alternative to gradual liquidation, impeded by stupendous interest charges, over a long stretch of years.[8] The levy would represent, of course, a special emergency effort, presumably never to be repeated. As has been pointed out, the plan became a major issue in the election of 1922, and was almost as prominent in that of 1923. The country, however, showed no liking for it, and in later years its authors have not pressed it. In the carefully prepared official program of the party adopted in 1928 it received no mention. Rather, the points now stressed—in addition to drastic reduction of expenditure upon armaments—are (1) greatly increased "death duties," or inheritance taxes, on large estates; (2) revision of the income tax rates upward upon larger and downward upon smaller incomes, with more differentiation than now between earned and unearned incomes, and in particular a graduated surtax on unearned incomes of more than £500 a year; (3) heavier imposts on land values; and (4) abolition of all taxes upon the necessaries of life, and of all existing protective duties."

Land Problems

Next comes the matter of agricultural and land policy. The broad facts of the existing rural situation are familiar to every one who knows England. Considerably less than half of the country (England and Wales) is under crops and grass; less than ten per cent of the people are regularly engaged in agriculture; the foodstuffs produced in an average year are sufficient to carry the population through hardly more than six weeks out of the fifty-two. Nevertheless, a full million and a half of able-bodied inhabitants are unemployed, a considerable proportion of them permanently, so far as their accustomed occupations are concerned. The Conservatives find here a rather embarrassing problem. Far the greater portion of the land is owned—most of it in the form of great estates—by more or

[8] *Labour and the War Debt; a Statement of Policy for the Redemption of War Debt by a Levy on Accumulated Wealth* (London, 1922) is the official party document on the subject. Cf. H. Dalton, *The Capital Levy Explained* (London, 1923).

[9] *Labour and the Nation* (rev. ed.), 39-43; H. Tracey (ed.), *The Book of the Labour Party,* II, Chaps. XV-XX.

less influential members of their party. Under the economic stress of the past few years, some of the estates have indeed been broken up; and the Conservatives have themselves been responsible for important legislation on land tenure which facilitates the process. They have also contributed something to such success as the small-holdings movement has had, and in 1923 they proposed as a feature of Mr. Baldwin's ill-fated fiscal program a bonus for all proprietors of land under cultivation. In general, they look to the increase of the number of independent landowners as the most hopeful line of improvement. It will hardly be denied, however, that the party has no very promising direct remedy to offer. Its program of national recovery looks, rather, to the rehabilitation of industry and trade, leaving the land situation in pretty much the form which the nineteenth century gave it.

Under the leadership of Mr. Lloyd George, the Liberals have given exceptional attention to the land problem, and through the instrumentality of the Land Committee already mentioned they have lately worked out a new agrarian policy based on a principle or method which they call "cultivating tenure." In essence, the plan is that the state shall be deemed to have resumed possession of specified types of land, which shall be entrusted by it to "cultivating tenants" competent to use it to the advantage of the community as a whole, and entitled to retain it only so long as they do so. The Committee proposed to put all cultivable land simultaneously under this arrangement, but the party has adopted the scheme only as applying to badly farmed land, poorly administered estates, land put up for sale, and such other land as the controlling county authorities might regard as necessary for making a success of the system. Dispossessed landowners would, of course, be allowed just compensation. The proposal, it will be observed, has the triple object of bringing more land under cultivation, securing more efficient husbandry, and increasing the number of holders.[10]

[10] "Holders," be it observed, not owners. Unlike the Conservatives, Liberals and Laborites alike favor (under conditions such as exist in Britain), not independent ownership, but some form of tenancy under the state. The agricultural situation is discussed, and the new Liberal plan is explained at length, in *The Land and the Nation* (London, 1925), which is the Committee's rural report. The proposals as modified and adopted by the National

The Labor party goes farther. It would nationalize all agricultural land "on equitable terms," and would follow this fundamental step with measures to establish security of tenure for efficient farmers, make both short and long term credit available on easy conditions, eliminate waste by the development of collective marketing, stabilize prices by the collective purchase of imported grain and meat, provide electrical power and transport in rural areas, and protect the agricultural worker by the establishment of an adequate minimum wage and of reasonable hours of labor. A reading of the clauses of the official program devoted to agriculture and rural life will show not only that the party is now giving attention as never before to the rural aspects of the national problem, but that it is bidding anxiously for the support of the agricultural worker.[11]

Social Services and Governmental Reform

Two other groups of issues may be spoken of more briefly. One relates to what may be termed social services and betterment; the other to reforms in the structure and workings of government. On a good many social subjects, the parties are not far apart. All, for example, were favorable to several features of poor law reform as carried out by the Conservatives in the Local Government Act of 1929.[12] All support old age pensions, health insurance, unemployment insurance, improved housing, and state-aided popular education. The records over a hundred years would show the achievements of the Conservatives in such domains to have been not greatly inferior to those of the Liberals. Naturally, Labor puts rather more stress upon these matters than do the others, notably upon measures to promote better housing, town and regional planning, increased maternal and school medical service, extension of health insurance to sections of the population not reached at present, improvement of elementary and secondary schools, and provision of easier access to universities and other insti-

Liberal Federation will be found in *Land Policy Proposals,* issued by the Liberal Publication Department. Cf. L. A. Atherley-Jones, "Mr. Lloyd George's Land Policy," *Fort. Rev.,* July, 1927; J. Corbett, "The Liberal Land Policy," *ibid.,* Oct., 1927.

[11] *Labour and the Nation* (rev. ed.), 30-32.

[12] See p. 645 below.

tutions of higher education. In particular, it urges that funds which at present go for armaments be diverted to purposes of social betterment.[13]

Party differences on matters relating to the form and character of the governmental system have come to light in earlier portions of this book and require here only to be recalled to memory. The House of Lords furnishes one of the main points at issue. As has appeared, the Conservatives would be willing to reconstruct the membership of that body, but would like also to restore its lost powers; the Liberals would support a change of membership, but would leave powers as they are; Labor would maintain unquestioned supremacy of the House of Commons and would offer "uncompromising resistance to the establishment of a second chamber with authority over finance and power to hamper the House of Commons and defeat democratic decisions." The famous Webb plan would do away with the House of Lords altogether,[14] and the party itself has expressed the desire that this be done, although the second chamber is nowhere mentioned by name in the latest adopted official program. There are plenty of conflicting views on further reform of the House of Commons, but hardly any of the questions have a clear-cut party aspect except that of plural voting. Labor calls for total suppression of this practice, and Liberalism's traditions commit it to the same position. Since 1918, however, the question has not been of major importance. Labor, and to a less extent Liberalism, formerly demanded equal suffrage for women. But that objective has been attained at the hands of a Conservative government. Home rule for Ireland is out of the picture. Labor, however, advocates the same thing, i.e., the creation of separate legislative assemblies with autonomous powers in local matters, for Scotland, Wales, and England. Liberals are traditionally more sympathetic toward such proposals than are Conservatives; but again the matter is not definitely a party issue. Labor urges full civil and political rights for civil servants, drastic legislation against corrupt

[13] *Labour and the Nation* (rev. ed.), 32-39; H. Tracey, *The Book of the Labour Party*, II, Chaps. ix-xiv. On Labor and education, see R. H. Tawney, *op. cit.*, Chap. v.

[14] See p. 334 above.

practices at elections, complete publicity of party funds, and "the termination of the practice of selling so-called political honors." [15]

The Party Outlook

The rise of the Labor party has dislocated and reoriented the entire political scene. For all that one can see, the shift is permanent; and for aught that one can say, it marks the beginning of a new and fundamentally different era in English political life. The party arose out of discontent centering about specific grievances having to do with hours of labor, compensation for injured workmen, relief during unemployment, establishment of a minimum wage, old age pensions, and reform of the poor law. At one time it appeared that when these concrete, and, after all, relatively minor, matters were disposed of, the party would have served its purpose and would be ready to pass off the stage. As the organization grew in numbers and resources, however, its conceptions of its mission steadily widened, its policies became less specific and local, its program envisaged broader and deeper forms of social and economic change stretching remotely into the future. The party's idealism appealed powerfully, even to men who did not accept, or even understand, all of its principles and policies; war-time conditions supplied a mighty impetus; and as a result we have no longer an organ or instrument of a class, working merely for

[15] Attention may be called here to certain hitherto unmentioned literature bearing generally on the positions and programs of the parties. (1) Conservative: W. Elliott, *Toryism and the Twentieth Century* (London, 1927); P. Loftus, *The Creed of a Tory* (London, 1926); W. J. Wilkinson, *Tory Democracy* (New York, 1925); N. Skelton, *Constructive Conservatism* (London, 1924); L. Rockow, "The Political Ideas of Contemporary Tory Democracy," *Amer. Polit. Sci. Rev.*, Feb., 1927. Three books containing speeches and writings of ex-Premier Baldwin are important in this connection, i.e., *Looking Ahead* (London, 1924); *Peace and Good-will in Industry* (London, 1925); and *On England* (London, 1926). (2) Liberal: H. L. Nathan and H. H. Williams (eds.), *Liberal Points of View* (London, 1927); *ibid., Liberalism and Some Problems of the Day* (London, 1929); J. M. Hogge, *The Policy of the Liberal Party* (London, 1925); R. Muir, *Politics and Progress* (London, 1923); H. Phillips, *The Liberal Outlook* (London, 1929); and G. Murray, "What Liberalism Stands For," *Contemp. Rev.*, Dec., 1925. (3) Labor: E. Benn, *If I Were a Labour Leader* (London, 1926), and A. Greenwood, *The Labour Outlook* (London, 1929).

immediate practical betterments, but a major political force confidently planning measures that would change the entire distribution of wealth, readjust the relations of the different social groups, recast the organization of industry, and quite upset the historic institution of property. "What lends interest to the recent successes of the Labor movement in England," writes a sober Labor adherent, "is the possibility that after several generations during which, in spite of many changes, English policy has been guided by broadly the same type of social interests, we may be on the edge of another watershed, analogous to that of the Reform Bill, whence new streams will descend to carve English political scenery into new shapes." [16]

Such wide-sweeping speculation aside, what does Labor's growth portend for the more immediate future of the British party system? The question is tantamount to asking whether in coming years there are to be three main parties or only two. This, in turn, is equivalent to inquiring whether the Liberal party is going to survive. For there can be no real doubt about the lasting qualities of its two principal competitors. There is in every country a place for a conservative (not necessarily reactionary) party—a party that is not so much an army on the march as a garrison holding the fort, a party that represents the eternal stand of the "haves" against the "have nots." There is equally a place, especially in a country with the social heritage and economic stresses of modern Britain, for a party which perpetually challenges the existing order and fights for liberalizing changes in it. As matters now stand in the British nation, these two rôles seem to be fully taken care of by Conservatism and Labor. What, if anything, is there left for Liberalism to do?

One view is decidedly negative. The party of Bright, Cobden, Gladstone, Morley, Rosebery, Asquith, Lloyd George, has had a long and splendid career. But its work is done; the great causes for which it fought have been won. Meanwhile there has risen alongside of it a new party born of twentieth, rather than eighteenth and nineteenth, century conditions, and possessed of the enthusiasm, vigor, and idealism which the Liberal party once displayed but has lost. Between the conservatism

[16] R. H. Tawney, *The British Labor Movement*, 9.

and immobility of the Tories and the progressivism and daring of Labor there is scant room for a middle-of-the-road attitude, policy, or party. There is a place, as Ramsay MacDonald never wearied of insisting during the campaign of 1924, for only two parties. Suspecting as much, Liberals have been drifting heavily into the Labor ranks, and only less heavily into the ranks of Toryism. Labor orators call loudly to what remains to close down and come over.

For the present, at all events, the Liberals that remain (and there are millions of them) do not admit the thesis of a dying party and are strongly bent upon going their own way. The party still has the ablest general staff, the most gifted group of thinkers, economists, and journalists. In Mr. Lloyd George it has a leader so brilliant that no one can ignore him, even if so mercurial that no one can trust him. It is well financed. Through its research activities it is doing more than any other party to get at the roots of the great problems that vex the nation, and through constructive reports such as those relating to the industrial and agricultural situation it is developing concrete solutions for the new questions of a new era. By suggesting such innovations as the nationalization of agricultural land and of minerals, it is showing capacity to readjust itself, and even to rival Labor in the novelty and boldness of the positions which it takes. Furthermore, plenty of older issues remain on which Liberalism has been accustomed to have something to say. Plural voting survives. The second chamber problem is as baffling, even if not quite as urgent, as in 1911. The much disliked Education Act of 1902 is still on the statute book. Disestablishment remains to be threshed out. Home rule for Scotland looms ahead. Free trade was never more menaced.

The proposal that the Liberal party simply give up the effort to keep going and join Labor *en masse* is too naïve to require discussion. The two parties indubitably have much in common; and the cautious, even conservative, trend of Labor policy under Mr. MacDonald's leadership—evidenced, for example, by the steady refusal to have anything to do with the Communists [17]

[17] Requests of the small but noisy Communist party to be allowed to join the Labor party have been rejected overwhelmingly at successive annual conferences, and the Communist aims and methods have been definitely

—would operate, as far as it went, to make coalition, and even amalgamation, easier.[18] But the ultimate Labor goal, the socialistic state, lies at the end of a road which the majority of Liberals have no mind to travel. They know that the present Labor policy is strongly disliked by important left-wing elements in the Labor party, notably the I.L.P., which still talk resolutely about attaining socialism and internationalism "in our time." Even if they subscribed to everything that the party now gives prominence in its published appeals to the nation, they could have no assurance that the radicalism of the Clydeside would not some day gain the upper hand.[19] They recognize, of course, that Liberalism can have only a barren future as a mere neutral zone, a half-way house, between Conservatism and Labor. But they believe that the party is successfully refashioning a faith of its own, and they conceive of the three parties of the future, not as standing to one another like three sections of the same straight line, with Liberalism in the central position, insensibly shading off into the other two, but as having the relation of the three angles of a triangle, each definitely opposed to the other two, yet each linked with the other two, and having some points of sympathy with both.[20]

As far as one can see, three main parties, rather than two, will continue to divide the field. That this opens the way for unusual and embarrassing political situations, experience has already shown. But for the present the nation will have to

and officially repudiated. See comment by Arthur Henderson in H. Tracey (ed.), *The Book of the Labour Party,* I, 28-32. Cf. A. Shadwell, *The Communist Movement* (London, 1925), and H. J. Laski, *Communism* (London, 1927).

[18] For a remarkable exposition of the nearness of Liberalism and Labor on the practical aspects of present-day politics, see an article by the eminent Liberal economist, J. A. Hobson, in the Liberal newspaper, the *Manchester Guardian* (weekly ed.), Feb. 8, 1929, and also the supporting editorial.

[19] C. R. Walker, "Those Wild Men of the Clyde," *Atlantic Month.,* May, 1926.

[20] R. Muir, *Politics and Progress,* 6. The lines on which the Liberal party might be rehabilitated, as they appeared to a young Liberal leader in 1923, are set forth in interesting fashion in this book. The periodical press abounds in discussions of the Liberal problem. Mention may be made of H. F. Spender, "The Liberal Task," *Fort. Rev.,* Jan., 1925; C. Hobhouse, "The Liberal Revival," *Contemp. Rev.,* Aug., 1927; and A. Hopkinson, "The Future of the Liberal Party," *Edinb. Rev.,* Jan., 1928.

make the best of it. One of six conditions must presumably exist at any given time: (1) The party in power will enjoy so heavy a preponderance that it will have an absolute majority both of the popular vote and of the seats in the House of Commons. This is a very improbable situation. Even the overwhelming victory of the Conservatives in 1924 did not give them a popular majority. (2) The party in power will have a majority in the House of Commons, but only a plurality of the popular vote. This is somewhat more likely to occur. Such a result was, indeed, produced by the general election of 1924. The odds against an absolute majority of seats in the possession of any one party are, however, heavy. In any event, the government would be a minority government so far as the country was concerned.[21] (3) The party in power will be a mere plurality party both in the country and in Parliament, in which event government will be even more decidedly by minority. (4) The party in power will have a plurality in the House of Commons, but not even that in the country. This was the position of the Labor party after the election of 1929. (5) The party in power will be—as the Labor party was in 1924—without a plurality, either in country or in Parliament, but ruling simply by virtue of rebuffs or defeats suffered by the other parties, though at the same time entirely by sufferance of one or both of them. This would be minority government pushed to its extreme. (6) A coalition will be entered into by two of the parties—not a mere passive agreement such as existed between Labor and Liberalism in 1924—but a real combination, with ministers drawn from both groups, and having at least a parliamentary majority, if not also a popular one.

The thoughtful Englishman finds little satisfaction in scanning this list. The first two possibilities, involving rule by single-party majority (at least in Parliament), promise to be attainable but rarely. The third, fourth, and fifth, involving various degrees of minority government, are undesirable save as mere stopgaps. The sixth, i.e., coalition, is exceedingly distasteful. If there is any unpleasant word in the Britisher's

[21] This could be, and at rare intervals was, true even under the bi-party system.

political vocabulary, it is the term "coalition." It cuts diametrically across his lines of political thinking; and the experience of a decade ago made its connotations not a whit more palatable.

Consequently it is not strange that there should have arisen some rather lively discussion of ways and means of extricating the country from the *impasse* into which the rise of Labor seems to have led it. The principal suggestions thus far offered have looked to the reconstruction of the mechanics of the electoral system—not, of course, with any expectation that this would solve all of the problems flowing from the existence of three parties, but with a view to removing as many as possible of the elements of luck and chance, especially those arising from three-cornered contests in single-member constituencies. The main concrete proposals are (1) the adoption of the Continental plan of large electoral areas, with proportional representation, and (2) introduction of the scheme of the "alternative vote." As has been observed, however, there is no present prospect that either of these changes will be made;[22] and even if either were to come about, the difficulty would be only partially alleviated. As long as three or more important parties exist side by side, the country will be in danger, whatever its electoral system, of finding coalition the only way of escape from minority government.

It all seems fundamentally un-English; and Englishmen are frankly troubled. Yet the bi-party system, with all its admitted advantages of simplicity and responsibility, has its unreasonable and illogical features. There is, after all, nothing sacred about it. Party systems are means, not ends. If the voters want to divide into no more than two groups, that is something to be thankful for. But if this division does not satisfy, it is futile to try to maintain it by traditions and manipulations. The English constitution has survived greater shocks than the collapse of bi-partyism, even granted—a thing by no means proved—that the collapse is real and lasting, and not merely a passing phase.

[22] See p. 312 above.

CHAPTER XXIV

PARTY ORGANIZATION

In view of the prolonged growth of English parties, and of the large place which they fill in the political system, one will not be surprised to find that they have developed extensive machinery for holding their membership together, formulating principles and policies, selecting candidates for office, and winning the electorate to their side whenever there is to be a contest at the polls. Continuous and effective organization is essential for party life and power everywhere. But it is especially necessary in a cabinet-government state, because there an election may be brought on at any time and by a turn of events largely or wholly unexpected. Members of the popular branch of Parliament have merely maximum, not definite and assured, terms; elections do not come at fixed and regular intervals; there are no dependable "off years," in which a party may relax, as an American party can and does. Rather, every party must stand at all times equipped for almost instant combat. In France, it is true, where the right of parliamentary dissolution exists but is never exercised,[1] national elections befall with the same regularity as in the United States. But in Great Britain dissolutions are common occurrences; two general elections have been known to take place within a single year, e.g., in 1910; elections—as, for example, that of 1923—sometimes take the country unawares, and parties must be ever ready.

Organization in Parliament

Speaking broadly, party machinery in Great Britain falls into two parts, i.e., that which is inside, and that which is outside, of Parliament. The parliamentary portion consists of three agencies or organs: the group of party members in Parliament (more particularly the House of Commons), considered as a

[1] See p. 463 above.

whole, and commonly referred to as the "parliamentary party;" the leaders within this group; and the whips. The extra-parliamentary portion comprises, mainly, the local party organizations in the constituencies and the national organization, including the "central office," built up by federating these local bodies.

In all parties the parliamentary members enjoy a high degree of immunity from control by any agency or authority of the party outside. Especially true is this of the Conservatives and Liberals. The parliamentary party, and not any congress or committee of the nation-wide party organization, chooses the leader, who, when the party is in power, is the prime minister and when it is not in power is the leader of the opposition; and while the commoners may individually, as candidates, have pledged themselves before their constituents to stand for certain principles and to support certain policies, the group as a whole is free at all times to determine its course of action, independently of any instructions either from constituents or from party organizations outside of Westminster. Members may, of course, be held to an accounting when they go back to their constituencies for reëlection. But there will be no disposition to deny them the legal and moral right to be guided by party decisions arrived at by the parliamentary group to which they belong. The situation in the Labor party is somewhat different, in that the party constitution requires the parliamentary representatives, singly and collectively, to "act in harmony with the constitution and standing orders of the party," and also enjoins that the national party executive and the Parliamentary Labor party shall confer at the opening of each parliamentary session, and at any other time when either body may desire such conference.[2] This undoubtedly imposes some restraint. In practice, however, the parliamentary group tends to be a free agent; it selects the party leader, appoints its whips, and chooses its tactics exactly as do the sitting members of the other parties.[3]

[2] Art. 7. The organization known as the Parliamentary Labor party dates from 1906.

[3] In 1925, when the left wing of the parliamentary party defied the party leader by persisting in opposing a special grant to meet the costs of a projected visit by the Prince of Wales to South Africa, the national executive took cognizance of the situation and considered ways of preventing the rift from permanently imperiling unified action by the group. A resolution

If the truth be told, it is not, in the case of any party, the parliamentary group as a whole that is specially important as a party agency, but rather the chiefs or leaders in that group. In the case of the party in power at any given time, this means the cabinet. It has been pointed out that the party system and the cabinet system arose simultaneously and in the closest possible relations. The earliest party organization was, indeed, the cabinet, and for the party in power the cabinet remains to this day the highest party authority. As such, it can brook no control by any outside organization. The parties out of power have, of course, no cabinet. But their parliamentary quotas contain an official leader and a number of other men of recognized importance who, if the party were to come into power, would compose the cabinet; and for purposes of party management these persons discharge substantially the same functions as if they were in ministerial office. The major fact about party organization in Parliament is, indeed, the absolute control of party policy by these leaders. In the case of lesser parties, the entire quota is occasionally convened in a caucus for deliberation on questions of policy. This was a common practice of the Labor group when it was small in numbers. But in the large parties this sort of thing is rare, being, indeed, almost unknown among the Conservatives. General meetings, are, indeed, sometimes held at one of the political clubs. They are commonly designed, however, only to give the leaders an opportunity to address, instruct, and inspire their followers, and rarely or never as occasions for general debate culminating in votes and decisions. The main exception to this rule arises when the formal chief of the party is to be selected. Even then, although general discussion takes place, the decision is likely to be made by a handful of the principal members.

Each group of leaders has, in each house, the assistance of the party whips. These are in all cases members of the house in which they perform their duties, although, by custom, they take no part in debate. The government whips in the House of Commons are usually four in number, i.e., the chief whip,

moved in the annual conference of 1925 to place the parliamentary party under the direction and control of the national executive was so lightly regarded that it was not even brought to a vote.

who holds the office of Parliamentary Secretary to the Treasury, and the three Junior Lords of the Treasury.[4] They are, of course, ministers, and, as such, are paid out of the public exchequer. The whips of the opposition parties, usually three in each case, are private members, named by the leaders, and unsalaried. The functions of the government whips consist, chiefly, in seeing that the ministry's supporters are at hand when a division on party lines is to be taken, keeping the ministers informed on the state of feeling among the party members in the house, bringing pressure to bear upon negligent or rebellious members, acting as intermediaries in making up slates for select committees, and serving as government tellers when a division is to be taken on party lines. "Stage managers," Ostrogorski calls these officials; "aides-de-camp, and intelligence department, of the leader of the House," they are termed by Lowell. The duties of the opposition whips are of similar nature, with allowance made for the differences arising from the fact that the leaders whom they serve are not in office but only hope to be.[5]

Organization Outside of Parliament—Local Machinery

An American writer has remarked that in Britain leadership counts for somewhat more, and organization for somewhat less, than in the United States.[6] It is undeniably true that party machinery—committees, caucuses, conventions, and what not—developed earlier on our side of the Atlantic than on the other. Local party machinery in the constituencies made its appearance in Britain only after the Reform Act of 1832: the first party organization to operate on a nation-wide scale was founded hardly more than sixty years ago.[7] In later decades,

[4] Conservatives and Liberals regularly have two whips each in the House of Lords.

[5] For good brief accounts of the whips, see M. Ostrogorski, *Democracy and the Organization of Political Parties,* I, 137-140, and A. L. Lowell, *Government of England,* I, 448-457. Cf. F. Gray, *The Confessions of a Candidate,* Chap. xiii, and Viscount Gladstone, "The Chief Whip in the British Parliament," *Amer. Polit. Sci. Rev.,* Aug., 1927.

[6] W. B. Munro, *Governments of Europe,* 258.

[7] Associations having a political character existed earlier but not definitely as party instrumentalities. See M. Ostrogorski, *Democracy and the Organization of Political Parties,* I, 117-134.

however, party organization, both national and local, has reached a high state of development, not only in the older Conservative and Liberal parties, but also—one is tempted to say especially—in the younger Labor party. It will be interesting to see something of the nature of the resulting machinery, beginning with that built up in the local communities, since it came first historically, and since, speaking broadly, the national organizations represent only associations or federations of the locally organized party groups.

The reasons for the dearth of party organization throughout the country prior to 1832 are not difficult to discern. Voters in both parliamentary and local elections in those days were few, and, in the counties at all events, scattered. As a rule, they had little of what we should call group consciousness. Parliamentary seats belonging to "rotten" and "pocket" boroughs were dispensed as patronage or sold to the highest bidder; in many other constituencies, county and borough, there was but a handful of voters; only here and there—as in the borough of Westminster—was the electorate large enough to form any real basis for party groupings. The act of 1832, however, changed the situation considerably. A half million persons were added to the electorate; the rule was introduced that no one might vote unless duly registered; and the constituencies were so reconstructed that the choice of representatives was thrown, in practically all cases, into the hands of a considerable number of people. In numerous places where elections had hitherto been merely a matter of form there were now to be real contests, with the difference between success and failure measured in terms of the number of qualified and registered voters who could be got to the polls. The lesson for party leaders and supporters, national and local, was obvious: agencies must be created which would see to it that the new voters were registered, canvassed, and, whenever necessary, stimulated to play their intended part when election time came round.

The device hit upon was the registration society, which thus became the earliest form of local party organization. Almost as soon as the Reform Act was on the statute book, societies of this nature, both Conservative and Liberal, appeared in certain constituencies, and by 1840 they were common throughout the country. At first they largely confined their activities to getting inexperienced, and often apathetic, voters on the parliamentary register and keeping them there, in so far as such voters could be depended on to support the candidates of the party. But presently they added canvassing voters (new and old) in their homes, supplying them with information about the candidates and the issues, persuading the hesitant, and rounding up the faithful at the voting places. When another million was added to the electorate in 1867 the responsibilities of these societies were augmented; and of course they were further increased in 1884. For a long time the societies did not attempt, except in isolated instances, to nominate candidates. Men were left to announce themselves to the voters; or, at most, the selections were made by a few influential leaders. Sooner or later, however, the local organization was bound to come to feel that this important function also lay within its province.

This development was fostered by the rise of the caucus. The term "caucus" has a somewhat sinister connotation in American politics; many movements on this side of the Atlantic conceived and carried out in the interest of popular control in government have had for their object the overthrow of some kind of a caucus. But whereas the American caucus has usually been of the nature of an oligarchy, the British caucus was from the first an agency of broader democracy. The initial appearance of the caucus in its British form was in the city of Birmingham, where, during the sixties, the Liberals adopted the plan of assembling all of the party members in each ward in a caucus, each such meeting choosing a ward committee, which, as the machinery was perfected, began sending delegates to a central convention representing the entire city. The principal author of this plan was Joseph Chamberlain, then a Liberal, although destined to play his rôle as a national statesman under the Conservative banner; and it is interesting to note that Chamberlain had visited America and had some acquaintance with conventions, caucuses, and other party devices on this side of the Atlantic. The new scheme was looked at askance by many Englishmen as likely to prove a first step toward the rule of rings and bosses then notoriously prevalent in American cities. But it was proceeded with, and the general election of 1868 afforded convincing demonstration of its effectiveness. It will be recalled that Birmingham was one of a limited number of towns in which, with a view to minority representation, the Reform Act of 1867 required electors to vote for fewer candidates than the number of seats to be filled. Through its general committee, the Liberals' central association both nominated the candidates of the party and guided the electors in distributing their votes in such a way that all three seats were captured, and not only these but also the city council and the school board. The upshot was that the Birmingham plan of caucus and convention—of local party organization on the basis of the full party membership, rather than simply of a small registration society, and with selection of candidates as well as promotion of their candidacy in the hands of the organization's central association—began spreading to all parts of the country, being taken up not only by the Liberals but also by the Conservatives, who were driven to it in self-defense.

Liberal organization on these lines naturally went forward faster in the towns than in the rural sections, because townspeople are more readily brought together and because the Liberal forces were predominantly urban. By the opening of the present century, however, there was a Liberal association in practically every constituency, rural and urban, in which the party was not in a hopeless minority; and this continues to be the case today. The National Liberal Federation, which in 1877 brought the local associations into a common nation-wide organization, guides and advises in the formation and conduct of the local units. Aside, however, from requiring that their government shall be based upon popular representation, it lays down no positive regulations; and it is especially to be observed that the state seeks to regulate in no way whatever either these local associations or any other party organizations. Naturally, there is a certain amount of variation. Yet, in general, every rural parish has a primary association; every small town has a similar association, with an elected executive committee; every parliamentary division of a county has a council and an executive committee; every parliamentary borough is organized by wards and has officers and committees on the plan of the Birmingham caucus. In some cases the associations are open to men and women alike; in others there are separate, but coöperating, organizations for the sexes.

In local organization the Conservatives were hardly behind their rivals, and in the formation of a nation-wide league of local societies they led by a full decade. Local Conservative associations were created in largest numbers in the years following the Reform Act of 1867, and by 1874, when the party secured its first majority in the House of Commons since 1841, England and Wales contained approximately four hundred and fifty. In the next two years the number was almost doubled. As has been noted, the effectiveness of the Birmingham caucus, and of the Liberal machinery generally, was not lost upon the Conservative organizers. Besides, many of the local organizations were composed mainly or entirely of workingmen. Hence, the representative principle was gradually given fuller play, and the agencies of local party control became no less democratic than those employed by the Liberals. It is not necessary to describe the machinery in detail. As in the case of the Liberals, the authorities of the national federation recommend certain forms of organization, embracing mass meetings, committees, councils, and officials in such combinations as seem most likely to meet the needs of parishes, wards, county divisions, boroughs, and other political areas; and, in the main, these recommendations are carried out. The Conservatives have had more money to spend on local organization than the Liberals, and they have covered the country rather more effectively. In earlier times, both parties had considerably more success in organizing their adherents in the boroughs than in the rural sections; concentration promoted coöperation and morale. Nowadays the difference is less marked.[8]

[8] Party organizations prior to the rise of the caucus are treated in M. Ostrogorski, *op. cit.*, I, 135-160, and the effects of the Reform Act of 1832 on party activities are described in C. Seymour, *Electoral Reform in England and Wales,* Chap. iv. Cf. A. Aspinwall, "English Party Organization in the Early Nineteenth Century," *Eng. Hist. Rev.*, July, 1926.

The rise of the caucus is dealt with in M. Ostrogorski, "The Introduction of the Caucus into England," *Polit. Sci. Quar.*, June, 1893. A much fuller acount is the same author's *Democracy and the Organization of Political Parties,* I, 161-240. The salient features are presented clearly in A. L. Lowell, *Government of England,* I, 469-478.

The National Union of Conservative and Constitutional Associations

It was natural that after a large number of local associations had grown up among the supporters of a given party an effort should be made to bring them together in some form of league or union. The Reform Act of 1867 supplied the cue, and the Conservatives—sponsors of the act, but frankly dubious about its consequences—led the way. The million new voters were mainly urban; being such, they were likely to lean rather strongly toward the Liberal party; to win any substantial proportion of them, the Conservatives must put forth unusual effort; and out of this situation arose (although other considerations played some part) the National Union of Conservative and Constitutional Associations, established at a conference held in the autumn of the year mentioned. The constitution as adopted provided for a purely federal organization. The members were to be, not persons, but associations, a characteristic retained not only by the Conservative national organization, but also by those of the Liberals and the Laborites, to this day. Any Conservative or Constitutional association might be admitted on payment of a guinea a year, and machinery was set up consisting of (1) a party congress, known as the Conference, composed (in addition to the officers of the Union) of delegates elected by the several member associations, two from each, (2) a Council, consisting of the officers of the Union, twenty-four persons elected by the Conference, and not more than twenty others chosen by the principal provincial associations, with provision for a few honorary members, and (3) a president, a treasurer, and a board of trustees, elected by the Conference.

The new organization was slow to get on its feet; in ten years fewer than one-third of the local associations joined, and the annual conferences were small affairs. However, it gradually proved its usefulness as an agency of stimulation and coördination, and after a reorganization in 1885-86 which broadened its basis and strengthened its machinery, it won the general support of the party. By 1888 the number of affiliated associations exceeded eleven hundred. One of the principal structural changes was the division of England and Wales into ten regions, each with a divisional organization resembling the organization of the Union itself. The divisional conferences failed to become important intermediate agencies of party deliberation, but the new machinery lent itself readily to party propaganda and discipline. The great deliberative agency of the party continued to be the Conference, meeting annually in some important city.[9] At first this body did not assume to give formal expression to its views on questions of public policy. But after 1885 it freely exercised the right not only to discuss such matters but to adopt resolutions concerning them. These expressions of principle were presumably for the guidance of the men who were directly responsible for the party's course in Parliament and before the country, namely, the ministers when the party was in power, the opposition leaders when it was not in power. If the truth be told, however, little attention was paid these pronouncements in parliamentary circles. The Conference repeatedly passed resolutions looking to preferential tariffs before 1903 without creating a ripple on the political sea; the same proposals, coming from the Colonial Secretary, raised a tempest. Again and again, prior to 1914, the Conference declared for woman suffrage, but without perceptible effect.

Gradually the lesson was learned that the Union's usefulness, even as also in the case of the local associations, lay in the direction of the voters rather than in that of the party leaders and lawmakers. It could not make "platforms" that would have much weight; it could not select the party chief who, when the party was in power, would be prime minister; it could not, in short, override the jealously guarded independence of the party organization in Parliament. But there were other and important things that it could do—things that had to be done if the party's morale was to be kept up and its strength maintained, and things for which the leaders at Westminster were glad enough to look to it. Finding its proper sphere, the Union set up at London a central office, with a paid staff, and built up what in effect came to be a great electioneering agency. Under

[9] The original plan of triennial meetings, to be held invariably at London, was abandoned in 1868.

the direction of a principal agent, a director of publicity, and other such officials, the organization nowadays helps establish new local associations where they are needed, aids and encourages associations which are beset with special difficulties, prepares suggestions and instructions for local party committees and workers, distributes literature, raises money, provides popular lectures, collects and broadcasts information having a party significance, and in sundry other ways keeps the local organization active and the whole party mechanism up to the level of efficiency required in a country where elections may come suddenly and unexpectedly. The central organization also compiles long lists of persons who would make acceptable candidates for parliamentary seats, and, as has been pointed out in another connection, not only advises organizations in the constituencies upon the choice of candidates, but stands ready to fit out a needy or embarrassed constituency with a candidate from some other part of the country, and, if necessary, to see that such candidacy is supported with speakers and funds.[10] The annual conference continues to be held, and earnest discussions of issues as well as of tactics take place. This is rather, however, with a view to sounding out opinion and whipping up interest than arriving at decisions that will bind the leaders, or anybody else, to a given course of action. The business of the Union is the winning of elections, not the formulation of principles and policies to be carried out by the party representatives, high or low, at Westminster.[11]

[10] Candidates in the constituencies continue to be selected (or accepted) nominally by the executive committee of the local party organization—a body of often three or four hundred delegates or representatives of different parishes or other areas in the constituency. In point of fact, however, they commonly owe their nomination to the advance decision of a handful of local party leaders, precisely as do candidates in the United States, whether chosen ostensibly at a direct primary or in a convention. As explained elsewhere (see p. 282 above), it is as difficult to get a nomination that means anything in Britain as in America, notwithstanding the ease with which the mere legal requirement—ten signatures on a nomination paper—can be met.

[11] The best accounts of the origin and earlier development of the National Union are A. L. Lowell, *op. cit.*, I, Chap. xxx, and M. Ostrogorski, *Democracy and the Organization of Political Parties,* I, 250-286. It may be added that in 1906 the divisional organization was remodeled and extended, and the Council—renamed the Central Council—enlarged to include (among

The National Liberal Federation

The triumph of the Conservatives in the general election of 1874 was attributed mainly to superior organization, and the idea took hold among Liberals that they, too, must organize nationally. The Birmingham caucus took the initiative, and a conference, attended by representatives of ninety-five local associations, was held at that city in 1887. A constitution was adopted; officers—chiefly residents of Birmingham, with Joseph Chamberlain as president—were elected; and, under the name of National Liberal Federation, an organization was launched which was intended not only to strengthen the party machinery throughout the country but to wield large, if not controlling, influence in shaping party policy. The principal difference, indeed, between the new Liberal organization and the Conservative National Union was that, whereas the latter was founded mainly for purposes of propaganda and morale, the former was intended to be largely, if not primarily, a policy-determining agency. In the words of Lowell, "it was expected to be, as Mr. Chamberlain expressed it, a Liberal parliament outside the imperial legislature; not, indeed, doing the work of that body, but arranging what work it should do, or rather what work the Liberal members should bring before it, and what attitude they should assume. By this process the initiative on all the greater issues, as far as the Liberal party was concerned, would be largely transferred from the Treasury Bench to the Federation." [12]

The government of the new organization was planned to be rather more democratic than that of the Conservative Union. The chief authority was the Council, which was a representative assembly composed of delegates from the local associations, not two from each as in the Conservative Conference, but from five to twenty according to population. At its annual meetings this body elected a president, a vice-president, a treasurer, and

other persons) one representative for every fifty thousand voters, or fraction thereof, in each county, and one for every twenty-five thousand in each parliamentary borough. It should be noted also that the National Union here described covers England and Wales only. Scotland and Northern Ireland have separate organizations.

[12] *Government of England,* I, 504.

an honorary secretary; and these officers, combined with from two to five delegates chosen by each local association, and with twenty-five persons named by the Committee itself, made up the General Committee. The Council was the "Liberal parliament," in which issues and policies were threshed out; the Committee (which established its headquarters at Birmingham) was an executive agency, charged mainly with organizing local associations and keeping up the party morale.

Like the Conservative Union, the Liberal Federation grew slowly. In the first year, not over a hundred local associations joined, and up to 1886 the number did not exceed 255. The breach within the party at this point on Gladstone's first home rule bill threatened complete disaster. The storm, however, was weathered; indeed, as has been observed, certain benefits resulted. The constitution was amended to make representation on the Council better proportioned to population; the offices were moved from Birmingham to London, and closer relations were established with Gladstone and other party chiefs in Parliament; and the new unity of the depleted party was evidenced by the gathering in of upwards of five hundred associations within two years.[13] As early as 1881 the Council began to try its hand at platform-making, and during the next decade it was continuously active in this direction, although it developed that what the body was usually expected to do was to ratify resolutions prepared in advance by committees, rather than to work out its own statements of policy.

The party out of office habitually talks freely about what it would do if it were in office, especially if it has no hope of being in office soon. This was the position of the Liberals for some years after 1886; and the Council's resolutions committed the party from year to year to a steadily lengthening list of reforms, culminating in the famous Newcastle Program of 1891, which, as one writer remarks, could hardly have been embodied in statutes in less than ten years by a cabinet with a large and homogeneous majority. The Gladstone and Rosebery governments of 1892-95 were considerably embarrassed because of being unable to do things that the nation had been led to believe that a Liberal government would do, and there-

[13] R. S. Watson, *The National Liberal Federation* (London, 1907), 54-82.

after the party leaders saw to it that the Council exercised its platform-making functions under a stronger sense of restraint. After 1896, indeed, the preparation of business for the General Committee, as well as for the Council, was entrusted to an Executive Committee, which, although including no members of Parliament, was designed to be a small body of men who could be depended upon not to bring embarrassment upon the parliamentary leaders. Thereupon the Council became hardly more than an annual meeting of party delegates to hear and approve announcements and proposals submitted by the General Committee, whose decisions, in turn, were really those of the smaller Executive Committee. Thus, equally with the less ambitious Conservative Union, the Liberal Federation failed to build up and maintain a great popular party legislature. Like its Tory counterpart, it developed a central office at London which became an active agency in promoting party organization, raising funds, selecting candidates, distributing literature, and supporting general party interests. But as an organ for the popular control of party policy and of the acts of the party representatives in Parliament, it too has been a sham. In neither party has a popular non-official organization been able to make headway against the bed-rock principle that in a cabinet system of government the parliamentary leaders must also be the party leaders.

As the National Liberal Federation stands today, it is a union of Liberal associations, each of which is free to adopt its own constitution and administer its own affairs. The Council consists of the national officers (president, treasurer, and chairman of the Executive Committee), the members of the Executive Committee, all Liberal members of Parliament, and representatives of the chief Liberal association in each of the parliamentary constituencies, in the ratio of one delegate for each six thousand electors, or major fraction thereof, in the constituency. The Council meets annually; and while no formal political program is submitted for general acceptance, there is full opportunity for discussion, in accordance with the Council's declared object, i.e., "to express by resolution or otherwise the opinions of the Liberal party on such questions as are deemed by general consent to be of the first importance, and generally to act as the authoritative and representative mouthpiece of the rank and file of the Liberal party throughout England and Wales." The Executive Committee consists of the president and treasurer of the Federation, elected by the district Liberal federations (members of Parliament being ineligible), and as many as six additional members selected by the Committee itself. The twenty-nine district representatives are allotted to the districts into which the country is divided for the purpose,[14] in the proportion of one representative for each twenty parliamentary constituencies or major fraction thereof. The old General Committee dropped out in 1923. In 1925, however, an Administrative Committee of eight members was created, with responsibility for the management of the party funds and for all matters of party organization, including the provision of candidates; and in the same year this agency, in turn, set up an Organization Committee of nine members which carries on the actual work of the party from the national headquarters at London, and is, to all intents and purposes, the central office in a new guise. The physical headquarters [15] are provided and maintained by the Liberal Central Organization, whose ex-officio chairman is the chief Liberal whip in the House of Commons. A Women's National Liberal Federation, given its present form in 1919 by a union of pre-existing women's organizations, links up some twelve hundred associations having an aggregate membership of 120,000. There is also a separate Scottish Liberal Federation, organized much like the English.[16]

[14] Each district has a regional federation, with a president, chairman, treasurer, several secretaries, and other officers. Thus there is a Devon and Cornwall Liberal Federation, an Eastern Counties Liberal Federation, a Home Counties Liberal Federation, a London Liberal Federation, etc. Other districts so organized include the Lancashire-Cheshire region, the Midlands, Northumberland and Durham, the Western Counties, and Wales.

[15] At 21 Abingdon St., Westminster, S.W. 1, London.

[16] On the earlier history of the National Liberal Federation, see A. L. Lowell, *Government of England,* I, Chap. xxix; M. Ostrogorski, *Democracy and the Organization of Political Parties,* I, 287-328; R. S. Watson, *The National Liberal Federation,* as cited, which covers the subject to 1906. Watson was president of the Federation from 1890 to 1902. His book, however, fails to give the intimate view of the organization's workings that might reasonably have been expected. Liberal organization as it exists today is outlined in *Liberal Year Book* (1928), 1-26.

Organization of the Labor Party

A stranger to English politics has been heard to say: "I can recognize your Tory party; I know where it begins and where it leaves off; the same is true of your Liberal party, though *it* spends most of its time in leaving off; but your Labor party is complicated. How does it work?" [17] Although it is doubtful whether the machinery of the Labor party was ever as complicated as that of either of the older parties, there was a time when perplexity on this score might well have been pardoned, even in a near at hand observer. Nowadays, however, the important lines are clear enough; and it will be interesting to see where they lie, and how the mechanism compares with that of the rival parties just described. The history of Labor party organization falls into two main periods or stages, divided by the year 1918. Prior to that date the party was not a broadly national organization, having branches open to individual members in every constituency; rather it was a federation, nationally and locally, of trade unions, trades councils, socialist societies, and a few local Labor parties, and one became a member of it only by joining one of these component organizations. In the great majority of constituencies there was no way by which a person who could not be, or did not care to be, a trade unionist, and who also did not want to identify himself with a socialist society, could become an effective Labor party supporter. The organizers of the Labor Representation Committee of 1900 and their successors in the management of the Labor party had conceived of the movement as of and for the "working classes;" and they had thought of the working classes as composed primarily, if not exclusively, of manual workers.

The quickening of the party resulting from war-time conditions brought, however, a broader view; and as soon as the Representation of the People Act of 1918 was on the statute-book a special conference was convened at Nottingham and a new constitution adopted in such form as to open a gateway into the party for old and new voters alike, and especially for women, who would have had scant access to the party ranks under the old arrangements. The membership clause of the

[17] Cited in H. Tracey (ed.), *The Book of the Labour Party,* I, 3.

new frame of government read as follows: "The Labor party shall consist of all its affiliated organizations, together with those men and women who are individual members of a local Labor party and who subscribe to the constitution and program of the party." Elsewhere the constitution made it clear that "workers by brain" were no less welcome than "workers by hand;" and any and all individuals who were prepared to endorse the principles of the party were to be encouraged to identify themselves with it by way of local Labor parties (neither trade unionist nor socialist as such), which were now organized in many additional constituencies. This departure marked a genuine rebirth of the party. The center of gravity was shifted perceptibly from the trade unions, hitherto completely dominant, in the direction of the local Labor parties; a party based on class gave way to a party grounded, as has been remarked, upon a broadly national constituency. Great accessions of numbers and strength followed, not only from the ranks of the new voters, but from people in all walks of life who for the first time saw their way clear, or found it possible, to enroll as Labor supporters.

These sweeping changes in the basis and structure of the party were accompanied by an appropriate and significant reconstruction of party machinery. In the counties and boroughs the main developments were the reorganization of the local Labor parties and the establishment of such parties in large numbers of constituencies previously devoid of them. The local party became a working alliance of individual members and of members of the affiliated trade unions and socialist societies in the constituency; [18] some voters belong simply as individuals, others by virtue of belonging to an affiliated union or socialist organization. Even yet there are constituencies in which there is no local Labor party, the functions of such an organization sometimes being performed by a local trades council. But the number of local Labor parties continues to grow, especially in the rural constituencies, where the national party management is now

[18] In 1927 the Coöperative Union Congress voted for a formal alliance with the Labor party, and thereupon local coöperative societies began to take their places as local units of the party along with the other types of organizations named.

spending most of its organization funds. Ample provision is made for women's sections of the local parties, and many such exist. A conspicuous feature of all British party organization is, indeed, the maintenance of separate committees, "sections," and even federations, for work among the female portions of the electorate.

The supreme governing authority of the national party is the Conference, which alone has power to amend the party constitution and standing orders. Like the Conservative Conference and the Liberal Council, the Labor Conference is a purely representative body, meeting once a year in a populous center selected by the national executive, though special meetings may be called, as was done in the late winter of 1917-18. Trade unions and other affiliated societies send one delegate for every thousand members on which fees are paid;[19] each local Labor party in a constituency, and also each trades council, sends one delegate; and an additional woman delegate may be sent from any constituency in which the number of affiliated and individual women members exceeds five hundred. All members of the National Executive, and of the Parliamentary Labor party, and all duly sanctioned parliamentary Labor candidates, are also members ex-officio, although with no right to vote unless sent as delegates. No delegate may represent more than one organization; all must be paid permanent officials or bona fide dues-paying members of the organization which they represent; and—although no formal pledge is exacted—all are honor bound to accept the constitution and principles of the Labor party. As in the conferences of other parties, proceedings are dominated by the executive—in American parlance, the machine. Except for business brought up by the Executive Committee or the Conference Arrangements Committee, discussions are restricted to matters arising out of the annual report of the Executive Committee, and to resolutions and amendments thereto submitted, in advance, in accordance with the standing orders. Notices of resolutions to be introduced must be given to the party secretary by April 1. These having been circulated among the affiliated societies and local parties, and notices of amendments having been received (up to May

[19] See p. 592 below.

16), the secretary prepares the final agenda. The work of the Conference eventuates in resolutions declaring the attitude and policy of the party on the matters covered, and as in the case of the other parties, these pronouncements are roughly tantamount to a party platform. As also in the case of the other parties, however, the parliamentary members will not permit their hands to be tied in any very specific way by such expressions of opinion and desire on the part of the rank and file.[20]

The National Executive, which is responsible for carrying on the general work of the party, consists, to all intents and purposes, of the Executive Committee and its auxiliary, the Central Office. The Executive Committee is elected annually by the Conference. Prior to 1918, eleven of the sixteen members represented the trade union element in the party. Since that date the body has had a broader basis, in accordance with the new form and character of the party itself. There are now twenty-three members, of whom thirteen represent national affiliated societies (trade unions and socialist organizations) and five represent local Labor parties, with four additional women representatives, and also the party treasurer ex-officio.[21]

[20] A word may be added as to the way in which the Labor party arrived at the broad statement of policy from which its platform in the general election of 1929 was extracted. At the Blackpool Conference of October, 1927, the Executive Committee was instructed, in view of the coming election, to prepare "a statement setting forth the broad proposals which from time to time have been approved by the party conference and which constitute a program of legislative and administrative action for a Labor government." Mr. MacDonald urged that the statement be a complete presentation of "the faith and works to which the Labor party is pledged." Others thought that it would be better to forego large announcements of ultimate ends and to prepare only a short program of immediate objectives which the party, if in office, could really hope to attain. The ex-premier's view prevailed, and the resulting document, *Labour and the Nation,* presented to the annual conference at Birmingham in October, 1928, and approved by it, became a fifty-page pamphlet setting forth some sixty-five articles of faith and comprising, as Mr. MacDonald said, "a survey of the whole of the problem which the Labor movement has been created to solve"—a structure on which the party could stand not only in 1928 but in all the years that must pass before the aim of "transforming Capitalism into Socialism" is eventually achieved.

[21] It is therefore possible now for the trade union element to be in a minority; and indeed in the Committee first elected after the reorganization it had only ten of the twenty-three members. Complaint continues, however,

Each affiliated national society is entitled to nominate one candidate for the first group (two, if the membership exceeds 500,000); each parliamentary constituency organization, through its local Labor party or trades council, may nominate one candidate for the second group; and each affiliated organization may nominate one woman candidate (two, if the membership exceeds 500,000) for the third group. All members, however, are finally elected by the full Conference, by secret ballot. The Conference also chooses the party treasurer, who, as has been indicated, becomes a member of the Executive Committee, and likewise the secretary, who serves as the principal permanent executive officer. The Committee sees to it that the party is represented by a properly constituted organization in every constituency where practicable; it gives effect to the decisions and orders of the Conference; it interprets the constitution and standing orders in cases of dispute, subject to a right of appeal to its superior, the Conference; it expels persons from membership and disaffiliates organizations which have violated the constitution or by-laws; and it supervises the multifarious work carried on at and through the party headquarters, i.e., the Central Office, at London. The Committee meets as a rule for two or three days each month, and subcommittees are set up for special purposes. The Central Office is under the immediate direction of the party secretary, with whom are associated (among other principal officials) an assistant secretary, a national agent, a chief woman organizer, and a finance officer, each with a suitable staff. Throughout the country, also, men and women district organizers and other agents work under Central Office direction.[22] Finally, there are special departments having to do with research and information, press and publicity, international relations, and legal advice. Until 1921, these belonged to the Labor party alone; in that year they became joint instrumentalities of the party and the Trades Union Congress; in 1926, however, the Con-

that the trade unions dominate the elections, and indeed the affairs of the party generally.

[22] There are nine districts. District J, or Scotland, has a special form of organization in which a Scottish Advisory Council, dating from 1915, serves in much the same capacity as the National Executive Committee in relation to the party as a whole.

gress withdrew its connection with all except the fourth.[23] The research department has sub-committees on such subjects as land and agriculture, education, public health, finance, justice, and local government, and furnishes most of the material which is put out through the press and publicity department. Publications take the form chiefly of handbooks, pamphlets, and leaflets, rather than substantial volumes such as those issued of late by the Liberals; and efforts to build up a vigorous newspaper press have not been notably successful. The only official Labor party daily paper, the *Daily Herald,* has never attained a large circulation, and its yearly deficits impose a heavy burden on its joint sponsors, the Labor party and the Trades Union Congress.

Coming within the purview of the Executive Committee and the Central Office is not only the supervision of party organization in the constituencies, the promotion of party propaganda, the support of a party press, and the management of party funds, but the approval, and upon occasion the selection, of parliamentary candidates. The local constituency organizations have, indeed, the right of initiative and choice. But the central organization must coöperate wherever desirable in finding the best candidates; it must see that every candidacy is strictly in accordance with the party constitution; and no candidate can finally be adopted until he or she has received the National Executive's express endorsement. It is not often that the central organization finds it necessary actually to wield the veto power; but the power clearly exists. The main requirements made of aspirants are: (1) that they go before the electorate under no other designation than that of "Labor candidate,"

[23] The Trades Union Congress represents the industrial, as the Labor party represents the political, side of the labor movement. The former was first upon the scene, and in the earlier years of the century there was some duplication of effort, and occasional unfriendliness. The reconstruction of the party in 1918, however, paved the way for more satisfactory relations. The Congress corresponds rather closely to the annual convention of the American Federation of Labor, differing from the latter chiefly in that, whereas the railroad brotherhoods and clothing workers stand outside of the Federation, there are no important British unions which do not participate in the Congress. The few unions outside are small local ones or professional associations which lie on the border between the middle class and the working class.

(2) that in any general election they include in their election addresses and emphasize in their campaigns the issues which the National Executive has selected from the general party program to be stressed in that particular contest, and (3) that they agree, if elected, to act in harmony with the party constitution and standing orders. Most of the candidates now selected by the constituencies are taken from a list endorsed by the national executive. Once seated at Westminster, successful candidates become members of the Parliamentary Labor party and subject to its discipline. They pass largely out of the control of the National Executive, and even of the Conference. They are, however, honor bound by the conditions and stipulations under which they have been accepted as candidates, and any tendency to insubordination ordinarily will be curbed by the thought that when another election comes round they will have no chance to be candidates again unless the National Executive is willing to give them the stamp of its approval.[24]

Party Finances

Although all parties manage to secure a good deal of unpaid service, they cannot carry on their multifold activities without large outlays of money. All have exchequers, more or less well filled, upon which salaries of officers and agents, office rentals, clerk hire, printing, postage, travel, assistance to local committees, and subsidies to candidates make heavy demands. The older parties have regularly relied for funds upon the contributions of members and supporters, made voluntarily, at least in theory, though often extracted from the donors by the importunity of whips or other workers. Neither the Conservatives nor the Liberals have ever had any system of assessment under which either local party organizations or individuals were required to contribute, or under which the party managers could know, other than very roughly, how much would be available for their use in any given year. Speaking broadly, however, neither of these parties was ever in dire straits for money—

[24] In his *A Policy for the Labour Party* (pp. 31-32) Ramsay MacDonald recognizes the danger that in constituencies in which particular trade unions are strong the idea may insensibly grow up that the seat belongs to the dominant union, resulting possibly in the selection of inferior candidates. He looks to the "good sense of the party" to obviate the difficulty.

except in the case of the Independent Liberals of the early post-war years, and perhaps the reunited Liberal party prior to the reëstablishment of the Lloyd George leadership in 1927. The Conservative party has the support today, as in the past, of most of the country's men of great wealth, and it has been accustomed to be financed by large (sometimes very large) contributions of landed magnates, brewers, bankers, and capitalists. The public has no way of knowing precisely what the party's resources are; but as a rule they afford every appearance of being ample, and an invariable accompaniment of parliamentary elections is the complaint of opposing parties that the Conservatives enjoy the huge advantage that comes from having fuller coffers.

Even in their palmier days, the Liberals had less to draw upon; the rank and file of the party contained fewer men of wealth, and evidences of frugality, if not parsimony, often appeared in the form, if not the effectiveness, of their organization throughout the country. But for one circumstance, they would indeed be at a disadvantage at the present time. That circumstance, already mentioned, is the fact that during the days of the Coalition government Mr. Lloyd George laid the foundations of a large political fund, which, through profitable investment in newspaper properties [25] (if not in other ways), has continued to grow, and a very considerable share of which he, in 1927, agreed to turn to the uses of the Liberal party. The precise sources of this fund have never been explained to everybody's satisfaction; notwithstanding somewhat ambiguous statements to the contrary, the notion persists that there is a connection between the fund and the lavish bestowal of honors in Coalition days. At all events, the Liberal party has been able to reconstruct its shattered machinery and was able to place a full quota of candidates in the field at the election of 1929 with assurance that they would be given generous financial support. Notwithstanding this windfall, the party rank and file continues, of course, to be appealed to for subscriptions.

One will not be surprised to be told that the Labor party has proceeded on quite different lines. Lacking sources from which

[27] Principally the *London Daily Chronicle,* which the enterprising Welshman bought for £600,000 and in a few years sold for £1,600,000.

to draw large voluntary contributions, it derives its income almost entirely from affiliation fees. Trade unions, socialist societies, coöperative societies, and other organizations directly affiliated to the party pay into the central party treasury 3*d.* per member per year, with a minimum payment of 30*s.* In the case of trade unions, the amount due is calculated, not on the total membership, but on the number of members contributing to the union's political fund; and it will be recalled that, whereas under the Trade Union Act of 1913 this meant all members not "contracting out,"i.e., not definitely refusing to contribute to the political fund, under the Trade Disputes and Trade Unions Act of 1927 it means only such members as specifically indicate their desire to make such contribution. Trades councils affiliated to the party pay 30*s.* a year. Local Labor parties must charge individuals enrolled as members a minimum of 1*s.* per annum in the case of males and 6*d.* per annum in the case of females, and from the sums realized must remit to the Central Office 2*d.* per member, with a minimum annual payment of 30*s.* By all odds the most important source of revenue is the trade unions; and local Labor parties, in selecting candidates, are sometimes obliged to pass over abler men for the simple reason that they lack trade union backing.[26] Trade union membership, however, fluctuates widely; the proportion of members contributing for political purposes has been sharply curtailed under the legislation of 1927: and the funds from this source yield nothing comparable with the large centralized war chests of the Liberals and Conservatives. Labor outlays on full-time agents and other propagandist machinery, although increasing, are relatively small.[27] On the other hand, Labor

[26] In 1928 the trade unions paid into the general fund £38,949; the local parties and trades councils, £1,673; the socialist societies and coöperative societies, £681. It may be noted that the "general fund" is made up of the contributions received from these sources, and that there is a separate "election" or "fighting" fund, raised by special appeals in advance of a general election, and also a "by-election" fund, secured by a levy on all constituencies and local parties whenever a by-election is impending. Some substantial gifts are made to the former fund, but the latter has not been very successful.

[27] For several years, organization work in the constituencies was encouraged by a grant of £40 a year out of the general fund to each constituency which maintained a full-time party agent or organizer. In 1926 a new

commands a greater amount of spirited unremunerated service than either of its competitors.

Auxiliary Organizations

No description of English party machinery would be complete without mention of the rôle played by organizations which, while not parts of the formal mechanism, are nevertheless agencies for keeping party spirit alive, promoting party morale, and otherwise serving party interests. First of all, there are political clubs, primarily social in character, yet having a frankly party basis. Oldest of these is the Carlton Club, established in 1831 as a center of Conservative life and activity in London. Its splendid building in Pall Mall is the place where Conservative members of Parliament commonly gather for consultations; there it was, for example, that the decision was reached in 1922 to withdraw support from the Lloyd George coalition government. Other Conservative clubs, e.g., the Constitutional and St. Stephens, will be found by any visitor to the Pall Mall district. The oldest Liberal organization of the kind, the Reform Club, ceased before the end of the nineteenth century to be a political club in the strict sense, but its place was taken by the National Liberal Club, which, along with other similar establishments in the capital, continues to serve all necessary purposes. There are also Conservative and Liberal clubs in principal cities throughout the country. Then there are ancillary leagues and societies. The most interesting of these is the Primrose League, founded in 1883 by Lord Randolph Churchill and named after what was supposed to be Disraeli's favorite flower. Elaborately organized, liberally financed, and supported by a membership of from one to two millions, it has been for almost half a century a prime agency of Conservative influence, especially at election time. There are also the Association of Conservative Clubs, the Young Conservatives' Union, the Junior Imperial League, and even the National Conservative Musical Union. The Liberals have the National Reform Union, the National League of Young Liberals, the Land and Nation League, the Eighty Club, and similar associa-

arrangement was adopted under which the subsidy is being gradually diminished.

tions. Several of these organizations, both Conservative and Liberal, enroll members of both sexes and of all social classes. The Labor party is not without similar auxiliaries. The National Labor Club, founded in 1924, serves as a main social center in the capital; while the Trades Union Congress, the Independent Labor party, the Fabian Society, and the Social Democratic Federation—in their respective spheres, and under special conditions entailed by the elements which they represent—play rôles comparable with those which the Conservative and Liberal auxiliaries have made familiar to every observer of British political life.[28]

[28] There is singularly little up-to-date and really informing literature on the general subject of party organization in Britain. M. Ostrogorski, *Democracy and the Organization of Political Parties* (trans. by F. Clarke, London, 1902), I, treats the subject historically; and A. L. Lowell, in Chaps. xxv-xxxiii of his *Government of England*, describes arrangements as they existed upwards of a quarter of a century ago. Information concerning present-day party machinery has to be pieced out chiefly from party yearbooks and other such publications, supplemented by items and articles in newspapers and magazines. One could wish that either a native Bryce or a foreign Ostrogorski would turn his attention to the broad subject as it lies today, or, short of that, that numbers of investigators would undertake first-hand studies of selected phases, eventuating in monographs comparable with some which deal with party matters in the United States. It may be added that a few topics—nominations, campaign expenditures, and the formation of public opinion—have very recently been studied by young American scholars, who, however, in most instances, have not yet published their results. One significant contribution of this character is J. M. Gaus, *Great Britain; A Study of Civic Loyalty* (Chicago, 1929).

CHAPTER XXV

THE SYSTEM OF ENGLISH LAW

For what purpose, chiefly, does government exist? Pressed for a reply, the man in the street would probably say, "to maintain law and order;" and he would have no lack of precedent and authority behind him. The barons who forced Magna Carta upon King John wanted the "law of the land" scrupulously observed; the framers of the Bill of Rights condemned James II for subverting the "laws and liberties" of the kingdom; Thomas Jefferson wrote into the Declaration of Independence a ringing indictment of George III for refusing his assent to laws, causing laws to be suspended, and obstructing the enforcement of laws. Law is, of course, only a means to an end—that end being what may be broadly termed justice. Furthermore, law has often been enforced by private individuals or agencies, and still is so enforced among some primitive peoples. But the primary business of the state is to interpret, apply, and execute law, and to some extent also, to make it; and no study of a governmental system can produce a correct impression which does not take some account, not only of the machinery for law-making and enforcement, but also of the sources and nature of the law itself—both (1) public law (e.g., constitutional and administrative), which regulates the activities of the government (or its agents) and the relations of the government and these agents with individuals and corporations, and (2) private law, both civil and criminal, in respect to which the government is not strictly a party but only a mediator charged with seeing that justice is done.

Some Fundamental Aspects

With peculiar aptness the vital principle of the English political system may be said to be the reign of law. The framework and procedure of the government do, indeed, as we have noticed, rest in no small degree upon extra-legal custom. But such custom has force only so long as it does not come into conflict with law, and it may be modified or superseded at any time by new legal enactments. As affecting the general body of the citizenry, two rules are fundamental: first, that no man may be deprived of life, liberty, property, or any other right, save on account of a breach of the law proved in court, and second, that no man stands above the law, and that for every violation of the law punishment may be inflicted or reparation exacted, whatever the station or connections of the offender.[1] Upon these hard-won and lofty principles a system of justice has been built up which lends the British nation one of its chief distinctions.

The English system of law[2] is, indeed, one of only two really great legal systems that mankind has evolved. The other is the Roman. Unlike as they were in many other respects, both Roman and Englishman had an unusual genius for law (as also for government in general), and one could travel widely over the world today without ever setting foot in a country where the legal system is not derived directly from either the civil law of Rome or the common law of England.[3] The law of practically all Continental Europe, of all Latin America, of Louisiana, Japan, and even Scotland, is at basis Roman; the law of Ireland, of the United States, of India, of the British dominions, and, of course, of England and Wales,

[1] The only exception to this general proposition is the sovereign, who may not be sued or prosecuted in the ordinary courts; but his immunity, as matters now stand, is of no practical importance. Mention has been made, in an earlier chapter, of certain recent tendencies to restrict the sphere of the rule of law, especially through the conferring of judicial or quasi-judicial functions upon administrative officers and tribunals. See pp. 203 ff. above; also A. V. Dicey, *Introduction to the Study of the Law of the Constitution* (8th ed.), pp. xxxviii-xliii. This development has not, however, gone far enough to invalidate the broad statement made above. On the rule of law in general, see W. S. Holdsworth, *Some Lessons from Our Legal History* (New York, 1928), Chap. iii; Dicey, *op. cit.*, Chap. iv; and J. A. R. Marriott, *The Mechanism of the Modern State*, II, Chap. xxxi.

[2] The law to be discussed in this chapter is private law only.

[3] The principal system aside from these two is the Mohammedan law (not itself entirely uninfluenced by the Roman), which prevails, in varying and somewhat confused forms, in Turkey, Arabia, and other Moslem lands.

is the English common law, modified and supplemented in varying degrees by statutes of local application.[4]

The two great systems were developed quite independently, and in their character, spirit, and implications are decidedly unlike. Starting in the *Jus Quiritium,* which found its earliest formal expression in the Twelve Tables of Appius Claudius, the civil law reached substantially its final form in the Justinian codes of the sixth century, at a time when Britain was only fairly beginning to be occupied by the Teutons from across seas. And although the indigenous Saxon (later English) law was subjected to powerful Roman influences in the Middle Ages, it never suffered any appreciable displacement or modification. "England is isolated in jurisprudence; she has solved her legal problems for herself." The dissimilarities of the two systems arise not merely from their independence in origin and growth, but also from the differing temperaments and propensities of the peoples who created them. Roman and Briton alike were practical-minded, but the former had a love of orderliness, coherence, and consistency which the latter largely lacked. We have seen that the Englishman has been content to go along with a system of government filled with anomalies and incongruities because those anomalies and incongruities have not

[4] J. Bryce, "The Extension of Roman and English Law," in *Studies in History and Jurisprudence,* 72-121. The persistence of English common law in the United States obviously gives the subject a peculiar interest for American students. "It is indeed noteworthy," remarks Lowell, "that the United States has kept in far closer touch with the legal than with the political thought of the mother country. English decisions have never ceased to be cited as authorities in American courts, while acts of Parliament have been copied with much less frequency, and political customs have scarcely been followed at all. The public institutions of the two countries are now very different, but their system of jurisprudence and their conceptions of law are essentially the same." *Government of England,* II, 472-473. The development and character of the Roman law can conveniently be compared with the growth of the English and other systems by use of J. Declareuil, *Rome, the Law-giver,* trans. by E. A. Parker (New York, 1926). Cf. J. Bryce, "The History of Legal Development at Rome and in England," in *Studies in History and Jurisprudence,* 745-781. On the geographical distribution of the world's great legal systems, see J. H. Wigmore, "A Map of the World's Law," *Geographic Rev.,* Jan., 1929, and for a full and vivid history of their rise and growth, the same author's *A Panorama of the World's Legal Systems,* 3 vols. (St. Paul, 1928). M. Smith, *The Development of European Law* (New York, 1928), is a valuable volume of essays.

kept the system from serving the purposes for which government exists. In like manner, he has not sought to whip his body of law into the symmetrical, polished scheme to be seen in the civil law, whether as it left the hands of the sixth-century codifiers or as it operates today, in its fundamentals, in France or Germany or Japan. Roman law (and modern law derived from it) has the smoothness, balance, and immobility of the pyramid of Cheops; English law has, rather, the deviousness and casualness of a labyrinth.

Other qualities the English law no less unmistakably possesses. Lack of certain artificial orderliness and symmetry does not mean the absence of unity and continuity. Formed originally of two streams—the Saxon and the Norman-French—which flowed together after the Conquest, the law developed thenceforth as a single national system with never a break to our own day; and one can read one's way backward in the textbooks and commentaries—Blackstone in the eighteenth century, Hale and Coke in the seventeenth, Fitzherbert in the sixteenth, Littleton in the fifteenth, Bracton in the thirteenth, and Glanvill in the twelfth—and find that although hardly a rule remains unaltered, one is always reading about the same great body of law. "Eventful though its life has been, it has had but a single life." And this suggests the second characteristic of the law, namely, that it is a living, ever-changing thing, dropping off here and taking on there, equally with that compound of rules and usages which, of course, is only a part of the law itself in the larger sense, i.e., the British constitution. "When we speak of a body of law," reads the opening sentence of a well-known history of the English system, "we use a metaphor so apt that it is hardly a metaphor. We picture to ourselves a being that lives and grows, that preserves its identity while every atom of which it is composed is subject to a ceaseless process of change, decay, and renewal." [5] The law is not an amorphous lump or mass; it is an organism.

But what *is* law? On this important point, too, the Englishman has his own ideas, even though he came by them relatively late and only after a deal of wavering between different opin-

[5] F. W. Maitland and F. C. Montague, *Sketch of English Legal History* (New York, 1915), p. 1.

ions. Continental peoples have made much of a law of nature, or natural law, which has, indeed, reflected many different concepts in different times and places, but in general has denoted a system of jurisprudence deduced by reason from the very nature of man and things, and existing anterior to and independent of principles or rules of man's own devising; and in Germany, France, and other lands of the civil law the relations between natural and positive law absorb much of the time and thought of the philosopher and jurist. The idea of a law of nature has not been unknown in England; indeed, in medieval days it was a common notion that statutes were void if they conflicted with natural law. This was a convenient doctrine when statutes emanated from an autocratic king, and as late as the seventeenth century John Locke gave it an approving philosophical exposition in the second of his *Treatises on Government.*[6] With the growth, however, of an omnipotent Parliament, whose acts were to be presumed to be the will of the people, the courts, and even the reformers, practically stopped talking about natural law, except in the general sense of principles of justice by which the judges should be guided in the decision of doubtful cases. As distinguished from such unformulated and somewhat intangible principles, *law* came definitely to be regarded as the rules, of whatever origin or character, which the courts will recognize and enforce. Principles or practices which the courts will not enforce may have a good deal of importance as custom, and perhaps as morality; but, for Englishmen at all events, they are not law.[7]

Rise and Growth of the Common Law

As thus defined, English law consists of two great elements, common law and statute law, with a third, on a somewhat dif-

[6] Bk. II, Chap. ii (ed. by Carpenter, pp. 118-124).

[7] "This doctrine, clearly stated by Hobbes (*Leviathan,* Pt. ii, Chap. 26), was given its fullest systematic treatment by Austin (*Jurisprudence,* Lect. I), and although his doctrine that the only source of law is command of a definite political superior, coupled with a sanction, has been very generally discarded, his sharp distinction between that which is actually law and that which ought to be law has remained unshaken. The latter he classed, not as law, but merely as positive morality." A. L. Lowell, *Government of England,* II, 476-477. The best brief analysis of the English conception of law and its effects is that by Lowell, *ibid.,* Chaps. lxi-lxii.

ferent basis of classification, i.e., equity. The rise and expansion of the common law forms one of the most interesting chapters in all legal history. The story goes back to the Saxon period, when, notwithstanding the primitive conditions of the times and the lack of national unity, certain legal usages and forms became common to the whole realm, or at all events the larger portions of it. Growing up in unwritten form, these customs were in part, from time to time, promulgated, or declared, as "dooms," or ordinances, by the king and his witan; though it was always characteristic of the common law, as it is today, that the great bulk of it was simply carried in men's minds without being written down, at any rate in any orderly manner. After the Conquest the displacement of local and diverse legal usages by customs general to the entire country went on at an accelerated pace, especially in the reigns of Henry II (1154-89) and his immediate successors. These were days of strong royal rule, when the king's government was reaching out in all directions for greater power, and, in particular, was establishing centralized authority in the important domains of finance and justice. Feudal and other local courts gave way to king's courts, conducted by royal judges—often men of real learning—who went out from London to all parts of the realm and dispensed justice in the king's name. Drawing their authority from a single source, forming a homogeneous staff, and with much incentive to and opportunity for interchange of information and ideas, these royal judges, even more than their less favorably situated predecessors of earlier days, sought to discover and apply the usages having the widest vogue. The decisions of one became precedents to be followed by others, and thus, woven of reiterated and respected judgments—in accordance with what the lawyers call *stare decisis,* i.e., the principle that the decision of a court sets up a presumptive basis of action in all analogous cases subsequently arising, especially when the same decision has been repeatedly made or affirmed over a long period of time—the common law became the great fabric of legal usage which, even by the thirteenth century, had grown to be one of the country's principal claims to distinction. It was a body of judge-made rules which, for the most part, had never been ordained by a king, or, of course, enacted by a legislature. Yet it had the royal authority behind it and was in every proper sense law, applied wherever the king's courts were held—which by the close of the Norman period meant every part of the land. Very different was the situation in France, where (partly because of the inferior power of the king in the earlier Middle Ages) elaborate bodies of local customary law arose, but nothing of the kind for the country as a whole, and where, indeed, law continued fundamentally regional rather than national until near the end of the eighteenth century.[8]

Other factors, of course, entered into the making of the great system of common law as handed down to modern times. There was a certain amount of influence from the Roman law, exerted not so much upon the actual content of the law, which always remained decidedly English, as in the direction of greater systematization and coherence.[9] There were contributions (also non-English in source) from the canon law, i.e., the legal system developed by the Western Christian Church, and from the "law merchant," which was a body of rules employed by European traders for the settlement of disputes among themselves. And, in particular, a good deal was added by the work

[8] The development of French and German law is described briefly in C. Ilbert, *Legislative Methods and Forms,* 8-19. Cf. J. A. R. Marriott, *The Mechanism of the Modern State,* II, Chap. xxxiv.

[9] The fact that the principles of Roman law found scant lodgment in the English common law is of much importance in relation to English constitutional development, because whereas the Roman law was grounded on the doctrine of the absolute authority of the prince, the common law recognized no such doctrine, but instead became the great bulwark of the defenders of parliamentary supremacy in the sixteenth and seventeenth centuries. "Little was known of that law [the Roman], less as time went on; but of this Englishmen were assured, that it presupposed a ruler above the law, while the king of England, though below no man, was held below the law. This reverence for the common law gained strength when, the baronage being crippled by civil strife, the king and commons stood face to face; and it finally justified itself when the royal power dashed against the law and fell back broken." F. W. Maitland, *Justice and Police* (London, 1885), 34. Cf. W. A. Dunning, *Political Theories from Luther to Montesquieu,* 197-200, 219-223; G. P. Gooch, *History of English Democratic Ideas in the Seventeenth Century,* Chaps. ii-iii. On the influence of Roman law in England, see F. Pollock and F. W. Maitland, *History of English Law to the Time of Edward I* (Cambridge, 1898), I, Chap. v; J. Bryce, *Studies in History and Jurisprudence,* 860-886; P. H. Winfield, *The Chief Sources of English Legal History* (Cambridge, 1926), Chap. iv; and C. P. Sherman, "The Romanization of English Law," *Yale Law Jour.,* Feb., 1914.

of the jurists and commentators. Sooner or later, legal-minded scholars were bound to find in this vast unassembled mass of principles and procedures a challenge to legal reporting and interpretation. As early as the twelfth century, Henry II's chief justiciar, Ranulf Glanvill, compiled a "treatise on the laws and customs of the English" (*Tractatus de Legibus et Consuetudines Anglorum*);[10] and in succeeding centuries other jurists—Bracton in the thirteenth (whose *De Legibus et Consuetudines Angliæ* has been termed "the crown and flower of English medieval jurisprudence"), Littleton in the fifteenth, Fitzherbert in the sixteenth, Hale and Coke in the seventeenth, and finally Blackstone, in his famous *Commentaries on the Laws of England*, in the nineteenth, gathered up the significant rules of common law that had developed by the time that each, respectively, wrote, commented on them, cited cases on which they were based, and thus helped both systematize the law and shape the lines of its future development.

Meanwhile the law kept on expanding steadily—finding a new application here and building out in a new direction there—as, indeed, it continues to do in our own time. There was never a break in its history; political revolutions only left it more strongly entrenched than before. Furthermore, when, in the seventeenth and eighteenth centuries, Englishmen began settling beyond seas, they carried the common law with them as perhaps their most priceless possession. To the colonists in America it was an Englishman's heritage, a bulwark against tyranny, a guarantee of liberties and rights—so precious, indeed, that the sturdy patriots who composed the First Continental Congress solemnly declared Americans to be "entitled to it by the immutable laws of nature." After the Revolution, it was no less valued than before, and, next only to language, it is no doubt today the most important joint possession of the United States and the mother land. For Englishmen themselves, it was, and is, the law and custom of the realm since the time when "the memory of man runneth not to the contrary." It still flows with pomp of waters unwithstood through all the tribunals where the English language is the language of the people.

[10] There is some question whether the *Tractatus* was not partly the work of Glanvill's nephew, Hubert Walter.

Statute Law and Its Relation to Common Law

During all of the time while the common law was taking form other law, however, was coming into being by a different process, i.e., by enactment. Common law merely grew up; statute law was *made*. For many centuries the king promulgated laws with only the advice and assistance of his council. After the rise of Parliament, however, statutes gradually became the handiwork of that body, even though to this day they describe themselves as being enacted by the "king, Lords, and Commons in parliament assembled." It is now more than six hundred years since Parliament began grinding out laws. Until a century or two ago, the bulk of this legislation was comparatively slight, and to this day Englishmen have restrained themselves in notable fashion from the orgies of law-making which fatten the statute-books in America. Changing social and economic conditions since the middle of the eighteenth century have, however, called for freer exercise of the legislative power, and for a long time now a substantial volume has been added to the Statutes of the Realm with every passing year, single laws not infrequently exceeding in bulk the entire legislative output of a medieval reign. Some of this statutory law deals with matters not covered at all by the common law. But a large share of it has to do with subjects that are so covered, at least in part; and hence the common law is constantly being not only supplemented by statute, but rounded out, qualified, clarified, codified, amended, or even repealed by it, as the case may be. Many important acts of Parliament are little more than statutory statements of law already built up by the courts. Others restate, but also amend, such law. Land law and criminal law, once great domains of common law, have now been cast very largely, though not entirely, in the form of parliamentary statute. For, treasured as the common law undoubtedly is, it enjoys no privilege or immunity as against Parliament. Enough has been said in earlier chapters about the powers of Parliament to make it clear that there is no principle or rule of common law which that body may not only reduce to statute but turn in a different direction or set aside altogether. When common law and statute conflict, statute always prevails; and no new development of common law can ever annul a statute. Hence, not only is common law cut into more and more deeply by statutory law as time goes on,[11] but, legally, all common law exists on sufferance, at the mercy of a national legislature which has unquestioned power to do with it as it chooses.[12]

All this would, however, give a totally false impression unless one hastened to add that by far the greater part of the law which the courts are called upon to enforce, in Britain and America alike, is common law; and so far as we can see, this will always be the case.[13] The common law is still the "tough legal fabric that envelops us all;" the statutes are only ornaments and trimmings. "The statutes," says an English writer, "assume the existence of the common law; they would have no meaning except by reference to the common law. If all the statutes of the realm were repealed, we should still have a system of law, though, it may be, an unworkable one; if we could imagine the common law swept away and the statute law preserved, we should have only disjointed rules torn from their context, and no provision at all for many of the most important relations of life." [14] Thus, no act of Parliament enjoins in general terms that a man shall pay his debts, or carry out his contracts, or pay damages for trespass or slander. Statutes do, indeed, have something to say about the modes by which these obligations shall be discharged, but the obligations themselves are derived only from the common law. Similarly, such time-honored principles as that a person shall be presumed innocent until he is proved guilty, that hearsay shall not be accepted as evidence, that a person shall not be compelled to incriminate

[11] Not necessarily rescinded, but at any rate taken off its original basis and merged in the growing body of statutory law.

[12] A good illustration—one of scores that could be cited—of how common law yields to statute is the legalizing of trade unions, long viewed by the common law as conspiracies in restraint of trade, by statutes of 1824-25 and later. See F. A. Ogg and W. R. Sharp, *The Economic Development of Modern Europe,* 401-406.

[13] Rather less of the common law, relatively, remains in our American states than in Britain, mainly because of the immoderate output of our legislatures. The situation is, of course, not the same in all states. Much pressure is constantly being brought to bear upon lawmakers to displace old and established rules of common law, which are alleged to be outworn, by legislation on more drastic or otherwise different lines.

[14] W. M. Geldart, *Elements of English Law* (London, 1912), 9.

himself, and that an accused shall be given the name of his accuser, spring only from the common law and have never, in Britain at all events, been laid down in any constitution, charter, or statute. In many parts of the domain of private law, Parliament has left the common law much to itself. Nine-tenths of each annual volume of statutes is concerned with public and administrative law; while at least that proportion of the rules which make up the law of torts, a great part of the law of contracts, and all the rules or doctrines of equity are common law, largely or wholly unaffected by legislative activity.[15]

Statute law, of course, invariably takes written form, and the acts of Parliament are to be found in imposing printed collections—the Statutes of the Realm—to which, as we have seen, a fresh volume is added every year. But where shall one look for the common law? It grew up independent of writing, and to this day there is no single code in which it is assembled, no text setting it forth in a comprehensive and authoritative way. This, however, does not mean that it cannot be taken down from the shelf and read, because in one way or another practically all parts of it have found their way into writing or print. The main source of it has been, of course, the decisions of judges, and ever since the reign of Edward I these have been "reported," i.e., recorded in writing—for two hundred years by lawyers who reported anonymously in the Year Books, and afterwards by others who reported under their own names in the Law Reports. Of almost equal importance are the works of learned jurists, commenting on the principles of the law and citing the cases from which they were derived or by which they were sustained—works of the nature of Coke's Commentary on Littleton's Tenures and Foster's eighteenth-century treatise on crown law. Of some importance, too, are the reported decisions of courts in other countries in which a system of law derived from the English is administered, such decisions naturally not having quite the weight of those handed down in Britain, but yet occasionally being very influential. In one way or another, the common law therefore turns out not to be unwritten law, except in the sense that it was never

[15] C. Ilbert, *Legislative Methods and Forms,* 6.

textually enacted as is a statute. Some small branches of the common law have, indeed, been codified and given statutory form, among them the law of partnership, the law of sales, and the law relating to bills of exchange.

Equity

A third great division of English law is equity; for although the lawyers speak of law *and* equity, they do not mean to imply that equity is not law. What equity is, and how it is related to the other parts of the law, will become clear, at least in a general way, if we note how the system came into existence. The story begins far back in Angevin, if not indeed Norman, times, when people who thought that the application of the rules of common law in cases in which they were interested had worked injustice, or when they felt that their cases were not covered, or were only imperfectly covered, by the common law, fell into the practice of petitioning the king for rulings and remedies suited to their particular situations. In days when the king was the maker of laws and in a very literal sense the fountain of justice, there was no reason why he should not take cases out of the hands of the regular courts and decide them himself—no reason except one, namely, that petitions poured in so fast that to attend to all of them would have meant an intolerable expenditure of time and energy. Solution of this difficulty was, however, readily found in arrangement for a proxy. The king had a chancellor who, as we have seen, was the principal secretary, and it was easy enough for him to turn over to this subordinate the actual examination of the petitions, and in time the answering of them as well. Not only was it easy, it was also logical; for the chancellor in those days was almost always a bishop or other ecclesiastic (hardly anybody else could qualify for secretarial duties in the Middle Ages), who might be presumed to be a specially good judge of questions of justice, morality, *equity,* such as were usually involved in the requests that came in. "Keeper of the king's conscience," the chancellor came to be called, even before the fourteenth century. Like the king himself, however, the chancellor had other things to do, so that presently it became necessary to appoint assistants, "masters in chancery," to aid him in the work. In the end, the natural thing happened—a regular court emerged known as the court of chancery.

The origin of the rules which form the present body of law known as equity can now be surmised. Precisely as the itinerant justices originally went out through the country deciding cases individually on their merits, but gradually developed rules of common law according to which cases of similar nature were regularly decided in the same way, so those who dispensed justice in the chancery built up rules of equity. Equity is case law, equally with the common law; indeed it is a species of common law—a sort of supplement or appendix to the common law, "filling up its defects, correcting abuses in the conduct of persons who resorted to it for fraudulent or oppressive purposes, and actually, though with caution, setting itself up as a rival to the common law courts by offering superior remedies, even in cases in which the common law professed to afford relief." [16] Beginning on relatively simple lines, it broadened out in time into a vast system of principles, rules, precedents, and implications, so intricate that a lawyer had to devote much hard study to the subject if he wanted to practice in an equity tribunal. In fact, at one time, chiefly the sixteenth century, equity waxed so important as to threaten the supremacy, if not the very existence, of the common law. It is still a huge body of living law, the subject of ponderous text-books, the theme of courses in law schools, the chosen domain of many a specialist in legal practice. It shows somewhat more influence of Roman legal principles than does the common law; it has a procedure largely its own; and although no longer administered in Britain in tribunals separate from the common law courts,[17] it is as distinct a body of law as it ever was.

If it be asked what the relation of equity now is to the rest of the law, the answer is: first, that it has no relation at all to the criminal law, being confined strictly to civil controversies; second, that it alone applies to certain kinds of civil cases, e.g., those arising out of the administration of property by a trustee; third, that the great bulk of other civil cases are dealt with normally under the rules of law rather than under those of

[16] E. Jenks, *The Book of English Law* (London, 1928), 41-42.

[17] See p. 610 below.

equity, the latter being appealed to, if at all, only with a view to correcting alleged omissions or injustices of the regular law courts; and fourth, that in several kinds of cases redress may be sought either at law or in equity as the plaintiff prefers.[18]

[18] The standard history of earlier English legal development is F. Pollock and F. W. Maitland, *History of English Law to the Time of Edward I*, 2 vols. (Cambridge, 1898). An equally notable work, covering practically the entire field chronologically, is W. S. Holdsworth, *History of English Law*, 9 vols. (2nd ed., London, 1922-26). The first volume of this great treatise contains a history of English courts from the Norman Conquest to the present day; the other volumes deal exhaustively with the development of legal doctrine and the general history of the law. Good single-volume histories include E. Jenks, *A Short History of English Law* (2nd ed., London, 1922); H. Potter, *An Introduction to the History of English Law* (2nd ed., London, 1926); and F. W. Maitland and F. C. Montague, *Sketch of English Legal History*, ed. by J. F. Colby (New York, 1915).

Excellent introductions to both the history and the content of the law are E. Jenks, *The Book of English Law*, as cited, and W. M. Geldart, *Elements of English Law* (London, 1912). Lord Justice Sankey, *The Principles and Practice of the Law Today* (London, 1928), is an authoritative brief survey; and F. W. Maitland's article on English law in the *Encyclopedia Britannica* (11th ed.), IX, 600-607, is a remarkably lucid account. W. S. Holdsworth, *Sources and Literature of English Law* (London, 1926), and *Some Lessons From Our Legal History* (New York, 1928), will be found instructive by lay readers.

The development and character of the common law are treated in G. B. Adams, *Council and Courts in Anglo-Norman England* (New Haven, 1926), Chap. v; R. Pound and T. F. T. Plunkett, *Readings on the History and Systems of the Common Law* (Rochester, 1928); R. Pound, *The Spirit of the Common Law* (Boston, 1922); and O. W. Holmes, *The Common Law* (Boston, 1881). "Judicial legislation" is discussed in A. V. Dicey, *Law and Public Opinion in England*, Lect. xi.

The beginnings of statute law are described in J. H. Beale, "The Early English Statutes," *Harvard Law Rev.*, Mar., 1922, and the character and forms of it are treated in C. Ilbert, *Legislative Methods and Forms*, 1-76, and P. H. Winfield, *The Chief Sources of English Legal History* (Cambridge, 1926), Chap. v.

On equity, see F. W. Maitland, *Lectures on Equity* (Cambridge, 1909); G. B. Adams, "The Origin of English Equity," *Columbia Law Rev.*, Feb., 1916, and "The Continuity of English Equity," *Yale Law Jour.*, May, 1917; and W. S. Holdsworth, "The Early History of Equity," *Mich. Law Rev.*, Feb., 1915.

C. K. Allen, *Law in the Making* (Oxford, 1927), is devoted to the processes by which rules come to be part of the law, especially in England.

CHAPTER XXVI

THE COURTS AND THE ADMINISTRATION OF JUSTICE

WHEN one turns to examine the judicial machinery through which this remarkable system of law is administered, the first thing that is discovered is that no single form of organization prevails throughout the entire United Kingdom. On the contrary, there is one arrangement of courts in England and Wales, another in Scotland, and still another in Northern Ireland, not to mention yet a different one in the region once belonging to the United Kingdom but now forming the Irish Free State. Scotland, whose law is modeled on the law of France, and hence rests back ultimately on the principles of civil or Roman jurisprudence, was guaranteed her separate system both of law and of courts by the Act of Union of 1707; and although since that date her criminal law has been gradually assimilated to the English, so that nowadays there is little difference between the two, her civil law remains very unlike the English, as, for example, in the almost total absence of rules of equity as distinguished from other rules of law.[1] Her judicial organization, too, is not on the English pattern. As for Ireland, she likewise was given the right, at the union of 1801, to keep her own law and courts. Her jurisprudence, however, was already being progressively remodeled on English lines. Long before 1922, the common law extended over the entire country; and the courts were fashioned after those across St. George's Channel, although with some important differences. Since the date mentioned, Northern Ireland has gone along without important change. The Free State, however, has so reorganized the judicial arrangements in the rest of the island as to make them

[1] W. E. Dodds, "A Few Comparisons between English and Scots Law," *Jour. of Compar. Legis. and Internat. Law,* Nov., 1926.

considerably less like the English than they once were. Except as otherwise stated, therefore, the court system described in the following pages is that of England and Wales alone.

The Judicial System as Reorganized in 1873-76

A glance at a diagram showing the more important tribunals and their interrelations may give the impression that the English system is a pretty complicated affair. It is, of course, not without its complexities. But at all events it is more highly integrated than our American system, which, as in federally organized countries generally, consists, in reality, of many separate and largely independent systems. Furthermore, it is very much simpler and more unified than it was up to half a century ago. In days that some men can still remember the country was cluttered up with courts, old and new, important and unimportant, generally with no sharply defined jurisdictions, overlapping and conflicting to the verge of chaos. There were civil courts and criminal courts, courts of equity and courts of common law, probate courts, divorce courts, ecclesiastical courts, and what not. All sorts of difficulties constantly arose. Cases multiplied in which it was difficult to determine which court had jurisdiction; each class of tribunals had its peculiar forms of practice and procedure; even the trained lawyer found his way through the maze with difficulty. The problem was keenly realized, and there was genuine desire for reform. But a solution came hard; more than fifty reports on the subject, official or professional, were drawn up during a half-century of almost continuous discussion.

Opinion finally became sufficiently crystallized to permit definite action, and, mainly between 1873 and 1876, the entire judicial establishment was reconstructed on simpler and more logical lines.[2] Practically all of the courts except those of petty jurisdiction were brought together in a single, centralized system. Tribunals which had been separate, and indeed rivals, became branches or subdivisions of a single Supreme Court of Judicature; law and equity jurisdictions were combined in the same courts; the lines of appeal, on both law and fact, were laid down with new definiteness; the fitness of the House of

[2] Chiefly by the Supreme Court of Judicature Act of 1873.

Lords for its judicial duties was increased by the addition of specially appointed lords of appeal in ordinary;[3] the work of justice in all of its phases and branches was toned up and re-integrated. Under the administrative direction of the Lord Chancellor, the Supreme Court of Judicature—divided into (1) a Court of Appeal and (2) a High Court of Justice, organized in three trial divisions, (a) Chancery, (b) King's Bench, and (c) Probate, Divorce, and Admiralty—was to perform combined appellate and trial functions, in both civil and criminal cases, which in other lands occupy a much larger number of tribunals. Beneath this Supreme Court a set of so-called county courts was assigned a definite and important place. At the top, the House of Lords, after temporarily losing its judicial functions altogether, became again the court of last resort for the hearing of appeals on questions of law from the highest tribunals of both civil and criminal jurisdiction. No major changes in the scheme have subsequently been found necessary.[4]

Absence of Administrative Courts

In one respect, the English judicial system had always been simpler than the systems in France, Germany, and other Continental states: it was (and still is) quite devoid of any separate set of administrative courts such as parallels the scheme of ordinary courts in Continental lands. This is not to say that there has been no development of administrative law in Britain and the English-speaking countries (including the United States) which follow the English usage. In point of fact, there has been built up, in Britain as well as in our own land, an impressive body of rules (developed to some extent by the judges and to a considerable extent by the administrative authorities) which, having to do with the legal relations existing between the government and its officers on the one hand and private citizens on the other, is of the very essence of admin-

[3] See p. 322 above.

[4] This does not mean that important legislation is not sometimes enacted introducing modifications which experience has shown to be desirable. In 1925 a great Supreme Court of Judicature (Consolidation) Act brought together in a single statute all of the measures passed since 1873 relating to the Supreme Court. A supplementary Administration of Justice Act was passed in 1928.

istrative law.[5] But the thing to be noted is that neither Britain nor the United States maintains a distinct set of courts in which these rules are interpreted and applied. Cases involving the acts of government officials—in so far as they are not adjudicated by purely administrative officers or agencies [6]—go to the same courts as cases of any other kind. An Englishman and a Frenchman are capable of debating from morn till eve the relative advantages of the two schemes. The Frenchman will say that the dignity and authority of the government require that its officers shall not be haled into the ordinary courts—that whether it be in the instance of a prefect who exceeds his powers by closing a factory because of unsanitary conditions or in that of a policeman who, pursuing an offender, injures an innocent bystander, the resulting dispute should be heard and adjusted by a tribunal under the control of the administrative, rather than the judicial, arm of the government, and by a procedure differing in various respects from that employed in the regular courts. The Englishman will boast that it is a token of liberty for the citizen to be able to summon public officials—any public official, indeed, except the king himself—before the ordinary courts, and will suggest that in a French administrative court, composed of administrative agents of the government, a plaintiff must surely find it difficult to get a sympathetic hearing of his grievance. To this the Frenchman will reply (quite correctly) that as a matter of actual experience the administrative tribunals on one side of the Channel render judgments against the government quite as freely as do the ordinary courts on the other side, and that (and, from a practical point of view, this is a decidedly important matter) if a plaintiff receives an award of damages

[5] K. B. Smellie, "Some Aspects of English Administrative Law," *Public Admin.*, July, 1927; G. E. Robinson, *Public Authorities and Legal Liability* (London, 1925); J. W. Garner, *La Conception Anglo-Américaine du Droit Administratif* (Paris, 1929); F. J. Port, *Administrative Law* (London, 1929). For some judicial decisions involving the rights and liabilities of servants of the crown, see B. A. Bicknell, *Cases on the Law of the Constitution*, 107-129.

[6] On the growing tendency to delegate judicial power to administrative authorities, see pp. 203-205 above. This development does not necessarily portend the eventual creation of administrative courts as such, but the question of its possible results is an interesting one.

under the French system, the judgment is against the government, and therefore enforceable, whereas an award rendered under the English system is only against the offending official personally, from whom as likely as not it is impossible to obtain actual redress. The unbiassed observer concludes that each system has its advantages, and that neither Britain nor France need be greatly troubled about its arrangements in this particular.[7]

Civil Actions and the Courts in Which They Proceed

It would be wearisome to describe, one by one, the many offices and courts that go to make up the English judicial system. The essential facts may better be brought out in another way, namely, by sketching the major processes by which justice, civil and criminal, is actually administered. For practical purposes, all cases that come before English courts may be classed as either civil or criminal; and the arrangement of the courts, as well as their procedure, is far more largely based on this distinction than in the United States, where the same court usually has jurisdiction in civil and criminal cases alike. A civil action is a proceeding brought by a private citizen, or by an official in his private capacity, to obtain redress from another person, official or private, for a wrong—slander, trespass, breach of contract, infringement of patents, and the like—alleged to have been committed against the bringer of the action, or "plaintiff," by the person against whom the action is brought, or "defendant." In such a proceeding the dispute is not between the crown and its subject (as it is in a criminal action), but between one of the crown's subjects and another, and the function of the public authorities is merely to judge,

[7] The pros and cons of the administrative court system are summarized in J. W. Garner, *Political Science and Government,* 785-791. A good brief account of the administrative courts of France will be found in E. M. Sait, *Government and Politics of France,* Chap. xi; of those of Germany, in F. F. Blachly and M. E. Oatman, *The Government and Administration of Germany,* Chap. xiv. In earlier editions of his *Law of the Constitution,* Mr. Dicey described the French system very unfavorably. In the edition now current (8th) he admits that his former views were based in part upon misinformation (see Chap. xii). In general, the Continental plan is regarded more favorably—at least is discussed more sympathetically—in English-speaking lands today than a generation ago.

i.e., to determine the merits of the controversy. The parties may at any time agree to give up litigation and reach a settlement out of court, a thing which can never be done in criminal proceedings.

The court in which a civil action will be brought depends mainly on the amount of the claim. If the sum is less than £100, or if, in equity cases, the value of the property about which the dispute arose is not more than £500, the suit will probably be instituted in a county court. The county courts of the present day, established by a parliamentary statute of 1846, replace, although they are not historically descended from, the ancient courts of the hundred and county. They are known as county courts, but in point of fact they are no part of the county organization and the area of their jurisdiction is a district which not only is smaller than the county but bears no relation to it. There are in England and Wales at present some four hundred and fifty of these districts, each with its own "court house," the object of maintaining such a number being to bring the agencies of justice close to the people and so to reduce the costs and delays incident to litigation. The volume of business to be transacted is very great; indeed, a million and a quarter cases are disposed of every year. Only a few of the most important of these cases, however, are actually handled by the county judges. The districts are grouped in fifty-five circuits, to each of which is assigned by the Lord Chancellor one judge, who holds court in each district of his circuit approximately once a month. But in every place where a county court sits there is a register in charge of the records of the court, and he disposes of the great majority of cases without referring them to the judge at all. Both judges and registers are paid out of the national treasury (the judges receive £1,500 a year) and hold office during good behavior.

Procedure in the county court is simple, both plaintiff and defendant frequently conducting their cases themselves. Where the amount in dispute exceeds £5, either party may demand a jury (which for this purpose consists of eight persons); but this is rarely done. Where there is a jury, it finds a verdict on the facts proved, under the direction of the judge; where there is none, the judge decides on the facts and on the law, and in either case he gives a judgment for the plaintiff or the defendant, which is enforced by seizure of the property of the party who fails to obey it, or even by imprisonment. The object of civil proceedings is, however, compensation, not punishment. On a point of law, an appeal can be taken to a "divisional sitting" of the High Court of Justice, though no further without leave of the latter or of the Court of Appeal. On matters of fact, there is technically no appeal from the verdict of a jury. An application may be, and often is, made, however, to a divisional court to order a new trial, on the ground that the judge instructed the jury wrongly, or that the jury's verdict was palpably not supported by the evidence before it.[8]

Where the plaintiff's claim exceeds the jurisdiction of the county court, he must, and, even if it does not, he may, bring his action first of all in the High Court of Justice. As already indicated, this High Court is organized in three divisions—Chancery, King's Bench, and Probate, Divorce, and Admiralty. In theory, any kind of civil action can be begun in any one of these divisions; and there is no limit to the importance of the actions that may be tried there. In practice, each division retains the kind of business that it inherited from the tribunals out of which it was formed. Under varying conditions, too complex to be detailed here, the judges (whose number is also variable) sit singly and in groups—although never as one body—at the capital [9] and on circuit. Appeals on points of law are carried from the divisional courts to the Court of Appeal. Technically, there is no appeal on questions of fact, but here again an application may be made—to the Court of Appeal, of course—to order a new trial. This last-mentioned exalted tribunal consists of the Lord Chancellor, three other high judicial personages sitting by ex-officio right, and, as the actual working members, six Lords Justices of Appeal specially appointed by the crown on nomination of the Lord Chancellor. All sittings take place at London, and usually in two sections, each consisting of three of the specially appointed judges; no witnesses

[8] On the county courts, see S. Rosenbaum, "Studies in English Civil Procedure: the County Courts," in *Pa. Law Rev.*, Feb., Mar., Apr., 1916; *Report of the Lord Chancellor's Committee on the County Courts,* Cmd. 431 (1919).

[9] At the Law Courts, in Fleet Street.

are heard; there is no jury; and the business, chiefly hearing appeals in civil cases from the different divisions of the High Court, is exclusively appellate. The decisions take the form of affirmation, reversal, or alteration of the judgment of the lower court. Beyond the Court of Appeals the dissatisfied litigant has still one more appeal on questions of law, if he can stand the delay and expense, i.e., to the House of Lords.

Criminal Actions—Magistrates and Courts

A criminal case is one in which the king (that is to say, in these days, the *government*), "prosecutes" a person who is alleged to have committed an offense, such as murder, theft, or forgery, in order that the accused, if found guilty, may be punished. Four distinct steps, or processes, are involved. First, there must be a definite accusation by a person who professes to know of the commission of the offense. Then there must be proof of the facts. After that there must be an authoritative statement of the rule which the offender is alleged to have broken. Finally, if the offense is proved, there must be condemnation and punishment. In primitive forms of justice, all of these steps are likely to be taken by the same person. The avenger is accuser, witness, judge, and executioner in one. In civilized justice, however, it is axiomatic that the several steps shall not only be separated in time, but shall also be taken by different persons. It is true that the government seems to be, and in the last analysis is, both prosecutor and judge; and throughout a long portion of the history of criminal justice in England the scales were on that account heavily weighted against the accused. The difficulty has in modern times been got round, however, by arrangements under which the government's (technically, the king's) functions in the two capacities are performed by entirely different sets of officials—by the "law officers of the crown" and other public prosecutors in the one instance, and by "His Majesty's judges" in the other. Whatever remained of the earlier stigma was completely removed by the Act of Settlement of 1701, which guaranteed judges security of tenure during good behavior and also salaries "ascertained and established." Under this protection, judges, although officers of the crown, may perform their duties in entire independence of the wishes of prosecutors, ministers, or king, and without risk of removal or reduction of salary.

When a person is accused of having committed a criminal offense, he is formally summoned, or arrested and brought, first of all, before one or more justices of the peace, or, in London and the larger boroughs, before a "stipendiary" magistrate (so called because, unlike the ordinary justice, he receives a salary).[10] Dating from the early fourteenth century, the office of justice of the peace has played a very important rôle in the development both of local administration and of justice. "The whole Christian world," declared Coke, "hath not the like office, if truly executed." The normal field of operations of the justices is the county, although certain boroughs have also a "commission of the peace;" and, aside from sundry persons who attain the office on an ex-officio basis,[11] the justices in any given county are appointed "at the pleasure of the crown," by the Lord Chancellor, usually on recommendation of the lord lieutenant of the county, who himself is chief of the justices and keeper of the county records.[12] In many counties the list of justices contains three or four hundred names; in Lancashire it reaches beyond eight hundred; and the number in the country as a whole is hardly short of twenty thousand. But almost half of the appointees never take the oath required to qualify them for magisterial service, and the actual work is performed in each county by a comparatively small number of persons. As has been indicated, the justices serve without pay; but the office carries much local distinction, and appointments are widely sought, Formerly, the justices were, in the main, country gentlemen; but men (and, since 1919, women also) are now appointed freely from all professions and social classes, with the result that the magistracy is far less aristocratic than even a genera-

[10] The stipendiary magistrates are barristers (see p. 628 below) and receive appointment from the Home Office. By virtue of their offices, they become justices of the peace. They have some powers not belonging to other justices.

[11] E.g., the mayor of a borough is a justice of the peace during his year of office and for twelve months afterwards.

[12] Until 1906, a property qualification (ownership of land, or occupation of a house worth £100 a year) was required of all save certain classes of appointees whose station was deemed a sufficient guarantee of fitness; but no such qualification is now imposed.

tion ago. The withdrawal of practically all administrative functions (chiefly in 1888) and the diminution of political influences on appointments have also made for improvement. Unlike judges, the justices do not, as a rule, have any particular professional or legal qualifications when appointed. Those of them, however, who actually render service gradually gain such qualifications from experience, and the system, although open to serious theoretical objections, admittedly works very satisfactorily.[13]

When the accused is brought before the "J. P." that official can himself dispose of the case if the offense is a minor one, e.g., neglecting to take out a license or riding a bicycle after dark without a light. But he cannot impose a higher penalty then twenty shillings or sentence to imprisonment for more than fourteen days. If the offense is of a more serious nature, the justice's duty is, in the first place, merely to see whether there is a prima facie case against the accused. For this purpose, he hears the evidence, usually sworn testimony, of the prosecutor and his witnesses. There is no jury, and the accused need not make any statement or offer any defense unless he likes. If, after the hearing, the justice feels that no prima facie case has been made out, i.e., that no jury would convict even if the prosecutor's evidence were unchallenged, he dismisses the charge, and the accused goes free. If, however, he thinks that a prima facie case has been established, he "commits the prisoner for trial," and decides whether to let him out on bail or to have him confined to await further proceedings. If the privilege of bail is refused, the prisoner may apply, by a writ of habeas corpus, to a judge of the High Court of Justice for an order compelling it to be granted.

The court in which the trial will take place is determined mainly by the seriousness of the case. A large and increasing number of offenses, including petty assaults and thefts, small breaches of public order, and other minor misdemeanors—and even graver offenses if the accused wishes, or if it is a first

[13] For a good brief account of the office of justice of the peace, see D. J. Medley, *Manual of English Constitutional History* (6th ed.), 419-427, and for full historical treatment, C. A. Beard, "The Office of Justice of the Peace in England," in *Columbia Univ. Studies in Hist., Econ., and Pub. Law,* xx, No. 1 (New York, 1904).

charge, or if he is under age—are "punishable on summary conviction." The court of summary conviction is composed of at least two justices of the peace (usually resident in the immediate neighborhood), and is known as "petty sessions." The trial is public and without a jury, and the accused is given full opportunity to be heard and to have the benefit of counsel. If the court finds the man guilty, it imposes a fine or a limited period of imprisonment. He may, however, appeal to "quarter sessions," which consists of all the justices in the county [14] (meeting quarterly) who have taken the oath and who care to go to the trouble of attending. Here his case will be heard again from beginning to end.[15]

In graver cases the accused is proceeded against by formal "indictment," or written statement charging him with a definite crime committed in a particular way; and he is entitled to a copy of this indictment before his trial. An indictment case is tried either before quarter sessions or "at assizes," assize courts being held three times a year in all counties and four times in certain cities, and presided over normally by a judge of the High Court of Justice who goes out "on circuit" for the purpose. Wherever the trial takes place, the accused is entitled to have his fate decided by a jury of twelve of his countrymen, chosen at random by the sheriff from a list of householders compiled by the local authorities; and he has an almost unlimited privilege of "challenging," i.e., objecting to, the jurors selected. It is the business of the judge (or judges) throughout the trial to see that the rules of procedure and evidence are followed; and after counsel for both sides have completed the examination of witnesses and have addressed the jury, the presiding judge sums up the case and gives the jurors any instructions about the law that may be necessary to enable them to arrive at a just verdict on the facts. If the jury finds the prisoner not guilty, he is forthwith discharged; and he can never again be tried on the same accusation. If, on the other hand, it finds him guilty, the judge pronounces the sentence provided by law; although, except in capital cases, he has considerable discretion,

[14] There are quarter sessions in some boroughs also.

[15] Petty sessions may also handle certain cases of a civil nature, chiefly disputes between employers and servants.

within fixed limits. If the jury cannot agree, there may be a new trial, with a different set of jurors.

Formerly there was no appeal from the verdict of a jury in a criminal trial, although appeal lay to the House of Lords on points of law. An act of 1907, however, set up a Court of Criminal Appeal consisting of not fewer than three judges of the King's (or Queen's) Bench; and a convicted person may now, as a matter of right, appeal to this tribunal on any question of law, and (with the permission of either the trial judge or of the Court of Criminal Appeal itself) on any question of fact, e.g., that the verdict of the jury was not justified by the evidence. If the appellate court thinks that there has been a serious miscarrage of justice, it can modify the sentence, or even quash the conviction altogether. There can be no appeal beyond the Court of Criminal Appeal, except to the House of Lords upon a point of law which one of the "law officers of the crown," the Attorney-General, certifies to be of public importance. Under no circumstances can the prosecutor appeal.[16]

The House of Lords as a Court

From the foregoing outline it is apparent that both civil and criminal cases may, under certain conditions, run a gamut which ends only in the House of Lords, so that the last word will be spoken by that august body. That Parliament as a whole was at one time primarily a court rather than a legislature supplies ample historical reason why the House of Lords should even today combine the most weighty judicial duties with law-making functions to which, as we have seen, it clings somewhat precariously.[17] Not so long ago, the House laid claim

[16] A standard treatise on English criminal justice is G. G. Alexander, *The Administration of Justice in Criminal Matters* (Cambridge, 1915). A good brief discussion from an American point of view is J. D. Lawson and E. R. Keedy, "Criminal Procedure in England," *Amer. Jour. of Crim. Law and Criminology,* Nov., 1910, and Jan., 1911. The latest major statute on criminal justice is the Criminal Justice Administration Act of 1914, although the Administration of Justice Act of 1928 made some important additions. American machinery and methods may be compared in detail by using R. Moley, *Politics and Criminal Prosecution* (New York, 1929), and *The Long Day in Court* (New York, 1929).

[17] The historical aspects of the judicial functions of Parliament are dealt with in thorough fashion in C. H. McIlwain, *The High Court of Parliament and Its Supremacy,* cited above.

to very great powers of original, as well as appellate, jurisdiction; and although the former is now largely restricted to matters pertaining to its own membership, and especially the claims of persons who seek to establish a right of membership,[18] a broad appellate jurisdiction—starting with control, through appeal, over the courts of common law in England, and expanding to embrace a similar supremacy in both civil and criminal actions over all British and Irish tribunals (and in civil, but not criminal, actions over all Scottish tribunals) except those of an ecclesiastical nature—is still maintained intact, save only that appeals from the courts of the recently created Irish Free State go, not to the House of Lords, but to the crown, and consequently are handled by the Judicial Committee of the Privy Council.[19]

On the ground that there was no guarantee that the House would contain judicial talent commensurate with its high responsibilities, a decision was reached in 1873 to abolish the body's appellate functions altogether; and the Judicature Act of that year contained a provision to this effect. Further consideration, however, led to a different solution of the problem. The statute was repealed before it took effect, and, as has been pointed out,[20] an Appellate Jurisdiction Act of 1876 introduced into the membership of the House two "lords of appeal in ordinary," who, being appointed for life (with salary) from men of high judicial standing, ensured the chamber against complete deficiency in legal knowledge and experience. The number of these special life members has since been increased to six; and in point of fact the judicial work of the House is now performed entirely by these half-dozen persons, together with the Lord Chancellor and occasionally other hereditary peers

[18] A privilege jealously maintained by the members of the House is, however, that of being tried in all cases of treason or felony (but not of misdemeanors) by their peers—which means by the second chamber itself, under the presidency of a Lord High Steward appointed by the crown if Parliament be sitting, otherwise by the court of the Steward, consisting of that official as judge, aided by a jury of peers summoned by him.

[19] This important agency, though not technically a court, fills a large place in the working judicial system. It functions principally in connection with appeals from the dominions and other overseas dependencies, and hence is dealt with in Chap. xxxi.

[20] See p. 328 above.

who hold, or have held, high judicial office. At least three of these "law lords" must hear and share in deciding any case that comes before the body. So far as the law goes, one member of the chamber has as much right to participate in judicial business as another. A sitting of the judicial members is technically a sitting of the House; the forms of procedure are those of a legislature, and not of a court; and all actions are entered in the Journal as part of the chamber's proceedings. Custom, however, though permitting visitors to look on from the galleries as during legislative sittings, decrees strictly that no members outside of the little group of law lords shall so much as be present at judicial sittings. The law lords, or any three of them, may sit and pronounce judgments at any time, regardless of whether Parliament is in session.[21] From such judgments there is no appeal; although, of course, they may be—but rarely are—in effect set aside by parliamentary legislation on lines contrary to those followed in the decisions.[22]

Reasons for the High Quality of British Justice

The British system of justice, both civil and criminal, deservedly enjoys an enviable reputation, both at home and abroad, for fairness, sureness, stability, and dignity. Foreign—especially American—lawyers and judges who go to England to observe its workings at close range rarely fail to return home

[21] When Parliament is in session the sittings of the law lords are held, as a rule, prior to the beginning of the regular sittings at 4:30 P.M.

[22] A good example of a House of Lords decision subsequently overridden in part by an act of Parliament is the Trade Unions and Trades Disputes Act of 1906 exempting trade unions from legal liabilities to which they were declared in the Taff Vale decision of 1901 to be subject. Another is the Trade Union Act of 1913 legalizing (with certain qualifications) political uses of trade union funds which the House of Lords, in the Osborne Judgment of 1909, had held improper. See F. A. Ogg and W. R. Sharp, *Economic Development of Modern Europe,* 412-418. It should be observed, of course, that the enactment of such subsequent legislation does not necessarily mean that the House of Lords has decided wrongly under the law existing at the time. It may mean only that a parliamentary majority, finding that the law, when tested in the highest court, has certain consequences, has concluded that the law itself ought to be changed.

On the House of Lords as a court see M. MacDonagh, *Book of Parliament,* 300-309; *ibid., The Pageant of Parliament,* II, 78-86; and W. S. Holdsworth, *History of English Law,* I, 170-193.

full of admiration for what they have seen.[23] There are other judicial systems, e.g., in France and Germany, which rest upon quite different principles, and for which much may be said. As systems developed by and for peoples with different backgrounds and ideas, they may be fully as defensible as the British. But if other evidence were lacking, the inherent excellence of the British system would be demonstrated by the close study of it, and large borrowings from it, made by peoples in all parts of the world, e.g., in Japan and China, who find it desirable to recast and modernize their inherited legal and judicial institutions. English law and justice have been hardly less influential in the world at large than English constitutional and governmental practice.

The explanation is to be found in three main phases or aspects of the system. The first has to do with the broad principles upon which justice is based, the second with the rules of procedure followed in the courts, and the third with the quality of bench and bar. A word may be said about each of these three matters.

Of underlying principles, some relate to the administration of justice generally, others to criminal justice particularly, and still others especially to civil justice. As viewed by an eminent English legal authority,[24] the rules of most general application are substantially as follows: 1. Judicial trials are held in open court, to which the public has free access. With the exception of a few opprobrious and short-lived tribunals such as the Elizabethan Court of High Commission, this practice has prevailed from time immemorial. There are many countries, however, in which judicial proceedings are conducted in secret.[25] 2. Both parties to a proceeding have a right to be represented by counsel, and to have their respective sides of the case heard by judge and jury. In some other systems of justice the accused, in criminal cases, is not necessarily entitled to be represented by

[23] See, for example, G. W. Alger, "The Irritating Efficacy of English Criminal Justice," *Atlantic Monthly,* Aug., 1928.

[24] E. Jenks, *The Book of English Law,* Chap. vii.

[25] The only surviving instances of the kind in Britain are cases in which children are required to give testimony involving decency or morality, cases involving trade processes unprotected by patents, and cases under certain "official secrets" acts.

skilled advisers. 3. The burden of proof rests, in almost every case, civil or criminal, on the accuser. 4. Guilt or innocence is established in accordance with a great body of recognized rules and maxims constituting "the law of evidence." 5. In all serious criminal cases the accused must be tried, not by a judge alone, but by a jury; and in civil cases involving an accusation against the moral character of either of the parties, that party may, if he desires, demand the verdict of a jury. 6. Judgment is rendered in open court, and, at least in the intermediate and higher courts, the judge or judges give the reasons for it. 7. In effect, if not in name, there is, in substantially all legal proceedings, at least one appeal to a higher tribunal from the decision of a court of first instance on a matter of law, and to a very large extent on matters of fact, so that the accused person, or, in civil cases, either party, has the right to submit his case to the judgment of at least two tribunals, acting independently of each other. The right of appeal has been widened considerably in our own times, notably by the creation of the Court of Criminal Appeals in 1907.

Examples of principles applicable only in criminal cases include: (1) before a person is formally placed on trial on a serious criminal charge, a preliminary inquiry is held before a magistrate (or magistrates) to determine whether there is a prima facie case against him; (2) with slight exceptions, no lapse of time operates to bar the crown from prosecuting, especially for serious offenses; (3) no accused person can be compelled to incriminate himself—a principle which follows logically from the English rule that an accused person is to be presumed innocent until proved guilty, but which is directly contrary to the inquisitorial method of justice employed in France and other Continental countries; and (4) legal aid must be assigned to "poor prisoners" at the county's expense. Similarly, examples of principles applicable only in civil cases are: (1) procedings may be begun without any preliminary inquiry as to the probability of the charges on which they are based being true; (2) proceedings, being of a purely private character, can be abandoned or compromised at any time by the parties, and without the permission of any court; and (3) after a comparatively short lapse of time, a plaintiff who has not enforced his rights is barred from doing so, e.g., by the rule of prescription in connection with the possession of land.

Not only do the British courts operate under salutary principles such as those enumerated, but they are favorably situated in the matter of rules of procedure. In the United States the rules which govern pleading, evidence, and all other aspects of court procedure emanate mainly—in many states entirely—from legislative bodies, not from the courts themselves. This means that they are made by men who not only have not had judicial experience but in many instances are not even lawyers, at all events of large experience and ability. The results are unsatisfactory, and there is a considerable movement for procedural regulation by court-made rules instead of by statutes.[26] In England, full power of rule-making is vested in a rules committee, consisting of the Lord Chancellor, seven other important judges, and four practicing lawyers—a decidedly expert body representing, as will be observed, both bench and bar. This very satisfactory arrangement dates from the judicial reforms of 1873. Originally, procedure was governed solely by the custom of the tribunal, and for a long time changes were made only by practice or by court-made rules, with Parliament occasionally intervening to create new remedial rights or to cut off old procedural abuses. In the nineteenth century, popular dislike of various features of existing procedure found expression in more vigorous regulation by the reformed Parliament.[27] A Civil Procedure Act of 1833 abolished a number of anomalies, and a Common Law Procedure Act of 1852 supplied a fairly complete procedural code. In these and other measures, however, the right of the judges to make such alterations in the rules of pleading and practice as they found desirable was fully recognized, and the Judicature Act of 1873 created the present rules committee and in effect turned over to it the entire task of rule-making. It is true that all new and revised rules must still be laid before Parliament, which, if it

[26] See a note on this subject by C. B. Whittier in *Amer. Polit. Sci. Rev.*, Nov., 1926. Cf. E. R. Sunderland, "Exercise of the Rule-Making Power," *Jour. of Amer. Judicature Soc.*, Oct., 1926, and R. Pound, "The Rule-Making Power of the Courts," *ibid.*, Dec., 1926.

[27] E. R. Sunderland, "The English Struggle for Procedural Reform," *Harvard Law Rev.*, Apr., 1926.

likes, may disallow them. But in point of fact the committee's work has been so well performed that no occasion for a parliamentary veto has ever arisen.[28]

The outstanding characteristics of the procedure thus developed and regulated are its expeditiousness, its indifference to mere technicalities, its emphasis upon the maintenance of an unobstructed road to substantial justice. The rules repose solidly on the principle that every action should proceed promptly to a decision on its merits, and that the parties ought never to be turned out of court because of some error in practice or procedure which in no way involves the merits of the controversy. "The relation of rules of practice to the work of justice," says a great English judge, "is intended to be that of handmaid rather than mistress, and the court ought not to be so far bound and tied by rules, which are after all intended only as general rules of procedure, as to be compelled to do what will cause injustice in a particular case." Herein is to be found the reason why less than one-half of one per cent of all cases are decided upon appeal on questions of practice and procedure. In the American states a great deal of trouble, and a considerable amount of injustice, arises not only from the pettifogging tactics of lawyers but from inflexible rules laid down by well-meaning but inexpert legislatures. There have been jurisdictions in which as high as fifty per cent of the cases reversed on appeal were decided upon questions of practice and procedure which in no way involved the merits of the controversy.

Needless to say, the superior adaptation of procedure to the ends in view is a main reason why justice is both surer and speedier in Britain than in most other countries. The calendars of the courts do not become clogged; a murder trial will often be carried through all of its stages while an American court would still be laboring over the empanelling of a jury. But there are other favorable circumstances, connected still more directly with the character of bench and bar. British judges are,

[28] Besides the formally enunciated rules—now grown bulky and often highly technical—there are numerous "rules of etiquette" which every member of bench and bar is expected to observe. There is no definite penalty for infraction of these rules; they are matters of courtesy and comity only. But there are practical ways of making life uncomfortable for persons who violate the professional code.

in general, of a high order of ability, independence, and integrity. One reason would seem to lie in the fact that the judiciary is entirely appointive; and not only the judges themselves, but court officers such as sheriffs and clerks. Not even the justices of the peace are elected. Nominated in the various counties by the lords lieutenant,[29] the latter are appointed by the Lord Chancellor, in the name of the king; and all members of the judiciary proper—of county courts, of High Court, of Court of Appeal—owe their positions to selection made primarily by the same powerful official. An elective judiciary did not work well in Revolutionary France and was soon given up; and it shows plenty of defects in most of our American states. Neither England nor any part of the British Empire has ever thought it wise to permit judges to be subjected to the political hazards and temptations that almost inevitably go along with an elective system. In France and Germany, judges are regularly appointed from among persons specifically and professionally trained for the bench. In Britain, as in the United States, this is not the case; judges are selected, rather, from among practicing lawyers. Under British usage, however, members of the county courts must be barristers of at least seven years' standing, which in the case of members of the High Court is increased to ten years, and in that of members of the Court of Appeal to fifteen years.

In the second place, the independence which flows from appointment rather than election is enhanced by life tenure,[30] and, further, by a security of position which arises from the fact that, while legally removals can be made by the Lord Chancellor, in practice none take place except on joint address of the two houses of Parliament. Removals are quite as rare as they are in the national judiciary of the United States, which, unlike the state judiciaries, is appointive as in Britain. In the third place, judicial positions in Britain are made attractive by much higher salaries than are paid in Continental Europe, or in the United States, even since the salary increases recently granted our federal judges. Judges of the county courts, whose jurisdiction includes all of the cases tried by the ordinary jus-

[29] See p. 653 below.

[30] The legal phrase is *quamdiu se bene gesserint*.

tice of the peace in the United States, receive £1,300 a year, which is more than is paid to most justices in the various state supreme courts of this country; while the salaries paid in the Supreme Court of Judicature range from £5,000 for the ordinary justice of the trial and appellate branches to £8,000 for the Lord Chief Justice and £10,000 for the Lord Chancellor—double or triple the salaries of justices of corresponding grade on this side of the Atlantic. Further dignity and distinction are lent by the practice of knighting judges upon their appointment. All this helps to secure and to retain brains, character, and energy.

On the side of the bar, a useful feature is the division of labor arising from the distinction between solicitors, or attorneys, who deal directly with clients and prepare cases, and barristers, who are engaged by the solicitors to conduct the cases for them before the courts. Each type of lawyer becomes expert in his special kind of work, and the results show in both the thoroughness with which cases are worked up and the skill with which they are handled after having been prepared. We have no arrangement of this sort in the United States, although of course it is not uncommon for certain members of a legal firm to devote themselves primarily to work in the office and others mainly to appearance in the court-room. In England a judge is master of his court-room, furthermore, to a greater extent than in America, and this makes for speed and efficiency as well as dignity.[31]

Judicial Review and Judge-made Law

The point has been sufficiently stressed elsewhere, but should not be overlooked here, that there is in Britain nothing analogous to what we know in the United States as judicial review. It is true that laws enacted in the overseas dominions, in India, in the Irish Free State, and in the non-self-governing colonies may be pronounced unconstitutional; the colonial courts may refuse to enforce them on that ground, and they may be declared void at London. But this judicial review is exercised only by the crown, through the Judicial Committee. Appeals

[31] The English legal profession is described in E. Jenks, *The Book of English Law,* Chap. vi.

involving overseas statutes do not reach any court, in the strict sense, in England; and as for the statutes under which the cases arise that *do* come to the English courts, they must be accepted and applied without question being raised as to their validity. Any act of Parliament is *ipso facto* law; the judges must take it for what it purports to be and enforce it as such, as long as it stands on the statute book. There is no exception to the rule, even in the important domain of private rights. The right of the courts to review, and to declare *ultra vires,* orders in council and administrative rules involves no contravention of this principle. These orders and rules may indeed be of a legislative nature. But they have validity only in so far as they are in accordance with superior law (statutory or otherwise), and the sole object of the judges in reviewing them is to uphold the supremacy of the law, itself non-reviewable, on which they purport to be grounded.

British courts are therefore relieved of a burden which rests heavily upon our higher tribunals in the United States, and which is falling upon the courts of Germany, Austria, and some other Continental countries in steadily increasing degree.[32] This does not mean, however, that their task is an altogether simple one. Like courts everywhere else, they still have a great deal to do with determining what the enforceable law really is. In the first place, the statutes have to be interpreted; and notwithstanding the rather exceptional clarity of the average British parliamentary measure, this power to construe often goes far toward making a statute mean much or little. It is not a matter merely of saying what Parliament intended when the measure was passed. A question presented by a case arising under a statute may manifestly not have been contemplated or envisaged by Parliament at all, and the statute may therefore have no conscious intent or meaning in relation to the matter in hand. In such a situation it falls to the judges to determine, not what the legislature meant, but what it probably would have meant if the question at issue had occurred to it—"to

[32] For a brief comparative survey of the development of judicial review, see J. W. Garner, *Political Science and Government,* 754-773. Cf. F. F. Blachly and M. E. Oatman, "Judicial Review of Legislative Acts in Germany," *Amer. Polit. Sci. Rev.,* Feb., 1927, and C. J. Friedrich, "The Issue of Judicial Review in Germany," *Polit. Sci. Quar.,* June, 1928.

guess what it would have intended on a point not present, if the point had been present." This, it will be perceived, is a difficult, not to say delicate, function. In discharging it, English judges, like judges everywhere, declare and in effect make law.[33] Finally, in the total absence of statutory provision directly, or even indirectly, covering a question at issue, it devolves upon the judges to decide what is the common law relating to the matter. The rules which are pertinent may, of course, be obvious and explicit. On the other hand, there may be room for doubt, in which event opportunity arises to influence by the decision made the entire future development of the common law upon the subject.

There is much difference of opinion upon the merits of judge-made law, and many English (and other) authorities prefer to speak of judges as "discovering" or "interpreting," rather than as "making," law. As Dicey remarks, however, while it is true that an English judge is primarily an interpreter, and not a maker, of law, he does, by interpretation, make law, and it is immaterial whether we call such law "judge-made" or something else.[34] As was pointed out earlier in the present chapter, the great body of English law originated, and has been continuously remodeled, at the hands of the judiciary. Not only that, but judges from one end of the land to the other are still busily reworking the legal fabric, equally with Parliament itself.[35]

[33] An interesting discussion of the possibilities of judicial construction in relation to a recent statute of prime importance will be found in A. T. Mason, "The British Trade Disputes Act of 1927," *Amer. Polit. Sci. Rev.*, Feb., 1928. Cf. H. J. Laski, "Judicial Review of Social Policy in England," *Harvard Law Rev.*, May, 1926.

[34] *Law and Public Opinion in England,* 359, note 2.

[35] The best treatises on the development of the English courts are W. S. Holdsworth, *History of English Law,* I, and A. T. Carter, *History of English Legal Institutions* (4th ed., London, 1910); to which may be added the latter author's briefer *History of the English Courts* (London, 1927). The origin of the courts of common law is treated in G. B. Adams, *Council and Courts in Anglo-Norman England,* Chap. viii, and the county court is dealt with in W. A. Morris, *The Early English County Court* (Berkeley, 1926). Useful brief accounts of the courts as they now are include A. L. Lowell, *Government of England,* II, Chaps. lix-lx; C. F. G. Masterman, *How England Is Governed,* Chaps. xi-xii; E. Jenks, *The Book of English Law,* Chaps. v-vii; and J. A. R. Marriott, *The Mechanism of the Modern*

State, II, Chap. xxxii. G. G. Alexander, *Administration of Justice* (Cambridge, 1915), describes court procedure, especially in criminal cases; and E. A. Parry, *The Law and the Poor* (New York, 1914), and C. Chapman, *The Poor Man's Court of Justice; Twenty-five Years as a Metropolitan Magistrate* (London, 1926), tell of the workings of the judicial system in first-hand and interesting fashion. The author of the last-mentioned book was for twenty years an English county court judge. W. E. Higgins, "English Courts and Procedure," *Jour. of Amer. Judicature Soc.,* VII, 185-234 (Apr., 1924), is a useful compendium. Comparisons with the American system may readily be made by using C. N. Callender, *American Courts; Their Organization and Procedure* (New York, 1927); and R. Pound, "Organization of Courts [English and American]," *Jour. of Amer. Judicature Soc.,* Oct., 1927, is an illuminating discussion. Comparisons with the French system may be made by using E. M. Sait, *The Government and Politics of France,* Chap. xii; with the German, by consulting F. F. Blachly and M. E. Oatman, *The Government and Administration of Germany,* Chap. xiii.

CHAPTER XXVII

LOCAL GOVERNMENT AND ADMINISTRATION: THE COUNTY

It is a curious commentary on human nature that most people take a livelier interest in the government of their country than in that of their home community. The average American knows more about the president than about the mayor of his city, follows the doings of Congress more closely than those of his county board of supervisors, is more likely to go to the polls when a senator is to be elected than a councilman, and could come nearer telling you what the navy costs per year than what is paid out for the public schools or the police establishment of his city. After all, this is, perhaps, not unnatural. The government of the nation is a big and impressive affair. It does things on a grand scale, challenging the attention and sometimes staggering the imagination. It gets the headlines in the newspapers. It appeals to pride and patriotism as local governments seldom do. Nevertheless, the government of one's home district—city, county, or what not—is really a matter of prime importance. The bulk of what one pays in taxes is spent within a few miles of the spot where it is paid. Schools, streets, roads, hospitals, parks and playgrounds are provided and managed principally by the authorities of the neighborhood. Life and property are protected by local police. Health is safeguarded mainly by local ordinances and officers. Furthermore, local government areas are the training grounds of efficient citizenship, the reservoirs from which talent and experience are drawn for the conduct of public affairs in their wider and loftier ranges.

Any one who sets about a study of the organization and character of local government in modern Britain comes at once upon two or three major facts. The first is that community feeling has always been strong and the people exceptionally interested in managing their local affairs in their own way. "The United Kingdom, and especially England," says a British writer, "was, at one time, emphatically a land of local institutions. Settled in the days when the means of intercourse over wide spaces were few and difficult, by a primitive people with no experience of civilized government, it naturally became a country of strong local interests, whose scattered little communities were absorbed in their own affairs, and knew little, if anything, beyond their own boundaries. Their isolation is attested by many unmistakable signs; one of the most striking being the fact that, until so late as the eleventh or twelfth century, one village might be in the throes of a famine, whilst another, not forty miles away, had a surplus of corn. People living in the east of England could hardly understand the speech of those living in the west. An old English poem speaks of it as a common practice to shoot at sight any stranger who came over the village boundary without blowing his horn. . . . Much of the Englishman's aptitude for self-government is, doubtless, due to this long history of local isolation."[1] However far these historical facts may go toward supplying the correct explanation, it is unquestionably true that devotion to and success in the art of self-government have characterized the Englishman not only in the home land but wherever else he has taken up his abode. We in America have, of course, profited enormously from his aptitude in this direction.

A second main fact is that while local government in the British Isles is older than the national government by hundreds of years, and has had an even more unbroken history, it has been progressively adapted to new conditions through the centuries and is today very different from what it was even a generation ago. Historic counties and boroughs survive, but their organization and functions have changed; the justices of the peace still flourish, but their once impressive administrative authority is practically gone; the gorgeously appareled sheriff lends picturesqueness to the scene as of yore, but not as the towering figure he once was. New jurisdictions have been laid out, new elective bodies called into being, new administrative

[1] E. Jenks, *Government of the British Empire,* 304.

offices created, new methods—often more prosaic, but presumably more efficient—introduced. Local government, like other parts of the constitutional system, has been a living, growing, changing thing, with the result, we may believe, of having become better suited in our day to the tasks devolving upon it than perhaps at any previous time. Furthermore, the local institutions of Britain give more play for initiative and control by the people who are governed under them than do those of France, Germany, and other Continental states. Some writers—for example, Freeman—have pictured English democracy in shire and borough with a good deal of exaggeration; certainly the democracy of most shires and boroughs, until rather recent days, was of a very restricted nature. Nevertheless, by and large, there was more local self-government in medieval and early modern Britain than was known elsewhere save perhaps in the Swiss cantons after the thirteenth century; and in our own day one would have to search far and wide to find a system of local government in which sound principles of popular rule—which does not necessarily mean a maximum amount of direct popular participation—operate more effectively. Though closely linked up with Whitehall and Westminster, English local institutions stand on their own feet in a sense in which the local institutions of France, Germany, and many other countries cannot be said to do so.

Finally, the system as we observe it today, while less symmetrical than the French, is uniform throughout England and Wales (except for special arrangements in metropolitan London),[2] and even in Scotland and Ireland it presents variations which for the most part are not fundamental. It is more complicated than the French, Belgian, or German, but no more so than the scheme found in some of our American states, and it is decidedly simpler than it was fifty or sixty years ago. The number of separate jurisdictions has been reduced, the interrelation of authorities made more clear, the guiding hand of the national government strengthened. The scheme can therefore be described with reasonable accuracy on general lines, without necessity of mentioning any large number of variations or exceptions.

[2] See pp. 673-677 below.

Local Government a Hundred Years Ago

One who proposes to trace the history of English local government is led all the way back to Anglo-Saxon times, when the country is first found covered over with shires, hundreds, townships, and boroughs, each with its own elected or appointed authorities. Those were days of large local independence—the "golden age of local government," they have been termed—for kingship was weak and centralized control almost unknown. After the Norman Conquest, things changed considerably. The Saxon shire became the Norman county; the hundreds gradually disappeared; many of the townships were converted into feudal manors; new units known as parishes—often also corresponding to old townships—made their appearance, first for uses of the church, but later becoming areas of civil government as well. In an era of strong royal power, furthermore, the local jurisdictions were brought under considerably closer control by the national government, especially in matters of finance and justice. After the fourteenth century, however, changes were relatively few for hundreds of years. The principal areas of local government continued to be the county, the borough, and the parish. Central control was at times stronger, and again weaker, but never pervasive enough to deprive the people locally of effective direction of their own affairs. In days of Tudor and Stuart autocracy, when for long stretches of time Parliament was never once called into session, local authorities continued to function, local elections to be held, and local bodies to make ordinances and levy imposts, keeping alive the principle of self-rule which, notwithstanding appearances to the contrary, still underlay the English constitutional system.

At the opening of the nineteenth century there were fifty-two counties, mostly of Saxon origin, although some dated from later extensions of the kingdom northward and westward or from other political or administrative changes. The last to be created were those of Wales. In Saxon times, and for many a day after, the chief figure in county affairs was the sheriff. He still existed when the nineteenth century opened, as an officer appointed by and representing the central government;

and there was a lord lieutenant, in charge of military matters, besides coroners and certain other officials. But as far back as the fourteenth century a new type of authority had been called into being, the justice of the peace; and by the days of which we are speaking county government was almost completely in the hands of these numerous and interesting local dignitaries. At first the justices were—as their name suggests—simply peace officers. But the king had found them increasingly serviceable in the administration of highways, poor relief, and similar matters, and practically all such functions had now been concentrated in their hands.[3] These justices were appointed by the crown, mainly from the ranks of the lesser landowners and the rural clergy, and of course represented the point of view of the gentry rather than of the lesser folk of the county. There was no provision for a council or other popular organ, so that by no stretch of the imagination could the government of the county be called democratic.[4]

A trace of democracy was, it is true, to be found in the management of affairs in the chief subdivision of the county, i.e., the civil parish, a unit which usually but not invariably coincided with the ecclesiastical parish.[5] The governing bodies of

[3] The law creating the office of justice of the peace, dating from the first year of Edward III's reign (1327), provided that in every county "good men and lawful" should be assigned to "keep the peace." Even before Edward's death, in 1377, the growth of the justices' administrative functions had actively begun; and so enormously did they multiply that by Queen Elizabeth's time complaint is heard that the backs of the justices were being broken by "not loads, but stacks, of statutes." "The justices of the peace," wrote the Elizabethan court secretary Thomas Smith, "be those . . . in whom the Prince putteth his special trust." By the creation and development of the office of justice of the peace, "it was decided that, for the future, local administration and jurisdiction in England should be entrusted, not to official delegates of the crown, sent like the *vice-comes* from the center of the state to its circumference, but to landed gentry or enfranchised burgesses living in the locality and only appointed by the central authority." J. Redlich and F. W. Hirst, *Local Government in England* (London, 1903), I, 13. The institution of the justices was thus a significant landmark in the struggle against the centralizing tendencies of government manifest in the Norman-Angevin period.

[4] The classic description of county government before the reforms of the nineteenth century is S. and B. Webb, *English Local Government from the Revolution to the Municipal Corporations Act: the Parish and the County* (London, 1906), Bk. II, Chaps. i-vi.

[5] In at least the southern and more densely populated parts of the coun-

the typical parish were two—the vestry (either open to all ratepayers or composed of elected representatives), which had general powers of administration, and the overseers of the poor, who, under an Elizabethan statute of 1601, were authorized to find employment for the able-bodied poor, to provide such other forms of relief as should be required, and to levy a local rate to meet the costs of their work. Since 1782, however, the parishes had been arranged in groups for poor-law purposes, and guardians appointed for these larger poor-law areas by the justices of the peace had come to be the real authorities in the administration of poor relief, as well as in most other essentially parochial matters. The abuses arising from poor-law administration were frequently appalling.[6]

The boroughs, numbering somewhat over two hundred at the opening of the century, were more or less populous places which in times past—in some cases as early as the twelfth and thirteenth centuries—had received charters from the crown, and accordingly had become separate and privileged areas of local government. There were no fixed principles of procedure in the matter, so that some boroughs were populous and others were not and some enjoyed much autonomy and others less. Speaking generally, however, they managed their purely local affairs with little check or restraint. They did not stand entirely apart from the county and parish organization; on the contrary, except in so far as they were specifically exempted by the terms of their charters, they were subject to the authority of the justices of the peace and of the governing agencies of the parishes within whose jurisdiction they lay. Their form of government was determined mainly by the provisions of their charters, and since in this respect, as well as in the matter of

try, the church had adopted the old Anglo-Saxon township as the district of the parson or "parish priest." Gradually, especially in the thirteenth and fourteenth centuries, this ecclesiastical parish took on functions of civil administration, and eventually the civil parish became clearly distinguishable from the ecclesiastical, even when, as commonly, the two were geographically one and the same. J. Redlich and F. W. Hirst, *op. cit.*, I, 28-31. The history of parish organization and functions is told with great fullness in S. and B. Webb, *The Parish and the County* (as cited), Bk. I, Chaps. i-vii.

[6] The principal work on poor-laws and their administration from the sixteenth century to 1834 is S. and B. Webb, *English Poor Law History: Part i, The Old Poor Law* (London, 1927).

powers, the instruments were drawn according to no definite plan, plenty of variation resulted. As a rule, however, the borough was governed by a close corporation composed of the "burgesses," or freemen, originally fairly numerous, but later narrowed until in most cases only an insignificant fraction of the inhabitants were included. These freemen, such as they were, chose the mayor, aldermen, and councillors. The system smacked strongly of oligarchy, but it was favored by the crown —if for no other reason, because it made the boroughs easier to control.[7]

The Reform of Borough Government

In the old days the arrangements that have been described seemed to give reasonable satisfaction. At all events, we do not hear of a great deal of complaint until the closing decades of the eighteenth century. Then, however, the inadequacy of the system (if such spontaneous and heterogeneous arrangements can properly be called a system) became a subject of much thought and discussion. A main reason was the change of conditions produced by the Industrial Revolution—a circumstance which, as we have seen, had much to do with stimulating the late eighteenth-century movement for reform of the House of Commons. Population shifted suddenly, in great masses, from country to town; old boroughs sprang into new importance; new urban centers grew up, with populations doubling in a decade or less. Under the impact of this tremendous social and economic readjustment, the old and simple devices of

[7] The history of English municipal institutions to 1835 is set forth in great detail in H. A. Merewether and A. J. Stephens, *History of the Boroughs and Municipal Corporations of the United Kingdom,* 3 vols. (London, 1835), and in S. and B. Webb, *English Local Government from the Revolution to the Municipal Corporations Act: the Manor and the Borough* (Parts i and ii bound separately, London, 1908). The first of these works was written to stir up interest in municipal reform, and is marred by occasional faulty conclusions. The second is balanced, fair, and especially exhaustive, Part ii containing easily the best existing history of borough government. Borough organization in the later Middle Ages may be studied in A. Ballard and J. Tait, *British Borough Charters* (London, 1923), and borough political development is outlined conveniently in C. W. Colby, "The Growth of Oligarchy in English Towns," *Eng. Hist. Rev.,* Oct., 1890. C. Gross, *Bibliography of British Municipal History* (New York, 1897) is an invaluable guide to the voluminous literature of a complicated subject.

local government—especially municipal government—crumpled up. Growing industrial cities called loudly for larger powers and more machinery for police protection, sanitation, water-supply, street-construction, public lighting, housing control, and other necessary services; Parliament was besieged for legislation in behalf of this or that locality—responding, as a rule, with measures improvising special arrangements, i.e., commissions, boards, etc., which perhaps served the immediate purpose but left the system as a whole more heterogeneous and confused than before. Added to all this was, of course, the slowly growing demand, already heard in relation to Parliament, for the placing of government upon a somewhat more popular basis.[8]

Like the reform of Parliament, the reconstruction of local government was held back by the Napoleonic wars, and by the revulsion of feeling produced by the Continental revolutions, and in a period when France and various states under French influence or control were overhauling their local government systems from the ground up, the English system underwent no changes except of the hand-to-mouth variety just described. In 1832, however, the ice was broken by the first great measure of parliamentary reform, and thereafter the country had not long to wait for the local government problem to be taken up, even though it was at first attacked at only one or two points and was in no sense completely solved until days that men still living can well remember. Cautious, gradual, piecemeal reform was the method, as it was in the democratization of the House of Commons, and as it usually is in matters of the sort when the Englishman is concerned.

A start was made with the boroughs, for the reason that they had been affected most by the new industrial developments and stood in greatest need of attention.[9] In 1833 Scotland was

[8] The effects of the Industrial Revolution upon the life of the people, especially in the towns, are described in A. Toynbee, *The Industrial Revolution* (London, 1896). See J. Redlich and F. W. Hirst, *Local Government in England,* I, 63-97, for an excellent résumé of the trend of politics and political opinion between 1688 and 1832.

[9] Poor-law administration was, however, taken up at about the same time; and after a royal commission had made a substantial report a highly important Poor Law (Amendment) Act was passed in 1834. See J. Redlich

given a new law on the subject; in the same year a royal commission was set to work studying the needs of England and Wales; and in 1835, after investigation had been made in 285 boroughs and had brought to light amazing anomalies and shortcomings, a Municipal Corporations Act was passed which can be looked back to today as fixing the basis of all borough organization—and, indirectly, of most other local government organization as well—south of the Clyde.[10] The new law applied to a total of 178 boroughs, leaving many minor municipalities untouched, and also leaving London, as being too large and important to deserve any but exceptional and individual treatment, out of the reckoning.[11] The arrangements now provided, however, for the large number of places covered were a great improvement upon the past. In the first place, all charters, privileges, customs, usages, and rights inconsistent with the new plan were swept away, and all boroughs to which the law extended, as well as all that might thereafter receive charters of incorporation, were put upon a common basis and given a uniform style of organization. The corporation was thenceforth to be "the legal personification of the local community," elected by, acting for, and responsible to the inhabitants; and the governing organ was to be a council composed of members chosen

and F. W. Hirst, *op. cit.*, I, 98-111. S. and B. Webb, *English Poor Law History:* Pt. ii, *The Last Hundred Years,* 2 vols. (London, 1929), carries down to date the monumental treatise of which the first portion is mentioned above (see p. 637, note 6). Cf. E. Abbott, "The Webbs on the Poor Law," *Social Service Rev.*, June, 1929. G. Nichols and T. McKay, *History of the English Poor Laws* (London, 1912), is another standard treatise on the subject.

[10] The commission's report was published in April, 1835, in five volumes. The first volume contained the report proper, which was brief but thorough and definite; the other four presented the evidence on which it was based. In 1837 a separate report was submitted, dealing with the government of London, though Parliament did not get round to a reorganization of the government of the metropolis until a full generation afterwards. See p. 674 below. For selected portions of the report of 1835, see T. H. Reed and P. Webbink, *Documents Illustrative of American Municipal Government* (New York, 1926), 3-29. Cf. J. Redlich and F. W. Hirst, *op. cit.*, I, 113-123.

[11] Some of the municipal corporations antedating 1835, and being neither included in the schedules to the act of that year nor subsequently dealt with by charter, continued unreformed until 1883, when an act of Parliament provided that any such corporation as should not have obtained a fresh charter by 1886 should be abolished. How London was later dealt with is explained below (pp. 673-677.)

for a three-year term by the equal and direct votes of all the local taxpayers. Municipal oligarchy was thus replaced by municipal democracy. In the second place, the sphere of municipal autonomy, together with the relations between central and municipal authorities, was defined anew; and while the government at London was given increased powers of supervision and control, local rights of raising and spending money, controlling police, disposing of municipal property, making by-laws or ordinances, and appointing officers were guaranteed and in some instances augmented. Without uprooting the system that had come down through the centuries, the new law brought it back into conformity with the theory on which it was originally based and put it in shape for extension to new and larger urban populations as fast as they should develop.[12] Not only that, but it mapped out a scheme of local organization and procedure which legislation of the next sixty years generalized for the entire country. Counties, rural districts, urban districts, parishes—all were in time given representative institutions of the municipal pattern, with only such modifications as essential differences of situation demanded. "Local government has been municipalized," became the Englishman's way of summarizing the long line of legislation which ended in the county, district, and parish councils as we know them today.

Aside from the new poor law of 1834, which abolished outdoor relief for the able-bodied and placed the administration of relief in the hands of boards of guardians serving in new groups of parishes known as poor-law unions, no other significant local government legislation dated from this period. County government, too, was aristocratic and antiquated enough. But the acuter difficulties felt in the towns did not extend to the rural areas; the new poor law had helped the situation somewhat; the conservative landholding gentry entrenched in the counties was content with things as they were; and after 1832 county ratepayers, from whom the impetus to reform must naturally come, had decidedly less voice in Parlia-

[12] Fuller treatment of the Municipal Corporations Act will be found in W. B. Munro, *The Government of European Cities* (rev. ed., New York, 1927), Chap. i; J. Redlich and F. W. Hirst, *op. cit.*, I, 123-133; and S. and B. Webb, *The Manor and the Borough*, Pt. ii, Chap. xi.

ment than did borough ratepayers. Accordingly, it is not surprising that some fifty more statutes, amending the Corporations Act of 1835, found their way upon the books, and that a monumental Municipal Corporations Consolidation Act became both a necessity and a reality (in 1882), before any noteworthy changes whatsoever in county government took place.[13]

The Reform of Rural Local Government

After the middle of the century legislation on local government matters amassed rapidly. Some of it, as just indicated, related to borough affairs, but a great deal of it had to do more broadly with highways and other improvements, burial grounds, sanitation, and education, and involved setting up multifold new administrative areas—"improvement act" districts, school districts, and what not, manned with highway boards, conservancy boards, improvement act commissioners, sanitary boards, burial boards, school boards, and other similar agencies. All that was attempted was to provide for each fresh need as it arose by creating special machinery to meet that particular need, and the arrangements made were seldom or never uniform throughout the country, nor did they bear any logical relation to arrangements already operative for other purposes. By 1870 the field of local government was crowded with an almost impenetrable undergrowth of conflicting jurisdictions; as Lowell puts it, the country was divided into counties, unions, and parishes, and spotted over with boroughs and with highway, burial, sanitary, improvement act, school, and other districts; and of these areas none save the parishes and unions bore any necessary relation to any of the rest.[14] In the effort to adapt the administrative system to the fast changing conditions of a rapidly growing population, Parliament piled act upon act, the result being a sheer jungle of interlacing jurisdictions, baffling to the student and fatal to orderly and economical administra-

[13] This was not, however, for lack of proposals on the subject. A "county board" bill, introduced in the House of Commons in 1836, following a report by a special commission on county finance, represented only the first of a long series of attempts to substitute an elective county authority for the appointive justices of the peace. See J. Redlich and F. W. Hirst, *op. cit.*, I, 164-169.

[14] *Government of England,* II, 135.

tion. It is computed that in 1883 there were in England and Wales no fewer than 27,069 independent local authorities,[15] and that ratepayers were liable for eighteen different kinds of taxes.

The Education Act of 1870, which introduced a new set of school board districts, may be said to have marked the end of the indiscriminate multiplication of local government jurisdictions. Already the need of simplification and consolidation was recognized widely. In 1871 the Poor Law Board (which in 1847 superseded the Poor Law Commission created in 1834) was converted into the Local Government Board, with the purpose of concentrating in a single department the supervision of the laws relating to public health, the relief of the poor, and local government generally; and when, in 1872, the entire country was divided into urban and rural sanitary districts, the work was done in such a way as to entail the least possible addition to the existing complexities of the administrative system.[16] The two measures, however, which, in the main, brought order out of confusion were the Local Government Act of 1888 and the District and Parish Councils Act of 1894.[17] The first

[15] These included 52 counties, 239 municipal boroughs, 70 improvement-act districts, 1,006 urban sanitary districts, 577 rural sanitary districts, 2,051 school board districts, 424 highway districts, 853 burial board districts, 649 poor-law unions, 14,946 poor-law parishes, 5,064 highway parishes not included in urban or highway districts, and 1,300 ecclesiastical parishes. For the situation in 1888, see G. L. Gomme, *Lectures on the Principles of Local Government* (London, 1897), 12-13. Cf. E. S. Griffith, *The Modern Development of City Government in the United Kingdom and the United States* (London, 1927), I, Chap. iv.

[16] The legislation of 1872 resulted from an extensive investigation by a Royal Sanitary Commission appointed in 1868. The commission's report, submitted in 1871, clearly revealed the imperfections, not only of existing health administration, but of the whole scheme of rural local government. All existing laws relating to public health were revised, codified, and consolidated in the great Public Health Act of 1875. J. Redlich and F. W. Hirst, *op. cit.*, I, Chap. iii.

[17] These measures applied only to England and Wales. But local government was reorganized in Scotland, on somewhat different lines, under Local Government (Scotland) Acts of 1889 and 1894. The first of these statutes replaced the old "commissioners of supply" by a system of county councils like the English; the second set up parish councils which, like the former boards of guardians in England, administer the poor laws in urban areas. See J. J. Clark, *Local Government in the United Kingdom* (4th ed., London, 1927), Chap. xxxi.

of these (commonly referred to as the County Councils Act) was the sequel of the Municipal Corporations Consolidation Act of 1882 and the Representation of the People Act of 1884, being designed to apply the principles of the reformed borough system to county government, and at the same time to invest the newly enfranchised rural population with a larger control of county affairs. The act created sixty-two administrative counties (some being coterminous with the preëxisting historic counties, others being subdivisions of them), and sixty-one "county boroughs," which were towns of more than 50,000 inhabitants.[18] In each county and county borough was set up a council elected by the people and endowed with large powers, including most of the administrative functions hitherto belonging to the justices of the peace. "The last entrenchment of class government had been stormed; the principles of representative democracy had now been extended over the whole field of English administration." [19]

The act of 1888 was compared by Gladstone to an outline map, the details of which remained to be filled in; and the reorganization of rural government so well begun by the Conservative ministry of Lord Salisbury was carried to substantial completion (until within our own day) by the District and Parish Councils Act, sponsored by the Liberal ministries of Gladstone and Rosebery in 1894. This measure provided (1) that every county should be divided into districts, urban and rural (not simply for sanitation purposes, as under the law of 1872, but for general local government purposes as well), and every district into parishes, and (2) that in every district, and in every rural parish with more than three hundred inhabitants, there should be an elected council, while in the smallest parishes there should be a primary assembly composed of all persons

[18] The number of county boroughs was gradually raised until in 1929 it was eighty-three. See p. 664 below.

[19] J. Redlich and F. W. Hirst, *op. cit.*, I, 203. For an excellent account of the movement leading up to the act of 1888, and also a full interpretation of the statute itself, see *ibid.*, I, Chap. iv. Of much interest in this connection is the discussion of county government to be found in J. S. Mill's *Considerations on Representative Government*, Chap. xv. Mill's chapter greatly influenced the development of opinion on the subject. Cf. C. H. Carter, *The Local Government Act, 1888* (London, 1924).

whose names appeared on the local government and parliamentary registers. To the parish councils and assemblies were transferred all of the civil functions of the vestries, leaving to those bodies the control of ecclesiastical matters only; while to the district councils, whether rural or urban, was committed control of sanitation, highways, and various other matters.[20]

The legislation of 1888 and 1894 had at least two major results. First, it put the local affairs of the rural portions of the country for the first time in the hands of popularly elected bodies. In the second place, it opened the way for the immediate or gradual abolition of all local governing authorities except the county, municipal, district, and parish councils, the boards of guardians, and the school boards, and thus contributed enormously to that progressive simplification of the local government system which is one of the most satisfactory developments of the past thirty years. The act of 1894 alone abolished eight thousand authorities. Since that date the consolidation of authorities and the elimination of areas have been carried considerably further, notably in the fields of educational and poor-law administration. Thus, in 1902 a monumental Education Act which, despite efforts to repeal it, still lies at the basis of the state-aided educational system, abolished the school districts created in 1870 and transferred the functions of the school boards to the councils of counties, boroughs, and districts. And a comprehensive Local Government Act of 1929, initiated principally with a view to readjusting the burden of local rates, abolished the historic poor-law unions and placed full responsibility for poor-law administration upon the councils of counties and county boroughs, and also transferred to the county councils all highway powers of rural district councils and certain main-highway responsibilities of urban districts and non-county boroughs, and admitted the same bodies to a share in the control of town planning enterprises. The suppression of the poor-law union had been urged for twenty years—in majority and minority reports of a poor-law commission in 1909, in a report of the Ministry of Reconstruction's local government committee in 1917, and in numberless discussions by

[20] J. Redlich and F. W. Hirst, *op. cit.*, I, 205-213.

students of administration and social reform.[21] The general tendency has been to eliminate minor local authorities charged with administration of particular services and to consolidate responsibility for such administration in the elective councils of the larger areas, i.e., the counties, county boroughs, and municipal boroughs; and impetus has been supplied not only by the desire to eliminate overlapping and waste, but especially by the purpose to relieve small areas which have found themselves financially overburdened by spreading local rating operations more equitably over larger districts.[22]

Central Control Over Local Government

Along with the developments described have gone important changes in the relations between local government authorities and the national government centering at London. Up to a century ago, the national government did not concern itself very much with purely local affairs. There was, of course, a certain amount of national legislation to be enforced locally, but in the main the pre-reform counties and boroughs went their several ways without much interference from the capital. The developments of the nineteenth century made it necessary to adopt a different policy—not at a stroke, of course, but by stages, as new economic and social conditions, new conceptions of public functions and obligations, drove the country, grudgingly enough, along the path of political reconstruction and reform. Boroughs were brought under a new uniform scheme of organ-

[21] *Report of the Royal Commission on Poor Law and Relief of Distress* (Cmd. 4499, 1909); *Report of the Machinery of Government Committee of the Ministry of Reconstruction* (Cmd. 9230, 1918). S. and B. Webb, *English Poor Law Policy* (2nd ed., London, 1913), is a history of the poor law from 1834 to the investigation of 1905-09. The same authors' *The Break-up of the Poor Law* (London, 1911) is Part i of the minority report of the Poor Law Commission.

[22] A readable and illuminating review of the whole course of local government development in Britain from the early eighteenth century to the date of publication is S. and B. Webb, *English Local Government: Statutory Authorities for Special Purposes* (London, 1922), Chaps. v-vi. The chapters referred to summarize the contents not only of the volume in which they occur but of the authors' *The Parish and the County* and *The Manor and the Borough,* already cited. The important act of 1929 is analyzed in I. G. Gibbon, "Recent Changes in the Local Government of England and Wales," *Amer. Polit. Sci. Rev.,* Aug., 1929.

ization; a nation-wide system of county organization was introduced; minor units of government and administration, even down to the parish, were rearranged and regularized; parliamentary statutes and orders in council took in hand important matters like public health and education, and prescribed in much detail the work to be done, and often how it was to be done, by county, borough, and district authorities; and national ministries, boards, and officials were set to supervise, and frequently to control, the local agencies, not alone as to matters that had been made the subjects of direct nation-wide regulation, but also as to many matters still considered as essentially of local, rather than national, concern. The result is that while there is still considerably less centralized control than in France and other Continental countries, there is a good deal more than we are accustomed to in the majority of our American states.

This central control is at once legislative, judicial, financial, and administrative. It is legislative in that Parliament enacts laws—many of them—prescribing what the areas of local government and administration shall be, what councils and officials (at all events as a minimum) these areas or units shall have, and what powers these authorities may or may not wield. It is legislative also in that orders in council issued by parliamentary authority grant charters of incorporation, fix dates for the taking effect of new statutes, and transfer powers of supervision from one executive department to another. It is judicial in that cases arising between public officials and corporations or private citizens are tried and decided in courts belonging to the national judicial establishment, over which the local governments have no direct, and but little indirect, control. It is financial in that, in recognition of the fact that much of the work done by local authorities is national in interest and benefit, grants are given them out of the national exchequer amounting, in such domains as police and education, to half, or approximately so, of the total outlays incurred—always on condition, however, that enough is voted locally, and sufficient care in expenditure is taken, to keep the subsidized services up to a satisfactory level of efficiency.[23] Finally, central control is administrative in that,

[23] On the general subject of grants in aid in Britain, see J. J. Clarke, *Local Government of the United Kingdom* (4th ed.), 169-175; F. O. White-

for purposes just mentioned or otherwise, almost every important act of a local government authority is subject either to supervision and review or to positive control at the hands of one or another of the central departments and boards operating from London.

Nearly all central departments touch local government at some point. Six, however, are of main importance in this connection. One, the Home Office, supervises police establishments and sees to the inspection of factories and mines.[24] A second, the Board of Education, supervises the local management of all elementary, secondary, technical, and collegiate schools which receive financial aid from the state. A third, the Ministry of Agriculture and Fisheries, directs the enforcement of laws relating to markets, food and drugs, diseases of animals, and numerous other matters. A fourth, the Ministry of Transport, has supervisory jurisdiction over roads, tramways, ferries, harbors, and docks, and (through statutory electricity commissioners) over electric lighting. A fifth, the Treasury, not only sanctions every grant of national funds for education, police, public health, highways, and other purposes, but must approve every advance of money made to municipal authorities by a subsidiary agency, the Public Works Loan Board, for housing

ley, "Contributions from the Central Authority Towards the Cost of Local Administrative Services," *Jour. of Public Admin.*, I, 259-285 (1923); and S. and B. Webb, *Grants in Aid* (new ed., London, 1920); and for purposes of comparison of grants in aid made by the national government of the United States to the several states, see A. F. MacDonald, *Federal Aid* (New York, 1928). The steady growth of grants in aid in Britain in later years has been a main cause of the increased control of the central government over the local authorities, precisely as a similar development in the United States has had a centralizing effect upon the relations between the national government at Washington and the governments of the states. The "derating" provisions of the Local Government Act of 1929 extensively rearranged the relations between national and local taxation and provided for discontinuance after March 31, 1930, of certain grants at present paid in aid of local services, substituting for these grants (and related local rates) an annual consolidated grant starting in 1930-31. For an explanation of these changes, see the article by Gibbon cited on p. 646 above.

[24] Half of the cost of the local police systems is borne by the national government in all cases in which the standards fixed by the Home Office are met. This, in effect, gives the department the power to prescribe organization, discipline, and equipment. In metropolitan London the police force is completely under Home Office control.

schemes and other public works. A fifth, the Ministry of Health, ranges most widely of all. As pointed out in an earlier chapter, it inherited, in 1919, practically all of the duties of the Local Government Board;[25] and while certain of these have since been transferred elsewhere, certain new ones have been added. In particular, this ministry has to do with public health, poor relief, old age pensions and other forms of social insurance—all highly important matters in local administration—besides auditing local accounts (except in the case of boroughs), approving certain forms of local borrowing, and supervising the management of municipally owned gas plants.[26] This dispersion of central supervision among many different ministries or departments is characteristic of, though hardly peculiar to, the British system. In many of our American states there is even a wider distribution, among such agencies as the department of education, the department of public health, the public utility commission, the tax commission, and the board of charities and corrections. In France and other European states, on the other hand, functions and powers of the kind are gathered largely in the hands of a single department, the ministry of the interior. The arrangements existing in Britain are confusing to the observer, and perchance to the administrator. But they afford distinct advantages of specialization; and, being flexible enough to be adapted easily to new needs and conditions, they serve the nation well. As has appeared, they are far from static. Functions and duties are constantly being transferred from one department to another.

It is also obvious that the dealings of the central departments with the local governments take various forms, ranging from supplying information and giving authoritative advice to imposing regulations and vetoing others locally made. The departments do not themselves undertake the work of county, district or borough administration, but in one direction or another they do about everything short of that. They inspect and hear complaints; they disallow local ordinances, even though as a rule only when a question of legality is involved;

[25] See p. 193 above.

[26] The Board of Trade also has functions in connection with the general matter of gas supply.

they assent or refuse to assent to the doing of many things by the local authorities which are allowed by the national laws to be done only with the approval of the appropriate central department; they avail themselves freely of the oft-granted power to lay down rules and regulations which the local authorities must observe; they audit local accounts, and, in the absence of anything like our municipal debt limits in the United States, keep local areas solvent by passing upon their proposals for borrowing—a power, incidentally, which gives them a great deal of control over what the English call "municipal trading," i.e., the public ownership and operation of gas and electric light plants, waterworks, tramways, and similar utilities. There is no single local agent through which this central administrative control is exercised in the fashion in which it is wielded in France through the prefect of the department.[27] But it is none the less real and effective. Often complained of as a species of paternalism inconsistent with the traditions of English local self-government, it is found, in practice, to be increasingly useful and necessary in a society growing ever more closely compacted under the effects of twentieth-century science and achievement.

The situation is saved, as a recent writer has pointed out, by the fact that, in the main, central control is administrative rather than legislative.[28] That is to say, the national laws under which regulation or supervision is carried on are, as a rule, general in their content, leaving the application to particular situations to be made by the central departments with a great deal of discretion. This distinguishes the system from our American plan of laying down minute legislative regulations which are made to apply whether or not the facts warrant application of them in individual instances. The English method is undoubtedly preferable; although, as Professor Munro rightly observes, it is feasible only where, as in Britain, the administrative authorities are responsible to the legislature, and therefore can be entrusted with the exercise of control which under our American scheme of separation of powers the legislature cannot allow to pass out of its own hands.[29]

[27] E. M. Sait, *Government and Politics of France,* 247-253.

[28] W. B. Munro, *The Governments of Europe,* 299-301.

[29] On the relations between the central and local agencies of government,

Local Government Today—the Historic County

The scheme of local government at which Britain has arrived is, as has been said, less logical and symmetrical than the French or other Continental systems, but it is decidedly more close-knit and coherent than the arrangements prevailing a few decades ago. Wherever one goes—outside of metropolitan London, which, like most national capitals, has an organization differing from that of ordinary cities—one finds substantially the same areas or units of local government, the same councils and officers, the same lines of supervision and control running out from the great central departments at Whitehall. Of governmental areas, there are five of chief importance, i.e., the county, the borough, the rural district, the urban district, and the parish. The country as a whole is divided into counties and county

see W. B. Munro, *Government of European Cities* (rev. ed.), Chap. iii; A. L. Lowell, *Government of England,* II, Chap. xlvi; J. J. Clarke, *Local Government of the United Kingdom* (4th ed.), Chap. ii; P. Ashley, *Local and Central Government,* Chap. i; and J. Redlich and F. W. Hirst, *op. cit.,* II, Pt. vi, Chaps. i-v. Much pertinent information is to be found in E. S. Griffith, *Modern Development of City Government in the United Kingdom and the United States,* I, Chap. vi, in which the history of British municipal government between 1900 and 1924 is reviewed in some detail. See also Vol. II, Chap. xi, of this same work. A few references may be added on sundry phases of national and local administration in general; e.g., (1) on taxation, E. Cannon, *History of Local Rates in England* (2nd ed., London, 1928); H. W. Horwill, "Problems of Local Taxation in England," *Polit. Sci. Quar.,* Dec., 1921; and R. S. Wright and H. Hobhouse, *Local Government and Local Taxation in England and Wales* (5th ed., London, 1922); (2) on accounting, J. H. Burton, *Local Authority Finance Accounts and Auditing* (London, 1923); (3) on borrowing, *ibid., Loans and Borrowing Powers of Local Authorities* (London, 1924); (4) on public health, B. G. Bannington, *English Public Health Administration* (new ed., London, 1928); (5) on municipal trading, A. L. Lowell, *Government of England,* II, Chap. xliv; J. J. Clarke, *Local Government in the United Kingdom* (4th ed.), Chap. xvii; D. Knoop, *Principles and Methods of Municipal Trading* (London, 1912), and G. B. Shaw, *The Common Sense of Municipal Trading* (London, 1912); (6) on police, F. W. Maitland, *Justice and Police* (London, 1885), and G. G. Alexander, *The Administration of Justice in Criminal Matters* (Cambridge, 1911); (7) on education, J. J. Clarke, *op. cit.,* Chap. xix; G. Balfour, *The Educational Systems of Great Britain and Ireland* (2nd ed., London, 1903); and H. Craik, *The State in Its Relation to Education* (London, 1914). References on poor relief are given on p. 646 above. For a much longer list on all of these and other subjects, see J. J. Clarke, *op. cit.* (4th ed.), 555-575.

boroughs;[30] the counties are divided into less populous rural and more populous urban districts, with also boroughs scattered here and there; districts and boroughs are subdivided into parishes. One hears of cities. But the term has no governmental or administrative significance. Under English nomenclature, a city is only a borough which, because of being the seat of a bishopric, or because of having received the title by royal patent (as in the case of Sheffield and Leeds), has a right to apply that honorable, but politically meaningless, designation to itself.[31]

The largest unit geographically for local government purposes, and certainly one of the most important, is the county. Here the inquirer encounters, however, one of the several surviving anomalies in the system: there are two complete sets of counties, one superimposed upon the other, instead of a single set as would be expected. This comes about through the fact that when, in 1888, the new administrative counties were created for purposes of reorganized local government, the fifty-two historic counties of England and Wales, many of them traceable back to Saxon shires, were left standing, with boundaries unchanged and with a few important functions, although no longer in any proper sense units of local government. At first glance, indeed, a map showing the administrative counties might be mistaken for one showing the historic divisions, for the exterior boundary lines do not differ widely except in some half-dozen instances.[32] Legally and functionally, however, the

[30] More populous boroughs which have been given all or most of the powers of an administrative county. See p. 664 below.

[31] For a list of "cities," see *Whitaker's Almanack* (1928), 574-578. The most important source material on the entire system of local government and administration as it stands today is the *First and Second Reports of the Royal Commission on Local Government* [Cmd. 2506 (1924) and Cmd. 3213 (1928)] and the *Minutes of Evidence taken before the Royal Commission on Local Government,* Parts i-xii (London, 1923-28). Excellent maps of all counties, with useful subsidiary matter, will be found in G. Philip, *Administrative Atlas of England and Wales* (London, 1928).

[32] The historic county of Sussex is divided into the two administrative counties of East Sussex and West Sussex. Cambridge, Hampshire, Northampton, and Suffolk are similarly partitioned. Each of three parts of Lincolnshire, and of the three historic "ridings" of Yorkshire, forms a separate administrative county. New administrative counties may be formed, existing ones may be divided, and boundaries may be otherwise changed

two sets of areas are quite distinct. Speaking broadly, the historic county[33] exists to serve certain uses of the national government; the administrative county has the same object in part, but in addition, and mainly, it exists to serve the purposes of local self-government. The historic county, in the first place, is the county of which we hear in connection with parliamentary elections. All county constituencies are geographical subdivisions of it, and one of its surviving officials, the sheriff, serves, as we have seen, as chief returning officer, in charge of carrying out the election of "county" members. In the second place, the historic county serves as the area for the administration of what the lawyers call "low," or petty, justice. The system of justices of the peace has been described elsewhere. The area to which these interesting local dignitaries are attached is, not the administrative, but the historic, county. Formerly, as we have seen, they had extensive administrative functions of a non-judicial nature; but in 1888 nearly all of these were transferred to freshly created authorities of the new set of administrative counties, leaving the justices substantially where they stand at the present day.

Along with the justices are found in each historic county a lord lieutenant and also, as already mentioned, a sheriff. Both are appointed by the crown; unlike the administrative county, the historic county, indeed, has no popularly elected governing authorities whatsoever. In earlier days the lord lieutenant was commander of the county militia, yeomanry, and volunteers; but this function was taken away from him in 1871, and nowadays he has little to do except keep certain county records,[34] nominate to the Lord Chancellor persons qualified to be appointed as justices of the peace, and serve personally as head of the "commission of the peace" within the county.

by provisional order of the Ministry of Health, confirmed by Parliament. Such changes, however, are rare. On the areas of county government, see F. Redlich and F. W. Hirst, *op. cit.*, Chap. i. Complete lists of historic, or "geographical," counties and administrative counties appear in *Whitaker's Almanack* (1928), 557.

[33] Often called in England a "geographical" county. The term "historic," however, seems preferable.

[34] In the capacity of *custos rotulorum*. As indicated below, however, the actual keeper of records is rather the clerk.

The office of sheriff ("shire-reeve") antedates the Norman Conquest. By the twelfth century the sheriff, as the principal local representative of the crown within the county, had become a very important personage, with a tendency even to make his position hereditary. Step by step his authority was pared down, until nowadays the office is only a pale image of what it once was. A sheriff in full regalia is still an imposing sight; but his duties—while important enough—are of a routine character, e.g., (1) conducting parliamentary elections, (2) receiving and attending judges on circuit, (3) summoning juries, and (4) executing the judgments, civil and criminal, of the courts of justice. The tenure is one year, and (as is true of all offices in the historic county) no salary is attached. "The whole history of English justice and police," comments Maitland, "might be brought under this rubric, the decline and fall of the sheriff." [35]

Finally, there are, in each historic county, a "clerk of the peace" and a coroner or coroners. Appointed formerly by the keeper of records as his deputy, the clerk is nowadays selected by a joint standing committee of the court of quarter sessions and the administrative county council; indeed, as will be mentioned again, he is ex-officio clerk of the latter body, which means that he is a busy and important functionary. As an official of the historic county, his principal duties are to take actual charge of the county records, to prepare and revise the voters' lists and registers for both parliamentary and local government elections, and to act (under the sheriff) as returning officer at parliamentary elections. Historically, the coroner belongs to the ancient county; and formerly he was elected by the freeholders. Nowadays, however, he is chosen by the council of the administrative county, and is, to all intents and purposes, an official of that area. His duties are to hold inquiries in cases of sudden death and of treasure trove, and to serve as a sheriff's deputy in summoning juries and executing writs.[36]

[35] *Justice and Police,* 69. The early history of the office is set forth in W. A. Morris, "The Office of Sheriff in the Anglo-Saxon Period," *Eng. Hist. Rev.,* Jan., 1916, and "The Office of Sheriff in the Early Norman Period," *ibid.,* Apr., 1918.

[36] Some counties have more than one coroner. For a general treatment of the subject, see T. Ottaway, *The Law and Practice Relating to Coroners* (London, 1927).

The Administrative County—the Council and Its Committees

Turning to the administrative county, we find a very different sort of thing—an area of real local self-government. The act of 1888 created sixty-three of these counties in England and Wales (including the county of London),[37] in addition to giving similar status to a number of boroughs thenceforth known as county boroughs and exempted from jurisdiction of the administrative county within whose bounds they happen to be situated.[38] Like the borough, but unlike the historic county, the administrative county is an incorporated territory, endowed with a legal personality, and possessing full powers of owning and disposing of property, and bringing suit in the courts, and of course capable of being sued. Furthermore, it has a full-orbed governmental system, not indeed created out of hand, but modeled closely upon that of the reformed boroughs of the period since 1835, with the result that (allowances being made for some rather important differences entailed by physical conditions) county government and borough government are pretty much of a pattern. In both cases the governing authority is an elected council consisting of a chairman, alderman, and councillors sitting as one body, and functioning administratively through clerks, treasurers, and other appropriate "permanent" officials appointed by the council and answerable to it.

The county councillors are elected, in single-member districts, for terms of three years. The requirements for voting in county and borough elections are the same; and since 1928 they have been, as in the case of the parliamentary suffrage, identical for men and women. On the other hand, they are not, and at no time have been, identical with those applying in parliamentary elections. As defined by the most recent legislation on the subject, i.e., the Representation of the People (Equal Franchise) Act of 1928, any person (man or woman) is entitled to be registered as a local government elector if (a) twenty-one years

[37] The number is now sixty-two, including London.

[38] As indicated above, there are now eighty-three of these county boroughs in England and Wales. They, of course, have a special status in relation to the administrative county only, not the historic county. New ones may be formed, existing ones may be united with administrative counties, and boundaries may be changed by provisional order of the Ministry of Health, confirmed by Parliament.

of age, (b) not subject to any legal incapacity, and (c) an occupier as owner or tenant,[39] on the last day of the qualifying period, of any land or premises in the local government area, and if, in addition, he or she (d) has during the whole of the qualifying period so occupied any land or premises, or (e) is the husband or wife, as the case may be, of a person entitled to be so registered. Plural voting is not permitted. Candidates are nominated substantially as are candidates for seats in the House of Commons, i.e., in writing, by two registered local government electors of the electoral division for which they stand, eight other such electors "assenting," and the nomination papers being filed at a place and time fixed by the returning officer. Campaign expenditures are regulated by statute,[40] on the basis of a maximum of £25 where the number of electors does not exceed 500, with *2d.* additional allowed for each elector above that number. Reports of expenditures must be made to the clerk of the council within twenty-eight days after the election.[41] Corrupt and illegal practices are defined and punished on the same lines as in parliamentary elections.

The number of councillors varies with the population of the county;[42] but whatever it is in an individual case, a newly elected council proceeds to choose, in addition, a quota of aldermen who will sit, not as a separate chamber, but in a single body along with the popularly chosen councillors. These aldermen may be selected from among the members of the council (in which case by-elections are necessary to fill the vacated positions) or from the outside; and they must be one-sixth as numerous as the ordinary councillors. The alderman's term being six years instead of three, half carry over and half are freshly elected whenever a new council begins its work. Except

[39] "Tenant" is so defined as to include lodgers who rent a room, or rooms, "in an unfurnished state."

[40] The Municipal Elections (Corrupt and Illegal Practices) Act of 1884, the Local Government Acts of 1888 and 1899, and the Local Elections (Expenses) Act of 1919.

[41] The same system obtains in connection with borough elections; but there are no limits, and no returns are required, in elections to rural and urban district councils or parish councils.

[42] The counties are of very unequal size and population. Aside from London, the most populous is Lancashire, with 1,746,418; the least populous, Rutland, with 18,368. Fourteen have a population of less than 100,000.

that he is elected differently, has a longer term, and on the average enjoys a little more prestige, an alderman differs in no respect from an ordinary councillor. The arrangement has the advantage, however, of ensuring somewhat greater experience in the council, and particularly of providing a way by which persons who for any reason are specially desirable as members, but who would be unwilling to become candidates at a popular election, or if candidates would probably fail at the polls, can be brought in. Councillors and aldermen together choose a county chairman, from their own number or from outside; and the whole group, numbering as a rule seventy-five or more persons, functions unitedly as "the council." In the choice both of ordinary councillors and of aldermen, party considerations play a comparatively minor rôle, and elections are frequently uncontested.[43] Members are drawn largely from the landowners, large farmers, and professional men, although representatives of the lower middle and laboring classes are far more numerous than they used to be, especially in populous counties where Labor has actively, and in several cases successfully, sought control. Since 1907 women have been eligible.[44]

It is not feasible to bring together so large a body very frequently. Hence the council meets, as a rule, only four times a year (the minimum required by law), and the greater part of the steadily increasing volume of business is taken care of by committees. Various parliamentary statutes, taken together, make it necessary for every council to have twelve different committees, e.g., on finance, education, small holdings, public assistance,[45] public health and housing, agriculture, and maternity and child welfare. But other committees are set up as each

[43] The generally non-partisan character of the elections is in many ways an advantage, but it is probably a main reason why, as a rule, only about fifty per cent of the qualified voters take part in county elections, whereas the proportion in parliamentary elections rarely falls below seventy-five per cent. The showing in borough elections is, on the average, not much better.

[44] To avoid repetition, it may be pointed out here, once for all, that a woman may now be a county councillor or alderman, a borough councillor or alderman, a district councillor, a parish councillor, a justice of the peace, and even a county council chairman or a borough mayor.

[45] This committee, required by the Local Government Act of 1929 which transferred poor-law administration to the county councils, is the most recent addition to the list.

council finds necessary, almost always including committees on main roads and bridges, weights and measures, and local government, besides an executive committee. Furthermore, there are joint committees composed of representatives of the county council and of other authorities, the most important being a standing joint committee for county police consisting of justices of the peace appointed by the court of quarter sessions, and of councillors, in equal numbers, and charged with selection of the chief constable and with general control of police.[46] The members of council committees are chosen by the council itself, a "slate" having, however, been previously prepared by a committee of selection, on the analogy of the practice prevailing in the House of Commons at London.[47] Most council committees, in county and borough alike, have sub-committees, and the demands of committee work upon the members are increasingly heavy.

The powers and duties of the county council are many and varied, and are still growing. In the act of 1888—which, as we have seen, transferred the administrative and financial powers of the justices of the peace to the new body, leaving to the justices little except their judicial functions—they are enumerated in sixteen categories, of which the most important are the raising, expending, and borrowing of money;[48] the care of county property, buildings, bridges, lunatic asylums, and reformatory and industrial schools; the appointment of administrative officials; the granting of certain licenses other than for the sale of liquor;[49] the care of main highways and the protec-

[46] E. Jenks, *Outline of English Local Government,* Chap. x.

[47] There is, however, a growing tendency in all local government committee organization toward coöptation, i.e., selection of a certain proportion of a committee's members by the committee itself. The object is to secure the services of experts, and sometimes to give a voice to persons directly affected. Illustrations are afforded by the committees on education, old age pensions, and maternity and child welfare.

[48] The county's sources of income include tolls, fees, rents, and subventions (especially for police, education, and health purposes) from the national exchequer. Any deficiency is provided for by the county "rate," or tax, levied by the council. Rates are assessed on all "rateable hereditaments," e.g., land, houses, mines, etc., and are payable by the occupier (as distinguished from the owner), except as otherwise provided by law. Certain lesser authorities are limited as to the amounts that they may raise by means of rates, but county and borough councils are not.

[49] Liquor licenses are granted by the justices of the peace.

tion of streams from pollution; and the enforcement of various regulations relating to animals, fish, birds, and insects. As noted elsewhere, the Education Act of 1902 made the council also the school authority throughout the country, except in the urban sections; and the Local Government Act of 1929 transferred to it the whole burden of poor-law administration, while at the same time increasing its responsibility for highways and town planning. The control of police within the county rests, as has been said, with a joint committee representing the council and the justices of the peace. Finally, the council may make by-laws for the county, supervise the work of the rural district councils, and even perform the tasks of these councils and their agents if they prove remiss.

Permanent Officials of the County

It goes without saying that the day-to-day administrative work of the county is carried on neither by the council as a whole nor by its committees. Even though most councils do occasionally give time to administrative details, their real business is to consider the general interests of the county and to formulate policies aimed at promoting them. The mass of administrative work is performed, rather, by a group of permanent officials, chosen by the council and answerable to it, and secure in their tenure as long as they render satisfactory service. These officials include, chiefly, a county clerk,[50] a treasurer, a surveyor (in charge of highway construction and repair), a land agent, an inspector of weights and measures, and a health officer. In the United States most of these officers would be elected by the people; they would be chosen primarily as Republicans or Democrats; and they would have to divide their time and energy between their administrative duties on the one hand and politics on the other. In Britain, where the "short ballot" has always prevailed, they are selected by the council, not, indeed, under formal civil service rules, but yet with reference almost entirely to their fitness for the work to be done;[51] although legally removable by the council at any

[50] Chosen, strictly, as an officer of the historic county by the joint standing committee of the court of quarter sessions and the county council, and serving ex-officio as clerk of the council.

[51] Cf. pp. 669-670 below.

time,[52] none are ever displaced for purely political reasons; and while the competence and public-mindedness of the councillors is a weighty factor, the conspicuous honesty and efficiency of county administration is to be credited largely to the capacity, experience, and security of the members of the permanent staff. Suitable pay, good opportunity for advancement, satisfactory arrangements for retirement on pension, as well as security of tenure, attract to the service men of considerably larger caliber than in earlier days.[53]

Districts and Parishes

Within the administrative county are various subdivisions which have governmental authorities and powers of their own. Most important, of course, are the boroughs; but there are also rural and urban districts, rural and urban parishes. The rural district is a subordinate area with an elective council which, under the statute of 1894 and amending acts, and subject to the general control of the county council, is responsible for matters such as water-supply, sanitation, and public health. Until 1929, it was charged also with the care of minor roads, but that function has now been transferred to the county council. Like the superior body, the district council has power to levy rates; like it, also, it appoints and controls a clerk, treasurer, surveyor, medical officer, sanitary inspectors, and other permanent salaried officials who carry on the routine administrative work. There are 663 of these rural districts in England and Wales. Some have a population of only a few hundred; others, of more than 50,000.

Then there are urban districts. When a rural district, or any other portion of an administrative county, attains a population

[52] A full-time health officer can ordinarily be removed only with the consent of the Ministry of Health. There are one or two other contingent exceptions.

[53] For fuller treatment of county government, the reader may be referred to E. Jenks, *An Outline of English Local Government* (6th ed., London, 1925), Chaps. viii-ix; R. S. Wright and H. Hobhouse, *An Outline of Local Government and Local Taxation in England and Wales* (5th ed., London, 1922), Chap. vi; and notably J. Redlich and F. W. Hirst, *op. cit.*, II, Pt. ii, Chaps. ii-v. Cf. W. Anderson, "How England Has Solved Some Familiar County Problems," *Nat. Munic. Rev.*, July, 1918, and H. Samuels, *The County Councillor* (London, 1925).

such that it needs special powers and functions, e.g., in connection with water-supply and fire protection, approaching those of a borough, the county council may erect the area into an urban district, which, like its rural counterpart, will find its place in the general scheme of local government rather minutely defined in the act of 1894 and later amendments. An urban district may in time become a borough; but as a district it has no charter and differs hardly at all from a rural district except in having certain special powers over sanitation, housing, licensing, and other matters, which are most appropriate in a thickly settled community.[54] As in the rural district, the council is elected from the parishes;[55] it meets monthly, utilizes committees, and elects its own chairman; and it appoints and employs a staff of permanent officials, organized to serve the somewhat more specialized purposes in hand. The number of urban districts in England and Wales is now 782.[56]

Until 1894, the kingdom was completely covered with a network of parishes, forming the smallest governmental units, and frequently, as in the case of the communes in France, having a history running back for centuries. The parishes are still there; everybody in the kingdom lives in some parish or other. In the boroughs and urban districts, however, they have lost their functions as units of civil government, and the vestries, once enjoying both civil and ecclesiastical authority, confine

[54] These powers are to some extent graduated according to the population of the district. More than a third have populations of less than 5,000, but a few exceed 100,000.

[55] In neither case are there aldermen as in the county and borough councils.

[56] On the rural and urban districts, see J. J. Clarke, *Local Government of the United Kingdom* (4th ed.), Chap. v; E. Jenks, *Outline of English Local Government* (6th ed.), Chap. vii; R. S. Wright and H. Hobhouse, *Local Government and Local Taxation* (5th ed.), Chaps. iii-iv; and especially J. Redlich and F. W. Hirst, *op. cit.*, II, Pt. iii, Chaps. i-ii. H. W. Wightwick, *District and Parish Councils* (London, 1926), is valuable. There are at present some districts which lie partly in one county and partly in another. The Local Government Act of 1929 provides an easy method by which county boundaries can be altered and such anomalies removed. It also requires every county council to make a review of all the districts wholly or partially within the county and before April 1, 1932, submit to the Minister of Health suitable proposals for alterations of boundaries, union of districts, formation of new districts, or conversion of rural districts into urban ones or *vice versa*.

their activities to electing church wardens and attending to other business of an ecclesiastical nature. Elsewhere the parish remains an area of civil government as well as a unit for church purposes—humble, to be sure, but in its way important.[57] Every such parish has a primary assembly, known as the parish meeting, in which all persons on the local government and parliamentary registers (including women, of course) are entitled to appear. What this little gathering of the people does depends on whether or not the parish also has a council; and this, in turn, depends largely on the parish's population. If the population is as much as three hundred, there must be a council; if less than that number, there may be one if the parish so desires—with the proviso that if the population is under one hundred, the consent of the county council is required. The council (if there be one) consists of from five to fifteen persons, elected for three years. In a parish with a council the parish meeting has little to do except choose the councillors and criticize their work; the council will appoint the "managers" of public elementary schools, the clerk, the treasurer, and such other petty functionaries as are needed. If there is no council, it falls, of course, to the "meeting" to perform these tasks. In the one case, the people come together once a year; in the other case, twice. There is really a good deal of work to be done, even though on a small scale. There is property to be managed, sanitary inspection to be attended to, provision to be made for public libraries, recreation grounds, and village greens. Formerly, whatever else might be necessary, a levy of rates was always to be made by the overseers of the poor, based on a valuation list of all rateable "hereditaments" in the parish, to satisfy the "precepts," or demands, addressed to them by the guardians of the poor and by the county authorities. An act of 1925, however, both abolished the historic office of overseer and transferred the statutory rating functions of the parish to the county, borough, and district councils.[58]

[57] In 1922 the number of rural parishes was 12,850.

[58] J. J. Clarke, *Local Government of the United Kingdom* (4th ed.), Chap. ix. On the parish in general, see E. Jenks, *Outline of English Local Government* (6th ed.), Chap. ii; R. S. Wright and H. Hobhouse, *Local Government and Local Taxation* (5th ed.), Chap. i; and, for very full treatment, J. Redlich and F. W. Hirst, *op. cit.*, II, Pt. iv, Chaps. i-iv.

CHAPTER XXVIII

MUNICIPAL GOVERNMENT

WE have yet to speak of the organization of the borough, where alone (outside of London) is to be found municipal government in the full sense of the term.[1] At the outset, it must be observed that the borough which we have in mind is the area or unit specially organized for municipal purposes, not the "parliamentary" borough, which is simply an electoral division. Legally, there is no connection between the two. It is true that when Parliament (which exclusively regulates the admission of boroughs to representation in the House of Commons) prescribes that such and such boroughs shall be entitled to elect members separately from the counties in which they are situated, it commonly designates local urban areas having borough governments. But many municipal boroughs—the smaller ones, naturally—have no separate representation in Parliament; and even in the case of the approximately 135 that have such representation,[2] the boundaries of the municipality and of the parliamentary division do not usually coincide exactly, and any extension or other change of the municipal borough's limits does not affect the parliamentary division unless Parliament makes alterations to correspond.[3] A municipal borough is now-

[1] So remarkably has Britain been urbanized in the past hundred years or more that well beyond three-fourths of the entire population now dwell in towns, and hence under the municipal governments to be described. In this connection, attention may be called to J. G. Thompson, *Urbanization; its Effects on Government and Society* (New York, 1927).

[2] Shown in G. Philips, *Administrative Atlas of England and Wales*, Plate 6.

[3] The Representation of the People Act of 1918, which overhauled the parliamentary constituencies, naturally brought about, temporarily at all events, a closer relation between the two sets of areas than had existed before. To ascertain the boundaries of a parliamentary borough, one consults the latest apportionment act of Parliament; of a municipal borough, the borough's own charter. See G. Philips, *op. cit.*

adays officially defined simply as any place for the time being organized and governed under the Municipal Corporations Consolidation Act of 1882 and its amendments. The original reform act of 1835 applied, as we have seen, to 178 boroughs in England and Wales. The number now organized according to the prescribed pattern is 253, besides eighty-three county boroughs.[4]

A borough differs from an urban district chiefly in having a charter and in being endowed with superior powers. The charter creates a corporation (consisting of the mayor, aldermen, and burgesses), and, in conformity with the general national law, prescribes a form of government and confers a body of powers similar to, although not in every respect identical with, those possessed by other boroughs. Charters of incorporation are granted by the crown. The first step to be taken, therefore, in case the people of an urban district or other area decide that they want a charter is to send in a petition addressed to the king and signed by a goodly number of resident householders. Contrary to what one might expect, there is no standard of population, or of rateable or assessable property, to be met before application can be made.[5] The petition is referred to a

[4] The distinction between county boroughs and ordinary boroughs is a matter, not of form or of organization, but of powers. The ordinary borough is governmentally, as well as geographically, a part of the administrative county in which it lies, whereas a county borough has been given all or most county powers and exempted almost entirely from county jurisdiction. Upon attaining a population of 75,000 (formerly 50,000), an ordinary borough may, under terms of a statute of 1926, seek from Parliament the passage of a private bill admitting it to the select circle of county boroughs. Most boroughs of more than 50,000 inhabitants are now county boroughs, although a few have not chosen to seek such status. For suggestive comment on the usefulness of the county borough system as a means of obviating the complicated and anomalous conditions commonly associated with city-county relations in the United States, see W. B. Munro, *Governments of Europe,* 289-290. Cf. J. Redlich and F. W. Hirst, *op. cit.,* II, Pt. ii, Chap. v. Certain disadvantages of the system are set forth in W. R. Barker, "Local Government Problems," *Edinburgh Rev.,* Jan., 1926. "The real reason," says this writer, "for deprecating the multiplication of independent urban areas is to be found, not in the incapacity of the comparatively small urban unit for self-government, but in the damage to the county which arises from the progressive denudation of its urban areas and its rateable values."

[5] More than a fourth of the present boroughs have a population of less than 5,000, which is smaller than that of half or more of the existing urban

small committee of the Privy Council, which employs an inspector to take evidence both for and against the proposal, and, if the report is favorable, publishes the proposed charter in the *London Gazette.* If at the end of a month no protest has been lodged, either by a local authority or by one-twentieth of the owners or ratepayers of the area affected, an order in council is issued granting the charter and fixing the boundaries of the new borough. If, however, protest is forthcoming, the grant can be made only in pursuance of an act of Parliament.[6]

The Borough Council

Borough government is constructed on the characteristic English plan of concentrating substantially all authority (subject, of course, to the ultimate control of the national government) in a single elective body, the council. The doctrine of the separation of legislative and executive powers, which is slowly being given up in American municipal circles, finds no more acceptance in the English borough than in the English county—or, for that matter, in the English national government itself. The borough council, and, indeed, the entire borough organization, is notably similar to that of the county, even though with a few important differences. The council consists of councillors, aldermen, and a mayor, sitting as one body. The councillors are elected directly by the people, under suffrage arrangements similar to those mentioned above as prevailing in the counties. In smaller boroughs they are commonly chosen on a general ticket; in larger ones, by districts or wards, each of which usually has three, though occasionally six, or even nine, representatives.[7] The term is three years, and, contrary to the plan in the counties, one-third of the councillors retire each year. Hence there is a municipal election every November —either the borough as a single constituency choosing one-

districts. In 1913 a new borough was created with a population of but slightly over 2,000. An English writer has remarked humorously that it is almost as difficult to discover why a town becomes a borough as it is to discover why a commoner becomes a peer.

[6] On charters and charter-making, see W. B. Munro, *The Government of European Cities* (rev. ed.), Chap. ii.

[7] The number of councillors is fixed for each borough by its charter, but under legislation of 1925 may be altered by an order in council.

third of the entire council, or the various wards choosing one, two, or three of their respective quotas. Women have been eligible since 1907, and many have been elected. Candidates for the borough council are nominated in the same way as those for the county council; and, so far as the ballots go, the election is non-partisan. Actually, however, party rivalry usually figures rather prominently, especially in boroughs where Labor is strong. In such boroughs—rapidly increasing in number—Conservative and Liberal forces not infrequently pool their strength in an effort (by no means always successful) to keep Labor from gaining control.[8]

Aldermen, to the number of one-third of the councillors,[9] are elected by ballot by the council from among the councillors or persons qualified to be councillors. The term is six years, and one-third retire biennially. As in the counties, by-elections are held to replace ordinary councillors who are chosen aldermen.

[8] Municipal suffrage and elections are described more fully in W. B. Munro, *The Government of European Cities* (rev. ed.), Chap. iv; A. S. Wright and E. H. Singleton, *Organization and Administration of the Town Clerk's Department,* etc., Chaps. iv-v; and J. Redlich and F. W. Hirst, *op. cit.,* I, Bk. II, Chaps. iv-v. The growing rôle of parties in municipal elections is set forth in Munro, *ibid.,* Chap. v. The rise of the Labor party is the chief explanation for the fact that, whereas twenty or thirty years ago, municipal elections rarely ran on party lines, they now do so in the great majority of cases. Quite a while before Labor counted for anything in Parliament it was electing municipal councillors in the industrial sections of the larger cities; during the World War its successes multiplied; and in the municipal elections of 1919-20 it captured one council after another and developed such strength that the Conservatives and Liberals were driven, not only to unwonted activity on party lines in municipal campaigns, but, as mentioned above, to enter into frequent coalitions as a means of preventing further Labor triumphs and of recovering some of the ground that had been lost. The period 1921-25 witnessed some recession of Labor control in borough councils, but the municipal elections of 1926-28 were marked by notable Labor victories. The number of Labor members of borough councils outside of London was, indeed, doubled by the elections of 1928 alone. On the party aspect of these elections, see J. K. Pollock, "Labor Party Gains in Municipal Elections in Britain," *Nat. Munic. Rev.,* Feb., 1928, and W. A. Robson, "The Recent Municipal Elections in England," *ibid.,* April, 1928. "The rise of the Labor party," writes Professor Munro, "has virtually put an end to the old notion that national issues should have no place in British municipal elections. In the rural communities . . . that notion still persists, but in the larger industrial towns it is gone." *Op. cit.,* 100.

[9] The number of councillors and aldermen is relatively large—in Liverpool, for example, 153 in all, and in Manchester, 141.

Again as in the counties, aldermen differ from the general run of councillors only in the manner of their election, in the length of their term, and in the fact that, being as a rule more experienced, they are likely to hold the principal committee chairmanships and to have most influence in the shaping of policy. Many good men who would not seek popular election, or would probably be beaten at the polls if they did so, are brought into the council in this way, although some people object to the check upon direct popular control which the system is deemed to involve.

The mayor—the counterpart of the council chairman in the county—is elected for one year by the council, usually from its own number, but occasionally from outside. He is not the head of a separate branch of government, as is the mayor of an American city (except in commission-governed municipalities), but merely the presiding officer of the council and the official representative of the borough on formal occasions. He cannot appoint or remove officers, control the departments, or veto ordinances.[10] Hence he need not be a man of executive ability or experience. As matters go, it is far more important that he be a person of some wealth, and of leisure; for the chief demands upon him will be of a social and philanthropic nature, and a salary is rarely provided.[11] If he is willing, he is likely to be reëlected a number of times. Reëlections of councillors and aldermen are also numerous, resulting in a continuity of service and an accumulation of experience rarely found in an American city council, where the doctrine of rotation in office still prevails.

The council meets in the town hall monthly, fortnightly, or weekly, according as the amount of business demands,[12] and

[10] He can, in fact, do so few things that it ought not to be difficult for him to measure up to the ideal of a recently elected mayor who promised in the conduct of his office to "avoid both partiality on the one hand and impartiality on the other!"

[11] It should be noted, however, that in these days of occasional Labor domination of borough councils there are mayors who are only wage-earners, and who, of course, are not looked to for the traditional gifts to every more or less worthy cause. All mayors are entitled to be reimbursed for their purely official expenses.

[12] The law requires only four meetings a year, as in the case of the county council. But no borough council finds it feasible to meet so infrequently.

carries on its deliberations under "orders," or rules of its own making. The larger part of its work, however, is transacted through committees, which are elected by the council and presided over by chairmen whom the committees themselves select. As in the case of the county council, there are certain "statutory" committees, i.e., committees which every council is required by national law to appoint. Conspicuous among these are a watch committee (which has charge of matters relating to the police force, the fire brigade, and licensing), a finance committee, a committee on education, a committee on old age pensions, and a committee on maternity and child welfare. In addition, there are committees which are appointed and maintained at the council's own discretion, the total number of committees running all the way from seven or eight to twenty or twenty-five, or even more. Practically all matters brought up in council meeting are referred to some committee; and since they are considered in a good deal of detail, and usually by the councillors who are best informed on the subject in hand, there is a strong tendency for committee findings and recommendations to be received favorably by the council and made the basis of its actions.[13]

The council constitutes, in the fullest sense, the government of the borough. Hence it exercises substantially all of the powers (save that of electing the councillors themselves) that come to the borough from the common law, from general and special acts of Parliament, and from provisional orders. These powers fall into three main classes: legislative, financial, and administrative. The council makes by-laws, or ordinances, relating to all sorts of matters—streets, police, health, traffic control, etc.—subject only to the power of the Ministry of Health to disallow ordinances on health and a few other subjects if that authority finds them objectionable. It acts as custodian of the "borough fund" (consisting of receipts from public property, franchises, fines, fees, etc.); levies "borough rates" of so many shillings or pence per pound on the rental value of real property, in order to obtain whatever additional revenue is

[13] Borough council committees are described in A. S. Wright and E. H. Singleton, *Organization and Administration of the Town Clerk's Department and the Justices' Clerk's Department* (London, 1925), Chap. iii.

needed;[14] draws up and adopts the annual budget; makes all appropriations; and borrows money on the credit of the municipality, in so far as the central authorities permit. Finally, it exercises control over all branches of strictly municipal administration. This it does, first, by appointing the staff of permanent salaried officers—clerk, treasurer, engineer, public analyst, chief constable, medical officer, etc.—who, with their respective staffs, carry on the daily work of the borough government, and, second, by continuous supervision of these same officials and their subordinates, exercised through the committees having to do with the various branches of municipal business.

Council Committees and the Municipal Service

This "municipal service," as it is termed to distinguish it from the national civil service, presents a number of interesting features. As already suggested, it falls into two main parts, the relatively small number of expert, professional, directing officials, and the larger clerical, non-professional, subordinate staff. As in the counties, the officials of the higher grades are selected exclusively by the council; none are elected by the people, and none are appointed by the mayor.[15] Candidates are not subjected to formal examination, but are scrutinized and selected very much as are applicants for responsible positions in the employ of private business establishments. The agency commonly used in the sifting process is the appropriate council committee. When, for example, a new borough treasurer is required, the finance committee looks over the field, receives applications, inquires into qualifications, and at length makes a recommendation to the council, which can usually be depended upon to ratify the committee's choice. It will not do to say that personal and partisan considerations never enter in; as between two candidates equally qualified but of different political faith, the choice is rather likely to fall upon the one whose

[14] Boroughs have, in general, the same kinds of revenues as counties (see p. 658), except that receipts from the operation of gas, electric, water, tramway, and other publicly owned utilities bulk very much larger.

[15] Except that one of three borough auditors is appointed by the mayor from among the members of the council and the other two are elected by the voters of the borough from among persons who are qualified to be, but are not, members.

political views coincide with those of the council majority. The selections are usually, however, of a high order. Not infrequently the man chosen will be one who has gained a reputation for efficient administration in another, perhaps less important, borough. Once in office, an appointee, although legally removable by the council at any time, is practically assured of being retained as long as he chooses to serve. There are occasional removals, of course, for incompetence, malfeasance, or neglect of duty. But partisan or other similar considerations seldom come into play.

The great mass of subordinate positions are filled by appointment by the head of the department concerned. The London County Council has set up, within its jurisdiction, a scheme of competitive examinations; and there is nothing to prevent an appointing authority anywhere from applying competitive or other sorts of tests as he may desire. There is no national law or rule, however, requiring competitive examination; there is, consequently, no uniform method; and, unlike the national service, the municipal service as a whole is not grounded upon any formal "merit" scheme. A few councils, without going as far as the London County Council, have laid down certain minimum requirements, and observers think that they discern a tendency toward wider adoption of the competitive test. As yet, however, there is plenty of room for patronage, as practiced by the chiefs of departments and by individual council members; and although it is the testimony of all students of the subject that the service is freer from the devastating effects of partisan and personal favoritism than the municipal services of the United States and most other countries, there remains a problem admittedly worthy of comparison with that which the nineteenth-century reformers so successfully solved in the domain of the national service.[16]

[16] W. A. Robson, *From Patronage to Proficiency in the Public Service*, 29-48; J. W. Dickins, L. C. Evans, H. Finer, and L. Hill, "Examinations for Local Officials," *Public Admin.*, VI (1928), 278-317. Finer says: "Perhaps less than ten per cent of the local administrative and clerical officials are recruited by reference to some public and objective test of quality; and in the main, with the exception of a few enlightened municipalities, the only attention paid to recruitment is of the negative sort, to avoid flagrant and scandalous inefficiency."

A notably strong feature of the British municipal system as a whole is the close working relations between the higher permanent officials and the council committees. The officials owe their positions to selection by the respective committees in the first instance; they have been chosen because the committees thought highly of their experience or their technical proficiency; and, once they are in office, the committees keep in close touch with them, not only with a view to supervising their work, but in order to avail themselves of the assistance that can be obtained in their own labors. The permanent officials attend the meetings of the committees and take an active part in them, though of course without a right to vote; and a major reason why committee recommendations carry so much weight as to be almost certain of adoption by the council is the knowledge of that body that such recommendations have been arrived at, not by mere deliberation of the committee as a group of laymen, but by full and free discussion of the technicalities involved, participated in by the persons best qualified to supply the necessary information and advice. There is relatively little of this sort of thing in American cities, where too frequently the relation between the council and its committees on the one hand and the heads of departments on the other is grounded upon jealousy and suspicion. The English committees play a decidedly more important rôle than the American, and the heads of departments and other principal administrative officials exert a greater influence upon municipal policy than they commonly do with us.

The steady growth of urban populations, coupled with the increasing complexity of modern life and the multiplying forms of service which governments, especially in municipal areas, are expected to render, imposes upon the borough council, its committees, and the permanent officials an ever-increasing burden of responsibility; and there are those who wonder whether borough government will not become so overloaded that it will break down, or at all events lose much of its present efficiency. There is no point to making predictions on this score, the less so by reason of the fact that the borough governments have shown much capacity in the past for taking on new functions, e.g., in relation to education, without apparent bad effects. The fact remains, however, that the number of things that a borough government has to do is rapidly growing, that borough officials and employees are multiplying proportionally, and that municipal expenditures are mounting. There is also to be considered the possible effect of future measures of devolution. As we have seen, the national government, particularly the national legislature, is acknowledged to be under excessive strain and stress at the present time. On that account—as well as because of a revival of the feeling of earlier days that the powers of government should be distributed widely, i.e., placed, as far as can well be contrived, in the local authorities, rather than concentrated in the nation as a whole—there is a perceptible tendency to devolve powers and tasks upon boroughs and counties. A great amount of such devolution has, indeed, been taking place quietly in the past quarter-century. Further experience may show the necessity of introducing new regional or other units and mechanisms to lighten the load at both the national and the local end of the present system. On the other hand, new and more expeditious ways of doing business may enable the existing machinery to go on meeting the demands made upon it. So far as the county and borough councils are concerned—and the problem is largely theirs—further development of the committee system on the lines described above would seem capable of enabling still heavier burdens of responsibility to be borne without unsatisfactory consequences.[17]

[17] The literature on borough government is voluminous. There is no better treatment of the subject than W. B. Munro, *Government of European Cities* (rev. ed.), Chaps. ii-viii. Other briefer accounts are A. L. Lowell, *Government of England,* II, Chaps. xxxix-xli; E. Jenks, *Outline of English Local Government* (6th ed.), Chaps. xi-xii; J. J. Clarke, *The Local Government of the United Kingdom,* Chap. vi, and much of Chaps. ix-xxix; and G. M. Harris, *Local Government in Many Lands* (London, 1926), Chap. xiii. More extensive treatment, though not entirely up to date, is J. Redlich and F. W. Hirst, *op. cit.,* I, Bk. II, Chaps. i-x. C. R. Atlee and W. A. Robson, *The Town Councillor* (London, 1925), is a convenient little book intended as a manual of information for persons engaged in municipal activities. Similarly, A. S. Wright and E. H. Singleton, *Organization and Administration of the Town Clerk's Department,* etc., is a practical guide to the multifold duties, functions, and relationships of the clerk's office. E. D. Simon, *A City Council from Within* (London, 1926), is an informing but rather dry record of the author's thirteen years of practical experience as a member of the Manchester city council, including a period of office as lord mayor.

The Government of London

Most of the world's great capitals—Paris, Berlin, Tokyo, Rome, Washington—have governments quite unlike those of other municipalities of the country in which they are located. This is true of London as well. The unique governmental arrangements found in this greatest of all urban centers represent a curious admixture of historical survival and the most up-to-date legislative regulation—legislation enacted almost entirely for London alone, since the capital has all along been dealt with quite apart from every other portion of the country.[18] Seventy-five years ago there was no London, for strictly governmental purposes, except the historic "City." This was a municipality somewhat more than a square mile in area situated on the left bank of the Thames, in the very heart of the metropolitan district, but politically unconnected with either the near-by "city" of Westminster or the hundred or more adjoining communities organized as self-governing parishes and districts. Long previously the City had largely ceased to be a residential region, becoming simply the business and financial center of the metropolis, and, indeed, of the nation; nowadays its population—consisting to a considerable extent of watchmen, janitors, and the like, does not exceed thirty thousand. But it had a proud history, stretching back even to pre-Roman times, and it clung, as it still clings, resolutely to its separate identity as a unit or area of government and administration.[19] The satellite areas had a population, when the nineteenth century dawned, of close to a million. But they were not linked up governmentally, either with the City or with one another. Each had its own authorities, levied its own rates, and provided its own public works and services. Powers were derived from some two hundred and fifty local acts of Parliament, as well as from general acts.

As we have seen, the Municipal Corporations Act of 1835 left London untouched; and although the royal commission

[18] It has even its own Public Health Act, Education Act, Building Acts, etc.

[19] For a full and interesting description of the City, as it was and in the main still is, see S. and B. Webb, *The Manor and the Borough,* Pt. ii, Chap. x.

whose report bore fruit in that great statute submitted a supplementary report dealing with the metropolis in 1837, it was not until 1855, after another commission had reported, that Parliament came to the point of enacting remedial legislation. Even then, not a great deal was done. The confusion and waste arising from independent street building, sewer construction, fire protection, and other such activities by a hundred separate but neighboring local governments led to the establishment of a metropolitan board of works of forty-six members representing the city corporation and the parish vestries. This helped somewhat. But a real solution came only as the century neared a close. In 1888, when the system of administrative counties and county councils was being adopted for the country at large, all extra-city London—an area of about 117 square miles, embracing populous portions of the five historic counties of Surrey, Kent, Essex, Middlesex, and Herts—was erected into the administrative county of London, with an elective council of large powers.[20] And in 1899 a Government of London Act further simplified the situation by sweeping away a mass of surviving parish and district authorities and jurisdictions and creating twenty-eight metropolitan boroughs, each with mayor, aldermen, and councillors such as any provincial borough possesses, although with powers somewhat differently defined and in certain directions, e.g., finance, considerably less extensive. As a glance at a map will show, these boroughs—Battersea, Bethnal Green, Chelsea, Greenwich, Holborn, Westminster, etc.—are very unequal in size, their boundaries having been marked off with a view to preserving various traditional lines.[21]

The situation today, therefore, is briefly this. At the center of the metropolitan area stands the historic City, which is, to all intents and purposes, a municipality within a municipality. It has a government of its own—a sort of government which, preserving as it does much of the old municipal system antedating the Corporation Act, is to be found nowhere else in the

[20] The Metropolitan Board of Works was abolished, or more properly superseded, by the new county council.

[21] Other boroughs, such as Hornsey and West Ham, are within the densely populated area commonly called "Greater London," but lie outside the bounds of the administrative county, and hence are not metropolitan boroughs in the technical sense.

realm. The corporation, or body of freemen and liverymen,[22] governs the city through a mayor and three "courts," or councils—a court of aldermen, elected for life by the freemen and liverymen of the twenty-six wards, a court of common council, chosen for one year by the same electorate, and a "court of common hall," which is, in effect, a primary assembly of the freemen, liverymen, and municipal officers charged with duties of an elective nature only. Here alone, among English local governments, the aldermen sit—though for certain purposes only—as a separate chamber. The court of common council, consisting of the lord mayor, the twenty-six aldermen, and 206 councillors, and meeting fortnightly, is the really important governing authority, its administrative work being handled, as in other municipalities, by standing committees and permanent officials. The lord mayor, who comes to his office by seniority from among the aldermen, is a mayor of an ordinary municipality raised to the topmost pinnacle of prestige and ceremonial splendor; but, like other English mayors, he has no independent powers. Obviously, the City is in these days an anachronism—a curious island of pre-reform municipal organization—which at first glance ought to be made to go the way of other medieval survivals; and there is considerable demand that it be assimilated to the remainder of the metropolis, not only from reformers who object to present arrangements as inconsistent with twentieth-century democracy, but from taxpayers who dislike to see the richest square mile of the metropolitan area exempted from contributing to the county rate. The undoubted efficiency of the existing government and the apparent contentment of the local ratepayers with things as they are, however, set up a rather formidable defense, and it seems likely that the City will stand its ground for a good while to come.[23]

[22] The liverymen are members of some seventy-five "companies," e.g., the Stationers' Company, the Grocers' Company, the Goldsmiths', and the Apothecaries', descended from medieval guilds. A ratepayer becomes a member of a company by making application and paying a fee of one guinea. This makes him a "freeman." If he wants to be a "liveryman" in the fullest sense, with a right to wear the livery or uniform of the company, he must pay five guineas.

[23] A. J. Glasspool, *The Corporation of the City of London: its Ceremonies and Importance* (London, 1924).

Flanking the City on all sides are the twenty-eight metropolitan boroughs, in organization and powers a cross between ordinary boroughs and urban districts. Coëxtensive with these geographically, and wielding a good deal of control over them in finance and other matters, is the administrative county of London, with its 124 councillors and its twenty aldermen, presided over by an elective chairman (who on ceremonial occasions is quite overshadowed by the lord mayor of the City), and endowed with powers broadly similar to those of county councils elsewhere, although differing also from them in a number of important respects. And sweeping far out into the surrounding regions are the jurisdictions of a Metropolitan Water Board (created in 1902) and a Metropolitan Police Board (dating from 1829), the authority of the latter extending, indeed, over all parishes within fifteen miles of Charing Cross—an area of almost seven hundred square miles.[24]

It goes without saying that the administrative county and the federated metropolitan boroughs have already accumulated an instructive history and present numerous features of interest to the student of local institutions. To bring out the differences between them and the counties and boroughs of the prevailing types as described in the earlier portions of this chapter would, however, require more space than is available here. Suffice it to say that elections to the L. C. C. (as the county council is colloquially termed) are contested keenly on party lines,[25] that the council is one of the most vigorous and industrious in the land, that its procedure bears a strong resemblance to that of the House of Commons, and that the body has many notable achievements—in public works, education, sanitation, etc.—to its credit; and, on the side of the boroughs, that an interesting though not very strong agency of correlation is found in a

[24] None of the municipal authorities heretofore mentioned has anything to do with police. Except that the city has its own separate arrangements, the entire police establishment of the district—the largest such organization in the world—is administered, under direct control of the Home Office, by a police commissioner appointed, on non-political grounds, by the crown. See R. B. Fosdick, *European Police Systems* (New York, 1915). Viscount Byng of Vimy, a former governor-general of Canada, was appointed commissioner in 1928.

[25] By the Municipal Reformers (largely Conservatives), the Progressives (mainly Liberals), and Labor.

"metropolitan boroughs standing joint committee" consisting of representatives of the City of London and of such metropolitan borough councils as choose to be represented,[26] and that in spite of some instances of extravagance, e.g., in Poplars, at the hands of councils dominated by Labor, the record achieved has generally been good.[27] There is complaint that the quality of municipal officials is not as high as it once was, and that the people of some of the boroughs take an insufficient interest in their local affairs; and so rapidly does the huge urban community grow that already there are dense populations on the county's borders encumbered with a jungle of jurisdictions and in need—even though they are usually rather hostile to the idea—of being brought under the L. C. C.'s jurisdiction. A royal commission on the government of the metropolis, reporting in 1923, was, however, unable to agree on any suggestion going farther than that the county council and the metropolitan borough councils should work out together some plan of reapportionment of functions already possessed.[28] Considering that the population of the metropolitan area has now come to be more than seven millions (which means, as a recent writer has reminded us, that one Englishman in every five is a Londoner), it is fair to assume that questions relating to the extension and improvement of the existing facilities for metropolitan government and administration will make large demands upon the thought and energies of the coming generation.[29]

[26] This body, meeting monthly, has no regulative power. It considers recommendations made to it by its executive committee, or by any of the boroughs, and passes resolutions for the information of the L. C. C. and the respective boroughs.

[27] See W. B. Munro, *The Government of European Cities* (rev. ed.), 187.

[28] *Report of the Commissioners Appointed to Inquire into the Local Government of Greater London.* Cmd. 1830 (1923).

[29] The best brief descriptions of London's government are W. B. Munro, *The Government of European Cities* (rev. ed.), Chap. ix; A. L. Lowell, *The Government of England,* II, Chaps. xlii-xliii; and J. J. Clarke, *Local Government of the United Kingdom* (4th ed.), Chap. xxx. A good general book on the subject is P. A. Harris, *London and its Government* (London, 1913). The physical development of the metropolis is discussed interestingly in A. Webb, *London of the Future* (London, 1921), and G. T. Forest, "London One Hundred Years Hence," *Public Admin.,* IV, 156-174 (1926). A. E. Davies, *The Story of the London County Council* (London, 1924), is a useful Fabian Society pamphlet. T. H. Reed and P. Webbink, *Documents Illustrative of American Municipal Government* (New York, 1926),

The Problem of Further Reconstruction of Local Government

Indeed, a good deal of attention is already given, not only to matters of metropolitan government, but to problems affecting the entire scheme of local government and administration as outlined in this and the preceding chapter; and some far-reaching proposals have been made. In the main, the existing system was either created or reformed in the nineteenth century, and it is the handiwork of the middle-class political elements, Conservative and Liberal, which controlled affairs in that period. To a considerable extent, it reflects the *laissez-faire* attitude then prevalent, even though the logic of events compelled such wide departures from that principle as to have endowed the local authorities with what look to many persons to be very extensive powers of regulation and collective enterprise. So far as those elements of society which created the system are concerned, further changes may be expected to proceed on the familiar lines—cautious, and usually belated, readjustments involving no very wide departures from tried and traditional arrangements. The newer social and political forces represented in the socialist movement and the Labor party come at the matter, however, with different ideas and in a different spirit. They consider that, although English local government is "unsurpassed for efficiency and excellence in many fields of utilitarian achievement," it is lamentably neglectful of the interests that make for cultural betterment; that the growing urbanization of the country will increasingly create situations which the present system is unfitted to meet; and that the system must be reconstructed from the ground up in the light of newer popular aspirations and needs, and no longer merely scrutinized by half-hearted royal commissions and tinkered with by conservative-minded and preoccupied parliamentarians.

A great deal could be written about the proposals that have come from earnest men and women who approach the problem from this angle. There would be danger of creating a somewhat exaggerated impression of the imminence of revolutionary

478-503, reproduces portions of a valuable statement by M. L. Gwyer appearing originally in the *Minutes of Evidence Taken Before the Royal Commission on London Government* (London, 1922), Part i. H. James, "The London Region," *Nat. Munic. Rev.*, Sept., 1928, is of some interest.

change; because, after all, no very wide departures from the existing order of things is to be expected unless Labor finds itself in power over a considerable period of time. Even then, the outcome would be uncertain. For not only has office a sobering effect, but in this matter of local government reorganization Labor men and women are themselves divided sharply. The party stands, in general, for the vigorous and progressive development of municipal activity, and in particular for the extension of social services such as education, public health, and housing. It is on record for a considerably larger measure of what we call in America municipal "home rule," and is sponsor for an important measure [30] which, if enacted—as it never will be except by a Labor-controlled Parliament—would permit local authorities to do everything not specifically reserved to the national government, thereby moving the whole center of gravity from London to the provinces, so far as local government is concerned, and not only relieving many local government matters from the necessity of passing through the bottleneck at Westminster, but liberating much of the time of the hard-pressed House of Commons. Beyond this, however, there is disagreement. Whether the existing scheme of counties, boroughs, and districts should be preserved is warmly debated. Mr. G. D. H. Cole has an ingenious plan for a total reorganization on regionalist lines; [31] Mr. and Mrs. Webb have a different plan; [32] Mr. Laski and other writers have still other ideas.[33] The discussion is interesting and stimulating. It emphasizes the truth, already voiced, that even local government is a fluid, flexible thing, never a static and finished product, and it points the way to practical reforms capable of being adopted quite independently of the larger and more idealistic programs in which they may be embedded—reforms of such character as have, indeed, already been adopted on highly important lines in the Local Government Act of 1929. It is impossible here, however, to do more than thus call attention to the existence of

[30] The Local Authorities (Enabling) Bill.

[31] *The Future of Local Government* (London, 1921).

[32] *A Constitution for the Socialist Commonwealth of Great Britain,* Pt. ii, Chap. iv.

[33] H. J. Laski, *The Grammar of Politics* (London, 1925), and *The Problem of Administrative Areas* (Northampton, 1918).

a tendency—now expressing itself in a more or less organized movement—which promises to bring the whole laboriously built plan of English local government under the severest scrutiny to which it has ever been subjected.[34]

[34] It should be emphasized that this chapter and the previous one deal with local government in England and Wales only. Scotland has its own system; so also do both Northern Ireland and the Irish Free State. On arrangements in the Free State, see pp. 734-737 below. The Scottish system, embracing counties, burghs, districts, and parishes, but with many peculiarities as to officials and powers, is described briefly in J. J. Clarke, *Local Government of the United Kingdom* (4th ed.), Chap. xxxi, and (in its municipal aspects) in W. B. Munro, *The Government of European Cities* (rev. ed.), 191-200, and very fully in W. E. Whyte, *Local Government in Scotland* (London, 1925). Arrangements in the two parts of Ireland are outlined in Clarke, *op. cit.*, Chap. xxxii, and touched upon in Munro, *op. cit.*, 200-204. Cf. J. J. Horgan, "Local Government in Ireland under the Free State," *Nat. Munic. Rev.*, Aug., 1926.

CHAPTER XXIX

THE UNITED KINGDOM—IRELAND TO 1914

THE constitution, government, and parties described in the foregoing chapters are those of England primarily. In varying degrees they are shared, however, by Wales, Scotland, and Ireland; and in order to get a rounded view even of English government in the narrower sense, to say nothing of British government on larger lines, it is necessary to give some attention to the political institutions of these once independent areas, and especially to the ways in which such institutions are geared up with the great central agencies of government at Whitehall and Westminster. Afterwards, and in closing, a word must be said about the Empire as a political unit, and about the scheme of imperial government generally.

Wales

Wales need not detain us, because for governmental purposes that historic principality has long been completely united with England. Edward I drew a large part of the country under English control in 1284, organized it in six counties on the English model, introduced the English judicial system, and—half with serious intent, half in jest—bestowed upon his son, in 1301, a title ever since borne by the recognized heir to the English crown, i.e., "prince of Wales." Henry VIII completed the work by setting up six more counties, giving both the counties and the leading towns the right to be represented in the House of Commons, and abolishing all local laws and customs which were at variance with the laws of England. Thenceforth the separate history of Wales, in so far as there was any, was cultural, not constitutional or political, and nowadays the system of government in the principality is in almost every respect identical with that in England itself. In 1747, indeed, it became a rule that in all acts of Parliament "England" should be construed to include Wales unless otherwise stipulated. There is a limited amount of legislation specially for Wales; but the great bulk of statutes applying to England apply equally, and without saying so, to the principality. One interesting divergence, which has a certain amount of political significance, arose in 1920, when, after prolonged agitation on the subject, an act of Parliament disestablished and disendowed the Anglican church in both Wales and the adjoining county of Monmouthshire.[1] It must be noted, too, that of late there has been somewhat of a movement for autonomy, with a local Welsh parliament, under a plan of devolution. This sentiment has been strongest in the north and west, where the population is most purely Welsh in speech and tradition and most aware of its special problems of labor, agriculture, and education.

Scotland and Its Government

To the north of England lies Scotland, separated from the larger country by no important physical barriers and seemingly destined by nature to form, in conjunction with it, one homogeneous state. Historical circumstances, however, made a political union between the two lands exceedingly difficult to bring about. Even yet there is not complete amalgamation; and growing talk of devolution suggests that existing bonds may in future be somewhat weakened rather than the reverse. Like Wales, Scotland long went its own way practically unmolested, although not entirely uninfluenced, by its more powerful neighbor. The Saxon conquerors of the southern parts of the island penetrated and to some extent settled in the nearer lowlands, but they never got a hold upon the highlands farther north, and their scant infusion did not prevent the gradual consolidation of the numerous Celtic tribes and clans into a Scottish kingdom, with Edinburgh as its capital, and with parliamentary institutions broadly similar to those which arose south of the

[1] As has been pointed out, this made Welsh bishops ineligible to sit in the House of Lords. "The Church in Wales" is now organized separately under an archbishop of Wales.

Tweed.[2] Toward the close of the thirteenth century, Edward I, the conqueror of Wales, undertook to settle a dispute over the succession to the Scottish throne, and from that step passed to an attempt to extend his own suzerainty over the country. For the time being he was successful. But when his son and successor became involved in a war with France, the Scots, led by the redoubtable Robert Bruce, rose in rebellion and in 1314, at historic Bannockburn, inflicted upon the English a defeat which broke their control and left the country once more completely independent. For three hundred years the two kingdoms lived on side by side, often far from friendly, but without any serious attempt by either to subjugate the other. As the weaker of the two, Scotland habitually made common cause with England's traditional enemy, France; and presently Scottish law and institutions are found showing effects of French influences which have by no means disappeared to this day.

In 1603, as every schoolboy knows, James VI of Scotland ascended the throne of England as James I and launched in that country the unhappy rule of the Stuarts. The union was a purely personal one through the crown, and so it remained for over a hundred years. James and each of his successors was at the same time king of England and king of Scotland. But the latter country continued to have its own parliament, its own established church, its own laws, its own courts, its own army, and its own system of finance. This sort of union was, of course, not very substantial. But the fact that it was able to withstand the strain of the Civil War, the Cromwellian dictatorship, the expulsion of James II, and the establishment of the Hanoverian dynasty, tended to make it more so; and circumstances were all the while ripening which dictated not only that it should be kept alive but that it should be made closer and more effective. On the one hand, the interest of the Scots slowly shifted from religion to industry and trade, and desire grew strong to end the tariff wars which England habitually turned to account in holding Scottish industry and other enterprise in check. On the other hand, England stood out resolutely

[2] The Scottish parliament always consisted, however, of a single chamber, in which the commoners enjoyed a greater share of power than in the English parliament of earlier times.

against admitting the Scots to an active trade with herself and her colonies unless they would give up their separate parliament and accept such other arrangements as would definitely convert the two realms into one. It was a hard decision for the doughty northerners to make, and it was reached only after long and furious debates at Edinburgh. But practical interest overrode sentiment; and after commissioners representing the two governments had worked out a treaty, the parliaments at Edinburgh and London gave it the form and authority of law. Early in 1707 the Act of Union with Scotland received the royal assent. That some step, either forward or backward, had become inevitable was indicated by the announcement of the Scottish parliament in 1704 that unless relief of some kind were found it would proceed to give the country a monarch of its own.[3]

Under the terms of union, the two countries were erected "forever" into a single kingdom, to be known as Great Britain. The Scottish parliament was abolished, and in lieu of it Scotland was given representation in the English—henceforth British—parliament at Westminster: forty-five commoners (thirty from the counties and fifteen from the boroughs), and sixteen peers, to be elected by the whole body of Scottish peers at the beginning of each parliament. These modest quotas did not assure the Scots much weight in legislation at Westminster; although it must be remembered that both branches of Parliament were then far smaller than now. But this did not so much matter because, in the first place, the Union fully guaranteed the coveted freedom of Scottish trade with England and the colonies, and because, in the second place, it similarly guaranteed the continuance of Scottish civil and criminal law —both common law and statutes—subject only to a necessary

[3] The text of the act of 1707 is printed in C. G. Robertson, *Select Statutes, Cases, and Documents,* 92-105, and in abridged form in G. B. Adams and H. M. Stephens, *Select Documents of English Constitutional History,* 479-483. J. Mackinnon, *The Union of England and Scotland* (London, 1896), is a scholarly volume covering principally the period 1695-1745; P. H. Brown, *The Legislative Union of England and Scotland* (Oxford, 1914), is an excellent series of lectures on the more immediate history of the act of 1707; and A. V. Dicey and R. S. Rait, *Thoughts on the Union Between England and Scotland* (London, 1920), is a systematic study of the circumstances, method, and results of the union.

ultimate power of revision by the common parliament. The Scottish judicial system, which was in some respects superior to the English, was to go on as before; the law establishing "the Protestant religion and Presbyterian church government" was "forever ratified, approved, and confirmed;" and arrangements for popular education—a field of activity entered by the Scottish government full two hundred years before the English government entered it—were left as they had previously been.[4]

From Queen Anne to our day, the political position of Scotland has continued substantially without change. Representation in the common parliament at Westminster remains what it was, except that, beginning in 1832, the number of commoners has been gradually brought up, to keep pace with the growth of population, to seventy-four. All general legislation for the country is, of course, enacted at Westminster. The bulk of it applies to Scotland, England, and Wales indistinguishably; and, as in the case of Wales, all acts of Parliament are construed to apply to Scotland unless they stipulate to the contrary. In the case of larger pieces of legislation, such as the parliamentary reform acts and the local government acts of the past hundred years, it is customary to give Scotland the benefit of a separate statute, in which such minor variations can be introduced as may seem desirable. And Scotland is further recognized as a distinct entity for legislative purposes by the arrangement, already described, under which all public bills relating exclusively to that area and referred to a standing committee in the House of Commons are assigned to a committee so constituted as to consist of all the members representing Scottish constituencies, with the addition of from ten to fifteen other members for the consideration of any particular bill. This Scottish committee may, perhaps, be thought of as a pale survival of the old Scots parliament.

For the supervision of Scottish administration, a new secretary of state for Scotland was created after the union. Following the Jacobite uprising of 1745, the function was transferred to the Secretary of State for Home Affairs. In 1885 it was

[4] The common school system of Scotland dates from a parliamentary statute of 1696 requiring an elementary school in every parish.

restored to a Secretary for Scotland, who, without being a "principal secretary," and without having a seat in the cabinet, exercised it under the same conditions as to appointment and responsibility that apply to other ministers. Finally, in 1926, a Secretaries of State Act abolished the secretaryship on this basis and created once more a principal Secretary of State for Scotland, who acquired equal rank with the previously existing principal secretaries, including a right always to have a seat in the cabinet. There are the usual under-secretaries; and various branches of administrative work are looked after by a lord advocate, a solicitor-general, a registrar-general, a board of health, a Privy Council committee on education, and other officers and boards corresponding broadly to those functioning in England and Wales.

Counties and boroughs serve as the principal local areas of administration and self-government. They differ at some points from those in England, but in general are organized under similar (though not identical) laws, and tend as time goes on to come gradually closer to the English model. At the union, as we have seen, Scotland retained its old system of law and justice, a system patterned largely on that of France. The scheme of courts is still very different from the English,[5] and the same is true of civil law and procedure, although the criminal law of the two countries is now practically identical.[6] An entirely separate ecclesiastical organization persists; likewise a distinct system of educational administration.[7]

The Scottish Home Rule Movement

On the whole, Scotland's experience with the union has been satisfactory. Many of her people were skeptical about tying up with "an auld enemy;" many joined Lockhart in the lament that April 30, 1707, was "the last day that Scotland was Scot-

[5] The justices of the peace, at the bottom of the scale, are rather similar to those in England; but the administration of justice in each county is in charge of a "sheriff-depute" who has no close counterpart in England, and the highest civil court, the Court of Session (from which appeal lies to the House of Lords at Westminster) rests back on the French *parlement* of Paris, rather than any English court, as a prototype.

[6] Criminal procedure is, however, in many respects different.

[7] On education, see A. L. Lowell, *Government of England,* II, Chap. 1.

land."[8] Repeal was mooted on sundry occasions; plots and incipient rebellions, especially in the highlands, kept the waters muddied until past the middle of the century. But, as DeFoe remarked, the union "was merely formed by the nature of things." Geographical proximity and trade necessities made it inevitable. And as the country, newly admitted to the profits of English and colonial trade, waxed prosperous and wealthy, regret gradually gave way to contentment, the more by reason of the fact that weight in governmental matters grew out of all proportion to numbers or square miles. There is a story of an Edinburgher who went to London and met no English because he called only on heads of departments. Facetiousness aside, the preponderance of Scots in all ranks of the government service has long been a matter of comment. Among recent premiers alone, Rosebery, Balfour, Campbell-Bannerman, and Ramsay MacDonald were Scots; Gladstone, too, was of Scotch ancestry. All in all, the Scot has rather ruled than been ruled.

This, however, has not prevented the growth in the last half-century of a considerable movement for Scottish "home rule." The example of Ireland has had something to do with it. Talk of devolution has contributed its share. The resurgence of nationalist feeling both before and after the World War has lent impetus. Dissatisfaction with defects of the existing situation, real or fancied, has found expression in the press, in local government bodies, and even on the floor of Parliament. Decades ago—in 1886, to be exact—a Scottish Home Rule Association came into existence to foster the ideal of "home rule all round," and, in particular, to agitate not only for restoration of a Scottish parliament, but for the creation of a national Scottish executive, or ministry, "to control the administration of Scottish affairs, subject to the Scottish parliament and to the Scottish parliament alone." Specifically, it is complained that legislation on matters of vital concern to Scottish well-being either fails to be enacted at all or comes only belatedly after it has long been needed; that progressive measures for

[8] Robert Burns sang:

> Farewell to a' our Scottish fame,
> Farewell our ancient glory,
> Farewell even to the Scottish name
> Sae famed in martial story!

Scotland are habitually overridden by Conservative English majorities; that it is anomalous for Scotland to have (in the office of the Secretary of State) what is in effect a national executive without a national parliament to exercise control over it; that as a rule the estimates for Scotland are passed in the House of Commons without any discussion whatsoever; that much so-called expenditure to which Scottish taxpayers contribute, while euphoniously called imperial expenditure, is really only English expenditure; that in many minor but nevertheless important matters Scotland, like a political Cinderella, is constantly being neglected and despised. Much might be said in rebuttal of these contentions—for example, that when great measures which it is desired to apply to both England and Scotland are under consideration, a separate act for Scotland is usually passed, in order to facilitate adaptation to Scottish needs and desires, even though much additional time is required from a hard-pressed Parliament.[9] The grievances that have been mentioned are not serious enough to have roused the whole people; nor—barring the adoption of some scheme of devolution applying generally throughout the realm—is there prospect of any important change in the present arrangements. It is, however, significant that upwards of a score of Scottish home rule motions and bills have been introduced at Westminster since 1889, and that in no instance have they failed to receive the support of a heavy majority of the Scottish members.[10]

Ireland to the Act of Union (1800)

Far less amicable and stable have been the relations between England (Great Britain since 1707) and Ireland. After all, Scotland joined hands with England voluntarily, because she saw that it was to her interest to do so. Ireland, however, was repeatedly invaded and conquered, held for centuries in involuntary dependence, and finally forced into a legislative union

[9] The most recent notable illustration is the Scottish Local Government Act of 1929.

[10] The case for Scottish home rule is presented, somewhat extravagantly, in *Home Rule for Scotland* (Glasgow, 1922), issued by the Scottish Home Rule Association. A review of Scottish home rule bills introduced in Parliament will be found in W. H. Chiao, *Devolution in Great Britain*, Chaps. iv-v. Cf. L. Spence, "The National Party of Scotland," *Edinb. Rev.*, July, 1928.

by a purely British decision backed up with clever political legerdemain. She may have derived some benefit from her English connections; in certain directions she undoubtedly did so. But she always regarded herself as a conquered and oppressed country, the prey of English landlords and tax-gatherers; and for hundreds of years her history was largely a story of efforts to confine British control within narrower limits, as the next best thing to eliminating it altogether. In our own day those efforts have so far succeeded that a sixth of the island has won the long-coveted "home rule," while the remainder, for which this concession had ceased to be an acceptable solution, has been erected into a "free state," autonomous and self-governing as are Canada, Australia, and the other dominions. During the World War, and for some time both before and after, the status of Ireland furnished one of the two or three most explosive and baffling constitutional questions with which harassed British statesmen were called upon to deal.

The remoter background of the problem must be explained briefly. English rule in Ireland began in the second half of the twelfth century, when the vigorous Henry II invaded the island, received the obeisance of various native princes, and organized the region around Dublin into a dependency long known as "the Pale." Englishmen settled in the territory in considerable numbers, but efforts to prevent them from becoming mixed with the natives proved a failure, and, except in the northern district of Ulster, where heavy English and Scottish settlement took place in the seventeenth century, the country remained decidedly Celtic. In the course of time a parliament arose. Until the sixteenth century, however, only English settlers were represented in it; and although Irish members were then admitted, they never counted for much. Catholics, indeed, were debarred from membership after the uprising of 1689-90, and later were excluded even from voting at parliamentary elections. Furthermore, Poynings' Law of 1494 gave all English laws, so far as applicable, force in Ireland, forbade the Irish parliament to meet without the English government's consent, and made all its acts subject to approval by the English crown. Later on (in 1720) the British parliament affirmed its right to legislate for Ireland on all matters whatsoever.

With a parliament thus shackled, and with executive power in the hands of an English lord lieutenant who was answerable to nobody except at London, Ireland passed along from century to century with hardly a shred of self-government. Her economic development was held in check, not only by recurring civil disorders, but by legislation enacted at or inspired from London; great sections of her territory were confiscated and turned over to English and Scotch proprietors and colonists, especially under James I, and again after Cromwell's suppression of the all but successful revolt precipitated by the English Civil War; further penalties were visited after the country had again guessed wrong and thrown its support to the deposed James II in his futile effort to regain his throne. By the opening of the eighteenth century the land was completely under alien control, and the people, if not broken in spirit, had at least lost hope of early relief. For almost three generations there were no further important developments.[11]

Toward the close of the century, however, Irish history once more began to be written rapidly. About 1780, when Britain was at bay, with most of Europe hostile or actually in arms against her, and with the most valuable of her colonial possessions about to slip from her grasp, a movement got under way which prompted the British Parliament in 1782 to repeal the declaratory act of 1720 and soon thereafter to rescind Poynings' Law and to concede the supremacy of the Irish parliament in strictly Irish affairs. This legislation was acclaimed loudly as giving Ireland virtual home rule. It, however, did nothing of the sort, because, in the first place, the parliament continued English in personnel rather than Irish, and, in the second place, it had no more control than before over the English-appointed and English-controlled executive. Disillusioned, and incited from France, the people once more, in 1798, embraced the hazards of open rebellion.[12]

It was the old story. British arms proved superior, and the

[11] The fullest and best account of Irish affairs in the eighteenth century will be found in various chapters of W. E. H. Lecky, *History of England in the Eighteenth Century,* 8 vols. (New York, 1878-90). A sympathetic but reliable guide to Irish history in general is S. Gwynn, *The History of Ireland* (London, 1922).

[12] France was, of course, now at war with Great Britain.

uprising was suppressed. Thereupon the government of the younger Pitt decided to wipe out what remained of Irish autonomy by merging the country with Britain under the terms of a legislative union similar to that of 1707 with Scotland. Locked in deadly combat with a powerful Continental foe, Britain, it was argued, must put an end to flank attacks through French encouragement of Irish rebellion. Besides, in almost two decades the rehabilitated island parliament had made little headway toward a solution of Irish problems, and it was time to try, as an alternative resource, a single consolidated parliament working from Westminster. Pitt was not unfriendly to the Irish people and must be credited with honestly believing that the proposed union would prove a benefit to them as well as a protection for Britain.

An act of union with Ireland, designed to "promote and secure the essential interests of Great Britain and Ireland, and to consolidate the strength, power, and resources of the British Empire," was accordingly drawn up and submitted to the two parliaments. Except in Ulster, it was strongly opposed by the people of the lesser island, and it was got through at Dublin only by notoriously corrupt methods, even though, as one writer has remarked, such methods were common enough in that day.[13] Votes were bought with peerages and offices; nearly a million pounds sterling in cold cash were spent; intimidation and coercion, in all their familiar forms, were brought freely into play. At last, early in 1800, the bill was passed. Five months later, similar action was taken at Westminster; and on January 1, 1801, the measure took effect. The two kingdoms were now "forever" merged in a single United Kingdom of Great Britain and Ireland. The separate parliament in Ireland became a thing of the past, and the island was given thirty-two seats in the House of Lords at Westminster ("four lords spiritual and twenty-eight lords temporal"), and 100 in the House of Commons (sixty-four for county constituencies, thirty-five for boroughs, and one for the University of Dublin). Executive authority was to be exercised through a viceroy, representing the crown. The Anglican Church of Ireland was consolidated with the established Church of England, under

[13] W. B. Munro, *Governments of Europe*, 320.

the name of the United Church of England and Ireland, although less than one-fifth of the island's inhabitants were adherents of it. Laws and courts were not to be affected, except as the joint parliament might later modify them; and equality of commercial privileges was guaranteed, although with certain reservations that had not been made in the case of Scotland. Great Britain and Ireland were to contribute to joint revenues in the proportion of fifteen to two.[14]

Ireland Under the Union

The union was in the nature of a solemn contract, and while the church was disestablished in 1869[15] and one or two lesser changes were made, in the main the arrangement stood intact until 1914, when, as we shall see, a home rule act passed over the veto of the House of Lords sought to turn back the pages of history and restore to the distracted island a separate parliament and various other instrumentalities and attributes of autonomy. Long before 1914, however,—indeed, almost before the ink was dry on the act of 1800—the union became the object of sullen opposition, punctuated with violent demonstrations;[16] particularly after 1850, the "Irish question," in one or another of its many phases, was, year in and year out, the most baffling problem with which successive governments at London were called upon to deal.

Through the earlier nineteenth century, the issue presented three main aspects. The first was religious. Descendants of Scottish and English settlers, grouped mainly in six northern and northeastern counties of the province of Ulster, were

[14] The text of the act of 1800 is printed in C. G. Robertson, *Select Statutes, Cases, and Documents*, 157-164, and in abridged form in G. B. Adams and H. M. Stephens, *Documents of English Constitutional History*, 497-506. On Ireland before the union, see T. E. May and F. Holland, *Constitutional History of England*, II, Chap. xvi; W. A. Phillips, *The Revolution in Ireland, 1906-1923* (New York, 1923), 1-26; and E. R. Turner, *Ireland and England* (New York, 1919), Chaps. iii-vi. A trustworthy account of the events leading to the Act of Union is J. R. Fisher, *The End of the Irish Parliament* (London, 1911).

[15] The four lords spiritual from Ireland thereupon dropped out of the House of Lords.

[16] Grattan's advice to his countrymen to "keep knocking at the union" may have been unwise, but it was followed to the letter. As early as 1803, protest was registered in a serious uprising known as Emmet's rebellion.

Protestants (Episcopalians or Presbyterians); the remainder of the population—nearly four-fifths—was almost entirely Catholic. Yet the Protestant "Church of England and Ireland" was the established church throughout the island, to whose support all of the people were required to contribute. The second aspect was agrarian. A long series of conquests and confiscations had brought almost all of the land into the hands of English proprietors, and the once independent and prosperous natives had sunk to the level of a poverty-stricken peasantry, living as tenants on the great estates, and enjoying scarcely any rights as against the powerful landlords. Large numbers of them migrated to America, especially after the potato famines of 1846-49, and the population of the island steadily dwindled. The third difficulty was political, arising out of the fact that the country had lost even the slender rights of self-government that it had enjoyed in the eighteenth century, and was now ruled from London practically as a crown colony. The religious grievance was, in the main, removed in 1869 by the act disestablishing and partially disendowing the church in Ireland,[17] and the land situation was slowly improved by legislation begun in 1870 and carried forward, by both Liberal and Conservative governments, until 1914, when the question could be regarded as practically settled.[18] The problem of government proved more baffing. A Catholic Emancipation Act of 1829, which made Catholics eligible for election to Parliament and for appointment to most public offices, gave some relief, but without touching the fundamental grievance, which, of course, was that Ireland did not have self-government.

A word about the kind of government that the island actually had. The titular head was a dignitary (already mentioned) known as the lord lieutenant, who, like the governor-general in an overseas dependency, was the immediate representative of the crown. In earlier days he had truly ruled the country. But since the rise of the cabinet system, he, like the king, had receded into honorable inactivity, and the real headship of the executive had passed to a minister, nominally his inferior,

[17] G. B. Adams and H. M. Stephens, *Select Documents of English Constitutional History,* 538.

[18] E. R. Turner, *Ireland and England,* 188-225.

known as the chief secretary for Ireland. This official was always a member of the cabinet,[19] and to a large extent he guided its Irish policy; nine months of every year he spent at London, and only three at Dublin. Practically all appointments in the various executive departments were made by the chief secretary, in the name of the lord lieutenant; and while as the nineteenth century advanced more posts in some of the departments went to Irishmen, the executive and higher administrative organization, though distinct from that to the east of St. George's Channel, was at all times mainly English in personnel, if not in outlook and spirit. The chief secretary and his subordinates were, of course, responsible, not to any Irish parliament or other organ of Irish opinion, but only to the parliament at Westminster, by which, also, all legislation for the country was enacted. For new laws, or improvements in old ones, Ireland thus had to look to a legislature which was mainly English, Welsh, and Scottish—even though it is true, as we have seen, that Ireland was not only represented in this legislature, but, after the great mid-century era of emigration, was distinctly over-represented, and that she therefore bore a share, and a disproportionate one, in the making of laws for England, Wales, and Scotland.

All in all, the system of government was neither so bad as it was generally painted by Irishmen nor so good as complacent Britishers were wont to regard it. After the opening of the offices to natives, the introduction of merit principles, and the popularizing of local government by a county councils act of 1898, the system was, indeed, not intrinsically bad at all. It stood in need merely of some changes of detail to be deserving of being regarded as both economical and efficient. Nevertheless it was not an *Irish* government; it was not even a government responsible to Irish opinion. Hence it was probably futile to expect it to satisfy the political instincts and longings of any considerable section of the Irish people.[20]

[19] Unless the lord lieutenant was a member, which was often the case in earlier days but seldom after the middle of the nineteenth century.

[20] For an interesting statement of the opinion that Ireland, down to the World War, was advancing rapidly in liberty and prosperity, see W. A. Phillips, *The Revolution in Ireland,* 44-45.

The Home Rule Movement in the Nineteenth Century

Under the leadership of Daniel O'Connell, who believed in "agitation within the law," a peaceful "home rule" movement was set on foot as early as 1834 with a view to the complete repeal of the Act of Union; a Repeal Association was founded in 1840. In 1843 the agitation was suppressed by the authorities; whereupon various insurrectionary efforts were made, with equal lack of success. In 1858 a Fenian Brotherhood, taking its name from *Fiana Eireann,* the old national militia, was organized by Irish refugees in the United States, and soon both England and Ireland were in the grip of a revolutionary movement, the aim of which was nothing less than to establish an independent Irish republic by a policy of terrorism. For thirty years Fenian outrages and drastic acts of suppression on the part of the government followed in dreary succession. Their net effect, however, was only to add to the accumulated misunderstandings between the two peoples.[21]

The methods of the Fenians were disapproved by the large numbers of Irishmen who, like O'Connell, believed in peaceful, lawful agitation, and in 1870 a meeting was held at Dublin at which, under the leadership of Isaac Butt, a young Protestant lawyer, a Home Government Association was organized with a view to upholding the Irish cause in a fashion better calculated to win the favorable consideration of the English people. The object of the new association, as set forth in the resolutions of the Dublin conference, was to secure for Ireland a parliament of her own, and to obtain for that parliament, under a federal arrangement, the right of legislating for, and regulating all matters relating to, the internal affairs of Ireland, and control over Irish resources and expenditure, "subject to the obligation of contributing our just proportion of the imperial expenditure." Butt himself advocated "the federation of the Empire on a basis of self-governed nations," on lines proposed

[21] The testimony of Gladstone should be noted, however, that the Fenian activities "produced among Englishmen an attitude of attention and preparedness which qualified them to embrace, in a manner foreign to their habits in other times, the vast importance of the Irish controversy." On the rise and character of the Fenian movement, see M. Davitt, *The Fall of Feudalism in Ireland* (London, 1904).

by later friends of devolution.[22] On the Dublin platform the Association (renamed, in 1873, the Irish Home Rule League) won several victories at by-elections; and at the general elections of 1874 it returned sixty members. The indifference with which the speeches of Butt and his colleagues in Parliament were greeted led the League to a more radical stand; by 1880 the full repeal of the legislation of 1800 had become the minimum program. Meanwhile Butt, whose sanity of views was not equaled by his capacity for leadership, was practically superseded, in 1877, by one of the most remarkable orators and parliamentarians of the time, Charles Stewart Parnell. Although barely thirty years of age, a Protestant, and a landlord, Parnell quickly transformed a disorganized faction into a compact and aggressive Nationalist party.[23] Fortified by an alliance with Michael Davitt's turbulent Land League, and wielding a rod of iron over the House of Commons by means of novel and startling obstructionist tactics,[24] the new leader brought the Irish question into the very center of the political stage.

Obviously, the success of the movement was conditioned upon the support of one or the other of the two great English parties. For a time—especially when, in 1885, Lord Salisbury selected for the post of lord lieutenant in Ireland a leading advocate of the federal idea—it seemed that the desired backing would come from the Conservatives; and at the elections of the year mentioned the Nationalists, while not abandoning their own campaign, worked openly for the success of various Conservative candidates. Conservative opinion on the subject had, however, undergone no real change, and the discovery quickly broke the alliance and left the Salisbury ministry without a majority. Now it appeared, however, that the Liberal leader, Gladstone, after long holding out, had been won over

[22] W. A. Phillips, *The Revolution in Ireland*, 47-50.

[23] R. B. O'Brien, *Life of Charles Stewart Parnell*, 2 vols. (New York, 1898). The standard history of the Nationalist party is F. H. O'Donnell, *History of the Irish Parliamentary Party*, 2 vols. (London, 1910). Of much value also are M. MacDonagh, *The Life of William O'Brien, the Irish Nationalist* (London, 1928), and T. P. O'Connor, *Memoirs of an Old Parliamentarian*, 2 vols. (London, 1929).

[24] How this feature of Irish policy led to the first adoption of closure in the House of Commons has been related elsewhere. See p. 405 above.

to the cause. Indeed, upon becoming prime minister, early in 1886, the new champion, as has been related elsewhere, brought in a bill setting up a separate parliament at Dublin and withdrawing Irish representation altogether from the House of Commons at Westminster.[25] Many Liberal members refused to support the measure, which failed to pass, even in the lower chamber. Furthermore, as has appeared, the bill permanently alienated large numbers of influential leaders and adherents of the party. But the rank and file which remained faithful to Gladstone's leadership now accepted home rule as one of its cardinal tenets; and when, in 1893, the Great Commoner's last ministry brought in another bill on the subject, the effort was unsuccessful only because of the hostility of the Unionist majority in the House of Lords.[26] During the following decade of Unionist government (1895-1905) the question was in abeyance. There was much excellent legislation for Ireland; but the party was unalterably opposed to home rule, and agitation on the subject was recognized to be practically useless.

The Home Rule Bill of 1912 and the Ulster Protest

When the Liberals regained power it was assumed that, sooner or later, they would renew the efforts of 1886 and 1893. That they did not do so for several years was due to the disinclination of the leaders to jeopardize the party's hard-won position, to the vast majority in the House of Commons which freed the party from any need of aid from the Nationalists, and to informal pledges given upon taking office that a home rule bill would not be introduced in the parliament elected in 1906. In time, however, the situation changed. The parliamentary elections of 1910 stripped the Asquith ministry of its huge majority and left it dependent upon the votes of the Nationalist

[25] See p. 490 above.

[26] Both of these home rule bills went on the rocks partly because of the unsatisfactory disposition made of the thorny question of Irish representation at Westminster. The bill of 1886 provided for no such representation in the House of Commons, although Ireland was to be taxed to pay one-seventeenth of all imperial expenses. The bill of 1893 assigned Ireland eighty seats in the House of Commons, but withheld from Irish members the right to vote on matters concerning only Great Britain or any part thereof, thus looking to an irregular arrangement under which such members were to be now in, now out of, the chamber.

and Labor groups. Like the Laborites, the Nationalists, now led by John Redmond, were prepared to make the most of their enhanced importance; and, naturally enough, they let it be understood that the price of their support would be nothing less than a new home rule bill.[27] Furthermore, whereas formerly such a measure would have been certain of defeat in the House of Lords, the Parliament Act of 1911 opened a way for home rule legislation regardless of Unionist opposition. The upshot was that in the spring of 1912, the prime minister introduced a carefully prepared home rule bill, the third great measure of the kind to be sponsored by his party.

Broadly, the new bill followed the lines of the unsuccessful measure of 1893. A bicameral Irish parliament (both houses elective) was to have power to make laws pertaining exclusively to the lesser island. The lord lieutenant, representing the crown, was to continue as chief executive,[28] but he was to act only on advice of an "executive committee," or cabinet, composed of the heads of the Irish departments, who in turn were to be responsible to the Irish House of Commons; in other words, Ireland was for the first time to have a real cabinet system. A long list of matters—defense, navigation, extradition, naturalization, coinage, weights and measures, foreign trade, patents and copyrights, etc.—were reserved exclusively to the parliament at Westminster, and any bill passed at Dublin might be vetoed by the lord lieutenant. Drastic restraints were imposed for the protection of Protestants; and while, in general, Ireland was to levy her own taxes, the revenues were to be collected, at all events for a time, by imperial agents and paid into the imperial treasury. As under the bill of 1893, but not that of 1886, Ireland was to continue to be represented in the House of Commons at Westminster. Her quota of seats was, however, to be reduced from the existing 103 to 42; and her representatives were to be debarred from voting on bills pertaining exclusively to England, Scotland, or Wales, under the "in and out" plan of 1893.

[27] "I believe the Liberals are sincerely friendly to home rule," declared Redmond in a speech before an American audience; "but, sincere or not, we have the power, and will make them toe the line." See W. B. Wells, *Life of John Redmond,* Chap. v.

[28] The office of chief secretary was to be abolished.

The British people had barely drawn a long breath following the fight of 1909-11 over budget proposals and second chamber reform before the home rule bill of 1912 brought them face to face with a far graver situation; the controversies stirred by the bills of 1886 and 1893, exciting as they seemed at the time, were tame compared with the conflict now precipitated. Liberals, Labor, and the bulk of the Nationalists warmly supported the measure;[29] Conservatives, dominant in the House of Lords and numerous in the House of Commons, bitterly opposed it, almost to a man. All the old arguments were heard again, and new ones, too, based especially on the novel angle presented by the danger of civil war if the plan were proceeded with. This danger rose out of the exceptionally determined and spectacular resistance offered by the Protestant, Unionist portions of the province of Ulster.

Ulster, as has been noted, became the seat of a considerable Protestant population in the early seventeenth century, when the subjugation of the northern parts of the island was completed by wholesale confiscations of land and by the settlement there of a hardy race of emigrants from the adjacent portions of England and Scotland. Thenceforth there were in the country, as a recent writer has said, two separate entities, almost two separate nationalities. "One was largely Celtic, Catholic, politically backward, and economically depressed, ignorant, poor, exploited by aliens, with hopeless outlook and fierce hatred for the despoiler. The other was Anglo-Saxon and Protestant, Episcopalian, Presbyterian, and dissenter, large proprietors or substantial artisans or farmers, under British authority ruling, or allied with the ruling class, always proud, sometimes prosperous and successful."[30] The somewhat softened British policy of the nineteenth century brought substantial improvement to both parts of the country. But whereas Ulster—especially the highly industrialized sections around Belfast—was drawn by its economic as well as by its cultural interests into closer relations with England, the remaining

[29] A group of Independent Nationalists, led by William O'Brien and objecting to financial and other features, held aloof. See M. MacDonagh, *Life of William O'Brien,* as cited.

[30] E. R. Turner, *Ireland and England,* 294.

provinces were not conciliated and moved rather in the opposite direction.

From the earliest mention of home rule, the Protestants of Ulster were apprehensive and hostile. They opposed the bill of 1886, and in 1893 they resolved in convention to refuse to recognize the authority of an Irish parliament if one were set up. When, therefore, in 1911, the Asquith government made known its intention to introduce a new bill on the subject, the Ulstermen, under the leadership of Sir Edward Carson, promptly began organizing opposition, asserting that they were prepared to go to extreme lengths, if necessary, to avoid subjection to a Catholic parliament—even to the setting up of a separate provisional government. Advocates of home rule did not fail to point out that in four, possibly five, of the nine counties composing the province, home rulers were in a majority;[31] and that the census of 1911 showed that, in the province as a whole, Protestants of all denominations outnumbered Catholics by rather less then 200,000;[32] and they urged that the fears of Ulstermen sprang from ancient prejudice rather than from candid weighing of the proposed legislation. But the dissentients insisted that under any scheme of separate government for Ireland whatsoever they would be the certain victims of economic subjection and religious oppression. Countenanced, and even openly encouraged, by Unionists in England (who urged that this was no ordinary political issue, to be decided entirely by the votes taken at Westminster), they held excited mass meetings, signed covenants never to submit to an Irish parliament, drew up plans for a provisional government, and made preparations for a war of resistance.

Home Rule Adopted but Suspended

Undeterred, the government pressed on with its bill, which was twice passed by the House of Commons in 1913, and

[31] The counties of Ulster, Armagh, Antrim, and Down were overwhelmingly Unionist; Cavan and Donegal were overwhelmingly Nationalist; Derry, Fermanagh, Monaghan, and Tyrone were more evenly divided.

[32] Protestants, almost 900,000; Catholics, 700,000. Ulster's thirty-one representatives in the House of Commons after the general election of December, 1910, included sixteen Unionists, thirteen Nationalists, one Independent Nationalist, and one Liberal.

twice rejected by the House of Lords. All that remained, under the terms of the Parliament Act, was for the popular chamber to pass it once more; and early in 1914 the measure was reintroduced with this in view. The bill, indeed, received its third passage in early summer. Before the royal assent was asked, however, an amending measure, supported by the government, was introduced in the House of Lords; with a view to overcoming the main difficulty, any Ulster county was to be allowed to vote itself out from under the new law for a period of six years if it so desired. This proposal only muddied the waters further: the Ulsterites and their Unionist sympathizers saw in it, at best, only a reprieve; the Nationalists, on their part, were of no mind to win home rule, only to behold the sections of the country that would pay the most taxes withdrawn from the scheme. Amid the clatter of warlike preparations in both north and south, the king, in mid-summer, took the unusual step of calling a conference of Liberal, Unionist, and Labor leaders at Buckingham Palace.[33] But even this was in vain; and meanwhile the House of Lords added fuel to the flames by passing the amending bill in such form as to exclude, not simply a few counties, but all of Ulster, and not for six years, but indefinitely.

The altered measure then went to the House of Commons and was under heated debate there when, suddenly, the whole political scene was changed by the outbreak of the World War. In the fierce glare of the terrific international struggle that had been brought upon the country, even the issue of Ireland paled. An all-round party truce was declared; Parliament turned to legislation instantly demanded by the new and greater crisis; controversial subjects were shelved. As for Ireland, the amending bill was dropped, and the government, promising that it would never impose home rule on Ulster by force, announced that the recently enacted measure would not take effect until the end of the war, or, in any case, until after one year, and that, indeed, it would be changed before ever being allowed to take effect at all. Amid dramatic scenes, this program was accepted all round; and some six weeks later the

[33] See documentary materials relating to the conference reprinted in E. M. Sait and D. P. Barrows, *British Politics in Transition,* 2-13.

long-awaited Government of Ireland Act received the royal assent.

After eighty years of agitation, a home rule act was on the statute-book; although, ironically enough, the men who had placed it there were under solemn pledge to see that it was changed into a different form of act before being allowed to go into operation. In point of fact, it never went into operation at all; for—to make the situation still more ironical—when at last the way was open to put a modified home rule statute into effect, the bulk of Ireland would have none of it.[34]

[34] The dramatic events of 1912-14 are sketched in F. L. Benns, *The Irish Question, 1912-1914* (New York, 1928); W. A. Phillips, *The Revolution in Ireland,* Chap. ii; and B. W. Wells, *Life of John Redmond,* Chaps. vi, viii. The position of Ulster is described in E. R. Turner, *Ireland and England,* 293-311, and R. MacNeill, *Ulster's Stand for Union* (London, 1921). For an able Unionist exposition, see E. W. Hamilton, *The Soul of Ulster* (New York, 1917). Useful articles are W. T. Laprade, "The Home Rule Bill of 1912," *Amer. Polit. Sci. Rev.,* Nov., 1912, and A. G. Porritt, "The Irish Home Rule Bill," *Polit. Sci. Quar.,* June, 1913. The relation of Irish home rule to proposals for "home rule all round," i.e., home rule for all constituent parts of the United Kingdom, is dealt with in W. H. Chiao, *Devolution in Great Britain,* Chaps. iv-v. Cf. A. V. Dicey, *Law of the Constitution* (8th ed.), pp. lxxxvii-xci.

CHAPTER XXX

THE IRISH FREE STATE

THE decisions of 1914 seemed to have disposed of the Irish question for at least as long as the war should last. The conflict, however, proved unexpectedly lengthy; besides, while the Nationalist leaders had entered into the truce in all sincerity, plenty of their countrymen, especially the younger and more volatile elements, could see in the situation nothing except one more splendid opportunity—such as the Napoleonic wars had at an earlier time been thought to present—to strike off the shackles of British connection and put upon the map a free and independent Irish nation. Even during the first year of the war, when unity seemed unimpaired, ambitions of this sort were cherished secretly; and in the second year they gave rise to a bold and open independence movement.

Sinn Fein and the Demand for Independence

Impetus and leadership were supplied mainly by an organization known as Sinn Fein,[1] a society which, as such, dated from 1905, although it was directly rooted in a series of efforts nearer the opening of the century to revive and perpetuate Gallic culture.[2] As a party, the Nationalists were prepared to be satisfied with home rule. But the Sinn Feiners, even before the war, thought of Ireland only as by right a sovereign state and were bent upon purging the land of every form of British influence and setting up an independent republic. Until 1912, their numbers were small and progress was slow; when the home rule bill of that year made its appearance, the Sinn Feiners were still thought of as only a noisy, misguided, and

[1] An old Irish term meaning "ourselves alone."

[2] This Irish revival is described in E. R. Turner, *Ireland and England,* Pt. iii, Chap. i. The Sinn Fein movement was inspired to no small degree by Irish secret societies in the United States.

irresponsible faction. Events from then on, however, worked greatly to the radicals' advantage, and by 1914 they were in a position to challenge the still relatively moderate Nationalist program at every turn. Outwardly, Sinn Fein subscribed to the truce. It is clear enough now, however, that its activities were but barely halted, and that, confident of German aid, the movement's leaders were, almost from the first, in the position of simply waiting for a favorable hour to strike. An armed insurrection in Dublin on the Monday after Easter, 1916, proved abortive, but the proclamation of an independent Irish republic and the election of a visionary schoolmaster as its president at least had the effect of showing a startled and war-ridden British nation what it would have to reckon with in its own household. From this point dates a state of quasi-warfare between the British government and Catholic Ireland which lasted full five years. Under the impetus of fiery leadership, reënforced by the effects of British measures of punishment and repression, Sinn Fein became a name to conjure with from Donegal to Cork, and long before Britain emerged from her gruelling struggle on the Continent, the center of gravity of the entire Irish problem had shifted from the issue of home rule to that of unconditional independence.[3]

How truly this was so was impressed by the results of the parliamentary election following the armistice. Although, as we have seen, interest in the campaign centered in questions of policy arising out of the great war just ended,[4] Ireland could by no means be left out of the reckoning. The Coalition leaders called for a settlement on the basis of self-government, but without coercion of Ulster, and certainly without liberation of any part of the island from its connection with Great Britain. The Independent Liberals urged that the home rule act of 1914 be immediately put into effect; Labor laid stress on Ire-

[3] Brief impartial accounts of the growth of Sinn Fein and of the Easter uprising will be found in E. R. Turner, *Ireland and England,* Pt. iii, Chaps. ii-iii, and W. A. Phillips, *The Revolution in Ireland,* Chaps. iii-iv. Cf. H. M. Pim, "Sinn Fein: Past, Present, and Future," *Nineteenth Cent.,* June, 1919. A fuller and very satisfactory history of Sinn Fein is R. M. Henry, *The Evolution of Sinn Fein* (London, 1920). S. Desmond, *The Drama of Sinn Fein* (London, 1923) is a readable journalistic account.

[4] See p. 495 above.

land's right to "freedom." In the island itself the contest, outside of Ulster, was, of course, almost entirely between the Nationalists and Sinn Fein. The new party, participating in its first general election, put up candidates for all but five of the 105 seats to which the island was then entitled, and the contest became one of the bitterest in the country's history. People who knew the situation expected substantial Sinn Fein successes. But not even the Sinn Fein leaders themselves looked for the landslide that resulted. The Unionists secured a total of twenty-five seats (in the northeastern counties, of course), thus practically holding their own. The Nationalists obtained seven, as compared with eighty-four in 1910; Sinn Fein captured the remaining seventy-three. The Nationalist party—the party of Butt and Parnell, of Redmond and Dillon—was not only defeated and repudiated; it was practically annihilated. Among the Sinn Fein victors was, as mentioned in an earlier chapter, the cultured Countess de Markievicz, English by birth and Polish by marriage, whose Dublin home had long been a center of Sinn Fein influence, and who thus became the first woman to be elected to Parliament.

During the campaign the Sinn Fein candidates openly proclaimed that, if elected, they would evince their scorn for everything British by refusing to take their seats in a British-controlled parliament; and this promise they faithfully kept. Instead of repairing to Westminster when the new parliament assembled, they—or such of them as were able to do so [5]—met in Dublin at the beginning of 1919, organized themselves as a *Dáil Eireann*, or national assembly, and turned their efforts to giving the country a republican government, with a parliament elected in the existing constituencies and executive authority lodged in a president and group of ministers. The principle of self-determination was declared no less applicable to Ireland than to Poland or Czechoslovakia, and fervid, although futile, appeals were repeatedly addressed to President Wilson, to French and Italian statesmen, and finally to the Peace Conference at Versailles, asking that Ireland be admitted to representation in the Conference on the same basis as Great Britain, or

[5] Thirty-seven were in jail when elected, and four others were under indictment in the United States.

at all events that her independence be promptly and unconditionally recognized. While all this was going on, Eamonn de Valera—elected "president" of the Irish republic while confined in an English prison—effected an escape, and, having appeared among his followers and encouraged them to keep up the fight, made his way to the United States, where he obtained some assistance for his cause, both financial and moral.[6]

The Government of Ireland Act of 1920

With five-sixths of Ireland in more or less open rebellion, an insurrectionary government boldly defying British authority, and a semblance of public order capable of being maintained only by armed repression, the harassed government at London cast about for a plan of settlement with which to replace the now impossible home rule act of 1914. The long awaited bill —the fourth historic measure of the kind to claim the attention of Parliament—reached the House of Commons early in 1920. It differed widely indeed from its predecessors. Repealing the dormant act of 1914, it provided for two separate governments, one for the six predominantly Protestant counties of Ulster,[7] the other for all remaining parts of the island. The lord lieutenant at Dublin was, indeed, to continue to serve as the king's representative for the entire country. But there was to be a distinct unicameral parliament in each section;[8] likewise a separate cabinet and a separate judiciary;[9] and full powers were conferred, subject to the reservation of foreign relations, defense, tariffs, coinage, naturalization, and certain other matters for regulation and management by imperial authority, and subject, further, to a number of explicit prohi-

[6] De Valera, "Ireland's Right to Independence," New York *Nation,* June 7, 1919. E. R. Turner, *Ireland and England,* 396-417, is a good brief account of developments in Ireland during the war years.

[7] Antrim, Down, Armagh, Londonderry, Fermanagh, and Tyrone, and the boroughs of Belfast and Londonderry. These did not constitute the whole of the historic province of Ulster. The important county of Donegal, for example, was not included. It was predominantly Catholic and has been identified throughout with the portion of the country that later became the Free State. See map, p. 713 below.

[8] Before the bill became law it was amended to provide for bicameral parliaments.

[9] There was, however, to be a high court of appeal for the entire country.

bitions upon the action of the subordinate governments within the fields allotted to them. The government at London was to apply no pressure to bring about a union of the two legislatures, although these bodies might themselves unite if they chose. Meanwhile, a joint agency, known as the Council of Ireland, and consisting of forty members elected in equal quotas by the two regional parliaments, was to exercise such harmonizing influence as it could, especially in relation to services, such as transportation, that were obviously of common interest.[10] As in the case of the home rule act of 1914, Ireland (as a whole) was to have forty-two representatives in the House of Commons at Westminster.

Defended by the ministry on the ground that it gave Ireland as much self-government as the general safety would permit and that it fitted in acceptably with an ultimate scheme of all-round devolution, the bill rested precariously in Parliament's hands during most of 1920. Ireland was an armed camp, and something heroic must be done. But Sinn Fein was unalterably opposed to the suggested plan; the Nationalists, on different grounds, were almost equally displeased; the Labor party and the Independent Liberals insisted on drastic amendments; many Unionist, and especially Liberal, adherents of the Coalition felt no enthusiasm for the government's proposals. In many quarters it was predicted that even if the bill became law the settlement would break down because of the refusal of Catholic Ireland to organize under it. The ministers, nevertheless, pressed on with the project, and near the end of the year the bill passed both houses and received the royal assent. For the first time in history, the House of Lords saw its way clear to put the stamp of its approval on a measure for Irish home rule.[11]

The new law was one for which much could be said. It gave the proposed Irish parliaments larger powers than Westminster had been willing to relinquish in 1914, and it provided means of preserving the essential unity of the country in spite of the partition. Machinery for conciliation is, however, useless

[10] One object in creating the Council was frankly stated, in the bill, to be "the eventual establishment of a parliament for the whole of Ireland."

[11] A full and satisfactory treatise on the act and its antecedents is A. Quekett, *The Constitution of Northern Ireland; Part i, The Origin and Development of the Constitution* (Belfast, 1928). See p. 717, note 26.

without the driving force of the spirit of conciliation; and, unhappily, this spirit was in the present case almost totally wanting. The turmoil in which the country had lived for years went on unabated; Sinn Fein continued as strongly bent as ever upon a single independent republic. In the North, the new system was, indeed, installed without serious difficulty. A parliament, heavily Unionist, was opened at Belfast in 1921, and a ministry was duly organized. From this point dates the North Ireland "home rule" government as we know it today. In the South, too, the forms were gone through. But when the new parliament was elected all but four of the members of the lower house turned out to be Sinn Feiners pledged not to take oath of allegiance to the crown, without which the assembly could not function. Legally, South Ireland had arrived at home rule; after many vicissitudes it now had a parliament of its own. But the concession had come too late, and the people would have none of it. Still more would have to be yielded—possibly independence itself—if intolerable anarchy on the one hand, and downright repression and extermination on the other, was to be avoided.

The Treaty of 1921

It might have seemed that the possibilities of negotiation had been exhausted. But in point of fact the time for sitting down around a table and working out a real settlement, on the plan of give and take, had only just arrived. Public sentiment in Britain, and even in parts of Ireland—to say nothing of the world at large—demanded a truer compromise than that embodied in the act of 1920; efforts of Sinn Fein to involve the United States in controversy with Great Britain over the matter had patently failed; financial aid hitherto drawn by the Irish extremists from American sympathizers was dwindling; Sinn Fein itself had become sharply divided between a wing, led by De Valera, that wanted to fight to the last ditch and the Griffith-Collins elements [12] which were ready to sacrifice something in order to get a settlement. A new period of negotiation, accord-

[12] Arthur Griffith, an able journalist and one of the founders of Sinn Fein, and Michael Collins, once called by Lloyd George "the bravest representative of a valiant race."

ingly, opened in early summer of 1921, when the British prime minister, Lloyd George, invited the Ulster prime minister and De Valera to attend a conference in London "to explore to the utmost the possibility of a settlement;" and it closed near the end of the year when an historic treaty was signed by representatives of Sinn Fein and the British government providing for the abrogation, in southern Ireland, of the abortive home rule scheme, and the erection of that section of the country into an Irish "free state" with substantially the status of Canada and other self-governing portions of the "community of nations known as the British Empire."[13] The new quasi-dominion was to include the whole of Ireland, unless within one month after final ratification of the free-state plan at London the Ulster parliament should signify to the crown that the northern counties desired to remain outside. There was little doubt that such a decision would be reached; in which case Northern Ireland was to go on unaffected, on a home rule basis and

[13] It is impossible to tell the story here, even in outline, of the prolonged, many-sided, oft-interrupted and oft-renewed discussions that led up, with unexpected success at the end, to the treaty. Notable incidents included the friendly mediation of the South African statesman, General Smuts, who frankly told the Sinn Feiners that they must be content with a status which was good enough for South Africa; the declaration of a "truce," July 10, which was reasonably well observed; a fresh appeal by De Valera to the sentiment of the world in behalf of Irish self-determination and independence; the British government's offer to Ireland, on July 20, of the status of a dominion; rejection of this offer, on August 10, as "illusory" unless the "right to secede" was fully guaranteed; Mr. Lloyd George's rejoinder, on August 13, that no right of secession could be admitted, and that the relations of northern and southern Ireland could not be allowed to be referred to foreign arbitration; the strong assertion of Ireland's *de jure* independence by the reassembled *Dáil Eireann,* followed by another election of De Valera to the presidency of the "republic" and the appointment of a new group of ministers; the assembling in London, on October 11, of a conference, after three months' parleying during which complete deadlock often threatened; and the working out of the comprehensive treaty to which signatures were affixed, at the close of a tense all-night session, on the morning of December 6. The Irish negotiators assented to a settlement stopping short of independence only because the British government had announced that it would not prolong the conference beyond the night of December 5, and because they knew that rejection of the dominion status plan would not only precipitate a contest of arms in which Ireland would be foredoomed to ruinous defeat but would cost the Irish the sympathy of the entire neutral world. Cf. W. A. Phillips, *The Revolution in Ireland,* Chap. xi.

as organized under the act of 1920.[14] Whatever its ultimate bounds territorially, the Free State was to have the constitutional status of Canada, with a parliament and a responsible ministry, a titular chief executive corresponding to the governor-general in the dominions, and, of course, no further representation in the House of Commons at Westminster.[15]

Tired of the subject, and feeling that no better settlement could be had, the British parliament approved the plan without delay. Ireland followed suit—first through ratification by the purely revolutionary *Dáil Eireann,* but later through similar action by the phantom parliament formerly chosen under the act of 1920. Early in 1922 a provisional government, created under terms of the treaty, took office; the British troops, released from their unpleasant labors, began returning home; the Free State, to all intents and purposes, became a reality. Catholic Ireland had been given her long-sought opportunity. Could she pull herself together and make such use of it as would justify her course in the eyes of the world? [16]

Adoption of the Free State Constitution

At the moment, the outlook was not promising. De Valera and his followers boycotted the provisional government, openly agitating for repudiation of the treaty; the *Dáil Eireann* refused to disband or to give up its pretense of being the legitimate parliament of a free Irish republic; civil war, thought to have been ended, went steadily on. Undaunted, however, the provisional government turned to the preparation of a permanent constitution, and by early summer the instrument, formulated by a committee under the chairmanship of Collins, was ready to be carried to London for approval. The broad out-

[14] Even if the northern counties decided not to exclude themselves from the Free State they were to constitute a segregated and privileged section thereof, retaining a separate local parliament.

[15] The text of the treaty will be found in D. Figgis, *The Irish Constitution* (Dublin, 1923), 96-99; *Encyclopædia Britannica* (11th ed.), XXXI, 587-588; and *London Times,* Dec. 7, 1921.

[16] The problem was to no small extent a psychological one. Government had long been, for the Irishman, a foreign and oppressive power; law, a restriction imposed from without. There was at least a possibility that the country might find government less interesting than grievances, the administration of law less thrilling than the defiance of it.

lines were, of course, already laid down in the treaty, and the British authorities' only concern was to see that the provisions of that document were duly observed. The first draft proved objectionable, because (1) the formula of the oath of allegiance to the king was not sufficiently explicit,[17] (2) the authority of the proposed governor-general was not recognized, (3) appeals were to be carried only to an Irish court of appeals and not to the Judicial Committee of the Privy Council, and (4) the Free State was to manage its own foreign affairs. The framers were, accordingly, required to try their hand again; and although some fresh difficulties came to light in the second draft, these were finally ironed out, and on June 15, 1922, the completed frame of government, fully assented to by the British cabinet, was given to the public.

It remained to secure approval of it by both the Free State and British parliaments. But inasmuch as the treaty had already passed both, and recent elections had brought into the Free State assembly a substantial majority favorable to the treaty and to the new basic law, this was achieved without great difficulty. At Dublin the Constitution Bill passed its third reading on October 25, and at London the final parliamentary sanction was given on November 29. The royal assent on December 5 completed the process. The members of the provisional parliament at Dublin became members of the new Chamber of Deputies; the provisional government became a cabinet, with William T. Cosgrave as "president," or prime minister; the members of the Senate were duly selected by a special procedure provided for this particular occasion, and held their first meeting on December 11; the last lord lieutenant gave up his thankless task; Timothy Healy, once a combative Nationalist, but popular with all elements on account of his shrewd wit and genial manners, was named governor-general; and on December 16 the last British regiments left the country. Presently, too, the new order received recognition in international circles when representatives of the Free State took their places, with acclamation, in the Assembly of the League of Nations. Meanwhile, on December 7, 1922, the Commons and Senate of Northern Ireland unanimously voted the six counties out of the

[17] Indeed, the king was not so much as mentioned.

Free State, Sir James Craig, the prime minister, declaring that, so far as could be foreseen, an absolute condition of Irish peace and well-being was the permanence of the separation. This action came as a disappointment, but hardly as a surprise.[18]

The New Régime Stabilized

With the taking effect of the Free State constitution and the decision of the northeastern counties to hold to their separate course, Ireland at last reached, presumably, the long-sought condition of constitutional equilibrium. "The constitution," said one of its authors (Arthur Griffith), "is that of a free and democratic state, and under it Ireland, for the first time in centuries, secured the power and opportunity to control and develop her own resources and to lead her own national life." It was unfortunate that a dismemberment of the country had proved a necessary preliminary; and no one was so naïve as to suppose that from this act would not flow serious disputes and a good many other practical disadvantages.[19] But there seemed to be no other way. Catholic Ireland was bent on thoroughgoing self-government, if full independence could not be had; Protestant Ulster was unalterably opposed to continued union with the rest of the country on any basis other than the perpetuation of the United Kingdom; Great Britain was determined alike that no part of Ireland should be independent and that Ulster should not be coerced. Accordingly, northern Ireland was to remain an integral part of the United Kingdom,[20] sending representatives to the parliament at Westminster, pay-

[18] The events from the ratification of the treaty to the withdrawal of the northern counties are described lucidly in W. A. Phillips, *The Revolution in Ireland,* Chaps. xii-xiii. Cf. A. C. White, *The Irish Free State; its Evolution and Possibilities* (London, 1923); E. Boyd, "Ireland, Resurgent and Insurgent," *Foreign Affairs,* Sept., 1922, and "Recent Irish History," *ibid.,* Dec., 1923; P. W. Wilson, "Ireland as a Free State," *Rev. of Revs.,* Jan., 1922, "The New Ireland," *World's Work,* Feb., 1922, and "The Irish Free State," *N. Amer. Rev.,* Mar., 1922.

[19] See p. 716 below.

[20] It has been noted that the term "United Kingdom," as used for official purposes, was presumed to be abandoned. See p. 100 above. It nevertheless persists in everyday speech, and even creeps into official, or semi-official, documents. With its altered meaning understood, it may still properly be employed.

ing taxes into the British treasury, relying upon the British army and navy for defense. Except for certain provincial rights conceded to its newly-established legislature in the act of 1920, its position was to be substantially as in the old days. On the other hand, southern Ireland was cut off from the United

Map of Ireland, showing the respective territories of the Irish Free State and Northern Ireland.

Kingdom and erected into a self-governing area with the internal affairs of which Great Britain was to have no right to interfere. It was required to assume its fair share of the general national debt;[21] but it was to have complete control over its own taxes, budgets, currency, and finances generally.

[21] In 1925 the treaty was so amended as to relieve the Free State of this obligation.

It must allow Great Britain, in time of war, strategic access to its coasts and harbors. But it was to maintain its own army and navy and to be primarily responsible for its own defense. It was to have its own flag. It was to have its own trade agents abroad, and might call them consuls if it liked. In short, its position was to be only slightly different from that which it would have occupied had it been simply a Newfoundland or a New Zealand, three thousand miles across seas.

Even after the decisions of 1922, much remained to be done before the two parts of the country should be fully stabilized and the relations between them put upon a tolerable working basis. Almost equally with the Free State territories, the north-eastern counties had been torn by political and religious animosities, the scene of chronic disorder; and a year or more was required to bring about a reasonable state of calm. The problem there, however, was simple as compared with that to be faced at Dublin. The Free State existed on paper; it had a skeleton political organization. But it presented the aspect rather of a mass of ruins than of a finished livable structure. Finances were in chaos; transportation was demoralized; education and poor relief needed overhauling; justice and local government awaited reorganization; scores of problems which through the long years had been neglected or dealt with in futile fashion at Westminster pressed for attention. One-third of the population of the country had been cut off, and with it most of the industries and taxable wealth. Propertied elements, such as there were, had long been migrating to safer habitats, and were still doing so. What remained was an almost purely agricultural population, less than three million in number, and for the most part wretchedly poor. Two years of exceptionally bad crops [22] produced conditions that were little better than famine, especially in the more populous counties of the west. With so many problems and such limited resources, the new government would have had an unenviable task even if complete unity and amity had prevailed. But there was far from being such a condition. At the very time when the new constitution was being put into operation, the Republicans—totally refusing to accept

[22] 1923-24.

the settlement arrived at—proclaimed an independent commonwealth, elected De Valera "president and foreign minister," and launched a fresh campaign of vilification, incendiarism, sabotage, and obstruction. For more than a year civil war went on between the supporters and opponents of the new régime, to an accompaniment of appalling lawlessness and destruction.

The government to which it now fell to take the situation in hand was, however, not British and "alien," but Irish; and it fortunately included many men not only of unimpeachable loyalty to Irish interests but of untiring energy, high purpose, and large constructive ability. Historians will undoubtedly agree that it made the best of a bad situation and in four or five years' time wrought a remarkable transformation. On the one hand, it planned and carried out, largely on a basis of consent, an extensive program of governmental reorganization and remedial legislation: taxation was readjusted; the educational system was reconstructed; an obsolete poor law was replaced by arrangements of a sort which Britain has herself just succeeded in effecting; agriculture, as the basic industry, was aided; local government was reformed; a bold step toward the expansion of manufacturing was taken by the electrification of the River Shannon. On the other hand, the government addressed itself to curbing the disaffected elements and building up national unity and morale. Even if the methods employed to this end were hardly less vigorous than those which British administrators had been accustomed to use, the troops and police set to repressing rebellion were native, not foreign; and gradually—with the successes and possibilities of the new order becoming daily more obvious—it dawned upon all except an irreconcilable element that, to all intents and purposes, Catholic Ireland now had what she had been fighting for, and that by keeping up domestic strife she was injuring nobody so much as herself. De Valera and his followers held out until 1927, to the extent, at least, of refusing to have anything to do with Parliament. But a good while before that date their opposition became largely passive; by 1925 the new régime could be regarded as definitely on its feet; and two years later—when Republican deputies at last consented to take their seats in the *Dáil*—it was possible for a leading writer on Irish affairs to speak truthfully of the event as marking the end of the first stage in the Free State's evolution.[23]

The Government of Northern Ireland

From these general aspects of the stabilization of the new arrangements we may turn to some description of the systems of government operating today in the two portions of the dissevered country. Closely bound to Great Britain, yet endowed with home rule, Northern Ireland stands, in the matter of autonomy, somewhere between the position of Scotland and that of the Free State.[24] It has it own parliament, as Scotland does not; but its powers of separate action fall considerably short of those of the Free State. The parliament consists of a House of Commons and a Senate. The former contains fifty-two members, chosen for a maximum of five years, in single-member constituencies, except that Queen's University, Belfast, returns four representatives under proportional representation. Formerly, the entire membership was chosen under the propor-

[23] S. Gwynn, *The Irish Free State, 1922-1927* (London, 1928), p. vii. This book is the best available review of the developments of the period covered. It may be added that prolonged and bitter controversy between the Free State and Northern Ireland over the fixing of the common boundary was brought to an end in 1925 by a settlement in which the London government itself bore a share, and which provided for a continuance of the temporary boundary recognized in 1920 when the Government of Ireland Act was framed, in lieu of a permanent boundary "compatible with economic and geographical conditions" which, according to the treaty, was to have been drawn by a boundary commission. The government of Northern Ireland, fearing losses of territory, refused to appoint boundary commissioners or to agree to a plebiscite. The boundary as it stands is still unsatisfactory, and the settlement is not regarded as final; but at any rate the tension was relieved. M. O. Hudson, "The Irish Boundary Question," *Amer. Jour. Int. Law,* Jan., 1925; "Macdara," "The Irish Boundary Settlement," *Fort. Rev.,* Apr., 1926. Cf. *Round Table,* Sept., Dec., 1924; Mar., 1925; Mar., 1926.

[24] It contains the six counties and two county boroughs named above (p. 706, note 7), with its capital at Belfast. The area is 5,263 square miles (a little more than the state of Connecticut), and the population by the census of 1926 was 1,255,881. The constitutional basis of the government is the Government of Ireland Act of 1920, as modified by the Irish Free State (Consequential Provisions) Act of 1922. The latter went into effect on the same day as the act providing for the Free State constitution, and contained various provisions which were to become operative in the event that Northern Ireland should vote itself out of the Free State. It repealed the Government of Ireland Act in so far as applicable to the parts of the country included in the Free State.

tional plan, but an act of 1929 abolished the system for all except university members and redistricted the country accordingly. The Senate consists of the lord mayor of Belfast and the mayor of Londonderry ex-officio and twenty-four other persons chosen by the House of Commons, according to the principle of proportional representation. The term is eight years, with half of the members retiring every four years. Two things are notable about the Senate: first, that despite the almost total absence of any desire in Ulster for such a body, it was provided for in 1920 in order to match the second chamber which had to be created for southern Ireland as a means of conciliating the Protestant minority in that quarter; and second, that it carries out more completely than any other second chamber in the British Empire the principle of election of the upper house by the lower one. The relations between the two houses, showing as they do strong influence of the Parliament Act of 1911, and of subsequent British discussion of the second chamber problem, are also interesting. If the two disagree upon a non-financial bill, the matter goes over to the next session. If then there is still disagreement, the governor, as chief executive, may call the two houses into joint session, whereupon the issue is decided by a majority vote, the commoners, of course, having twice the potential voting strength of the senators. In the case of money bills, the second chamber may reject but not amend. If, however, the Commons refuses to acquiesce, a joint sitting, which settles the fate of the measure, takes place in the same session. All executive power continues to be vested in the king, but is exercised by a governor [25] through a group of responsible ministers constituting a cabinet, on the plan familiar throughout the Empire. A new supreme court of judicature for Northern Ireland, in two divisions, heads up the reorganized judicial system; and civil and criminal law have been brought into closer harmony with English law than they previously were.[26]

[25] This title, superseding "lord lieutenant," was adopted in 1922.

[26] A. S. Quekett, *The Constitution of Northern Ireland;* Pt. i, *The Origin and Development of the Constitution,* cited above. This is by all odds the most accurate and informing treatise on the subject. The author is parliamentary draftsman to the Belfast government, and he proposes to follow up the present book with another containing an annotated edition of all constitutional enactments of and relating to Northern Ireland.

Nature of the Free State Constitution

As in the case of Canada, Australia, and the other dominions, the people of the Free State had the privilege of making their own constitution.[27] There were, of course, restrictions. As in the other instances named, the completed instrument could not become operative until it had been approved at London; and there was the special qualification in the case of the Free State that the constitution must adhere faithfully to a solemn and comprehensive agreement previously entered into, i.e., the treaty of December 6, 1922. It was, indeed, stipulated in the preamble that if any of the constitution's provisions or amendments, or any laws enacted thereunder, should at any time be found repugnant to the treaty, they should, so far as such repugnancy extended, be considered void and inoperative. The matters with which the treaty dealt, and upon which, accordingly, the framers' hands were tied, related, however, almost exclusively to the status of the Free State within "the community of nations forming the British Commonwealth of Nations," the relations to be sustained with the parliament and government at London, and the powers which the new government might exercise, conditionally or otherwise. Upon internal governmental organization, it wisely had little to say. There was to be a parliament and a "government," i.e., a cabinet, and, of course, a governor-general representing the crown. But how the members of parliament were to be chosen, whether there should be one house or two, what executive departments should exist, how central and local governments should be tied up together—these and many other important things were left untouched. Within the rather broad outside limits fixed by the treaty, therefore, the form and characteristics of the Free State political system are such as the Irish chose to make them. The result is a frame of government which, while departing by no means entirely from traditional English lines, is nevertheless in many of its features quite unlike any to be found

[27] The Free State consists of the provinces of Leinster, Munster, and Connaught and the Ulster counties of Cavan, Donegal, and Monaghan, with its capital at Dublin. The total area is 26,592 square miles (somewhat more than three times the area of Massachusetts), and the population in 1926 was estimated at 2,972,802.

elsewhere in the English-speaking world. American influence is scarcely perceptible; likewise, Canadian and Australian. This is not to criticize the plan, but only to emphasize its interest for the student of comparative institutions.[28]

It may be true, as an American writer remarks, that the Free State constitution is "rather academic in tone, and smacks of the lamp." [29] Coming from a people as emotional as the Irish, however, it keeps remarkably close to earth, being, on the whole, quite as practical a document as the German republican constitution of 1919. Its first section is in the nature of a bill of rights. But this does not go beyond (a) declaring the Free State a co-equal member of the British Commonwealth of Nations, (b) proclaiming that all powers of government are derived from the people, (c) defining citizenship, (d) guaranteeing men and women equal rights as citizens, (e) making the Irish language the "national" tongue, while yet recognizing English as equally an official language, and (f) guaranteeing the good old English rights (naturally, without calling them such) of habeas corpus and freedom of speech and assembly. Under strict treaty injunction, freedom of conscience and worship is pledged to all the people; while other interesting clauses, with a distinctly modern sound, proclaim the right to form associations or unions and the right to share in free elementary education. In short, the rights and liberties guaranteed to the citizenry follow the lines marked out in the newer constitutions of the world generally, but without a trace of anything bolshevistic or otherwise ultra-radical.

[28] As will appear, the Free State constitution as it stands today, after various changes dictated by a few years of experience, bears rather more resemblance to the British constitution than it did originally. See, for example, the altered basis of the cabinet (p. 732 below). The constitution is outlined and commented on briefly in D. Figgis, *The Irish Constitution,* already cited, and S. Gwynn, *The Irish Free State, 1922-1927,* Chap. iii, and more fully in J. G. S. MacNeill, *Studies in the Constitution of the Irish Free State* (Dublin, 1925). Cf. MacNeill, "Thoughts on the Constitution of Ireland," *Jour. of Compar. Legis. and Int. Law,* Feb., 1923; W. P. M. Kennedy, "The Significance of the Irish Free State," *No. Amer. Rev.,* Sept., 1923; and H. Kennedy, "The Character and Sources of the Constitution of the Irish Free State," *Amer. Bar Assoc. Jour.,* Aug., Sept., 1928. The relation of the Free State and British constitutions is considered at some length in the introduction to MacNeill's volume.

[29] W. B. Munro, *Governments of Europe,* 326.

The Governmental System—Chamber of Deputies

These fundamentals duly taken care of, the constitution proceeds to outline the structure and powers of the government—first the legislature, then the executive, and finally (very briefly) the judiciary. The legislature (*Oireachtas*) consists of "the king and two houses": a Chamber of Deputies (*Dáil Eireann*) and a Senate (*Seanad Eireann*).[30] The Senate is formed on more novel lines than the Chamber; yet the latter is not without interest. It consists of (a) representatives chosen in multi-member constituencies, by secret ballot and proportional representation,[31] for five-year terms,[32] subject, however, to right of dissolution by the governor-general acting on advice of the executive council, and (b) three members each for Dublin University and the newer National University, elected by the degree-holders. The number of members is to be determined by legislative act "from time to time," in such manner that there will never be less than one representative for each thirty thousand, nor more than one for each twenty thousand, of the population—subject to the further requirement (for which, as we have seen, there is no analogy in the United Kingdom) that a reapportionment of seats shall be made at least once in every ten years. The present membership of 153 includes 127 representatives from the counties, twenty from three boroughs, and six from the two universities.

All citizens twenty-one years of age and over, without dis-

[30] *Oireachtas* is pronounced "urrigktas;" *Dáil Eireann,* "dawil eerin;" *Seanad Eireann,* "shānad eerin." The national name of the Free State, *Saorstát Eireann,* is pronounced "sharestat eerin."

[31] According to the Hare system, with single transferable vote. See p. 312, note 77.

[32] The constitution originally specified four years as the maximum life of a parliament. An amendment of 1927 [Constitution (Amendment No. 4) Act] changed this to six years "or such shorter period as may be fixed by legislation," and Parliament thereupon passed a law establishing a five-year period, which, of course, is the same as in Britain. Americans, whose congressmen have terms of two years only, will be interested to note that the change in Ireland from four years to five was dictated by the feeling that the shorter period did not give members time enough in which to accustom themselves to parliamentary procedure or to carry to fruition large projects of legislation. The constitutional six-year provision would enable a parliament to prolong its own life for a year by simple legislative act.

tinction of sex, who "comply with the provisions of the prevailing electoral laws," e.g., as to registration, may vote for representatives, and also take part in initiatives and referenda.[33] A qualified person may register and vote where he resides, where he occupies business premises, or in a university constituency, but in only one of the three (selected by himself), in case he can qualify in more than one constituency. Plural voting, which, as we have seen, survives to a limited extent in Great Britain, is totally excluded from the Free State system. Candidates for the *Dáil* are nominated in the same way as candidates for the House of Commons in Britain, and a money deposit is required, as in Britain, except that in the Free State the amount is £100 and the candidate is required to poll one-third of the number of votes requisite to elect him if he is to recover his money.[34] Nominations may be made up to the eighth day after the proclamation of a general election, and the polling—which takes place on the same day throughout the country—must be fixed for from six to fourteen days after the closing day for nominations. There are absent-voting provisions; also ample regulations, broadly similar to the British, designed to protect the purity and orderliness of elections.[35] All in all, so far as constitutional and legal stipulations go, the Chamber of Deputies is very much the usual sort of popular legislative branch, shaped according to the most approved notions of European post-war democracy.

The Senate

For the choice of senators, the constitution's framers brought into play a unique scheme of indirect popular election. For direct popular election, such as prevails in the United States and Australia and is soon to come into operation in New Zealand, they did not care. There were no states whose legisla-

[33] Except that members of the police establishment throughout the country are debarred, as were police and certain other public officers at one time in England.

[34] Cf. p. 281 above.

[35] These regulations, covering both corrupt and illegal practices, are laid down chiefly in the Electoral Abuses Act of 1923. The Ministry of Local Government and Public Health is responsible for all arrangements in connection with elections.

tures could be empowered to elect, as under the original system in the United States. Something on the order of the French plan of election by local electoral colleges composed of persons participating in an ex-officio capacity might have been adopted, but did not materialize. Appointment, whether for life, as in Canada, or for a term of years, as heretofore in New Zealand, was hardly considered. The decision reached was dictated mainly by the conception that prevailed as to the kind of a body that the Senate should be, and especially of the kind of persons who were to be enabled to find their way into it. "The Senate," says the constitution, "shall be composed of citizens who have done honor to the nation by reason of useful public service, or who, because of special qualifications or attainments, represent important aspects of the nation's life."[36] Such persons, it was assumed, would not, as a rule, get into the Chamber of Deputies even if they tried. Yet their services as legislators were greatly to be desired; and, as the chief architect of the constitution explains, the method of electing senators was shaped definitely with a view to encouraging the choice of such "senatorial persons."[37]

The plan (as will be indicated below, it has since been changed) was briefly as follows. The Senate was to consist of sixty members, elected for twelve years.[38] Four members were to sit for and be elected by the universities.[39] The remaining fifty-six were to be elected directly by the registered voters of the country, under an arrangement whereby one-fourth, i.e., fourteen, should vacate their seats every three years, an equivalent number accordingly being elected triennially.[40] The electorate for senatorial purposes was, however, to be different from that for the choice of deputies, in that the voting age was to be thirty instead of twenty-one. It was also to function differently, in that, while, for purposes of convenience, the *Dáil* constituencies and their returning officers were to be made use of in Senate elections, the entire electorate was in effect to

[36] Art. 29.

[37] Darrell Figgis, *The Irish Constitution,* 27-28.

[38] It will be recalled that this was the term which the Bryce Report proposed for members of the House of Lords at Westminster.

[39] Two for the National University and two for Dublin.

[40] One member was to be elected by each university every six years.

constitute a single constituency.[41] Proportional representation was to prevail, as in the choice of deputies. In order to procure the right kind of candidates, it was provided that, while the people should elect, they should make their choice only from a panel of candidates, made up, in the case of each triennial election, as follows: (1) twenty-eight nominated by the Chamber of Deputies, (2) fourteen nominated by the Senate,[42] and (3) persons who, having at any time been members of the Senate (including members about to retire), should indicate their desire to be included. This meant that whenever the people should come to the election of a group of fourteen senators, they were to make their choice from a panel of forty-two nominees, plus such number as might have got on the list under the last provision mentioned. The plan thus combined the principles of selection by the houses of parliament, direct popular election, and proportional representation in a scheme which contributed a hitherto untried experiment to the solution of the second chamber problem.

In making up the original Senate, temporary and entirely different devices were employed, and several years would have been required to bring into full operation the regular system as laid down in the constitution. Before that time arrived, the system was changed. When the first popular senatorial election was held, in 1925, the results were regarded as unsatisfactory; three-quarters of the candidates turned out to be people, if not of doubtful qualifications, at all events quite unknown to the voters of the country at large.[43] Accordingly, in 1928, in anticipation of the election of the next quota, a constitutional amendment shortened the senatorial term from twelve years to nine (one-third of the members being elected every three years), and provided that instead of the people making the choice, election should be by an electoral college consisting of the

[41] In addition, there was to be a general returning officer, appointed by the Minister of Local Government and Public Health, who was to be responsible for the final count of votes and for reporting the results to the clerk of the Senate.

[42] Each of these quotas being selected according to the principle of proportional representation.

[43] H. F. Gosnell, "An Irish Free State Senate Election," *Amer. Polit. Sci. Rev.*, Feb., 1926.

senators and deputies sitting as one body;[44] and the senatorial election of December, 1928, was carried out on that basis. Although the new plan was generally understood to be supported by De Valera and his party with a view to making the second chamber unpopular and bringing about an early abolition of it, the government party assumed responsibility for it, thus giving it the appearance of meeting an almost unanimous popular and official desire. Whether the departure was really for the better was doubted seriously by outside observers. Certainly the election of 1928 was conducted on purely party lines, and the candidates nominated were mostly mere party politicians.

Relations Between the Two Houses

The relations between the two houses, and, in turn, between Parliament and the electorate, present features which at some points reveal strong influence of British parliamentary experience and at others show wide departure from anything Britain has known. Parliament is required to hold at least one session each year. The members must take an oath of allegiance to the constitution and of fidelity to the crown;[45] and they are ex-

[44] Constitution (Amendment No. 7) Act. Proportional representation continues.

[45] Ever since 1922 this oath of allegiance has been a main obstacle to political unity and peace in the country. The form of the oath is prescribed in Art. 17 of the constitution, and is as follows: "I ———— do solemnly swear true faith and allegiance to the constitution of the Irish Free State as by law established, and that I will be faithful to His Majesty King George V, his heirs and successors by law, in virtue of the common citizenship of Ireland with Great Britain and her adherence to and membership of the group of nations forming the British Commonwealth of Nations." The Republican followers of De Valera have steadily demanded that the oath be expunged from the constitution, and when in 1927 their duly elected deputies finally yielded to it in order to take their seats in the *Dáil,* they still protested that they regarded it as only an empty formula. In the same year the objectors invoked the popular initiative as a means of bringing about a rescinding of the oath, and the requisite number of signatures was obtained. Lack of the necessary machinery for procuring action on measures so initiated, however, prevented the matter from going further; and, as is indicated below, the controversy resulted in constitutional changes abolishing not only the abortive popular initiative but the popular referendum on laws as well (see p. 727). De Valera's contention was that the treaty of 1921 did not impose upon members of Parliament the necessity of taking the oath in question—that it merely prescribed the form of oath to be used if the members took any oath at all. The Dublin government, however, has consistently refused to entertain any proposals looking to either the

tended the customary privileges and immunities, together with a guarantee of financial remuneration for their services.[46] Money bills must originate in the Chamber of Deputies; other measures may start in either house. Every bill passing one branch must be sent to the other. But the powers of the two bodies are entirely different. In the case of a money bill, the Senate may make "recommendations." But within fourteen days the measure must be returned to the Chamber of Deputies, which may pass it again, accepting or rejecting any or all of the other chamber's proposals, and thereupon the bill, as the constitution rather naïvely says, is "deemed to have passed both houses." Attempt is made to specify precisely what shall be regarded as a money bill;[47] but it is recognized that in individual cases there may be doubt, and hence provision is made for a definitive ruling by a committee of privileges consisting of three members elected by each house, with a judge of the Supreme Court acting as chairman.[48] Appropriations may be voted only if they have, in the same session, been recommended by a message from the governor-general, acting on advice of the executive council.[49]

Bills other than money bills can also be enacted into law without the assent of the Senate, and by a procedure rather quicker and easier than that required for attainment of the same end at Westminster. If the Senate proposes amendments to a bill passed by the Chamber, and the latter accepts them, the measure, of course, prevails in the revised form. But if the Chamber chooses not to accept the alterations, the bill, at the expiration of eighteen months may be sent to the Senate a second time, and at the expiration of sixty days more may be made law whether the second chamber has agreed to it or not.[50]

omission or amendment of the oath. See S. Gwynn, *The Irish Free State, 1922-1927*, Chap. iv.

[46] This was fixed in 1923, for members of both houses alike, at £30 a month, with free travel between Dublin and the constituencies.

[47] Art. 34.

[48] This is reminiscent of the Bryce Report and the government resolutions of 1922. See pp. 351-352 above.

[49] Art. 36.

[50] The constitution originally enabled the *Dáil* to enact a law over the head of the Senate after an interval of only 270 days. The rule in its present form dates from 1928.

The framers of the constitution wanted a Senate that should have talent and experience, but they had no intention of giving it any great amount of power; and various proposals in more recent days, looking to strengthening the chamber's position, e.g., that senators be made eligible to hold ministerial posts,[51] have fallen upon deaf ears. A novel feature of some significance, however, appears in the right of the second chamber to request a joint sitting of the members of both houses for the purpose of debating, although not of voting upon, any bill except a money bill. The value of such a sitting lies principally, of course, in the opportunity that it affords for the points of view and arguments which have prevailed in one house to be heard at first hand by the members of the other house.[52] Having passed Parliament, bills are presented to the representative of the king, i.e., the governor-general, who (acting according to the "law, practice, and constitutional usage" regulating such matters in Canada) may signify the sovereign's assent, impose a veto, or reserve the measure "for the signification of the king's pleasure at a later date."

The constitution was framed under strong democratic impulse, and it is not surprising to find that direct provision was made for one of those twin devices of direct democracy which we know as the referendum and the initiative, and contingent provision for the other. On written demand of two-fifths of the members of the Chamber, or of a majority of the members of the Senate, any bill passed by both houses (except a money bill or a bill declared by both houses to be an emergency measure) might be suspended for a period of ninety days, and if within that time a popular referendum on it was demanded, either by three-fifths of the members of the Senate or by one-twentieth of the electors then on the national register, the measure must be submitted to the people, whose decision was to be conclusive.[53] Furthermore, while amendments to the constitution were to be adopted during the first eight years (i.e., until 1930) by ordinary legislation, after this period they were to become effective only in pursuance of a referendum partici-

[51] See p. 730 below.

[52] The speaker of the Chamber presides, or, in his absence, the chairman of the Senate.

[53] Art. 47.

pated in by a majority of the voters, and in which a favorable vote was cast either by a majority of the voters or, in lieu of that, by two-thirds of those actually voting. Finally—still following the provisions of the original constitution—Parliament was given two years in which to make suitable arrangements under which both laws and constitutional amendments might be popularly initiated on petition of fifty thousand voters; and it was stipulated that if such provision were not made within this period, the people themselves, by petition of not less than seventy-five thousand electors, might require the houses to act, or at any rate to submit the matter to a popular vote. The British constitution, of course, knows nothing of either the referendum or the initiative in the forms contemplated in these provisions, and it is doubtful whether there was any genuine demand for them in Ireland. At all events, their history there has been far from impressive. No provision was ever made for bringing the initiative into effect; the referendum was invoked only as a futile weapon of partisan warfare, chiefly by the disgruntled Republicans; and in 1928, under impetus supplied principally by President Cosgrave and his supporters, a constitutional amendment struck completely from the fundamental law both of the articles (47 and 48) relating to the two subjects and made the necessary consequential changes in other articles.[54] There is, therefore, now no provision whatever for the popular initiative, and none for the popular referendum except as that device may later come into operation in connection with the adoption of constitutional amendments.

Parliamentary Organization and Procedure

A word may be said about parliamentary organization and procedure. In the main, this is regulated by standing orders of each of the two houses, supplemented by an elaborate body of standing orders on private bills adopted by both bodies in 1923. The principal officer is, of course, the speaker of the Chamber of Deputies, whose powers and general position closely resemble

[54] Constitution (Amendment No. 10) Act, 1928. De Valera demanded a referendum on this measure, but the president countered by getting the *Dáil* to declare that the bill was one involving the public safety, which declaration, under constitutional provision, shut out the right to ask for a polling of the electorate.

those of his counterpart at Westminster. The one official no less than the other is designed to be an impartial, non-political moderator; and since under the Irish system of proportional representation there would be no such guarantee of the speaker's reëlection to Parliament as exists under the British single-member-district plan, notwithstanding that his reëlection might be regarded as indispensable by the *Dáil* as a whole, a constitutional amendment of 1927 [55] stipulates that the chairman of the Chamber preceding a dissolution shall (unless he announces his desire not to be reëlected) be deemed reëlected from the constituency for which he previously sat without actually being voted for at all.[56] The new Chamber is not, of course, bound to reëlect the previous speaker, and in case of its failure to do so he would find himself in a somewhat anomalous position. Reëlection, however, is practically assured. The same speaker, in point of fact, has held office since the Free State government came into existence.[57] Unlike the practice at Westminster, the speaker presides both in general sittings and in committee of the whole. A standing committee system has only begun to develop, but special committees are used freely. Proceedings in both Chamber and Senate are carried on mainly in English, but Irish may be used; and official documents, including published statutes, regularly appear in both languages. Public bills are handled very much as at Westminster, except that those not disposed of at the end of a session may, by resolution, be carried over in any completed stage to the next session. Private bill procedure presents an unusual feature, in that all such bills, and also bills to confirm provisional orders, must originate in the Senate. Private acts, of course, require the concurrence of the Chamber; but the whole procedure is shaped with a view to saving the time of that body. That the Chamber is still the more heavily burdened is indicated by the fact that

[55] Constitution (Amendment No. 2) Act.

[56] That is, he is regarded as returned automatically, and the number of members from the constituency elected by regular process is reduced by one. It is interesting to observe that this plan was suggested by the Senate as an alternative to a somewhat different one brought forward by the government. See S. Gwynn, *The Irish Free State, 1922-1927,* pp. 133-134.

[57] Michael Hayes, an ardent young Sinn Feiner and once a lecturer in University College, Dublin. He sits for the National University.

its journals for the first five years fill eighteen substantial volumes, whereas those of the Senate occupy only seven volumes half as large. Considering that practically all of the members of the Chamber in its earlier days were entirely without experience in parliamentary work, and that large legislative tasks had to be undertaken under conditions of peculiar difficulty, the body has achieved a very honorable record.[58]

Executive and Judicial Arrangements

The executive part of the Free State government also presents some unusual and interesting features. The intent of the constitution as adopted was that arrangements should be similar to those prevailing in Canada and other dominions: executive authority was to be vested in the crown as represented at Dublin in the person of a governor-general, but to be exercised through a group of ministers responsible to the Chamber; and the governor-general, appointed by the king on the advice of the cabinet at London, was to be the regular intermediary through which communications should pass between the British and Free State governments. For four years the system operated on this basis; and even yet the fundamentals continue unchanged. Since the Imperial Conference of 1926, however, the governor-general's position has become different, not only in the Free State but also in the dominions generally. From having been the representative of the crown, which really meant "His Majesty's Government," i.e., the ministry, at London, he has come to be only the representative of the sovereign, i.e., a viceroy; from having been *instructed* by the cabinet at London, he has come to be *advised* wholly by the executive council at Dublin; from having been chosen presumably at Whitehall with no more than the courtesy of consultation with Irish authorities, his appointment has come to be controlled entirely, except as a matter of pure form, by Dublin;[59] communications no longer pass through his hands,

[58] The record is reviewed briefly in S. Gwynn, *op. cit.*, Chap. xiii, and at length in Justice Hanna, *The Statute Law of the Irish Free State* (Dublin, 1929).

[59] In point of fact, the Irish leaders practically dictated the selection of the first incumbent, Timothy Healy, in 1922. The British government had contemplated appointing a distinguished peer.

but go straight from government to government, i.e., from prime minister to prime minister; and while he still retains certain powers, e.g., of appointment and veto, they are only such as the king himself retains at London—which means that, so far as discretionary actions are concerned, they amount in practice to virtually nothing at all. From the old lord lieutenant to the present governor-general is truly a long descent. The first governor-general, Timothy Healy, by reason of his rich experience, his vigorous personality, and his long association with the men to whom it fell to organize the new régime, made the office one of large influence and power; more than once he was accused of overstepping the strictly legal proprieties associated with it.[60] His successor, James MacNeill, who took the post, in its new form, at the end of 1927, has necessarily occupied a less conspicuous place in the picture.[61]

The framers of the constitution took over the principle of the cabinet system; and the work of the executive is carried on, as in other cabinet-government countries, by a group of ministers. Some interesting variations, however, were introduced. It was desired that the executive council, in effect the cabinet, should be kept small, and as provided for in the original constitution, it was restricted to the president, i.e., prime minister, the vice-president, and two other ministers—though the number might be increased by legislative act by one, two, or three, but not more. These "political" members of the ministry were to be selected for their posts exactly as are the prime minister and all other ministers in Britain, Canada, and Australia; all were to be members of the Chamber (in no case the Senate); and, failing of support in that body, they were to resign, as do ministers similarly situated in cabinet governments elsewhere. Thus far, the arrangement was only the conventional sort of thing. A challenging element of novelty, however, was introduced in connection with the remaining ministers. These eight (or fewer, as the case might be, since the total number of ministers was not to exceed twelve) were to be "non-political;" instead of being selected by the prime minister, they were to be chosen by a committee of the Chamber, with a view to their

[60] L. O'Flaherty, *The Life of Tim Healy* (London, 1927).
[61] S. Gwynn, *The Irish Free State, 1922-1927,* Chap. v.

"suitability to office" and to representation of the "Free State as a whole rather than of groups or parties;" they were to be members of neither house of Parliament, though they might attend sittings of the Chamber and take part in debate; and, barring removal by the Chamber for malfeasance or incompetence, they were to remain in office throughout the term of the Chamber existing at the time of their appointment, or for such other period as might be fixed by law.[62]

A scheme under which the prime minister had control over the selection of less than half of his colleagues, less than half sat in Parliament, all of these sat in one house only, and some ministers remained secure in office while others were being forced out by a hostile Chamber, represented, obviously, a cabinet system of a highly modified type. There was nothing like it elsewhere in the world. It attempted to preserve the regular plan of ministerial responsibility, while at the same time placing most of the departments in the hands of permanent, non-political, and presumably more or less expert, "extern" officials. The latter were put in substantially the same position that all ministers occupy in Switzerland, where the seven members of the Federal Council are chosen as a collegial executive by the popular branch of Parliament, but have no seats in that body and if found in disagreement with it merely modify their policy instead of giving up office.[63] The system works well at Berne; and the plan is supposed to have been adopted for Dublin through influence of the Swiss example. But of course the Swiss have not attempted the same sort of combination that the Irish plan involved, and there was certainly room for doubt whether a scheme that was at the same time a cabinet system and not a cabinet system could, in the long run, be made to work. The object was to place limits upon party government by securing the management of certain departments, e.g., Agriculture, the activities of which are of a relatively technical and routine character, by persons presumably selected without reference to politics. It was at least debatable, however, in the first place, whether party govern-

[62] Arts. 50-52.

[63] R. C. Brooks, *Government and Politics of Switzerland* (Yonkers, 1918), Chap. v.

ment is, after all, a thing to be shunned, and in the second place, whether a scheme of "internal" and "external" ministers does not contain within itself the seeds of intolerable friction and confusion.[64]

Five years of experience confirmed the fears of the doubters and led, in 1927, to a constitutional amendment introducing a significant change. As might have been expected, non-political ministers chosen by the Chamber felt themselves under no compelling obligation to support the measures of their political colleagues, and special difficulty was encountered with one such minister, occupying the postmaster-generalship, who used his position to criticize the general policy of the government. The prime minister therefore proposed that the maximum membership of the executive council be increased from seven to twelve, so that in future it would be possible for more, or even all, of the ministers to be selected by the premier and to be assimilated in other respects to the political portion of the group. The plan was opposed on the ground that the existing scheme had not been sufficiently tried. On the other hand, it was contended that the popular mind had never adjusted itself to the conception that what was called "the government" should not be responsible for the entire sphere of administration, and that probably it never would do so. In the end, the amendment prevailed, and a long step was taken toward bringing in the cabinet system in its traditional form.[65] At the date of writing (1928) that culmination seemed altogether probable, although the entire distance had not yet been covered. It may be added that efforts of the Senate to procure a provision enabling ministers to sit in that body were unsuccessful. A senator may, of course, accept appointment as a minister, but in doing so he automatically vacates his seat.

The permanent civil service is organized on lines broadly similar to those that have been worked out on the opposite side of St. George's Channel. It rests upon a Civil Service Regulation Act of 1924, which provided for a civil service commission of three members appointed by the executive council and en-

[64] The plan is criticized severely by Darrell Figgis in his *Irish Constitution*, Chap. v.

[65] Constitution (Amendment No. 5) Act, 1927.

dowed with extensive powers to conduct competitive examinations and certify candidates. Corresponding closely to the control exercised by the Treasury at London is the authority vested in the Minister of Finance. He alone may make regulations concerning the classification and remuneration of civil servants, together with the terms and conditions of their work, and also may revoke such regulations at any time; [66] he fixes the pay and chooses the assistants of the civil service commission; in collaboration with the head of the department concerned, he may dispense with examinations for particular positions or groups of positions. Promotions, on the other hand, are controlled by the heads of departments. Naturally, the workings of the system thus far have been considerably affected by the necessity of carrying over a large part of the service which was in existence in the troubled period before the Free State was created.

One of the major tasks of the Free State government in the first days was to organize a new judicial system. Sinn Fein courts had long challenged the authority of such British-established courts as survived, and the treaty did not fail to lay down the lines on which an integrated judiciary should be developed. As duly created by act of the Free State parliament, the present judicial establishment consists of courts of first instance—including a High Court—and a court of final appeal, known as the Supreme Court. Judges are appointed by the governor-general, on recommendation of the executive council, and are guaranteed full independence and security of tenure during good behavior. In all cases in which the validity of a law, "having regard to the provisions of the constitution," is brought into question, the High Court alone exercises original jurisdiction; and thus is recognized, contrary to the practice of Britain, but in line with that in the dominions and in the United States, the principle of judicial review. Subject to such exceptions as may be provided by law (but not extending to cases which involve the validity of a statute), all decisions of the High Court can be appealed to the Supreme Court, whose decisions, in turn, are not reviewable by any other tribunal,

[66] Subject to disallowance by Parliament within a period of twenty-one days.

saving only the right of any person to appeal therefrom to "His Majesty in Council," i.e., to the Judicial Committee at London.[67]

Local Government and Administration

When the Free State was created, Ireland had a system of local government very similar to the English—for the very good reason that it had been created and developed under laws passed at Westminster, mainly since the middle of the nineteenth century.[68] An (Irish) Local Government Act of 1898 divided the whole country into administrative counties, thirty-three in number, and set up elective county councils endowed with extensive fiscal and other powers; there were a few incorporated boroughs, with mayors, aldermen, and councillors, as on the opposite side of St. George's Channel; and there were rural and urban districts, with councils (also dating from 1898), though no parishes or parish councils. An act of 1919 brought arrangements still more closely into line with those

[67] This provision for appeal to the Judicial Committee continues a sore point with most Free State people. As indicated elsewhere, it was omitted from the constitution as originally drafted, and was later inserted only as a prerequisite to the British government's endorsement of the instrument. A test of sentiment arose in 1925, when the Committee entertained an appeal from a decision of the Irish High Court, sustained by the Supreme Court, in an unimportant case brought under a land act passed two years previously. The Free State government took the position not only that it was inconsistent with the spirit of the constitution for the Committee to consent to receive appeals in any except cases of grave public concern, but that assurances had been given in 1922 that it would not do so; and, in order to challenge the Committee's action the more dramatically, it brought in and carried without division a retrospective land bill upholding at every point the decision of the Irish courts in the recent case. A fuller account of this episode will be found in S. Gwynn, *op. cit.*, Chap. vi. In 1928 the issue was reopened by a Privy Council ruling, in a case pending in various forms since 1924, to the effect that Free State civil servants were entitled to a larger retiring allowance than had been granted to them. Appeals going to the Judicial Committee were discussed on general lines in the Imperial Conference of 1926. The question of some immediate change in the rules governing appeals from the Free State was not pressed, but it was made clear that the right was reserved to bring it up again at the next Conference. See D. Figgis, "Ireland and the Privy Council," *Fortnightly Rev.*, Nov., 1923; J. F. Davidson, "The Irish Free State and Appeals to the Privy Council," *Canadian Bar Rev.*, May, 1928.

[68] This legislation really started with the Municipal Corporations Act of 1840, which popularized Irish urban government on the lines followed in England in the act of 1835.

familiar in England, except for the difference involved in the use of proportional representation in the election of the local bodies.

Save for a reorganization of the administration of education in 1923, the structure of local government in the North has continued unchanged since the partition of the island—for that matter, since the legislation of 1898. The six administrative counties have the customary councils; Belfast and Londonderry have the usual governments of county boroughs; thirty urban districts have councils, with the power, among others, of levying rates; thirty-two rural districts also have councils, but without rating power; poor relief is administered by boards of guardians in poor-law unions.[69] In the parts of the country included in the Free State there has naturally been more change. Under the agreement by which the Free State was created, all local government areas and authorities were to be continued until changed by the new Dublin parliament; and the constitution of 1922 gives this parliament a free hand in making such alterations as it likes. In its larger features, the system of earlier days stands intact, even though, as a system, it was not built up by the Irish themselves but was imposed from without as an incident of English rule. There are twenty-seven administrative counties, each with its council elected by proportional representation. There are four county boroughs (Dublin, Limerick, Waterford, and Cork) and five ordinary municipal boroughs, each also with its council consisting of mayor, aldermen, and councillors. There are sixty-two urban districts, each with a council but no aldermen or mayor; and twenty-four towns have town commissioners under an old statute of 1854. On the other hand, an act of 1923 made the county the unit for the administration of poor relief, and a statute of two years later abolished the rural district councils and the boards of guardians and amalgamated their areas to form a county health district with a board of health as the chief sanitary, and also poor relief, authority. Under the Free State system, education is kept out of the hands of the local bodies.[70]

[69] G. M. Harris, *Local Government in Many Lands,* 197-202.
[70] *Jour. of Compar. Legis. and Int. Law,* May, 1927, pp. 36-38.

As a result of innovations dating from the troubled years after 1918, and of a considerable amount of legislation enacted since 1922, the system as it now stands presents several interesting features. One is the use of proportional representation, already mentioned, in the election of all county and borough councils. Another is the election, in the boroughs, of all aldermen and councillors simultaneously and for terms of three years. Aldermen are chosen directly by the people, not by the councillors as in England; they have no longer term than the councillors, being, indeed, distinguished from the latter only in that they are the members who polled the heaviest votes at the election. A third fact worthy of note is that the borough councils have rather wider powers than those in England. Equally interesting are certain aspects of central administration and control, arising no doubt from the fact that for the first time in history Irish local government is under the direct control of an Irish national government. For one thing, there is at Dublin, as there is not at London, a minister of local government—strictly, a minister of local government and public health.[71] This of itself tends to give greater unity to central supervision. In the second place, the bulk of the permanent officials of counties, boroughs, and districts are selected, not by the councils of those areas, as in England, but by a national authority at Dublin known as the Local Appointments Commission. This is a truly extraordinary arrangement, involving a degree of centralization which can hardly be met with elsewhere. The commission in question consists of the secretaries of the three ministries of local government, finance, and education, and under the terms of the law it prescribes (with the consent of the appropriate minister) the qualifications for all permanent local offices to which the act applies, examines candidates for appointment (employing competitive examinations in so far as feasible), and makes the final selections—with no participation whatever by the local governments themselves. Not only that, but while the local authorities may suspend a

[71] As has appeared, however, the Local Government Board at London, abolished in 1919, was of the nature of a local government department, and has been succeeded in that character, to a considerable extent, by the Ministry of Health. See p. 193 above.

permanent official, pending inquiry, none may be removed except by the executive council, or cabinet, at Dublin, on recommendation of the Minister of Local Government and Public Health. Like a good many other features of the present local government system, this plan of appointments and removals, absolutely reversing all English local government practice, represents an experiment. It has been in operation only since 1926, and may or may not endure. But no bolder attempt to ensure competent administration of local affairs is on record.

A further interesting phase of the system—aimed also at securing honest and efficient local government—is the power of the Minister of Local Government and Public Health, under a law of 1923, to dissolve any local authority found to be negligent, insubordinate, or corrupt, and to appoint paid national commissioners in its stead. This power has been exercised in several instances, notably in connection with the county-borough councils of Dublin and Cork. Indeed there is some likelihood that Dublin, as the national capital, will pass permanently under the management of a group of three commissioners, just as did our own District of Columbia fifty years ago. Significant, too, is the power given all councils, by the same act of 1923, to delegate their powers voluntarily to commissioners, or to a manager—a provision which may contain the germ of a local government development on the lines of the American city-managership. The ease and success with which commission or manager government has been operated where thus far installed is, indeed, the most hopeful aspect of Irish local government in the last five years, and may perhaps be relied upon to correct the errors that have too often been made, with the encouragement of the local government department, in the direction of setting up excessively large and unwieldly councils.[72]

[72] Local government in the Free State is described somewhat more fully in S. Gwynn, *The Irish Free State, 1922-1927,* Chap. xxv; J. J. Clarke, *Local Government of the United Kingdom* (4th ed.), Chap. xxxii; and J. J. Horgan, "Local Government in Ireland under the Free State," *Nat. Munic. Rev.,* Aug., 1926. Cf. the last-mentioned author's "The Cork City-Manager Plan; an Irish Experiment," *ibid.,* May, 1929, describing what may fairly be termed the first application of the American manager plan to a European city. The act providing for the experiment was drafted by Mr. Horgan.

Progress of Constitutional Amendment

The provision of the constitution already noted whereby for a period of eight years the instrument was capable of being amended (in any manner consistent with the treaty) by simple legislative act was undoubtedly a wise one; and we have seen that changes which experience proved desirable have been made in considerable number. One such change cleared the way for at least a temporary adjustment of the boundary question. Another made it possible for the *Dáil* to avail itself of the services of the same speaker as long as it likes. Another enabled external ministers to be brought into the executive council. Another suppressed the referendum on laws, and the abortive initiative. Still another abolished popular election of senators. Not all amendments that have been proposed, even by the government, have been adopted. De Valera's demand that the Senate be abolished has gone unheeded, even though the mode of electing senators has been altered; keen hostility to proportional representation has not yet prevailed.[73] Further changes will certainly be made, even after the procedure is tightened up by the coming into effect of the compulsory referendum on constitutional amendments in 1930. Indeed, there has been, and still is, a good deal of interest in the oft-made proposal that in the year mentioned, or at some other early date, a joint committee of the Chamber and Senate, or a similar representative agency, be set the task of going over the entire constitution and, in the light of the considerable experience that has now been had, recommending changes calculated to put the instrument into better working shape. At the date of writing (April, 1929) no arrangements looking to a general revision of this nature have been announced. Unless some carefully defined limitations were agreed upon in advance, the undertaking would be arduous, and perhaps hazardous. It goes without saying, however, that in one fashion or another the fundamental law will continue to adjust itself to changing conditions and proved needs, both through formal amendment of the document of 1922 and through the growth of enveloping custom and convention.

[73] See p. 741 below.

Parties and Elections

The years which have witnessed the gradual stabilization of the new constitutional order have also embraced the initial stages in the development of a party system. The conditions under which the Free State was established foreordained that, for some time to come at all events, there would be two main political elements in the country, one supporting the settlement and the other opposing it; and to this day there have been two major parties, corresponding respectively to these attitudes—the *Cumann no nGaedheal,* or Government party, and the *Fianna Fáil,* or Republican party. The one took its stand on the treaty and, although numbering a good many adherents who had once supported the independence movement, pledged itself to the loyal carrying out of the arrangements made under that instrument; the other refused to recognize the treaty and demanded complete separation from Great Britain as a preliminary to the independent Irish republic so often vainly proclaimed. For a time, as we have seen, the warfare of these two parties was by no means confined to the platform and the ballot-box. Republicans engaged in marauding expeditions and other disorders, not stopping at sabotage and assassination; the government met them with severe measures, imprisoning thousands and executing considerable numbers. Gradually the authorities got the upper hand, and by 1925 order was restored, although feeling still ran high, as no doubt it will—at intervals, at all events—for many a day to come. Meanwhile, as one would have expected, sundry minor parties made their appearance, corresponding in most instances more or less closely to particular economic interests, e.g., a Labor party and a Farmer party. A National League also set up as a party; and in addition there were various moderately stable groups of "independents."

There have been three general elections—one in 1923 and two in 1927. At the first one the Government party polled about a fourth more popular votes than the Republicans and secured sixty-three seats as compared with their forty-four. Inasmuch, however, as thirty-three of the Republican members-elect were in prison and the remainder refused to take the oath of allegiance, and hence were not seated, the government found itself confronted with no important opposition in the Chamber. That situation continued, indeed, until after the general election of June, 1927, when the new group of Republican members abandoned the policy of boycott and was seated. This gave the apparently waning Republican cause a fresh lease of life, and at the elections which came on in September of the same year—largely because of the stalemate in which the preceding contest had resulted—the party ran the Government a close race.[74] The campaign witnessed a good deal of effort to bring various parties together, and while no formal unions took place, there arose an alignment—Government party, Farmer's party, and Independents against the Republicans, Labor, and the National League—which to some observers seemed to forecast the ultimate rise of a bi-party system. Certainly the entrance of the Republicans into the *Dáil* as a constitutional opposition led thousands of Labor and National League voters to transfer their allegiance to that party, with the result that these, as other, minor parties emerged weaker than before, and suggesting that under the stress of another general election some of the lesser groups might disappear altogether.

The whole situation, however, was—and is—much too fluid to warrant confident prediction. As someone has remarked, Ireland is a land where the inevitable never happens and the impossible always occurs. The only thing definitely assured is that the Republicans have come to be almost as strong as the Government party, and that the chief party battles of the next few years will be, as in the past, between these two great portions of the electorate. One may venture the prophecy, however, that with the passing of the Republican leadership of the dark and bloody days of 1916-21, and under the ameliorating influence of the concession of larger autonomy at the Imperial

[74] The results were as follows:

Party	Popular Vote	No. of Seats
Government	453,064	61
Republicans	411,833	57
Labor	105,271	13
Independents	104,059	12
Farmers	74,723	6
National League	19,000	2
Communists	12,473	1

Conference of 1926, the party will gradually reorient itself in the direction of acceptance of the Free State solution, will become interested in new issues (such as protective tariffs), and, if brought into power, will press only for certain modifications of the country's present status, rather than for the absolute independence once so ardently sought. This would be a transformation indeed; but things even more strange are recorded in the annals of party politics. The decision of the Republican deputies in 1927 to give up the non-participating policy of the past four or five years may have been only a tactical move, dictated by confidence of being able before long to dominate the Chamber and upset the new order. But again it may prove to have been, rather, a step in the conversion of an irreconcilable faction into a moderate constitutional party.[75]

[75] For interesting comment, see *Manchester Guardian* (weekly ed.), Dec. 28, 1928, p. 509. It may be added that proportional representation as an electoral device is distinctly on trial in the Free State and that developments are being watched with much interest in Britain and elsewhere. The continued lack of a party majority in the Chamber of Deputies is ascribed to the workings of the proportional principle, and during the second electoral campaign of 1927 the Government party pledged itself to modify or abolish the system if returned to power. The party certainly found no cause to alter its position in the fact that whereas it polled, at this election, the largest vote in seventeen out of the twenty-nine contested constituencies, as compared with a Republican preponderance in only nine, it secured only four more seats than did its rival. To date, however, it has not found itself in a position to do anything about the matter. There is no question that in every Free State general election thus far held the mind of the electorate, as indicated by the distribution of the popular vote, has been mirrored with rather remarkable accuracy; not a constituency but has returned a multi-party delegation. If this is the thing to be sought in a representative system, the present scheme serves the purpose. Mr. Cosgrave (president of the council) and other government leaders, however, hold that effective government is possible only when the ministers have behind them a homogeneous parliamentary majority such as is rarely or never obtainable under the proportional system. The abolition of the proportional scheme is unlikely, but the constituencies, which almost every one now concedes to be too large, will probably be made smaller and more numerous, J. K. Pollock, "The Irish Free State Elections of September, 1927," *Amer. Polit. Sci. Rev.*, Feb., 1928; J. H. Humphreys, "The Irish Free State Election, 1923," *Contemp. Rev.*, Oct., 1923, and "Elections in the Irish Free State," *ibid.*, Aug., 1927.

The literature dealing with the government and public affairs of the Free State is voluminous. In addition to titles already cited, it will suffice to mention the *Round Table* and *Current History* as magazines containing periodic notes on the course of political events in the country, and to call

The Free State and Dominion Status

A word may be added concerning the Free State's imperial and international position. Following the lines marked out by the treaty, the constitution describes the new political unit as "a co-equal member of the British Commonwealth of Nations;" and not only has the Free State fully vindicated its claim on this score but its authorities have induced the government at London to adopt an attitude which has established precedents affecting members of the Commonwealth everywhere. By further provision of the treaty, the Free State's position is that of a dominion—in particular, Canada. This does not mean that the Free State *is* a dominion. Technically, it is not such; it merely has dominion status. This, however, is largely a distinction without a difference, as it is also in the case of Newfoundland, which officially is only a colony but in substance is a dominion; and in time the term "dominion" is likely to be employed officially, as it already is in everyday speech, especially by Irishmen. To have the status of a dominion meant much in 1922. Today, it means more. Even before the Imperial Conference of 1926, it meant the right not only to make laws with a minimum of interference from London, to levy taxes and float loans independently, and to be separately represented in international conferences, but also to have independent membership in the League of Nations and to maintain diplomatic representatives at foreign capitals. Since the occasion referred to, it has meant still fuller freedom, under a new formula expressly recognizing the autonomy of the members of the Commonwealth and their equality with one another.[76] Manifestations of this newer status include, among other things, the change of the royal title and of the position of

attention to S. Gwynn, "Ireland, One and Divisible," *For. Affairs,* Dec., 1924, as a sane discussion of the outlook for Irish reunion, and to H. Plunkett, "Ireland's Economic Outlook," *ibid.,* Jan., 1927, as a vivid description of the bearings of the economic situation on the country's political future. A valuable book by a foreigner who has long interested himself in Irish affairs is L. Paul-Dubois, *Le drame irlandais et l'Irlande nouvelle* (Paris, 1927). A very informing summary of Free State legislation during the transitional years 1922-24 will be found in *Jour. of Compar. Legis. and Internat. Law,* May, 1926, pp. 19-53.

[76] See p. 761 below.

the governor-general described above; also the newly-won privilege of initiating and negotiating treaties of all kinds with foreign states, so long as Great Britain and all other members of the Commonwealth are informed of what is being done and are not subjected to any direct or consequential obligations.

On the basis of these growing rights accruing from its dominion status, the Free State sought, and in 1923 obtained, membership in the League of Nations; in 1924 it set the pace—being followed by Canada in 1927—by accrediting an envoy extraordinary and minister plenipotentiary to the president of the United States, and in receiving, in return, a minister from this country; in 1926 it participated on terms of full equality in the Imperial Conference, and played a highly important rôle. A ministry of external affairs at Dublin functions very much like the foreign offices at London, Paris, and Berlin; while in London a Free State high commissioner, like similar representatives of the dominions, has received official recognition as of a rank virtually equal to that of the ambassadors of the great independent states.

As might be expected, these developments have contributed a good deal toward reconciling the Free State population to a continued connection with the British Empire. Irrespective of the treaty, remarked a Free State minister fresh from the Imperial Conference of 1926, Ireland must be a member of some group, and her natural relationship is with the British Commonwealth. "It is just as much an Irish Empire as an English one," asserted a member of the *Dáil* exuberantly after his return from a tour of the Irish colonies in the dominions.[77] This is not to say that everybody is satisfied with the existing arrangements. On the contrary, there is strong Free State demand for some rather important changes. The fundamentals of the new régime, however, seem pretty well stabilized. "On the one hand," says an Irish writer already quoted, "there is a general disposition to abandon the demand for complete independence of all connection with the British Commonwealth of Nations, and a growing realization of the advantages to be gained by strengthening and utilizing that connection. On the other hand, there has been, even among those who have striven

[77] *Round Table,* Mar., 1927, p. 346.

hardest and most successfully to reorganize the country on the basis of dominion independence, a distinct tendency to extend further the claim for immunity from interference by the imperial government, and to demand—in coöperation with the leaders of other dominions—the abolition of the formal symbols of imperial sovereignty, such as the original duties of the governor-general, or the privileges of the Judicial Committee of the Privy Council, or the oath of allegiance." [78] In a period of rapid imperial reorientation, the ultimate position of the Free State in the Commonwealth, and in the world, will be worked out as the resultant of these two significant, but not necessarily incompatible, tendencies.[79]

[78] S. Gwynn, *op. cit.*, pp. xv-xvi.

[79] S. Gwynn, "The Irish Free State and Dominion Status," *Nineteenth Cent.*, Aug., 1926, and *The Irish Free State, 1922-1927,* Chaps. vii-viii; T. A. Smiddy, "The Position of the Irish Free State in the British Commonwealth of Nations," in *Great Britain and the Dominions* (Lectures on the Harris Foundation, Chicago, 1928). For references on dominion status generally, see next chapter.

CHAPTER XXXI

SOME ASPECTS OF IMPERIAL AFFAIRS

THE most imposing and altogether remarkable political structure of modern times is the British Empire. This is not merely because it includes from one-sixth to one-fifth of the habitable surface of the globe, or because one person out of every four to five the world over acknowledges allegiance to the British crown. It is also because of the great variety of peoples and civilizations embraced in the Empire, the unique political machinery which holds it together, and perhaps most of all the presence within its bounds of no less than half a dozen broad dominions with extensive rights of self-government and substantial national autonomy. Books have been written comparing it with great empires of the past.[1] As a recent writer connected with the British Foreign Office has remarked, however, such efforts are rather useless, because hardly one significant point in common can be found.[2] Three hundred fifty years of empire-building, haphazard and desultory as it was, has resulted in a political establishment which, a committee of the Imperial Conference of 1926 rightly said, "defies classification and bears no real resemblance to any other political organization which now exists or has ever been tried."

There is no intention to enter upon a description of the Empire in this book. A separate, and even larger, volume would be required for the purpose. Besides, such volumes already happily exist. Somewhat curiously, British writers have met this need far more generously than the need for comprehensive and up-to-date treatises on the political system of Britain herself. It must have become apparent, however, that the powers and activities of the government centering in Whitehall and

[1] For example, C. P. Lucas, *Greater Rome and Greater Britain* (Oxford, 1912).

[2] J. B. Hurst, in *Great Britain and the Dominions* (Chicago, 1928), 3.

Westminster reach far beyond the British shores and cannot be understood thoroughly unless some attention is paid to their overseas aspects. To bring into view the outstanding points of contact between the governmental system previously described and the outlying areas of the Empire is the object of the present brief chapter. Nothing will be said about the Empire's history, and only enough about the internal political arrangements of the various types of dependencies to give some impression of the complexity of the problems with which British and colonial statesmen and administrators in our time are called upon to deal.[3]

Political Areas in the Empire

The Empire's heterogeneity is indicated not only by the diversity of race, language, and institutions within its bounds, but by the fact that there is not even a common term by which the component units, or entities, can be called.[4] Perhaps the comprehensive word already used, i.e., "dependencies," comes nearest to serving the purpose. The caption, however, is distasteful to the more autonomous areas, and in any event it must be employed with so many different meanings as to have little value. "Colonies" is even less accurate; "possessions," still more repugnant to self-governing populations. The point is not worth quibbling over; the British themselves have not been troubled about it. Any particular area always has an

[3] Convenient single-volume accounts of the Empire's growth include H. Robinson, *The Development of the British Empire* (Boston, 1922); A. Demangeon, *The British Empire*, trans. by E. F. Row (New York, 1925); C. S. S. Higham, *History of the British Empire* (London, 1921); J. A. Williamson, *A Short History of British Expansion* (New York, 1922), and C. Lucas, *The Story of the Empire* (London, 1924), in H. Gunn (ed.), *The British Empire*, a survey in 12 vols. Extensive works containing much descriptive matter, though not wholly up to date, are C. Lucas, *Historical Geography of the British Colonies*, 12 vols. (London, 1886-1916), and A. J. Herbertson and O. J. Howarth (eds.), *The Oxford Survey of the British Empire*, 6 vols. (Oxford, 1914), especially Vol. vi, *General Survey*. C. Wittke, *A History of Canada* (New York, 1928); E. A. Walker, *A History of South Africa* (London, 1927); and E. Scott, *A Short History of Australia* (London, 1916), are convenient brief histories of particular colonies.

[4] The heterogeneity of the Empire is pictured vividly in A. J. Toynbee, *The Conduct of British Empire Foreign Relations Since the Peace Settlement* (London, 1928), 3-8.

official designation—dominion, colony, protectorate, mandate—which fairly describes its character. Beyond that, it has not been found necessary to go.

From the point of view of governmental status or relations, the Empire's make-up is a matter of at least five or six main categories or classes of territories, each with certain obvious general characteristics, yet without any claim to complete symmetry or uniformity. First, there are the dominions, often referred to also as self-governing colonies. Canada, Australia, New Zealand, and South Africa are officially in this class. Newfoundland, although officially a colony, is in fact, as has been said, a dominion; likewise the Irish Free State, which, while not technically a dominion, has been granted dominion status. Since 1923 Southern Rhodesia has been rapidly approximating dominion status; and the list is likely to be lengthened as time goes on. A dominion of East Africa is already being talked about, and the Labor party would make a dominion out of India. Except the Irish Free State, all of the existing dominions, it will be observed, have been peopled primarily from the British Isles and are today, in the main, English-speaking countries.[5] Naturally, therefore, it is in these that the right of self-government has been carried farthest. Precisely how far it has been carried will appear when we turn to consider the relations which the dominions sustain with the political authorities at London. Suffice it to say here that all are, in effect, autonomous republics.

The student of comparative government can discover many interesting and significant differences among the dominion governments, but for purposes of a bird's-eye view all are pretty much of a pattern. In every case there is a written constitution, drawn up and adopted locally, though effective only by virtue of having been enacted by the imperial parliament in the form of a statute, and subject to amendment, in important respects, only with the consent of London.[6] In every case the

[5] In Canada, however, almost one-third of the population is of French descent.

[6] Canada, indeed, cannot independently amend its constitution in any particular. This is not true of the other dominions, though Professor Keith considers that even in Australia, where ostensibly there is the greatest freedom of constitutional change, no amendments may be made without

king is represented by a governor or governor-general, who since the Imperial Conference of 1926 bears, as we have seen, precisely the same legal relations to the dominion government that the king himself sustains with the imperial government. In every case the cabinet system exists and operates on lines substantially like those prevailing at London. In every case there is a bicameral parliament. The second chamber is made up variously: in Canada its members are appointed for life; in South Africa they are elected for ten years by the provincial parliaments; in Australia they are elected for six years by direct vote of the people. The Irish Free State has tried different systems; and, as has been noted elsewhere, the second chamber problem, taken at large, has by no means been solved, particularly in Canada. The popular branch of the legislature is in every instance about what a person familiar with English political traditions would expect. Leaving out of account native populations, manhood suffrage prevails; women have been enfranchised; and indeed some cautious provision is being made for representation of colored inhabitants. One rather fundamental difference of form appears. Some of the dominions have unitary governments, some federal. Newfoundland, New Zealand, and the Irish Free State have known no trace of federalism; South Africa was created by uniting separate political areas, but has a government that does not quite qualify as federal; Canada and Australia, likewise sprung from union of separate colonial areas or units, are truly federal. Students of the workings and problems of federal institutions find the last-mentioned countries almost as fruitful fields of observation as the United States.[7]

imperial consent except such as fall clearly "within the framework of a federal constitution." *Responsible Government in the Dominions* (2nd ed., Oxford, 1928), II, 1146.

[7] The monumental work on the dominion governments is A. B. Keith, *Responsible Government in the Dominions,* already cited. Among numerous other important books may be mentioned: *ibid., The Constitution, Administration, and Laws of the Empire* (London, 1924), and *War Government of the British Dominions* (London, 1921); J. Bryce, *Modern Democracies* (New York, 1921), I, Chaps. xxxiii-xxxvii (Canada), II, Chaps. xlvi-lvii (Australia and New Zealand); H. E. Egerton, *Federations and Unions Within the British Empire* (London, 1911); W. P. M. Kennedy, *The Constitution of Canada* (London, 1922); E. Porritt, *Evolution of the Dominion of Canada* (Yonkers, 1928); W. H. Moore, *The Constitution of the*

A second general class of dependencies includes certain ones that may be described as semi-autonomous. The principal examples are two of very unequal extent, i.e., India and Malta. Under the new constitution of 1919, the "dependent empire" of India has a curious hybrid style of government which, without giving autonomy, permits of a broad division of offices, powers, and functions between British and native authorities and marks a definite step in the "gradual development of self-governing institutions" to which the imperial government has of late been pledged. The division which is carried out in the fifteen provinces between "reserved" subjects, such as justice and police, and "transferred" subjects, such as education, public health, and local government, has brought into use the old Roman term *dyarchy* as fittingly describing the dual or bifurcated basis on which the system reposes.[8]

Then there are the so-called crown colonies. The term is less useful than it once was, because wide differences of political organization have grown up among the dependencies to which it is applied. Speaking broadly, these numerous dependencies are alike in that they have comparatively few inhabitants of European descent and are not considered capable of self-government on approved British lines. But, as in the case of Bermuda and the Bahamas, they may have an elective lower chamber and an appointive upper one; like Jamaica, Cyprus, and Ceylon, they may have a legislative council of a single house, partly elective and partly appointive; like Trinidad and British Honduras, they may have such a council which is wholly appointive; finally, like Gibraltar and St. Helena, they may have no legislative body at all. There is a tendency for such colonies to rise in the scale. But progress is slow, and military or naval considerations frequently play as important a part as anything else in determining the status assigned them.

Commonwealth of Australia (2nd ed., Melbourne, 1910); E. Sweetman, *Australian Constitutional Development* (London, 1925); and W. B. Worsfold, *The Union of South Africa* (London, 1912).

[8] A. B. Keith, *Constitution, Administration, and Laws of the Empire,* Pt. ii, Chap. v; C. P. Ilbert, *The Government of India* (Oxford, 1922); L. Curtis, *Dyarchy* (Oxford, 1920); V. Chirol, *India, Old and New* (London, 1921); D. N. Banarjee, *The Indian Constitution and Its Actual Working* (London, 1926).

Much of their legislation comes from London in the form of orders in council; and it goes without saying that the governor, as instructed and directed by the Colonial Office, is the principal figure in their political life.[9]

Next may be mentioned the protectorates. Of these, there were formerly more than at present. Various developing African territories have passed through this stage into something else; Egypt, indeed, after existing unwillingly as a protectorate from 1914 to 1922, was finally recognized as an independent state. But a large number of "protected states" in India still fall in this class; also various African territories, notably Uganda, Kenya, Nyasaland, and Somaliland. In theory, at least, the protectorates are simply native states which are safeguarded by British arms and taken care of in their international relations by British diplomacy. Actually, some of them are accustomed to a large amount of British control over their domestic affairs.[10]

The peace arrangements at the close of the World War added still another class of territories for which some degree of responsibility is assumed, i.e., the mandates. Mandates, too, differ among themselves; but the general principle underlying them is that the mandatory state shall be responsible for the peace, development, and general well-being of the areas assigned to it, and shall make periodic reports of its trusteeship to the League of Nations. Some mandates associated with British authority are under the direct control of the London government, for example, Palestine, Tanganyika, and British Togoland. Others are assigned to certain of the dominions, for example, former German Southwest Africa to the Union of South Africa and former German New Guinea to Australia.[11]

As if the varied arrangements described were not complicated enough, accuracy requires it to be stated that there are

[9] A. B. Keith, *Constitution, Administration, and Laws of the Empire*, Pt. ii, Chap. vi; H. Wrong, *Government of the West Indies* (Oxford, 1923).

[10] A. B. Keith, *op. cit.*, Pt. ii, Chap. vii.

[11] The mandate system in general is described briefly in A. B. Keith, *op. cit.*, Pt. ii, Chap. viii, and more fully in F. White, *Mandates* (London, 1926). The dominion mandates are dealt with in A. B. Keith, *Responsible Government in the Dominions* (2nd ed.), II, 1049-1064.

also areas which are held in condominium by Great Britain and some associated power. Thus the Egyptian Sudan is, at least technically, governed by Great Britain and Egypt jointly, and the New Hebrides by Great Britain and France.

The Empire as a Political Unit

The Empire is a heterogeneous collection of separate entities; and yet it is a political unit. Lines of connection, and of more or less control, run out from London to every red spot on the map; cross lines bind the different areas by political as well as economic ties. There is no written constitution for the Empire, just as there is none for Great Britain; and the Imperial Conference of 1926 was of the opinion that nothing would be gained by attempting to fabricate one. But there is a substantial body of imperial constitutional law, under which an integrated, even if widely ramifying, imperial government is carried on. Some idea of the political interconnections that exist will be gained if we call to mind the principal agencies or instrumentalities through which control from London is exerted—first legislative, then executive and administrative, and finally judicial.

Legislative control naturally takes two main forms: (1) legislation at London for the overseas empire, and (2) imperial veto, in some form, of measures enacted in the dependencies. Both are matters of a good deal of complexity. So far as legislation from London is concerned, the fundamental fact is that in legal theory there is full right to make any and all laws for any and all dependencies. Even the constitutions of the dominions are in form statutes of the Imperial Parliament, which legally could repeal or amend any of them, and could assume to itself any amount of other law-making authority. The actual situation is that most imperial legislation for the non-self-governing parts of the Empire is allowed to take the form of orders in council, and that relatively few statutes affecting the dominions are enacted except such as come from their own parliamentary bodies. There are, however, numerous older imperial statutes which apply equally in the dominions and in the home land; and to them is occasionally added new and important legislation touching matters on which the dominions are not themselves competent to legislate or matters of Empire importance which need to be regulated on a uniform basis. An example of the former is the Demise of the Crown Act of 1901 providing that no office should thenceforth be vacated by such demise. Examples of the latter are the Fugitive Offenders Act of 1881, the Copyright Act of 1911, the Nationality and Status of Aliens Acts of 1914 and 1922, and the Indemnity Act of 1920. There is an accepted convention that imperial legislation affecting the dominions ought to be passed only after consultation with the dominion governments, and it is normally acted upon. Such legislation, however, will not necessarily be prevented by dominion indifference or opposition. The general principle holds that no legislation is to be regarded as applying to the dominions unless it is so stipulated. Some imperial legislation is made applicable in the dominions only if they adopt it by a ratifying act; some applies there only in case there is no dominion legislation on the subject. The Army Act and the complementary Naval Discipline Act necessarily extend to the entire Empire, since the imperial forces could not be permitted to fall under non-imperial control if stationed in any dominion or colony.

Turning to imperial control over legislation enacted in the dependencies, one finds that while the imperial government has surrendered to full dominion regulation great areas of activity with which it has no desire to interfere, it wields active checking power in the non-self-governing colonies, and that even in the dominions it has never relaxed control in any matter deemed vital to the Empire and may still assert its superior authority at any and all times. There are four principal modes by which imperial control over colonial legislation may be exercised, not only in the less free dependencies (in so far as there applicable), but also in the dominions. One is outright veto by the governor or governor-general, acting at his own discretion, or, perchance, on the advice of the ministers. In the dominions, this power is now rarely or never exercised. It is not as nearly extinct as the royal veto in Britain, but it would be very unlikely to be used unless, for example, a bill should accidentally pass the two houses in an obviously imperfect form. The second mode is disallowance from London after a bill has received the governor-general's assent, and has perhaps taken effect. This power of disallowance exists in connection with all of the dominions and colonies except the Irish Free State. In actual use, it would, however, be more objectionable from the colonial point of view than any of the others, and it, too, is seldom or never brought into play, especially as affecting legislation in the dominions. There is usually a fixed period of one or two years within which disallowance, if contemplated, must take place; and, with slight exceptions, the rule is that an act, if disallowed, must be disallowed as a whole and not simply in respect to certain of its provisions.

A third mode, which is the usual one, is to postpone the taking effect of a measure until the "pleasure of the crown"—which, of course, means the attitude of the cabinet at London—can be ascertained. The governor-general may so "reserve" a measure on his own initiative. Or the measure may itself contain a suspending clause of similar purport. A common practice in Canada when any serious question of approval from London arises is to provide in the statute that it shall become operative only upon being proclaimed. If the imperial government dissents, no proclamation is issued. A bill reserved for signification of the royal pleasure lapses after a stipulated period if assent is not announced. In Canada and Australia the interval is two years; in most other dominions and colonies, one year. Finally, the imperial government may influence the course of dominion legislation by making proposals and expressing its wishes to the dominion authorities, and even to all intents and purposes ordering that legislation of a given nature be, or be not, enacted. The immigration legislation of the dominions, for example, has been quite generally recast to meet imperial objections and requests.[12]

On the side of executive and administrative relationships, the agencies chiefly to be noted are the king, the cabinet, certain of the ministries or executive departments, and, in the dominion or colony, the governor-general or governor. Much is heard, in

[12] On the general subject of imperial control over legislation, see A. B. Keith, *Responsible Government in the Dominions* (2nd ed.), II, 748-770, 1032-1040, and especially R. L. Schuyler, *Parliament and the British Empire; Some Constitutional Controversies Concerning Imperial Legislative Jurisdiction* (New York, 1929).

this connection, of the "crown." Common allegiance to the crown is the cement which holds the Empire together; many of the dependencies are "crown colonies;" the crown appoints governors, instructs them, lays down regulations, and dispatches troops for purposes of defense. It is hardly necessary to say, however, that "crown" means here almost precisely what it means in relation to the British government itself. The king personally has no more to do with colonial affairs than with war office matters or finance. The cabinet, naturally, has much to do with them, on lines of policy relating to particular dependencies, or classes of dependencies, or the Empire as a whole. And, of course, three of the great executive departments—the Colonial Office, the Dominions Office, and the India Office—as described in an earlier chapter, give all of their time and effort to the affairs of those portions of the Empire which have been assigned to them respectively. In carrying on dealings with the self-governing colonies, some assistance is lent by high commissioners maintained in London by the dominions, although the functions of these agents are more largely commercial than political.

In the non-self-governing areas—even India—administrative direction and control are real and extensive, although varying from class to class of dependencies, and indeed from colony to colony. In the dominions, authority of the kind is small and indirect, and is tending still further to diminish. No administrators, save only the governor-general, are sent out from London to Canada or Australia or the Irish Free State; and, except at a few relatively unimportant points, not even the governor-general can cause an administrative policy in which the imperial government may be interested to be carried out unless he can find dominion ministers who, with the support of the dominion parliament, will perform the acts necessary for the purpose. The governor-general may, of course, dismiss a ministry. But if the ministers are strong in public confidence, it is worse than useless to do so. Should the imperial government be determined upon carrying out an executive policy which the dominion ministers persistently refuse to support, the only mode of breaking the deadlock, as a leading authority suggests, is the enactment of imperial legislation covering the matter, or even a recall of the governor-general "in order to test the desire of the dominion to remain a part of the Empire." [13]

At the Imperial Conference of 1926 an inter-imperial relations committee recommended that as "an essential consequence of the equality of status existing among the British Commonwealth of Nations," the governor-general of a dominion should henceforth be regarded, not as a representative or agent of "His Majesty's Government in Great Britain or of any department of that government," but as the representative of the crown, "holding in all essential respects the same position in relation to the administration of public affairs in a dominion as is held by His Majesty the King in Great Britain." This principle was approved. When, however, it was proposed further that the governor-general should cease to be the formal official channel of communication between the British government and the government of his dominion, and that communication should thenceforth be between government and government direct, it was decided to leave the matter to be adjusted with the several dominion governments according to their preferences. In point of fact, correspondence between British and dominion prime ministers had long been taking place.

Judicial Appeals—The Judicial Committee of the Privy Council

The relations between Britain and the dependencies have also a judicial aspect. Speaking broadly, the judicial establishments of the non-self-governing colonies are created and regulated by imperial law, and the judiciary is largely recruited from the governing country. The dominions, on the other hand, have courts and procedures which, although derived mainly from earlier imperial precedent and regulation, are nowadays quite independent; and dominion judges are, of course, almost invariably dominion men. The most interesting institution that one encounters in this connection is one which has already

[13] A. B. Keith, *Responsible Government in the Dominions* (2nd ed.), II, 748. Newfoundland regulations inconsistent with a *modus vivendi* between Great Britain and the United States relative to fishing rights had to be overridden by imperial order in council in 1907.

been mentioned a number of times, i.e., the Judicial Committee of the Privy Council—an agency which, in the absence of any single system of law or of law courts throughout the Empire as a whole, nevertheless links up the legal and judicial systems of the far-flung colonies and possessions under a common appellate authority at London. A remote forerunner of the present Judicial Committee was the Privy Council's committee for trade and plantations, set up in 1668, which was instructed to hear all causes that came "by way of appeals" from the islands of Jersey and Guernsey. Subsequently there were, from time to time, other Council committees with more or less extensive appellate functions; and the Judicial Committee as it now stands was created in 1833 to take over jurisdiction (mainly, but not exclusively, civil) formerly exercised, in a rather loose manner, either by these committees or, more frequently, by the Council as a whole. As composed today, the Committee includes the Lord Chancellor and any former incumbents of his office, the six lords of appeal in ordinary, the Lord President of the Council, the privy councillors who hold (or have held) high judicial positions, and varying numbers of judges from overseas superior courts [14]—altogether an imposing group of judicial dignitaries, twenty or more in number.

The principal function of the Committee is to hear appeals from certain kinds of courts and from courts in certain places, i.e., ecclesiastical courts,[15] prize courts,[16] courts in the Chan-

[14] Courts of India as well as of the dominions. Until 1928, the number of dominion judges who might be members of the Judicial Committee was limited to seven. It is now unrestricted.

[15] These are courts maintained by the Anglican Church for the enforcement of church law, which, it must be observed, is a part of the law of the land. They range from the court of the archdeacon at the bottom up through the consistory court, or court of the bishop, to the provincial court, or court of the archbishop. Formerly they enjoyed a very extensive jurisdiction, embracing wills, marriage and divorce, perjury, defamation, "brawling," etc. Since 1857 all of the subjects named and various others have been removed to the secular courts, notably the Probate, Divorce, and Admiralty Division of the High Court. Nowadays the ecclesiastical tribunals have to do with little aside from discipline among the clergy, including offenses against morality and against doctrine and ritual. See A. L. Lowell, *Government of England,* II, Chap. li, and W. R. Anson, *Law and Custom of the Constitution* (3rd ed.), II, Pt. ii, 275-281.

[16] These deal with condemnation of vessels and cargoes captured in time of war.

nel Islands and the Isle of Man, courts in India, the dominions (including the Irish Free State), and the colonies, and English courts established by treaty in foreign countries, notably China.[17] In form, these appeals are addressed to the crown, for hearing and advice, and—still following the theory—are turned over by the Council to its special agency for such work, i.e., the Judicial Committee. Actually, however, the petition goes straight to the Committee; and, although, not being a court, that body cannot render a judgment, but can only recommend to the crown that the appeal be granted or denied, i.e., that the judgment against which protest is made be sustained or reversed, the Committee's recommendation invariably eventuates in an order in council in which the finding is given validity as a judgment.[18] To all intents and purposes, therefore, the Committee serves as a supreme court for all British and British-controlled jurisdictions for which that function is not fulfilled by the House of Lords. As remarked by a recent writer, its jurisdiction is geographically more extensive than that of any other judicial or quasi-judicial body.[19]

In the main, the labors of the Committee are performed by the Lord Chancellor and the six lords of appeal in ordinary, assisted, in cases coming from India and the colonies, by members representing the overseas territory concerned in each instance. Leaving these overseas members out of account, the Committee therefore differs hardly at all, in its working personnel, from the House of Lords when sitting as a court. Indeed, it is commonly taken for granted that if, as a result of further changes in the House of Lords, the appellate juris-

[17] The *principal* function, because under the act of 1833 the king-in-council may refer any matters—not simply appeals—to the Committee for advice. It is customary, for example, so to refer any question as to the removal of a colonial judge.

[18] The Committee's recommendations bear some resemblance to what are commonly known as advisory opinions. English judges of higher grades also give advisory opinions on questions of law when requested by either the executive or the legislature. See V. Veeder, "Advisory Opinions of the Judges of England," *Harvard Law Rev.*, Jan., 1900. The principle of the advisory opinion finds recognition in Canada, Austria, Sweden, and several other countries; also in at least thirteen states of the American union, although not in connection with the national judiciary.

[19] W. B. Munro, *Governments of Europe*, 275-276.

diction of that body should be taken away, it would simply be transferred to the Judicial Committee, somewhat enlarged, perhaps, to equip it for its added duties.[20] Appeals pour in from the four corners of the earth, so that it becomes necessary to expedite matters by organizing the Committee into two divisions, one of which hears the numerous petitions from India, and the other, those from the rest of the Empire. The sittings are held in a fine old oak-paneled room in Downing Street, five members commonly hearing each appeal[21] and reaching decisions which, unlike the judgments of the House of Lords, must be unanimous. Not being judges—at all events when acting in this particular capacity—the members do not wear wigs or robes; and the proceedings are of an informal, almost conversational, character. Unlimited argument is allowed, and immediate oral indication is sometimes given to the waiting counsel as to what the recommendation to the crown will be. In arriving at such recommendations, the councillors are not rigidly bound to follow their earlier judgments; nor are they bound by the decisions of the House of Lords. In the course of a year the legal knowledge of the members is likely to be tested to the utmost, for appeals requiring attention turn upon points in the most diverse systems of law—Hindu, Buddhist, Mohammedan, French, Roman, Dutch, besides, of course, the English common law. It is this aspect of the work that makes the services of the overseas jurists especially valuable, if not indispensable.

The range of the Judicial Committee's jurisdiction requires an additional word of comment. Some appeals are brought "of right," that is, because the amounts involved or the interests in question clearly fall within bounds prescribed by orders in council or by statutes. But many—all, indeed, in the case of Canada, Australia, and South Africa—can be brought only by virtue of permission granted in advance, by the court from whose judgment the appeal is taken (almost invariably the

[20] Proposals that a single imperial court of appeal be created by merging the judicial functions of the House of Lords and the Judicial Committee have several times been discussed—by a special conference on the subject at London in 1901 and by later Imperial Conferences—but without result. Australia has generally been favorable, Canada unfavorable.

[21] At least three, exclusive of the Lord President, must be present.

highest appellate court in the colony), or by the Committee itself. A Judicial Committee Act of 1844 gave statutory validity to the right of the crown to hear appeals from any court of justice in any British colony or possession; and this broadly defined authority still exists except in so far as restricted by later imperial legislation. In the case of two of the dominions, i.e., Australia and South Africa, restrictions have been imposed; in all other instances there are none. In Canada, various attempts to bring about curtailment, e.g., a statute of 1888 undertaking to cut off appeal in criminal cases, have been unsuccessful. Appeals from Canadian courts are numerous (one of the Committee's divisions devotes at least two months to them every summer); and they have included many cases involving important questions of a constitutional nature.[22] The constitution of Australia, as first drafted, aimed not only to cut off appeals outside of the country on constitutional questions, but to empower the Commonwealth parliament to prohibit such appeals on all other kinds of questions as well. The parliament at London, however, was unwilling to approve these features, and appeals even on constitutional matters are possible today with the assent of the Australian High Court—although it must be added that that tribunal has made it known that permission will normally be refused. In South Africa, appeals have been restricted to cases decided in the appellate division of the Supreme Court, and permission to appeal is not granted freely. In connection with the setting up of the Irish Free State in 1922-23, strong effort was made to procure an agreement under which all judicial actions should terminate in Ireland. Once more the authorities at London successfully insisted that the right of appeal to the crown, on constitutional as well as other questions, be preserved; although, as indicated above, appeals that have been carried have aroused no end of discussion and friction, and some readjustment not touching the fundamental right may possibly be made.[23] In the case of India and the non-self-governing

[22] R. Cameron (ed.), *The Canadian Constitution as Interpreted by the Judicial Committee of the Privy Council* (Winnipeg, 1915), is a useful collection of documents.

[23] D. Figgis, "Ireland and the Privy Council," *Fort. Rev.*, Nov., 1923. Cf. p. 734 above. At the Imperial Conference of 1926 the Free State's demand

colonies, appeal is limited only by the Judicial Committee's discretion. Leave to appeal is almost always refused in criminal cases, and the readiness with which it is granted in civil cases tends to vary inversely with the stage of perfection reached by the judicial institutions of the various dependencies. The territories within the Empire which are in the earlier stages of their development are prone to make extensive use of the Committee's services. As for the self-governing areas, although, as has appeared, they are inclined to feel that it is beneath their dignity to allow cases to be carried from their own courts to even as able and impartial a body as the Judicial Committee, there is no unanimity of opinion among them, and no evidence that Westminster will relax its historic policy in the matter. "All the expressions of good will and desire to meet dominion wishes at successive imperial conferences," notes a recent writer, "do not include a single offer to abolish the appeal." [24]

The Dominions and Their International Status

The Empire is a single state, in both municipal and international law. There is a common British citizenship, based on the uniform allegiance of "subjects" to a single crown; a considerable body of law applies equally in every part of the domain; and it is not possible for any community of British subjects to be at peace with a foreign country with which the Empire is at

for abolition of appeal was abandoned only on the understanding that the right was reserved to bring up the matter at the next Imperial Conference.

[24] A. B. Keith, *Responsible Government in the Dominions* (2nd ed.), II, 1149. The legal profession in the dominions generally favors the continuance of appeals. But some people charge that this is mainly for reasons of professional gain. For an excellent account of the Judicial Committee by a jurist who rendered long service as a member, see Viscount Haldane, "The Judicial Committee of the Privy Council," *Empire Rev.*, July, 1923. See also A. B. Keith, *op. cit.* (2nd ed.), II, 1087-1109; C. J. Tarrington, *Chapters on the Law Relating to the Colonies* (4th ed., London, 1914), containing interesting lists of cases appealed; N. Bentwich, *The Practice of the Privy Council in Judicial Matters* (2nd ed., London, 1926); A. H. Robinson, *Appeals to the Privy Council in Constitutional Cases* (London, 1921); W. E. Raney, "The Appeal to the Privy Council," *Canadian Bar Rev.*, Sept., 1927, and "The Finality of Privy Council Decisions," *ibid.*, May, 1926, and G. Kelly, "The Dominions and the Judicial Committee," *Nineteenth Cent.*, Feb., 1929. For a recent Privy Council decision adjusting a long-standing boundary dispute in America, see J. R. Hayden, "Newfoundland Gains 100,000 Square Miles," *Curr. Hist.*, May, 1927.

war, or to be at war with a country with which the Empire is at peace. Nevertheless, the dominions have gradually gained a status, especially since the World War, which yields them not only a plenitude of self-government to be found elsewhere only in sovereign states, but also a large degree of actual independence, and which, as has been observed, constitutes one of the Empire's chief claims to distinction. The matter is a complicated one, and it is not feasible to go far into it here. But a few salient facts may be brought to view.

In the first place, by unanimous declaration of the Imperial Conference in 1926, the dominions are "autonomous communities within the British Empire, equal in status, in no way subordinate one to another in any respect of their domestic or internal affairs, though united by a common allegiance to the crown, and freely associated as members of the British Commonwealth of Nations.[25] Each dominion, according to language employed freely by high and responsible officials during the meeting referred to, is "master of its own destiny," and, in fact if not always in form, "subject to no compulsion whatever." Great Britain herself remains, as Lord Grey has remarked, the nerve-center of the Empire; but so far as Britain and the dominions are concerned, equality of status is the root principle governing all inter-imperial relations. Such equality of status was long talked about on the basis of formal federation. Geographical and other conditions made it impossible of attainment in that way. But it has nevertheless been arrived at along the road of autonomy.[26]

From this follows naturally the independent membership of the dominions (and, indeed, of India as well) in the League of Nations. The dominions were represented separately in the Peace Conference of Paris in 1919,[27] and their representatives

[25] *Imperial Conference, 1926. Summary of Proceedings.* Cmd. 2768.

[26] South African Nationalists and other elements formerly unfriendly to the Empire as a sort of superstate have, since the Conference of 1926, adopted a more favorable attitude, feeling, as General Hertzog expresses it, that there is "no question any longer of domination or superiority over the dominions." *London Times,* Dec. 18, 1926.

[27] This of itself was enough to open a new epoch in the constitutional history of the Empire. The dominions were the only communities without titular sovereignty and independence represented in the Conference. But already their status was such that, added to the part which they had played

there, with the full concurrence and support of the British government, decided to claim and secure admission to separate membership, in their own rights, in the League. The claim, although provocative of misgivings in non-British quarters, including the United States,[28] could not be denied, and Canada, Australia, New Zealand, South Africa, and India took their places among the original members of the League in 1920, with the addition of the Irish Free State in 1923. Some people construed this as an evidence that the British Empire was breaking up, and the impression was strengthened when dominion representatives at Geneva began taking independent and contrary lines of action when they did not happen to be in agreement with the policy of the government at London. Such freedom of action was, however, taken for granted in British and dominion circles, and has, indeed, been hailed by the well-informed as a source of imperial strength, in the sense, at all events, that any attempt to compress all parts of the Commonwealth into a single channel of action would certainly be provocative of protest and dissension. Some of the dominions have played a prominent rôle in League affairs, and in 1927 Canada was elected to a seat in the League Council.

With respect to the conduct of foreign affairs generally, the Imperial Conference of 1926 frankly recognized that in this sphere, as in the sphere of defense, "the major share of responsibility rests now, and must for some time continue to rest, with His Majesty's Government in Great Britain." [29] It was recognized also, however, that all of the dominions are actually engaged to some extent, and some to a considerable extent, in the conduct of foreign relations, particularly with foreign states on their borders. The growing activities of Canada in relation to the United States were cited, and the opinion was expressed that such dominion management of external relations must be permitted to continue, subject only to the general

in the war, they could not be excluded by such a technicality as the lack of formal sovereign independence.

[28] It will be recalled that Greater Britain's six votes in the League Assembly (seven after 1923) was a principal ground of objection in this country to membership in the League.

[29] *Imperial Conference, 1926. Summary of Proceedings.* Cmd. 2768, pp. 25-26.

principle that neither Great Britain nor any dominion may be committed to the acceptance of active obligations except with the definite assent of its own government. In this connection it is to be noted that the dominions, with full British assent, have begun to send diplomatic representatives to foreign countries. As has been observed, the Irish Free State set the pace in 1924 by accrediting an envoy extraordinary and minister plenipotentiary to the United States, receiving, in return, a minister from this country. After prolonged consideration of the matter, Canada took a similar step in 1926-27.[30] In each instance, the envoy from the dominion is the ordinary channel of communication with the Washington government on all affairs relating only to the particular dominion which he represents; while matters of imperial concern, or which affect other dominions in the Commonwealth, continue to be handled by the British embassy. The Irish and Canadian ministers have been accorded full recognition by the diplomatic corps at Washington, and occupy separate places in the order of precedence. As a recent writer has remarked, the arrangement affords an excellent example of the unity in diversity characteristic of the British Commonwealth.[31] In 1928 the Canadian government arranged also with the French and Japanese governments for reciprocal diplomatic representation; and it has been announced that the Irish Free State will soon provide for diplomatic representation at both Paris and Berlin. On the other hand, Australia, New Zealand, and South Africa give no sign of following the Irish and Canadian precedents.

One will not be surprised to be told that treaty-making raises a number of difficult questions. Treaties are ordinarily supposed to be made only by sovereign and independent states, and yet from the general international position which the dominions have acquired it might be inferred that they may make treaties independently so long as the interests of no other parts of the Empire are affected. Such a claim was, indeed,

[30] The power was given Canada by an agreement announced in 1920, but, it so happened, was not taken advantage of by that dominion until after the Free State, by virtue of the equality of its status with that of Canada, had taken action of the sort.

[31] A. L. Lowell and H. D. Hall, *The British Commonwealth of Nations* (Boston, 1927), 604. See *ibid.*, 652-655, for pertinent documents.

set up by Canada in connection with the famous halibut-fisheries treaty of 1922 with the United States, and was made good to the extent that that agreement, as being of concern solely to Canada and the United States, was signed only by a Canadian, and not a British, representative.[32] The procedure followed in this case has prevailed in a number of subsequent Canadian treaties, both with the United States and with various European countries, and in the Imperial Conference of 1923 the general principle was laid down that treaties, whether commercial or political, may be negotiated, signed, and ratified separately by any dominion government, provided that no other part of the Empire is affected and that any other government in the Empire likely to be interested is consulted. The limitation specified is, of course, of great importance. Practically, it becomes necessary for any dominion proposing to conclude a treaty with a foreign power to obtain the imperial government's consent; and it remains true that, legally, a treaty can be signed and ratified only in virtue of full powers issued by the king on the recommendation of a British minister. It is difficult, however, to accept the dictum of a leading authority that the "alleged concession" of the treaty right to the dominions in 1923, and even in 1926, is "a mere chimera." [33]

Bilateral treaties, although certainly raising questions, are a relatively simple matter. But how about multilateral treaties, especially treaties negotiated at international conferences? On this point, the Imperial Conference of 1926, although it considered the subject at length, could arrive at no single or fixed rule. Much must depend on the circumstances—whether the dominions participated separately in making the treaty, whether all or only some are affected, whether the treaty itself contains any stipulations on the manner of ratification, and other determining conditions. The Conference made some recommendations, which are too extensive and technical to be presented here.[34] But time will be required to mature definite and agreed lines of policy. Indeed, the important and difficult problem of

[32] For the documents, see A. L. Lowell and H. D. Hall, *op. cit.*, 639-645.
[33] A. B. Keith, *Responsible Government in the Dominions* (2nd ed.), II, 1150.
[34] *Ibid.*, II, 607-613, 663-669.

dominion representation in international conferences remains largely unsolved.[35]

It has been stated that it is impossible for a community of British subjects to be at peace with a foreign country with which the Empire is at war, or to be at war with a country with which the Empire is at peace; and this solidarity in belligerency and neutrality seems as strong evidence as is needed of the Empire's essential unity in international law. The force of the argument is, however, considerably weakened by the doctrine, already established empirically before 1926 and definitely formulated and accepted in that year, that there is both an "active" and a "passive" belligerency, and that while it is true that when the Empire is at war every portion of it, including the dominions, is passively belligerent, a dominion is the sole judge of the nature and extent of its own coöperation—that is, of whether it will be an active belligerent as well. The constitution of the Irish Free State categorically provides that "save in the case of actual invasion, the Free State shall not be committed to actual participation in any war without the consent of its parliament." [36] On paper, the theoretical distinction between passive and active belligerency reconciles the unitary character of the Empire in relation to foreign states with the full autonomy and equality of the members of the Commonwealth in regard to one another; and it is to be borne in mind that common membership in the League of Nations goes far toward committing Great Britain and the dominions to solidarity of action in world affairs. Nevertheless, the attempted distinction might in practice lead to very embarrassing situations. It did, indeed, produce such a situation in connection with the Chanaq incident of 1922, when, Great Britain being on the brink of a renewal of war with Turkey, South Africa and Canada gave evidence of being unwilling to be drawn into the conflict in any active way.[37] One can imagine circumstances under which one

[35] A. J. Toynbee, *op. cit.,* 83-99. Naturally, the dominions are not represented when they are not invited, as was true in the case of the Washington Conference of 1921-22. Dominion representatives were, however, attached to the British—perhaps more properly the imperial—delegation in the instance mentioned.

[36] Art. 49.

[37] Hostilities were averted at the eleventh hour. This crisis became the

or more of the dominions might withhold active participation in a war entered upon by Great Britain without causing ill feeling; such a case would be Canada's abstention from a war between Great Britain and, let us say, Afghanistan.[38] But if the war were one of larger proportions, there could hardly fail to be resentment toward any member of the Commonwealth seeking to remain aloof. Since there can be no guarantee that in the event of a recurrence of war on a large scale every dominion would be prepared to take an active part, and since a division of policy in the matter would bring the unity and perpetuity of the Empire into jeopardy, it is obviously to the interest of the Commonwealth in a very special sense that the danger of international war be reduced to a minimum.[39]

immediate occasion of the downfall of the Lloyd George coalition government. See p. 501 above. For an account of the affair, including the attitude of the dominions, see A. J. Toynbee, *op. cit.*, 46-52.

[38] As a matter of fact, in the Anglo-Afghan war of 1919 it was never suggested that the overseas dominions should take part.

[39] The best recent discussions of the dominions and their international status are A. B. Keith, *Responsible Government in the Dominions* (2nd ed.), II, 840-926, and *The Constitution, Administration, and Laws of the Empire*, Pt. i, Chaps. iii-iv; A. J. Toynbee, *The Conduct of British Empire Foreign Relations Since the Peace Settlement*, previously cited; M. Nathan, *Empire Government* (London, 1928); and L. L. Minty, *Constitutional Laws of the British Empire* (London, 1928). Other useful references include A. L. Lowell and H. D. Hall, *The British Commonwealth of Nations*, previously cited; the volume of lectures, already mentioned, entitled *Great Britain and the Dominions* (Chicago, 1928); P. N. Baker, *The Status of British Dominions* (London, 1929); J. B. Scott, "The British Commonwealth of Nations," *Amer. Jour. Internat. Law*, Jan., 1917; V. K. Johnston, "Dominion Status in International Law," *ibid.*, July, 1927; W. H. Moore, "The Dominions and Treaties," *Jour. Compar. Legis. and Internat. Law*, Feb., 1926; A. B. Keith, "The Imperial Conference, 1926," *ibid.*, Feb., 1927; C. D. Allin, "International Status of the British Dominions," *Amer. Polit. Sci. Rev.*, Nov., 1923; *ibid.*, "Proposals for the Neutrality of the British Dominions," *Polit. Sci. Quar.*, Sept., 1922; and *ibid.*, "Recent Developments in the Constitutional and International Status of the British Dominions," *Minn. Law Rev.*, Jan., 1928. Canada's international position is considered in R. Borden, *Canada in the Commonwealth* (London, 1928); P. E. Corbett and H. A. Smith, *Canada and World Politics* (London, 1928); H. L. Keenleyside, *Canada and the United States* (New York, 1929); C. Martin, *Empire and Commonwealth; Studies in Governance and Self-Governance in Canada* (Oxford, 1929); C. D. Allin, "Canada's Treaty-Making Power," *Mich. Law Rev.*, Jan., 1926; and J. S. Evart, "Canada, the Empire, and the United States," *Foreign Affairs*, Oct., 1927.

The Future of the Empire

Seventy-five years ago there was a good deal of doubt among Englishmen as to whether the Empire as it then stood would endure. The loss of the American colonies suggested that when other possessions reached a somewhat advanced stage in their growth they too would claim and receive independence; disappointing experiences with Canada and the shock of the Indian Mutiny begat pessimism; the necessity of granting the principal colonies tariff autonomy threatened to lessen their commercial value; undeniably the overseas territories required heavy outlays of money and entailed constant risk of war. The "wretched colonies," wrote Disraeli in 1854, "will all be independent in a few years and are a millstone round our necks." Canada, said the *London Times,* might as well be ceded to the United States first as last. This low ebb of British colonial zeal was, however, only a passing phase. The last quarter of the nineteenth century saw a shift of opinion which brought appreciation of and interest in the overseas empire once more to a lofty pitch. Increased pressure for markets and for raw materials gave a new point of view; capital seeking investment outside of the British Isles coveted the protection of the British flag; the rise of French, German, and Italian imperialism, and especially the rapid partition of Africa, supplied impetus; the deep-seated tradition of sea-power lent support; writers like Sir John Seeley and Rudyard Kipling exploited the idea that the settled colonies were essentially an extension of England, argued that their connection with the United Kingdom was natural and vital, and appealed to patriotism and pride as sustaining forces in further imperial endeavor. From a period of apathy and retrenchment, the country passed, between 1875 and 1890, into an epoch of annexations and consolidations —from the days of the "Little Englanders" to those of Beaconsfield, Chamberlain, and Curzon.[40]

[40] The mid-century stage of inactivity is dealt with in illuminating fashion in R. L. Schuyler, "The Rise of Anti-Imperialism," *Polit. Sci. Quar.*, Sept., 1922, and "The Climax of Anti-Imperialism in England," *ibid.*, Dec., 1921. The outburst of colonial zeal, especially after 1878, is sketched in R. Muir, *The Expansion of Europe* (Boston, 1917), Chaps. vii-viii. Seeley's famous book, *The Expansion of England,* was published in 1883.

Through many vicissitudes, and with many momentary backward swings of opinion, the British people's devotion to the Empire has been kept not only alive but ardent to this day. There are still Little Englanders, just as there are still men who, entirely accepting the imperial ideal, can see no escape from the Empire's eventual collapse. But one will search in vain through the official pronouncements of the three great political parties for proposals or promises looking to the setting adrift of crown colonies, or of India, or even of the dominions. The Labor party—certainly the least "imperialistic" of the three—calls in its program as outlined in 1928 for "the closest coöperation between Great Britain and the dominions, for the elevation of India to equality in the Commonwealth with the dominions, and for the preparation of "indigenous peoples" for "full self-government at the earliest practicable date." [41] But it nowhere suggests dismantling the Empire. The emphasis all along the line, in all parties and in all sober discussion, official and otherwise, is upon ways and means of readjusting the internal and external arrangements of the Empire in better accordance with the new world conditions of the twentieth century, and particularly of the post-war period. That the Empire, however changed in form, will go on, is taken for granted.

Nothing is more obvious than that the problems of empire are now quite different from what they formerly were. The dominions have grown, in some cases with startling rapidity, into self-governing quasi-republics; trade has shifted into new channels and assumed new forms; immigration has taken on an altered character and significance; new ideas as to what is right or expedient in dealing with "backward" peoples have won acceptance; the League of Nations has introduced a new framework of international, and even of inter-imperial, relations. The situation in which the Empire of today finds itself fairly bristles with unsolved problems. Some of these—the foreign relations of the dominions, the dominions and treaty-making, the dominions and war—we have mentioned. Many others, especially as connected with trade and other aspects of economic life, have not been, and cannot be, touched upon. The

[41] *Labour and the Nation* (1928), *passim.*

future of the Empire, it is scarcely necessary to remark, hangs on the manner in which, and the success with which, these challenges to constructive statesmanship are met.

We have said that there is no written imperial constitution. It is doubtful whether there ever will be one. But this does not mean that there is not a great and growing body of imperial constitutional law—to say nothing of imperial conventions or customs as well. How such law and custom develop must be evident from the foregoing pages. Take, for example, the matter of dominion participation in the management of foreign relations. As recently as 1911 Prime Minister Asquith stoutly maintained that the responsibility of the British government in such weighty matters as formulating foreign policy, making treaties, declaring war, concluding peace, and, indeed, in all forms of relations with foreign powers, could not be shared. The experiences of the World War led, however, to the adoption of a different attitude. The Imperial War Conference of 1917 declared all of these activities to be of common concern to the whole Empire, and therefore matters in which action was to be common. The resolution of the Conference to this effect was accepted by the British government as a working principle; whereupon the Imperial Conferences of 1923 and 1926 took the next logical step of working out rules and methods for giving effect to the plan, the government again accepting them and thereby placing upon them the stamp of legal validity. Within the space of a decade the entire scheme of imperial foreign relations was revolutionized—not by formal act of Parliament, nor yet by unilateral action of the London executive authorities, but by conference, resolution, and informal assent.[42]

[42] The Imperial Conference, mentioned often in the preceding pages, calls for a word of comment. Historically, it arose out of experience with a series of colonial conferences, starting on the occasion of Queen Victoria's jubilee in 1887, and devoted principally to discussions of schemes of "imperial federation." These meetings failed to attain their chief objective, i.e., the development of some sort of all-empire council or parliament; and eventually such a piece of machinery was given up as impracticable. It was recognized as desirable, however, that there should continue to be gatherings of official spokesmen of Britain and the major dependencies for the consideration of problems of mutual interest, and the result has been a series of Imperial Conferences—in 1911, 1917, 1918, 1923, and 1926—and the

In similar fashion have come most other recent changes in inter-imperial relationships, and from the same process must be expected to flow all of the greater understandings and readjustments by which the Empire will continue to preserve the harmony, and also build the machinery, necessary to its survival. Thus the Empire feels its way along the tortuous path of its existence, developing its rules of action as it goes. Its scheme of life at any given moment contains much that is illogical, and even incongruous. But readers of our earlier chapters will recognize in the procedure the same practical-minded meeting of problems as they arise which made the living, expanding British constitution what it is today, and will understand that logic and symmetry are—in the Britisher's world, at all events—not essential to serviceableness and durability.[43]

acceptance of the Imperial Conference as, indeed, a regular and established institution. Meetings are attended by representatives—the prime ministers and others—of Great Britain, the dominions, and India, with the British prime minister in the chair; agenda are prepared in advance by a permanent secretariat, each government being at liberty to suggest topics for discussion; sub-committees are assigned various subjects for examination and report; sessions are private, though the conclusions and resolutions are published as a parliamentary paper; and decisions are reached on a basis of unanimity rather than by mere majority vote. The Conference is purely a consultative and advisory body. It has no power to bind a single government or parliament. Since, however, every prime minister has concurred in every resolution passed, its actions are practically certain of ratification at London, Ottawa, Canberra, and the other capitals; and such ratification vests them with full legal sanction. Any proposal which fails to meet with unanimous approval of the participating governments falls to the ground. All matters of common interest come within the scope of the Conference, but naturally the subjects receiving most attention are foreign relations, defense, and trade. A full account of the earlier colonial and later imperial conferences will be found in A. B. Keith, *Responsible Government in the Dominions* (2nd ed.), II, 1176-1245.

[43] The present character and outlook of the Empire are dealt with from various points of view in A. Zimmern, *The Third British Empire* (London, 1927); R. Jebb, *The Empire in Eclipse* (London, 1925); W. P. Hall, *Empire to Commonwealth* (New York, 1928); H. D. Hall, *The British Commonwealth of Nations; A Study of the Past and Future Development* (London, 1920); H. E. Egerton, *British Colonial Policy in the Twentieth Century* (London, 1922); and L. H. Guest, *The New British Empire* (London, 1929). L. Curtis, *The Problem of the Commonwealth* (London, 1916), and A. B. Keith, *Imperial Unity and the Dominions* (Oxford, 1916), are older but still important. *The Round Table,* a quarterly review published in London since 1911, is indispensable for students of Commonwealth politics.

INDEX

INDEX